# Anthropology

# Anthropology

*What Does It Mean to Be Human?*

Robert H. Lavenda
Emily A. Schultz
Cynthia Zutter

*Canadian Edition*

OXFORD
UNIVERSITY PRESS

## OXFORD
### UNIVERSITY PRESS

Oxford University Press is a department of the University of Oxford.
It furthers the University's objective of excellence in research, scholarship,
and education by publishing worldwide. Oxford is a registered trade mark of
Oxford University Press in the UK and in certain other countries.

Published in Canada by
Oxford University Press
8 Sampson Mews, Suite 204,
Don Mills, Ontario  M3C 0H5 Canada

www.oupcanada.com

**Library and Archives Canada Cataloguing in Publication**

Lavenda, Robert H., author Anthropology : what does it mean to be human? /
Robert H. Lavenda, Emily A. Schultz, Cynthia Zutter. — First Canadian edition.

Includes bibliographical references and index.
ISBN 978–0–19–901286–2 (paperback)

1. Anthropology.  I. Schultz, Emily A. (Emily Ann), 1949–,
author II. Zutter, Cynthia Marnie, 1965–, author III. Title.

GN25.L38 2016          301          C2015-908505-5

Cover image: Peter Stuckings/Getty Images

# Contents in Brief

# Contents

**FOCUS ON FOUR FIELDS**
**Biological Anthropology: Bioarchaeology and the Analysis of Human Remains**   162

**FOCUS ON FOUR FIELDS**
**Archaeology: Dating Methods in Archaeology and Paleoanthropology**   194

## 14 | *What Can Anthropology Tell Us about Social Inequality?* 392

## 15 | *What Can Anthropology Tell Us about Globalization?* 426

# Preface

This original US version of this book emerged out of Robert Lavenda's and Emily Schultz's increasing dissatisfaction with all the available general anthropology texts. The authors found that these texts either overwhelmed beginning students with detail and the sheer volume of material or else provided overly brief introductions that failed to convey the richness of the field. They therefore set out to write a book that introduces this broad field concisely yet thoroughly, providing diverse perspectives and examples to foster not only an appreciation of anthropology but also a deeper engagement with it—one that helps students better understand themselves and the world around them. Anthropology professors (and their students) needed a general anthropology text that struck the right balance, fit into a 15-week semester, and came with a complete package of ancillary materials.

In preparing this first Canadian edition, Cynthia Zutter has focused on two central themes, both of which Lavenda and Schultz strongly support. First, she has incorporated Canadian ideas and practices in as many ways as possible. Throughout the text, she has added discussions that focus on Canadian topics such as multiculturalism, bilingualism, same-sex marriage, and cultural resource management. She has also included many examples from across Canada, covering concerns such as how Canadian laws and policies affect people's everyday lives, how ethnicity and indigeneity are recognized, how Indigenous languages are being revitalized, and how French is being preserved in Acadia. In addition, Zutter has incorporated a wide variety of anthropological research carried out by Canadian anthropologists, both within Canada and in other regions—from Madagascar to Taiwan to Brazil. Second, like previous US editions of this text, this Canadian edition continues to address the central issues of the discipline, highlighting the controversies and commitments that shape contemporary anthropology in North America and around the world, and that make it interesting and exciting.

## Approach

This book may be concise, but we cover the field effectively. We take a question-oriented approach that illuminates major concepts for students and shows them the relevance of anthropology in today's world. Structuring each chapter around an important question and its subquestions, we explore what it means to be human, incorporating answers from all four major subfields of anthropology—biological anthropology, archaeology, linguistic anthropology, and cultural anthropology—as well as from applied anthropology. We have made every effort to provide a balanced perspective, both in the level of detail we present and in our coverage of the major subfields.

The questioning approach not only sparks curiosity but orients students' reading and comprehension of each chapter, highlighting the concepts every student should take away from a general anthropology course. For example, students need to know about evolutionary theory, human variation, and the biological, social, and cultural critique of the concept of race, since knowledge in these areas is one of the great achievements of the discipline of anthropology. No other discipline (and possibly no other course) will teach about these matters the way anthropologists do, focusing on the idea of humans as biocultural organisms. Students need to know about the fossil evidence for the evolution of *Homo sapiens*, which they are not likely to learn about elsewhere. Students need to know what archaeology can tell us about the human past, as well as what ethnography can teach us about social complexity and inequality. They need to know that culture is more than just cultural festivals, regional foods, and interesting traditional costumes. They need to know about language and cognition and the central role of learning and play in human development. They need to understand the wellsprings of human creativity and imagination. It is valuable for them to see the many forms of human relatedness, and how people organize themselves. They need to know about globalization from the bottom up and not just the top down. They need to see how all the subfields of anthropology together can provide important, unique insights into all these topics, and how anthropology can provide a vital foundation for their university education.

The world we face as anthropologists has changed dramatically in the last quarter century, and anthropology has changed, too. We have always felt it necessary to present students with a view of what contemporary anthropologists are doing; we therefore address the most current issues in the field and have thoroughly updated the text accordingly for this edition. Students will take away from the book an appreciation of how these areas of specialization have developed over time, and how they contribute to our understanding of the world in the twenty-first century.

## Organization

Divided into fifteen chapters and four "Focus" features, this book is the ideal length for a one-semester course. Chapters 1 and 2 introduce the entire field and the concept of culture, which intersects all aspects of the discipline of anthropology. Following this comprehensive introduction, six chapters are devoted to biological anthropology and archaeology: evolutionary theory (Chapter 3); human variation (Chapter 4); the primates (Chapter 5); the fossil record and human origins (Chapter 6); the human past (Chapter 7); and the first farmers, cities, and states (Chapter 8). Topics in linguistic and cultural anthropology are covered in chapters on language and communication (Chapter 9); symbolic practices (Chapter 10, covering play, art, myth, ritual, and religion); economics (Chapter 11); politics (Chapter 12); kinship, marriage, and sexuality (Chapter 13); social inequality (Chapter 14, covering gender, class, caste, race, ethnicity, and nationalism); and globalization (Chapter 15). Throughout, the book incorporates discussions of indigeneity and gender, while paying special attention to issues of power and inequality in Canada and the contemporary world.

In the Canadian edition, Zutter placed the chapter on culture immediately after the introductory chapter to highlight the important role that culture plays in all aspects of anthropology, including biological anthropology and archaeology. She has also included additional emphasis on the biocultural nature of human organisms throughout, to facilitate the integration of biological and cultural approaches in anthropology.

In addition, brief "Focus" features (after chapters 6, 7, 9, and 13) explore key concerns, methods, and approaches within each of the four major subfields of anthropology in greater depth, focusing on bioarchaeology and the stories that our skeletons hold (biological anthropology); methods for dating archaeological remains and hominin fossils (archaeology); the study of language use and the components of language (linguistic anthropology); and ethnographic methods commonly used in fieldwork (cultural anthropology).

—Robert H. Lavenda, Emily A. Schultz, and Cynthia Zutter

# *Acknowledgements*

My thanks goes out to all of the many people who helped me throughout the development of this Canadian edition of Robert Lavenda and Emily Schultz's *Anthropology: What Does It Mean to Be Human?* The editors at Oxford University Press have been a pleasure to work with, especially Tanuja Weerasooriya and Janice Evans, both of whom were patient and provided sage advice as they guided me through the creation of this project, and the entire production team. As well, I would like to extend a note of gratitude to Caroline Starr, who initiated and championed this project from its initial stages. Editorial assistance was provided by Rose Lorentzen, whose organizational skills were extremely helpful. My students at MacEwan University guided the project with their valuable comments and suggestions. In addition, I'd like to extend my gratitude to Robert Lavenda and Emily Schultz for providing me with such a wonderful opportunity to combine their exceptional textbook with Canadian content.

Individual contributions from Canadian anthropologists form some of the key additions to this text, and I am grateful to those who provided personal explanations of their current research. My thanks goes out to Michel Bouchard, Carly Dokis, Linda Fedigan, Jennifer Lui, April Nowell, Christine Schreyer, Sarah Shulist, Kisha Supernant, and Andrew Walsh. I appreciate their generosity in sharing their work for this project.

I would also like to extend my thanks to the following reviewers, as well as those who wish to remain anonymous:

Alexis Dolphin, Western University
Maciej Domanski, Dawson College
Nick Gabrilopoulos, Dawson College
Michael Gregg, Mount Allison University
Helen R. Haines, Trent University
David Hopwood, Vancouver Island University
Nicole Kilburn, Camosun College
Erin McGuire, University of Victoria
Hugh McKenzie, MacEwan University
Mark Prentice, Vanier College
Robbyn Seller, John Abbott College
Tara Tudor, Camosun College

Their insightful comments and suggestions contributed to the outcome of this Canadian edition.

This edition is dedicated to my family, including my siblings and my children, Kris, Troy, and Matthew. Their support and understanding throughout this process has been enduring. I am grateful to my husband, Mike, as well, for sharing in my journey as a Canadian anthropologist.

—Cynthia Zutter

# From the Publisher

Oxford University Press is delighted to present the first Canadian edition of *Anthropology: What Does It Mean to Be Human?* This thought-provoking work offers an informative, practical, and comprehensive introduction to the discipline—one that not only reveals the richness of anthropological study but also fosters a deeper understanding of the many factors shaping human experience. Discussing issues and examples from across the globe, this engrossing text shows Canadian students the relevance of anthropology in today's world—both at home and abroad.

# Key Features

## 11 Why Do Anthropologists Study Economic Relations?

▲ A vegetable market in Chichicastenango, Guatemala. Photo: AWL Images/Getty Images

### Chapter Outline

- How Do Anthropologists Study Economic Relations?
- How Do Anthropologists Study Production, Distribution, and Consumption?
- How Are Goods Distributed and Exchanged?
- Does Production Drive Economic Activities?
- Why Do People Consume What They Do?
- The Anthropology of Food and Nutrition
- Chapter Summary
- For Review
- Key Terms
- Suggested Readings

*A questions-oriented approach.* Structuring each chapter around an important question and its subquestions, the authors illuminate major concepts, incorporating answers from the main subfields of anthropology—biological anthropology, archaeology, linguistic anthropology, and cultural anthropology—as well as applied anthropology. This engaging approach sparks students' curiosity while focussing their learning around key topics in the field.

FIGURE 10.8 | A crowd of hockey fans cheers on Team Canada during the 2010 Winter Olympic Games in Vancouver. These kinds of mass public events can create a feeling of communitas in today's nation-states.

The ritual frame is more rigid than the play frame. Consequently, ritual is the most stable liminal domain, whereas play is the most flexible. Players can move with relative ease into and out of play, but such is not the case with ritual.

Finally, play usually has little effect on the social order of ordinary life; as a result, play can safely create a wide range of commentary on the social order. Ritual is different: its role is explicitly to maintain the status quo, including the prescribed ritual transformations. Societies differ in the extent to which ritual behaviour alternates with everyday, non-ritual behaviour. When nearly every act of everyday life is ritualized and other forms of behaviour are strongly discouraged, we sometimes speak of **orthopraxy** ("correct practice"). Traditionally observant Jews and Muslims, for example, lead a highly ritualized daily life, attempting from the moment they awaken until the moment they fall asleep to carry out even the humblest of activities in a manner that is ritually correct. In their view, ritual correctness is the result of God's law, and it is their duty and joy to conform their every action to God's will.

Margaret Drewal (1992) argues that, at least among the Yoruba, play and ritual overlap (see EthnoProfile 10.3: Yoruba on page 287). Yoruba rituals combine spectacle, festival, play, sacrifice, and so on and integrate diverse media—music, dance, poetry, theatre, sculpture (Drewal 1992, 198). They are events that require improvisatory, spontaneous individual moves; as a result, the mundane

order is not only inverted and reversed but may also be subverted through power play and gender play. For example, gender roles are rigidly structured in Yoruba society. Yoruba rituals, however, allow some cross-dressing by both men and women, providing institutionalized opportunities for men and women to cross gender boundaries and to express the traits that the Yoruba consider to be characteristic of the opposite sex, sometimes as parody but some[...] (Drewal 1992, 190).

## How Are Wo[...]
## Symbolic Pra[...]

Our previous discuss[...] and ritual provided [...] human beings use cul[...] ings of everyday expe[...] on those insights and [...] cultural creativity to [...] a more comprehensiv[...] passing pictures of rea[...]

**orthopraxy** "Correct [...] from approved forms of b[...]

**world views** Encompas[...] members of societies.

difficult. The ethnographic evidence suggests that matrilineages must be examined on a case-by-case basis.

The Haida of Canada's northwest coast are a matrilineal people (see EthnoProfile 13.2: Haida), with each matrilineage belonging to either the Raven or the Eagle *k'waalaa* (clan). Strong feelings of reciprocity and social responsibility exist between the Ravens and the Eagles, and membership in a particular matrilineage and its *k'waalaa* shapes individuals' identities as well as social relationships (Krmpotich 2010). The Haida use matrilineal identity to navigate such matters as their participation in potlatches, their use of property, whom they should marry, their social status, and whom they can ask for economic support. As all things in Haida society are either owned by or a part of either the Raven or the Eagle *k'waalaa*, belonging to a matrilineage is both humbling and empowering.

A Haida matrilineage can be thought of as a broad network of families linked through ancestry, property, and common social responsibilities. The most closely related members of a matrilineage tend to share the strongest bonds, which are based on love, friendship, history, obligations, shared work, and commitment. Indeed, matrilineal kin form the basis of each person's sense of family, and they play integral roles in major life events—for example, by leading rites of passage; by preparing feasts, potlatches, weddings, and other celebrations; and by mourning the deceased (Krmpotich 2010, 162). At the same time, individuals are generally encouraged to marry outside of their *k'waalaa*, a practice that facilitates non-matrilineal kinship bonds (e.g., between children and fathers).

Haida often wear crests to represent the matrilineage to which they belong. The designs of these crests are owned and inherited by members of the *k'waalaa* to which they correspond, and they can be painted or embroidered onto garments and even tattooed onto a person (Figure 13.6). These material expressions perpetuate a sense of belonging and continuity of family and lineages. A significant factor in Haida kinship is the relationships between the living and the dead. Ancestors are often considered as guides for the living, providing opportunities and companionship.

**EthnoProfile 13.2**

**Haida**

**Region:** Northwest coast of North America

**Nation:** Canada

**Population:** 60,000

**Environment:** Maritime, cool

**Livelihood:** Fishing, whaling, collecting plants

**Political organization:** Traditionally, clans, public consensus; today, a tribal council within a modern nation-state

**For more information:** Boelscher, Marianne. 1988. *The Curtain within: Haida Social and Political Discourse.* Vancouver: University of British Columbia Press.

FIGURE 13.6 | Haida wear crests to physically represent the matrilineages to which they belong. Here, Haida elders wear full ceremonial regalia at the dedication ceremony for a new canoe on Graham Island, part of the Queen Charlotte Islands in British Columbia.

*Canadian focus.* An array of Canadian examples makes the text highly relevant and accessible to students in Canada. Canadian scholarship and perspectives throughout also give readers insight into the many Canadian contributions to the field.

FIGURE 8.2 |
Industrial agriculture converts acres of habitat into a uniform agroecology for growing commercial crops. These constructed niches offer protection from disease, drought, and insect infestations that the plants would be highly susceptible to in other environments. Canola, one of Canada's most economically valuable crops, is planted and harvested on more than 5 million hectares of land across the country.

patterns of habitation experienced by earlier hominins. It is important to recognize that people do not have to become farmers to become sedentary. The sedentary adaptations of the Indigenous peoples of the northwest coast of Canada (e.g., the Haida people of Haida Gwaii) depended not on agriculture but on seasonally re-occurring salmon runs. These reliable sources of food were "harvested" as regularly as crops but involved

For a discussion of how sedentism and agricultural practices contributed to the spread of malaria-carrying mosquitoes in tropical regions, see Chapter 4, pp. 75–6.

FIGURE 8.3 | In Australia, hunter-gatherers burn vegetation to encourage the growth of certain types of plants.

minimal ecological interference and no processes of domestication.

Sedentism is probably more usefully understood as a consequence of humans choosing to depend on resources in particular kinds of constructed niches. Sedentism is a key element that modifies the selection pressures of those who come to depend on subsistence resources in a fixed location, be it a riverbank or a cultivated field or a pasture. Human beings who f[...] port larger populatio[...] periodic famine. At [...] to a variety of new s[...]

A very popular term these days is *globalization*. But what does it mean? In this chapter, we will look at how anthropologists study globalization by following global flows of information, people, and commodities. You will learn how anthropologists approach debates about such contemporary matters as international migration, multiculturalism, and human rights. We will also show how cultural anthropology's traditional ethnographic focus can make unique contributions to our understanding of globalization.

In this chapter, we take up again the story of relations between the West and the rest of the world, how those relations have changed over the last fifty or so years, and with what consequences. We look at ourselves as much as we look at the traditional subjects of anthropological research.

## What Happened to the Global Economy after the Cold War?

In 1989, the Cold War came to an end. The Soviet Union and its satellite states collapsed, and China began to encourage some capitalist economic practices. These radical changes in the global political economy left no part of the world unaffected. For some, this period of uncertainty offered a chance to challenge long-unquestioned truths about development and underdevelopment that had guided

government policies throughout the Cold War. From new social movements such as the *rondas campesinas* of Peru to squatter movements in cities to movements defending the rights of women and various minority groups to movements to preserve rain forests, people attempted to construct entirely new social institutions that often bypassed national governments or development agencies (see Figure 15.1). Anthropologist Arturo Escobar (1992) argued that the new social movements in Latin America were struggles over meanings as well as over material conditions.

This work promoted the hope that new social movements might succeed in promoting less exploitative forms of society in generations to come. But the world toward which such arguments were aimed was already disappearing. The breakdown of communism led to a crisis of confidence among many who had been inspired by key tenets of Marxist thought. At the same

MAP 15.1 | Location of societies whose EthnoProfiles appear in Chapter 15.

*Global approach.* Providing a broad context for analysis, the text features examples from around the world, includes a substantial chapter on globalization, and highlights how the spread of capitalism has drastically shaped how people everywhere live their lives.

### In Their Own Words

### Dowry Too High. Lose Bride and Go to Jail

*In some parts of the world, discussions of bridewealth or dowry seem so divorced from reality as to appear "academic." But elsewhere, these topics remain significant indeed. In May 2003, news media all over the world reported the story of a bride in India who called the police when a battle erupted over demands for additional dowry payments at her wedding. The* New York Times *reports.*

Noida, India, 16 May—The musicians were playing, the 2000 guests were dining, the Hindu priest was preparing the ceremony, and the bride was dressed in red, her hands and feet festively painted with henna.

Then, the bride's family says, the groom's family moved in for the kill. The dowry of two televisions, two home theatre sets, two refrigerators, two air-conditioners, and one car was too cheap. They wanted $25,000 in rupees, now, under the wedding tent.

As a free-for-all erupted between the two families, the bartered bride put her hennaed foot down. She reached for the royal blue cellphone and dialed 100. By calling the police, Nisha Sharma, a 21-year-old computer student, saw her potential groom land in jail and herself land in the national spotlight as India's new overnight sensation.

"Are they marrying with money, or marrying with me?" Ms Sharma asked today, her dark eyes glaring under arched eyebrows. In the next room a fresh wave of repor-

Nisha Sharma, surrounded by some of the dowry with which her family had intended to endow her.

propelled Nisha Sharma to Hindi stardom. One television station set up a service allowing viewers to "send a message to Nisha." In the first two days, 1500 messages came in.

Illegal for many decades in India, dowries are now often disguised by families as gifts to give the newlyweds a start in life. More than a media creation, Ms Sharma and her dowry defiance struck a chord in this nation, whose expanding middle class is rebelling against a dowry tradition that is being overfed by a new commercialism.

"Advertisements now show parents giving things to make their daughters happy in life," Brinda Karat, general secretary of the All India Democratic Women's Association, a private group, said, referring to television commercials for products commonly given in dowries.

"It is the most modern aspects of information technology married to the most backward concepts of subordination of women," Ms Karat continued in a telephone interview. Last year, she said, her group surveyed 10,000 people in 18 of India's 26 states. "We found an across-the-board increase in dowry demand," she said.

Much of the dowry greed is new, Ms Karat added. In a survey 40 years ago, she noted, almost two-thirds of

FIGURE 13.15 | As migration from the Dominican Republic to the United States has increased, more Dominicans are staying and bringing their families or creating families in the United States. Such celebrations of ethnic pride as the Dominican Day Parade in New York City have increased in recent years.

heavy psychological burden of separation. Although he might be working in a hotel in New York, for example, the husband was still the breadwinner and the main decision maker in the household. He communicated by visits, letters, and occasional telephone calls. Despite

the strains of migration, moreover, the divorce rate was actually slightly lower in migrant families than in families whose members never migrated. This was in part because the exchange of information between Los Pinos and New York was both dense and frequent but also because strong ties of affection connected many couples. Finally, "the goal of the overwhelming majority of the migrants [from Los Pinos] I spoke with was permanent return to the Dominican Republic. Achievement of this goal was hastened by sponsoring the migration of dependents, both wives and children, so that they could work and save as part of the reconstituted household in the United States" (Georges 1990, 201). This pressure also helped keep families together.

In recent years, the Internet has come to play an increasingly important role in the lives of families that are separated by migration, education, work, and so on. Daniel Miller and Don Slater (2000) studied Internet use in Trinidad, finding that email and instant messaging have considerably strengthened both nuclear and extended families, allowing closer relations between distant parents and children, among siblings, and among other relatives.

### Anthropology in the Contemporary World

#### Caring for Infibulated Women Giving Birth in Norway

Female genital cutting (FGC) has generated enormous publicity—and enormous conflict. Coping with this practice across difference is complex. People in Western societies often have very little grasp of how the operation fits into the cultural practices of those who perform it. Even women from societies with the tradition find themselves on opposing sides: Some seek asylum to avoid it, while others are prosecuted because they seek to have it performed on their daughters. Many governments have declared it a human rights violation.

Norway has struggled with these issues ever since 1991, when it became the home of a large number of refugees from civil war in Somalia. Norwegian health care is free, and Norway has one of the lowest infant mortality rates in the world. Nevertheless, despite the efforts of dedicated health care workers to be culturally sensitive, outcomes for Somali women are not always optimal.

Medical anthropologist R. Elise B. Johansen tried to find out why (Johansen 2006, 516).

In contemporary Norway, Johansen reports, giving birth is considered a positive, "natural" process that women are expected to be able to handle with minimal medical intervention. As a result, "midwives are preferred to obstetricians, medication and incisions are avoided whenever possible, partners are allowed to be present in the delivery room to support the birthing mother, newborns are immediately placed on the mother's belly, and mothers are encouraged to breast feed immediately" (2006, 521). At the same time, Norwegian health workers believe that giving birth "naturally" is hard for Norwegian women, because their "natural female essence" is "buried under layers of modernity" (521). Norwegian women nevertheless support "natural" birth practices out of concern for the health of the child, and they expect to manage

*Coverage of gender and feminist anthropology.* The authors tightly weave the topic of gender into the fabric of the text. Discussion of issues such as gender inequality, feminist archeology, and varieties of human sexual practice offers students insight into important areas of study within anthropology.

## Inequality and Structural Violence in Haiti

The entire world focused on Haiti in January 2010, when a devastating earthquake struck the country, killing more than a thousand people, rendering more than a million people homeless, and turning much of the built environment to rubble. Paul Farmer is an anthropologist and medical doctor who has been involved with aid work in Haiti since 1983. The organization he co-founded, Partners in Health (PIH), provided care to many who suffered in the earthquake and is active in efforts to rebuild and improve medical facilities that were lost (see PIH's website for details: www.pih.org/country/haiti/; also see PIH Canada's website for information on how Canadians are contributing to PIH's efforts in Haiti: http://pihcanada.org/our-work/haiti). Today, the organization continues to be involved in strengthening Haiti's health care systems in various ways, including partnering with the Haitian government to help build the University Hospital in Mirebalais and train a new generation of doctors, nurses, and health care workers.

One reason the effects of the earthquake were so devastating is that most Haitians live under precarious circumstances, with child mortality rates around 87 per 1000 live births. Farmer's activities as a physician have exposed him to extreme forms of human suffering that have long been taken-for-granted aspects of everyday life for those at the bottom of Haitian society (see Figure 14.1 and EthnoProfile 14.1: Haiti). Farmer describes this suffering as the outcome of structural violence. Structural violence is a product of the way that political and economic forces structure people's risks for various forms of suffering within a population. Much structural violence takes the form of infectious and parasitic disease. But it can also include other forms of extreme suffering, such as hunger, torture, and rape (Farmer 2002, 424). Structural violence circumscribes the spaces in which the poorest and least powerful members of Haitian society must live and subjects them to highly intensified risks of all kinds. The *structural* aspect of this violence must be emphasized because most Western outside observers (even those who want to alleviate suffering) often focus only on individuals

> **structural violence** Violence that results from the way that political and economic forces structure risk for various forms of suffering within a population.

**FIGURE 14.1 |** Dr. Paul Farmer with an AIDS patient at a medical clinic in a rural Haitian village. Political and economic forces structure people's risks for various forms of suffering in Haiti as elsewhere.

### EthnoProfile 14.1

**Haiti**

**Region:** Caribbean
**Nation:** Haiti
**Population:** 7,500,000
**Environment:** Rough, mountainous terrain; tropical to semiarid climate
**Livelihood:** Varied about 80 per cent poverty
**Political organiza**
*For more informa and Accusation: Ha Berkeley: Universit*

and their personal
to blame the victim

Farmer's work
first-hand the suff
including one you
one young man wh
the course of a bea
these two individua
fashion," and he re
violence operating
class, and race con

is to the family business (2002, 190). Ong notes, however, that flexible citizenship informed by a postnational ethos is not an option for non-elite migrants: "whereas for bankers, boundaries are always flexible, for migrant workers, boat people, persecuted intellectuals and artists, and other kinds of less well-heeled refugees, this ... is a harder act to follow" (190).

She points out that, on the way to their success, contemporary Chinese merchants "have also revived premodern forms of child, gender, and class oppression, as well as strengthened authoritarianist regimes in Asia" (2002, 190). Yet, neither the positives nor the negatives should, she insists, be attributed to any "Chinese" essence; instead, she thinks these strategies are better understood as "the expressions of a habitus that is finely tuned to the turbulence of late capitalism" (191).

### Are Human Rights Universal?

Globalization has stimulated discussions about human rights: powers, privileges, or material resources to which people everywhere, by virtue of being human, are justly entitled. Rapidly circulating capital, images, people, things, and ideologies juxtapose different understandings about what it means to be human or what kinds of rights people may be entitled to. The context within which human-rights discourse becomes relevant is often described as multiculturalism: living permanently in settings surrounded by people with cultural backgrounds different from your own and struggling to define with them the degree to which the wider society should accord respect and recognition to the cultural beliefs and practices of different groups. It is precisely in multicultural settings—found everywhere in today's globalized world—that questions of rights become salient and different cultural understandings of what it means to be human, and what rights humans are entitled to, become the focus of contention.

Essentially, the ideology of multiculturalism defines Canada as a modern nation-state. Canada was

> **human rights** Powers, privileges, or material resources to which people everywhere, by virtue of being human, are justly entitled.

> **multiculturalism** Living permanently in settings surrounded by people with cultural backgrounds different from one's own and struggling to define with them the degree to which the cultural beliefs and practices of different groups should or should not be accorded respect and recognition by the wider society.

**FIGURE 15.7 |** In 2013, demonstrators in Quebec marched against the province's proposed Charter of Values, which sought to prohibit public-sector employees from wearing or displaying religious symbols, including the hijab. Many people opposed the bill on the grounds that a number of its provisions violated individuals' fundamental rights to religious freedom and expression of beliefs.

one of the first countries in the world to introduce a federal multiculturalism policy (in 1971), and as a result Canada's version of multiculturalism has been adopted internationally. Over the past forty years, Canada's culturally inclusive immigrant-integration policies have become the cornerstone for maintaining the country's economic success and growth. Yet, as in other multicultural societies, the close proximity of people with different cultural values and beliefs has led to various debates over what constitute a "human right" (Figure 15.7).

#### Human-Rights Discourse as the Global Language of Social Justice

Discourses about human rights have proliferated in recent decades, stimulated by the original UN Universal Declaration of Human Rights in 1948 and followed by numerous subsequent declarations. For example, in 1992, the Convention on the Elimination of All Forms of Discrimination against Women (CEDAW) declared that violence against women was a form of gender discrimination that violated the human rights of women. This declaration was adopted by the UN General Assembly in 1993 and became part of the rights platform at the Fourth World Conference on Women in Beijing, China, in 1995. Anthropologist Sally Merry (2001, 36–7) observes that this declaration "dramatically demonstrates the creation of new rights—rights which depend on the state's failure to protect women rather than its

*Current anthropological approaches to power and inequality.* In-depth treatment of issues such as nationalism, racism, class, caste, and human rights helps students understand how power is manifested, deployed, resisted, and transformed.

## Focus on Four Fields

### Biological Anthropology: Bioarchaeology and the Analysis of Human Remains

#### What Secrets Do Our Skeletons Hold?

The study of human remains can be traced back to the development of anthropology as an academic discipline in the nineteenth century. Today, this study typically falls under the umbrella of biological anthropology, a major component of which is bioarchaeology. However, the lines that separate different anthropological specialties are often flexible, and paleoanthropologists, archaeologists, and other types of scientists are also often involved in the analysis of human remains. In this section, we will focus on the methods and techniques typically used by bioarchaeologists.

Bioarchaeology can be thought of as the archaeology of human death, since it relies on the remains left behind by individuals long after they have died. Death is a fact of life and an unavoidable topic for anthropologists who study humans both past and present (Rubertone 2007). The topic intersects with questions about social issues and population dynamics, such as inequalities in wealth, health status, and the occurrence of disease. The analysis and interpretation of mortuary remains reminds us that humans are biocultural organisms. After all, this analysis can reveal a great deal about not only an individual's physical characteristics (e.g., height, weight, sex) but also the cultural practices of the society in which she or he lived (e.g., religious or spiritual practices and the structure of rituals) (ibid., 256).

The excavation and analysis of human remains often involves a systematic set of procedures that begins with surveying, both on foot and with non-invasive techniques like ground-penetrating radar, to locate graves. Once a grave has been located and prior to any excavation, researchers must apply for permission from local governments and request the consent of any known relatives who are still living. In Canada, this

latter requirement of
First Nations or Inuit
of burials requires
respectful of those w
ing relatives. Each c
for obtaining permis
remains. In the Uni
established by feder
ally set out by the p
the remains are loc
Chapter 7, p. 182.)

If and when p
excavation can begir
retrieving biological
associated with the g
and beliefs influence
are buried, and wha
ials. Bioarchaeologis
tices by recording as
uncover. What is the
back, or front? Is it "f
ition) or laid out flat
of only one individu
the graves oriented a
axis? Are the remain
or coffins)? What typ
graves? Is there any
or tools? The combin
sources of data can
tion about the indivi

#### Excavating I

What sorts of confl
after the excavatio
cumstances might l
to observe religious
ing the remains? Wh
become an issue? If
whom do they belo

> **bioarchaeology** The study of human remains from prehistory to provide information about the human past.

#### Analysis of Skeletal Remains

Bioarchaeologists often use skeletal remains to look at patterns of age and sex, genetic markers, health status, evidence of disease, and even the types of food the individual consumed while he or she was alive. But where do they begin?

The first step is to look at the skeletal remains and any other biological indicators that are present in the grave. The individual's age at death is usually one of the first characteristics that a researcher identifies. Skeletal size is typically a reliable indicator of age at death for youths up to approximately 12 years of age. For older individuals, analysis of the long bones of the skeleton can provide useful clues. All long bones are composed of a diaphysis (i.e., a shaft) and two epiphyses (i.e., ends). In children and adolescents, the area between the diaphysis and the epiphyses consists of a layer of cartilage known as a "growth plate" or an epiphyseal plate. The epiphyseal plates of different long bones fuse to their diaphysis at different ages. In females, the epiphyseal plates begin to fuse from 12 to 17 years of age; in males, they begin to fuse from 15 to 21 years of age (Bass 1995, 17). As a general guide, the stages of fusion can be used to determine the approximate age of adolescents. If all epiphyses are fused, the individual is likely an adult. Because the aging process beyond early adulthood causes the internal structures of bones to thin and become brittle, researchers can use bone density to estimate the age at death for adults.

Dentition is another key indicator of age at death. The presence of baby (or "milk") teeth indicates a young child, generally under the age of 6 or 7. As a general rule, the first permanent molars erupt at age 6, the second at age 12, and the third (better known as "wisdom

teeth") between the ages of 18 and 21. Estimations of older individuals are generally based on the loss of and wear patterns on teeth, and on evidence of dental disease. Different rates of dental disease typically appear in different age groups, with the oldest members of a population generally being most affected by dental disease (such as cavities and abscess) and tooth loss. Teeth can also be used to identify family and relations. For example, the absence of teeth (e.g., no wisdom teeth) or the presence of more teeth than is typical is often associated with genetic markers.

In addition to discovering an individual's age at death, bioarchaeologists also try to determine the sex of the skeleton. Although it is almost impossible to determine the sex of pre-adolescent skeletons based on their physical characteristics, the sex of adult skeletons is generally apparent by looking at the shape of the pelvis (Figure F1.1). Females tend to have larger and more *U*-shaped hips, which facilitates childbirth, while males' hips tend to be narrower.

The structure of the skull also differs between males and females (Figure F1.2). Most notably, eye sockets tend to be more squared in males and more rounded in females. In addition, the chin is more *U*-shaped in males and more *V*-shaped in females. Finally, the occipital condyle (the bump at the rear base of the skull) is much more pronounced in males than in females.

Bioarchaeologists also often look at the skeleton for evidence of health and disease. Children who have been subject to times of stress, like severe fever or malnutrition, often have linear features on their bones indicating that the bones stopped growing. These are known as Harris lines. Children who lack sufficient vitamin D can develop a bone disease known as rickets, which causes

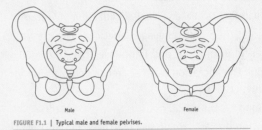

Male      Female

FIGURE F1.1 | Typical male and female pelvises.

*"Focus on Four Fields" features.* Engaging modules introduce students to the methods and approaches anthropologists use to conduct research within their various subfields.

## List of "Anthropology in the Contemporary World" Boxes

*"Anthropology in the Contemporary World" boxes.* A range of fascinating examples and cases help students see the many ways in which anthropology is relevant today.

## List of "EthnoProfile" Boxes

*EthnoProfiles.* Brief overviews of geographic, linguistic, demographic, and organizational information offer students context regarding various societies discussed in the text.

## List of "In Their Own Words" Boxes

*"In Their Own Words" boxes.* Short commentaries capture diverse voices—including those of anthropologists, non-anthropologists, and indigenous peoples—providing students with fresh perspectives on interesting topics related to chapter content.

was the emergence of culture, which can be defined as sets of learned behaviour and ideas that human beings acquire as members of society. Human beings use culture to adapt to and transform the world in which they live.

Human beings are more dependent than any other species on learning for survival because they have no instincts that automatically protect us and help us find food and shelter. Instead, we have come to use our large and complex brains to learn from other members of society what we need to know to survive. Learning is a primary focus of childhood, which is longer for humans than for any other species.

From the anthropological perspective, the concept of *culture* is central to explanations of why human beings are what they are and why they do what they do. Anthropologists are frequently able to show that members of a particular social group behave in a particular way *not* because the behaviour was programmed by their genes, but because they observed other people and copied what they did. For example, North Americans typically do not eat insects, but this behaviour is not the result of genetic programming. Rather, North Americans have never seen any of their friends or family eat insects, have been told as children that eating insects is horrible, and do not eat insects themselves. Yet North Americans can eat insects with no ill effects. This dietary behaviour can be explained in terms of cul-

ways of thinking and acting that help us find food, shelter, and mates and that teach us how to rear our children. Our biological endowment, rich as it is, does not provide us with instincts that would automatically take care of these survival needs. Human biology makes culture possible; human culture makes human biological survival possible.

For further discussion of how humans use culture to adapt to and transform the world in which they live, see Chapter 2, p. 23.

## What Makes Anthropology a Cross-Disciplinary Discipline?

Because of its diversity, anthropology does not easily fit into any of the standard academic classifications. The discipline is usually listed as a social science, but it spans the natural sciences and the humanities as well. What it is *not*, as we will see, is the study of the "*exotic*," the "*primitive*," or the "*savage*," terms originally used in colonial times that anthropologists rejected long ago. Figure 1.2 illustrates the variety of interests that fall under the anthropological umbrella.

Traditionally, North American anthropology has been divided into four subfields: *biological anthropology*, *cultural anthropology*, *linguistic anthropology*, and

# 5 | What Can the Study of Primates Tell Us about Human Beings?

▲ A mother orangutan expresses affection toward her daughter. Photo: olga_gl/Shutterstock

### Chapter Outline

- What Are Primates?
- How Do Anthropologists Classify Primates?
- What Do We Know about the Kinds of Primates Living Today?
- Are There Patterns in Primate Evolution?
- How Do Paleoanthropologists Reconstruct Primate Evolutionary History?

- Chapter Summary
- For Review
- Key Terms
- Suggested Readings

unication" (107) rtist's audience. dience in mind, as if the works heir response is cal. In addition, an just the end attention needs h some product pointed out, for Nigeria do not ut rather enjoy 0.1: Margi). by "transforma- he link between ary. This means e object or idea own sake. They different mean- entation depend sts that they be tion-representa- maker makes a for example, he the hero in his ee-dimensional at puppet made tyle, inclination e internal state

of the hero at a specific moment (Figure 10.2). At the same time, he is carrying out this work more or less skillfully and is representing in his work the meanings that Arjuna carries for his Javanese audience.

Alland's definition of art attempts to capture something universal about human beings and cultural creativity. Similarly, anthropologist Shelly Errington (1998, 84) observes that all human cultures have "symbolic forms': artifacts, activities, or even aspects of the landscape that humans view as densely meaningful." One dramatic example of this in Canada is the National War Memorial in Ottawa, which has a profound emotional impact on hundreds of thousands of people who visit it each year (see Figure 10.3). The memorial continues

For more on the people of Java, see EthnoProfile 9.1, on p. 247.

**FIGURE 10.2** | One of the great mythic heroes of Javanese *wajang* is represented here in a beautifully painted flat leather shadow puppet. The colour of the image, the angle of the head, the shape of the eye, the position of the fingers, and the style, colour, and quantity of the clothing all represent the inner state of the hero.

ngdoms;

2006.

*The Mandara Margi: A Society Living on the Cerge.* www.indiana.edu/~margi

## Chapter Summary

1. Anthropology aims to describe in the broadest sense what it means to be human. The anthropological perspective is holistic, comparative, and evolutionary and has relied on the concept of culture to explain the diversity of human ways of life. Human beings depend on cultural learning for successful biological survival and reproduction, which is why anthropologists consider human beings to be biocultural organisms. Anthropology is also a field-based discipline. In North America today, anthropology is considered to have four major subfields: biological anthropology, archaeology, cultural anthropology, and linguistic anthropology; many people also consider applied anthropology to be a fifth major subfield.

2. Biological anthropology began as an attempt to classify all the world's populations into different races. By the early twentieth century, however, most anthropologists had rejected racial classifications as scientifically unjustifiable and objected to the ways in which racial classifications were used to justify the social practice of racism. Contemporary anthropologists who are interested in human biology include biological anthropologists, primatologists, and paleoanthropologists.

3. Cultural anthropologists study cultural diversity in all living human societies, including their own. Linguistic anthropologists approach cultural diversity by relating varied forms of language to their cultural contexts. Both gather information through fieldwork, by participating with their informants in social activities, and by observing those activities as outsiders. They publish accounts of their research in ethnographies.

4. Archaeology is the cultural anthropology of the human past, with interests ranging from the earliest stone tools to twenty-first-century garbage dumps. Archaeologists focus on understanding how humans lived in the past, how past societies interacted with one another, and how cultures changed over time. Archaeologists are stewards of human prehistory, and they rely on historic preservation laws to protect archaeological remains from looting and destruction.

5. Applied anthropologists, who are frequently referred to as practising anthropologists, often use information from the other anthropological specialties to solve practical cross-cultural problems. Medical anthropology connects biological anthropology, cultural anthropology, and applied anthropology, focusing on cultural perceptions of health and illness, suffering, and well-being.

## For Review

1. What is anthropology? What makes it different from the other social sciences? What do the qualities of being *holistic*, *comparative*, *field based*, and *evolutionary* contribute to the discipline?

2. How do anthropologists define culture? In what ways is this definition different from other, less specialized definitions of *culture*? How would the anthropological definition of culture inform the way that anthropologists view data?

3. What makes anthropology a cross-disciplinary discipline? Why is a cross-disciplinary approach advantageous to anthropologists?

4. Describe the main subfields of modern anthropology. Include one area of study for each subfield. What sorts of research projects might require anthropologists from two or more of these subfields to work together?

5. Identify three aspects of biological anthropology that appeal to you, and describe why you think they are interesting.

6. What are some [...]
   anthropology? [...]
   most? Why?

7. Summarize the [...]
   ethnology.

8. How do linguis[...]
   languages? Wh[...]
   ogists' conduc[...]
   need to develo[...]
   Christine Schre[...]

9. What are some [...]
   study? Which o[...]
   interesting? W[...]

10. What are the [...]
    ogy and the oth[...]
    advantages of [...]

11. Why is critical [...]
    of focus withi[...]
    examples of th[...]

## Key Terms

| | | |
|---|---|---|
| anthropology 3 | ethnography 11 | material culture 14 |
| applied anthropology 15 | ethnology 11 | medical anthropology 16 |
| archaeology 14 | evolution 4 | paleoanthropology 8 |
| biocultural organisms 5 | fieldwork 11 | primatology 8 |
| biological anthropology | gender 10 | races 6 |
| (or physical anthropology) 8 | holism 3 | racism 8 |
| comparison 4 | informants 11 | sex 10 |
| cultural anthropology 9 | language 12 | |
| culture 5 | linguistic anthropology 12 | |

## Suggested Readings

Ashmore, Wendy, and Robert J. Sharer. 2013. *Discovering Our Past: A Brief Introduction to Archaeology*. 6th ed. New York: McGraw-Hill. *An engaging introduction to the techniques, assumptions, interests, and findings of modern archaeology.*

Feder, Kenneth. 2014. *Frauds, Myths, and Mysteries: Science and Pseudoscience in Archaeology*. 8th ed. New York: McGraw-Hill. *An entertaining and informative exploration of fascinating frauds and genuine archaeological mysteries that also explains the scientific method.*

Harrison, Julia, and Regna Darnell, eds. 2006. *Historicizing Canadian Anthropology*. Vancouver: UBC Press. *An overview of the history of Canadian anthropology that outlines the progression of the field here in Canada as it developed into the current multi-faceted discipline with distinctively Canadian perspectives.*

Hedican, Edward. 2012. *Social Anthropology: Canadian Perspectives on Culture and Society*. Toronto: Canadian Scholars Press. *An introduction to cultural anthropology from a Canadian perspective, featuring many examples from Canadian anthropologists.*

Hirsch, Jennifer S., Holly Wardlow, Daniel Jordan Smith, Harriet M. Phinney, Shanti Parikh, and Constance A. Nathanson. 2010. *The Secret: Love, Marriage and HIV*. Nashville: Vanderbilt University Press. *An analysis of the cross-cultural social organization of extramarital sexual practices in Mexico, Nigeria, Uganda, Vietnam, and Papua New Guinea and the implications of those practices for married women's HIV risk in those settings.*

Kidder, Tracy. 2004. *Mountains beyond Mountains: The Quest of Dr Paul Farmer, a Man Who Would Cure the World*. New York: Random House. *A highly readable account of anthropologist and physician Paul Farmer's efforts to enlist powerful funders, the World Health Organization, and ordinary people in neglected communities in a quest to bring the best modern medicine to those who need it most.*

Relethford, John. 2012. *The Human Species: An Introduction to Biological Anthropology*. 9th ed. New York: McGraw-Hill. *An excellent, clear introduction to biological anthropology.*

Strang, Veronica. 2009. *What Anthropologists Do*. Oxford: Berg. *An exploration and explanation of the many ways anthropology is being used in everyday life, written specifically for students.*

*Engaging learning tools.* Chapter outlines, marginal definitions of key terms, chapter summaries, questions for review, annotated suggestions for further reading, lists of related websites, and a glossary help students synthesize concepts and offer avenues for further exploration.

# A Full Complement of Ancillaries

This text is supported by an array of supplementary resources, for both students and instructors, designed to enrich the learning experience. The companion websites for *Anthropology* can be found at

**www.oupcanada.com/Lavenda**

## For the Student

- **Student study guide.** An extensive package of review material—including chapter outlines, learning objectives, and multiple choice, true/false, and essay questions, as well as lists of relevant readings, websites, films, and video links—is designed to reinforce and enhance student learning.

## For the Instructor

- **Instructor's manual.** This comprehensive resource features a sample syllabus, chapter summaries, questions for discussion and debate, suggested activities and assignments, and lists of suggested readings, web links, and films.
- **PowerPoint slides.** Dynamic lecture slides summarize key points from each chapter and incorporate figures and tables from the text.
- **Image bank.** This expansive resource contains a wealth of full-colour figures, photographs, and tables that will make classroom lectures engaging and relevant for students.
- **Test generator.** A comprehensive bank of test questions provides hundreds of multiple choice, true/false, and short-answer questions.

**COMPANION WEBSITE**

Robert H. Lavenda, Emily A. Schultz and Cynthia Zutter

*What Does it Mean to Be Human? Canadian Edition*
ISBN 13: 9780199012862

Inspection copy request

Ordering information

Contact & Comments

**About the Book**

*Anthropology* asks what it means to be human, incorporating answers from all four major subfields of anthropology - biological anthropology, archaeology, linguistic anthropology, and cultural anthropology - as well as applied anthropology. Fully conveying the richness of the discipline, this detailed yet accessible introduction helps students gain a deeper understanding of the human condition by looking at themselves and the world around them through an anthropological lens.

**Sample Material**

Get Adobe PDF reader [ US | UK ]

**Instructor Resources**

You need a password to access these resources. Please contact your local Sales and Editorial Representative for more information.

**Student Resources**

# 1 What Is Anthropology?

▲ Women on their way to market, Amhara Region, northern Ethiopia. Photo: Buena Vista Images/Getty Images

## Chapter Outline

This chapter introduces the field of anthropology. We look at what anthropology is and explore its four main subfields: biological anthropology, cultural anthropology, linguistic anthropology, and archaeology. We touch on anthropology's key concept—culture—as well as its key research method—fieldwork. We conclude with a discussion of the ways anthropological insights are relevant in everyday life.

In early 1976, two of the authors of this book (Robert H. Lavenda and Emily A. Schultz) travelled to northern Cameroon, in western Africa, to study social relations in the town of Guider, where they rented a small house. In the first weeks they lived there, Lavenda and Schultz enjoyed spending the warm evenings of the dry season reading and writing in the glow of the house's brightest electric fixture, which illuminated a large, unscreened veranda. After a short time, however, the rains began, and with them appeared swarms of winged termites. These slow-moving insects with fat, two-inch abdomens were attracted to the light on the veranda, and the anthropologists soon found themselves spending more time swatting at the insects than reading or writing. One evening, in a fit of desperation, they rolled up old copies of the international edition of *Newsweek* and began an all-out assault, determined to rid the veranda of every single termite.

The rent Lavenda and Schultz paid for this house included the services of a night watchman. As they launched their attack on the termites, the night watchman suddenly appeared beside the veranda carrying an empty powdered milk tin. When he asked if he could have the insects they had been killing, Lavenda and Schultz were a bit taken aback but warmly invited him to help himself. He moved onto the veranda, quickly collected the corpses of fallen insects, and then joined the anthropologists in going after those termites that were still airborne. Although Lavenda and Schultz became skilled at thwacking the insects with their rolled-up magazines, their skills paled beside those of the night watchman, who simply snatched the termites out of the air with his hand, squeezed them gently, and dropped them into his rapidly filling tin can. The three individuals managed to clear the air of insects—and fill the night watchman's tin—in about ten minutes. The night watchman thanked Lavenda and Schultz and returned to his post, and the anthropologists returned to their books.

The following evening, soon after Lavenda and Schultz took up their usual places on the veranda, the watchman appeared at the steps bearing a tray with two covered dishes. He explained that his wife had prepared the food for them in exchange for their help in collecting termites. The anthropologists accepted the food and carefully lifted the lids. One dish contained *nyiri*, a stiff paste made of red sorghum, a staple of the local diet. The other dish contained another pasty substance with a speckled, salt-and-pepper appearance, which Lavenda and Schultz realized was termite paste prepared from the insects they and the watchman had killed the previous night.

The night watchman waited at the foot of the veranda steps, an expectant smile on his face. Clearly, he did not intend to leave until the others tasted the food his wife had prepared. Lavenda and Schultz looked at each other. They had never eaten insects before or considered them edible in the North American, middle-class diet they were used to. To be sure, "delicacies" like chocolate-covered ants exist, but such items are considered by most North Americans to be food fit only for eccentrics. However, the anthropologists understood the importance of not insulting the night watchman and his wife, who were being so generous. They knew that insects were a favoured food in many human societies and that eating them brought no ill effects (Figure 1.1). So they reached into the dish of *nyiri*, pulling off a small amount. They then used the ball of *nyiri* to scoop up a small portion of termite paste, brought the mixture to their mouths, ate, chewed, and swallowed. The watchman beamed, bid them goodnight, and returned to his post.

Lavenda and Schultz looked at each other in wonder. The sorghum paste had a grainy tang that was rather pleasant. The termite paste tasted mild, like chicken, not unpleasant at all. The anthropologists later wrote to their families about this experience. When their families wrote back, they described how they had told friends about Lavenda and Schultz's experience. Most of their friends had strong negative reactions. But one friend, a home economist, was not shocked at all. She simply commented that termites are a good source of clean protein.

**FIGURE 1.1 |** Many people around the world eat insects. Here, a restaurant worker in Bangkok, Thailand, prepares grubs for cooking.

## What Is Anthropology?

The above anecdote illustrates some of the central elements of the anthropological experience. Anthropologists want to learn about as many different human ways of life as they can. The people they come to know are members of their own society or live on a different continent, in cities or in rural areas. Their ways of life may involve patterns of regular movement across international borders, or they may make permanent homes in the borderlands themselves. Archaeologists reconstruct ancient ways of life from traces left behind in the earth that are hundreds or thousands of years old; anthropologists who strive to reconstruct the origin of the human species itself make use of fossil remains that reach back millions of years into the past. Whatever the case may be, anthropologists are sometimes exposed to practices that startle them. However, as they take the risk of getting to know such ways of life better, they are often treated to the sweet discovery of familiarity. This shock of the unfamiliar becoming familiar—as well as the familiar becoming unfamiliar—is something anthropologists come to expect and is one of the real pleasures of the field. In this book, we share aspects of the anthropological experience in the hope that you, too, will come to find pleasure, insight, and self-recognition from an involvement with the unfamiliar.

**Anthropology** can be defined as the study of human nature, human society, human language, and the human past (adapted from Greenwood and Stini 1977). It is a scholarly discipline that aims to describe in the broadest possible sense what it means to be human. Anthropologists are not alone in focusing their attention on human beings and their creations. Human biology, literature, art, history, linguistics, sociology, political science, economics—all these scholarly disciplines and many more—concentrate on one or another aspect of human life.

What is distinctive about the way anthropologists study human life? As we shall see, anthropology is *holistic, comparative, field based,* and *evolutionary.* First, anthropology emphasizes that all the aspects of human life intersect with one another in complex ways and become integrated with one another over time. Anthropology is thus the *holistic* study of human nature, human society, human language, and the human past. This holism draws together anthropologists whose specializations might otherwise divide them. At the most inclusive

**anthropology** The study of human nature, human society, human language, and the human past.

**holism** A characteristic of the anthropological perspective that describes, at the highest and most inclusive level, how anthropology tries to integrate all that is known about human beings and their activities.

For an alternative definition and use of the term *holism*, see Chapter 2, p. 26.

level, we may thus think of anthropology as the unified (or holistic) study of humans.

Second, in addition to being holistic, anthropology is a discipline interested in comparison. To generalize about human nature, human society, human language, and the human past requires evidence from the widest possible range of human societies. It is not enough, for example, to observe only our own social group, discover that we do not eat insects, and conclude that human beings as a species do not eat insects. When we compare human diets in different societies, we discover that insect eating is quite common and that our North American aversion to eating insects is nothing more than a dietary practice specific to our own society. Indeed, upon reflection we can identify some of our own dietary practices that may seem strange to people in other societies. For example, Canadians have a strong affinity for a gooey liquid that flows from certain trees. Every year, thousands of trees in Quebec and Ontario are used to make some of the best maple syrup in the world, yet not all societies would recognize processed tree sap as a part of their regular diet.

Third, anthropology is also a field-based discipline. That is, for almost all anthropologists, the actual practice of anthropology—its data collection—takes place away from the office and in direct contact with the people, the sites, or the animals that are of interest. Whether they are biological anthropologists studying capuchins in Costa Rica, archaeologists excavating a site high in the Canadian Arctic, linguistic anthropologists learning an unwritten language in the rainforest of Colombia, or cultural anthropologists studying ethnic identity in small-town festivals in Quebec, anthropologists are in direct contact with the sources of their data. For most anthropologists, the richness and complexity of this immersion in other patterns of life is one of our discipline's most distinctive features. Field research

connects anthropologists directly with the lived experiences of other people or other primates or to the material evidence that humans have left behind. Academic anthropologists intersperse field research with the other tasks they perform as university professors. Other anthropologists—applied or practising anthropologists—regularly spend most or all of their time interacting with communities in the field. All anthropology begins with a specific group of people (or primates) and always returns to them as well.

Lastly, anthropologists look for characteristics that unite all of humanity and that are valid across space and time. Because anthropologists are interested in documenting and explaining change in the human past, evolution is at the core of the anthropological perspective. Anthropologists examine both *biological and cultural evolution* of the human species. *Biological evolution* looks at how the physical features and life processes of human beings have changed over time. It also examines human origins and the genetic variation and inheritance in living human populations. *Cultural evolution* concerns change over time in beliefs, behaviours, and material objects that shape human development and social life.

As we will see in Chapter 7, early anthropologists' discussions of cultural evolution emphasized a series of universal stages. However, this approach has been rejected by contemporary anthropologists who talk about cultural evolution, like William Durham (1991) and Robert Boyd (e.g., Richerson and Boyd 2005). Currently, there are lively theoretical debates in anthropology and other related fields like evolutionary biology and developmental psychology concerning culture change and whether or not it should be referred to as "cultural evolution." In the midst of this debate, one of anthropology's most important contributions to the study of human evolution remains the demonstration that biological evolution is not the same as cultural evolution. Distinction between the two remains important as a way of demonstrating the fallacies and incoherence of arguments claiming that everything people do or think can be explained biologically, for example, in terms of "genes" or "race" or "sex."

comparison A characteristic of the anthropological perspective that requires anthropologists to study similarities and differences across as many human societies as possible before generalizing about human beings and their activities.

evolution A characteristic of the anthropological perspective that requires anthropologists to place their observations about human beings and their activities in a temporal framework that takes into consideration change over time.

## What Is the Concept of Culture?

A consequence of human evolution that had the most profound impact on human nature and human society was the emergence of culture, which can be defined as sets of learned behaviour and ideas that human beings acquire as members of society. Human beings use culture to adapt to and transform the world in which they live.

Human beings are more dependent than any other species on learning for survival because they have no instincts that automatically protect us and help us find food and shelter. Instead, we have come to use our large and complex brains to learn from other members of society what we need to know to survive. Learning is a primary focus of childhood, which is longer for humans than for any other species.

From the anthropological perspective, the concept of *culture* is central to explanations of why human beings are what they are and why they do what they do. Anthropologists are frequently able to show that members of a particular social group behave in a particular way *not* because the behaviour was programmed by their genes, but because they observed other people and copied what they did. For example, North Americans typically do not eat insects, but this behaviour is not the result of genetic programming. Rather, North Americans have never seen any of their friends or family eat insects, have been told as children that eating insects is horrible, and do not eat insects themselves. Yet North Americans can eat insects with no ill effects. This dietary behaviour can be explained in terms of culture rather than biology.

However, to understand the power of culture, anthropologists must also consider human biology. Anthropologists in North America traditionally have been trained in both areas so that they can understand how living organisms work and become acquainted with comparative information about a wide range of human societies. As a result, they can better evaluate how biology and culture contribute to different forms of human behaviour. Indeed, most anthropologists reject explanations of human behaviour that force them to choose either biology or culture as the cause. Instead, they emphasize that human beings are biocultural organisms. Our biological makeup—our brain, nervous system, and anatomy—is the outcome of developmental processes to which our genes and cellular chemistry contribute in fundamental ways. It also makes us organisms capable of creating and using culture. Without these biological endowments, human culture as we know it would not exist. At the same time, our survival as biological organisms depends on learned

ways of thinking and acting that help us find food, shelter, and mates and that teach us how to rear our children. Our biological endowment, rich as it is, does not provide us with instincts that would automatically take care of these survival needs. Human biology makes culture possible; human culture makes human biological survival possible.

For further discussion of how humans use culture to adapt to and transform the world in which they live, see Chapter 2, p. 23.

## What Makes Anthropology a Cross-Disciplinary Discipline?

Because of its diversity, anthropology does not easily fit into any of the standard academic classifications. The discipline is usually listed as a social science, but it spans the natural sciences and the humanities as well. What it is *not*, as we will see, is the study of the "*exotic*," the "*primitive*," or the "*savage*," terms originally used in colonial times that anthropologists rejected long ago. Figure 1.2 illustrates the variety of interests that fall under the anthropological umbrella.

Traditionally, North American anthropology has been divided into four subfields: *biological anthropology*, *cultural anthropology*, *linguistic anthropology*, and *archaeology*. Because of their commitment to holism, many anthropology departments try to represent most or all of the subfields in their academic programs. However, universities in other parts of the world, such as Europe, usually do not bring all these specialties together. Many North American anthropologists, however, associate holistic four-field North American anthropology with the successful repudiation of nineteenth-century scientific racism by Franz Boas and other early twentieth-century anthropologists. They also value four-field anthropology as a protected "trading zone" within which anthropologists are encouraged to bring together fresh concepts and knowledge from a variety of research traditions. Canadian anthropologist Regna Darnell, a distinguished professor at Western University, has intensively reviewed, documented, and

culture Sets of learned behaviour and ideas that human beings acquire as members of society.

biocultural organisms Organisms (in this case, human beings) whose defining features are codetermined by biological and cultural factors.

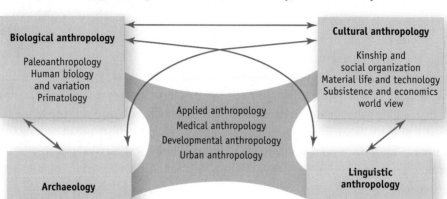

**Anthropology**
The integrated study of human nature, human society, and human history.

FIGURE 1.2 | In the United States and Canada, anthropology is traditionally divided into four specialties: biological anthropology, cultural anthropology, linguistic anthropology, and archaeology. Applied anthropology draws on information provided by the other four specialties.

analyzed the successful integration of the four fields of anthropology in academia throughout North America (1992, 1998, 2000; see also Harrison and Darnell 2006 for an overview of the history of anthropology in Canada).

Anthropological holism is attractive even to those who were not trained in North America. British anthropologist Tim Ingold (1994, xvii), for example, argues, "The best anthropological writing is distinguished by its receptiveness to ideas springing from work in subjects far beyond its conventional boundaries, and by its ability to connect these ideas in ways that would not have occurred to their originators, who may be more enclosed in their particular disciplinary frameworks." We share the views of Darnell and Ingold: trained in holistic four-field anthropology, we continue to value the unique perspective it brings to the study of human nature and human society. Indeed, as the organizers of a relatively recent anthropological conference observed, "Even those who were the least persuaded that the traditional four-field organization of [North] American anthropology was still viable (if it ever was) came away with

races  Social groupings that allegedly reflect biological differences.

a strong sense that the subfields had a great deal to say to one another and indeed needed one another" (McKinnon and Silverman 2005, viii).

## Biological Anthropology

Since the nineteenth century, when anthropology was developing as an academic field, anthropologists have studied human beings as living organisms in order to discover what makes them different from or similar to other animals. Early interest in these matters was a by-product of centuries of exploration and colonial expansion. Western Europeans found tremendous variation in the physical appearance of peoples around the world and tried to make sense of these differences. Some researchers developed a series of elaborate techniques to measure different observable features of human populations, including skin colour, hair type, and skull shape, hoping to find scientific evidence that would allow them to classify all the peoples of the world into a set of unambiguous categories based on distinct sets of biological attributes. Such categories were called **races**, and many scientists were convinced that clearcut criteria for racial classification would be discovered if careful measurements were made on enough people from a range of different populations.

## In Their Own Words

## Anthropology as a Vocation

*Michel Bouchard, an associate professor at the University of Northern British Columbia, describes his personal journey as an anthropologist. Moving throughout the circumpolar region and Canada, Bouchard has investigated a variety of topics, ranging from individual and group identity formation to associations between language and status to interpretations of nationalism across different populations.*

From a small town in northern Alberta to the distant tundra beyond the Arctic Circle of Russia, I have sought to understand identity, what makes us "Us," and how and why we distinguish between this "Us" and an "Other." This journey entailed trying to understand how language is used within communities, but also how the mundane rituals of daily life define us. Thus, I have analyzed Russian animated children's movies and visited graveyards in a largely Russian-speaking community on the margins of the Republic of Estonia to understand Russian nationalism, and I have sought to understand why in my home community of Falher, Alberta, it is "natural" to speak to babies and dogs in French, while English is used whenever there is a unilingual English-speaker within earshot because it is "polite."

After completing my BA at the University of Toronto, I continued on to the Université Laval in Québec to pursue my graduate research. Not having much funding, I chose to return home to live in my parents' basement while I conducted a study of my own community. I was a fourth-generation French-speaker from Alberta who had grown up in a small region where the French language was still the dominant language throughout the community. Yet in other areas of Alberta, the province in which both my parents and I had been born, I was made to feel a stranger, as most Albertans believed that all French-speakers lived in Québec. As I conducted my research, I came to grips with issues of status and stigma, and how these issues influence the use of

language and language maintenance. Even before they start school, children know which language is dominant, which group has high status, and they act accordingly. Today I continue to investigate such themes as I conduct new research, in an attempt to understand how such feelings of stigma can be countered to ensure that minority languages are not lost.

From Falher I pushed into the Baltics and then Russia to better understand issues of nation and nationalism. There, I hit a roadblock, as the existing theory did not truly allow a nuanced explanation of how nation was understood and identity formulated. For over a decade, I have been working to develop a new, more relevant theoretical construct of nation—one that recognizes how nations are continually reconstituted in narrative in an act that I call *curating*—while acknowledging that nations are not modern inventions, but rather constructs that took root during the medieval period.

Recently, I have begun exploring a new topic, Métis ethnogenesis (i.e., the process by which Métis people have formed—and continue to form—a collective ethnic identity). This latest research seeks to understand how the emergence of a Métis identity is tied to the earlier Canadien identity that was adopted by the French-speakers born in the colony of New France in the seventeenth century. I continue to use historical documents with an anthropological gaze to see how communities emerge and are shaped over time.

Source: Courtesy of Michel Bouchard, Professor at the University of Northern British Columbia.

European scientists first applied racial categories to the peoples of Europe itself, but their classifications soon included non-European peoples, who were coming under increasing political and economic domination through colonial expansion by European and European American capitalist societies. These peoples differed from "white" Europeans not only because of their darker skin colour but also because of their unfamiliar languages and customs. In most cases, their technologies were also no match for the potent armaments of the West. In the early eighteenth century, the European biologist Carolus Linnaeus (Carl von Linné, 1707–1778) classified known human populations into four races (Amerindian, European, Asian, and Negro) based on skin colour (reddish, white, yellow, and black, respectively). Linnaeus also connected racial membership with the mental and moral attributes of group members. Thus, he wrote, Europeans were "fickle, sanguine, blue-eyed, gentle, and governed by laws," whereas Negros were "choleric, obstinate, contented, and regulated by custom" and Asians were "grave, avaricious, dignified, and ruled by opinion" (Molnar 2001, 5–6).

In the nineteenth century, influential natural scientists such as Louis Agassiz (1807–1873), Samuel George Morton (1799–1851), Francis Galton (1822–1911), and Paul Broca (1824–1880) built on this idea of race, ranking different populations of the world in terms of skull size; they found the brains of "white" Europeans and North Americans to be larger and saw the other "races" as representing varying grades of inferiority, with the two lowest grades being represented by Amerindians and Africans (Gould 1996). These findings were used to validate the social practice of racism: the systematic oppression of members of one or more socially defined "races" by members of another socially defined "race" that is justified in terms of the supposed inherent biological superiority of the rulers and the supposed inherent biological inferiority of those they rule.

For expanded discussion of the methods anthropologists use to study human variation without using the term *race*, see Chapter 4, pp. 80–9. For a discussion of present-day racism and associated social issues in Canada, see Chapter 14, p. 404.

Biological or physical anthropology as a separate discipline had its origins in the work of scholars like these, whose training was in some other discipline, often medicine. Johann Blumenbach (1752–1840), for example, whom some have called the "father of physical anthropology," was trained as a physician. Blumenbach identified five different races (Caucasoid, Mongoloid, American, Ethiopian, and Malayan), and his classification was influential in the later nineteenth and twentieth centuries (Molnar 2001, 6). He and his contemporaries

racism  The systematic oppression of members of one or more socially defined "races" by members of another socially defined "race" that is justified in terms of the supposed inherent biological superiority of the rulers and the supposed inherent biological inferiority of those they rule.

biological anthropology (or physical anthropology)  The specialty of anthropology that looks at human beings as biological organisms and tries to discover what characteristics make them different from other organisms and what characteristics they share.

primatology  The study of non-human primates, the closest living relatives of human beings.

paleoanthropology  The study of human fossils and associated remains to understand our evolutionary history.

assumed that the races of "mankind" (as they would have said) were fixed and unchanging subdivisions of humanity.

However, as scientists learned more about biological variation in human populations, some of them came to realize that traits traditionally used to identify races, such as skin colour, did not correlate well with other physical and biological traits, let alone mental and moral traits. Indeed, scientists could not even agree about how many human races there were or where the boundaries between them should be drawn.

By the early twentieth century, some anthropologists and biologists were arguing that "race" was a cultural label invented by human beings to sort people into groups and that races with distinct sets of biological attributes simply did not exist. Anthropologists like Franz Boas (1858–1942), for example, who in the early 1900s founded the first department of anthropology in North America, at Columbia University in New York, had long been uncomfortable with racial classifications in anthropology. Boas and his students devoted much energy to debunking racist stereotypes, using both their knowledge of biology and their understanding of culture. As the discipline of anthropology developed in the United States and later in Canada, students were trained in both human biology and human culture to provide them with the tools to fight racial stereotyping. After World War II, this position gained increasing strength in North American anthropology, under the forceful leadership of anthropologist Sherwood Washburn (1911–2000). The "new" physical anthropology Washburn developed at the University of California, Berkeley, repudiated racial classification and shifted attention to patterns of variation and adaptation within the human species as a whole. This shift in emphasis led many of Washburn's followers to define their specialty as biological anthropology, a move that highlighted their differences with the older "physical anthropology" devoted to racial classification.

Some biological anthropologists work in the fields of primatology (the study of the closest living relatives of human beings, the non-human primates), paleoanthropology (the study of fossilized bones and teeth of our earliest ancestors), and human skeletal biology (measuring and comparing the shapes and sizes—or morphology—of human bones and teeth using skeletal remains from different human populations) (Figure 1.3).

FIGURE 1.3 | Some biological anthropologists are primatologists, such as Linda Fedigan, who studies capuchins, spider monkeys, and other primates in their natural habitats and teaches at the University of Calgary (a). Other biological anthropologists are paleoanthropologists, such as Pamela Willoughby, who studies ancient human ancestors and teaches at the University of Alberta (b).

Newer specialties focus on human adaptability in different ecological settings, on human growth and development, or on the connections between a population's evolutionary history and its susceptibility to disease (e.g., paleodemography). Recent genetic studies in Quebec, for example, have investigated the link between certain medical issues occurring among current populations and similar issues among those who settled New France generations ago (Bherer et al. 2011). In addition, forensic anthropologists use their knowledge of human skeletal anatomy to aid human rights investigations in places like Bosnia and Herzegovina (Skinner et al. 2002) or assist law enforcers with the identification of human remains (Mayne Correia and Beattie 2002). In both of these cases, biological anthropologists are participating in applied anthropology (see the discussion of applied anthropology below).

And molecular anthropologists trace chemical similarities and differences in the immune system, an interest that has led to active research on the virus that causes HIV/AIDS.

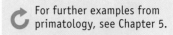 For further examples from primatology, see Chapter 5.

Whether they study human biology, primates, or the fossils of our ancestors, biological anthropologists clearly share many methods and theories used in the natural sciences—primarily biology, ecology, chemistry, and geology. What tends to set biological anthropologists apart from their non-anthropological colleagues is the holistic, comparative, and evolutionary perspective that has been part of their anthropological training. That perspective reminds them always to consider their work as only part of the overall study of human nature, human society, and the human past.

## Cultural Anthropology

The second specialty within anthropology is **cultural anthropology**, which is sometimes called *sociocultural anthropology*, *social anthropology*, or *ethnology*. By the early twentieth century, anthropologists realized that racial biology could not be used to explain why everyone in the world did not dress the same, speak the same language, pray to the same god, or eat insects for dinner. About the same time, anthropologists such as Margaret Mead (1901–1978) (Figure 1.4) were showing that the biology of sexual difference could not be used to predict how men and women might behave or what tasks they would perform in any given society. Anthropologists concluded that something other than biology had to be responsible for these variations. They suggested that this "something else" was culture.

Many anthropologists did significant research throughout the twentieth century to separate human biological variation from human cultural practices, showing that these practices could not be reduced to "racial" difference. By the latter part of the twentieth century, anthropologists also regularly distinguished

**cultural anthropology** The specialty of anthropology that shows how variation in the beliefs and behaviours of members of different human groups is shaped by sets of learned behaviours and ideas that human beings acquire as members of society—that is, by culture.

**FIGURE 1.4 |** Margaret Mead on the island of Samoa in the 1920s. In the early twentieth century, Mead and other cultural anthropologists worked to identify and describe the difference between biological sex and culturally determined gender roles.

between the biological **sex** of an individual and the culturally shaped **gender** roles considered appropriate for members of each sex in a given society. Many anthropological studies have highlighted how gender roles shape social changes in our global world; for example, Canadian anthropologist Marie-France Labrecque, at Université Laval, has spent many years researching the importance of women's roles in Latin America (see

**sex** Observable physical characteristics that distinguish two kinds of humans, females and males, needed for biological reproduction.

**gender** The cultural construction of beliefs and behaviours considered appropriate for each sex.

Labrecque 2012, 222). As we shall see throughout the text, attention to gender has become an integral part of all anthropological work.

Because people everywhere use culture to adapt to and transform everything in the wider world in which they live, the field of cultural anthropology is vast. Cultural anthropologists tend to specialize in one or another domain of human cultural activity. Some study the ways particular groups of human beings organize themselves to carry out collective tasks, whether economic, political, or spiritual. This focus within cultural anthropology bears the closest resemblance to the discipline of sociology, and from it has come the identification of anthropology as one of the social sciences.

Sociology and anthropology developed during the same period and share similar interests in social organization. What differentiated anthropology from sociology was the anthropological interest in comparing varieties of human social life around the globe. In the racist framework of nineteenth- and early-twentieth-century European and North American societies, some people viewed sociology as the study of "civilized" industrial societies and labelled anthropology as the study of all other societies, lumped together as "primitive." Today, by contrast, anthropologists are concerned with studying *all* human societies, and they reject the labels *civilized* and *primitive* for the same reason they reject the term *race*. Contemporary anthropologists do research in urban and rural settings around the world and among members of all societies, including their own.

Anthropologists discovered that people in many non-Western societies do not organize themselves into bureaucracies, yet they still manage to carry out successfully the full range of human activity because they developed institutions of relatedness that enabled them to organize social groups through which they could live their lives. One form of relatedness, called *kinship*, links people to one another on the basis of birth, marriage, and nurturance. The study of kinship has become highly developed in anthropology and remains a focus of interest today. In addition, anthropologists have described a variety of forms of social groups organized according to different principles, such as secret societies, age sets, and numerous forms of complex political organization, including states. In recent years, cultural anthropologists have studied contemporary issues of gender and sexuality, transnational labour migration, urbanization, globalization, the post–Cold War resurgence of ethnicity and nationalism around the globe, and debates about human rights.

Cultural anthropologists have investigated the patterns of material life found in different human groups. Among the most striking are worldwide variations in clothing, housing, tools, and techniques for getting food and making material goods. Some anthropologists specialize in the study of technologies in different societies or in the evolution of technology over time. Those interested in material life also describe the natural setting for which technologies have been developed and analyze the way technologies and environments shape each other. Others have investigated the way non-Western people have responded to the political and economic challenges of colonialism and the capitalist industrial technology that accompanied it.

People everywhere are increasingly making use of material goods and technologies produced outside their own societies. Anthropologists have been able to show that, contrary to many expectations, non-Western people do not slavishly imitate Western ways. Instead, they make use of Western technologies in ways that are creative and often unanticipated but that make sense in their own local cultural context. For example, some anthropologists are currently tracing the various ways in which populations both inside and outside the West make use of cyber technologies for their own social and cultural purposes.

As cultural anthropologists have become increasingly aware of the sociocultural influences that stretch across space to affect local communities, they have also become sensitive to those that stretch over time. As a result, many contemporary cultural anthropologists make serious efforts to place their cultural analyses in detailed historical context. Cultural anthropologists who do comparative studies of language, music, dance, art, poetry, philosophy, religion, or ritual often share many of the interests of specialists in the disciplines of fine arts and humanities.

Cultural anthropologists, no matter what their area of specialization, ordinarily collect their data during an extended period of close involvement with the people in whose way of life they are interested. This period of research, called fieldwork, has as its central feature the anthropologists' involvement in the everyday routine of those among whom they live (Figure 1.5). People who share information about their

FIGURE 1.5 | Cultural anthropologist Robert Laughlin with members of the Sna Jtz'ibajom puppet theatre troupe in San Cristóbal de las Casas, Mexico. Cultural anthropologists talk to many people, observe their actions, and participate as fully as possible in a group's way of life.

culture with anthropologists have traditionally been called informants; however, some anthropologists object to the use of this term because it suggests a role that is limited to supplying information for the benefit of the researcher. Therefore, some contemporary anthropologists prefer to describe these individuals as *respondents*, *collaborators*, *teachers*, *friends*, or simply *the people I work with* because these terms emphasize a relationship of equality and reciprocity. Fieldworkers gain insight into another culture by participating in social activities with members of that culture and by observing those activities as outsiders. This research method, known as *participant-observation*, is central to cultural anthropology.

Cultural anthropologists write about what they have learned in scholarly articles or books and sometimes document the lives of the people they work with on film or video. An ethnography is a description of "the customary social behaviours of an identifiable group of people" (Wolcott 1999, 252–3); ethnology is the

**fieldwork** An extended period of close involvement with the people in whose way of life anthropologists are interested, during which anthropologists ordinarily collect most of their data.

**informants** People in a particular culture who work with anthropologists and provide them with insights about the local way of life. Also called *respondents, collaborators, teachers,* or *friends*.

**ethnography** An anthropologist's written or otherwise recorded description of a particular culture.

**ethnology** The comparative study of two or more cultures.

comparative study of two or more such groups. Thus, cultural anthropologists who write ethnographies are sometimes called *ethnographers*, and anthropologists who compare ethnographic information on many different cultural practices are sometimes called *ethnologists*. But not all anthropological writing is ethnographic. Some anthropologists specialize in reconstructing the history of our discipline, tracing, for example, how anthropologists' fieldwork practices have changed over time and how these changes may be related to wider political, economic, and social changes within the societies from which they came and within which they did their research.

## Linguistic Anthropology

Perhaps the most striking cultural feature of our species is language: the system of arbitrary vocal symbols we use to encode our experience of the world and of one another. People use language to talk about all areas of their lives, from material to spiritual. Linguistic anthropology therefore studies language, not only as a form of symbolic communication, but also as a major carrier of important cultural information. In the early twentieth century, the focus of many anthropologists was to transcribe non-Western languages and to produce grammars and dictionaries of those languages as a means of preserving them from being lost. This sort of preservation remains important today as many languages are being lost around the world as modernization and rapid globalization require the use of European languages in place of traditional languages. Today, many of these traditional languages are being taught in schools to the younger generations of Indigenous peoples to revitalize and maintain traditional knowledge and cultural practices.

Contemporary linguistic anthropologists and their counterparts in sociology (called *sociolinguists*) study the way language differences correlate with differences in gender, race, class, or ethnic identity.

---

language   The system of arbitrary vocal symbols used to encode one's experience of the world and of others.

linguistic anthropology   The specialty of anthropology concerned with the study of human languages.

---

Some have specialized in studying what happens when speakers are fluent in more than one language and must choose which language to use under what circumstances. Others have written about what happens when speakers of unrelated languages are forced to communicate with one another, producing languages called *pidgins*. Some linguistic anthropologists study sign languages. Others look at the ways children learn language or the styles and strategies followed by fluent speakers engaged in conversation. More recently, linguistic anthropologists have paid attention to the way political ideas in a society contribute to people's ideas of what may or may not be said and the strategies speakers devise to escape these forms of censorship. Some take part in policy discussions about literacy and language standardization and address the challenges faced by speakers of languages that are being displaced by international languages of commerce and technology such as English. Some linguistic anthropologists and others who study language even apply their knowledge to help create new languages for movies and TV shows like Klingon in *Star Trek* or Valyrian in *Game of Thrones* (Figure 1.6) (see the "Anthropology in the Contemporary World" box).

In all these cases, linguistic anthropologists try to understand language in relation to the broader cultural and historical contexts that make it possible. For example, in Canada, the interplay between our

FIGURE 1.6   |   Some linguistic anthropologists have helped to create new languages for movies and TV shows. Canadian linguistic anthropologist Christine Schreyer, shown here, developed a written form of Kryptonian for the 2013 movie *Man of Steel*.

## Anthropology in the Contemporary World

### Language Revitalization: What Can We Learn from Conlang Communities?

It is not every day that an anthropologist finds herself on the set of a big-budget Hollywood movie production. Yet this is what happened to Canadian linguistic anthropologist Christine Schreyer, an assistant professor at the University of British Columbia's Okanagan campus. Schreyer was asked by the studio in charge of production to develop the written form of Superman's alien language, Kryptonian, for the 2013 movie *Man of Steel*.

Schreyer's training as an anthropologist equipped her with an intimate understanding of the interdependence that exists between language and culture, as each influences and shapes the other. Her work for *Man of Steel* was successful because she constructed the language in relation to the characteristics of Kryptonian culture that had been developed in past Superman comic books and movies. Yet the principles involved in creating and transmitting this fictional language have even greater significance for language revitalization in the real world, a pressing issue among linguistic anthropologists today.

For years before she became involved with *Man of Steel*, Schreyer had been studying conlangs (constructed languages) in order to grasp how and why these linguistic creations have become established forms of communication among fandoms the world over. Indeed, many conlangs—such as those used in *Star Trek* and *The Lord of the Rings* trilogy—have grown substantial user communities since their creation. Schreyer decided to focus on speakers of the Na'vi language, which was created to be spoken by the aliens in the 2009 movie *Avatar*. In addition to learning about the Na'vi-speaking community itself, Schreyer was interested in discovering what threatened or endangered language communities might be able to learn from the successful spread of Na'vi.

Schreyer quickly discovered that conlang users have made expert use of social media and IT to build up their communities. While these mediums have not always been useful to minority communities endeavouring to revitalize their traditional languages, Schreyer believes that there is potential for them to be more productive in the future. The key lies in analyzing why conlangs have been so successful and then applying the principles behind that success to endangered languages.

At least part of the answer seems to lie in the perceived prestige associated with each language. Conlangs draw their prestige from the lore surrounding the characters who use them in fictional realities. People generally wish to learn conlangs because of their attachment to a larger universe of wonder and fantasy. Similarly, a lingua franca such as English or Portuguese gains its prestige from dominating the economic marketplace—a realm that many people perceive as offering great economic and other benefits. Where do minority languages draw their prestige from? Predominately, this prestige originates in tradition and a sense of belonging to a culture—a sense of identity. Finding a way to increase the level of prestige attached to an endangered language, to increase its appeal to potential users, is vital to revitalization. How this can be achieved depends on the community in question.

Language revitalization is a very current, very critical issue in linguistic anthropology today. As different societies converge in the increasingly globalized marketplace, there seems to be little room for traditional languages. Yet these languages remain key to individual and group identities, and their preservation is important to the promotion of equal human rights across the globe. While not yet fully explored, the question of why some people are willing to spend so much time and energy learning conlangs may one day lead to new and creative solutions to this important issue.

*To read the original interview on which this piece is based, see http://blog.wennergren.org/2014/08. See also Schreyer 2011.*

two official languages is deeply affected by past and present tensions between French- and English-speaking Canadians. Because highly specialized training in linguistics as well as anthropology is required for people who practise it, linguistic anthropology has long been recognized as a separate subfield of anthropology. Contemporary linguistic anthropologists continue to be trained in this way, and many cultural anthropologists also receive linguistics training as part of their professional preparation.

# Archaeology

**Archaeology** is another major specialty within anthropology. It is sometimes referred to as the cultural anthropology of the human past. Archaeologists are committed to the discovery and systematic study of the remnants of our past—everything from piles of bones and stones to the foundations of early great cities like Teotihuacan in Mexico. Through the analysis of **material culture**, archaeologists focus on reconstructing human prehistory, the long stretch of time before the development of writing. Archaeologists seek to understand past human cultural activity using a variety of methods. They conduct surveys of areas to understand where people lived; they try to reconstruct the types of houses in which people dwelled; they study prehistoric garbage to understand what people ate; and they look closely at and even recreate prehistoric tools people made to survive. And of course, archaeologists also excavate or dig archaeological *sites* (i.e., areas with high concentrations of human cultural remains) to recover *artifacts* (i.e., portable objects created or modified by humans).

Archaeologists rarely work alone. The complexity and vastness of human prehistory often requires a large team (or crew) of specialists working alongside archaeologists to assist in carrying out archaeological research. These teams may consist of geologists, botanists, wildlife biologists, metallurgists, pottery specialists, or others. Together, these experts work to better understand how humans lived in the past, what they ate to survive, how they manufactured their tools, and even what the environment was like when the site was occupied.

Archaeologists often work alongside paleoanthropologists as well, especially where human remains or burial sites are discovered, and their findings often complement each other. For example, archaeological information regarding successive stone-tool traditions in a particular region may correlate with human fossils that indicate ancient humans' prehistoric occupation of that region. In order to make these correlations,

archaeologists must establish a clear sequence of events, or a timeline, for the artifacts and sites. To do this, they use a wide variety of dating techniques to establish the approximate ages of the *artifacts* (see the "Focus on Four Fields" feature on pp. 162–5 for more information).

Surveys of geographical areas are also important to create distribution maps of sites and artifacts across space. From this information, archaeologists can generate hypotheses about when certain societies existed, what their territorial ranges were, and what patterns of sociocultural change they experienced. For example, archaeologists often compare the appearance of certain cultural artifacts, like pottery or stone tools, at one site to the appearance of those artifacts at another site, which allows them to hypothesize about the nature and degree of social contact between different peoples in the past. The sites and artifacts that archaeologists investigate sometimes relate to relatively recent events in the human past. For example, some archaeologists study what remains of seventeenth- and eighteenth-century fur-trade posts or explorers' ships (see Figure 1.7) or abandoned nineteenth-century industrial sites. Some contemporary archaeologists even dig through layers of garbage deposited by human beings within the last two or three decades, often uncovering surprising information about contemporary consumption patterns.

It is important to note here that, unlike most fictional archaeologists like Indiana Jones and Lara Croft, anthropological archaeologists have ethical responsibilities to maintain and conserve the artifacts of human prehistory. For-profit looting of artifacts, along with the destruction of archaeological sites caused by industrial development, are still very common, especially in countries with political unrest and widespread poverty. To combat such harmful actions, historic preservation laws exist throughout the world; these laws require archaeologists to seek government permission to excavate sites and to follow specific protocols for preserving and curating artifacts. Archaeologists are considered stewards of the past and accountable to the public for the interpretation, conservation, and preservation of human prehistory. Shared ethics and methods regarding the discovery of archaeological sites and artifacts are explicitly outlined on the websites for the Society for American Archaeology (SAA) and the Canadian Archaeological

---

**archaeology** The specialty of anthropology that studies the human past by analyzing material remains left behind by earlier societies.

**material culture** Objects created or shaped by humans and given meaning through cultural practices.

FIGURE 1.8 | Some applied forensic anthropologists use their knowledge of skeletal anatomy to aid in human rights investigations. Here, a forensic expert working with the International Commission on Missing Persons (ICMP) checks human remains found in a mass grave in the village of Tomasica in Bosnia and Herzegovina.

FIGURE 1.7 | Canadian anthropologist Owen Beattie's work in the Canadian Arctic has led to a greater understanding of what became of the members of the "lost" Franklin expedition, which disappeared only months after beginning its search for the Northwest Passage in 1845.

Association (CAA). A final note: the majority of professional archaeologists work in the field of cultural resource management (CRM), which is also known as salvage archaeology. These archaeologists work alongside environmental scientists to assess locations that are slated to be developed for industry and infrastructure projects. As a result, thousands of new sites are documented annually, and our knowledge of the human past is growing exponentially.

## Applied Anthropology

**Applied anthropology** is the subfield of anthropology in which anthropologists use information gathered from the other anthropological specialties to propose solutions to practical cross-cultural problems (Figure 1.8). Some may use a particular group of people's ideas about illness and health to introduce new public health practices in a way that makes sense to and will be accepted by members of the group. Others may use knowledge of traditional social organization to ease the problems of refugees trying to settle in a new land. Yet others may apply this knowledge to help communities adapt to changing local circumstances. A great example of this is the work being done by Mark Nuttall, from the

University of Alberta, regarding the varied perceptions of northern Indigenous peoples to climate change and how policy makers can work with these groups to facilitate their successful adaptation to their changing environments (2009; see also Crate and Nuttall 2009). Still other applied anthropologists may use their knowledge of traditional and Western methods of cultivation to help farmers increase their crop yields. Given the growing concern throughout the world with the effects of different technologies on the environment, this kind of applied anthropology holds promise as a way of bringing together Western and non-Western knowledge in order to create sustainable technologies that minimize pollution and environmental degradation. In addition, some applied anthropologists have become management consultants or carry out market research, and their findings may contribute to the design of new products.

In recent decades, some anthropologists have become involved in policy issues, actively participating in social processes that attempt to shape the future of those people among whom they work (Moore 2005, 3). This development has involved a change in our understanding of what applied anthropology is. Anthropologists in Canada have a long history of

**applied anthropology** The subfield of anthropology in which anthropologists use information gathered from the other anthropological specialties to solve practical cross-cultural problems.

working with First Nations bands to assist with government negotiations regarding land use and resource development as well as self-government. In fact, this focus on collaborating with First Nations communities is what makes Canadian anthropology unique in North America (Waldram 2010). In his overview of the intersection between applied anthropology and Aboriginal issues in Canada, Edward Hedican (2008) describes the many instances in which anthropologists have been employed by various bands to mediate development issues like the James Bay hydroelectric dam in Quebec (Salisbury et. al 1972) and the proposed MacKenzie Valley Pipeline through the Northwest Territories (Salisbury et. al 1974). Additionally, in Canada and elsewhere, applied anthropologists often work in the legal arena, providing their expertise to support tribal groups' efforts to claim official self-government status (e.g., Weaver 1997), or to defend Indigenous peoples' land rights (e.g., Asch 1984, 2014).

Although many anthropologists believe that applied work can be done within any of the traditional four fields of anthropology, increasing numbers in recent years have come to view applied anthropology as a separate field of professional specialization (see Figure 1.2). More and more universities in Canada and the United States have begun to develop courses and programs in a variety of forms of applied anthropology. Anthropologists who work for government agencies or non-profit organizations or in other non-university settings often describe what they do as the *anthropology of practice*. In the twenty-first century, it has been predicted that more than half of all new PhDs in anthropology will become applied or practising anthropologists rather than take up positions as faculty in university departments of anthropology.

## Medical Anthropology

**Medical anthropology** is one of the most rapidly growing branches of applied anthropology. Over the past half century or so, it has developed into an important anthropological specialty that has offered

new ways to link biological and cultural anthropology. Medical anthropology concerns itself with human health—the factors that contribute to disease or illness and the ways that human populations deal with disease or illness (Baer, Singer, and Susser 2003, 3). In many cases, medical anthropologists have cross-appointments with schools of medicine and may have been trained as either nurses or medical doctors. Some early work done in Canada in this field was led by Emőke Szathmáry (1986), who examined the high incidence of diabetes among the Dene, suggesting that there is a connection between the introduction of processed, westernized foods and the rise of diabetes in this population. Medical anthropologists may consider the physiological and cultural variables that are involved with the perception of human health and disease, the environmental features that affect human well-being, and the way the human body adapts to various environments. Contemporary medical anthropologists engage in work that directly addresses the anthropological proposition that human beings must be understood as biocultural organisms (Figure 1.9).

Particularly significant has been the development of *critical medical anthropology*, which links questions of human health and illness in local

For further discussion of human illness in relation to social inequality, see Chapter 14, pp. 394–6.

settings to social, economic, and political processes operating on a regional, national, or global scale. A good example is the work of Dr Sandra Hyde (2007) from McGill University, who has studied the spread of HIV/AIDS in China, including how political forces in China have shaped public perception and response to the disease, and how the rise of HIV/AIDS has affected various groups throughout the country. Critical medical anthropologists have been among the most vocal in pointing out how various forms of suffering and disease cannot be explained only by the presence of microbes in a diseased body, but may depend on—or be made worse by—the presence of social inequality and a lack of access to health care. According to anthropologist Merrill Singer (1998, 195), critical medical anthropology "is committed to the 'making social' and the 'making political' of health and medicine." Thus, critical medical anthropologists pay attention to the way social divisions based on class, "race," gender, and

**medical anthropology** The specialty of anthropology that concerns itself with human health—the factors that contribute to disease or illness and the ways that human populations deal with disease or illness.

FIGURE 1.9 | Medical anthropologist Andrea Wiley is shown here in a high-altitude setting in the Himalayas of Ladakh, India, where she studied maternal and child health. Working directly with informants in the field gives medical anthropologists the opportunity to study the cultural as well as biological factors that impact human health.

ethnicity can block access to medical attention or make people more vulnerable to disease and suffering. They draw attention to the way traditional Western biomedicine "encourages people to fight disease rather than to make the changes necessary to prevent it," for example, by linking low birth weight in newborn babies to poor nutrition, but failing to note that poor nutrition "may be a major health factor among impoverished social classes and oppressed ethnic groups in developed countries despite an abundance of food in society generally" (Singer 1998, 106, 109).

One of the most important insights of critical medical anthropologists has been to point out that "various practices that bioculturalist anthropologists have traditionally called 'adaptations' might better be analyzed as social adjustments to the consequences of oppressive sociopolitical relationships" (M. Singer 1998, 115). Anthropologists Gavin Smith and R. Brooke Thomas (1998, 466), for example, draw attention to situations where "social relations compromise people's options" for attaining biological well-being and cultural satisfaction but where people do not passively accept this situation and choose instead to "try to escape or change these relations"; Smith and Thomas call these practices "adaptations of resistance." In later chapters we cite case studies by medical anthropologists that illustrate the complex and nuanced views these anthropologists are able to bring to the explanation and treatment of human suffering.

## The Uses of Anthropology

Why take a course in anthropology? An immediate answer might be that human fossils or broken bits of ancient pots or the customs of faraway peoples inspire a fascination that is its own reward. But the experience of being dazzled by seemingly exotic places and peoples carries with it a risk. As you become increasingly aware of the range of anthropological data, including the many options that exist for living a satisfying human life, you may find yourself wondering about the life you are living. Contact with the unfamiliar can be liberating, but it can also be threatening if it undermines your confidence in the absolute truth and universal rightness of your previous understanding of the way the world works.

The contemporary world is increasingly interconnected. As people from different cultural backgrounds come into contact with one another, learning to cope with cultural differences becomes crucial. Anthropologists experience both the rewards and the risks of getting to know how other people live, and their work has helped to dispel many harmful stereotypes that sometimes make cross-cultural contact dangerous or impossible. Studying anthropology may help prepare you for some of the shocks you will encounter in dealing with people who look different from you, speak a different language, or do not agree that the world works exactly the way you think it does.

Anthropology involves learning about the kinds of living organisms we human beings are, the various ways we live our lives, and how we make sense of our experiences. Studying anthropology can equip you to deal with people with different cultural backgrounds in a less threatened, more tolerant manner. You may never be called on to eat termite paste. Still, you may one day encounter a situation in which none of the old rules seem to apply. As you struggle to make sense of what is happening, what you learned in anthropology class may help you relax and dare to try something totally new to you. If you do so, perhaps you too will discover the rewards of an encounter with the unfamiliar that is at the same time unaccountably familiar. We hope you will savour the experience.

## *In Their Own Words*

## What Can You Learn from an Anthropology Major?

*The Career Development Center at SUNY Plattsburgh developed a document that highlights what students typically learn from a major in anthropology.*

| | | |
|---|---|---|
| 1. | Social agility | In an unfamiliar social or career-related setting, you learn to quickly size up the rules of the game. You can become accepted more quickly than you could without this anthropological skill. |
| 2. | Observation | You must often learn about a culture from within it, so you learn how to interview and observe as a participant. |
| 3. | Analysis and planning | You learn how to find patterns in the behaviour of a cultural group. This awareness of patterns allows you to generalize about the group's behaviour and predict what they might do in a given situation. |
| 4. | Social sensitivity | Although other people's ways of doing things may be different from your own, you learn the importance of events and conditions that have contributed to this difference. You also recognize that other cultures view your ways as strange. You learn the value of behaving toward others with appropriate preparation, care, and understanding. |
| 5. | Accuracy in interpreting behaviour | You become familiar with the range of behaviour in different cultures. You learn how to look at cultural causes of behaviour before assigning causes yourself. |
| 6. | Ability to appropriately challenge conclusions | You learn that analyses of human behaviour are open to challenge. You learn how to use new knowledge to test past conclusions. |
| 7. | Insightful interpretation of information | You learn how to use data collected by others, reorganizing or interpreting the data to reach original conclusions. |
| 8. | Simplification of information | Because anthropology is conducted among publics as well as about them, you learn how to simplify technical information for communication to non-technical people. |
| 9. | Contextualization | Although attention to details is a trait of anthropology, you learn that any given detail might not be as important as its context and can even be misleading when the context is ignored. |
| 10. | Problem solving | Because you often function within a cultural group or act on culturally sensitive issues, you learn to approach problems with care. Before acting, you identify the problem, set your goals, decide on the actions you will take, and calculate possible effects on other people. |
| 11. | Persuasive writing | Anthropologists strive to represent the behaviour of one group to another group and continually need to engage in interpretation. You learn the value of bringing someone else to share—or at least understand—your view through written argument. |
| 12. | Assumption of a social perspective | You learn how to perceive the acts of individuals and local groups as both shaping and being shaped by larger sociocultural systems. The perception enables you to "act locally and think globally." |

Source: Omohundro 2000.

## Chapter Summary

1. Anthropology aims to describe in the broadest sense what it means to be human. The anthropological perspective is holistic, comparative, and evolutionary and has relied on the concept of culture to explain the diversity of human ways of life. Human beings depend on cultural learning for successful biological survival and reproduction, which is why anthropologists consider human beings to be biocultural organisms. Anthropology is also a field-based discipline. In North America today, anthropology is considered to have four major subfields: biological anthropology, archaeology, cultural anthropology, and linguistic anthropology; many people also consider applied anthropology to be a fifth major subfield.

2. Biological anthropology began as an attempt to classify all the world's populations into different races. By the early twentieth century, however, most anthropologists had rejected racial classifications as scientifically unjustifiable and objected to the ways in which racial classifications were used to justify the social practice of racism. Contemporary anthropologists who are interested in human biology include biological anthropologists, primatologists, and paleoanthropologists.

3. Cultural anthropologists study cultural diversity in all living human societies, including their own. Linguistic anthropologists approach cultural diversity by relating varied forms of language to their cultural contexts. Both gather information through fieldwork, by participating with their informants in social activities, and by observing those activities as outsiders. They publish accounts of their research in ethnographies.

4. Archaeology is the cultural anthropology of the human past, with interests ranging from the earliest stone tools to twenty-first-century garbage dumps. Archaeologists focus on understanding how humans lived in the past, how past societies interacted with one another, and how cultures changed over time. Archaeologists are stewards of human prehistory, and they rely on historic preservation laws to protect archaeological remains from looting and destruction.

5. Applied anthropologists, who are frequently referred to as practising anthropologists, often use information from the other anthropological specialties to solve practical cross-cultural problems. Medical anthropology connects biological anthropology, cultural anthropology, and applied anthropology, focusing on cultural perceptions of health and illness, suffering, and well-being.

## For Review

1. What is anthropology? What makes it different from the other social sciences? What do the qualities of being *holistic*, *comparative*, *field based*, and *evolutionary* contribute to the discipline?

2. How do anthropologists define culture? In what ways is this definition different from other, less specialized definitions of *culture*? How would the anthropological definition of culture inform the way that anthropologists view data?

3. What makes anthropology a cross-disciplinary discipline? Why is a cross-disciplinary approach advantageous to anthropologists?

4. Describe the main subfields of modern anthropology. Include one area of study for each subfield. What sorts of research projects might require anthropologists from two or more of these subfields to work together?

5. Identify three aspects of biological anthropology that appeal to you, and describe why you think they are interesting.

6. What are some of the main topics of interest in cultural anthropology? Which of these topics appeal to you the most? Why?

7. Summarize the difference between ethnography and ethnology.

8. How do linguistic anthropologists learn about human languages? What types of research do these anthropologists' conduct? What knowledge and skills would you need to develop in order to create a new language like Christine Schreyer did for *Man of Steel*?

9. What are some of the topics or things archaeologists study? Which of these topics or things do you find most interesting? Why?

10. What are the connections between applied anthropology and the other branches of anthropology? Outline the advantages of applied anthropology.

11. Why is critical medical anthropology an important area of focus within applied anthropology? What are some examples of this type of research?

## Key Terms

anthropology  3
applied anthropology  15
archaeology  14
biocultural organisms  5
biological anthropology
   (or physical anthropology)  8
comparison  4
cultural anthropology  9
culture  5

ethnography  11
ethnology  11
evolution  4
fieldwork  11
gender  10
holism  3
informants  11
language  12
linguistic anthropology  12

material culture  14
medical anthropology  16
paleoanthropology  8
primatology  8
races  6
racism  8
sex  10

## Suggested Readings

Ashmore, Wendy, and Robert J. Sharer. 2013. *Discovering Our Past: A Brief Introduction to Archaeology.* 6th ed. New York: McGraw-Hill. *An engaging introduction to the techniques, assumptions, interests, and findings of modern archaeology.*

Feder, Kenneth. 2014. *Frauds, Myths, and Mysteries: Science and Pseudoscience in Archaeology.* 8th ed. New York: McGraw-Hill. *An entertaining and informative exploration of fascinating frauds and genuine archaeological mysteries that also explains the scientific method.*

Harrison, Julia, and Regna Darnell, eds. 2006. *Historicizing Canadian Anthropology.* Vancouver: UBC Press. *An overview of the history of Canadian anthropology that outlines the progression of the field here in Canada as it developed into the current multi-faceted discipline with distinctively Canadian perspectives.*

Hedican, Edward. 2012. *Social Anthropology: Canadian Perspectives on Culture and Society.* Toronto: Canadian Scholars Press. *An introduction to cultural anthropology from a Canadian perspective, featuring many examples from Canadian anthropologists.*

Hirsch, Jennifer S., Holly Wardlow, Daniel Jordan Smith, Harriet M. Phinney, Shanti Parikh, and Constance A. Nathanson. 2010. *The Secret: Love, Marriage and HIV.* Nashville: Vanderbilt University Press. *An analysis of the cross-cultural social organization of extramarital sexual practices in Mexico, Nigeria, Uganda, Vietnam, and Papua New Guinea and the implications of those practices for married women's HIV risk in those settings.*

Kidder, Tracy. 2004. *Mountains beyond Mountains: The Quest of Dr Paul Farmer, a Man Who Would Cure the World.* New York: Random House. *A highly readable account of anthropologist and physician Paul Farmer's efforts to enlist powerful funders, the World Health Organization, and ordinary people in neglected communities in a quest to bring the best modern medicine to those who need it most.*

Relethford, John. 2012. *The Human Species: An Introduction to Biological Anthropology.* 9th ed. New York: McGraw-Hill. *An excellent, clear introduction to biological anthropology.*

Strang, Veronica. 2009. *What Anthropologists Do.* Oxford: Berg. *An exploration and explanation of the many ways anthropology is being used in everyday life, written specifically for students.*

# 2  Why Is the Concept of Culture Important?

▲ A young girl receives her first bronze neck rings, traditionally worn by women of the Kayan Lahwi tribe, Kayah State, Myanmar. Photo: © Marc Dozier/Corbis

## Chapter Outline

- How Do Anthropologists Define Culture?
- Culture, History, and Human Agency
- Why Do Cultural Differences Matter?
- How Can Cultural Relativity Improve Our Understanding of Controversial Cultural Practices?
- Does Culture Explain Everything?

- The Promise of the Anthropological Perspective
- Chapter Summary
- For Review
- Key Terms
- Suggested Readings

In this chapter, you will examine in greater detail the concept of culture, one of the most influential ideas that anthropologists have developed. We will survey different ways that anthropologists have used the culture concept to expose the fallacies of biological determinism. We will also discuss the reasons some anthropologists believe that continuing to use the culture concept today may be a problem.

Anthropologists have long argued that the human condition is distinguished from the condition of other living species by culture. Other living species learn, but the extent to which human beings depend on learning is unique in the animal kingdom. Because our brains are capable of open symbolic thought and our hands are capable of manipulating matter powerfully or delicately, we interact with the wider world in a way that is distinct from that of any other species.

## How Do Anthropologists Define Culture?

In Chapter 1, we defined *culture* as patterns of learned behaviour and ideas that humans acquire as members of a society, together with the artifacts and structures we create and use. Culture is not reinvented by each generation; rather, we learn it from other members of the social groups we belong to, although we may later modify this heritage in some way. Children use their own bodies and brains to explore their world. At the same time, other people actively work to steer their activity and attention in particular directions. Consequently, children's exploration of the world is not merely trial and error. The path is cleared for them by others who shape their experiences. We use two terms in the social sciences to refer to this process of culturally and socially shaped learning. The first, *socialization*, is the process of learning to live as a member of a group. This involves mastering the skills of appropriate interaction with others and learning how to cope with the behavioural rules established by that group. The second term, *enculturation*, refers to the cognitive challenges facing humans who live together and must come to terms with the ways of thinking and feeling considered appropriate to their respective cultures.

Because children learn to act, think, feel, and speak at the same time, we will use the term *socialization/enculturation* to represent this holistic experience. *Socialization/enculturation* produces a socially and culturally constructed individual capable of functioning successfully in society. So culture is *shared* as well as *learned*. But many things we learn, such as table manners and what is good to eat and where people are supposed to sleep, are never explicitly taught but rather are absorbed in the course of practical daily living. French anthropologist Pierre Bourdieu called this kind of cultural learning *habitus*, and it is heavily influenced by our interactions with material culture. According to Daniel Miller (2010, 53), Bourdieu's theory "gives shape and form to the idea that objects make people. . . . We walk around the rice terraces or road systems, the housing and gardens that are effectively ancestral. These unconsciously direct our footsteps, and are the landscape of our imagination, as well as the cultural environment to which we adapt." The cultural practices shared within social groups always encompass the varied knowledge and skills of many different individuals. For example, space flight is part of North American culture, and yet no individual North American could build a space shuttle in his or her backyard.

Human cultures also appear *patterned*; that is, related cultural beliefs and practices show up repeatedly in different areas of social life. For example, in North America, individualism is highly valued, and its influence can be seen in child-rearing practices (babies are expected to sleep alone, and children are reared with the expectation that they will be independent

**socialization** The process by which humans as material organisms, living together with other similar organisms, cope with the behavioural rules established by their respective societies.

**enculturation** The process by which humans living with one another must learn to come to terms with the ways of thinking and feeling that are considered appropriate in their respective cultures.

at the age of 18), economic practices (individuals are urged to get a job, to save their money, and not to count on other people or institutions to take care of them; many people would prefer to be in business for themselves; far more people commute to work by themselves in their own cars than carpool), and religious practices (the Christian emphasis on personal salvation and individual accountability before God). Cultural patterns can be traced through time: that English and French are widely spoken in Canada, whereas Fulfulde (a language spoken in West Africa) is not, is connected to the colonial conquest and domination of Canada by speakers of English and French in past centuries. Cultural patterns also vary across space: For example, the English of Newfoundland differs from the English of other provinces in style, rhythm, and vocabulary (Figure 2.1).

It is this patterned cultural variation that allows anthropologists (and others) to distinguish different "cultural traditions" from one another. But separate cultural traditions are often hard to delineate. That is because, in addition to any unique elements of their own, all contain contradictory elements, and all also share elements with other traditions. First, customs in one domain of culture may contradict customs in another domain, as when religion tells us to share with others and economics tells us to look out for ourselves alone. Second, people have always borrowed cultural elements from their neighbours, and many increasingly refuse to be limited in the present

**FIGURE 2.1** | A street sign in St John's, Newfoundland, poses a friendly question to passersby. While the language on this sign would seem perfectly natural to most Newfoundlanders, it would seem strange to people living in other parts of Canada.

by cultural practices of the past. Why, for example, should literacy not be seen as part of Ju/'hoansi culture once the children of illiterate Ju/'hoansi foragers learn to read and write? Thus, cultural patterns can be useful as a kind of shorthand, but it is important to remember that the boundaries between cultural traditions are always fuzzy. Ultimately, they rest on someone's judgment about how different one set of customs is from another set of customs. As we will see shortly, these kinds of contradictions and challenges are not uncommon, leading some anthropologists to think of culture not in terms of specific customs but in terms of rules that become "established ways of bringing ideas from different domains together" (Strathern 1992, 3).

For more on the Ju/'hoansi, see EthnoProfile 11.5, on p. 314.

So far we have seen that culture is learned, shared, and patterned. Cultural traditions are also reconstructed and enriched, generation after generation, primarily because human biological survival depends on culture. Thus, culture is also *adaptive*. Human newborns are not born with "instincts" that would enable them to survive on their own. On the contrary, they depend utterly on support and nurturance from adults and other members of the group in which they live. It is by learning the cultural practices of those around them that human beings come to master appropriate ways of thinking and acting that promote their own survival as biological organisms (Figure 2.2). And in addition to helping us to adapt to our surroundings, culture allows us to transform the environments in which we live so that they can better meet our needs.

Finally, culture is *symbolic*. A symbol is something that stands for something else. The letters of an alphabet, for example, symbolize the sounds of a spoken language. There is no necessary connection between the shape of a particular letter and the speech sound it represents. Indeed, the same or similar sounds are represented symbolically by very different letters in the Latin, Cyrillic, Hebrew, Arabic, and Greek alphabets, to name but five. Even the sounds of spoken language are symbols for meanings a speaker tries to express. The fact that we can translate from one language to another suggests that the same

**symbol** Something that stands for something else.

**FIGURE 2.2** | Of all living organisms, humans are the most dependent on learning for their survival. From a young age, girls in northern Cameroon learn to carry heavy loads on their heads and also learn to get water for their families.

or similar meanings can be expressed by different symbols in different languages. But language is not the only domain of culture that depends on symbols. Everything we do in society has a symbolic dimension, from how we conduct ourselves at the dinner table to how we bury the dead. It is our heavy dependence on symbolic learning that sets human culture apart from the apparently non-symbolic learning on which other species rely.

Human culture, then, is *learned*, *shared*, *patterned*, *adaptive*, and *symbolic*. And the contemporary human capacity for culture has also evolved, over millions of years. Culture's beginnings can perhaps be glimpsed among Japanese macaque monkeys who invented the custom of washing sweet potatoes and among wild chimpanzees who invented different grooming postures or techniques to crack open nuts or to gain access to termites or water (Boesch-Achermann and Boesch 1994; Leca, Huffman, and Vasey 2012; Wolfe 1995, 162–63; see Figure 2.3). Our apelike ancestors surely shared similar aptitudes when they started walking on two legs some 6 million years ago. By 2.5 million years ago, their descendants were making stone tools. Thereafter, our **hominin**

**hominins** Humans and their immediate ancestors.

lineage gave birth to a number of additional species, all of whom depended on culture more than their ancestors had. Culture, then, is not something that appeared suddenly with the arrival of *Homo sapiens*. Rather, culture had long been an integral part of our evolutionary heritage by the time *Homo sapiens* appeared some 200,000 years ago. As such, paleoanthropological and archaeological work can offer startling insight into how past cultures functioned, survived, and changed.

For more on human biological and cultural evolution, see Chapter 6. For more on how researchers use paleoanthropological and archaeological techniques to learn about these past cultures, see Chapter 7, pp. 167–74.

Thus, as Rick Potts (1996, 197) puts it, "an evolutionary bridge exists between the human and animal realms of behaviour. . . . Culture represents continuity." Potts proposes that modern human symbolic culture and the social institutions that depend on it rest on other, more basic abilities that emerged at different times in our evolutionary past. Monkeys and apes possess many of these abilities to varying degrees, which is the reason they may be said to possess simple cultural traditions. Certainly our earliest hominin ancestors were no different.

Apes apparently also possess a rudimentary capacity for symbolic coding, or symbolic representation, something our ancestors undoubtedly possessed as well. But new species can evolve new capacities not found in their ancestors. This occurred in the human past when our ancestors first developed a capacity for complex symbolic representation, including the ability to communicate freely about the past, the future, and the invisible. This ability distinguishes human symbolic language, for example, from the vocal communication systems of apes. Biological anthropologist Terrence Deacon (1997, 413, 416) argues that evolution produced in *Homo sapiens* a brain "that has been significantly overbuilt for learning symbolic associations" such that "we cannot help but see the world in symbolic categories." Complex symbolic representation apparently was of great adaptive value for our ancestors. It created selective pressures that increased human symbolic capacities over time. Put another way, culture and the human brain coevolved, each adapting to key features of the environment (Deacon 1997, 44;

**FIGURE 2.3** | A chimpanzee uses a stick to get termites out of a hole in a large rock.

Odling-Smee 1994). We have used our complex symbolic abilities, moreover, to create institutions—complex, variable, and enduring forms of cultural practice that organize social life, also unique to our species. As a result, for *Homo sapiens*, culture has become "the predominant manner in which human groups vary from one another . . . it swamps the biological differences among populations" (Marks 1995, 200). It is because of this coevolution of human biology (in particular, the human brain) and culture that anthropologists refer to humans as *biocultural organisms*.

> For a more thorough description of human language and other communication systems, see Chapter 9.

## Culture, History, and Human Agency

The human condition is rooted in time and shaped by history. As part of the human condition, culture is also historical, being worked out and reconstructed in every generation. Culture is also part of our biological heritage. Our biocultural heritage has produced a living species that uses culture to surmount biological and individual limitations and is even capable of studying itself and its own biocultural evolution.

This realization, however, raises another question: Just how free from limitations are humans?

Opinion in Western societies often polarizes around one of two extremes: Either we have free will and may do just as we please, or our behaviour is completely determined by forces beyond our control. Many social scientists, however, are convinced that a more realistic description of human freedom was offered by Karl Marx (1963, 15), who wrote, "Men make their own history, but they do not make it just as they please; they do not make it under circumstances chosen by themselves, but under circumstances directly encountered, given, and transmitted by the past." That is, people regularly struggle, often against great odds, to exercise some control over their lives. Human beings active in this way are called *agents*. Human agents cannot escape the cultural and historical context within which they act. However, they must frequently select a course of action when the "correct" choice is unclear and the outcome uncertain. Some anthropologists even liken human existence to a minefield that we must painstakingly try to cross without blowing ourselves up. It is in such contexts, with their ragged edges, that human beings exercise their **human agency** by making interpretations, formulating goals, and setting out in pursuit of those goals (Figure 2.4).

**human agency** Human beings' ability to exercise of at least some control over their lives.

## In Their Own Words

### The Nature/Culture of Genetic Facts

*Anthropology can tell us a lot about human biology and heredity. However, as biological anthropologist Jonathan Marks testifies, it is important to realize that "natural facts" have cultural information (values, meanings) integrated into them.*

Anthropology is positioned to try to explain why groups of scientists do and say the things they do, in parallel with why groups of Natives do and say the things they do (Franklin 1995). The basic explanation lies in a significant contribution of twentieth-century anthropology, namely, the discovery that human facts are fundamentally biocultural. . . . Consequently, we are now understanding the facts of human biology not so much as facts of nature, but as facts of "nature/culture." . . . After all, "innate" and "learned" are not antonyms, for the most fundamentally hard-wired human adaptations—walking and talking—are actively learned by every person, every generation.

The facts of human biology are, of necessity, facts of human culture in three ways. First, our evolutionary lineage has been coevolving with technology for millions of years, and consequently the environment into which our own species evolved and adapted was necessarily a cultural one. . . . Second, as individuals, we develop within environments that are profoundly cultural. . . . And third, these facts have always been produced in a context of conflicting interests of patronage, political ideologies of diverse kinds, professional aspirations, and cultural expectations. . . . [For example, a]rchaeological facts are often produced in the service of nationalism . . . , for they may authorize the historical identity of a nation. . . . The problem is not that culture corrupts our understanding of nature; it is that culture is integral to understanding nature (Franklin 1995, 2003). One literally cannot understand natural facts any way other than culturally.

Source: Marks 2013, 249. © 2013 by Annual Reviews, http://www.annualreviews.org.

Many anthropologists insist that it is possible to develop a view of human beings that finds room for culture, history, and human agency. The anthropological point of view called **holism** assumes that no sharp boundaries separate mind from body, body from environment, individual from society, my ideas from our ideas, or their traditions from our traditions. Rather, holism assumes that mind and body, body and environment, and so on, interpenetrate each other and even define each other. From a holistic perspective, attempts to divide reality into mind and matter are unsuccessful because of the complex nature of reality, which resists isolation and dissection. Anthropologists who have struggled to develop this holistic perspective on the human condition have made a contribution of unique and lasting value. Holism holds great appeal for those who seek a theory of human nature that is rich enough to do justice to its complex subject matter.

In anthropology, holism is traditionally understood as a perspective on the human condition in which the whole (for example, a human being, a society, a cultural tradition) is understood to be greater than the sum of its parts. For example, from a holistic perspective, human beings are complex, dynamic living entities shaped by genes, culture, and experience into entities whose properties cannot be reduced to the materials out of which they were constructed. To be sure, human organisms are closed off from the wider world in some ways by how our cells, tissues,

For an alternative definition and use of the term *holism*, see Chapter 1, p. 3.

**holism** A perspective on the human condition that assumes that mind and body, individuals and society, and individuals and the environment interpenetrate and even define one another.

**FIGURE 2.4** | People regularly struggle, often against great odds, to exercise some control over their lives. During the "Dirty War" in Argentina in the 1970s and early 1980s, women whose children had been "disappeared" by secret right-wing death squads began, at great personal risk, to stand every Thursday in the Plaza de Mayo, the central square of Buenos Aires, with photographs of their missing children. Called the Mothers of the Plaza de Mayo, they continue their weekly vigil today. They were a powerful rebuke to the dictatorship and to subsequent governments that were not forthcoming about providing information about the disappeared.

and organs are bound into a single body. At the same time, like all living organisms, human beings are open to the world in other ways: we breathe, eat, harbour colonies of intestinal bacteria to aid our digestion, excrete waste products, and learn from experience (see Deacon 2003, 296–7). Similarly, a society is not just the sum of its individual members; people in groups develop dynamic relationships that facilitate collective actions impossible for individuals to bring about on their own. And cultural traditions are not just a list of beliefs, values, and practices; rather, different dimensions of cultural activity, such as economics and politics and religion, are knotted together in complex ways. To understand any human community requires untangling those cultural threads in order to reveal the full range of factors that shape particular cultural practices in that community.

Human beings who develop and live together in groups shaped by cultural patterns are deeply affected by shared cultural experiences. They become different from what they would have been had they matured in isolation; they also become different from other people who have been shaped by different social and cultural patterns. Social scientists have long known that human beings who grow up isolated from meaningful social interactions with others do not behave in ways that appear recognizably human. As anthropologist Clifford Geertz (1973, 40) observed long ago, such human beings would be neither failed apes nor "natural" people stripped of their veneer of culture; they would be "mental basket cases." Social living and cultural sharing are necessary for individual human beings to develop what we recognize as a human nature.

One useful way of thinking about the relationships among the parts that make up a whole is in terms of coevolution. A coevolutionary approach to the human condition emphasizes that human organisms, their physical environments, and their symbolic practices codetermine one another; with the passage of time, they can also coevolve with one another. A coevolutionary view of the human condition also sees human beings as organisms whose bodies, brains, actions, and thoughts are equally involved in shaping what they become. Coevolution produces a human nature connected to a wider world and profoundly shaped by culture. These connections make us vulnerable over the courses of our lives to influences that our ancestors never experienced. The open, symbolic, meaning-making properties of human culture make it possible for us to respond to those influences in ways that our ancestors could not have anticipated.

## Why Do Cultural Differences Matter?

The same objects, actions, or events frequently mean different things to people with different cultures. In fact, what counts as an object or event in one tradition may not be recognized as such in another. This powerful lesson of anthropology was

**coevolution** The interconnected relationship between biological processes and symbolic cultural processes, in which each makes up an important part of the environment to which the other must adapt.

illustrated by the experience of some volunteers working with the United States' Peace Corps in southern Africa.

In the early 1970s, the Peace Corps office in Botswana was concerned by the number of volunteers who seemed to be "burned out," failing in their assignments, leaving the assigned villages, and increasingly hostile to their Tswana hosts. (See Map 2.1 and EthnoProfile 2.1: Tswana.) The Peace Corps asked American anthropologist Hoyt Alverson, who was familiar with Tswana culture and society, for advice. Alverson (1977) discovered that one major problem the Peace Corps volunteers were having involved exactly this issue of similar actions having very different meanings. The volunteers complained that the Tswana would never leave them alone. Whenever they tried to get away and sit by themselves for a few minutes to have some private time, one or more Tswana would quickly join them. This made the Americans angry. From their perspective, everyone is entitled to a certain amount of privacy

and time alone. To the Tswana, however, human life is social life; the only people who want to be alone are witches and the insane. Because these young Americans did not seem to be either, the Tswana who saw them sitting alone naturally assumed that there had been a breakdown in hospitality and that the volunteers would welcome some company. Here, one behaviour—a person walking out into a field and sitting by himself or herself—had two very different meanings (Figure 2.5).

From this example we can see that human experience is inherently ambiguous. Even within a single cultural tradition, the meaning of an object or an action may differ, depending on the context. Quoting philosopher Gilbert Ryle, anthropologist Clifford Geertz (1973, 6) noted that there is a world of difference between a wink and a blink, as anyone who has ever mistaken one for the other has undoubtedly learned. To resolve the ambiguity, experience must be interpreted, and human beings regularly turn to their own cultural traditions in search of an interpretation that makes sense. They do this daily as they go about life among others with whom they share traditions. Serious misunderstandings may arise, however, when individuals confront the same

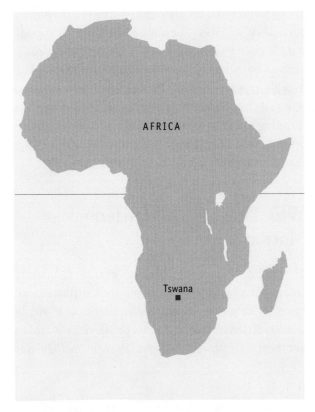

**MAP 2.1 | Location of Tswana. For more information, see EthnoProfile 2.1.**

## EthnoProfile 2.1

### Tswana

**Region:** Southern Africa

**Nation:** Botswana

**Population:** 1,200,000 (also 1,500,000 in South Africa)

**Environment:** Savannah to desert

**Livelihood:** Cattle raising, farming

**Political organization:** Traditionally, chiefs and headmen; today, part of a modern nation-state

**For more information:** Comaroff, Jean. 1985. *Body of Power, Spirit of Resistance: The Culture and History of a South African People*. Chicago: University of Chicago Press.

**FIGURE 2.5 |** For Tswana, human life is social life, and only witches or the mentally ill would choose to spend time isolated from others. For most Westerners, in contrast, alone or "private" time is a highly valued part of everyday life. These sorts of cultural differences can lead to misunderstandings when members of different cultural traditions come into close contact with one another.

ambiguous situation without realizing that their cultural ground rules differ.

## What Is Ethnocentrism?

*Ethnocentrism* is the term anthropologists use to describe the opinion that one's own way of life is natural or correct, indeed the only way of being fully human. Ethnocentrism is one solution to the inevitable tension that arises when people with different cultural backgrounds come into contact. It reduces the other way of life to a version of one's own. Sometimes

we correctly identify meaningful areas of cultural overlap. But other times, we are shocked by the differences we encounter. We may conclude that if our way is right, then their way can only be wrong. (Of course, from their perspective, our way of life may seem to be a distortion of theirs.)

The members of one society may go beyond merely interpreting another way of life in ethnocentric terms. They may decide to do something about the discrepancies they observe. They may conclude that the other way of life is wrong but not fundamentally evil and that the members of the other group need to be converted to their own way of doing things. If the others are unwilling to change their ways, however, the failed attempt at conversion may enlarge into an active dualism: us versus them, civilization versus savagery, good versus evil. The ultimate result may be war and genocide—the deliberate attempt to exterminate an entire group based on race, religion, national origin, or other cultural features.

## Is It Possible to Avoid Ethnocentric Bias?

One way to address the question of whether it is possible to avoid ethnocentric bias is to view relationships between individuals with different cultural backgrounds as not being fundamentally different from relationships between individuals with very similar cultural backgrounds. Even people with little in common can learn to get along, even if it is not always easy. Like all human relationships, relationships between individuals with different cultural backgrounds affect all parties involved, changing them as they learn about each other. People with a cultural background very different from your own may help you see possibilities for belief and action that are drastically at odds with everything your tradition considers possible. By becoming aware of these unsuspected possibilities, you become a different person. People from cultural backgrounds different from yours are likely to be affected in the same way.

**ethnocentrism** The opinion that one's own way of life is natural or correct and, indeed, the only true way of being fully human.

For a more in-depth discussion of ethnocentrism in the context of social inequality, see Chapter 14, p. 410.

Learning about other cultures is at once enormously hopeful and immensely threatening; once it occurs, we can no longer claim that any single culture has a monopoly on truth. Although this does not mean that the traditions in question must therefore be based entirely on illusion or falsehood, it does mean that the truth embodied in any

cultural tradition is bound to be partial, approximate, and open to further insight and growth.

## What Is Cultural Relativism?

Anthropologists must come to terms with the tensions produced by cultural differences as they do their fieldwork. One result has been the formulation of the concept of **cultural relativism**. Definitions of cultural relativism have varied as different anthropologists have tried to draw conclusions based on their own experience of other ways of life. For example, cultural relativism can be defined as "understanding another culture

**cultural relativism** Understanding another culture in its own terms sympathetically enough so that the culture appears to be a coherent and meaningful design for living.

---

## In Their Own Words

### The Paradox of Ethnocentrism

*Ethnocentrism is usually described in thoroughly negative terms. As anthropologist Ivan Karp points out, however, ethnocentrism is a more complex phenomenon than we might expect.*

Anthropologists usually argue that ethnocentrism is both wrong and harmful, especially when it is tied to racial, cultural, and social prejudices. Ideas and feelings about the inferiority of blacks, the cupidity of Jews, or the lack of cultural sophistication of farmers are surely to be condemned. But can we do without ethnocentrism? If we stopped to examine every custom and practice in our cultural repertoire, how would we get on? For example, if we always regarded marriage as something that can vary from society to society, would we be concerned about filling out the proper marriage documents, or would we even get married at all? Most of the time we suspend a quizzical stance toward our own customs and simply live life.

Yet many of our own practices are peculiar when viewed through the lenses of other cultures. Periodically, for over fifteen years, I have worked with and lived among an African people. They are as amazed at our marriage customs as my students are at theirs. Both [North] American students and the Iteso of Kenya find it difficult to imagine how the other culture survives with the bizarre, exotic practices that are part of their respective marriage customs. Ethnocentrism works both ways. It can be practised as much by other cultures as by our own.

Paradoxically, ethnographic literature combats ethnocentrism by showing that the practices of cultures (including our own) are "natural" in their own setting. What appears natural in one setting appears so because it was constructed in that setting—made and produced by human beings who could have done it some other way. Ethnography is a means of recording the range of human creativity and of demonstrating how universally shared capacities can produce cultural and social differences.

This anthropological way of looking at other cultures—and, by implication, at ourselves—constitutes a major reason for reading ethnography. The anthropological lens teaches us to question what we assume to be unquestionable. Ethnography teaches us that human potentiality provides alternative means of organizing our lives and alternative modes of experiencing the world. Reading ethnographies trains us to question the received wisdom of our society and makes us receptive to change. In this sense, anthropology might be called the subversive science. We read ethnographies in order to learn about how other peoples produce their world and about how we might change our own patterns of production.

Source: Karp, Ivan. 1990. Guest editorial in *Cultural Anthropology: A Perspective on the Human Condition*, by Emily Schultz and Robert Lavenda, 2nd edn. St. Paul, MN: West. Excerpt from pp. 74–5.

in its own terms sympathetically enough so that the culture appears to be a coherent and meaningful design for living" (Greenwood and Stini 1977, 182). According to this holistic definition, the goal of cultural relativism is to promote understanding of cultural practices, particularly of those that an outsider finds puzzling, incoherent, or morally troubling. These practices range from trivial (like eating insects) to horrifying (like genocide), but most are likely to be located somewhere between these extremes.

## How Can Cultural Relativity Improve Our Understanding of Controversial Cultural Practices?

Rituals initiating girls and boys into adulthood are widely practised throughout the world. In some parts of Africa, this ritual includes genital cutting (Figure 2.6). For example, ritual experts may cut off the foreskins of the penises of adolescent boys, who are expected to endure this operation without showing fear or pain. In the case of girls, ritual cutting may involve little more than nicking the clitoris with a

**FIGURE 2.6** | Among many East African people, including the Maasai, female genital cutting is an important part of the transformation of girls into women. These young Maasai women are recovering from the operation. After undergoing the operation, Maasai women are proud of their new status as adults. Do you think this practice is a violation of human rights? Why, or why not?

knife blade to draw blood. In other cases, however, the surgery is more extreme. The clitoris itself may be cut off (or excised), a procedure called *clitoridectomy*. In some parts of eastern Africa, however, the surgery is even more extreme: The labia are excised along with the clitoris, and the remaining skin is fastened together, forming scar tissue that partially closes the vaginal opening. This version is often called *pharaonic circumcision* or *infibulation*. When young women who have undergone this operation marry, they may require further surgery to widen the vaginal opening. Surgery may be necessary again to widen the vaginal opening when a woman gives birth; and after she has delivered her child, she may expect to be closed up again. Many women who have undergone these procedures repeatedly can develop serious medical complications involving the bladder and the colon later in life.

The removal of the male foreskin—or circumcision—has long been a familiar practice in Western societies, not only among observant Jews, who perform it for religious reasons, but also among physicians, who have encouraged circumcision of male newborns as a hygienic measure. The ritual practice of female genital cutting (FGC), by contrast, has been unfamiliar to most people in Western societies until recently.

### Genital Cutting, Gender, and Human Rights

In 1978, radical feminist Mary Daly grouped "African female genital mutilation" together with practices such as foot binding in China and witch burning in medieval Europe and labelled all these practices patriarchal "Sado-Rituals" that destroy "the Self-affirming being of women" (111). Feminists and other cultural critics in Western societies spoke out against such practices in the 1980s. In 1992, African American novelist Alice Walker published a bestselling novel, *Possessing the Secret of Joy*, in which the heroine is an African woman who undergoes the operation, suffers psychologically and physically, and eventually pursues the female elder who performed the ritual on her. Walker also made a film, called *Warrior Marks*, that condemned female genital cutting. Although many Western readers continue to regard the positions taken by Daly and Walker as formidable and necessary feminist assertions of women's resistance against patriarchal oppression, other readers—particularly women from societies in which female genital cutting is an ongoing practice—have responded with far less enthusiasm.

Does this mean that these women are in favour of female genital cutting? Not necessarily; in fact, many of them are actively working to discourage the practice in their own societies. But they find that when outsiders publicly condemn traditional African rituals like clitoridectomy and infibulation, their efforts may do more harm than good. Women anthropologists who come from African societies where female genital cutting is traditional point out that Western women who want to help are likely to be more effective if they pay closer attention to what the African women themselves have to say about the meaning of these customs: "Careful listening to women helps us to recognize them as political actors forging their own communities of resistance. It also helps us to learn how and when to provide strategic support that would be welcomed by women who are struggling to challenge such traditions within their own cultures" (Abusharaf 2000).

A better understanding of female genital cutting is badly needed in places like Canada, the United States, and the European Union, where some immigrants and refugees from Africa have brought traditions of female genital cutting with them. Since the mid-1990s, growing awareness and public condemnation of the practice has led to the passage of laws that criminalize female genital cutting in 18 African states and 12 industrialized nations, including Canada and the United States (Center for Reproductive Rights 2015). Non-profit advocacy organizations such as the Center for Reproductive Rights consider female genital cutting (which they call "female genital mutilation," or "FGM") a human rights violation. They acknowledge: "Although FGM is not undertaken with the intention of inflicting harm, its damaging physical, sexual, and psychological effects make it an act of violence against women and children" (Center for Reproductive Rights 2015). Similarly, the United Nations (UN) has stated that FGM "is recognized internationally as a violation of the human rights of girls and women"; it has even proclaimed 6 February International Day of Zero Tolerance for Female Genital Mutilation to encourage the elimination of FGM worldwide (UN 2015a).

Some women have been able successfully to claim asylum or have avoided deportation by claiming that they have fled their home countries to avoid the operation. However, efforts to protect women and girls may become increasingly complicated when immigrant or refugee mothers in Canada and the United States who seek to have their daughters ritually cut are stigmatized in the media as "mutilators" or "child abusers" and find that this practice is considered a felony punishable by up to five years in prison (Abusharaf 2000). A startling example of this is presented by cultural anthropologist Janice Boddy (2007) of the University of Toronto, who recalls that during her study of Sudanese immigrant women in Toronto, her university ethics board required her to report any young women with FGC to the police. Boddy suggests that this criminalization of FGC is part of the Western "climate of fear" where cultural practices from other nations are often misunderstood.

For more on differing views of FGC, see the "Anthropology in the Contemporary World" box in Chapter 13, on p. 376.

## Genital Cutting as a Valued Ritual

Female genital cutting is clearly a controversial practice about which many people have already made up their minds. In such circumstances, is there any role to be played by anthropologists? Anthropologist Rogaia Mustafa Abusharaf thinks there is. She writes: "Debates swirling around circumcision must be restructured in ways that are neither condemnatory nor demeaning, but that foster perceptions illuminated by careful study of the nuanced complexities of culture" (Abusharaf 2000, 17).

One ethnographic study that aims to achieve these goals has been written by Janice Boddy, who has carried out field research since 1976 in a small Muslim village that she calls Hofriyat in rural Sudan, where female genital surgery is traditionally performed in childhood. She writes that "nothing . . . had adequately prepared me for what I was to witness" when she first observed the operation; nevertheless, "as time passed in the village and understanding deepened I came to regard this form of female circumcision in a very different light" (1997, 309). Circumcisions in Hofriyat were traditionally performed on both boys and girls, but the ritual had a different meaning for boys than it did for girls. Once circumcised, a boy takes a step toward manhood, but a girl will not become a woman until she marries. Female circumcision is required, however, to make a girl marriageable, making it possible for her "to use her one great gift, fertility" (310).

Boddy encountered a number of different explanations by scholars and other observers about the purpose of female genital cutting. In Hofriyat, female circumcision traditionally involved infibulation, the most extreme version of genital cutting. Among the justifications offered for infibulation, she found that preserving chastity and curbing female sexual desire made the most sense in rural Sudan, where women's sexual conduct is the symbol of family honour. In practical terms, infibulation ensures "that a girl is a virgin when she marries for the first time" (1997, 313). Women who undergo the procedure do indeed suffer a lot, not only at the time of circumcision, but whenever they engage in sexual intercourse, whenever they give birth, and, over time, as they become subject to recurring urinary infections and difficulties with menstruation. What cultural explanation could make all this suffering meaningful to women?

The answer lies in the connection rural Sudanese villagers make between the infibulated female body and female fertility. Boddy believes that the women she knew equated the category of "virgin" more with fertility than with lack of sexual experience and believed that a woman's virginity and her fertility could be renewed and protected by the act of reinfibulation after giving birth. Women she knew described infibulated female bodies as clean and smooth and pure (1997, 313). Boddy concluded that the ritual was best understood as a way of socializing female fertility "by dramatically de-emphasizing [women's] inherent sexuality" and turning infibulated women into potential "mothers of men" (314). This means they are eligible, with their husbands, to found a new lineage section by giving birth to sons. Women who become "mothers of men" are more than mere sexual partners or servants of their husbands and may attain high status, with their name remembered in village genealogies.

Boddy also discovered that the purity, cleanliness, and smoothness associated with the infibulated female body is also associated with other activities, concepts, and objects in everyday village customs. For example, she discovered that "clean" water birds, "clean food" such as eggs, ostrich eggshells, and gourds shaped like ostrich eggshells all were associated with female fertility. Indeed, "the shape of an ostrich egg, with its tiny orifice, corresponds to the idealized shape of the circumcised woman's womb" (1997, 317). Fetching water is traditionally considered women's work, and the ability of an object to retain moisture is likened to its ability to retain fertility. A dried egg-shaped gourd with seeds

that rattle inside it is like the womb of an infibulated woman that contains and mixes her husband's semen with her own blood. The traditional house in Hofriyat itself seems to be a symbol for the womb, which is called the "house of childbirth" (321). In the same way that the household enclosure "protects a man's descendants, so the enclosed womb protects a woman's fertility . . . the womb of an infibulated woman is an oasis, the locus of appropriate human fertility" (321).

Evidence like this leads Boddy to insist that, for the women of Hofriyat, *infibulation* is "an assertive symbolic act." The experience of infibulation, as well as other traditional curing practices, teaches girls to associate pure female bodies with heat and pain, making them meaningful. Such experiences become associated with the chief purpose women strive for—to become mothers of men—and the lesson is taught to them repeatedly in a variety of ways when they look at water birds or eggs or make food or move around the village. Boddy's relativistic account demonstrates how the meanings associated with female infibulation are reinforced by so many different aspects of everyday life that girls who grow up, marry, and bear children in Hofriyat come to consider the operation a dangerous but profoundly necessary and justifiable procedure that enables them to help sustain all that is most valued in their own world.

## Culture and Moral Reasoning

A relativistic understanding of female genital cutting, therefore, accomplishes several things. It makes the practice comprehensible and even coherent. It reveals how a physically dangerous procedure can appear perfectly acceptable—even indispensable— when placed in a particular context of meaning. It can help us see how some of the cultural practices that we take for granted, such as the promotion of weight loss and cosmetic surgery among women in our own society, are equally dangerous. In a relatively recent issue of the *New York Times*, for example, reporter Natasha Singer (2007, E3) observes, "Before braces, crooked teeth were the norm. Is wrinkle removal the new orthodontics?" Media and marketing pressure for cosmetic treatments that stop the visible signs of aging bombard middle-aged women. People are living longer, and treatments like Botox injections are becoming more easily available, with the result that "the way pop culture perceives the aging face"

**FIGURE 2.7 | Cultural context** can help to render a physically dangerous procedure comprehensible. Above, plastic surgery advertisements are displayed along a staircase at the entrance to a subway station in the Gangnam district in Seoul, South Korea. In what ways can the wide acceptance and popularity of cosmetic surgery in countries like South Korea function as an analogue for the acceptance of female genital cutting in Sudan and other African nations?

is changing, leaving women "grappling with the idea of what 60 looks like" (2007, E3). Moreover, pressure to undergo anti-aging treatments, including plastic surgery, is not simply a matter of vanity. "At the very least, wrinkles are being repositioned as the new gray hair—another means to judge attractiveness, romantic viability, professional competitiveness, and social status" (2007, E3). Singer quotes a 33-year-old real estate broker who has had Botox injections, chemical peels, and laser treatments who said, "If you want to sell a million-dollar house, you have to look good . . . and you have to have confidence that you look good" (2007, E3). In Sudan, people say that virgins are "made, not born" (Boddy 1997, 313); perhaps in Canada, youth is also "made, not born." In Canada and in many other countries around the world today, the media message to women is that success in life requires not an infibulated body, but a face and a body that never age (Figure 2.7). In both cases, cultural practices recommend surgical intervention in the female life cycle to render permanent certain aspects of youthful female bodies that are otherwise transient (fertility and unlined faces, respectively).

## Did Their Culture Make Them Do It?

Do these examples imply that women support harmful practices simply because "their culture makes them do it?" For some people, this kind of explanation is plausible, even preferable, to alternative explanations, because it absolves individual people of blame. How can one justify accusing immigrant African women of being mutilators or abusers of children and throw them into prison if they had no choice in the matter, if their cultures conditioned them into believing that female circumcision was necessary and proper and they are powerless to resist?

Nevertheless, such an explanation is too simplistic to account for the continued practice of infibulation in Hofriyat. First, the villages of Sudan are not sealed off from a wider, more diverse world. Sudan has experienced a lively and often violent history as different groups of outsiders, including the British, have struggled to control the land. Boddy describes the way rural men regularly leave the village as migrant workers and mix with people whose customs—including sexual customs—are very different from the ones they left behind; and outsiders, like anthropologists, also may come to the village and establish long-lasting relationships with those whom they meet. Second, Boddy's account makes clear that the culture of Hofriyat allows people more than one way to interpret their experiences. For example, she notes that although men in Sudan and Egypt are supposed to enjoy sexual intercourse with infibulated women more than with non-infibulated women, in fact these men regularly visit brothels where they encounter prostitutes who have not undergone the surgery.

Third, and perhaps most significantly, Boddy (1997, 312) observes that a less radical form of the operation began to gain acceptance after 1969, and "men are now marrying—and what is more, saying that they prefer to marry—women who have been less severely mutilated," at least in part because they find sexual relations with these women to be more satisfying. Finally, as these observations also show, Boddy's account emphatically rejects the view that women or men in Hofriyat are passive beings, helpless to resist cultural indoctrination. As Abusharaf (2000, 18) would wish, Boddy listened to women in Hofriyat and recognized them "as political actors forging their own communities of resistance." Specifically, Boddy showed how increasing numbers of women (and men) continued to connect female genital cutting with properly socialized female fertility—but they no longer believed that infibulation was the only procedure capable of achieving that goal.

Understanding something is not the same as approving of it or excusing it. People everywhere may be repelled by unfamiliar cultural practices when they first encounter them. Sometimes when they understand these practices better, they change their minds. They may conclude that the practices in question are more suitable for the people who employ them than their own practices would be. They might even recommend incorporating practices from other cultures into their own society. But the opposite may also be the case. It is possible to understand perfectly the cultural rationale behind such practices as slavery, infanticide, headhunting, and genocide—and still refuse to approve of these practices. Insiders and outsiders alike may not be persuaded by the reasons offered to justify these practices, or they may be aware of alternative arrangements that could achieve the desired outcome via less drastic methods. In fact, changing practices of female circumcision in Hofriyat seem to be based precisely on the realization that less extreme forms of surgery can achieve the same valued cultural goals. This should not surprise us: It is likely that any cultural practice with far-reaching consequences for human life will have critics as well as supporters within the society where it is practised. This is certainly the case in Canada, where abortion and euthanasia remain controversial issues. Indeed, the Supreme Court of Canada's 2015 ruling that allows doctor-assisted suicide in some cases demonstrates how cultural practices are open to change as well as how controversial such change can be.

A sensitive ethnographic account of a controversial cultural practice, like Boddy's account of infibulation in Hofriyat, will address both the meaningful dimensions of the practice and the contradictions it involves. As Boddy (1997, 322) concludes,

> Those who work to eradicate female circumcision must, I assert, cultivate an awareness of the custom's local significances and of how much they are asking people to relinquish as well as gain. The stakes are high and it is hardly surprising that efforts to date have met with little success. It is, however, ironic that a practice that—at least in Hofriyat—emphasizes female fertility at a cultural level can be so destructive of it physiologically and so damaging to women's health overall. That paradox has analogies elsewhere, in a world considered "civilized," seemingly far removed from the "barbarous East." Here too, in the West from where I speak, feminine selfhood is often attained at the expense of female well-being. In parallels like these there lies the germ of an enlightened approach to the problem.

Cultural relativism makes moral reasoning more complex. It does not, however, require us to abandon every value our own society has taught us. Every cultural tradition offers more than one way of evaluating experience. Exposure to the interpretations of an unfamiliar culture forces us to reconsider the possibilities our own tradition recognizes in a new light and to search for areas of intersection as well as areas of disagreement. What cultural relativism does discourage is the easy solution of refusing to consider alternatives from the outset. It also does not free us from sometimes facing difficult choices between alternatives whose rightness or wrongness is less than clear-cut. In this sense, "cultural relativism is a 'toughminded' philosophy" (Herskovits 1973, 37).

## In Their Own Words

### Human-Rights Law and the Demonization of Culture

*Sally Engle Merry is a professor of anthropology at New York University.*

Why is the idea of cultural relativism anathema to many human-rights activists? Is it related to the way international human-rights lawyers and journalists think about culture? Does this affect how they think about anthropology? I think one explanation for the tension between anthropology and human-rights activists is the very different conceptions of culture that these two groups hold. An incident demonstrated this for me vividly a few months ago. I received a phone call from a prominent radio show asking if I would be willing to talk about the recent incident in Pakistan that resulted in the gang rape of a young woman, an assault apparently authorized by a local tribal council. Since I am working on human rights and violence against women, I was happy to explain my position that this was an inexcusable act, that many Pakistani feminists condemned the rape, but that it was probably connected to local political struggles and class differences. It should not be seen as an expression of Pakistani "culture." In fact, it was the local Islamic religious leader who first made the incident known to the world, according to news stories I had read.

The interviewer was distressed. She wanted me to defend the value of respecting Pakistani culture at all costs, despite the tribal council's imposition of a sentence of rape. When I told her that I could not do that, she wanted to know if I knew of any other anthropologists who would. I could think of none, but I began to wonder what she thought about anthropologists.

Anthropologists, apparently, made no moral judgments about "cultures" and failed to recognize the contestation and changes taking place within contemporary local communities around the world. This also led me to wonder how she imagined anthropologists thought about culture. She seemed to assume that anthropologists viewed culture as a coherent, static, and unchanging set of values. Apparently cultures have no contact with the expansion of capitalism, the arming of various groups by transnational superpowers using them for proxy wars, or the cultural possibilities of human rights as an emancipatory discourse. I found this interviewer's view of culture wrongheaded and her opinion of anthropology discouraging. But perhaps it was just one journalist, I thought.

However, the recent article "From Skepticism to Embrace: Human Rights and the American Anthropological Association" by Karen Engle in *Human Rights Quarterly* (2001) paints another odd portrait of anthropology and its understanding of culture. In this piece, a law professor talks about the continuing "embarrassment" of anthropologists about the 1947 statement of the AAA [American Anthropological Association] Executive Board, which raised concerns about the Universal Declaration of Human Rights. Engle claims that the statement has caused the AAA "great shame" over the last fifty years (542). Anthropologists are embarrassed, she argues, because the statement asserted tolerance without limits. While many anthropologists now embrace human rights, they do so primarily in terms of the protection of culture (citing 1999 AAA Statement on Human Rights at www.aaanet.org). Tensions over how to be a cultural relativist and still make overt political judgments that the 1947 Board confronted remain. She does acknowledge that not all anthropologists think about culture this way. But relativism, as she describes it, is primarily about tolerance for difference and is incompatible with making moral judgments about other societies.

But this incompatibility depends on how one theorizes culture. If culture is homogenous, integrated, and consensual, it must be accepted as a whole. But anthropology has developed a far more complex way of understanding culture over the last two decades, focusing on its historical production, its porosity to outside influences and pressures, and its incorporation of competing repertoires of meaning and action. Were this conception more widely recognized within

## Does Culture Explain Everything?

We believe that our view of the concept of culture as presented in this chapter is widely shared among contemporary cultural anthropologists. Nevertheless, in recent years the concept of culture has been critically re-examined as patterns of human life have undergone major dislocations and reconfigurations. The issues are complex and are more fully explored in later chapters, popular culture as well as among journalists and human-rights activists, it could shift the terms of the intractable debate between universalism and relativism. Instead, culture is increasingly understood as a barrier to the realization of human rights by activists and a tool for legitimating non-compliance with human rights by conservatives.

One manifestation of the understanding of culture prevalent in human-rights law is the concept of harmful traditional practices. Originally developed to describe female genital mutilation or cutting, this term describes practices that have some cultural legitimacy yet are designated harmful to women, particularly to their health. In 1990, the committee monitoring the Convention on the Elimination of All Forms of Discrimination Against Women (CEDAW), an international convention ratified by most of the nations of the world, said that they were gravely concerned "that there are continuing cultural, traditional, and economic pressures which help to perpetuate harmful practices, such as female circumcision," and adopted General Recommendation 14, which suggested that state parties should take measures to eradicate the practice of female circumcision. Culture equals tradition and is juxtaposed to women's human rights to equality. It is not surprising, given this evolving understanding of culture within human-rights discourse, that cultural relativism is seen in such a negative light. The tendency for national elites to defend practices oppressive to women in the name of culture exacerbates this negative view of culture.

Human-rights activists and journalists have misinterpreted anthropology's position about relativism and difference because they misunderstand anthropology's position about culture. Claims to cultural relativism appear to be defences of holistic and static entities. This conception of culture comes from older anthropological usages, such as the separation of values and social action advocated in the 1950s by Talcott Parsons. Since "culture" was defined only as values, it was considered inappropriate to judge one ethical system by another one. For Melville Herskovits, the leader of the AAA's relativist criticism of the Universal Declaration of Human Rights in 1947, cultural relativism meant protecting the holistic cultures of small communities from colonial intrusion (AAA 1947 Statement, AA 49: 539–43).

If culture is understood this way, it is not surprising that cultural relativism appears to be a retrograde position to human-rights lawyers. Nor is it puzzling that they find anthropology irrelevant. As human-rights law demonizes culture, it misunderstands anthropology as well. The holistic conception of culture provides no space for change, contestation, or the analysis of the links between power, practices, and values. Instead, it becomes a barrier to the reformist project of universal human rights. From the legal perspective on human rights, it is the texts, the documents, and compliance that matter. Universalism is essential while relativism is bad. There is a sense of moral certainty which taking account of culture disrupts. This means, however, that the moral principle of tolerance for difference is lost.

When corporate executives in the US steal millions of dollars through accounting fraud, we do not criticize American culture as a whole. We recognize that these actions come from the greed of a few along with sloppy institutional arrangements that allow them to get away with it. Similarly, the actions of a single tribal council in Pakistan should not indict the entire culture, as if it were a homogeneous entity. Although Pakistan and many of its communities have practices and laws that subordinate women, these are neither homogeneous nor ancient. Pakistan as a "culture" can be indicted by this particular council's encouragement to rape only if culture is understood as a homogeneous entity whose rules evoke universal compliance. Adopting a more sophisticated and dynamic understanding of culture not only promotes human-rights activism, but also relocates anthropological theorizing to the centre of these issues rather than to the margins, where it has been banished.

Source: Merry 2003. Reproduced by permission of the American Anthropological Association from *Anthropology News*, Volume 44, Issue 2, Pages 4–5, February 2003. Not for sale or further reproduction.

but we offer here a brief account to provide some historical context.

For at least the past fifty years, many anthropologists have distinguished between *Culture* (with a capital *C*) and *cultures* (plural with a lowercase *c*). The term *Culture* has been used to describe an attribute of the human species as a whole—its members' ability, in the absence of highly specific genetic programming, to create and to imitate patterned, symbolically mediated ideas and activities that promote the survival of our species. By contrast, the term *cultures* has been used to refer to particular, learned ways of life belonging to specific groups of human beings. Given this distinction, the human species as a whole can be said to have Culture as a defining attribute, but actual human beings have access to particular human cultures—either their own or other people's.

It is the plural use of *cultures* with a lowercase *c* that has been challenged. The challenge may seem puzzling, however, because many anthropologists have viewed the plural use of the culture concept not only as analytically helpful but also as politically progressive. Their view reflects a struggle that developed in nineteenth-century Europe: Supporters of the supposedly progressive, universal civilization of the Enlightenment, inaugurated by the French Revolution and spread by Napoleonic conquest, were challenged by inhabitants of other European nations, who resisted both Napoleon and the Enlightenment in what has been called the Romantic Counter-Enlightenment. Romantic intellectuals in nations like Germany rejected what they considered to be the imposition of "artificial" Enlightenment civilization on the "natural" spiritual traditions of their own distinct national cultures (Kuper 1999; Crehan 2002).

This political dynamic, which pits a steamroller civilization against vulnerable local cultures, carried over into the usage that later developed in anthropology, particularly in North America. The last decades of the 1800s and the first few decades of the 1900s marked a period of expanding European colonial empires as well as westward consolidation of control in North America by European settlers. At that time, the social sciences were becoming established in universities, and different fields were assigned different tasks. Anthropology was allocated what Michel-Rolph Trouillot (1991) has called "the savage slot"—that is, the so-called "primitive" world that was the target of colonization. Early Canadian anthropologists, such as George Mercer Dawson, Diamond Jenness, and Marius Barbeau, were often charged with documenting and preserving the "disappearing savages," which included conducting intensive research of these supposedly "dying cultures." Moreover, since these early anthropologists were often employed by the National Museum of Canada, First Nations relics and artifacts were often taken without permission,

colonization The act of settling a region, establishing control over the Indigenous peoples who live there, and appropriating local lands and resources for one's own use.

under the guise of "cultural preservation." In these and other cases, anthropologists became the official academic experts on societies whose members suffered racist denigration as "primitives" and whose ways of life were being undermined by contact with Western colonial "civilization."

Anthropologists were determined to denounce these practices and to demonstrate that the "primitive" stereotype was false. Some found inspiration in the work of English anthropologist E.B. Tylor, who, in 1871, had defined "culture or civilization" as "that complex whole which includes knowledge, belief, art, morals, law, custom, and any other capabilities and habits acquired by man as a member of society" ([1871] 1958, 1). This definition had the virtue of blurring the difference between "civilization" and "culture," and it encouraged the view that even "primitives" possessed "capabilities and habits" that merited respect. Thus, in response to stereotypes of "primitives" as irrational, disorganized, insensitive, or promiscuous, anthropologists like Franz Boas and Bronislaw Malinowski were able to show that, on the contrary, so-called "primitives" possessed "cultures" that were reasonable, orderly, artistically developed, and morally disciplined (Figure 2.8). The plural use of *culture* allowed them to argue that, in their own ways, "primitives" were as fully human as "civilized" people were.

By the end of the twentieth century, however, some anthropologists became concerned about the way the plural concept of culture was being used. That is, the boundary that was once thought to protect vulnerability was starting to look more like a prison wall, condemning those within it to live according to "their" culture, just as their ancestors had done, like exhibits in a living museum, whether they wanted to or not. But if some group members criticize a practice, such as female

FIGURE 2.8 | Anthropologists like Franz Boas—seen here demonstrating a position in the Kwakiutl (Kwakwaka'wakw) Hamatsa dance ritual in 1894—showed that so-called "primitives" possessed reasonable and developed "cultures."

genital cutting, that is part of their cultural tradition, does this mean that the critics are no longer "authentic" members of their own culture? To come to such a conclusion overlooks the possibility that alternatives to a controversial practice might already exist within the cultural tradition and that followers of that tradition may themselves decide that some alternatives make more sense than others in today's world. The issue then becomes not just which traditions have been inherited from the past—as if "authentic" cultures were monolithic and unchanging—but, rather, which traditional practices ought to continue in a contemporary world, and who is entitled to make that decision.

## Culture Change and Cultural Authenticity

It is no secret that colonizing states have regularly attempted to determine the cultural priorities of those whom they conquered. Sending missionaries to convert colonized peoples to Christianity is one of the best-known practices of Western cultural imperialism. For example, in the nineteenth and twentieth centuries, missionaries were sent to the far northeast of the Canadian Arctic to assist in "civilizing" the Inuit. Although these missionaries were initially resisted, eventually they made many converts. Indeed, the Inuit have incorporated many aspects of Christianity into their cultural traditions, and today most Inuit consider it to be part of their cultural heritage (Laugrand and Oosten 2010, 36). But how should this religious conversion be understood?

Doesn't the fact that most Inuit today are Christians demonstrate that federal officials and missionaries succeeded in their policies of Western Christian cultural imperialism? Maybe not: "When Christianity was adopted, [Inuit] shamanism was no longer publicly performed, but many beliefs and practices continued. Inuit showed amazing creativity in integrating new beliefs and practices into their culture and, conversely, in integrating Inuit traditions into Christian beliefs and practices" (Laugrand and Oosten 2010, 36). Despite the prevailing perceptions that these so-called "primitive societies" would die off with the expansion of the dominant Western civilization, the Inuit continued to thrive. Moreover, they adopted Western technologies and adapted to new cultural practices that helped ease the challenges of living in one of the most isolated and inhospitable environments in the world. As Canadian anthropologists Frédéric Laugrand and

Jarich Oosten (2010, 36) note: "The period from the transition to Christianity until the establishment of modern Nunavut was not just a time of cultural loss, but also a time of great cultural innovation."

The Inuit combined their traditional beliefs and practices with those of Christianity. Many prominent elders, including Inuit shamans (*angakkuit*), adopted Christianity and were trained as missionaries and ministers, making Christianity highly attractive to others. Missionaries, in turn, actively sought to adapt Christian practices to traditional Inuit ways. For example, Anglican missionaries translated hymns and scriptures into the Inuktitut language of the Inuit using syllabics, and they distributed these translations in the form of "little red books" (Remie and Oosten 2002). These books were central to Christianizing the Inuit, and they became so popular that they often reached Inuit in isolated areas even before missionaries had established missions there. Another outcome of the creation of the "little red books" was that the Inuit rapidly learned to read and write using these texts, resulting in Inuit's literacy rate matching that of many European countries by the end of the nineteenth century (Remie and Oosten 2002, 112).

It might be as accurate to say that the Inuit "Inuitized" Christianity, therefore, as it would be to say that missionaries "Christianized" the Inuit. For example, the shape of the cross can be recognized in the inukshuk represented on the Nunavut flag, and the traditional Inuit Sedna feast has become integrated with Christmas celebrations (Laugrand and Oosten 2010, 327). In addition, many of the shamans and elders who became lay preachers and ministers continued to practise traditional healing and divination in secret, combining integral Inuit traditions with Christian practice. Interestingly, the evangelical and Pentecostal movement known as Canada Awakening Ministries that has spread to Nunavut in recent years evokes many aspects of the elders' shamanism. For example, speaking in tongues, which is common to Pentecostalism, recalls shamanistic behaviour (Laugrand and Oosten 2010, 341).

By integrating Western traditions into their own culture, Inuit Christians have been able to convert what began as an exercise in cultural imperialism into a reaffirmation of traditional Inuit values. For example, by transforming the inukshuk into a symbol of the cross, they have effectively made the cross an Inuit symbol that encourages people to follow their ancestors in a modern context (Laugrand and Oosten 2010,

377). This challenges the presumption that "authentic cultures" never change. Such an inflexible concept of culture can accommodate neither the agency of Inuit Christians nor the validity of the ongoing and continually unfolding cultural traditions they produce.

Today, a variety of groups, from Indigenous activists in Amazonia to immigrant activists in Europe, have incorporated the plural use of *culture* into their own self-definitions, and in some cases anthropologists defend this move as valuable and progressive. In addition, scholarly disciplines outside anthropology, from cultural studies to cognitive science, have incorporated *culture* into their own technical vocabularies. On the one hand, this can be seen (perhaps ironically) as a measure of the success of earlier generations of anthropologists in demonstrating the value of the culture concept. On the other hand, it means that today, *culture* is sometimes used in ways that anthropologists find objectionable but that they cannot control.

⟳ For more information on anthropological approaches to ethnicity, globalization, and identity, see chapters 12, 14 and 15.

## The Promise of the Anthropological Perspective

The anthropological perspective on the human condition is not easy to maintain. It forces us to question the common-sense assumptions with which we are most comfortable. It compels us to consider the cultural contexts that influence how "scientific experts" conduct their research. It only increases the difficulty we encounter when faced with moral and political decisions. It does not allow us an easy retreat, for once we are exposed to the kinds of experience that the anthropological undertaking makes possible, we are changed. We cannot easily pretend that these new experiences never happened to us. There is no going back to ethnocentrism when the going gets rough, except in bad faith. So anthropology is guaranteed to complicate your life. Nevertheless, the anthropological perspective can give you a broader understanding of human nature and the wider world, of society, culture, and history, and thus it can help you construct more realistic and authentic ways of coping with those complications.

## Chapter Summary

1. Anthropologists have argued that culture distinguishes the human condition from the condition of other living species. Human culture is learned, shared, patterned, adaptive, and symbolic. It did not emerge all at once but evolved over time. Our biological evolution aligns with cultural influences, making our species essentially biocultural.

2. Many anthropologists have long thought holistically about human culture. Anthropological holism argues that objects and environments interpenetrate and even define each other. Thus, the whole is more than the sum of its parts. Human beings and human societies are open systems that cannot be reduced to the parts that make them up. The parts and the whole mutually define, or codetermine, each other and coevolve. This book adopts a coevolutionary approach to human nature, human society, and the human past. Human beings depend on symbolic cultural understandings to help them resolve the ambiguities inherent in everyday human experience.

3. Anthropologists believe that ethnocentrism can be countered by a commitment to cultural relativism, an attempt to understand the cultural underpinnings of behaviour. Cultural relativism does not require us to abandon every value our society has taught us; however, it does discourage the easy solution of refusing to consider alternatives from the outset. Cultural relativism makes moral decisions more difficult because it requires us to take many things into account before we make up our minds.

4. Human history is an essential aspect of the human story. Culture is worked out over time and passed on from one generation to the next. The cultural beliefs and practices we inherit from the past or borrow from other people in the present make some things easier for us and other things more difficult. At the same time, culture provides resources human beings can make use of in the pursuit of their own goals. Thus, the anthropological understanding of human life recognizes the importance of human agency.

5. Many anthropologists have criticized the use of the term *cultures* to refer to particular, learned ways of life belonging to specific groups of human beings. Critics argue that this way of talking about culture seems to endorse a kind of oppressive cultural determinism. Supporters, however, argue that in some cases this version of the culture concept can be used to defend vulnerable social groups against exploitation and oppression by outsiders.

## For Review

1. Consider the five key attributes of human culture highlighted in this chapter. How do you experience these in your day-to-day life? Why is it important that culture is adaptive?

2. What are complex symbolic representation and institutions, and why are they especially important to human culture? Provide an example of one institution that you are involved in every day. How you do think that institution shapes your life?

3. What is human agency? How does attention to human agency affect the way anthropologists interpret cultural phenomena? How does Marx's quote on p. 25 pertain to your life? Do you agree with him?

4. What do anthropologists mean by *holism*? How do different factors combine to produce different human societies?

5. Describe the problems US Peace Corps volunteers were having in Botswana in the early 1970s and the explanation that was provided by anthropologist Hoyt Alverson. Have you ever experienced a misunderstanding with someone from a different culture? Analyze what happened. Do you think that there is a cultural explanation for your problem?

6. Explain the effects of ethnocentrism and cultural relativism on an individual's perception of another culture. Is there a cultural practice that you do not understand? Could cultural relativity help you understand this practice?

7. Some cultural practices, such as female genital cutting, are highly contentious. Discuss the issues at stake and think about how cultural relativism changes the discussion. Why is it important to remain culturally relative when discussing sensitive issues?

8. Distinguish between *Culture* (with a capital *C*) and *culture(s)* (with a lowercase *c*) by providing an example of each. What does this difference reflect for anthropologists?

9. Summarize the case study on Inuit Christianity with the five key attributes of culture in mind. Which attributes are discussed, and how does the case study highlight them?

## Key Terms

coevolution   27
colonization   38
cultural relativism   30
culture   25

enculturation   22
ethnocentrism   29
holism   26
hominins   24

human agency   25
socialization   22
symbol   23

## Suggested Readings

Gamst, Frederick C., and Edward Norbeck. 1976. *Ideas of Culture: Sources and Uses.* New York: Holt, Rinehart, and Winston. *A useful collection of important articles about culture. The articles are arranged according to different basic approaches to culture.*

Geertz, Clifford. 1973. "Thick Description: Toward an Interpretive Theory of Culture" and "The Impact of the Concept of Culture on the Concept of Man." In *The Interpretation of Cultures: Selected Essays*, pp. 3–30 and 33–54. New York: Basic Books. *Two classic discussions of culture from a major figure in North American anthropology. These works have done much to shape the discourse about culture in anthropology.*

Kuper, Adam. 1999. *Culture: The Anthropologists' Account.* Cambridge, MA: Harvard University Press. *A critical history of the use of the culture concept in anthropology, which traces its links to earlier Western ideas about culture and analyzes the work of several late twentieth-century anthropologists who made the concept central to their scholarship. Based on his experience with the abuse of the culture concept in apartheid South Africa, Kuper recommends that anthropologists drop the term entirely from their professional vocabulary.*

Sapir, Edward. 2002. *The Psychology of Culture: A Course of Lectures.* 2nd ed. Reconstructed and edited by Judith T. Irvine. Berlin: Mouton de Gruyter. *A collection of noted anthropologist Edward Sapir's contributions to anthropology, including the intersections of culture theory, psychology, and linguistics.*

Voget, Fred. 1975. *A History of Ethnology.* New York: Holt, Rinehart, & Winston. *A massive, thorough, and detailed work best suited for students seeking a challenging read.*

# 3 *Why Is Evolution Important to Anthropologists?*

▲ A cactus finch (*left*) and a medium ground finch (*right*) on a branch, Floreana Island, Galápagos National Park, Ecuador. These specimens showcase the sort of variation between species of finches Darwin observed and considered while developing his theory of natural selection. Photo: Joel Sartore/Getty Images

## Chapter Outline

The question of why evolution is important to anthropologists is fundamental to contemporary anthropology and is a topic of great significance in wider scientific discussions. As introduced in Chapter 1, humans are considered biocultural organisms; as such, we are subject to the evolutionary processes that affect all life on earth. In this chapter, we will look at how the living world was understood before the nineteenth century, where Darwin's ideas came from, how they have been further elaborated since his time, and why evolutionary theory continues to be our most powerful tool for understanding biological processes today.

Philosopher of science Philip Kitcher (1982) has suggested that successful scientific theories are testable, unified, and fruitful. A theory is testable when its hypotheses can be independently matched up against nature. A theory is unified when it offers just one or a few basic problem-solving strategies that make sense of a wide range of material evidence. And a theory is fruitful when its central principles suggest new and promising possibilities for further research. The modern theory of biological evolution possesses all three characteristics. Evolutionary hypotheses are highly testable in a number of ways. As we shall see, material evidence from widely diverse sources has consistently fit evolutionary predictions. Because it is based on a few central concepts and assumptions, the evolutionary research program is also highly unified. Charles Darwin's *On the Origin of Species by Means of Natural Selection* appeared in 1859. As Kitcher (1982, 48) puts it, Darwin "gave structure to our ignorance." After that date, biologists could borrow Darwin's methods to guide them in new and promising directions. The study of life has not been the same since. As we begin our study of human evolution, you may be surprised at the number of terms and concepts that you are learning from biology, genetics, and ecology. The theory of evolution has engaged the efforts of many scientists for over a hundred and fifty years. Their work has produced a still-developing, powerful, multi-stranded theory. To understand the arguments made by modern evolutionary biologists, we have to learn the language of evolution. The payoff will be a nuanced view of what the theory of evolution is really about and how powerful it really is.

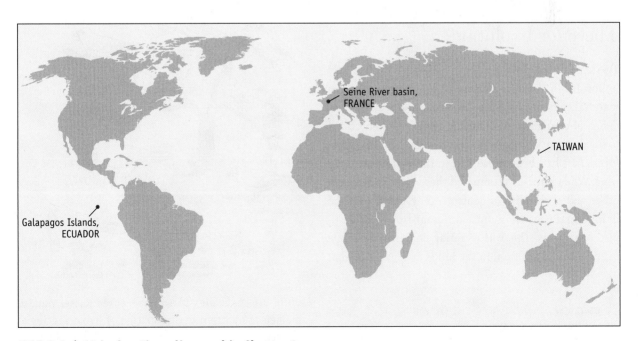

**MAP 3.1** | Major locations discussed in Chapter 3.

## What Is Evolutionary Theory?

**Evolutionary theory** claims that living species can change over time and give rise to new kinds of species, with the result that all organisms ultimately share a common ancestry. Because of this common ancestry, information about biological variation in finches or genetic transmission in fruit flies can help us understand the roles of biological variation and genetics in human evolution.

Niles Eldredge and Ian Tattersall (1982, 2) observe that evolution "is as highly verified a thesis as can be found in science. Subjected to close scrutiny from all angles for over a century now, evolution emerges as the only naturalistic explanation we have of the twin patterns of similarity and diversity that pervade all life." Steven Stanley (1981, xv), an evolutionary biologist, states that "the theory of evolution is not just getting older, it is getting better. Like any scientific concept that has long withstood the test of time, this one has suffered setbacks, but, time and again, has rebounded to become richer and stronger." More than thirty years later, evolutionary thinkers remain convinced that the story they propose to tell about the history of life on earth is more persuasive than any of its rivals. To what do they owe this sense of confidence?

## What Material Evidence Is There for Evolution?

Two kinds of material evidence have been particularly important in the development of evolutionary theory: material evidence of change over time and material evidence of change across space. Geological research led to the discovery of the fossil record—the remains of life forms that had been preserved in the earth for a long time. When scientists compared these fossils with each other and with living organisms, they noted that the living organisms were quite different from the fossilized organisms. This was material evidence of change over time, or **evolution**, in the kinds of organisms that

have lived on the earth. Any persuasive biological theory would have to find a way to explain this material evidence.

Equally important material evidence for the development of evolutionary theory came from the study of living organisms. Darwin himself was most interested in explaining the pattern of distribution of living species of organisms. In one of his best-known studies, Darwin noted that neighbouring geographic areas on the islands of the Galápagos archipelago were inhabited by species of finch different from the finch species found on the Ecuadorian mainland. At the same time, the various Galápagos species resembled one another closely and resembled mainland finch species (Figure 3.1). Species distribution patterns of this kind suggested change over space, which, again, any persuasive biological theory would have to explain.

In the centuries before Darwin, however, the fossil record was mostly unknown, and many of those concerned with biology did not see the pattern of distribution of living species as evidence for past change. To understand why Darwin's ideas had such a powerful impact requires an understanding of pre-Darwinian views of the natural world (Table 3.1).

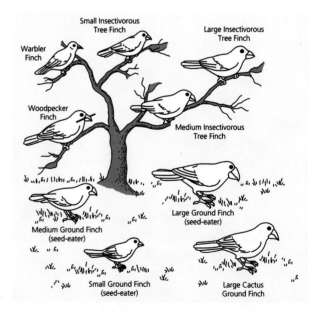

**FIGURE 3.1** | Charles Darwin and Alfred Russel Wallace explained the pattern of distribution of living species of organisms (such as the various species of finches living on the Galápagos Islands) by arguing that all the variants had evolved from a single ancestral species.

---

**evolutionary theory** The set of testable hypotheses that assert that living organisms can change over time and give rise to new kinds of organisms, with the result that all organisms ultimately share a common ancestry.

**evolution** The process of change over time.

**TABLE 3.1** | Pre-Darwinian Views of the Natural World

| View | Key Features |
| --- | --- |
| Essentialism | Each "natural kind" of living thing is characterized by an unchanging, perfect core of features that separates it from all other natural things. Based on ideas derived from Plato. |
| Great Chain of Being | A comprehensive framework used in the Middle Ages based on Aristotelian principles that linked all living things in an elaborate chain. It was based on three principles:<br>1. *Continuity*: Attributes of one kind of organism always overlap to some extent with the attributes of organisms closest to it in the classification.<br>2. *Plentitude*: A world of organisms created by a benevolent God can have no gaps but must include all logically conceivable organisms.<br>3. *Unilinear gradation*: All organisms can be arranged in a single hierarchy based on various degrees to which they depart from divine perfection. |
| Catastrophism | The notion that natural disasters, such as floods, are responsible for the extinction of species, which are then replaced by new species. Introduced by French scientist Georges Cuvier. |
| Uniformitarianism | The belief that the natural processes (such as erosion or volcanism) that affect the earth's surface today were at work in the past. Thus, we can use our understanding of current processes to reconstruct the history of the earth. Popularized by British geologist Charles Lyell. |
| Transformational evolution | Assuming essentialist species and a uniformly changing environment, proponents argued that all members of a species transform themselves in identical ways in order to adapt to commonly experienced changes in the environment. To explain why, they invoked (1) the law of use and disuse and (2) the inheritance of acquired characters. Introduced by French naturalist Jean-Baptiste de Monet de Lamarck. |

# Pre-Darwinian Views of the Natural World

In the Western societies of antiquity, the Greeks thought the world had been, and would be, around forever; in the Judeo-Christian tradition, it was thought that the world was young and would end soon. Both traditions saw the world as fixed and unchanging.

## Essentialism

If the world does not change, then the various forms of life that are part of it also do not change. We can trace this view back to the ancient Greek philosopher Plato (*c.* 429–*c.* 347 BCE). A central element of Plato's philosophy was a belief in an ideal world of perfect, eternal, unchanging forms that exist apart from the imperfect, changeable, physical world of living things. Plato believed that these two worlds—ideal and material—were linked and that every ideal form was represented in the physical, material world by a number of imperfect but recognizable forms—for example, the ideal form of "cowness" was represented by living cows of varying sizes, colours, temperaments, and so on. Plato also believed that when observers looked at living cows and saw their similarities despite all this variation, what they were really seeing was the ideal form, or essence, of "cowness" that each individual cow incarnated.

According to Plato, all living things that share the same essence belong to the same "natural kind," and there are many natural kinds in the world, each of which is the result of the imperfect incarnation in the physical world of one or another eternal form or ideal ("cowness," "humanness," "ratness," and the like). This view is called essentialism. For essentialists, as Ernst Mayr (1982, 256) explains, "each species is characterized by its unchanging essence . . . and separated from all other species by a sharp discontinuity. Essentialism assumes that the diversity of inanimate as well as of organic nature is the reflection of a limited number of unchanging universals. . . . All those objects belong to the same species that share the same essence." That essence is what made every individual cow a cow and not, say, a deer.

## The Great Chain of Being

Greek ideas were adopted and adapted by thinkers in the Judeo-Christian religious tradition. By the Middle Ages, many scholars thought they could describe the organizing principles responsible for harmony in nature. According to Arthur Lovejoy ([1936] 1960), they reasoned as follows: the ancient Greek philosopher Aristotle (384–322 BCE) suggested that kinds of organisms could be arranged in a single line from most primitive to most advanced. Aristotle further argued that the attributes of one kind of organism always overlap to some extent with the attributes of organisms closest to it in the classification so that the differences between adjacent organisms were very slight. Together, these ideas constituted a principle of continuity. Logically implied by the principle of continuity is the principle of plenitude, or fullness, which states that a world of organisms created by a benevolent God can have no gaps but must include all logically conceivable organisms. Finally, the assumption that God alone is self-sufficient and perfect, which was held by a variety of ancient and medieval philosophers, implied that each of God's creatures must lack, to a greater or lesser degree, some part of divine perfection. As a result, the various kinds of organisms can be arranged in a single hierarchy, or unilinear gradation, like a ladder or a chain, based on the degrees to which they depart from the divine ideal.

When the notion of unilinear gradation was combined with the notions of continuity and plenitude, the result was called the Great Chain of Being, a comprehensive framework for interpreting the natural world. This framework suggested that the entire cosmos was composed "of an immense, or of an infinite, number of links . . . every one of them differing from that immediately above and that immediately below it by the 'least possible' degree of difference" (Lovejoy [1936] 1960, 59). Degrees of difference were understood in theological terms to be degrees of excellence. Creatures farthest away from divine perfection were lowest in the hierarchy, whereas creatures most like God (such as the angels) ranked highest (Figure 3.2). Human beings occupied a unique position in the chain. Their material bodies linked them to other material beings; but unlike other material creatures, they also possessed souls and were thereby linked to the spiritual realm by a God who had created them in his image.

For several hundred years—from the Middle Ages through to the eighteenth century—the Great Chain of Being was the framework in the Western world within which all discussions of living organisms were set. This framework of ideas continued as late as the mid-eighteenth century, influencing even Carolus Linnaeus (1707–1778), who is the father of modern biological **taxonomy** or classification (Figure 3.3). Linnaeus was committed to an essentialist definition of natural kinds. He focused on what modern taxonomists call the **genus** (plural *genera*) and used the form and structure of reproductive organs to define the "essence" of a genus (Mayr 1982, 178). (The term *species*, which modern biologists assign to subpopulations of the same genus that share certain specific attributes, was used more loosely in the past by essentialists and by non-essentialists.) Essentialists like Linnaeus knew that individuals sometimes differ markedly from what is considered "normal" for others of their kind. But these deviations were thought of as accidents, or "degradations," that could not affect the unity of the natural kind.

## Catastrophism and Uniformitarianism

In the eighteenth century, unprecedented social and scientific discoveries gradually raised doubts about the Great Chain of Being. The principle of continuity was criticized by French scientist Georges Cuvier (1769–1832), a pioneer in modern anatomy who also

**FIGURE 3.2** | In the Great Chain of Being, creatures were ranked according to their degree of divine perfection. Plants and fungi, which lack mobility and sensory organs, were ranked below animals, which were in turn ranked below human beings.

**taxonomy** In biology, a classification system used to organize various kinds of organisms.

**genus** The level of the Linnaean taxonomy in which different species are grouped together on the basis of their similarities to one another. In modern taxonomies, genus is ranked between family (less specific) and species (more specific).

**species** For Linnaeus, a Platonic "natural kind" defined in terms of its essence. For modern biologists, a reproductive community of populations (reproductively isolated from others) that occupies a specific niche in nature.

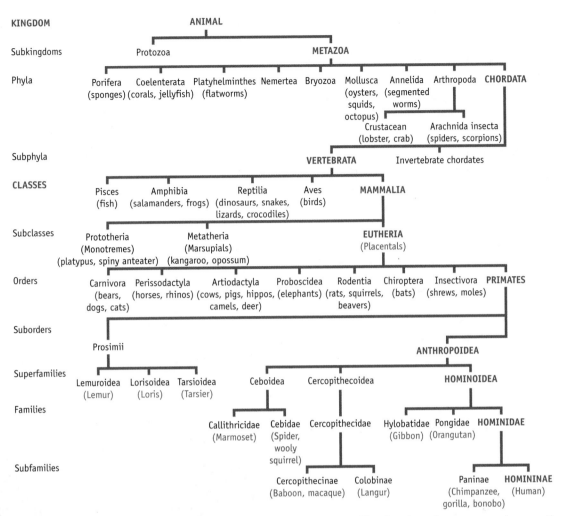

**FIGURE 3.3 |** A modern biological taxonomy based on the Linnaean classification (popular names are in parentheses). Organisms sharing structural similarities are still grouped together, but their similarities are understood to be the result of common ancestry, indicated by the horizontal line connecting them. Thus, Paninae (chimpanzees, gorillas, and bonobos) and Homininae (human beings) all share a recent common ancestor.

carried out some of the first important excavations of fossils in the Seine River basin near Paris. He was a firm believer in the essentialist definition of natural kinds, but his anatomical studies convinced him that there were only four natural categories of living things. Each category was excellently adapted to its way of life but had no connection to any of the others. Cuvier's studies of the fossil record convinced him that, over time, some species had been abruptly wiped out and replaced, equally abruptly, by new species from somewhere else. He called these abrupt transitions "revolutions," although this term was translated into English as "catastrophe." Hence, the term *catastrophism* came to refer to the notion that natural disasters, such as floods, are responsible for the extinction of some natural kinds, which are later replaced by new natural kinds.

In some ways, Cuvier's ideas were perfectly traditional: he did not reject the essentialist understanding of species and never suggested that new species were simply old species that had changed. Yet, his idea that some species might disappear in mass extinctions was quite radical because, according to Judeo-Christian theology, God had created all possible forms of life only once. In the same way, Cuvier's assertion in 1812 that there were no connections whatsoever among the four basic categories of living things seriously undermined the principle of unilinear gradation. That is, if the four categories had nothing in common with one another, then they could not be arranged in a simple chain of natural kinds, each precisely placed between the one slightly less advanced and the one slightly more advanced. Ernst Mayr (1982, 201) concluded that this argument dealt the Great Chain of Being its death blow.

But the Great Chain of Being did not die gently, because its principles had become inextricably intertwined with Judeo-Christian beliefs about the natural world. By the late eighteenth and early nineteenth centuries, one result of this process of amalgamation was the development of an approach arguing that the perfection of each organism's adaptation could only be the result of intentional design by a benevolent creator. One group of thinkers, known as "catastrophists," modified Cuvier's theory and argued that the new species that replaced old ones had been specially created by God. Others subscribed to a position known as *uniformitarianism*, which stressed nature's overall harmonious integration as evidence for God's handiwork. These "uniformitarians" criticized the ideas of Cuvier and the catastrophists. God might allow the world to change, they admitted, but a benevolent God's blueprint for creation could not include sharp breaks between different forms of life and the abrupt disappearance of species through extinction. The uniformitarian position gained powerful support from the book *Principles of Geology* by Charles Lyell (1797–1875), published between 1830 and 1833. Lyell argued that the same gradual processes of erosion and volcanism that change the earth's surface today had also been at work in the past. Assuming the uniformity of these processes, he contended that our understanding of current processes could be used to reconstruct the past history of the earth.

The quarrel between catastrophists and uniformitarians has often been portrayed as a conflict between narrow-minded dogmatism (identified with the catastrophists) and open-minded, empirical science (identified with the uniformitarians). But, as Stephen Jay Gould (1987) demonstrated, this portrayal misrepresents the nature of their disagreement. Both Cuvier and Lyell were empirical scientists: the former, a leading anatomist and excavator of fossils; the latter, a fieldworking geologist. Both confronted much of the same material evidence; however, as Gould points out, they interpreted that evidence in very different ways. Catastrophists were willing to accept a view of earth's history that permitted ruptures of harmony in order to preserve their belief that history, guided by divine intervention, was going somewhere. By contrast, the harmonious, non-directional view of the uniformitarians was rooted in their belief that time was cyclic, like the changing seasons. Uniformitarians promoted the view that God's creation was the "incarnation of rationality"—that is, that God's creation unfolded in accordance with God's

laws, without requiring subsequent divine intervention or a fixed historical trajectory.

## Transformational Evolution

Thus, by the early years of the nineteenth century, traditional ideas about the natural world had been challenged by new material evidence and conflicting interpretations of that evidence. In the ferment of this period, French naturalist Jean-Baptiste de Monet de Lamarck (1744–1829) grappled with the inconsistencies described above, dealing the first serious blow against essentialism (Figure 3.4). Lamarck wanted to preserve the traditional view of a harmonious living world. One of the most serious challenges to that view was the problem of extinction. How could perfectly adapted creatures suddenly be wiped out, and where did their replacements come from? Some suggested that the extinctions were the result of the biblical Noah's flood, but this could not explain how aquatic animals had become extinct. Others suggested that extinctions were

**FIGURE 3.4** | Jean-Baptiste de Monet de Lamarck. Lamarck wanted to preserve the traditional view of a harmonious living world, but his interpretation of the evidence of fossils eventually undermined exactly the view he was trying to defend.

the result of human hunting, possibly explaining why mastodons no longer roamed the earth. Some hoped that natural kinds believed to be extinct might yet be found inhabiting an unexplored area of the globe.

Lamarck suggested an original interpretation of the material evidence that had been used to argue in favour of extinction. Noticing that many fossil species bore a close resemblance to living species, he suggested in 1809 that perhaps fossil forms were the ancestors of living forms. Fossil forms looked different from their descendants, he believed, because ancestral features had been modified over time to suit their descendants to changing climate and geography. Such a process would prove that nature was harmonious after all—that, although the world was a changing world, living organisms possessed the capacity to change along with it.

Many elements of the Great Chain of Being could be made to fit with Lamarck's scheme. Lamarck believed that once a natural kind had come into existence, it had the capacity to evolve over time into increasingly complex (or "perfect") forms. This could happen, Lamarck suggested, because all organisms have two attributes: (1) the ability to change physically in response to environmental demands and (2) the capacity to activate this ability whenever environmental change makes the organism's previous response obsolete. Otherwise, the resulting lack of fit between organisms and environment would create disharmony in nature. Lamarck never suggested that a species might adapt to change by splitting into two or more new species; rather, he suggested that every member of every species is engaged in its own individual adaptive transformation over time. This is why Lamarckian evolution has also been called *transformational evolution*.

Lamarck proposed two "laws" to explain how such transformation occurs. First, he said, an organ is strengthened by use and weakened by disuse (an early statement of "use it or lose it"). If environmental changes cause members of a species to rely more heavily on some organs than on others, the former will become enhanced and the latter reduced. This was known as the law of use and disuse. Lamarck further argued that this first law had evolutionary consequences because the physical result of use or disuse could be passed from one generation to the next, which resulted in his second law: the inheritance of acquired characteristics.

Consider the following example: modern pandas possess an oversized, elongated wrist bone that aids them in stripping bamboo leaves, their favourite food,

**FIGURE 3.5** | Lamarckian transformational evolution and Darwinian variational evolution offer two different explanations for how the panda got its "thumb." The "thumb" is actually an elongated wrist bone that aids pandas in stripping bamboo leaves, their favourite food, from bamboo stalks.

from bamboo stalks (Figure 3.5). This bone has been called the panda's "thumb," although pandas retain all five digits on each paw. Had Lamarck known about the panda's "thumb," he might have explained its origin as follows: suppose that pandas originally had wrist bones like those of other bears. Then the environment changed, obliging pandas to become dependent on bamboo for food. Pandas, unable to survive on bamboo unless they found an efficient way to strip the leaves off the stalk, were forced to use their forepaws more intensively (the law of use and disuse) in order to remove enough bamboo leaves to satisfy their appetite. Continual exercise of their wrists caused their wrist bones to enlarge and lengthen into a shape resembling a thumb. After acquiring "thumbs" through strenuous activity, pandas gave birth to offspring with elongated wrist bones (the law of inheritance of acquired characters). Thus, Lamarck's laws could explain how each species builds up new, more complex organs and attains, over many generations, higher levels of "perfection."

Because transformational evolution works through the efforts of individual members of a species, what would prevent different individuals from transforming themselves in different directions? Part of the answer is that Lamarck expected a changing environment to affect all individuals of the same species in the same way, leading to identical responses in terms of use and disuse. But the rest of the answer lies with the fact that Lamarck still accepted the essentialist belief that every individual member of a species was identical in essence to every other member. Only if this were so could all members of the same species respond in the same ways to the same environmental pressures and retain their species identity over time.

Lamarck's transformational theory of biological evolution was rejected by biologists in the early twentieth century, when geneticists were able to demonstrate that neither the law of use and disuse nor the law of inheritance of acquired characters applied to genes. In the early nineteenth century, however, Lamarck's speculations opened the door for new ideas about how organisms develop and change through time.

## What Is Natural Selection?

Lamarck had argued that a species could vary over time. Contemporaries of Lamarck, observing living organisms in the wild in Europe, the Americas, Africa, and Asia, had demonstrated that species could vary over space as well. Where did all this mutually coexisting but previously unknown living variation come from?

The mystery of geographical variation in living organisms was particularly vexing to Charles Darwin (1809–1882, Figure 3.6) and Alfred Russel Wallace (1823–1913), whose field observations made it impossible to ignore. Wallace reasoned that the relationship between similar but distinct species in the wild could be explained if all the similar species were related to one another biologically—that is, if they were considered daughter (or sibling) species of some other parental species. Darwin, comparing the finches on the Galápagos Islands with finches on the Ecuadorian mainland, reasoned that the similarities linking the finches could be explained if all of them had descended from a single parental finch population. Both men concluded independently that similar species must descend from a common ancestor, meaning that any species might split into a number of new species given enough time. But how much time? In the 1650s, James Ussher, the Anglican archbishop of Ireland, used information in the Bible to calculate that

**FIGURE 3.6** | Charles Darwin (1809–1882).

God created the earth on 23 October 4004 BCE, a date that was still widely accepted. Charles Lyell and other geologists, however, claimed that the earth was much more than 6000 years old (indeed, it is about 4.5 billion years old). If the geologists were right, there had been ample time for what Darwin called "descent with modification" to have produced the species diversity we find in the world today.

Darwin had refrained from publishing his work on evolution for years but was moved to action when Lyell warned him that Wallace was ready to publish his ideas. As a result, Darwin and Wallace first published their views in a scientific paper carrying both their names. Darwin became better known than Wallace in later years, in part because of the mass of material evidence he collected in support of his theory together with his refined theoretical interpretations of that evidence.

The theory of **common ancestry**—"the first Darwinian revolution" (Mayr 1982, 116)—was in itself scandalous, because it went far beyond Lamarck's modest suggestion that species can change without losing their essential integrity. Not only did Darwin propose that similar species can be traced to a common ancestor, but he also offered a straightforward, mechanistic explanation of how such descent with modification takes place. His explanation, the theory of **natural selection**,

**common ancestry** Darwin's claim that similar living species must all have had a common ancestor.

**natural selection** A two-step, mechanistic explanation of how descent with modification takes place: (1) every generation, variant individuals are generated within a species because of genetic mutation, and (2) those variant individuals best suited to the current environment survive and produce more offspring than do other variants.

was "the second Darwinian revolution." That natural selection remains central to modern evolutionary theory is testimony to the power of Darwin's insight, because it has been tested and reformulated for more than 150 years and remains the best explanation we have today for the diversity of life on earth.

Charles Darwin's theory of evolution was possible only because he was able to think about species in a new way. Although Lamarck had begun to do this when he suggested that species could change, Darwin completed the job. If organisms could change, then they did not have a fixed essence. This, in turn, meant that variation—or differences—among individual members of a species might be extremely important.

Thus, Darwin turned the essentialist definition of *species* on its head. He argued that the important thing about individual members of a species is not what they have in common but how they are different. The Darwinian theory of evolution by natural selection argued that variation, not a unitary essence, is the central condition of life. This is why it is called **variational evolution**, in contrast to the transformational evolution of Lamarck (see, e.g., Lewontin 1982). The idea of variational evolution depends on what Ernst Mayr (1982) calls "population thinking"—that is, seeing the populations that make up a species as composed of biological individuals whose differences from one another are genuine and important.

## Population Thinking

Darwin combined this new view of species with other observations about the natural world. Consider, for example, frogs in a pond. Nobody would deny that new frogs hatch from hundreds of eggs laid by mature females every breeding season, yet the size of the population of adult frogs in a given pond rarely changes much from one season to the next. Clearly, the great potential fertility represented by all those eggs is never realized or the pond would shortly be overrun by frogs. Something must keep all those eggs from maturing into adults. In order to explain this phenomenon, Darwin used the mainstream nineteenth-century capitalistic ideas of Thomas Malthus, who suggested that population numbers are limited by resource availability (Figure 3.7). Darwin noted that there was a limited food supply in the pond, which means that the hatchlings are forced to compete with one another for food. Darwin

**FIGURE 3.7 |** Darwin used mainstream ideas about capitalism to explain the concept of fitness. Even though female turtles produce many offspring, such as those seen here, only those whose variant traits best equip them to compete for limited resources will survive to adulthood and reproduce.

wondered what factors determined which hatchlings win and which lose. Pointing to the variation among all individuals of the species, he argued that those individuals whose variant traits better equip them to compete in the struggle for existence are more likely to survive and reproduce than those who lack such traits. Individuals who leave greater numbers of offspring are said to have superior fitness.

Such an argument makes no sense, of course, unless species are understood in variational terms. For an essentialist, the individual members of a species are

**variational evolution** The Darwinian theory of evolution, which assumes that variant members of a species respond differently to environmental challenges. Those variants that are more successful ("fitter") survive and reproduce more offspring, who inherit the traits that made their parents fit.

identical to one another because they share the same essence; it makes no difference which or how many of them survive and reproduce. From an essentialist point of view, therefore, competition can occur only between different species because only the differences between entire species (not between a species' individual members) matter. Once we think of a species in variational terms, however, the notion that competition for resources "is 'dog eat dog' rather than 'dog eat cat'" begins to make sense (Depew and Weber 1989, 257).

When Darwin interpreted his observations, he came up with the following explanation of how biological evolution occurs. Levins and Lewontin (1985, 31ff.) summarize his theory in three principles and one driving force that sets the process in motion:

1. The principle of variation. No two individuals in a species are identical in all respects; they vary in such features as size, colour, and so on.
2. The principle of heredity. Offspring tend to resemble their parents.
3. The principle of natural selection. Different variants leave different numbers of offspring.

The driving force, Darwin suggested, was the struggle for existence. In a later edition of *On the Origin of Species*, he borrowed a phrase coined by sociologist Herbert Spencer and described the outcome of the struggle for existence as "survival of the fittest."

## Natural Selection in Action

To illustrate the operation of natural selection, let us return to the problem of how pandas got their "thumbs." Lamarck would explain this phenomenon by arguing that individual pandas all used their wrists intensively to obtain enough bamboo leaves to survive, causing their wrist bones to lengthen, a trait they passed on to their offspring. Darwin, by contrast, would explain this phenomenon by focusing attention not on individual

**aptation**  The shaping of any useful feature of an organism, regardless of that feature's origin.

**adaptation**  The shaping of a useful feature of an organism by natural selection for the function it now performs.

**exaptation**  The shaping of a useful feature of an organism by natural selection to perform one function and the later reshaping of that feature by different selection pressures to perform a new function.

pandas, but on a *population* of pandas and the ways in which members of that population differed from one another. He would argue that originally there must have been a population of pandas with wrist bones of different lengths (the principle of variation). Because offspring tend to resemble their parents, pandas with long wrist bones gave birth to offspring with long wrist bones and pandas with short wrist bones gave birth to offspring with short wrist bones (the principle of heredity). When the climate changed such that pandas became dependent upon bamboo leaves for food, pandas with wrist bones of different lengths had to compete with one another to get enough leaves to survive (the struggle for existence).

Note that, in this example, "the struggle for existence" does not imply that the pandas were necessarily *fighting* with one another over access to bamboo. The pandas with long wrist bones functioning as "thumbs" for stripping bamboo stalks were simply more successful than pandas who lacked such a "thumb"; that is, in this new environment, their elongated wrist bones made them fitter than pandas with short wrist bones. Thus, pandas with "thumbs" survived and left more offspring than did those without "thumbs." As a result, the proportion of pandas in the population with elongated wrist bones in the next generation was larger than it had been in the previous generation and the proportion of pandas in the population with short wrist bones was smaller. If these selective pressures were severe enough, pandas with short wrist bones might not leave any offspring at all, resulting at some point in a population made up entirely of pandas with "thumbs."

In Darwinian terms, adaptation has been traditionally understood as the process by which an organism "is engineered to be in harmony with the natural environment" as a result of natural selection (Little 1995, 123). However, this concept contains ambiguities that can confuse the *process* of adaptation with its *outcomes* (also often called "adaptations"). In 1982, paleontologists Stephen Jay Gould and Elisabeth Vrba helped to resolve this confusion by distinguishing among **aptation**, **adaptation**, and **exaptation**. An *aptation* refers to any useful feature of an organism, regardless of its origin. An *adaptation* refers to a useful feature of an organism that was shaped by natural selection for the function it now performs.

For a discussion of these concepts in relation to human variation, see Chapter 4, pp. 80–6.

An *exaptation*, by contrast, refers to a useful feature of an organism that was originally shaped by natural selection to perform one function but later reshaped by different selection pressures to perform a new function.

The distinction between adaptation and exaptation is important because mistaking one for the other can lead to evolutionary misinterpretations. For example, it has been standard practice to explain an organism's current form (e.g., an insect's wing shape) as an adaptation for the function it currently carries out (i.e., flight). This kind of explanation, however, raises problems. If insect wings evolved gradually via natural selection, then the first modest appendages on which selection would operate could not have looked like—or worked like—the wings of living insects. As a result, those early appendages could not have been used for flying. But what adaptive advantage could something that was not yet a wing confer on insect ancestors? Gould and Vrba (1982) showed that appendages that were not yet wings could have been adaptive for reasons having nothing to do with flying. For example, the original adaptive function of insect appendages was body cooling, but these appendages were later exapted for the function of flying, once they had reached a certain size or shape (Figure 3.8). Specialists in human evolution like Pam Willoughby (2007) use the concepts of adaptation and exaptation to explain some of the twists and turns in human evolutionary history.

Darwin's theory of evolution by natural selection is elegant and dramatic. As generations of biologists have tested its components in their own research, they have come to examine it critically. For example, much debate has been generated about the concept of fitness. Some people have assumed that the biggest, strongest, toughest individuals must be, by definition, fitter than the smaller, weaker, gentler members of their species. Strictly speaking, however, Darwinian, or biological, fitness is nothing more (and nothing less) than an individual's ability to survive and leave offspring. There is no such thing as "absolute" fitness. In a given environment, those who leave more offspring behind are fitter than those who leave fewer offspring behind. But any organism that manages to reproduce in that environment is fit. As geneticist Richard Lewontin (1982, 150) puts it, "In evolutionary terms, an Olympic athlete who never has any children has a fitness of zero, whereas J.S. Bach, who was sedentary and very much overweight, had an unusually high Darwinian fitness by virtue of his having been the father of twenty children."

Clearly, Darwinian theory has been challenged to show that biological heredity operates to produce ever-renewing variation and to explain how such variation is generated and passed on from parents to offspring. Darwin's original formulation of the theory of evolution by natural selection was virtually silent about these matters. Darwin was convinced on the basis of considerable evidence that heritable variation must exist, but he and his colleagues were completely ignorant about the sources of variation. Not until the beginning of the twentieth century did knowledge about these matters begin to accumulate, and not until the 1930s did a new evolutionary synthesis of Darwinian principles and genetics become established.

## How Did Biologists Learn about Genes?

Offspring tend to look like their parents, which suggests that something unchanging is passed on from one generation to the next. At the same time, offspring are not identical to their parents, which raises the possibility that whatever the parents pass on may be modified by environmental forces. The question of whether biological inheritance was stable or modifiable, or both, challenged Darwin and his contemporaries.

In the absence of scientific knowledge about heredity, Darwin and many of his contemporaries adopted a theory of heredity that had roots in antiquity: the theory of pangenesis. **Pangenesis** was a theory of inheritance

**FIGURE 3.8 |** How did wings evolve for flight? Gould and Vrba (1982) suggest that appendages on early insects were for body cooling but later exapted for flying once those appendages had reached a certain size or shape.

in which multiple particles from both parents blended in their offspring. That is, it claimed that an organism's physical traits are passed on from one generation to the next in the form of distinct particles. Supporters of pangenesis argued that all the organs of both mother and father gave off multiple particles that were somehow transmitted, in different proportions, to each of their offspring. For example, suppose that a child resembled her father more than her mother in a particular trait— say, hair colour. Pangenesis explained this by arguing that the child had received more "hair colour particles" from her father than from her mother. The particles inherited from both parents were believed to blend in their offspring. Thus, the child's hair colour would be closer to her father's shade than to her mother's.

As we know today, heredity is not the result of pangenesis. In the years since Darwin conducted his research, biologists have discovered that physical differences in offspring result from the way new sets of chromosomes form during fertilization. To arrive at this discovery, they first had to realize that living cells reproduce by undergoing two kinds of division. The first kind, mitosis, is simply the way body cells split and make exact copies of themselves. The second kind, meiosis, is more central to the question of how offspring inherit traits from their parents. In meiosis, a cell divides its chromosome pairs in half, producing "sex cells" or "germ cells" (sperm and eggs) that contain only half of the genetic material contained in the original cell. When sperm and egg join, the individual

chromosomes from both parents combine to create new paired chromosomes, resulting in a unique individual. A major contribution toward our modern understanding of genetic inheritance came from the experiments Gregor Mendel conducted in the nineteenth century.

## Mendel's Experiments

The notion of particulate inheritance was already common in the middle of the nineteenth century when the Austrian monk Gregor Mendel (1822–1884) began conducting plant-breeding experiments in the garden of his monastery. His great contribution was to provide evidence in favour of non-blending, single-particle inheritance, called Mendelian inheritance. When Mendel crossed peas with strikingly different traits, some of those traits did not appear in offspring of the first generation ($F_1$) (Figure 3.9). They did, however, reappear in their original form in the next generation ($F_2$). Had the particles blended, all the offspring of plants with red flowers and plants with white flowers should have been some shade of pink; but this did not happen, providing strong evidence that the particles responsible for the trait did not blend in offspring but remained discrete.

When Mendel carefully counted the number of offspring in the $F_2$ generation that showed each trait, he consistently came up with a 3:1 ratio of one form to the other, a factor nobody before him had noticed. This ratio recurred whenever Mendel repeated his experiments. If pangenesis were correct, no such ratios would have occurred because each individual would have inherited an unpredictable number of particles from each parent. However, the 3:1 ratio made excellent sense if, as Mendel assumed, each individual inherited only one particle from each parent (Mayr 1982, 721).

The results of his breeding experiments suggested to Mendel something else as well—that the particle responsible for one form of a particular trait (e.g., flower colour) could be present in an organism but go unexpressed. Those particles whose traits are expressed in an organism are said to be *dominant*; those whose traits are not expressed are said to be *recessive*. (We now know that sometimes both traits can be expressed, in which case they are said to be *codominant*.) Mendel thus concluded that the particles responsible for a particular trait, such as the pea's flower colour, occur in pairs. An individual gets one particle for each trait (i.e., one-half of the pair) from

pangenesis  A theory of heredity suggesting that an organism's physical traits are passed on from one generation to the next in the form of multiple distinct particles given off by all parts of the organism, different proportions of which get passed on to offspring via sperm or egg.

chromosomes  Sets of paired bodies in the nucleus of cells that are made of DNA and contain the hereditary genetic information that organisms pass on to their offspring.

mitosis  The way body cells make copies of themselves. The pairs of chromosomes in the nucleus of the cell duplicate and line up along the centre of the cell. The cell then divides, each daughter cell taking one full set of paired chromosomes.

meiosis  The way sex cells make copies of themselves, which begins like mitosis, with chromosome duplication and the formation of two daughter cells. However, each daughter cell then divides again without chromosome duplication and, as a result, contains only a single set of chromosomes rather than the paired set typical of body cells.

Mendelian inheritance  The view that heredity is based on non-blending, single-particle genetic inheritance.

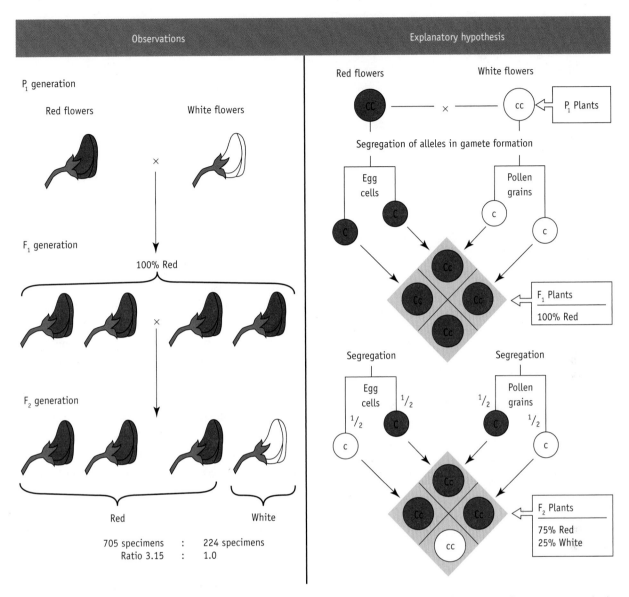

**FIGURE 3.9** | Mendel crossbred peas with red flowers and peas with white flowers (the parental, or P$_1$, generation). This produced a generation (F$_1$) of only red flowers. When Mendel crossed red-flowered peas from the F$_1$ generation, they produced the F$_2$ generation of peas, in which there were approximately three red-flowered plants for every one plant with white flowers. This 3:1 ratio of red to white flowers, together with the reappearance of white flowers, could be explained if each plant had two genetic factors and the factor for red flowers was dominant. Only a plant with two factors for white flowers would produce white flowers, whereas red flowers would appear in every plant that had at least one factor for red.

each parent. This is the **principle of segregation**. Mendel further argued that each pair of particles separates independently of every other pair when what he called "germ cells" (egg and sperm) are formed. This is the **principle of independent assortment**. As a result, each sperm and ovum is virtually guaranteed to be different from all others produced by an individual because the collection of particles that each contains will be distinct. Moreover, the pairs of particles that come together in any individual offspring are random,

depending on which egg and which sperm happened to unite to form that individual.

**principle of segregation** A principle of Mendelian inheritance in which an individual gets one particle (gene) for each trait (i.e., one-half of the required pair) from each parent.

**principle of independent assortment** A principle of Mendelian inheritance in which each pair of particles (genes) separates independently of every other pair when germ cells (egg and sperm) are formed.

## The Emergence of Genetics

Mendel's insights were ignored for nearly 35 years until three biologists rediscovered them at the beginning of the twentieth century, resulting in an explosion of research and vast growth of scientific knowledge about heredity. The British scientist William Bateson coined the term *genetics* in 1908 to describe the new science being built on Mendelian principles. He invented the term *homozygous* to describe a fertilized egg that receives the same particle from both parents for a particular trait and the term *heterozygous* to describe a fertilized egg that receives a different particle from each parent for the same trait.

In 1909, the Danish geneticist W.L. Johannsen suggested the term *gene* to refer to the particle itself. Although genes occur in pairs in any individual, geneticists discovered that there might be many more than two forms of a given gene. Bateson used the term *alleles* to refer to all the different forms that a particular gene might take.

At first, nobody knew what physical structures corresponded to the genes and alleles they had been describing. However, advances in cell biology led some scientists to suggest that the chromosomes in the cell nucleus might play an important role. These sets of paired bodies were easy to see under the microscope because they accepted a coloured stain very well (hence their name, from Greek, meaning "coloured bodies"). Animals of different species have different numbers of chromosomes (humans have 46), but all chromosomes are found in pairs (humans have 23 pairs).

## Genes and Traits

Geneticists originally thought (and many non-scientists still believe) that one gene equals one trait. Sometimes a single allele does appear to govern a single physical trait. This may be true of many physical traits that show discontinuous variation—that is, sharp breaks from one individual to the next. Recall that the flowers on Mendel's pea plants were either red or white; they did not come in various shades of pink. This observation led Mendel to conclude that a single dominant particle (or two identical recessive particles) determines flower colour.

Early research, however, showed that one gene–one trait was too simplistic an explanation for many hereditary traits. Sometimes many genes are responsible for producing a single trait, such as skin colour; such traits are thus said to be the result of polygeny. Traits like skin colour in human beings are different from traits like flower colour in Mendel's peas because they show continuous variation. That is, the expression of the trait grades imperceptibly from one individual to another, without sharp breaks. The discovery of polygenic inheritance showed that Mendelian concepts could be used to explain discontinuous and continuous variation alike.

Perhaps even more surprising than polygenic activity was the discovery that a single gene may affect more than one trait, a phenomenon called pleiotropy. For example, the *S* allele that gives human red blood cells increased resistance to malarial parasites also reduces the amount of oxygen these cells can carry (Rothwell 1977, 18). Similarly, the allele that causes the feathers of chickens to be white also works to slow down their body growth (Lerner and Libby 1976). The discovery of pleiotropy showed that genes do not produce traits in isolation. Many geneticists came to focus attention on what the Russian geneticist Sergei Chetverikov called the "genetic milieu," investigating the effects that different genes could have on one another (Figure 3.10). For example, geneticist Theodosius Dobzhansky was able to demonstrate that "certain genes or chromosomes could convey superior fitness in some combinations, and be lethal in combination with other chromosomes" (Mayr 1982, 580).

genetics  The scientific study of biological heredity.

homozygous  Describes a fertilized egg that receives the same particle (or allele) from each parent for a particular trait.

heterozygous  Describes a fertilized egg that receives a different particle (or allele) from each parent for the same trait.

gene  The portion or portions of the DNA molecule that code for proteins that shape phenotypic traits.

alleles  All the different forms that a particular gene might take.

discontinuous variation  A pattern of phenotypic variation in which the phenotype (e.g., flower colour) exhibits sharp breaks from one member of the population to the next.

polygeny  The phenomenon whereby many genes are responsible for producing a phenotypic trait, such as skin colour.

continuous variation  A pattern of variation involving polygeny in which phenotypic traits grade imperceptibly from one member of the population to another without sharp breaks.

pleiotropy  The phenomenon whereby a single gene may affect more than one phenotypic trait.

For more on the connection between pleiotropy and human variation, see Chapter 4, p. 80.

## In Their Own Words

### Culture: The Silent Language Geneticists Must Learn

*The following is an excerpt from a speech that Roderick McInnes, professor of genetics and biochemistry at McGill University, gave at a meeting of the American Society of Human Genetics in 2010. In this speech, McInnes describes how important it is for human geneticists to consider the role of culture in their research and how it is essential to create respectful community-based research initiatives with Indigenous peoples.*

The subject of my address, "Culture: The Silent Language Geneticists Must Learn," occurred to me when I recently discovered a reprint of a favourite book, *The Silent Language*, by Edward T. Hall, first published in 1959. The silent language referred to in the title is culture. He wrote that ". . . cultural patterns are literally unique, and therefore they are not universal. . . . Consequently, difficulties in intercultural communication are seldom seen for what they are." As geneticists and genomicists have reached out to study the world's populations, . . . the opportunities for cultural misunderstanding have grown. In some instances, remarkable progress has been made, both in doing research with Indigenous communities and [in] doing it in ways welcomed by them. In others, the cultural perspective of the researchers, and their more powerful cultural position in society, has prevented them from fully considering the priorities of the study population, . . . and the population under study has been left with a sense of mistrust, stigmatization, or weakened political authority (Manson 1989; Dukepoo 1999). . . .

A geneticist's first impression of an Indigenous culture is similar to viewing an iceberg: what you see isn't what you get. The obvious differences—the visible one-seventh of the iceberg above the water—are only a small fraction of all the distinct features of the Indigenous culture. These surface features poorly represent the larger substratum of profound differences hidden beneath the surface.

My first goal [in giving this speech] is to increase your awareness of the perspectives and concerns of Indigenous populations regarding genetic research. . . . Perhaps the predominant reality for Indigenous populations, with respect to research, is the fact that we, geneticists from Western-oriented cultures, are from the dominant [i.e., more powerful] culture. . . . This fact generally permeates almost all interactions between researchers and Indigenous populations. As exemplified by the experience of Mohatt and his colleagues in conducting research with Alaskan Natives, the researcher must . . . avoid unconsciously sending the "message that the researcher, as someone holding specialized knowledge and language,

could tell the community what was right . . . " (Mohatt et al. 2004). The power differential may be unwittingly and unfavourably tilted against the . . . Indigenous culture before even a word has been spoken.

My second goal is to present examples of both successful and unsuccessful research studies of Indigenous populations and to consider why some succeeded and others failed. Third, I will emphasize that the culture, priorities, values, and jurisdiction of the Indigenous community must be respected and that, in successful studies, they have been. The take-home message is that we must do "culturally competent" research; research that respects the Indigenous community's beliefs, their desire for self-determination, their desire to benefit from the research, and their wish to retain intellectual property rights and ownership of samples of DNA, tissues, and body fluids. One can visualize the ideal dynamic between researchers and Indigenous communities schematically: imagine that a large circle is us, the dominant culture, and that the Indigenous culture is a very much smaller circle within or partially within our culture (see below). The equality of the reach and influence of the Indigenous population over the whole research project can be represented by the arrows radiating out from the small central circle of the Indigenous community to the perimeter of the large circle. . .

One of the first unfortunate interactions between geneticists and an Indigenous population occurred in Canada and involved the Nuu-chah-nulth, a tribe whose people live on the west coast of Vancouver Island in British Columbia (Pullman and Arbour 2009). The Nuu-chah-nulth have a high frequency of rheumatoid arthritis. In the early 1980s, Dr R.H. Ward, at the time at the University of British Columbia, approached the tribal leaders about undertaking a search for HLA alleles that might be linked to the arthritis in this tribe. A study of 900 participants failed to demonstrate linkage. These studies were conducted according to ethical guidelines of the time. . . . The problems arose later. Between 1985 and up to 2000, the DNA was moved to other research centres without the

Continued

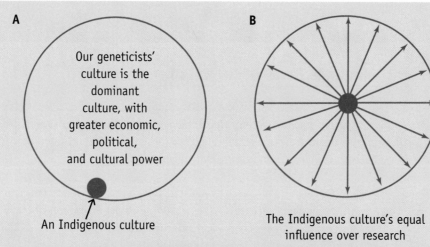

The relationship between the dominant Western culture and an Indigenous population. (a) The view of our culture from the perspective of an Indigenous culture. (b) The ideal equality of an Indigenous culture's influence over research is represented by the arrows reaching to the full perimeter of the dominant culture's circle of influence.

knowledge or consent of the tribe and was used for research that hadn't been authorized. . . . Such misuse of DNA samples for studies outside the original research question has been a recurrent problem for Indigenous populations (Lee et al. 2009; Royal et al. 2010). . . .

The perception of researchers that DNA collected for research becomes their property is actually a common problem: once the DNA is taken, . . . it can be difficult for [the Indigenous community] to recover the samples. . . . Regrettably, the outcome for the Nuu-chah-nulth was a sense of betrayal and a loss of trust in researchers. But the tribe responded to this sense of mistrust with action. The elected chief formed a committee to establish conditions to be followed by researchers who wished to carry out research with their community. Subsequently, the Nuu-chah-nulth made important contributions to the development of the Canadian guidelines on research with Indigenous populations (CIHR 2010). . . .

One of the recurrent complaints of Indigenous people about research is that it benefits the researchers and not the population being studied. An Alaskan Native saying perfectly captures the resentment bred of experiences like those of the Nuu-chah-nulth: "Researchers are like mosquitoes; they suck your blood and leave" (Cochran et al. 2008). . . .

[In response to such negative outcomes in the field, m]any Canadian researchers realized that our "investigator-driven" paradigm had to be changed for studies with Indigenous populations. The outcome was the *Guidelines for Health Research Involving Aboriginal People* developed by the Canadian Institutes of Health

Research [CIHR]. The community-based participatory approach outlined in these guidelines, and that all of us would be well advised to use, is exemplified by a study undertaken by Laura Arbour and her colleagues in northern British Columbia with the Gitxsan people (Arbour et al. 2008). In the Gitxsan community, the long QT syndrome and sudden [infant] death are very prevalent. . . . Community members brought this problem to the attention of university researchers. To provide advice and govern the research, the Gitxsan Health Society formed a local research advisory committee consisting of lay community members and medical personnel. Laura's studies showed that up to approximately 1 out of 100 individuals carry [the mutation that is associated with the long QT syndrome]. This prevalence is about 50 fold greater than that found in the general population. . . .

The features of the Gitxsan long QT syndrome research that were characteristic of participatory research were that the Gitxsan initiated the research, participated in the development of the research protocol, and maintained an ongoing advisory and governance role. In addition, there were tribal research assistants, the community reviewed the results with the investigators, reviewed the paper before it was submitted for publication, and agreed with the decision to use their tribal name in the publication. . . .

With respect to genetic research with Indigenous populations, I suggest that we must now be invited into the metaphorical tent of the Indigenous communities. . . . If we succeed, both genetics and the populations of the world will be the richer.

Source: Reprinted from McInnes, Roderick, R. "Culture: The Silent Language Geneticists Must Learn." *American Journal of Human Genetics* 88 (3); 254–61, 2011, with permission from Elsevier.

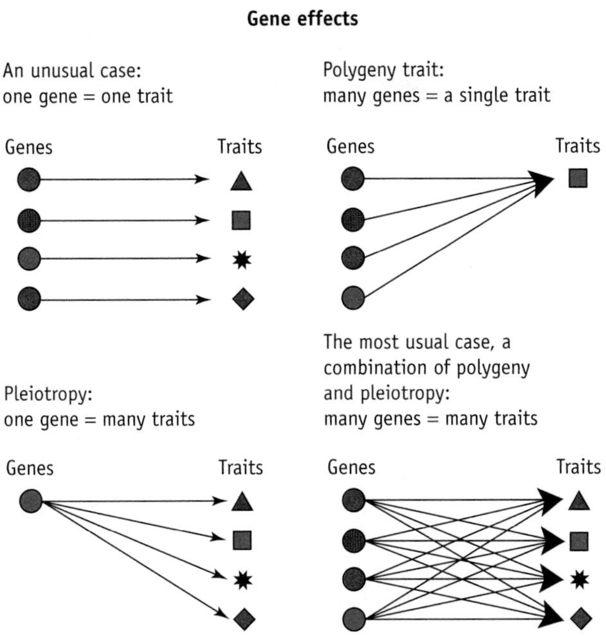

**Gene effects**

An unusual case:
one gene = one trait

Genes      Traits

Polygeny trait:
many genes = a single trait

Genes      Traits

The most usual case, a
combination of polygeny
and pleiotropy:
many genes = many traits

Pleiotropy:
one gene = many traits

Genes      Traits

Genes      Traits

**FIGURE 3.10** | Only rarely is a single physical trait the result of the action of a single gene. Many traits are the result of gene interaction, involving polygeny, pleiotropy, or, as is usually the case, both.

## Mutation

Early in the twentieth century, geneticists discovered that very occasionally a new allele can result when the old form of a gene suddenly changes (or undergoes a **mutation**) but that, otherwise, genes are stable. Mutation thus explains how genetic inheritance can be unchanging and still produce the variation that makes evolutionary change possible (Mayr 1982, 755). Being part of a process of stable inheritance means, however, that the occurrence of genetic mutations is random with respect to the adaptive challenges facing the organism in which it occurs: mutations do not occur because the organism "needs" them. Mutations can be harmful or helpful, but they may also have no effect at all (Figure 3.11). Mutations that neither help nor harm an organism are called "neutral" mutations.

Modern genetics, by contrast, assumes that, apart from mutation, genes are inherited unchanged from parent organisms and that it is impossible for an organism's experiences or "needs" to feed back and reshape the genetic information in the sex cells. Natural selection can act only on randomly produced variation, which makes evolution by natural selection a two-step process. First, random genetic variation is produced. Second, those organisms whose variant traits better

**FIGURE 3.11** | The pale coloration of the white Bengal tiger is caused by a mutation in a protein called SLC45A2. How might this sort of visible mutation be either helpful or harmful?

equip them to meet environmental challenges survive and produce more offspring than those whose traits equip them less well.

It is important to emphasize that, from a Darwinian point of view, *individual organisms* do not evolve genetically. Barring mutations (or the interventions of genetic engineering), individual organisms are stuck with the genes they are born with. However, the *populations* to which individuals belong *can evolve* as each generation contributes different numbers of offspring to the generation that comes after it. Put another way, from a Darwinian perspective, the only *biological* effect an individual can have on its population's evolution is in terms of the *number of offspring* that it bequeaths to the next generation. More (or fewer) offspring mean more (or fewer) copies of parental genes in the next generation. This is why Darwinian population biologists traditionally track evolutionary change by measuring changes in gene frequencies over time.

For more information on the connection between mutation and patterns of human variation, see Chapter 4, p. 78

## DNA and the Genome

The discovery in the early 1950s of the structure of chromosomes greatly expanded our understanding of

**mutation** The creation of a new allele for a gene when the portion of the DNA molecule to which it corresponds is suddenly altered.

## In Their Own Words

### Science, Democracy, and Taiwanese Stem Cells

*Jennifer Liu, of the University of Waterloo, discusses her work on the processes and progress of stem-cell research in Taiwan, highlighting an alternative perspective on how science and genomic research is conducted in Taiwanese culture.*

In the early years of the new millennium, stem cells were being touted as the next big thing in human DNA analysis. These cells, it seemed, had the potential to regenerate all kinds of human cells and to treat a variety of seemingly intractable diseases. My own research started with a spark of anger at media stories in North America that seemed to suggest that East Asian countries would race ahead in stem-cell research because, as I heard phrased in various ways, "they don't care about the ethics." Informed by an anthropological sensibility that is suspect of essentializing discourses and that insists that cultural forms and norms must be examined in their specific contexts, I set about to study stem-cell research and its ethics in Taiwan.

Since I'm also interested in the relationship between science and democracy, Taiwan seemed an ideal site. Its complex modern political history includes 50 years as a colony of Japan (1895–1945), followed by 38 years of martial law (1949–1987), the longest period of sustained

martial law in history. Full electoral democracy was established in 1996. Although Taiwan governs autonomously, it is claimed by the Chinese government as a province of China. While many on the island support closer relations with China, many also strenuously resist, and an independence movement flourishes.

Elsewhere, I write about the ways that stem-cell and related genomic research are used by some to articulate a uniquely Taiwanese identity in a biological register. I write about the morning I awoke in Taipei to headlines that Taiwanese researchers had created fluorescent pigs that glowed green "all the way through"; these became a kind of model animal for some kinds of stem-cell research there. I write about how policy was made in ways that conform to international standards of scientific research and democratic governance, and how Taiwanese scientists are, in many ways, transnational scientists, among other things. What I found in Taiwan did not at all support a

genetic mutation. We now know that chromosomes are made up largely of long molecules of deoxyribonucleic acid, or **DNA**, parts of which are used by living cells as templates for the construction, or *synthesis*, of proteins that make up most of the tissues and organs of any living organism. The DNA molecule, assembled in the shape of a double helix, resembles a twisted ladder, the rungs of which are made up of chemical components called "bases." Although there are many bases, DNA ordinarily makes use of only four: guanine, cytosine, adenine, and thymine. Each rung of the DNA ladder is made up of two of these bases: guanine always links to cytosine, and adenine always links to thymine.

The sum total of all the genetic material in the cell nucleus is called the **genome**. We know today that the human genome contains approximately 20,500 genes,

but these account for less than 2 per cent of the entire genome. Geneticists know that some non-coding DNA in the genome is involved in regulatory functions, but we remain ignorant of the functions played by much of it. Recent work on DNA and stem cells has the potential to lead to a cure for many human diseases, but it is also ethically risky, as this form of research threatens to modify and even replicate the human genome. Anthropologist Jennifer Liu provides some insight into the practice and promise of stem-cell research and how it is being done in Taiwan (see the "In Their Own Words" box).

Discovery of the structure and operation of DNA solidified the rejection of Lamarckian views by geneticists. Simply put, no matter how useful or valuable a particular adaptation might be to an organism, genetic inheritance provides no mechanism whereby such information could be directly transmitted through that organism's tissues and cells in order to restructure the organism's DNA in a more "adaptive" form. At the same time, knowledge of DNA explained what mutations were: changes in the structure of the DNA molecule. Cosmic radiation, heat, and chemicals can all alter the

**DNA (deoxyribonucleic acid)** The structure that carries the genetic heritage of an organism as a kind of blueprint for the organism's construction and development.

**genome** The sum total of all the genetic information about an organism, carried on the chromosomes in the cell nucleus.

claim that "they don't care about the ethics." The stem-cell scientific community cares deeply about ethics, but ethics are not necessarily configured in the same way as they are in North America.

Below, I introduce two Taiwanese human embryonic stem-cell scientists working in Taiwan and their respective ethics. They both operate in an ethical frame, but the right thing to do is configured differently and results in different practices for each. They each prioritize different values—on the one hand, of *biomedical* progress and Taiwanese inclusion, and on the other, of specific *bioethical* considerations.

Dr Lee had been recruited back to Taiwan specifically for his expertise in human embryonic stem-cell research. Before returning to Taiwan, he had used human embryos in his research almost without thinking, but after years back home he still has not used a single human embryo. Dr Pan, on the other hand, expands his quest to produce "Taiwanese" stem-cell lines. Both scientists are working on projects of ethical significance for both their science and their people, but they possess distinctly different views and approaches.

For Dr Pan, it involves pushing forward scientifically to develop "Taiwanese" stem-cell lines to include his people, with their unique genetics, in the promise of stem-cell therapeutics. This is made all the more urgent because several medical concerns in Taiwan are perceived as receiving inadequate attention in Western-dominated biomedical sciences.

For Dr Lee, this means delaying his research as he searches for bioethical clarity; this involves both personal reflection and active participation in the development of national policy. He was a member of several committees working on ethics and research protocols, regularly attended meetings, and helped to establish the regulatory structure for biomedical research. For Dr Lee, scientific progress means slowing his bench research in order to get the bioethical and institutional elements in order. His concern is with the inclusion of Taiwanese publics in an explicitly *bioethical* register. He wants to know, of a general public, of Buddhist groups, among others, "what do they *really* think?" and "do they *all* really think this?"

Source: Jennifer Liu, Assistant Professor at the University of Waterloo. For more information, see Liu 2012a and 2012b.

---

structure of DNA; and when these alterations occur in the sex cells, they can be passed on to offspring.

## Genotype, Phenotype, and the Norm of Reaction

Geneticists realized long ago that the molecular structure of genes (or genotype) had to be distinguished from the observable, measurable, overt characteristics of an organism that genes help to produce (its phenotype). For example, the sequences of bases on a stretch of DNA (genotypes) are used by living cells to assemble strings of amino acids that bond to form proteins (phenotypes), but bases are not the same thing as protein molecules. How does a genotype get realized in a phenotype? The question is not idle because fertilized eggs do not turn into organisms in a vacuum. Living organisms grow in a physical environment that provides them with nourishment, protection, and other vital resources to support their development over time until they are mature and

able to reproduce their own offspring. Without the raw materials for protein synthesis supplied by the ovum, and later by food, genotypes can do nothing. At the same time, just as one gene does not equal one trait, different genotypes may be associated with the same phenotype. Mendel first showed this when he was able to demonstrate the existence of recessive genes. That is, red flowers could be produced by homozygous dominant parents (i.e., both red) as well as by heterozygous parents (i.e., one red and one white); but only one in every four offspring of heterozygous parents would have the chance of producing white flowers (i.e., if it received a recessive white gene from each parent). Nevertheless, individuals with the same genotype—identical twins, for example, or cuttings from a single plant or cloned animals—may also develop a range of different phenotypes (Figure 3.12).

> genotype  The genetic information about particular biological traits encoded in an organism's DNA.

> phenotype  The observable, measurable, overt characteristics of an organism.

**FIGURE 3.12** | Individuals with the same genotype may exhibit a range of different phenotypes. Identical twins, for example, develop unique fingerprints due to exposure to different environmental stressors in the womb.

To understand how we get from an organism's genotype to its phenotype, we must consider both genotype and phenotype in relation to the environment in which that organism developed. Biologists compare the phenotypic outcomes of organisms with the same genotype in different environments and with different genotypes in the same environment, and they plot these outcomes on what is called a **norm of reaction**. Levins and Lewontin (1985, 90–1) define the norm of reaction as "a table or graph of correspondence between the phenotypic outcome of development and the environment in

**norm of reaction** A table or graph that displays the possible range of phenotypic outcomes for a given genotype in different environments.

**niche construction** When organisms actively perturb the environment in ways that modify the selection pressures experienced by subsequent generations of organisms.

which the development took place. Each genotype has its own norm of reaction, specifying how the developing organism will respond to various environments. In general, a genotype cannot be characterized by a unique phenotype."

Different genotypes can produce the same phenotype in some environments, and the same genotype can produce different phenotypes in different environments. Despite very different genotypes, the eyes of newborn babies all tend to be the same colour, as does hair colour as we age. Indeed, the phenotype of a single individual can vary markedly from one environment to the next. As Lewontin (1982, 20) points out, "People who 'tend to be fat' on 5500 calories a day 'tend to be thin' on 2000. Families with both 'tendencies' will be found living in the same towns in Northeastern Brazil, where two-thirds of the families live on less than what is considered a minimum subsistence diet by the World Health Organization."

Increasing numbers of biologists are addressing not only the ways in which the organism's phenotype is shaped by the environment in which it develops, but also how organisms shape the environments in which they develop. For example, in their book *Niche Construction*, F. John Odling-Smee, Kevin Laland, and Marcus Feldman (2003, 1) argue that organisms play two roles in evolution, carrying genes and interacting with environments.

Specifically, organisms interact with environments, take energy and resources from environments, make micro- and macrohabitat choices with respect to environments, construct artifacts, emit detritus and die in environments, and by doing all these things, modify at least some of the natural selection pressures in their own and in each other's local environments. This second role for phenotypes in evolution is not well described or understood by evolutionary biologists and has not been subject to a great deal of investigation. We call it "niche construction."

**Niche construction** is understood to occur either when an organism actively perturbs the environment or when it actively moves into a different environment (Odling-Smee et al. 2003, 41). If the physical, environmental consequences of niche construction are erased between generations, this process can have no long-term effects on evolution. But if these consequences endure, they feed back into the evolutionary process, *modifying the selection pressures* experienced by subsequent generations of organisms (Figure 3.13). Odling-Smee et al. (2003, 50–115) provide numerous examples taken from all taxonomic groups of living organisms, including blue-green algae, earthworms, dam-building beavers, burrowing rodents, and nest-building birds. Their most controversial proposal is that niche construction be incorporated into evolutionary theory as an additional adaptive process alongside natural selection and that non-genetic "legacies of modified natural selection pressures" be recognized in addition to the genetic legacies passed on in the egg and sperm. In their view, a suitably extended evolutionary theory would recognize both niche construction and natural selection as evolutionary processes contributing together to the dynamic adaptive match between organisms and environments (2–3).

Taking niche construction into account encourages biologists to look at organisms in a new way. Rather than picturing them as passively staying in place, subject to selection pressures they cannot affect, organisms are now seen as sometimes capable of actively intervening in their evolutionary fate by *modifying the environment*: Odling-Smee et al. (2003, 298) predict that "those members of the population that are least fit relative to the imposed selective regime will be the individuals that

**FIGURE 3.13** | Many species, including beavers, construct key features of their own ecological niches. Beaver dams modify selection pressures experienced by beavers, but they also alter selection pressures experienced by neighbouring species whose own niches are altered by the presence of the beaver dam in their habitats.

exhibit the strongest evidence for niche construction." Alternatively, organisms that *move into a new environment* with different selection pressures can no longer be automatically identified as the unquestionable losers in evolutionary competition in their former environment. Niche construction portrays all organisms (not just human organisms) as active agents living in environments that are vulnerable to the consequences of their activities, contributing in potentially significant ways to the evolutionary histories of their own and other species.

According to Odling-Smee et al. (2003, 3), acknowledging niche construction as an adaptive process offers a way to link evolutionary theory and ecosystem ecology, and it also alters the relationship between evolutionary theory and the human sciences. They regard human beings as "virtuoso niche constructors" (367), and their arguments should be of great interest to anthropologists, especially cultural anthropologists who insist that any explanation of social and culture change must make room for human agency: the way people struggle, often against great odds, to exercise some control over their lives. The agency of organisms as niche constructors matters in evolution "because it introduces feedback into the evolutionary dynamic [which] significantly modifies the selection pressures [on organisms]" (Odling-Smee et al. 2003, 2; see also Deacon 2003). As we will see in later chapters,

> ↻ For a thorough discussion of the connection between human niche construction and the cultural process of domestication, see Chapter 8, pp. 204–9.

we as humans are never free to do exactly as we please but always have options for action. And the actions we choose to undertake can sometimes reshape the selective pressures we experience, exactly as niche construction theorists would predict.

## What Does Evolution Mean to Anthropologists?

Ever since Darwin, evolutionary theory has been subjected to repeat testing. Although the results of those tests have led to modifications of the theory in certain respects, none of them has ever called the concept of evolution itself into question. Indeed, the power of evolutionary theory is illustrated by how the work of Linnaeus, Darwin, and Mendel meshes together so beautifully, even though each of them worked independently. Modern biologists agree that no process other than evolution can explain nearly as much about the history of life on earth.

The study of evolution in contemporary biology is very lively. New evidence and new ways of interpreting evidence have led many evolutionists to question the adequacy of their old ways of understanding and to develop different perspectives on the evolutionary process. They are keenly aware that a phenomenon as complex as evolution requires theoretical pluralism—that is, the recognition that a variety of processes operating at different levels work together to produce the similarities and differences that characterizes the living world. As evolutionary theorists Peter Richerson, Robert Boyd, and Joseph Henrich (2003, 366) remind us, "Evolutionary theory prescribes a method, not an answer, and a wide range of hypotheses can be cast in an evolutionary framework. . . . Darwinism as a method is not at all committed to any particular picture of how evolution works or what it produces. Any sentence that starts with 'evolutionary theory predicts' should be regarded with caution."

Life has a comprehensible history for modern evolutionists. How it is likely to change next, however, cannot be predicted with any certainty because random factors continue to play an important evolutionary role. Human biologists have been forced to rethink the place of their own species in the web of life. Unquestionably, the result has been to dislodge human beings from the centre. Most contemporary evolutionists would probably agree with Steven Stanley (1981, 151) that "not all paths lead toward *Homo sapiens*, and possibly no persistent path led directly toward him." Indeed, the very notion that organisms are "going somewhere" along a linear evolutionary "path" has been questioned. Stephen Jay Gould (1996, 162) has argued that apparent directional trends in evolution such as increasing body size are "really random evolution away from small size, not directed evolution toward large size." He suggests that a more appropriate way to think of the history of life is in terms of expansion or contraction over time in the total range of variation in living forms (i.e., life's "full house"). To do so is to recognize that bacteria have always been the most common form of life on this planet. Organisms of extreme complexity (such as human beings) were bound to appear as the range of variation expanded, but the kind of organisms they turned out to be "is utterly unpredictable, partly random, and entirely contingent—not at all foreordained by the mechanisms of evolution. . . . Humans are here by the luck of the draw, not the inevitability of life's direction or evolution's mechanism" (Gould 1996, 174–5).

Moreover, once we consider our own species alongside other species whose comings and goings have been so well documented in the fossil record, we cannot avoid grappling with the following well-known facts:

> The only certainty about the future of our species is that it is limited. Of all the species that have ever existed 99.999 per cent are extinct. The average lifetime of a carnivore genus is only 10 million years, and the average lifetime of a species is much shorter. Indeed, life on earth is nearly half over: Fossil evidence shows that life began about 3 billion years ago, and the sun is due to become a red giant about 4 billion years from now, consuming life (and eventually the whole earth) in its fire. (Lewontin 1982, 169)

On the other hand, the story of our species has many unique twists and turns and is far from over. Compared to many living organisms on the earth, we are a relatively "recent" species; yet we have coevolved within changing environments for millions of years using our creative cultural tendencies to modify the world around us. And who knows? Perhaps we will find a way to spread beyond our solar system, and our descendants may escape the grim fate that awaits our planet in 4 billion years or so. In the meantime, we remain on earth, searching for answers about who we are and how we are to live our lives.

## Chapter Summary

1. Evolutionary theory is a testable, unified, and fruitful scientific theory. Material evidence of evolutionary change over time can be found in the fossil record and in the pattern of distribution of living species of organisms.

2. Before Darwin, European thinkers divided living things into natural kinds, each of which was thought to have its own unchanging essence. The Great Chain of Being was understood as God's creation, naturally harmonious and without gaps, and it inspired Linnaeus's important eighteenth-century taxonomy of living organisms.

3. In the nineteenth century, catastrophism and uniformitarianism undermined the Great Chain of Being. Catastrophism was based on the ideas of Georges Cuvier, who argued that some species had become extinct in massive natural disasters, after which new species were introduced from elsewhere. Uniformitarianism was promoted by geologist Charles Lyell, who argued that the same processes of erosion and uplift that can be observed to change the earth's surface today had been at work in the past. Uniformitarianism implied that changes in life forms were as gradual and reversible as changes in the earth's surface.

4. Lamarck tried to preserve the view of a harmonious Great Chain of Being by claiming that fossil species had not become extinct. Lamarck argued that individual members of a species are all able to transform themselves in the same way when facing the same environmental pressures. Lamarckian transformational evolution has been rejected by contemporary evolutionary researchers. In contrast to Lamarck, Darwin and Wallace concluded that the similarities shared by distinct living species could be explained if all such species had descended from a single parental species that had lived in the past. In addition, Darwin proposed that such "descent with modification" could occur as a result of the straightforward, mechanistic process of natural selection.

5. Darwin's theory of evolution by natural selection (or variational evolution) was based on the principle of variation, the principle of heredity, and the principle of natural selection. Variational evolution was driven by what Darwin called the "struggle for existence" between individuals of the same species to survive and reproduce. In a given environment, those variant individuals who survive and leave greater numbers of offspring are said to have greater fitness than other members of their species who leave fewer offspring. There is no such thing as "absolute" fitness.

6. Evolutionary theorists use the concept of adaptation to refer both to a process of mutual adjustment between organisms and their environments and to the phenotypic features of organisms that are produced by this process. Reconstructing accurate evolutionary histories of organisms requires distinguishing adaptations from exaptations.

7. Darwin did not know why offspring tend to resemble their parents, nor did he understand how variation was introduced into populations. Answers to these questions were developed in the field of genetics. Genes are associated with particular portions of the DNA molecules located on the chromosomes in the cell nucleus. The machinery of the cell uses DNA to synthesize proteins necessary for life processes and makes it possible for chromosomes to be copied before cells divide. Gene interaction helps explain how continuous traits, such as skin colour or hair colour, are the result of unchanging inheritance. Different genotypes may produce the same phenotype, and the same genotype may produce different phenotypes, depending on the kinds of environments in which organisms possessing these genotypes live and grow. That is, each genotype has its own norm of reaction.

8. The study of evolution in contemporary biology is very lively. Modern biologists agree that life on earth has evolved, but they have different views about how evolutionary processes work. Many evolutionary thinkers are increasingly convinced that a phenomenon as complex as biological evolution requires theoretical pluralism.

## For Review

1. How has the theory of evolution been important in shaping how anthropologists view human history?

2. Explain the kinds of material evidence that have been important in the development of evolutionary theory.

3. What are the beliefs that influenced essentialism and the Great Chain of Being? Provide an example from each theory that exhibits these beliefs.

4. Explain the difference between transformational (Lamarckian) evolution and variational (Darwinian) evolution.

5.  Using the principles of natural selection, explain to a friend why pandas have thumbs. How does the role of populations factor into the Darwinian explanation of why pandas have thumbs?

6.  Distinguish among aptation, adaptation, and exaptation. Provide an example of each.

7.  Why is the principle of variation so important in evolutionary theory?

8.  Explain non-blending, single-particle inheritance (Mendelian inheritance). Why are Mendel's experiments still important today?

9.  What is the difference between discontinuous variation and continuous variation? What is meant by the "genetic milieu"?

10. What are the differences between genotype and phenotype? Why are these differences important?

11. What is a norm of reaction? Explain its significance for the evolution of human populations.

12. It is clear that an environment can have a profound effect on the evolution of a population, but what part, if any, does a population have in shaping its environment? Discuss Odling-Smee et al.'s "most controversial proposal." Make sure to discuss the main components of niche construction in your discussion.

## Key Terms

adaptation   52
alleles   56
aptation   52
chromosomes   54
common ancestry   50
continuous variation   56
discontinuous variation   56
DNA (deoxyribonucleic acid)   60
evolution   44
evolutionary theory   44
exaptation   52
gene   56

genetics   56
genome   61
genotype   61
genus   46
heterozygous   56
homozygous   56
meiosis   54
Mendelian inheritance   54
mitosis   54
mutation   59
natural selection   50
niche construction   62

norm of reaction   62
pangenesis   54
phenotype   61
pleiotropy   56
polygeny   56
principle of independent assortment   55
principle of segregation   55
species   46
taxonomy   46
variational evolution   51

## Suggested Readings

Ayala, Francisco J., and John C. Avise, eds. 2014. *Essential Readings in Evolutionary Biology.* Baltimore: John Hopkins University Press. *This book is a bit challenging to students new to evolutionary biology, but it is a marvellous compendium of 48 excerpts by influential evolutionary thinkers, from Darwin to the present day, including theoretical developments connected with the rise of genetics, the negotiation of evolutionary synthesis, the discovery of the structure of DNA, and more.*

Crawford, Michael H., ed. 2006. *Anthropological Genetics: Theory, Methods, and Applications.* Cambridge: Cambridge University Press. *An overview of current practices and advances in anthropological genetics with contributions from leading researchers in this emerging field.*

Gould, Stephen Jay. 1987. *Time's Arrow, Time's Cycle: Myth and Metaphor in the Discovery of Geological Time.* Cambridge, MA: Harvard University Press. *A fascinating account of the historical and cultural context out of which catastrophism and uniformitarianism were forged in the nineteenth century.*

———. 1996. *Full House: The Spread of Excellence from Plato to Darwin.* New York: Harmony Books. *An eloquent and entertaining defence of the view that human beings were not the end point of biological evolution and that bacteria are more properly regarded as the dominant life forms on earth.*

Kevles, Daniel J., and Leroy Hood, eds. 1992. *The Code of Codes: Scientific and Social Issues in the Human Genome Project.* Cambridge, MA: Harvard University Press. *This edited collection contains a wide range of articles by geneticists, molecular biologists, biochemists, historians of science, and social scientists who examine the prospects and consequences of mapping all the genes in the human body. The book offers a range of opinions on how fully we will know what it means to be human if we one day learn all there is to know about our genes.*

Lewontin, Richard. 1991. *Biology as Ideology: The Doctrine of DNA.* New York: Harper Perennial. *The text of this book began as a series of radio broadcasts for the Canadian Broadcasting Company (CBC) and is supplemented with an article Lewontin published in* the *New York Review of Books. Lewontin's accessible and hard-hitting essay addresses excessive claims that are sometimes made in the name of human genetics and offers incisive criticism of current efforts by geneticists to map all the genes in the human body.*

——. 2001. *The Triple Helix: Gene, Organism, and Environment.* Cambridge, MA: Harvard University Press. *Lewontin reminds biologists not to forget the role of organisms and environment in discussions of evolution; these are often ignored in discussions that attribute everything to genes.*

Lovejoy, Arthur O. (1936) 1960. *The Great Chain of Being.* New York: Harper Torchbooks. *Originally published in 1936, this classic is as fresh and relevant as anything being written about evolution today. A marvellously clear and detailed account of pre-Darwinian thinking about life on earth.*

Marks, Jonathan. 1995. *Human Biodiversity: Genes, Race, and History.* New York: Aldine. *Marks is a biological anthropologist with a strong commitment to a biocultural approach to human nature. This book is an excellent introduction to biological anthropology.*

Pálsson, Gísli. 2007. *Anthropology and the New Genetics. New Departures in Anthropology.* Cambridge: Cambridge University Press. *Pálsson introduces and clearly outlines the issues and fallacies that are aligned with genetic studies and human evolution.*

# 4 What Can Evolutionary Theory Tell Us about Human Variation?

▲ A Ju/'hoansi San family using sticks to dig for nutritious roots, Tsumkwe, Otjozondjupa Region, Namibia. Recent research shows that the San are the most genetically diverse people on earth. Photo: David Cayless/Getty Images

## Chapter Outline

Not everyone looks the same. Why is that? Does it make a difference? Do the differences cluster together? In this chapter, we will look at the way evolutionary theory explains patterns of human biological variation. In particular, we will show why anthropologists have concluded that these patterns cannot be explained by the cultural concept of "race."

Chapter 3 presented some of the central concepts of modern evolutionary theory. Continuing on the theme of evolution, this chapter investigates how biologists and anthropologists have used evolutionary theory in their research. This chapter will focus on research looking at human evolution and variation, both of which are important components of biological anthropology. Evolutionary studies can be divided into two major subfields: microevolution and macroevolution. Microevolution devotes attention to short-term evolutionary changes that occur within a given species over relatively few generations. It involves what is sometimes called "ecological time," or the pace of time as experienced by organisms living in and adapting to their ecological settings. Macroevolution, by contrast, focuses on long-term evolutionary changes, especially the origins of new species and their diversification across space and over millions of years. Macroevolutionary events are measured in geological time, spanning many generations of organisms along with the development and decay of many different ecological settings.

## What Is Microevolution?

### The Modern Evolutionary Synthesis and Its Legacy

In the 1930s and 1940s, biologists and geneticists worked to formulate a new way of thinking about evolution that combined Darwinian natural selection and Mendelian ideas about heredity. Until recently, this approach (called the "modern evolutionary synthesis" or "neo-Darwinism") dominated research and thinking in biology. As we saw in the last chapter, contemporary evolutionary theorists have challenged, expanded, and enriched this neo-Darwinian research program, much the way the formulators of the modern synthesis had earlier challenged, expanded, and enriched the contributions made by Darwin, Mendel, and other early evolutionary thinkers. But some achievements of the modern synthesis remain fundamental to our understandings of living organisms. In anthropology, perhaps the most significant contribution of neo-Darwinism was

the way it undermined the nineteenth-century anthropological misconception of "biological race," refocusing attention on a new understanding of biological species. After World War II, many anthropologists rejected the biased, race-based physical anthropology of the nineteenth and early twentieth centuries and replaced it with a "new physical anthropology" or "biological anthropology." Research in biological anthropology took for granted the common membership of all human beings in a single species, considered humans as biocultural organisms, and addressed human variation using concepts and methods drawn from neo-Darwinism (Strum et al. 1999).

For further discussion of the links between race, biological anthropology, and culture, see Chapter 1, for in-depth treatment of race and social stratification, see Chapter 14, pp. 403–10.

Biologists have proposed alternative definitions of *species* that attempt to respect the purpose of Darwinian taxonomy, which is to represent scientists' best current understanding of the relationships between and among organisms. As biological anthropologist John Fleagle (2013, 2) points out, "Most biologists agree that a species is a distinct segment of an evolutionary lineage, and many of the differences among species concepts reflect attempts to find criteria that can be used to identify species based on different types of information." Neo-Darwinians defined a species as "a reproductive community of populations (reproductively isolated from others) that occupies a specific niche in nature" (Mayr 1982, 273). This definition, commonly referred to as the *biological species concept*, has been useful to field biologists studying populations of living organisms. However, this definition has been less useful

**microevolution** A subfield of evolutionary studies that devotes attention to short-term evolutionary changes that occur within a given species over relatively few generations of ecological time.

**macroevolution** A subfield of evolutionary studies that focuses on long-term evolutionary changes, especially the origins of new species and their diversification across space and over millions of years of geological time.

for scientists studying fossils. In fact, Fleagle notes that the biological species concept has been losing favour even among field biologists because "as more and more 'species' have been sampled genetically, it has become clear that hybridization between presumed species has been very common in primate evolution" (2013, 1; see also Stringer 2012, 34).

As we will see in Chapter 5, many taxonomists working with living primates prefer to use the *phylogenetic species concept*, which identifies species on the basis of a set of unique features (morphological or genetic) that distinguish their members from other, related species. Contemporary paleoanthropologists also often rely on this concept of species, as we will see in Chapter 6, although they also sometimes apply a *phenetic fossil species concept*. Users of the phenetic fossil species concept first attempt to calculate the measureable morphological differences between living species. They then assume that similar degrees of morphological difference may also be used to distinguish species in the fossil record. Fleagle (2013, 2) observes that this concept can be a useful way to sort fossils in a continuously changing lineage "in which the endpoints may be very different but individual samples overlap."

Species normally are subdivided into *populations* that are more or less scattered, although the separation is not complete. That is, populations of the same species (or individual members of those populations) may be separated at one time but may merge together again, and successfully reproduce, at a later time. Evolutionary theorists Ian Tattersall and Rob DeSalle (2011, 50) describe this process of species differentiation and reintegration as "reticulation." They emphasize that reticulation takes place *within* a species and that the "resulting web-like pattern of relationships is very different from the dichotomous pattern *among* species" on which the phylogenetic species concept is based. For example, prior to the rise of the great ancient civilizations, the human species was made up of widely scattered populations. Those populations living in North America had been separated from populations in Europe for thousands of years, until the European explorations of the Americas began in the fifteenth century. However, when Europeans and the Indigenous peoples of North America did come into contact, they were able to interbreed and produce viable, fertile offspring. From the perspective of the biological species concept, this ability to interbreed and produce fertile offspring indicates that members of these different populations belong to the same reproductive community and hence the same species. Proponents of the phylogenetic species concept can specify the set of unique features that distinguish all successfully interbreeding populations of the human species from populations of other related species.

Finally Darwinian population thinking requires biologists to recognize the distinctiveness of each individual *organism* that belongs to a particular population of a given species. It is variation among individual organisms in particular populations in particular environmental circumstances that engenders the Darwinian struggle for existence. To follow arguments made by evolutionary biologists, therefore, these three nesting concepts— *species* made up of *populations* made up of *organisms*— must be kept distinct from one another. It is also important to remember that even if individual organisms from populations of different species occasionally mate with one another, such matings do not necessarily dissolve the species boundary. For instance, horses and donkeys can interbreed to produce mules, but mules are infertile, so the species boundary between horses and donkeys is unaffected by these matings.

> For a related discussion of evidence of cross-species hybridization in the human fossil record, see Chapter 6, p. 139.

Neo-Darwinians were also concerned about the genetic makeup of species. They introduced the concept of the gene pool, which includes all of the genes in the bodies of all members of a given species (or a population of a species). Using mathematical models, evolutionary theorists can estimate the gene frequency of particular genes—that is, the frequency of occurrence of gene variants or alleles within a particular gene pool. Measuring the stability or change of gene frequencies in populations over time allowed geneticists to trace short-term evolutionary change, in a new field called population genetics. Once population geneticists had identified a target population, they analyzed its gene pool by calculating the frequencies of various alleles within that gene pool and trying to figure out what

**gene pool** All the genes in the bodies of all members of a given species (or a population of a species).

**gene frequency** The frequency of occurrence of the variants of particular genes (i.e., of alleles) within the gene pool.

**population genetics** A field that uses statistical analysis to study short-term evolutionary change in large populations.

would happen to those frequencies if the carriers of the various alleles were subjected to particular selection pressures (Table 4.1). Some evolutionary geneticists tested these predictions on such organisms as fruit flies, but others concentrated on human beings.

The ability of human beings from anywhere in the world to interbreed successfully is the most important measure of membership in our species. However, comparing our genotypes provides additional evidence of our biological closeness. As we discussed in Chapter 3, most alleles come in a range of different forms (i.e., are polymorphous), and known polymorphous variants fall into one of two groups. The first group, polymorphic alleles, accounts for most genetic variation across populations. Populations differ not because they have mutually exclusive sets of alleles but because they possess different *proportions* of the same set of alleles. An example is the ABO blood groups: the polymorphic alleles *A*, *B*, and *O* are found in all human populations, but the frequency of each allele differs from population to population. The second group, private polymorphisms, includes alleles that are found in the genotypes of some, but usually not all, members of a particular population. One example is a genetically determined blood cell antigen known as the "Diego antigen." The Diego antigen occurs only in Asian and African populations, although 60 to 90 per cent of the members of these populations do not have it (Marks 1995, 165).

Such results support the inescapable conclusion that the traditional Western concept of "race" is biologically and genetically meaningless. There is not a simple line that can be drawn to distinguish groups of humans based on their genetic makeup. Racial thinking is essentialistic. However, evolutionary geneticist Richard Lewontin (1972) demonstrated more than four decades ago that more genetic variation could be found within conventionally identified racial groups than could be found between them. These results, based on population thinking, make it clear that "humankind...is not divided into a series of genetically distinct units" (Jones 1986, 324). Ian Tattersall and Rob DeSalle (2011, 141) point out that Lewontin's claims have successfully withstood attempts to reject them experimentally for more than forty years. This means that the boundaries said to define human "races" have been culturally imposed on shifting and unstable clusters of alleles (Marks 1995, 117).

It turns out that genetic variation in human populations is mostly a matter of differences in the relative proportions of the same sets of alleles. In fact, the distribution of particular phenotypes shifts gradually from place to place across populations as the frequencies of some alleles increase while those of others decrease or stay the same. Moreover, the distributions of some traits (like skin colour) do not match the distributions of other traits (like hair type). This sort of gradual intergradation of genetic variation from population to population is called a cline. Clines can be represented on maps, as in Map 4.1, which

**polymorphous**  Describes alleles that come in a range of different forms.

**cline**  The gradual intergradation of genetic variation from population to population.

**TABLE 4.1 | Example of Allele Frequency Computation**

Imagine you have just collected information on *MN* blood group genotypes for 250 humans in a given population. Your data are the following:

Number of *MM* genotype = 40

Number of *MN* genotype = 120

Number of *NN* genotype = 90

The allele frequencies are computed as follows:

| Genotype | Number of People | Total Number of Alleles | Number of *M* Alleles | Number of *N* Alleles |
|---|---|---|---|---|
| *MM* | 40 | 80 | 80 | 0 |
| *MN* | 120 | 240 | 120 | 120 |
| *NN* | 90 | 180 | 0 | 180 |
| **Total** | 250 | 500 | 200 | 300 |

The relative frequency of the *M* allele is computed as the number of *M* alleles divided by the total number of alleles: 200/500 = 0.4.

The relative frequency of the *N* allele is computed as the number of *N* alleles divided by the total number of alleles: 300/500 = 0.6.

As a check, note that the relative frequencies of the alleles must add up to 1.0 (0.4 + 0.6 = 1.0).

Source: Relethford 2008, 74.

**MAP 4.1** | This map illustrates the continuum or cline of skin colours exhibited among Indigenous peoples around the world. What evolutionary, environmental, and/or cultural forces might have contributed to the development of this cline?

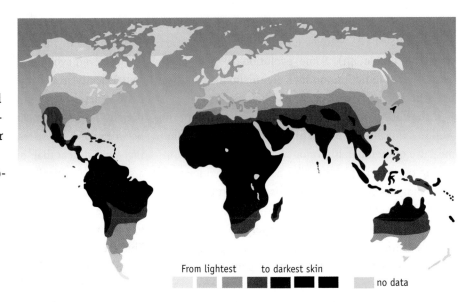

From lightest     to darkest skin                    no data

shows the gradually shifting distribution of differences in human skin colours from the equator to the poles.

If you were to walk from Stockholm, Sweden, to Kampala, Uganda, you would perceive gradual changes in average skin colour as you moved from north to south (or vice versa). Evolutionary biologists argue that skin pigmentation is distributed in this way as a consequence of natural selection: in regions close to the equator, individuals with darker skin pigmentation had a selective advantage over individuals with lighter pigmentation. By contrast, populations farther away from the equator faced less intense selection pressure for darkly pigmented skin and perhaps even selective pressures in favour of lighter skins. But *different* selection pressures would have been at work on other traits, such as stature or hair type, within the same population, which is why the geographical distributions of these traits do *not* match up neatly with the distribution of skin pigmentation. To make things even more complex, different genes may be involved in the production of similar phenotypic traits in different populations: for example, although different ancestral populations of humans living near the equator have dark skin, the identity and the number of alleles involved in the production of this phenotypic trait may be different in different populations.

These sorts of observations about global variations in human phenotypes led biological anthropologist Frank Livingstone (1964, 279) to declare over fifty years ago that "There are no races, there are only clines." Clinal variation explains why people searching for "races" have never been able to agree on how many there

are or how they can be identified. *Clines are not groups.* The only group involved in clinal mapping is the entire human species. Each cline is a map of the distribution of a *single* trait. Biologists might compare the clinal maps of trait A and trait B to see if they overlap and, if so, by how much. But the more clines they superimpose, the more obvious it becomes that the trait distributions they map *do not coincide* in ways that neatly subdivide into distinct human subpopulations. Since the biological concept of "race" predicts exactly such overlap, it cannot be correct. In other words, *clinal analysis tests the biological concept of "race" and finds nothing in nature to match it.* And if biological races cannot be found, then the so-called races identified over the years can only be symbolic constructs, based on cultural elaboration of a few superficial phenotypic differences—skin colour, hair type and quantity, skin folds, lip shape, and the like. In short, early race theorists "weren't extracting races from their set of data, they were imposing races upon it" (Marks 1995, 132).

## The Molecularization of Race?

During the 1960s and 1970s, anthropologists and others explained that there was no biological basis for race; in other words, all humans are part of a single species. Although there is internal variation within the species, it does not easily fall into the cultural categories of "race" as they had been defined. In the past thirty years, however, there has been a resurgence of attempts to explain distinct genetic groupings in terms of "race."

Further descriptions of the history of race and racism can be found in Chapter 1, on p. 8, and in Chapter 14, on pp. 404–6.

For example, controversial books such as *The Bell Curve: Intelligence and Class Structure in American Life* (Herrnstein and Murray 1994) or *A Troublesome Inheritance: Genes, Race, and Human History* (Wade 2014) attempt to align genetic traits with behaviours "innate" to specific biological "races."

Perhaps no more complicated set of questions has been raised about race in the twenty-first century than those that have emerged following the completion of the Human Genome Project (HGP) in 2003. The goals of the project were as follows:

- to identify all the approximately 20,500 genes in human DNA;
- to determine the sequences of the 3 billion chemical base pairs that make up human DNA;
- to store this information in databases;
- to improve tools for data analysis;
- to transfer related technologies to the private sector; and
- to address the ethical, legal, and social issues that may arise from the project (US Department of Energy 2014).

As anthropologist Nadia Abu El-Haj (2007) has suggested, some molecular biologists quickly mobilized the information produced by the HGP to attempt to develop forms of medical treatment based on the identification of genes associated with particular diseases. Some formed private biomedical research companies that promised to help create a future of *personalized medicine*: therapies based on knowledge of individuals' genomes that were precisely tailored to a particular individual's degree of genetic risk for a particular disease.

In recent years, the cost of sequencing individual genomes has been dropping; Tattersall and DeSalle (2011, 184) predict that "with the $1000 genome on the horizon, we will soon have the ultimate tool for individualized medicine." However, the cost has been high enough that many researchers have used genetic data from other members of populations to which individuals belong to stand in for certain parts of an individual's particular genome. For example, if your mother's brother suffers from a particular disease with a genetic component, researchers may conclude that you and other biological

relatives have an increased risk for that disease. In this case, information about your biological family stands in for information about you. As Abu El-Haj (2007) explains, some biomedical researchers also use information about "racial" groups' genetics to stand in for genetic information particular to individuals who consider themselves to be members of such groups. The thinking is that if a disease marker shows up in the genomes of some people said to be members of a particular "race," then this may be an indication that other people classified in the same "race" might also be at risk for the disease.

Does this pragmatic use of race in medical research mean that researchers are committed to the doctrines associated with scientific racism? Abu El-Haj (2007, 284) says no, for two reasons. First, the old race concept focused on the classification of *phenotypes*, whereas the new race concept classifies *genotypes*. The transition from a phenotypic to a genotypic view of race came about, she says, as a consequence of changing historical understandings of sickle-cell anemia in North America. In the first part of the twentieth century, sickle-cell anemia was identified as a disease of "black" people—of people with African ancestors. But later, its cause was traced to molecular genes: the presence of an abnormal "sickling" hemoglobin allele at a particular locus on a chromosome. "At the meeting point between these two definitions of the disease . . . the commitment to race as a molecular attribute took form," leading over time to "the correlation of disease risk and racial difference" (Abu El-Haj 2007, 287).

Second, nineteenth-century race science aimed to discover how many races existed and to assign all individuals to their "true race." The commercial technologies used by biomedical researchers do distinguish human populations in terms of the continents from which their ancestors presumably came. But all these technologies assume that everyone has a mixed ancestry of some kind; the goal is to measure how much of which ancestry markers are present in each population, thereby determining the degree of risk that members of that population face for genetic diseases associated with particular ancestries. As Abu El-Haj says, ancestry markers "are not used to discover one's 'true' race. . . . Instead, ancestry markers are used, for example, to understand the Puerto Rican population's risk for asthma" (Abu El-Haj 2007, 288). That is, if genome analysis determined that some ancestral population contributed genes to contemporary Puerto Rican populations that enhanced their risk for developing asthma, this information would be crucial in devising personalized drugs precisely keyed to individuals with different risks for asthma.

Perhaps the best-known example of a biomedical treatment designed to treat members of a particular "race" comes from the United States—the development and distribution of the drug BiDil. On its BiDil website, Arbor Pharmaceuticals (2015), the current manufacturer of BiDil, describes this drug as "a fixed-dose combination medicine consisting of isosorbide dinitrate and hydralazine hydrochloride. It is approved by the FDA for the treatment of heart failure in self-identified African American patients when added to standard heart failure medicines." Approval from the US Food and Drug Administration (FDA), the site reports, was based on results of the African-American Heart Failure Trial (or A-HeFT), which "studied 1050 self-identified African American patients with heart failure: It is the largest number of African American patients ever studied in a major heart failure trial. . . . A-HeFT was started on May 29, 2001, and the study was halted early in July 2004 due to a significant survival benefit seen with BiDil as compared to standard therapy alone."

Even though neither the researchers who developed the drug nor the FDA endorses nineteenth-century racial categories, there were clear problems with the original A-HeFT study. Most notably, the drug trial involved only "self-identified" African American subjects, which the FDA agrees is a "highly imperfect" but "useful proxy" for whatever factors are responsible for the observed "racial differences." The FDA admits that other individuals besides self-identified African Americans might well benefit from BiDil, but this was not demonstrated by the A-HeFT drug trial, because all of its participants were African American. In other words, the drug was proven only to work on African Americans because it was tested only on African Americans. This is a circular argument that has led to much controversy surrounding the drug as well as the financial collapse of the drug's original developer, NitroMed.

Abu El-Haj (2007, 293) notes that the successful production and marketing of drugs such as BiDil have transformed race into "a potentially profitable commodity." Moreover, "giving federal recognition to a drug like BiDil implies recognizing the biological reality of race." The current situation is perplexing, to say the least: such notions as "race" and "biology" are still with us, but their meanings appear to have changed, producing consequences that seem to be both positive and negative. She concludes that "Nature, too . . . has a history," and that history "may well differ not just across time but between the various disciplines. . . . The same of course is true of race" (294).

Biological evidence has not in the past and will not in the future dismantle oppressive sociopolitical structures created as a result of racist ideologies, but it can provide an important component in the struggle to eliminate these practices from our societies. Anthropologists need to be vigilant, emphasizing in no uncertain terms the lack of biological justification for the racial categories promoted by scientific racists. As Jonathan Marks (1995, 117) reminds us, it was the recognition that human variation did not come in neat divisions called "races" that "began to convert racial studies into studies of human microevolution."

## Human Variation and the Four Evolutionary Processes

What controls the patterns of gene frequencies that characterize a given population? Modern evolutionists recognize four evolutionary processes that can alter the frequencies at which genes occur in a given population: *natural selection*, *mutation*, *gene flow*, and *genetic drift*. To understand how these processes work, let's begin by considering an example that involves the first two, natural selection and mutation, which were introduced in Chapter 3.

Mutation is responsible for variant alleles that may be present at a single locus on a chromosome. Some of these mutations are mobilized during development to help produce specific physical traits. When a trait proves helpful, evolutionary theory predicts that the frequency of the alleles involved in its production will be increased by natural selection. Perhaps the best-known instance of microevolution of such a trait by means of natural selection concerns a variant of hemoglobin, one of the proteins in red blood cells.

In many human populations, only one allele—hemoglobin A (*HbA*)—is present. In other populations, however, mutant forms of hemoglobin A may also be present. One such mutant allele, known as *HbS*, alters the structure of red blood cells, distorting them into a characteristic sickle shape and reducing their ability to carry oxygen (Figure 4.1). When individuals inherit the *HbS* allele from both parents, they develop sickle-cell anemia. About 85 per cent of those with the *HbS/HbS* genotype do

Because the *HbS* allele seems to be harmful, we would expect it to be eliminated through natural selection. But in some populations of the world, it has a frequency of up to 20 per cent in the gene pool. Why should that be? It turns out that the *HbS* allele also conveys an evolutionary advantage—higher resistance to malaria. Research has shown that people exposed to malaria have a better chance of resisting the parasite if their hemoglobin genotype is *HbA/HbS* rather than the normal *HbA/HbA*. Thus, in regions of the world where malaria is common, having the *HbS* allele is advantageous to survival; not surprisingly, it is in these same regions that the *HbS* allele appears in its highest frequencies.

The *HbA/HbS* genotype is an example of what geneticists call a "balanced polymorphism," in which the heterozygous genotype is fitter than either of the homozygous genotypes. In Mendelian terms, we would say that the *HbA* and *HbS* alleles are codominant, with the result that a single *HbS* allele changes the structure of red blood cells enough to inhibit malarial parasites but not enough to cause sickle-cell anemia.

The rise of malarial infection in human beings appears to have begun only a few thousand years ago (Livingstone 1958). Before that time, the people who lived where malaria is now found gathered and hunted wild foods for a living. This way of life kept forests intact, leaving few open areas where water could collect and malaria-carrying mosquitoes could breed in large numbers. As these inhabitants began to cultivate plants for food, however, they needed to clear large tracts of forest for their fields, creating large open spaces where rainwater could collect in stagnant pools, providing ideal breeding conditions for mosquitoes. And as the population of cultivators grew, so grew the number of hosts for the malaria parasite.

If the *HbS* allele first appeared in the populations of gatherers and hunters, it probably had a low frequency. But once cultivation began, selection pressures changed. At that point, individuals with the *HbA/HbS* genotype were fitter because they had a greater probability of surviving and reproducing than individuals with *HbA/HbA* or *HbS/HbS*. As a result, the frequency of *HbS* increased in the population, despite the fact that in a double dose it was generally lethal. This example also illustrates the way niche construction—the enduring consequences of efforts organisms make to modify the environments in which they live—can reshape the selection pressures that a population experiences. In this case, a switch from one pattern of food acquisition to another created new

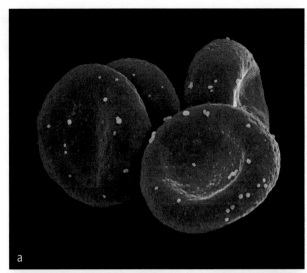

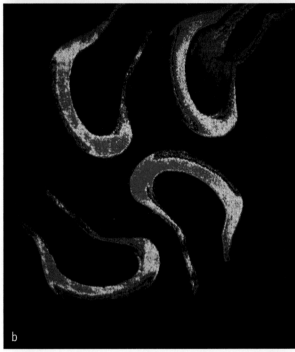

**FIGURE 4.1** | Normal red blood cells (a) look very different from the distorted, "sickled" red blood cells (b). Sickled red blood cells carry less oxygen than do normal red blood cells; however, they also offer an evolutionary advantage to populations living in some regions of the world.

not survive to adulthood and, hence, do not reproduce. Although many people in the United States think that sickle-cell anemia affects only people with ancestors who came from Africa, in fact many people in India, Saudi Arabia, and Mediterranean countries such as Turkey, Greece, and Italy also suffer from the disease.

For more background on the processes of natural selection and mutation, see Chapter 3, pp. 50–1 and 59.

## In Their Own Words

## Riding the Migration Wave of French Colonization in Quebec

*The genetic consequences of demographic migrations are not clearly known. Using church registries and genetic records, Claudia Moreau et al. examined the expansion of colonies in Quebec from 1686 to 1960, noting that females along the initial "wave front" of settlement (i.e., those who arrived first and settled the area) had significantly higher fitness (reproductive success) than did women in the "range core" (i.e., those who lived in settlements that had already been established). Laurent Excoffier, one of Moreau's colleagues on the project, explains the concept of a "wave front" as follows: "The wave front is a moving edge . . . always at the periphery of the range. So individuals begin by colonizing a given region, which becomes the wave front by definition. Then, people send migrants toward new regions, which become the wave front in turn . . . and when a given territory has been fully settled, the wave front disappears since there is no wave of advance anymore" (qtd in Bryn, 2011).*

Deep-rooted human genealogies in recently expanded populations may offer an opportunity to study the wave front demographics and its genetic consequences on present-day populations. We studied the genealogies reconstructed from Quebec parish registers that document the [relatively] recent temporal and spatial expansion of the settlement of the Charlevoix Saguenay Lac-Saint-Jean (ChSLSJ) region, northeast of Quebec City, Canada: a prime example of a [relatively] recent, fast, and well-documented range expansion [see the map below]. The European colonization of Quebec was initiated in 1608 with the foundation of Quebec City, and the colony was well established by the end of the seventeenth century. The peopling of the Charlevoix region started from Baie-Saint-Paul, and both a rapid demographic growth and the development of the timber industry promoted further expansions after 1838 up the Saguenay River and the Lac-Saint-Jean region (SLSJ). The spatial and temporal dynamics of the peopling of the whole ChSLSJ region can be reconstructed by tracing back the founding events of new localities. As shown in [the map page 77], the inferred colonization process is a mixture of long-distance settlements creating an irregular wave front, followed by further,

more progressive, short-range expansions, which then filled gaps and created a more regular wave front.

On the basis of the computation of a wave front index (WFI), we find that the ancestors of the Saguenay and the Lac-Saint-Jean people lived more often on or close to the wave front than expected by chance. . . . In contrast, WFI is significantly lower in the Charlevoix region. . . . These results are consistent with different colonization dynamics of SLSJ and Charlevoix. The wave front was always widespread in SLSJ where new localities were continuously settled, whereas it was much smaller in Charlevoix where most localities remained in the range core until the twentieth century [see the map above]. New immigrants from outside ChSLSJ constituted an important minority of the people getting married, with a greater proportion of immigrants settling on the wave front than on the range core, especially before 1900 (up to 20 per cent on the wave front and up to 10 per cent in the range core). . . .

We computed the expected number of genes left by a given ancestor to the current generation [its genetic contribution (GC)] for all ancestors of ChSLSJ, distinguishing between those having reproduced on the wave front and those in the range core. We find that over the entire studied

niches for humans, mosquitoes, and malaria parasites, simultaneously reshaping the selection pressures experienced by all three populations (Odling-Smee et al. 2003).

The above example illustrates how gene frequencies are most commonly altered within a relatively

**gene flow**  The exchange of genes that occurs when a given population experiences a sudden expansion due to in-migration of outsiders from another population of the species.

**genetic drift**  Random changes in gene frequencies from one generation to the next due to a sudden reduction in population size as a result of disaster, disease, or the out-migration of a small subgroup from a larger population.

closed, relatively stable population. However, gene frequencies can also be altered—often quite drastically—if a given population experiences a sudden expansion due to the in-migration of outsiders from another population of the species, which is called gene flow. A population can also undergo genetic drift—random changes in gene frequencies from one generation to the next. Genetic drift may have little effect on the gene frequencies of large, stable populations, but it can have a dramatic impact on populations that are suddenly reduced in size by disease or disaster (the *bottleneck effect*) or on small subgroups that establish themselves apart from

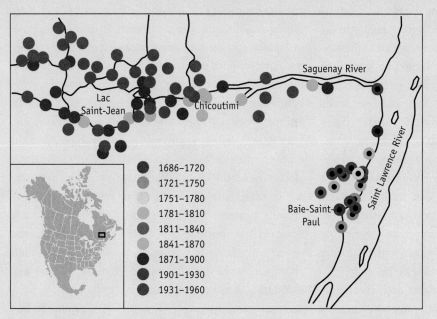

Map of the Charlevoix Saguenay Lac-Saint-Jean region showing the range expansion dynamics and the wave front at different periods. Each filled circle represents a locality, and its colour indicates its age. Localities from the Charlevoix region are indicated by a black dot.

period, individuals on the front have contributed significantly more genes to the present generation than [have] those in the core, in line with the theory predicting that surfing alleles should be traced back to ancestors living on or close to the wave front. We find similar results when we restrict the analysis to the SLSJ region, which has been colonized more recently. Overall, ancestors on the edge contributed 1.2 to 3.9 times more genes to the current generation than [did] ancestors from the core, the oldest ancestors generally passing on more genes than more recent ones, in keeping with previous results. In addition, 40.2 per cent of all ancestors of the ChSLSJ living between 1686 and 1930 were on the wave front, reaching 45.1 per cent for the SLSJ region. For SLSJ, the number of ancestors living directly on the front

or just one generation away from it even reaches 81 per cent, showing the importance of this moving edge for this region.

We compared the reproductive success of women on the edge to [that of] the ones in the core, considering both the number of their children [family size (FS)] and the number of their married children [effective family size (EFS)]. SLSJ female ancestors living on the edge had on average 15 per cent more children than core SLSJ female ancestors . . . and 20 per cent more married children. . . . These results show that women's fertility was significantly higher on the wave front than in the range core and that the larger genetic contribution of ancestors reproducing on the wave front is likely not due purely to a neutral surfing process but also to a net effect of positive selection on the front.

Source: Moreau et al. 2011, 1148–9. Published online 3 November 2011. Reprinted with permission from AAAS.

a larger population (the *founder effect*). Both of these effects accidentally eliminate large numbers of alleles.

The effects of genetic drift have been studied in relation to the French Canadian population of Quebec. Today, this population consists of approximately 6 million people, most of whom are descendants of the approximately 8500 French settlers who arrived in New France in the period from the early seventeenth century to the late eighteenth century (Laberge et al. 2005). The availability of both genomic and genealogical data for this population has allowed researchers to distinguish several founder events and establish related indices (see

Moreau et al. 2011; Roy-Gagnon et al. 2011). For example, Laberge et al. (2005) have found evidence that the various migrations of these settlers and their early descendants led to a series of regional founder effects, the genetic implications of which are reflected in the geographical distribution of certain genetic diseases among French Canadians in Quebec today. In their study, Laberge et al. identified conditions that had never before been uncovered in any other population as well as conditions that were far more common among French Canadians than among members of the wider Canadian population. Other studies have identified certain groups within past

French Canadian populations whose relatively high fertility rates have had a disproportionately high impact on the genetic makeup of the current population. (See the "In Their Own Words" box highlighting the work of Claudia Moreau and her colleagues at the University of Montreal).

In review, modern evolutionists recognize four evolutionary processes: mutation, natural selection, gene flow, and genetic drift. Chance plays a role in each. The occurrence of a mutation is random, and there is no guarantee that a useful mutation will occur when it is needed; many mutations are neutral, neither helping nor harming the organisms in which they occur. Nor is there any way to predict the factors that make population migrations possible or to foresee the natural accidents that diminish populations. Unpredictable changes in the environment can modify the selection pressures on a given population, affecting its genetic makeup. Moreover, as we discussed in Chapter 3, *niche construction* can sometimes alter the selection pressures that individuals, their descendants, and other neighbouring organisms experience in those environments. For example, control of fire and the invention of clothing made it possible for early humans to colonize cold environments that were inaccessible to earlier ancestors, who lacked these cultural skills. Niche construction of this kind buffers us from experiencing some selection pressures, but it simultaneously exposes us to others (see Creanza, Fogarty, and Feldman 2013).

For more information on the process of niche construction, see Chapter 3, p. 62–3.

Today, many biologists and anthropologists agree that the most intense selection pressures our species faces come from disease organisms that target our immune systems and from human-made environmental threats, such as pollution and the ozone hole (Leslie and Little 2003; Farmer 2003; Figure 4.2). Evidence that microorganisms are a major predatory danger to humans comes from research on the connection between infectious diseases and polymorphic blood groups (i.e., blood groups that have two or more genetic variants within a population). Biological anthropologists James Mielke, Lyle Konigsberg, and John Relethford (2011) point out, for example, that the diseases human beings have suffered from have not always been the same. When our ancestors were living in small foraging bands, they were susceptible to chronic parasitic infections, such as pinworms, and diseases transmitted from animals. After the domestication of plants and animals, however, human diets changed, settled life in towns and cities increased, and sanitation worsened. Populations expanded, individuals had more frequent contact with one another, and the stage was set for the rise and spread of *endemic* diseases (i.e., diseases particular to a population) that could persist in a population without repeated introduction from elsewhere. As a result,

the increase in endemic diseases started to apply selective pressures that were different from those exerted by chronic diseases. These diseases usually select individuals out of the population before they reach reproductive age. Differential mortality (natural selection)

FIGURE 4.2 | Some of the most intense selection pressures faced by humans today are human-made. In countries such as China, air pollution is believed to be the cause behind the unusually high rates of asthma and other respiratory problems among children.

based on genetic variation in the blood types would be expected to influence genetic polymorphisms. Thus recurrent epidemics of diseases such as smallpox, cholera, plague, and measles, which swept through continents, undoubtedly contributed to the shaping of the genetic landscape. (Mielke et al. 2011, 105–6)

This was especially true during the colonization of the Americas, when these European diseases killed thousands of North American Indigenous peoples, drastically reducing their populations and their genetic diversity.

Several evolutionary processes may affect a population at the same time. For example, a rare, helpful allele might appear in a population through mutation. However, if a natural disaster such as an earthquake struck the population while the new allele was still very rare, it might be completely lost if its few carriers were among those who perished (genetic drift). Alternatively, the frequency of a harmful new allele might increase in subsequent generations if its carriers survived such a disaster and if they introduced the new allele into a larger population through interbreeding (gene flow). Niche construction could also be implicated if, for example, gene flow were enabled or intensified as a result of persisting, environment-modifying activities of the populations exchanging genes.

Measuring the interaction among these evolutionary processes allows population geneticists to predict the probable effects of inbreeding and outbreeding on a population's gene pool. Inbreeding tends to increase the proportion of homozygous combinations of alleles already present in a population. If some of these alleles are harmful in a double dose, inbreeding increases the probability that a double dose will occur in future generations and thus decrease fitness. If helpful combinations of alleles occur in an inbreeding population, their proportions can increase in a similar way.

At the same time, inbreeding over several generations tends to reduce genetic variation. Natural selection on genes has a better chance of shaping organisms to changed environments if it has a wider range of genetic variation to act on. Perhaps for this reason, mating with individuals from outgroups is widely observed in the animal kingdom. Monkeys and apes, for example, regularly transfer into a new social group before they begin to reproduce (Figure 4.3). Human beings ordinarily do the same thing, except that our reproductive practices are shaped by culture; people in different societies draw the boundaries around in-groups and outgroups differently. In one society, the children of brothers and sisters may be considered members of the same "family" and, thus, off limits for marriage; in another, they may be considered members of different "families" and, thus, ideal marriage partners. However, cultural rules forbidding *incest*, or sexual relations with close kin, do not always succeed in preventing such relations from occurring.

**FIGURE 4.3** | Among rhesus monkeys, young adult males will typically leave the group in which they were born to enter another social group before mating.

**TABLE 4.2** | Effects of the Four Evolutionary Processes on Variation within and between Populations

| Evolutionary Process | Variation within Populations | Variation between Populations |
|---|---|---|
| Mutation | Increases | Increases |
| Gene Flow | Increases | Decreases |
| Genetic Drift | Decreases | Increases |
| Natural Selection | Increases or decreases | Increases *or* decreases |

Table 4.2 summarizes the effects of the four standard evolutionary processes on gene frequencies within and between populations.

## Adaptation and Human Variation

One of the breakthroughs of modern genetics was the discovery of *gene interaction*. That is, a single gene may contribute to the production of more than one phenotypic feature (*pleiotropy*), and many genes may combine forces to produce a single phenotypic feature (*polygeny*). Pleiotropy and polygeny help explain how it is that genes, which are discrete, could influence phenotypic traits such as body size or skin colour, which show continuous gradations. Traits that are the product of multiple genes offer multiple and varied opportunities for natural selection to shape phenotypic traits in ways that are adaptive for the organisms in which they are found.

In discussions of gene action, biologists commonly distinguish between genes of major effect and polygenes of intermediate or minor effect. A gene of major effect is a gene at one locus whose expression has a critical effect on the phenotype. The *HbS* allele that produces the sickling trait in red blood cells is an example of a gene of major effect. But phenotypic traits that depend on one or a few genes of major effect are rare. The evolution of a phenotypic trait may begin with selection on genes of major effect, but the products of such genes may be pleiotropic, producing adaptive as well as harmful consequences for the organism. Further selection on multiple polygenes of intermediate or minor effect that also affect the trait, however, may modify or eliminate those harmful consequences (West-Eberhard 2003, 101–4). Finally, because gene expression does not take place in an environmental vacuum, many phenotypic traits in organisms are even more finely tuned for their adaptive functions by inputs from environmental

**phenotypic plasticity** Physiological flexibility that allows organisms to respond to environmental stresses, such as temperature changes.

factors such as nutrients, temperature, humidity, altitude, or day length. Human phenotypic traits such as body size or skin colour, for example, are the outcome of complex interactions among multiple gene products and environmental influences throughout the life cycle.

Many students of human genetics have devoted attention to the way natural selection may mold complex human phenotypic traits, better adapting human populations to their specific environments. More recently, developmental biologists have been able to show how the responsiveness of organisms to their environments also contributes to the abilities of those organisms to adapt to their environments. A fertilized human egg (or zygote) has its own phenotype, and the zygote's phenotype can respond to environmental influences—such as those encountered in a woman's uterus—*even before its own genes are active*. This responsiveness is called **phenotypic plasticity**: "the ability of an organism to react to an environmental input with a change in form, state, movement, or rate of activity" (West-Eberhard 2003, 35). Because all living organisms exhibit phenotypic plasticity, it is *incorrect* to assume that genes "direct" the development of organisms or "determine" the production of phenotypic traits. Indeed, much of the "action" that goes into producing adult organisms with distinctive phenotypes goes on during development.

It is important to stress that acknowledging the phenotypic plasticity of organisms has nothing to do with Lamarckian ideas of use and disuse and the inheritance of acquired characteristics, neither of which is accepted by modern evolutionary biologists. As West-Eberhard (2003, 29) points out,

> There is no hint of direct (Lamarckian) influence of environment on genome in this scheme—it is entirely consistent with conventional genetics and inheritance. By the view adopted here, evolutionary change depends upon the genetic component of phenotypic variation screened by selection,

whether phenotypic variants are genetically or environmentally induced. It is the genetic *variation* in a response (to mutation or environment) that produces a response to selection and cross-generational, cumulative change in the gene pool.

Some of the most exciting work in evolutionary biology today involves linking new understandings about developmental influences on phenotypes with understandings of traditional evolutionary processes like mutation, gene flow, genetic drift, and natural selection (West-Eberhard 2003; Gould 2002; Oyama et al. 2001).

Adaptation as a process refers to the mutual shaping of organisms and their environments. However, the term *adaptation* can also be used to refer to the phenotypic traits that are the outcome of adaptive processes (see Chapter 3). Biological anthropologists traditionally distinguish three levels of phenotypic adaptation: genetic adaptations, short-term adaptations, and developmental adaptations. Each of these shows differing degrees of phenotypic plasticity. The sickling trait in hemoglobin described in the previous section is a classic example of a genetic adaptation because the form of the hemoglobin molecule is the phenotypic product of a single-locus gene of major effect. Most human phenotypic traits, however, are the product of pleiotropy, polygeny, and inputs from the environment.

Often the environmental input operates as a triggering mechanism for an adaptive response. This is the case for the shivering response, an adaptive physiological response in human beings sometimes called "short-term acclimatization." Human beings are warm-blooded organisms who need to maintain a constant internal body temperature to function properly. When the surrounding temperature drops, however, and threatens to cool our internal organs below this threshold temperature (roughly 37°C, or 98.6°F), this temperature drop triggers a twitching response in the muscles that surround our vital organs, as a way of generating heat. If we are able to increase our body temperature above the threshold—by going indoors, putting on clothes, or moving closer to the fire—the shivering stops.

Other forms of acclimatization are longer lasting than the shivering response and take shape over the course of many months or years as human beings

are born, grow up, or come to spend much of their lives in particular environments. The physiological or morphological changes these individuals undergo are consequences of human phenotypic plasticity, not genetic variation. For example, among northern peoples, there are a number of physiological changes that have allowed them to be exposed to cold temperatures for long periods of time without sustaining major cold-related injuries. One such change is the development of a higher-than-average basal metabolic rate (BMR), which contributes to a higher body temperature. Another is the development of a superior "hunters' response"—the process by which blood vessels alternately constrict and then dilate, in a cyclical pattern, in response to exposure to the cold (see Figure 4.4). This response protects core body temperature as well as maintaining blood flow to the extremities, thus protecting against frostbite (see So 1980, 69; Steegman 1977).

Another form of acclimatization is found among peoples who live in mountain environments such as the highlands of the Andes in South America. Human populations who live at these high altitudes are subject to hypoxia, a deficiency in the amount of oxygen in the blood, because less oxygen is available to breathe than at lower altitudes. Studies have shown that people who grow up in high altitudes adapt to lower oxygen levels by developing greater chest dimensions and lung capacities than do people living at low attitudes. Studies have also shown that individuals who were not born in such an environment increased in chest dimensions and lung capacity the longer they lived in such an environment and the younger they were when they moved there (Greska 1990). These sorts of changes, sometimes called "developmental acclimatization," are consequences of human phenotypic plasticity that occur when the human body is challenged—in this case, by a low level of oxygen in the environment.

### Skin Colour

Skin colour is a highly visible, complex, continuous phenotypic trait in human populations (Figure 4.5). Variation in skin colour seems to be the product of a few

---

**adaptation** The mutual shaping of organisms and their environments.

**acclimatization** A change in the way the body functions in response to physical stress.

## Anthropology in the Contemporary World

### Examining the Remains of Richard III

One way to learn about our present and our future is by exploring our past. Nowhere is this approach more prevalent than in the anthropological study of genetics. The sequencing of ancient genomes allows researchers to explore not only the lives of persons in the past but also the lives that we are living today. Below is one example of a DNA-sequencing project that promises to change the way we think about life, both past and present.

In 2012, archaeologists found skeletal remains while excavating a parking lot in Leicester, England. While they were hoping to find the remains of a monastery that was said to be buried beneath hundreds of years of infrastructure, they found much more than they were expecting: skeletal remains that were later identified as those of Richard III, England's last king to die in battle. His remains have since been reinterred, but not before his entire genome was sequenced by Canadian geneticist Turi King and her colleagues at the University of Leicester. In King's own words, this project is important because it "will help to teach us not only about him, but ferment discussion about how our DNA informs our sense of identity, our past and our future" (quoted in Wellcome Trust 2014). Because of King's work, Richard III's DNA will be accessible to future researchers in all disciplines.

The positive identification of Richard III's skeletal remains was an exceptional find for geneticists, as researchers are rarely given the chance to examine DNA from an ancient person whose identity is known to them. Moreover, Richard is one of only a limited group of ancient humans whose DNA has been sequenced. Others include Neanderthal specimens, hunter-gatherers from Spain, an Inuit ancestor from Greenland, and Ötzi the Iceman

The identification of Richard III's remains would not have been possible without modern gene-sequencing technologies and access to Richard III's distant living relatives. King was able to retrieve mitochondrial DNA (mtDNA) from two know descendants of Richard's sister, Canadian-born Michael Ibsen and Australian Wendy Duldig, who were tracked down using a variety of historical documents. King found that the mtDNA of both Ibsen and Duldig matched that of the skeleton excavated from the Leicester parking lot. Thus, according to King, "there is, at its most conservative, a 99.999 per cent probability that these are indeed the remains of Richard III" (quoted in Treble 2015).

Sequencing ancient mtDNA is no small feat, as an individual's biological material becomes degraded as the body decomposes. Only after numerous hours of painstakingly intricate work was King able to compare the mtDNA from Ibsen and Duldig to that from the skeleton found under the parking lot. Her results were then independently scrutinized by two other laboratories that specialize in working with ancient DNA. In both cases, King's results were verified. Richard III had been discovered more than five hundred years after his death.

The data King and her colleagues have uncovered provides biological anthropologists, archaeologists, and historians with concrete facts that can be used to verify or refute written accounts and other historic documents from the period in which Richard III lived. For example, Richard III had been described by some, including his rival and successor, Henry Tudor, as a "poisonous hunchback'd toad"; other contemporaries described him as having a bodily shape of low stature. These descriptions fit with the story told by the skeletal remains recovered from the parking lot, as the remains show clear signs of scoliosis, which deforms the spine into an *S* shape. Thus, while King's findings cannot offer insight into Richard's historical reputation of being a vile, untrustworthy murderer, they do provide physical evidence of what his body was like in life and in death and, by extension, how he lived and died.

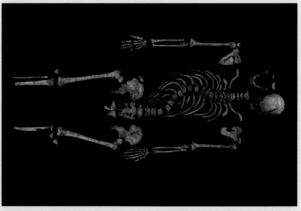

The skeletal remains of Richard III shows a curvature of the spine due to scoliosis.

*Source*: Adapted from Wellcome Trust 2014 and Treble 2015. For more information on the results of King's research, see King et al. 2014.

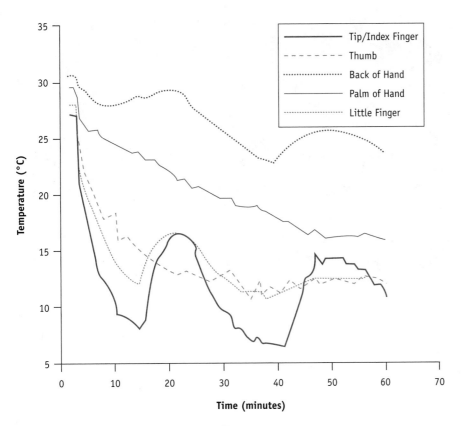

FIGURE 4.4 | Over time, extremities exposed to very cold temperatures experience alternating vasoconstriction and vasodilation, which results in a cyclical rise and fall in tissue temperature. The line in this graph represents the change in temperature in the tip of a finger exposed to extreme cold.

genes of major effect, additional polygenes of intermediate or minor effect, and input from the environment. As Nina Jablonski (2004, 613) suggests, "determination of the relative roles of variant genes and varying environments has proven extremely challenging"; in addition, it is not clear how many alleles are involved or whether identical genes are responsible for the dark skin of apparently unrelated human populations (Marks 1995, 167–8). Biological anthropologists agree that skin colour is adaptive and related to the degree of ultraviolet radiation (UVR) that human populations have experienced in particular regions of the globe.

It is important to emphasize that "similar skin colours have evolved independently in human populations inhabiting similar environments," making skin colour "useless as a marker for membership in a unique group or 'race'" (Jablonski 2004, 615). Indeed, some of the most striking features of human skin are clearly consequences of developmental and phenotypic plasticity: variations in skin thickness are a function of age and history of sun exposure; the outer layers of the skin in darkly pigmented or heavily tanned people have more, and more compact, cell layers, making the skin more effective as a barrier to sun damage. The overall intensity of skin colour is thus determined by a combination of morphological, physiological, environmental, and developmental factors. When the intricate articulation of these factors is destabilized, the outcome can be anomalous skin conditions such as *albinism* (an absence of pigmentation), abnormally intense pigmentation, or a patchy spotting of light and dark skin (Jablonski 2004, 590).

Human skin colour exhibits clinal variation, with average pigmentation growing gradually lighter in populations that live closer to the poles (Map 4.1). The pigments in human skin (melanins) protect the skin against sunburn by absorbing and scattering UVR and by protecting DNA from damage that can lead to cancer (Jablonski 2004, 590). Of course, as humans we are at risk of sun damage to the skin because we do not grow fur coats, as our closest primate relatives do. Dark fur coats can actually protect primates from tropical heat by absorbing short-wave radiation (UVB) near the surface of the coat and reflecting much long-wave radiation (UVA) away before it reaches the skin (598).

These advantages of fur, however, are reduced if the fur is wet with sweat, which can happen if the temperature rises or the organism's activity level increases.

**FIGURE 4.5** | Skin colour in human populations is a very complex phenotypic trait that shows continuous variation-different skin shades grade imperceptibly into one another without sharp breaks. This variation results from the interaction of a few genes of major effect, various polygenes of intermediate or minor effect, and input from the environment.

Under these conditions, "thermal sweating as a method of cooling becomes more important," and it is "greatly facilitated by the loss of body hair" (Jablonski 2004, 599). It is now hypothesized that the last common ancestor of humans and chimpanzees probably had light skin covered with dark hair, like other Old World primates. However, the loss of hair created new selection pressures in favour of increasingly darker skin, such that by 1.2 million years ago, early members of the genus *Homo* would have had darkly pigmented skin (Rogers et al. 2004).

Exposure of human skin to solar radiation has complex and contradictory consequences. Too much sunlight produces sunburn and destroys folic acid, which is a crucial factor in healthy cell division. At the same time, solar radiation also has positive consequences: it stimulates the synthesis of vitamin D in human skin. Vitamin D is crucial for healthy bone development and other cellular processes. According to Jablonski and Chaplin (2000), these selective pressures have produced two opposing clines of skin pigmentation. The first cline grades from dark skin at the equator to light skin at the poles and is an adaptive protection against sun damage. The second cline grades from light pigmentation at the poles to dark pigmentation at the equator and is an adaptive response favouring vitamin D production. In the middle of these two clines, they argue, natural selection favoured populations with enhanced phenotypic plasticity who could tan more easily during hot, sunny seasons but easily lose their tans in seasons when temperature and sunlight levels decreased.

Jablonski (2004, 604) concludes that "the longer wavelengths of UVR, which are capable of penetrating deep into the dermis of the skin, have been the most important agents of natural selection in connection with the evolution of skin pigmentation." At the same time, because people have always migrated, different populations vary in the numbers of generations exposed to the selective pressures of any single regime of solar radiation. Human cultural practices (wearing clothes, using sun block, staying indoors) have shaped the levels of pigmentation and levels of vitamin D production in particular individuals or populations. Gene flow following the interbreeding of human populations with different selective histories would further complicate the relationship between the skin colours of their offspring and selection pressures imposed by local levels of solar radiation.

Many of these factors may explain why the skin colours of the Native peoples of South America are lighter than those of Native populations in Asia or Europe who live at similar latitudes. Most anthropologists estimate these populations migrated from the Old World perhaps 10,000 to 15,000 years ago, which means they have had far less time to experience the selective pressures associated with local solar radiation levels anywhere on the continent. In addition, these migrants were modern humans with many cultural adaptations to help them modify the negative effects of solar radiation, including both protective clothing and a vitamin D–rich diet. Obtaining vitamin D from food rather than sunlight has thus altered selection pressures that otherwise would have favoured lighter skin. Thus, the darker skin pigmentation of circumpolar peoples may be the consequence of selection pressures for darker skin as a protection against solar radiation reflected from snow and ice (Jablonski 2004, 612).

### Intelligence

Intelligence may be the most striking attribute of human beings. However, attempts to define and measure "intelligence" have a long history of controversy. Is intelligence a single, general, unitary "thing" that people have more or less of? If not, what attributes and skills ought to count? Psychologist Howard Gardner (2000, 1) points out that "Every society features its ideal human being." In his view, "the intelligent person" in modern Western societies has been exemplified by individuals who could do well at formal schooling and succeed in commerce. It is perhaps not surprising, then, that tests developed in Western societies purporting to measure individuals' intelligence quotient (IQ) traditionally have equated high scores on verbal and mathematical reasoning with high intelligence.

But these are not the only areas in which humans display differing levels of ability or skill. Gardner, for example, has long argued that in addition to linguistic and logico-mathematical intelligence, human beings possess different types of intelligence, including bodily–kinesthetic intelligence (displayed by exceptional athletes and dancers), interpersonal or intrapersonal intelligence (displayed by individuals with exceptional understanding of social relations or their own psyches), musical intelligence, spatial intelligence, and naturalist intelligence (which attunes us to plants and animals in the world around us). In Gardner's view, these types of intelligence can probably be enhanced in all individuals, given the right kind of environmental support (Figure 4.6). Indeed, even linguistic intelligence and logico-mathematical intelligence require the proper environmental support—long-term training and practice in rich cultural settings—to produce the highest levels of achievement.

Because the definition of intelligence is so controversial, and because not all forms of intelligence are equally rewarded in Canada and the United States, great controversy results when attempts to measure intelligence are applied not only to individuals but also to entire social groups, defined on the basis of gender, class, or "race." The former president of Harvard University was subjected to strong criticism when he acknowledged that fewer women than men become scientists and suggested, in the face of massive evidence to the contrary, that perhaps this meant that women simply had less "intrinsic aptitude" for science and engineering

FIGURE 4.6 | According to Howard Gardner, there are multiple types of intelligence that human beings can display, and each of these types can be enhanced with the right environmental support. Here, children in Brazil learn to play the recorder, helping to enhance their musical skill.

than men did (Summers 2005). Controversies have been as great or greater when ideas about intelligence have been linked to ideas about race. In Canada, for example, people tend to assign each other to "races" on the basis of phenotypic criteria like skin colour. As we have seen, such "races" are then often regarded as different natural kinds, each sharing its own biological essence. From this assumption, it is a short step to conclude that differences between races must include differences in intelligence. Some scientists have devised IQ tests that they claim can measure intelligence, the results of such testing repeatedly showing, for example, that the average IQ score for African North Americans and Native North Americans is below that of European North Americans, which is below that of Asian North Americans, a false premise that only perpetuates inequality and racist attitudes.

Do IQ scores show that racial differences in intelligence are clear-cut and genetically determined? They do not. First, the idea that races are natural kinds assumes that racial boundaries are clear and that traits essential to racial identity (e.g., skin colour) are discrete and non-overlapping. However, as we noted above, skin colour is a continuously varying phenotypic trait, both among members of the so-called racial groups as well as across the boundaries of those groups. Particular shades of skin colour cannot be assigned exclusively to particular socially defined races, nor can they be used to infer any other so-called racial attribute, such as intelligence or athletic ability.

Second, it is far from clear that there is a single, accurately measurable substance called "intelligence" that some people have more of than others. Performing well on paper-and-pencil tests tells us very little about practical problem-solving skills and creativity, which might equally deserve to be called "intelligence." Third, even if intelligence is such a measurable substance, we do not know that IQ tests actually measure it. People can score badly on an IQ test for many reasons that have nothing to do with intelligence: they may be hungry or ill or anxious, for example. When different social groups within a society consistently score differently as groups, however, we may suspect that the test itself is to blame. Arguing that IQ tests measure cultural knowledge far more than they measure intelligence, many critics contend that the vocabulary items used on most IQ tests reflect experiences typical of European North American middle-class culture. People from different cultural backgrounds do poorly on the test because their experiences have not provided them with the knowledge being tested. In Canada, for example, research has shown that Aboriginal Canadian students' poor performance on standardized intelligence tests reflects differences in cultural understanding and language barriers, not intelligence (Common and Frost 1988). When researchers have looked at more culturally sensitive mechanisms of measuring intelligence and learning, Aboriginal Canadian children match closely with other Canadian children (Wilgosh et al. 1986).

Many studies have shown that how an individual will do on an IQ test is more accurately predicted by social class and educational background than by "race." When students of different "racial" backgrounds are compared in this way, "race"-based differences in IQ scores are not apparent. In the United States, for example, when African American and European American students are matched by class and educational background, the differences in average IQ scores disappear (Molnar 1992). Similarly, African American children adopted by middle-class European American parents tend to score significantly higher on IQ tests compared to African American children living in lower-income communities (Woodward 1992). Studies like these demonstrate repeatedly that IQ scores are not phenotypic traits uniquely determined by genes; rather, they are individual traits that are powerfully affected by a range of environmental factors over the course of the human life cycle.

## Phenotype, Environment, and Culture

In recent years, many evolutionary biologists and biological anthropologists have recognized that trying to attribute every phenotypic trait of an organism to adaptation is problematic. Sometimes an adaptive explanation seems transparently obvious, as with body shape in fish and whales or wing shape in bats and birds, which equips these animals for efficient movement through water and air. Other times, adaptive explanations seem less obvious, or even contrived. As we saw in Chapter 3, the wings of contemporary insects are better understood as an exaptation, when appendages that evolved as an adaptation to one set of selective

For more information on exaptation and adaptation, see Chapter 3, pp. 52–3.

pressures began at some point to serve an entirely different function.

In other words, the trait an organism possesses today may not be the direct result of adaptation but, instead, may be the by-product of some other feature that was being shaped by natural selection. It may also be the consequence of random effects. Jonathan Marks (1995) has observed, for example, that anthropologists have tried, without notable success, to offer adaptive explanations for the large, protruding brow ridges found in populations of human ancestors. He suggests that brow ridges might well have appeared "for no reason at all—simply as a passive consequence of growing a fairly large face attached to a skull of a small frontal region" (190).

We must also remember that phenotypes are shaped by environment as well as by genes. For example, some have argued that slow growth in height, weight, and body composition and delayed onset of adolescence among Guatemalan Mayan children constitute a genetic adaptation to a harsh natural environment. However, by comparing measurements of these traits in populations of Mayans who migrated to the United States with similar measurements in those in Guatemala, Barry Bogin (1995, 65) was able to disprove these claims, for "the United States–living Maya are significantly taller, heavier, and carry more fat and muscle mass than Mayan children in Guatemala." Similarly, other biological anthropologists working in the Andean highlands have refuted the hypothesis that hypoxia is responsible for poor growth among some Indigenous populations (de Meer et al. 1993, Leonard et al. 1990). They point out that the genetic explanation fails to consider the effects that poverty and political marginalization can have on human health and maturation rates.

For more information on the connections among poverty, political marginalization, and health, see Chapter 14, pp. 394–6.

At the beginning of the twenty-first century, it has become fashionable for many writers, particularly in the popular media, to treat genes as the ultimate explanation for all features of the human phenotype. Given the great achievements by molecular biology that followed the discovery of the structure of the DNA molecule, this enthusiasm is perhaps understandable. But

discussions of human adaptive patterns that invoke natural selection on genetic variation alone are extremely unsatisfactory. For one thing, they mischaracterize the role genes play in living organisms. Speaking as if there were a separate gene for each identifiable phenotypic trait ignores pleiotropy and polygeny, as well as phenotypic plasticity. It also ignores the contribution of the other classic evolutionary processes of genetic drift and gene flow, as well as the influences of historical and cultural factors on human development (as in the case of the Mayan migrants). Researchers in the Human Genome Project originally expected that, given our phenotypic complexity, the human genome would contain at least 100,000 genes; today, we know that the actual number is closer to 20,500, which is remarkably close to the number of genes in the genome of the roundworm Caenorhabditis elegans, one of the simplest organisms that exists. Clearly, the number of genes possessed by an organism is not coupled in any straightforward way to its phenotypic complexity.

The gene-centred approach gained considerable influence in anthropology after 1975, because of the widespread theoretical impact of a school of evolutionary thought called "sociobiology." Sociobiology attracted some anthropologists who proposed explanations of human adaptations based on sociobiological principles. Other anthropologists have been highly critical of sociobiology. However, after forty or so years, some proposals emerging from this debate have come a long way toward meeting the objections of sociobiology's original critics.

It is important to understand that much of this research is based on **formal models**. These models are "formal" because scientists use the tools of formal logic or mathematics to find answers to particular questions about the evolution of human behaviour. For example, evolutionary psychologists typically assume that the psychological abilities possessed by modern human beings are adaptations that were shaped by specific environmental challenges early in our species' evolutionary history. They employ formal psychological tests on contemporary human subjects to demonstrate the presence of these abilities and then use logical deduction to "reverse engineer" from these contemporary

**formal models** Mathematical formulas to predict outcomes of particular kinds of human interactions under different hypothesized conditions.

abilities back to the hypothetical selective pressures that would have shaped these abilities. By contrast, scientists who study gene–culture coevolution, cultural group selection, or niche construction use mathematical formulas to predict outcomes of particular kinds of human interactions under different hypothesized conditions. Computers allow them to simulate, for example, what happens when certain behavioural patterns are repeated for many generations. The researchers then examine the reports of ethnographers or other social scientists to see if any of the outcomes produced by their mathematical calculations match the actual behaviour patterns found in real human societies.

No beginning anthropology textbook can offer an in-depth introduction to formal modelling of human biological and cultural evolutionary processes (Table 4.3). But students should be aware of this dynamic and contentious field of research, in which anthropologists, biologists, ecologists, psychologists, and other scientists collaborate.

Students should also be aware that many anthropologists—cultural anthropologists in particular—are highly critical of formal models, especially formal models of cultural evolution. They point out that formal modelling cannot work unless actual human interactions, which are messy and complex, are tidied up and simplified so that they can be represented by variables in mathematical equations. Reverse engineering has also been criticized for being overly reliant on logical deduction, rather than empirical evidence, in the generation of hypotheses about the human past. Critics argue that these approaches produce nothing more than cartoon versions of everyday life that often reveal systematic Western ethnocentric bias.

In our view, the perspective with the most promise is that of niche construction, which articulates in unusually clear language a point of view many anthropologists and others have held for a very long time. And they are not the only ones. As ecologist Richard Levins and biologist Richard Lewontin (1985, 259) pointed out,

**TABLE 4.3** | Formal Models in the Study of Human Biological and Cultural Evolution

| Theoretical Perspective | Key Features |
|---|---|
| Sociobiology | • Defined by E.O. Wilson (1980, 322), one of its founders, as "the systematic study of the biological basis of all social behaviour." Originally focused on explaining the evolution of *altruism*—the willingness to give up benefits for oneself in order to help someone else. Sociobiologists argued that altruism makes sense if we pay attention not to individuals but to the genes they carry. |
| | • Organisms share the most genes with their close relatives; therefore, sociobiologists hypothesize, natural selection will preserve altruistic behaviours if the altruists sacrifice themselves for close kin, a concept known as *kin selection*. Some anthropologists adopted the sociobiological approach to human societies, whereas others viewed sociobiology as a pernicious perspective that threatened to resurrect nineteenth-century racism. |
| Behavioural Ecology | • A school of thought based on sociobiological reasoning that accepts the importance of natural selection on human adaptations, but rejects sociobiology's genetic determinism. Behavioural ecologists accept the view that human adaptations depend on cultural learning rather than on genetic control, but they insist that the cultural behaviour human beings develop is closely circumscribed by the selection pressures imposed upon us by the ecological features of the environments in which human populations have lived (see Cheverud 2004; Sussman and Garber 2004). |
| Evolutionary Psychology | • Like earlier sociobiologists, evolutionary psychologists insist that human adaptations are phenotypes under close genetic control. Unlike earlier sociobiologists, however, evolutionary psychologists do not invoke natural selection on genes to explain human behaviour patterns as adaptations to present-day conditions. Rather, they argue that natural selection on human genes was most significant millions of years ago, in the environment in which our ancestors lived when they were first evolving away from the other African apes (called the "environment of evolutionary adaptedness" or EEA). |
| | • Evolutionary psychologists argue that natural selection in the EEA produced a human brain consisting of a set of sealed-off "mental modules," each of which was designed by natural selection to solve a different adaptive problem (see Barkow, Cosmides, and Tooby 1992). |

**TABLE 4.3** | (continued)

| Theoretical Perspective | Key Features |
|---|---|
| Gene–Culture Coevolution | • An analysis of the origin and significance of culture in human evolution that is critical of standard sociobiological accounts. The version developed by Robert Boyd and Peter Richerson (1985) argues that human behaviour is shaped by two inheritance systems, one genetic and one cultural. Cultural traits are passed on by learning, not via the chromosomes, but since these traits vary, are passed on from individual to individual, and confer differential fitness on those who use them, they can undergo natural selection. |
| | • The two inheritance systems are interconnected: human biological evolution creates the possibility for cultural creativity and learning, while human cultural traditions create the environment that allows human biological processes to continue, even as culture creates selection pressures of its own that shape human biological evolution. This is why the process is called gene–culture *coevolution* (see also Durham 1991; Cavalli-Sforza and Feldman 1981). |
| Cultural Group Selection | • Sociobiologists argue that group selection cannot occur as the outcome of natural selection operating on genes unless group members are biological kin who share genes (see the explanation of *kin selection*, above). If group members do not share genes, the good of the individual and the good of the group no longer coincide; this means that individuals who sacrificed themselves for other group members would take their "group selection" genes with them to the grave. |
| | • But if behaviours are shaped by cultural inheritance rather than genetic inheritance (as in gene–culture coevolution), this argument may not hold. When the forces of cultural learning are powerful enough, the fitness of an individual may come to depend on the behaviours of other individuals in a local group. This is known as cultural group selection. Once the forces of cultural transmission take hold, it is usually easier and cheaper to behave the way the group dictates than to strike out on one's own (Richerson and Boyd 2005; D.S. Wilson 2002). |
| Niche Construction | • Odling-Smee, Laland, and Feldman (2003) argue that human evolution depends not just on our genetic heritage and our cultural heritage but also on an additional heritage of modified selection pressures which we pass on to our descendants in the form of a constructed niche. They use the concept of "artifact" to represent these environmental modifications: artifacts include birds' nests and rodents' burrows as well as human artifacts like clothing and furnaces. Odling-Smee et al. argue that their "triple-inheritance" theory offers a more satisfactory explanation of the evolutionary histories of organisms than do accounts focusing on genes and culture alone. |

[using] cultural mechanisms to control our own temperature has made it possible for our species to survive in almost all climates, but it has also created new kinds of vulnerability. Our body temperature now depends on the price of clothing or fuel, whether we control our own furnaces or have them set by landlords, whether we work indoors or outdoors, our freedom to avoid or leave places with stressful temperature regimes. . . . Thus our temperature regime is not a simple consequence of thermal needs but rather a consequence of social and economic conditions.

# What Is Macroevolution?

Unlike microevolution, which studies changes within a single species over relatively short stretches of ecological time, macroevolution studies evolution at or above the species level over extremely long stretches of geological time and is concerned with tracing (and explaining) the extinction of old species and the origin of new species. Evidence for these processes comes from close study of fossils and of the comparative anatomy of living organisms. As we shall see, the way we understand macroevolution shapes our understanding of human evolution.

Until about 25 years ago, most evolutionary biologists were more or less convinced that the problems of macroevolution had been solved in a satisfactory manner by Darwin himself. Darwin claimed, and neo-Darwinians agreed, that macroevolution—the origin of new species—is simply what happens when microevolution continues over a long enough period of time. Such a view seemed plausible because, as we have seen, all these evolutionary thinkers assumed that, over time, genetic and environmental changes are inevitable. Mutation (if unchecked by natural selection) inevitably changes a species' physical attributes over time in the same way that the natural environment, perpetually subject to uniformitarian processes of erosion and uplift, never remains constant. Evolution was thought to occur when independent processes of genetic change and environmental change intersect in the phenotypes of organisms living in a particular habitat.

In his final formulation of the theory of natural selection, Darwin argued that there is no such thing as a fixed species, precisely because evolution is gradual. And evolution is gradual because environments change slowly.

> **anagenesis**  The slow, gradual transformation of a single species over time.
>
> **phyletic gradualism**  A theory arguing that one species gradually transforms itself into a new species over time, yet the actual boundary between species can never be detected but only drawn arbitrarily.
>
> **cladogenesis**  The birth of a variety of descendant species from a single ancestral species.

Lamarck's concept of long-term evolutionary change was also gradualistic, except that he pictured *individual members* of a long-lived natural kind (and their offspring) tracking the changing environment over a long period of time. For Darwin, however, one species gradually transforms itself over time into a new species, a process called anagenesis, although the actual boundary between species can never be detected but only drawn arbitrarily. Darwin's theory of the origin of new species is called phyletic gradualism (Figure 4.7 and Table 4.4).

Arguing for phyletic gradualism made a lot of sense in Darwin's day, given the kind of opposition he faced; and it has many defenders today. But some biologists have argued that phyletic gradualism does not explain a number of things that evolutionary theory must explain. In particular, it cannot explain the fact that a single fossil species often seems to have given birth to a number of descendant species, a process called cladogenesis. What about those breaks in the fossil record that led Georges Cuvier to argue that old species disappeared and new species appeared with what, from the point of view of geological time, was extreme rapidity? Is this just the result of poor preservation of intermediate forms, or do new species arise suddenly without having to go through any drawn-out intermediate stages? Or do the fossils that we thought represented intermediate stages in the anagenesis of a single species actually belong to several different species that resulted from the process of cladogenesis?

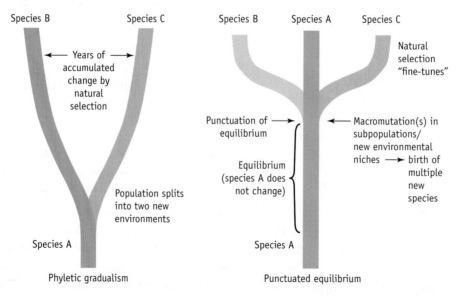

**FIGURE 4.7 | Two models of macroevolution: phyletic gradualism (left) and punctuated equilibrium (right). Research and theories about punctuated equilibrium have challenged the common neo-Darwinian understanding of speciation by means of phyletic gradualism.**

**TABLE 4.4** | Models of Macroevolution

|  | Phyletic Gradualism | Punctuated Equilibrium |
|---|---|---|
| **Originator(s)** | Charles Darwin (in the late 1800s) | Stephen Jay Gould and Niles Eldredge (in the 1970s) |
| **Macroevolution** | A uniform process, the eventual outcome of microevolution, given enough time | *Different* from microevolution, not a uniform process |
| **Motor of Speciation** | The result of *anagenesis*, the gradual transformation of one species into another species | The result of *cladogenesis*, the rapid production of multiple new species alongside parent species |
| **Species Boundary** | Species boundaries are arbitrary | Species boundaries are real |
| **Consequences** | No sharp breaks in fossil record between old and new species | Speciation achieves the shifting of "genetic and morphological centres of gravity of parent and daughter species" such that "each species is now free to accumulate more variation and hence more potential species differences" (Tattersall 1998, 163) |

In the early 1970s, these problems led evolutionists Stephen Jay Gould and Niles Eldredge to propose that the rate and manner of evolutionary change may differ at the level of genes, of organisms, and of species. They argued that patterns in the fossil record (including the patterns Cuvier had recognized) suggest that phyletic gradualism might not explain all cases of evolutionary change. Between the breaks in the fossil record, many fossil species show little—if any—change for millions of years. Moreover, it is often the case that new species appear in the fossil record alongside their unchanged ancestors (Eldredge and Tattersall 1982, 8). We find evidence of this phenomenon when we compare ourselves to the other living primates. Gould and Eldredge (1977) contended that evolutionary change is not a uniform process but rather that most of evolutionary history has been characterized by relatively stable species coexisting in equilibrium (plural, *equilibria*). Occasionally, however, that equilibrium is punctuated by sudden bursts of speciation, when extinctions are widespread and many new species appear. This view is called the theory of **punctuated equilibrium** (see Figure 4.7 and Table 4.4). They claimed "that speciation is orders of magnitude more important than phyletic evolution as a mode of evolutionary change" (116).

The similarities between living primates and humans are outlined in Chapter 5, on p. 98.

But if phyletic gradualism is not the rule, where do new species come from? Gould and Eldredge (1977) argue that drastic changes in the natural environment trigger extinction and speciation by destroying habitats and breaking reproductive communities apart. When this happens, the populations that remain have both a radically modified gene pool and the opportunity to construct a new niche in a radically modified environment. When adaptive equilibria are punctuated this way, speciation is still thought to require thousands or hundreds of thousands of years to be completed. From the perspective of ecological time, the process still appears "gradual," but from the perspective of geological time, speciation appears "rapid" when compared to the long periods of stasis that precede and follow it.

Research and theorizing about punctuated equilibria have challenged the common neo-Darwinian understanding of speciation by means of anagenesis. Punctuationists view speciation as the outcome of cladogenesis, which had always been recognized as part of the neo-Darwinian synthesis but had never been given the important role that punctuationists assign it. Punctuationists also reject neo-Darwinian descriptions of speciation as the outcome of changing gene frequencies, insisting that speciation itself triggers adaptive change (Eldredge and Tattersall 1982, 62). Finally, punctuationists propose that natural selection may operate among variant, related species within a single genus, family, or order, a process called **species selection**. Just like natural selection among individuals of the same species, however, species selection is subject to random forces.

**punctuated equilibrium** A theory claiming that most of evolutionary history has been characterized by relatively stable species coexisting in an equilibrium that is occasionally punctuated by sudden bursts of speciation, when extinctions are widespread and many new species appear.

**species selection** A process in which natural selection is seen to operate among variant, related species within a single genus, family, or order.

Some species flourish simply because they tend to form new species at a high rate. Sometimes, however, none of the variant species is able to survive in the changed environment, and the entire group—genus, family, or order—may become extinct (Stanley 1981, 187–8). If speciation events occur rapidly in small, isolated populations, punctuationists predict that fossil evidence of intermediate forms between parent species and descendant species may not survive or may be hard to find, although occasionally paleontologists might get lucky (see also Eldredge 1985).

Geneticists have not yet been able to pinpoint the genetic changes involved in speciation, but one hypothesis links speciation to mutations in genes involved in the timing of interrelated biological processes, which have major pleiotropic effects. Ernst Mayr (1982, 605–6) argued, however, that only a few such mutations might be sufficient if the population undergoing speciation was small and isolated, involving few reproducing individuals and thus subject to the force of genetic drift. This is, in fact, the sort of speciation scenario the punctuationists also imagine, the setting in which cladogenesis has long been presumed to occur. As Steven Stanley (1981, 127) observed, "It is estimated that 98 or 99 per cent of the protein structures of humans and chimpanzees are the same! Clearly, evolution is reshaping animals in major ways without drastically remodelling the genetic code."

Thinking about evolution in terms of punctuated equilibria fundamentally restructures our view of life. As Stanley (1981, 5) explains, "the punctuational view implies, among other things, that evolution is often ineffective at perfecting the adaptations of animals and plants; that there is no real ecological balance of nature; that most large-scale evolutionary trends are not produced by the gradual reshaping of established species, but are the net result of many rapid steps of evolution, not all of which have moved in the same direction." He later observes that the theory of punctuated equilibrium "accentuates the unpredictability of large-scale evolution" and interprets speciation as "a kind of experimentation, but experimentation without a plan" (181).

Needless to say, these suggestions remain highly controversial. Many modern evolutionary biologists remain convinced that phyletic gradualism is well supported by the fossil records of many species.

For examples of phyletic gradualism in hominin evolution, see Chapter 6, pp. 136–7.

# Can We Predict the Future of Human Evolution?

Current arguments among evolutionary biologists illustrate these researchers' varied attempts to grasp the meaning of evolution. How we classify the natural world matters not only to scientists, who want to be sure their classifications match what they find when they go to nature, but also to non-scientists. How we make sense of evolution is important because people of all societies see a connection between the way they make sense of the natural world and the way they make sense of their own lives. Many people believe that human morality is, or ought to be, based on what is natural. For such people, evolutionary interpretations of nature can be threatening even if they portray a natural world that is orderly. If nature's order is dog-eat-dog and if human morality must be based on nature's order, then survival at any cost must be morally correct because it is "natural." This is clearly why many people find the more extreme claims of human sociobiology so repugnant. For those who want to root compassion and generosity in human nature, sociobiology offers a portrait of human nature in which such behaviour has little or no value.

But perhaps the uncontrolled and uncontrollable pursuit of food and sex is no more natural in our species than sharing, compassion, and non-violent resolution of differences. As we will see in Chapter 5, many primatologists have evidence to show that, most of the time, most apes and monkeys do not live by the "law of the jungle." Possibly, the law of the jungle is not a law after all.

Human beings, like all living organisms, are subject to evolutionary processes. Like other organisms, our species shares a gene pool whose different combinations, together with environmental input, create different phenotypes that are able, within certain limits, to allow a certain range of adaptive responses. But we are not like other organisms in all respects, and this is what makes the study of human nature, human society, and the human past necessary. In order to adapt to our environments—to make a living and replace ourselves—we have options that do not exist for other organisms: cultural adaptations that are passed on by learning, even when there is no biological reproduction (see Figure 4.8).

**FIGURE 4.8** | An individual may have high cultural fitness and no genetic fitness at all. Here, a religious teacher who is celibate (thereby reducing her genetic fitness to zero) passes cultural knowledge to a new generation of other people's offspring.

The rich heritage of human culture is the source of much wisdom to guide us in our moral dealings with one another. The more we learn about biology, however, the more we realize that neither genotypes nor phenotypes nor environmental pressures provide obvious answers to our questions about how to live. If anything, "nature" offers us mixed messages about what is, or is not, likely to promote survival and reproduction. And in any case, with the development of culture, human beings have long been concerned not only with survival and reproduction but also with what it takes to lead a meaningful life. This search for a meaningful life has been part of the human condition for millennia and is likely to remain with us long after our contemporary scientific debates have become history.

## Chapter Summary

1. The neo-Darwinian evolutionary synthesis of the 1930s and 1940s combined Darwinian natural selection with Mendelian ideas about heredity. Neo-Darwinians studied populations of reproductively isolated species, concentrating on the population's gene pool, estimating the frequency of occurrence of different alleles of a particular gene, and predicting how those gene frequencies might be affected by different selection pressures.

2. Human population genetics has shown that different human populations from all over the world share basically the same range of genotypic variation, no matter how different they may appear phenotypically, reinforcing the position that the concept of "race" is biologically meaningless.

3. Natural selection, mutation, gene flow, and genetic drift are four evolutionary processes that can affect change in gene frequencies in a population over time. Sometimes one evolutionary process may work to increase the frequency of a particular allele while a different process is working to decrease its frequency. Inbreeding over several generations can be harmful because it decreases genetic variation and increases the probability that any alleles for deleterious traits will be inherited in a double dose, one from each parent.

4. Natural selection seems to have molded many complex human phenotypic traits, better adapting human populations to their environments. Anthropologists have studied how variations in traits such as skin colour appear to have been shaped by natural selection. Anthropologists have also shown how variations in IQ test scores reflect variations in cultural background, social class, and educational background rather than "race."

5. Many evolutionary biologists and biological anthropologists recognize that trying to attribute every phenotypic trait of an organism to adaptation is problematic. Some traits may not be the result of adaptation but the

by-product of some other feature that was shaped by natural selection—or even the consequence of random effects.

6. Gene-centred explanations of human evolution gained considerable influence in anthropology after 1975, because of the widespread theoretical impact of a school of evolutionary thought called "sociobiology." Sociobiologists have used formal mathematical models borrowed from population genetics and game theory to back up some of their claims. However, critics have also used formal models to test sociobiological principles.

7. Anthropologists have been involved in the development of formal models critical of sociobiological models. The most influential critical models include those of gene–culture coevolution, cultural group selection, and niche construction. Anthropologists still face the challenge of deciding how to situate such critical formal models within broader anthropological discussions of human culture and history.

8. Until fairly recently, most evolutionists were phyletic gradualists, who thought that microevolutionary anagenesis led to macroevolutionary speciation, given enough time. Gould and Eldredge, however, proposed that most of evolutionary history has consisted of relatively stable species coexisting in equilibrium. Macroevolution occurs, in their view, when this equilibrium is punctuated by a burst of speciation by cladogenesis. They further propose that species selection may operate among variant, related species. Debate between phyletic gradualists and punctuationists has been lively.

## For Review

1. Distinguish between microevolution and macroevolution. Explain why this distinction is important to anthropologists.

2. How did neo-Darwinians define a species? What is the significance of a "reproductive community" in regard to different human populations?

3. Explain what a cline is and why it is important. Consider the example of a cline discussed in this chapter and explain it to one of your friends.

4. Explain what is meant by the "molecularization of race." How has the human genome project changed the scientific discussion of "race"?

5. What are the four evolutionary processes outlined in this chapter? In what ways can they overlap to affect one another? Provide examples.

6. Describe how natural selection explains why a high proportion of the sickling allele is maintained in certain human populations but not others.

7. What is phenotypic plasticity, and why is it important?

8. Explain the difference between short-term acclimatization and developmental acclimatization.

9. What factors influence IQ? Why do anthropologists and many other scholars insist that IQ is not determined by genes alone.

10. Explain why natural selection on genetic variation alone is not sufficient to explain the range of human adaptive patterns revealed by archaeology, ethnography, and history.

11. Compare and contrast phyletic gradualism and punctuated equilibria. Which theory do you find more convincing?

12. Define *cladogenesis* and explain how evolutionary biologists might use it to develop taxonomies of species.

## Key Terms

acclimatization   81
adaptation   81
anagenesis   90
cladogenesis   90
cline   71
formal models   87

gene flow   76
gene frequency   70
gene pool   70
genetic drift   76
macroevolution   69
microevolution   69

phenotypic plasticity   80
phyletic gradualism   90
polymorphous   71
population genetics   70
punctuated equilibrium   91
species selection   91

## Suggested Readings

Anemone, Robert L. 2011. *Race and Human Diversity: A Biocultural Approach*. New Jersey: Pearson. *A concise text for the introduction of human biological variation and diversity. The history of race is also well laid out, and current cultural constructions of race are outlined.*

Gould, Stephen Jay. 1989. *Wonderful Life: The Burgess Shale and the Nature of History*. New York: Norton. *In this now-classic account of the discovery and interpretation of an important paleontological site, Gould analyzes what that site tells us about the nature of evolution and sciences that study history.*

Keenleyside, Anne, and Richard Lazenby. 2011. *A Human Voyage: Exploring Biological Anthropology*. Toronto: Nelson. *A great introductory biological anthropology textbook written by Canadians that outlines the development of biological anthropology in Canada as well as current perspectives from Canadian researchers.*

Marks, Jonathan. 2011. *The Alternative Introduction to Biological Anthropology*. New York: Oxford University Press. *An up-to-date introduction to the subfield, raising critical issues that are often sidestepped in introductory textbooks. This text is especially strong in its coverage of the value of the anthropology of science for biological and cultural anthropology.*

Mielke, James H., Lyle W. Konigsberg, and John H. Relethford. 2011. *Human Biological Variation*, 2nd ed. New York: Oxford University Press. *A thorough and contemporary overview of our biological diversity that integrates real-world examples on interesting topics, including genetic testing, lactose intolerance, dyslexia, IQ, and same-sex attraction.*

Relethford, John H. 2013. *The Human Species: An Introduction to Biological Anthropology*, 9th ed. New York: McGraw-Hill. *A fine introduction to modern biological anthropology, with up-to-date reviews of current research on human variation as well as chapters on primatology and human evolution.*

Robins, Ashley. H. 1991. *Biological Perspectives on Human Pigmentation*. Cambridge: Cambridge University Press. *A concise survey of what is known about the biological factors responsible for human pigmentation as well as the possible evolutionary significance of variation in pigmentation in different human populations.*

Stanley, Steven M. 1981. *The New Evolutionary Timetable*. New York: Basic Books. *A classic, accessible introduction (by a punctuationist) to the debate between phyletic gradualists and punctuationists.*

# 5 What Can the Study of Primates Tell Us about Human Beings?

▲ A mother orangutan expresses affection toward her daughter. Photo: olga_gl/Shutterstock

## Chapter Outline

- What Are Primates?
- How Do Anthropologists Classify Primates?
- What Do We Know about the Kinds of Primates Living Today?
- Are There Patterns in Primate Evolution?
- How Do Paleoanthropologists Reconstruct Primate Evolutionary History?

- Chapter Summary
- For Review
- Key Terms
- Suggested Readings

Our closest animal relatives are the primates. This chapter introduces you to the richness and variety of primate ways of life, and it provides an overview of primate evolution. Primates are fascinating in their own right, but they also can help us understand more about what it means to be human.

Human beings are primates, and the evolution of human beings constitutes one strand of the broader evolutionary history of the primate order. Because knowledge of living primate species offers important clues to their evolutionary past, this chapter begins with an overview of what we know about living primates. Because modern primates have their own evolutionary history but also share an evolutionary history with human beings, we then turn to a brief look at their evolution.

## What Are Primates?

Western Europeans first learned about African apes in the seventeenth century. Ever since, these animals have been used as a mirror to reflect on and speculate about human nature. But the results of this exercise have been contradictory. The physical characteristics that humans share with primates have led many observers to assume that these primates also share our feelings and attitudes. This is called **anthropomorphism**, the attribution of human characteristics to non-human animals. In the twentieth century alone, Westerners vacillated between viewing primates as innocent and comical versions of human beings (e.g., Curious George) and as brutish and degraded versions of human beings (e.g., King Kong, Figure 5.1). When studying primates, we must remain aware of how our own human interests can distort what we see (Haraway 1989). If you think humans are basically kind and generous, primates will look kind and generous; if you think humans are basically nasty and selfish, primates will look nasty and selfish. Pamela Asquith, a primatologist from the University of Victoria, has been studying the role of anthropomorphism in primatological studies for over thirty years, and she points out that awareness of anthropomorphism has enhanced our studies of primates, adding a more nuanced understanding of their lives (Asquith 2011, 243). She also insists on continued discussions of this topic in order to avoid either romanticizing or demonizing primates, so that we might be able to understand these animals in their own right.

**anthropomorphism** The attribution of human characteristics to non-human animals.

**FIGURE 5.1** | In the West, primates are often portrayed in ways that embody human fears and anxieties. In the 1930s, the giant ape in the original *King Kong* (a) embodied a racial threat to the power of white males and the sexual virtue of white females. Since that time, our shifting interests and understandings seem to have influenced the 2005 remake of *King Kong* (b), in which the white human heroine and the giant ape become allies in an effort to evade greedy, abusive, and exploitative white males.

# How Do Anthropologists Classify Primates?

The first step in understanding primates is to address the variety they exhibit. Primatologists, like other biologists, turn for assistance to modern biological taxonomy, the foundations of which were laid by Linnaeus in the eighteenth century. Current practice involves taxonomists grouping organisms together on the basis of morphological traits, behavioural traits, and geographical distribution (Mayr 1982, 192). The laboratory technique of DNA hybridization allows researchers to combine single strands of DNA from two species to see how closely they match. When human DNA is compared to primate DNA, these strands all match very closely. In fact, the similarity between human DNA and our closest primate relative, the chimpanzee, is as high as 99 per cent (Chimpanzee Sequencing and Analysis Consortium 2005). As we will see in Chapter 6, these kinds of comparisons are no longer limited to the DNA of living primates. New laboratory techniques that permit the recovery of ancient DNA from fossilized bones tens of thousands of years old are making it possible to reconstruct evolutionary continuity and divergence as measured in similarities and differences in the DNA of living species and their extinct relatives (Brown and Brown 2013).

For more on Linnaeus and early taxonomies, see Chapter 3, p. 46.

Taxonomists classify organisms by assigning them to groups and arranging the groups in a hierarchy based on the seven levels originally recognized by Linnaeus: kingdom, phylum, class, order, family, genus, and species. Biologists continue to assign Latin names to species (e.g., *Homo sapiens*). The species name consists of (1) a generic name (always capitalized) that refers to the genus in which the species is classified and (2) a specific name that identifies particular species (any distinguishing name will do, including the Latinized name of the person who first identified the species). Genus and species names are always italicized. The taxonomy recognized by modern biologists is an inclusive hierarchy. That is, related lower groups are combined to make higher groups: related species make up a genus, related genera make up a family, and so on. Each species—and each set of related species grouped at any level of the hierarchy—is called a taxon (plural, *taxa*). For example, *H. sapiens* is a taxon, as is Hominoidea (the superfamily to which humans and apes belong) and Mammalia (the class to which primates and all other mammals belong) (see Figure 3.3).

Contemporary taxonomies are designed to reflect the evolutionary relationships that modern biologists believe were responsible for similarities and differences among species, and taxonomists debate which kinds of similarities and differences they ought to emphasize. Traditional evolutionary taxonomies focused on the morphology of organisms—the shapes and sizes of their anatomical features—and related these to the adaptations the organisms had developed. Organisms that seemed to have developed similar adaptations at a similar level of complexity in similar environments were classified together in the same evolutionary grade. In traditional systems, primates are classified into four evolutionary grades: the least complex grade is represented by prosimians ("pre-monkeys") and includes lemurs, lorises, and tarsiers; anthropoids (monkeys, apes, and humans) represent a more advanced grade; hominoids (apes and humans) represent an even more advanced grade; and the most advanced grade is the hominins (humans). The lesser apes (gibbons) are distinguished from the great apes (gorillas, chimpanzees, orangutans, and bonobos) on the grounds that the great apes have achieved a more complex adaptation than the lesser apes have. For the same reason, the great apes are grouped together on the grounds that their adaptations are more similar to one another than to those of human beings.

This traditional approach to taxonomy has much to recommend it—especially to paleontologists because fossils are often so few and so incomplete that any classification more precise than "grade" is likely to be misleading. Paleontologists realize that adaptive morphological similarity by itself is not a foolproof indicator of evolutionary relatedness. This is because similarity can arise in one of two ways: (1) members of different

taxon  Each species, as well as each group of species related at any level in a taxonomic hierarchy.

morphology  The physical shape and size of an organism or its body parts.

prosimian  The least complex evolutionary grade of the primates, which includes lemurs, lorises, and tarsiers.

anthropoid  The primate evolutionary grade that includes monkeys, apes, and humans.

hominoid  The primate evolutionary grade that includes apes and humans.

species inherit common features from a common ancestor (homology), or (2) members of different species with very different evolutionary histories develop similar physical features as a result of adapting to similar environments (homoplasy, or convergent evolution). Examples of homoplastic traits include wings in birds and in bats and long, hydrodynamic body shapes in fishes and in whales.

To avoid confusing homology with homoplasy, some twentieth-century taxonomists developed an alter-native taxonomic method called *cladistics* that is based on homology alone (that is, on evolutionary relatedness alone). Cladistics attempts to reconstruct the degrees of similarity and difference that result from cladogenesis (the formation of one or more new species from an older species). First, cladists must distinguish between homologous and analogous physical traits, focusing on homologous traits only. Then, they must determine which of the homologous traits shared by a group of organisms belonged to the ancestral population out of which they all evolved. These traits are called "primitive traits."

To trace later evolutionary developments, cladists identify phenotypic features shared by some, but not all, of the descendant organisms. A group of organisms possessing such a set of shared, derived features constitutes a natural group called a *clade* that must be recognized in the taxonomy. Finally, if cladists find derived features that are unique to a given group, this too requires taxonomic recognition. A group of organisms sharing a set of unique, derived features that sets them apart from other such groups within the same genus would qualify as a species (Figure 5.2). This way of defining species exemplifies the *phylogenetic species concept*. In recent years, cladistic methods have been widely adopted by primatologists and human paleontologists, and the following discussion uses cladistic categories.

> For a discussion of the phylogenetic species concept and other species concepts that have been proposed, see Chapter 4, p. 70.

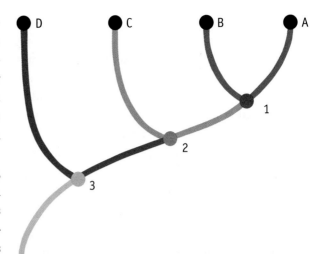

**FIGURE 5.2** | This cladogram shows the relationships among four hypothetical species: A, B, C, and D. Each is assigned separate species status on the basis of unique, derived traits. A and B together possess shared, derived traits not found among C or D, indicating that A and B share a recent common ancestor (1). A, B, and C together possess shared, derived traits that distinguish them from D, indicating that they, too, share a common—but more distant—ancestor (2). A, B, C, and D are grouped together for analysis on the basis of shared, primitive traits common to them all or shared, derived traits that distinguish their common ancestor (3) from an out-group not shown in the cladogram.

## What Do We Know about the Kinds of Primates Living Today?

Primates are found today throughout the world, most often in the tropical regions. Some species, such as the Japanese macaque, have moved out of the tropics and into temperate climates. Primates are unusual, however, because, unlike most mammalian groups, their many and varied species are nearly all found in the tropics. Primates are studied in laboratories, in captive populations in zoos or research facilities, and in the wild. Primatologists must gather and compare information from all these settings to construct a picture of primate life that does justice to its richness and diversity.

And primate life is tremendously diverse. Different species live in different habitats, eat different kinds of food, organize themselves into different kinds of social configurations, and observe different patterns of mating and raising offspring. In light of all this diversity, most primatologists would probably caution against taking any single primate species as a model of early

**homology** Genetic inheritance resulting from common ancestry.

**homoplasy** Convergent, or parallel, evolution, as when two species with very different evolutionary histories develop similar physical features as a result of adapting to a similar environment.

human social life (Cheney et al. 1987, 2). Alison Jolly (1985, 36) points out that any species' way of life—what it eats and how it finds mates, raises its young, relates to companions, and protects itself from predators—defines that species' ecological niche. And, she adds, "With primates, much of the interest lies in guessing how our ancestors evolved from narrow confinement in a particular niche into our present cosmopolitan state."

## Strepsirrhines

Strepsirrhines include lemurs, lorises, and galagos (see Figure 5.3), the prosimians that have a rhinarium (a wet-looking, grooved nose) and a cleft upper lip that is attached to their gums by a web of skin (think of a dog's or a cat's nose and upper lip). Other shared, derived features that unite strepsirrhines include the tooth comb (forward-tilting lower incisors and canine teeth used for grooming), a grooming claw on the second digit of their feet, and an ankle bone (or talus) that flares to the side (Fleagle 2013, 57). Strepsirrhine dentition (the sizes, shapes, and numbers of their teeth) displays the dental formula 2.1.3.3 (that is, each side of both upper and lower jaws has two incisors, one canine, three premolars, and

> **ecological niche** A species' unique position within the ecosystem in which it exists, which is shaped by its way of life (e.g., what it eats and how it finds mates, raises its young, relates to companions, and protects itself from predators).
>
> **dentition** The sizes, shapes, and number of an animal's teeth.
>
> **nocturnal** Active during the night.

three molars). Females have a bicornuate ("two-horned") uterus and a primitive form of placenta in which the blood of the mother and the blood of the fetus are more separated from one another than they are in other primates. Ancient and contemporary DNA comparisons indicate that all the Madagascar species (including the mouse lemur, the smallest living primate) form a clade separate from lorises and galagos, although more detailed relations among many species remain unclear (Fleagle 2013, 82).

Today, lemurs (Figure 5.4) are found only on the island of Madagascar, off the east coast of Africa, where they were isolated from competition from later-evolving primate species on the African mainland. They have been classified into 2 superfamilies, 5 families, and 15 genera (Fleagle 2013, 5). There is evidence that different species of brown lemurs are able to successfully interbreed with one another, although they have different numbers of chromosomes; different species of sportive lemurs are also able to interbreed despite chromosome differences that distinguish them (Fleagle 2013, 63, 67). Humans first arrived in Madagascar about 2000 years ago, and it appears that they were responsible for the extinction of a number of large-bodied lemur species, either by hunting or by destroying their habitats (Fleagle 2013, 73).

Lorises are found in Africa and Asia, and their close relatives, the galagos, are found in Africa. These groups possess features in their cranium that differentiate them from lemurs. Both groups live in trees and are nocturnal (active at night), but they differ in their

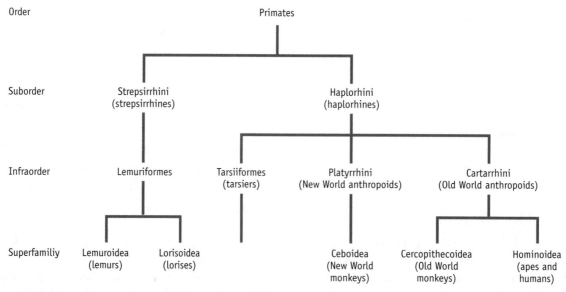

**FIGURE 5.3 |** Cladistic taxonomy of the primates.

FIGURE 5.4 | The striking black-and-white tail of the ring-tailed lemur lacks prehensile capabilities (i.e., the ability to grasp), but it serves another important function. During mating season, males compete for dominance via "stink wars" in which they cover their tails with an odorous secretion and wave them at their opponents.

characteristic styles of movement: lorises are slow climbers, whereas galagos are leapers (Fleagle 2013, 78).

## Haplorhines

Haplorhines include tarsiers and anthropoids, primates with a dry-looking nose that is separate from their lips (rather than a rhinarium) and a continuous upper lip that is not attached directly to their gums (think of your own nose and upper lip). Some taxonomists emphasize the features all Haplorhini share, and they recognize in their taxonomies three Haplorhini infraorders: Tarsiiformes (tarsiers), Platyrrhini (New World anthropoids), and Catarrhini (Old World anthropoids) (see Figure 5.3). Other taxonomists, who judge that anthropoids have more in common with each other than they do with tarsiers, treat Haplorhini and Anthropoidea as semiorders, place Tarsiiformes in Haplorhini, and classify Platyrrhini and Catarrhini as two infraorders in Anthropoidea.

### *Tarsiers*

Tarsiers (Figure 5.5) are small nocturnal primates that eat only animal food, such as insects, birds, bats, and snakes. Tarsiers used to be grouped with lemurs and lorises, but cladists have argued persuasively that

FIGURE 5.5 | Although tarsiers used to be grouped together with lemurs and lorises on phenetic grounds, cladists point out that tarsiers share a number of derived traits with the anthropoids.

they belong in the same clade as anthropoids. This is because they share a number of derived traits with the anthropoids, including dry noses, detached upper lips, a similarly structured placenta (and heavier infants), and a structure in their skulls called the "postorbital partition" (Bearder 1987; Aiello 1986).

Tarsier body morphology—a tiny body and enormous eyes and feet—is quite distinctive. Tarsier dentition is also unusual: tarsiers have no tooth comb but resemble lemurs and lorises in the upper jaw (2.1.3.3), although not the lower jaw (1.1.3.3). In other respects, tarsier tooth morphology resembles that of anthropoids (Fleagle 2013, 85).

### *Anthropoids*

Anthropoids include New World monkeys, Old World monkeys, apes, and humans. New World monkeys are called platyrrhines, a term referring to their broad, flat

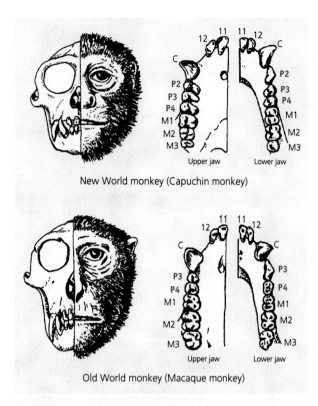

**FIGURE 5.6** | New World monkeys, such as the capuchin, have flat noses with nostrils pointing sideways and three premolars (P2, P3, and P4). By contrast, Old World anthropoids, including Old World monkeys such as the macaque (see Figure 5.3 also), have noses with downward-pointing nostrils and only two premolars (P3 and P4).

**FIGURE 5.7** | A well-known species of New World monkeys is the spider monkey. These monkeys' tails function much like a fifth limb, helping them to suspend themselves in the trees.

noses; Old World monkeys, apes, and humans are called catarrhines in reference to their downward-pointing nostrils (Figure 5.6). Platyrrhines also differ from catarrhines in dentition: the platyrrhine dental formula is 2.1.3.3, whereas the catarrhine dental formula is 2.1.2.3. In other words, platyrrhines have three premolars, while catarrhines have two. Some platyrrhines have prehensile, or grasping, tails, whereas no catarrhines do. Finally, all platyrrhines are tree dwellers, whereas some catarrhine species live permanently on the ground. John Fleagle (2013, 90) reminds us that all these anthropoid features did not appear at once but rather evolved in a piecemeal fashion over millions of years.

New World monkeys are the only clade of anthropoids that evolved in Central and South America. It happens that some New World monkeys have evolved lemur-like adaptations and some have evolved ape-like adaptations, but other adaptations are unique

prehensile  The ability to grasp, with fingers, toes, or tail.

(Fleagle 2013, 92). Platyrrhini are classified into 2 superfamilies, 7 subfamilies, and 18 genera (Fleagle 2013, 5). Titi monkeys are the least specialized of all New World monkeys and may bear the closest resemblance to the earliest platyrrhines (Fleagle 2013, 93). Capuchins (or organ-grinder monkeys) are well known outside their habitats in the South American rainforest. Some populations in open habitats in Brazil have been observed walking on their hind legs and using tools to break open palm nuts (Fleagle 2013, 104). Owl monkeys, found throughout South America, are the only nocturnal anthropoid species (Fleagle 2013, 106). The largest New World monkeys are atelids like the spider monkey, which have prehensile tails (Figure 5.7). Their tails function much like a fifth limb, helping them to suspend themselves in the trees. These are the New World monkeys whose adaptations, aside from their tails, most resemble those of Old World apes (Fleagle 2013, 98). Overall, the adaptive diversity of New World monkeys is impressive. There is no evidence of hybridization among species of New World monkeys (Fleagle 2013, 116).

Old World monkeys include two major groups: the colobines and the cercopithecines. Colobines, including the langurs of Asia and the red colobus monkeys of Africa, are all diurnal (active during the day) and primarily adapted to arboreal life, although they have been observed to travel on the ground between tracts of forest. Colobines have four-chambered stomachs, presumably an adaptation to a heavy diet of leaves (Struhsaker and Leland 1987). Sorting out the phylogenetic connections among colobines in Africa and Asia has been difficult; it appears that much hybridization has occurred among them in the past (Fleagle 2013, 135). Indeed, hybridization seems to have happened regularly among many Old World monkey species, which makes it difficult for taxonomists to agree about how to classify them (Fleagle 2013, 148). Cercopithecines include some species adapted to live in the trees and others adapted to live on the ground. Those species living in forests, such as African guenons, are often found in one-male breeding groups; females remain in the groups where they were born, while males ordinarily transfer out at puberty. Groups of more than one species are often found feeding and travelling together (Cords 1987).

Ground-dwelling cercopithecines include several species of baboons, perhaps the best known of all Old World monkeys. Hamadryas baboons (*Papio hamadryas*) and gelada baboons (*Theropithecus gelada*) are found in Africa. Although they belong to different genera, they both live in social groups that possess a single breeding male. However, this superficial similarity turns out to be the result of very different social processes. Hamadryas males build up their one-male units by enticing females away from other units or by "adopting" immature females and caring for them until they are ready to breed (Figure 5.8). They carefully police the females in their units, punishing those that stray with a ritualized neck bite. In addition, hamadryas males thought to be kin form bonds to create a higher-level social unit known as a "clan." Several one-male units, several clans, and some individual males congregate in a band to forage together, and three or four bands may sleep together at night in a troop. By contrast, gelada baboons construct their one-male units on a core of strongly bonded female relatives that are closely influenced by the dominant female and that stay together even if the male of their group is removed (Stammbach 1987).

The most widely distributed primate genus in the world is *Macaca*—or the macaques—of which there are

FIGURE 5.8 | Hamadryas baboons live in highly complex, multi-levelled societies. At the lowest level are reproductive units, which consist of one male and several females, followed by clans, bands, troops, and communities.

FIGURE 5.9 | The Japanese macaques of Arashiyama, Japan, are one of the longest continuously studied primate populations in the world. Informal observations began as early as 1948, with formalized studies beginning around 1954; these studies have led to numerous longitudinal primate studies (Leca, Huffman, and Vasey 2012).

over twenty species (Figure 5.9). Their habitat ranges from Gibraltar and North Africa to Southeast Asia. All macaque species live in large multi-male groups with complex internal social structures. They do well in a wide variety of habitats and have been especially successful living in habitats disturbed by humans, with whom they have a long history of interaction in many parts of the world (Fleagle 2013, 123).

diurnal Active during the day.

Hominoidea is the superfamily of catarrhines that includes apes and humans. Apes can be distinguished from Old World monkeys by morphological features such as dentition (reduced canine size, changes in jaw shape and molar shape) and the absence of a tail. Traditional taxonomies divide living apes into three grades, or families: the lesser apes (gibbons), the great apes (orangutans, gorillas, and chimpanzees), and the hominids (humans). As we noted earlier, this taxonomic judgment was based on the differences in the kinds of adaptations each grade of anthropoid had developed. In recent years, however, many cladists have argued that classification within the great ape and human categories must be revised to reflect the results of biochemical and DNA testing, which show that humans and African apes (gorillas and chimpanzees) are far more closely related to one another than they are to orangutans. Moreover, because chimpanzees and humans share more than 98 per cent of their DNA, more and more taxonomists have concluded that these genetic similarities require placing chimpanzees and humans together in the same family, Hominidae; humans and their immediate ancestors are then grouped into a subfamily called Homininae and are called *hominins* (Bailey et al. 1991; Goodman et al. 1990). This usage, now adopted by many leading authorities (e.g., Klein 2009, 74–5; Stringer and Andrews 2005, 16), will be followed in this book.

However, some biological anthropologists object that using genetics alone to determine taxonomy ignores important evolutionary information. For instance, emphasizing the genetic similarities between chimps and humans ignores wide adaptive differences between these taxa that illustrate Darwinian "descent with modification." These differences help explain why chimps and other apes are on the verge of extinction, largely as a consequence of human adaptive success. Biological anthropologist Jonathan Marks (2013, 251) asks:

> Who would say "nature" is reducible to "genetics" (aside from self-interested geneticists)? Certainly not the evolutionary "synthetic theorists" of the mid-twentieth century (Huxley 1947; Simpson 1949). If "evolution" refers to the naturalistic production of difference, then to say that we are apes is equivalent to denying that we have evolved. Or to

sexual dimorphism Observable phenotypic differences between males and females of the same species.

put it another way, if evolution is descent with modification, then our ape identity implies descent without modification.

Both traditionalists and cladists agree that gibbons belong in their own family, Hylobatidae. Gibbons, the smallest of the apes, are found in the tropical rainforests of southeastern Asia. Most primate species show sexual dimorphism in size; that is, individuals of one sex (usually the males) are larger than individuals of the other sex. Gibbons, however, show no sexual dimorphism in size, although in some species males and females have different coat colours. Gibbons are monogamous, neither male nor female is consistently dominant, and males contribute a great deal of care to their offspring. Gibbon groups usually comprise the mated pair and one or two offspring, all of whom spend comparatively little time in social interactions with one another. Gibbon pairs defend their joint territory, usually by vocalizing together to warn off intruders, but occasionally by engaging in physical encounters. Establishing a territory appears to be difficult for newly mated pairs, and there is some evidence that parents may assist offspring in this effort. Evidence also suggests that some young male gibbons inherit the territory of their parents by pairing with their widowed mothers, although these pairs do not seem to breed (Leighton 1987).

Orangutans are found today only in the rainforests of Sumatra and Borneo in southeastern Asia. Their dentition is different from that of chimpanzees and gorillas. Orangutans are an extremely solitary species whose way of life has made them difficult to study in the wild. Adult female orangutans and their offspring occupy overlapping ranges that also overlap the ranges of more than one male. Orangutan males come in two different adult forms, unflanged and flanged. Unflanged males are the size of females, whereas flanged males grow protruding fleshy jowls, called flanges, and may be twice as large. Some orangutan populations have been documented demonstrating cultural differences in tool use and vocalization (Fleagle 2013, 158–9). Biruté Galdikas, from Simon Fraser University, has spent most of her career studying these fascinating primates and has established a foundation (Orangutan Foundation International) to aid in the conservation of their ranges, which are becoming very limited as deforestation threatens to destroy their rainforest habitats (see the

## Anthropology in the Contemporary World

### Orangutan Conservation in Borneo

Globalization and economic growth have often come at a cost to various species, and in many cases primates in particular have suffered disastrous consequences. Primatologists such as Biruté Galdikas of Simon Fraser University have devoted their lives to the study and protection of endangered great apes like orangutans. Galdikas began working with the orangutans of Borneo in 1971, and in 1986 she founded the Orangutan Foundation International (OFI) to protect and revitalize dwindling orangutan populations. The OFI supports reforestation and rehabilitation programs and reintroduces back into their natural habitat orangutans that were captured and sold as pets. The foundation also provides information sessions to the inhabitants of Borneo to help curb poaching and deforestation. These sessions are guided by decades of research that have been completed by Galdikas and her colleagues.

While mature orangutans are extremely solitary—particularly males, who can roam over a range of up to forty kilometres—juvenile orangutans are highly dependent on their mothers. Orangutans depend on their mothers much longer than do any other primates, staying up to ten years at their mothers' sides before becoming a reclusive individual at maturity. During these years, juvenile orangutans learn all they need to know to survive on their own. The rehabilitation program run by the OFI provides support for orangutans that have been taken and removed during this crucial time. Introduction back into the wild can be difficult for any animal that has been removed from its habitat for a long period, but this process is particularly challenging for one that has been taken away before it has reached maturity.

In 1971, when Galdikas first arrived, poaching was widespread because various orangutan body parts were being used locally in medicinal products or sold as souvenirs to tourists. At the same time, kidnapping was common because orangutans, like many other primates, are desired as household pets and are often illegally exported to be sold as such. Poaching and kidnapping become easier as deforestation encroaches on orangutans' territory. As plant life is removed and the ecology of the tropical forests shifts, the fruits that orangutans depend upon grow less plentiful, causing individuals to forage farther in order to maintain a healthy diet. The removal of trees and forest cover also exposes orangutans to more predators and makes them vulnerable to human interference.

Since the early 1970s, Galdikas's extensive research has been instrumental in the development and success of the OFI. The reserve where Galdikas has maintained her long-term research project has been designated as a national park, known as the Tanjung Puting National Park. This development is a result of her intensive lobbying efforts in which she advocated for the preservation of the orangutans' natural habitat. From her first field season, Galdikas has done what was popularly believed to be impossible to do: she has cultivated a wealth of knowledge about orangutans, including their habits and their ecology, all the while preserving for future populations of orangutans the swampy lowlands in which they live.

Whether by design or by chance, Galdikas conducted much of her research through forming intimate relationships with orphaned orangutans that took her as a mother. These unlikely children went everywhere with Galdikas, as would infant orangutans with their biological mothers. From these interactions, Galdikas created long-term connections with creatures that are commonly very solitary and often difficult to spot in their forested homes. As the pressures of ever-intensifying globalization lead to deforestation, such efforts to understand species' needs and behaviours in the wild remain essential to finding ways of mitigating the harm too often brought on by human activity.

Biruté Galdikas with orangutans in Tanjung Puting National Park, located in Indonesian Borneo.

*Source*: Adapted from Yin 2011.

"Anthropology in the Contemporary World" box about orangutan conservation in Borneo).

There are five living subspecies of gorillas, all of which are found in Africa: the western lowland gorilla, the Cross River gorilla, the eastern lowland gorilla (also known as Grauer's gorilla), the Bwindi gorilla, and the mountain gorilla. The rarest subspecies, the mountain gorilla, is probably the best known, thanks to the work of American primatologist Dian Fossey, whose experiences have been popularized in books and film. Mountain gorillas eat mostly leaves. Like the New World howler monkeys, both male and female gorillas transfer out of the group in which they were born before they start breeding. The transfer, which does not appear forced, may occur more than once in a female's life. An adult female gorilla may produce three surviving offspring in her lifetime. Gorillas are highly sexually dimorphic, and the dominant male often determines group activity and the direction of travel. Immature gorillas are attracted to dominant males, who ordinarily treat them with tolerance and protect them in dangerous situations (Stewart and Harcourt 1987; Whitten 1987).

Chimpanzees (*Pan troglodytes*) are probably the most studied of all the apes. British primatologist Jane Goodall and her associates in Gombe, Tanzania, have followed some chimpanzee groups for over fifty years. Other long-term field research on chimpanzees has been carried out elsewhere in eastern and western Africa as well (Boesch-Achermann and Boesch 1994). In recent years, a second species belonging to the genus Pan, *Pan paniscus*, known as

the bonobo (Figure 5.10), has received increasing attention, both in the wild and in captivity. Bonobos are found only in central Africa south of the Zaire River and may number fewer than 100,000; forest destruction, human predation, and capture for illegal sale all threaten their survival (de Waal 1989, 177). The two species differ morphologically: bonobos have less rugged builds, shorter upper limbs, and longer lower limbs than chimpanzees and sport a distinctive coiffure. Both species share a fluid social structure; that is, temporary smaller groups form within the framework of a larger community (de Waal 1989, 180; Nishida and Hiraiwa-Hasegawa 1987, 172). Their patterns of social interactions differ, however. Bands of unrelated adult males are very common among chimpanzees but rare among bonobos. Bonds formed between unrelated females are relatively weak among chimpanzees but strong among bonobos. Bonds between the sexes are much stronger among bonobos as well. This means that female bonobos play a more central role in their society than female chimpanzees play in theirs (de Waal 1989, 180).

Chimpanzees and bonobos eat both plant and animal foods. Indeed, one of Goodall's famous early discoveries was that chimpanzees deliberately make tools to help them find food. They have been observed preparing sticks to fish for insects in termite mounds or anthills, using leaf sponges to obtain water from tree hollows, and using rocks to smash open nuts. Indeed, patterns of tool use seem to vary regionally, suggesting the existence of separate cultural traditions in different

**FIGURE 5.10 |** Although they belong to the same genus, chimpanzees and bonobos differ markedly in social and behavioural characteristics. Unlike female chimpanzees, female bonobos have higher social status than males and develop strong social bonds with other females, even those who are unrelated. Here a female stands in the centre of a group feeding on palm nuts.

chimpanzee groups. Male chimpanzees have been observed hunting for meat and sharing their kill with other members of the group; interestingly, forest-dwelling chimpanzees are more likely to hunt in groups, presumably because the foliage makes their prey harder to secure (Boesch-Achermann and Boesch 1994).

Bonobos have never been observed using tools in their native habitats (Nishida and Hiraiwa-Hasegawa 1987, 166). However, the sexual life of chimpanzees cannot compare with the highly eroticized social interactions typical of bonobos. Bonobo females are able and willing to mate during much of their monthly cycle, but researchers have also observed a high degree of mounting behaviour and sexual play between all members of bonobo groups, young and old, involving individuals of the same sex and of the opposite sexes. Studying a captive colony of bonobos in the San Diego Zoo, Frans de Waal and his assistants observed 600 mounts, fewer than 200 of which involved sexually mature individuals. Although this might be a function of life in captivity, it does not appear to be contradicted by data gathered in the wild. Nishida and Hiraiwa-Hasegawa (1987, 173), who refer to material gathered under both conditions, conclude that elaborate bonobo sexual behaviour is "apparently used to manipulate relationships rather than to increase reproductive rates." De Waal (1989, 212) agrees, suggesting that "conflict resolution is the more fundamental and pervasive function of bonobo

sex." Wolfe (1995) notes that same-sex mounting behaviour has been observed in 11 different primate species. Also of note in a discussion of same-sex sexual behaviour among primates is the research conducted by Paul Vasey, who has studied this sort of behaviour among Japanese female macaques over the past two decades. In his recent work, Vasey clearly outlines the differences between sexual behaviour in primates and sexual orientation in humans, cautioning against using these studies as any type of evolutionary model for human sexuality or sexual behaviour (Vasey and VanderLaan 2012, 168).

When we try to summarize what makes primate life unique, we are struck by its flexibility, resilience, and creativity. Primates can get by under difficult circumstances, survive injuries, try out new foods or new social arrangements, and take advantage of the random processes of history and demography to do what none has done before (Jolly 1985, 80–81, 242, 319). Simplistic models of primate behaviour assuming that all primates are fundamentally alike, with few behavioural options, are no longer plausible. As Mary Ellen Morbeck (1997, 14) observes, "Most current models are inadequate when applied to the complex lives of large-bodied, long-lived, group-living mammals, primates, and humans with big brains and good memories." Overall, it seems quite clear that flexibility is the hallmark of primate adaptations.

## Anthropology in the Contemporary World

### Why Do Female Humans Experience Menopause?

Evolutionary theory posits that an individual's main driving force is to be reproductively successful. This is true across all species, yet female humans, unlike all other female primates, experience the end of menstrual cycles—and therefore cease being able to reproduce—decades before death. In contrast, other female primates continue producing viable offspring throughout their entire lives, even when they live to a relatively old age. What, then, might account for such early menopause in humans?

Primatologist Linda Fedigan, Canada Research Chair in primatology and professor at the University of Calgary, has investigated this question in some depth. While studying

Japanese macaques, she became interested in the differences between the reproductive capabilities of female humans and those of female primates. She noted that female macaques reproduce throughout their entire lives, which is not the case for female humans, who enter menopause on average between 52 and 54 years of age and then continue to live for many more years. After discovering these differences, Fedigan combined her work with data from long term studies on seven different primate species from around the world and compared it to ethnographic information on traditional societies such as that of the Ju/'hoansi of the Kalahari Desert (EthnoProfile 11.5).

Continued

Fedigan sought to establish whether the presence of modern medicine was affecting the time difference between reproductive cessation and death in female humans. However, her results showed that this was not the case. What, then, might account for these differences?

Fedigan notes that there are currently two proposed explanations that might provide the answer. Both have connections to evolutionary theory.

One explanation is known as the "grandmother hypothesis." This hypothesis notes that while it is true that reproductive success is the driving force of all species, the means to this end can differ greatly depending on the life cycle of the species in question. Human offspring are incredibly dependent for a significant portion of their early lives; therefore, they require a great amount of attention from their caregivers—first and foremost their mothers, followed by their fathers and other relatives. Cross-culturally, grandparents play a strong supportive role in caring for children. Thus, for humans, ceasing to reproduce around the age of 40 to 50 and instead focusing on existing children and grandchildren may be the best way to ensure the survival of future generations—to achieve reproductive success. In fact, some evidence gathered from hunter-gatherer populations suggests that young children have better survival rates when grandmothers are actively involved in their care. In evolutionary terms, the grandmother hypothesis suggests that as humans evolved, those who were invested in maintaining the longevity of a few offspring would have been more reproductively successful than those who were interested only in producing as many offspring as possible. This is a great example of "less is more."

The other explanation—and the one that Fedigan believes her research supports—is referred to as the "shelf-life of eggs hypothesis." The basis of this explanation is that because female primates are born with all of the eggs that they will ever have, and because those eggs deteriorate throughout a female's life, there are only a finite number of years that a female primate is capable of reproducing. Evidence to support this hypothesis comes from the fact that both female humans and female great apes—our closest primate relatives—cease to reproduce in their early fifties (on average, between 50 and 52 for great apes and between 52 and 54 for humans). In fact, no female mammal reproduces much beyond 54 years of age. The difference, however, is that while humans tend to live far beyond their early to mid-fifties, great apes do not. Thus, it seems that human females do not actually experience "early menopause," but rather "delayed death." From an evolutionary perspective, the shelf-life of eggs hypothesis proposes that while certain evolutionary pressures led to longer lifespans in humans, there was no accompanying increase in the number or longevity of eggs in female humans.

Ultimately, both theories have their merits. Moreover, it may be that aspects of both are correct. While we cannot yet draw any conclusions about why there is such a long gap between the end of women's reproductive lives and the end of their biological lives, comparative studies such as Fedigan's have offered us new insights and new ways of thinking about human reproduction. This observation reflects the more general value of studying primates from an anthropological perspective—to help us understand not only where we have come from but where we are today and even where we are headed as a species.

Sources: Adapted from Montgomery 2014 and Racknow 2013.

## Are There Patterns in Primate Evolution?

How do we begin to trace evolutionary developments within the primate order? The first step is to create a framework for comparison. For example, to trace the evolution of the mammalian skeleton, paleontologists collect samples of fossil mammal bones that span a long stretch of geological time, and they distinguish the bones of the animal's head—the skull, or cranium (plural, crania), and lower jaw, or mandible—from the rest of the animal's bones, its postcranial skeleton. Homologous bones of different ages can then be compared for similarities and differences. The fossilized and living species grouped together in the primate order share no single attribute that sets all of them apart from other living creatures. What does distinguish primates, living and extinct, are three different sets of features: ancestral characteristics (often called "primitive characteristics"), past evolutionary trends, and unique prehensile features (Table 5.1). In addition, primates are unusual because they are "distinguished mainly by a tendency to retain specific parts that other

cranium   The bones of the head, excluding the jaw.

mandible   The lower jaw.

postcranial skeleton   The bones of the body, excluding those of the head.

**TABLE 5.1** | Primates' Distinguishing Characteristics

| Ancestral Characteristics | Evolutionary Trends | Unique Prehensile Features |
|---|---|---|
| • Five digits on hands and feet<br>• Clavicle for flexible shoulders<br>• Walking with the palms of the hands and the feet flat on the ground (plantigrade locomotion) | • Increased relative brain size<br>• Reduced facial projection and reliance on smell<br>• Increased dependence on sight and development of stereoscopic vision<br>• Reduced number of teeth<br>• Increased infant dependency<br>• Greater dependence on learned behaviour | • Opposable thumbs and toes<br>• Nails instead of claws<br>• Sensitive pads on tips of fingers and toes<br>• Dermal ridges (finger prints) on digits, soles, palms, and underside of prehensile tails |

*Source*: Following Le Gros Clark (1963) and others.

animals have lost during their evolution" (Klein 2009, 68). This is why primates are often described as generalized organisms that can live in varied environments. So even though primates have adaptive features suited to arboreal ecosystems, they can survive in terrestrial ones as well (for example, baboons).

Ancestral characteristics that primates inherited from their earlier non-primate mammalian ancestors appear in their generalized postcranial skeletons. These characteristics include the following:

- the presence of five digits on the hands and the feet;
- the presence of the clavicle, or collar bone, allowing for flexibility in the shoulder joint; and
- the use of the palms of the hands and the feet (rather than the toes) for walking, called plantigrade locomotion.

W.E. Le Gros Clark (1963) identified four evolutionary trends that can be traced across the primate order since the first primates evolved away from their primitive mammalian ancestors:

- an increase in brain size, relative to body size, and an increase in the complexity of the neocortex (or new brain);
- a reduction of both the projection of the face and the reliance on the sense of smell;
- an increasing dependence on the sense of sight, resulting in the relocation of the eyes onto the same plane on the front of the face so that the visual field of each eye overlaps, producing depth perception (or stereoscopic vision) (Figure 5.11); and
- a reduction in the number of teeth.

Some scholars have suggested two additional evolutionary trends: an increasing period of infant dependence and a greater dependence on learned behaviour.

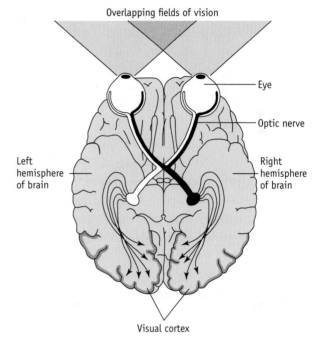

**FIGURE 5.11** | Primates have stereoscopic vision, which means that their fields of vision overlap, and the optic nerve from each eye travels to both hemispheres of the brain. The result is true depth perception.

Finally, primates' unique prehensile morphological features include the following:

- opposable thumbs (i.e., the thumb is opposite the other fingers and can be "opposed to" the other fingers for grasping; most primates, aside from humans, also have opposable great toes);
- nails rather than claws on at least some digits;

**stereoscopic vision** A form of vision in which the visual field of each eye of a two-eyed (binocular) animal overlaps with the other, producing depth perception.

- pads at the tips of fingers and toes that are rich in nerve endings; and
- dermal ridges, or friction skin, on the digits, soles, palms, and underside of prehensile tails.

Le Gros Clark (1963) argued that primate evolutionary trends and unique features were the outcome of an arboreal adaptation—that is, adaptation to life in the trees. In his view, creatures with excellent grasping abilities, acute binocular vision, and a superior brain are well suited to an arboreal habitat. However, many other organisms (e.g., squirrels) have adapted to life in the trees without having evolved such traits. Matt Cartmill (1972) offered the "visual predation hypothesis." He suggested that many of these traits derive from an ancestral adaptation to feeding on insects at the ends of tree branches in the lower levels of tropical forests. Selective pressure for improved vision may have resulted from the fact that these ancestral primates fed at night and relied on sight to locate their prey. More recently, Robert Sussman (1991) and Katherine Milton (1993) have argued that switching from insect predation to consumption of edible plant parts and fruit set the stage for future primate evolution leading to grasping hands, visual acuity (including colour vision), larger brains, and increased behavioural flexibility. Combined, these evolutionary trends and unique features are all important when looking at primates.

It is important to remember that while past evolutionary trends apply to the primate order as a whole, all primate species were not affected by these trends in the same way. R.D. Martin (1986, 13) pointed out that lessened reliance on smell probably developed only in primates that were diurnal rather than those that were nocturnal. Some living primates are still nocturnal and continue to rely heavily on a well-developed sense of smell. These matters continue to be debated, but, as Fleagle (2013, 225) concludes, "Unfortunately, until we have a better fossil record . . . the details of primate origins will remain hidden."

# How Do Paleoanthropologists Reconstruct Primate Evolutionary History?

The following survey of primate evolution begins approximately 65 million years ago (mya) with the onset of the Cenozoic geological era and continues throughout the subsequent six epochs until the current one,

known as the Holocene. The Cenozoic era is divided into six geological epochs, known as the Paleocene, the Eocene, the Oligocene, the Miocene, the Pliocene, and the Pleistocene, listed from oldest to most recent (Figure 5.12). During these millions of years, the earth's continents moved significantly to end up where they are today (Figure 5.13). Consequences of this continental drift include the creation of new land masses (e.g., islands like Madagascar and Iceland) along with new landforms (e.g., the Himalayan mountains and the Mediterranean Sea). In conjunction with these changes to the land, climate shifted from a warmer, more moderate, wet global climate to a cooler, more temperate climate with seasonal fluctuations. Combined, these modifications to the world and its climate had direct impact on the evolution of primates, with those primates best suited to their environment continuing to create new generations.

## Primates of the Paleocene

The Paleocene lasted from about 65 to 55 mya. Evidence about early primate evolution in this period is growing but remains complex and subject to debate. Based on DNA evidence from living mammals, it now seems that primates, tree shrews, and so-called "flying lemurs" (gliding mammals from Southeast Asia with tooth combs) are more closely related to one another than they are to other mammals. All three have been placed together into the superorder Euarchonta, which also includes a group of Paleocene fossils known as plesiadapiforms (Fleagle 2013, 212). Plesiadapiforms were numerous, varied, and successful during the Paleocene and early Eocene of Europe and North America (Fleagle 2013, 213–4). But taxonomists disagree about their connection to primates, and the relation of Euarchonta to primates remains unclear (Fleagle 2013, 224). The best current candidate for the oldest probable primate is *Altiatlasius*, whose fragmentary fossils have been found in late Paleocene deposits in North Africa. Too little is known about *Altiatlasius*, however, to relate it clearly to later primate taxa; indeed, exactly where the first primates evolved is still unknown (Rose 1994; Fleagle 2013, 231).

## Primates of the Eocene

The first undisputed primates appeared during the Eocene epoch, which lasted from about 55 to about 38 mya. Most of the fossils we have from these primates are jaws and teeth, but skulls, limb bones, and even some

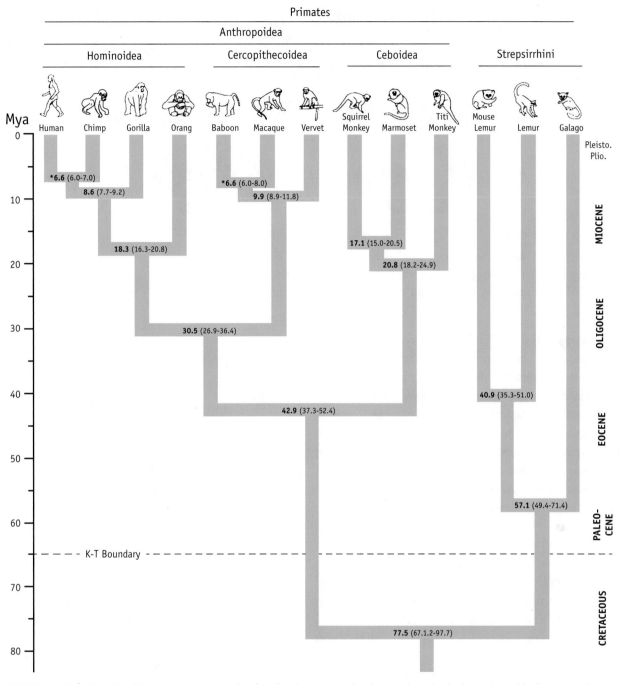

**FIGURE 5.12** | This timeline arranges the major fossil primate taxa by date and geological epoch and indicates estimated divergence dates in millions of years.

nearly complete skeletons have also been recovered. The best-known Eocene primates fall into two basic groups. The first group, *adapids*, looks a lot like living lemurs. However, a number of morphological features—dentition in particular—distinguish them from their modern counterparts. Eocene adapids had four premolars, whereas modern lemurs have only three; and their lower incisors and canines were generalized, whereas modern lemurs possess a specialized tooth comb. The

second group, the *omomyids*, resembles living tarsiers (Figure 5.14). Most omomyids were much smaller than adapids. Adapted for climbing, clinging, and leaping, omomyids appear to have been nocturnal, feeding on insects, fruit, or gum (Rose 1994). A tiny primate from the early Eocene of Mongolia called *Altanius orlovi* may be ancestral to both adapids and omomyids (Fleagle 2013, 231). Linking later omomyids fossils to living tarsiers, however, is not straightforward because different

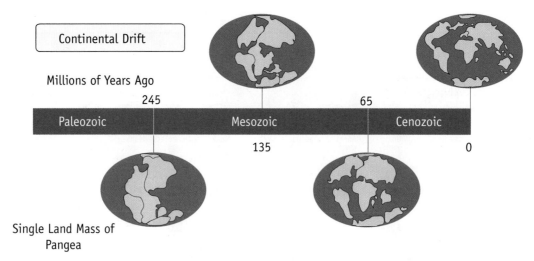

**FIGURE 5.13** | Across the history of the earth, the land masses that we recognize today as continents and islands have undergone a shift known as "continental drift." By the beginning of the Cenozoic era, the continents had completed much of their separation, but they had not yet arrived in their current positions.

features evolved at different times, and parallel evolution seems to have been common. "Nevertheless, omomyoids, tarsiers, and anthropoids all share a number of features that lead almost all researchers to group them together in the semiorder Haplorhini" (Fleagle 2013, 256). Currently, taxonomists are working to reconcile contradictions between older biomolecular estimates of the period that strepsirrhines split from haplorhines with more recent dates provided from the fossil record (Fleagle 2013, 259).

The early ancestors of later anthropoids began to appear in the period of transition between the late Eocene and early Oligocene, perhaps 44 to 40 mya (Martin 1993; Simons and Rasmussen 1994). The *parapithecids* are the most primitive early anthropoid group from this period, with a dental formula of 2.1.3.3., which, as we saw, is found in platyrrhines (Fleagle 2013, 267). However, parapithecids may well not be direct ancestors of New World monkeys because this and

other shared attributes may be primitive traits retained from earlier ancestors (ibid., 273). We still do not know how the earliest platyrrhines reached the New World (ibid., 291).

## Primates of the Oligocene

The Oligocene epoch lasted from about 38 to about 23 mya. During this period, temperatures cooled and environments dried out. Those adapids whose ancestors made it to the island of Madagascar evolved into modern lemurs, unwittingly finding a safe refuge from evolutionary competition elsewhere. Everywhere else the early anthropoids and their descendants flourished.

Oligocene layers at the Fayum, in Egypt, dating from between 35 and 31 mya have long been our richest source of information about anthropoid evolution. The best-represented group of early anthropoids is the

**FIGURE 5.14** | The fossil omomyid *Necrolemur* (left) belongs to the superfamily Omomyidae, thought to be ancestral to the modern tarsier (right).

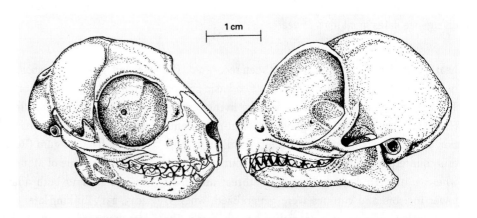

*propliopithecids*, which were larger than the parapithecids and had the 2.1.2.3 dental formula characteristic of all later catarrhines. However, many features of their anatomy are more primitive than those found in Old World monkeys and apes (Fleagle 2013, 273).

*Aegyptopithecus zeuxis*, the largest of the Oligocene anthropoids, is well known from numerous fossilized teeth, skulls, and limb bones, and it appears ancestral to later Old World anthropoids, or catarrhines (Figure 5.15). *A. zeuxis* lived 35 mya and looked very much like a primitive monkey (Simons 1985, 40). The bones of its lower jaw and upper cranium are fused along the midlines, and the eye orbits are closed off from the brain by a bony plate. Nevertheless, its limb bones show none of the features that allow modern apes to hang upright or swing from the branches of trees. Its cranium also shows some primitive characteristics: its brain was smaller, its snout projected more, its eye orbits did not face as fully to the front, and its ear was not as fully developed.

*A. zeuxis* had two premolars (a diagnostic catarrhine [Old World monkey] feature), and it also had Y-5 molars. A Y-5 molar is a tooth with five cusps that are separated by a *Y*-shaped furrow (Figure 5.16). Later Old World monkeys (cercopithecoids) have bilophodont molars with four cusps arranged in pairs, each of which is joined by a ridge of enamel called a "loph." Early Miocene fossils, 17 to 19 million years old, of undoubted cercopithecoid monkeys have molars with a fifth cusp and incomplete lophs. Thus, "the bilophodont teeth of Old World monkeys are derived from an ancestor with

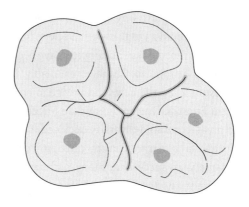

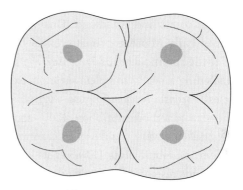

**FIGURE 5.16 |** The upper molar shows the characteristic Y-5 pattern of apes and humans; the lower molar exhibits the bilophodont pattern of Old World cercopithecoid monkeys. Current evidence suggests that the Y-5 molar was primitive for all Old World anthropoids and that the bilophodont molar of the cercopithecoids developed later.

more ape-like teeth" (Fleagle 2013, 348), and the Y-5 pattern was primitive for all Old World anthropoids, making *A. zeuxis* and other Oligocene catarrhines likely ancestors of both Old World monkeys and hominoids (apes and humans) (Fleagle 2013, 273; Stringer and Andrews 2005, 84).

The earliest known hominoid fossils date from the middle to late Oligocene (29 mya) and come from western Saudi Arabia and northern Kenya (Fleagle 2013, 313). It was during the Miocene, however, that hominoid evolution took off.

## Primates of the Miocene

The Miocene lasted from about 23 to about 5 mya. Between 18 and 17 mya, the continents finally arrived at their present positions, when the African plate (which includes the Arabian Peninsula) contacted the Eurasian

**FIGURE 5.15 |** *Aegyptopithecus zeuxis* is the largest of the Oligocene fossil anthropoids and may be ancestral to all catarrhines (Old World monkeys, apes, and humans).

plate. This helps explain why fossil hominoids from the early Miocene (about 23 to 16 mya) have been found only in Africa. More recent fossil hominoids have been found from western Europe to China, presumably because their ancestors used the new land bridge to cross from Africa into Eurasia. During the middle Miocene (about 16 to 10 mya), hominoid diversity declined. During the late Miocene (about 9 to 5 mya), cercopithecoid monkeys became very successful, many hominoid species became extinct, and the first members of a new lineage, the hominins, appeared.

In the early Miocene, eastern Africa was covered with tropical forest and woodland. One well-known collection of early Miocene primate fossils has been assigned to the hominoid genus *Proconsul*. The best evidence, including a nearly complete skeleton, exists for the species *Proconsul heseloni* (Figure 5.17), which was about the size of a modern gibbon (Klein 2009, 117). *Proconsul heseloni* is very apelike in its cranium, teeth, and shoulder and elbow joints. However, its long trunk, arms, and hands resemble those of modern monkeys. It appears to have been a fruit-eating, tree-dwelling, four-footed (four-handed?) proto-ape that may have lacked a tail. Some argue that it is also generalized enough in its morphology to have been ancestral to later hominoids, including modern apes and human beings, although this is debated (Fleagle 1995). *Proconsul* and other early Miocene hominoids were confined to Africa and the Arabian Peninsula.

Most taxonomists agree, however, that *P. heseloni* and other early-Miocene hominoids were outside the modern hominoid clade (Fleagle 2013, 320). These early hominoids also retained many primitive catarrhine features lost by later cercopithecoid monkeys, showing that "Old World monkeys are a very specialized group of higher primates" (Fleagle 2013, 322).

The land bridge connecting Africa to Eurasia was formed during the middle Miocene (16 to 10 mya).

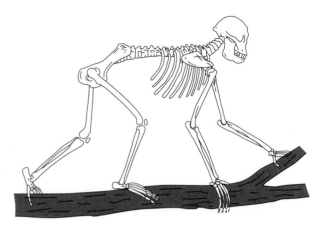

**FIGURE 5.17 |** *Proconsul,* perhaps the best known of the earliest African hominoids. Some argue that *Proconsul* is generalized enough in its morphology to have been ancestral to later hominoids, including modern apes and human beings, although this is debated.

The earliest fossils assigned to the modern hominoid clade date to the middle and late Miocene (10 to 5 mya) and come mostly from Africa, although one genus, *Kenyapithecus*, is also represented by a second species from Turkey (Fleagle 2013, 320). Once hominoids made it out of Africa, they experience a rapid radiation throughout many parts of the Old World, and their fossils remain difficult to classify (Fleagle 2013, 326). Unfortunately, very few African hominoid fossils of any kind date from the late Miocene (10 to 5 mya) or the early Pliocene (5 to 2.5 mya) (Benefit and McCrossin 1995, 251).

In the absence of hard data, attempts to identify either the last common ancestor of the African apes and human beings or the earliest ancestors of chimpanzees and gorillas must be based on educated speculation (Stringer and Andrews 2005, 114). Nevertheless, we know that it was during the late Miocene that the first ancestors in our own lineage appeared. Tracing their evolutionary history is the topic of the next chapter.

## Chapter Summary

1.  If we avoid anthropomorphism, careful comparison between human beings and primate species has the potential to offer enormous insight into our evolutionary past. Primatologists attempt to make sense of primate diversity by creating primate taxonomies. Traditional taxonomies of primates compared the phenotypes and adaptations of primates and recognized four primate grades. Cladistic taxonomies ignore adaptation and the fossil record and classify organisms only on the basis of homologous evolutionary traits found in living species. Many primatologists combine features of both kinds of taxonomies

to demonstrate relations of evolutionary relatedness between species.

2. Strepsirrhines include lemurs and lorises. Haplorhines include tarsiers and anthropoids. Anthropoids include New World and Old World forms. New World monkeys evolved separately from Old World anthropoids and differ from them in nose shape and the number of premolars; in addition, some New World monkeys evolved prehensile tails. All New World monkey species are tree dwellers.

3. Old World anthropoids include species of monkeys and apes, as well as human beings; all share the same nose shape and the same number of premolars. Apes are distinguished from Old World monkeys by dentition, skeletal shape and size, and the absence of a tail. The African apes are far more closely related to one another than to gibbons or orangutans, and human beings are more closely related to chimpanzees than to any other ape species. Chimpanzees deliberately make simple tools to help them find food. Bonobos are known for their highly eroticized social interactions and for the central role females play in their society.

4. Primates are distinguished from other species through a number of ancestral characteristics, evolutionary trends, and unique features associated with prehensility. These evolutionary developments have not affected all primate species in the same way.

5. Paleontologists assign primate fossils to various categories after examining and comparing cranial and postcranial skeletal material. They have concluded that the first undisputed primates appeared during the Eocene. The best-known Eocene primates are the adapids, which resemble living lemurs, and the omomyids, which resemble living tarsiers. The early ancestors of later anthropoids ( monkeys, apes, and humans) appeared in the late Eocene and are known from sites in northern Africa and Asia. Some Oligocene primate fossils look like possible ancestors to modern New World anthropoids; others, like *Aegyptopithecus zeuxis*, appear ancestral to all later Old World anthropoids.

6. The first hominoids that evolved in Africa during the early Miocene were very diverse. One of the best-known examples is *Proconsul heseloni*, which is generalized enough to have been ancestral to later apes and human beings. During the middle Miocene, hominoids rapidly spread and diversified, and their fossils are found from Europe to eastern Asia. In the late Miocene, many hominoid species became extinct. Paleoanthropologists agree that chimpanzees, gorillas, and human beings shared a common ancestor in the late Miocene.

## For Review

1. How do biologists classify primates? What are the advantages and disadvantages of the major approaches to taxonomy discussed at the beginning of this chapter?

2. Distinguish between homology and homoplasy. Comparing different species, what might be some examples of each?

3. What are clades? Illustrate with examples.

4. Summarize the features used to distinguish different kinds of primates from each other. What is distinctive about the anthropoids?

5. Discuss the differences and similarities of chimpanzees and bonobos.

6. In what ways do ancestral characteristics, evolutionary trends, and unique morphological features distinguish primates from other species? What are some examples?

7. What adaptive explanations do paleoanthropologists give for the unique prehensile features of primates? Do you find these explanations convincing?

8. Prepare a table or chart that displays what is currently known about key developments in primate evolution, from the Paleocene to the Miocene.

9. As our closest evolutionary cousins, primates are often viewed by humans as living insights into our own evolutionary history. But what are some dangers of ascribing human traits to primates, and vice versa?

## Key Terms

anthropoid  98
anthropomorphism  97
cranium  108
dentition  100
diurnal  103
ecological niche  100

hominoid  98
homology  99
homoplasy  99
mandible  108
morphology  98
nocturnal  100

postcranial skeleton  108
prehensile  102
prosimian  98
sexual dimorphism  104
stereoscopic vision  109
taxon  98

## Suggested Readings

Campbell, Christina J., Agustín Fuentes, Katherine C. MacKinnon, Simon K. Bearder, and Rebecca M. Stumpf. 2010. *Primates in Perspective*. 2nd ed. New York: Oxford University Press. *A comprehensive overview of the primates and what we know about them.*

de Waal, Frans. 2003. *My Family Album: Thirty Years of Primate Photography*. Berkeley: University of California Press. *In addition to being an influential primatologist, de Waal is a superb photographer. These images are an excellent visual introduction to the various primate species he has studied.*

Fleagle, John G. 2013. *Primate Adaptation and Evolution*. 3rd ed. Amsterdam: Elsevier. *A detailed, up-to-date, and engaging introduction to primatology. The chapters cover both living primates and the fossil record of primate evolution, including that of Homo sapiens. This text also addresses current issues in primate conservation.*

Fossey, Dian. 1983. *Gorillas in the Mist*. Boston: Houghton Mifflin. *Dian Fossey's account of research among the mountain gorillas of Rwanda over a 13-year period; it includes many colour photographs. Fossey was murdered at her field station in 1985. This book inspired a major motion picture of the same name.*

Goodall, Jane. 1986. *The Chimpanzees of Gombe: Patterns of Behavior*. Cambridge, MA: Harvard University Press. *This volume presents the results of a quarter of a century of scientific research among chimpanzees in Gombe, Tanzania.*

——. 2010. *Jane Goodall: 50 Years at Gombe*. New York: Stewart, Tabori, and Chang. *After 1986, Jane Goodall shifted the emphasis of her work from scientific observation to rescuing and rehabilitating laboratory animals and working for environmental causes, as have many primatologists concerned about threats to the continued viability of the species they have studied.*

Haraway, Donna. 1989. *Primate Visions: Gender, Race, and Nature in the World of Modern Science*. New York: Routledge. *This volume, a major landmark in primate studies, contains a series of essays by a feminist historian of science who describes the way Western cultural assumptions about gender, race, and nature have shaped how primates are studied.*

International Union for Conservation of Nature (IUCN). *The IUCN Red List of Threatened Species*. www.iucnredlist.org. *The IUCN manages a website that contains updated lists of endangered animal species, estimating the degree of endangerment and explaining the sources of endangerment. Entering "primates" into their search engine brings up a list of endangered primate species as well as a wealth of information about the taxonomic status of primate species, their life histories, their habitats, and where their populations can be found.*

Primate Conservation, Inc. *All the World's Primates*. www.all-theworldsprimates.org. *This website, which describes itself as "the comprehensive online resource for primate information," provides information on all primate species currently recognized by the International Union for Conservation of Nature (IUCN). It also presents contributions on living and fossil primates by researchers including Jane Goodall, Richard Leakey, and John Fleagle.*

Smuts, Barbara B., Dorothy L. Cheney, Robert M. Seyfarth, and Richard W. Wrangham, eds. 1987. *Primate Societies*. Chicago: University of Chicago Press. *A classic, comprehensive survey of research on primates from all over the world, with articles by 46 contributors.*

Strier, Karen B. 2013. *Primate Ethnographies*. Toronto: Pearson. *A collection of first-hand accounts of long-term primatological research that reveals the interplay among primates, people, and institutions. Essays discuss such topics as field studies on lemurs, New World monkeys, Old World monkeys, and apes. This is a great introduction to the challenges and excitement of primate field research.*

Tudge, Colin, with Josh Young. 2009. *The Link: Uncovering Our Earliest Ancestors*. New York: Little, Brown. *This volume was written in connection with a film, The Link, broadcast on several television channels worldwide. Science writer Colin Tudge wrote chapters 3 to 8, plus the epilogue, and he provides a brief, solid, reader-friendly introduction to contemporary work in primate evolution. Josh Young, who wrote chapters 1, 2, and 9, describes how fossils have become valuable commodities in twenty-first-century antiquities markets. He also shows the high stakes facing scientists who introduce new primate fossils to a media-saturated world.*

# 6  What Can the Fossil Record Tell Us about Human Origins?

▲ A researcher measures the mandible of an *Australopithecus garhi* in the Laboratory of Paleontology in Addis Ababa, Ethiopia. Photo: Daniel Herard/Science Source

## Chapter Outline

Anthropology has made major contributions to our understanding of human biological and cultural evolution. This chapter tells the story of what we have learned from fossils, stone tools, and other cultural remains, from the appearance of our earliest known ancestors about 6 million years ago through to the appearance of modern *Homo sapiens* about 200,000 years ago. It also examines our ancestors' migrations and innovative adaptations to every corner of the planet.

## What Is Hominin Evolution?

About 10 million years ago (mya), when the Miocene epoch was drawing to a close, grasslands increased at the expense of forests, and many species of hominoids became extinct throughout Europe, Asia, and Africa. Some African hominoids seem to have adapted to the changed conditions by spending more time on the ground, a move that apparently exposed them to new selective pressures favouring bipedalism—walking on two feet rather than four. *Hominins* (bipedal hominoids) first appeared in Africa at the end of the Miocene or beginning of the Pliocene, between 10 and 5 mya.

As we saw in Chapter 5, contemporary taxonomists classify the African great apes and humans together as *hominoids*; and within the hominoid category, they separate out humans and their bipedal ancestors, who are classified together as *hominins*. Within the hominin category, a further distinction is also commonly made between recent hominin species assigned to the genus *Homo* and earlier hominin species assigned to such genera as *Ardipithecus*, *Australopithecus*, or *Paranthropus*. Several authorities informally refer to all the earlier hominins as "australopiths" (Tattersall 2012; Klein 2009, 131), and that is what we will do here.

Fossil hominins are grouped together with living human beings because of a set of skeletal features that indicate habitual bipedalism, a feature that seems to be the first of our distinctive anatomical traits to have appeared (Figure 6.1). Hominin evolution has also been marked by additional evolutionary changes in dentition. Finally, some hominins developed an expanded brain

and ultimately came to depend on tools and language—that is, on culture—for their survival (Table 6.1). These developments did not occur all at once but were the result of mosaic evolution (different traits evolving at different rates). For this reason, anthropologists speak of the evolution of our species as a process, not an event, using the term *human origins* (Silcox 2013).

## Who Were the First Hominins (6–3 mya)?

### The Origin of Bipedalism

The skeletons of all primates allow upright posture when sitting or swinging from the branches of trees. Many primates often stand upright and occasionally walk on their hind limbs for short distances. Because bipedalism requires upright posture, primates have already, so to speak, taken a step in the right direction. Put another way, we could say that hominoid morphology for upright posture that evolved in an arboreal context was exapted for hominin bipedalism in a terrestrial context.

What sort of selective pressures might have favoured bipedal locomotion in hominoids? To answer this question, paleoanthropologists examine the advantages bipedalism would have conferred. Moving easily on the ground might have improved hominoids' ability to exploit food resources outside the protective cover of the shrinking Miocene forests. Upright posture would have made it easier for them to spot potential predators in open country, and skillful bipedal locomotion would have made it easier for them to escape. Finally, walking upright simultaneously reduces the amount of skin surface exposed to the sun, allows greater distances to be covered (albeit at slow speeds), and is more energy-efficient (Day 1986, 189; R. Foley 1995, 143). Using 3-D computer-generated models, Alan Cross and his colleagues at Simon Fraser University (2008, 2011) have examined energy use and heat regulation during

---

**bipedalism**  Walking on two feet.

**australopiths**  An informal term used to refer to all hominins that appeared before those of the genus *Homo*.

**mosaic evolution**  A process of change over time in which different phenotypic traits, responding to different selection pressures, may evolve at different rates.

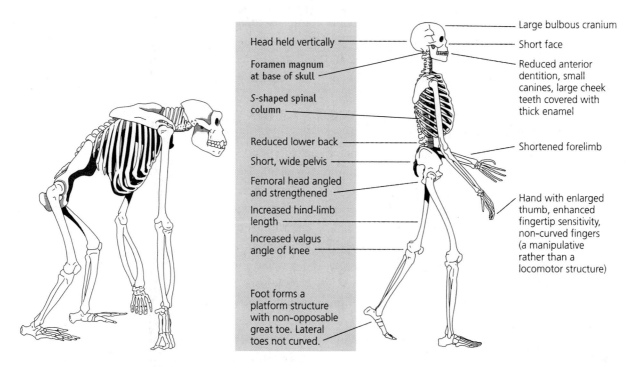

Head held vertically

Foramen magnum at base of skull

*S*-shaped spinal column

Reduced lower back

Short, wide pelvis

Femoral head angled and strengthened

Increased hind-limb length

Increased valgus angle of knee

Foot forms a platform structure with non-opposable great toe. Lateral toes not curved.

Large bulbous cranium

Short face

Reduced anterior dentition, small canines, large cheek teeth covered with thick enamel

Shortened forelimb

Hand with enlarged thumb, enhanced fingertip sensitivity, non-curved fingers (a manipulative rather than a locomotor structure)

**FIGURE 6.1** | Apes (*left*) are adapted anatomically for a form of quadrupedal locomotion called knuckle walking, although they often stand upright and occasionally may even walk on their hind limbs for short distances. A human skeleton (*right*) shows the kinds of reshaping natural selection performed to produce the hominin anatomy, which is adapted to habitual bipedalism.

bipedal locomotion of hominins. Their work supports the energy-efficiency theory of bipedalism in hominins.

Michael Day (1986, 190) suggests that the greater stamina bipedal hominins would have achieved may have permitted them to become "endurance hunters," slowly tracking game over long distances as they moved into the previously vacant ecological niche of daylight hunting. However, endurance walking would have been equally important in enabling the first hominins to cover long distances between widely scattered sources of plant food or water. Indeed, the teeth of these hominins suggest that they were probably omnivorous, not carnivorous; that is, they ate a wide range of plant

and animal foods. Equipped with just a simple digging stick, their diet might have included "berries, fruits, nuts, buds, shoots, shallow-growing roots and tubers, fruiting bodies of fungi, most terrestrial and the smaller aquatic reptiles, eggs, nesting birds, some fish, mollusks, insects, and all small mammals, including the burrowing ones. This diverse diet . . . is very close to that of the Gombe National Park chimpanzees . . . and living gatherer/hunters" (Mann 1981, 34). As the forests retreated and stands of trees became smaller and more widely scattered, groups of bipedal hominins

**omnivorous** Eating a wide range of plant and animal foods.

**TABLE 6.1** | Four Major Trends in Hominin Evolution

| Trend | Development | Dates |
|-------|-------------|-------|
| **Bipedalism** | Evidence of bipedalism marks the appearance of the hominin line. | Between 10 and 5 mya |
| **Distinctive Dentition** | The development of huge cheek teeth (molars) and much smaller front teeth was characteristic of the australopiths. | 4 to 2 mya |
| **Expanded Brain** | Brain expansion beyond the 350 to 550 cm³ of the australopiths was characteristic of the genus *Homo*. | Beginning 2.4 mya |
| **Culture** | Greater reliance on learned and shared patterns of behaviour and thought. Use of stone tools. Later, communication through spoken language. Combined, these are key building blocks for human culture. | Beginning 2.5 mya |

appear to have ranged over a variety of environments (Isaac and Crader 1981, 89; see also Freeman 1981; Mann 1981). They would have been able to carry infants, food, and eventually tools in their newly freed hands (Lewin 1989, 67–68).

The oldest known hominins are the australopiths, and their fossils come from Africa (Map 6.1), some dating back into the Miocene. The oldest remains are fragmentary, however, and their significance for later hominin evolution is still being debated. The most noteworthy of recent australopith finds are *Sabelanthropus tchadensis* (6 to 7 million years old), from Chad (Brunet et al. 2002, 6); *Orrorin tugenensis* (6 million years old), from Kenya (Senut et al. 2001); and *Ardipithecus kadabba* (5.2 to 5.5 million years old) and *Ardipithecus ramidus* (4.4 to 5.8 million years old), from Ethiopia (White et al. 2009; Haile-Selassie et al. 2004; Haile-Selassie 2001; T.D. White et al. 1994). After 15 years of reconstruction and analysis, American paleoanthropologist Tim White

and his colleagues formally announced in 2009 the discovery of "Ardi," a relatively complete skeleton of *Ar. ramidus*, which apparently could walk bipedally on the ground, although in a manner different from later australopiths and members of the genus *Homo* (see Figure 6.2). Most paleoanthropologists have traditionally viewed bipedal locomotion as an adaptation to life in open African grasslands called *savannah*. However, *Ar. ramidus* apparently lived in a wooded environment. Richard Potts, an expert in ancient environments, reviewed evidence about the environment in which *Ar. ramidus* would have lived in Ethopia. He also looked at biomolecular information about the kinds of plants *Ar. ramidus* ate, based on analysis of teeth from five different fossil individuals. Potts (2012, 157) concluded that "combined evidence from the two sites thus appears to indicate a certain degree of spatial and possibly temporal variability in the proportion of grass versus trees." Potts also expressed concern that "the term *savanna* can be

**MAP 6.1** | Major sites in eastern and southern Africa from which fossils of australopiths and early *Homo* have been recovered.

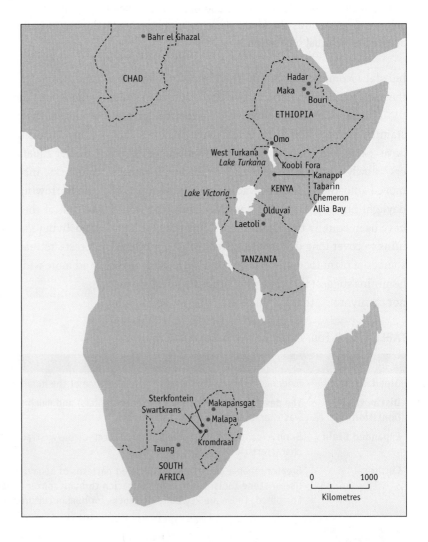

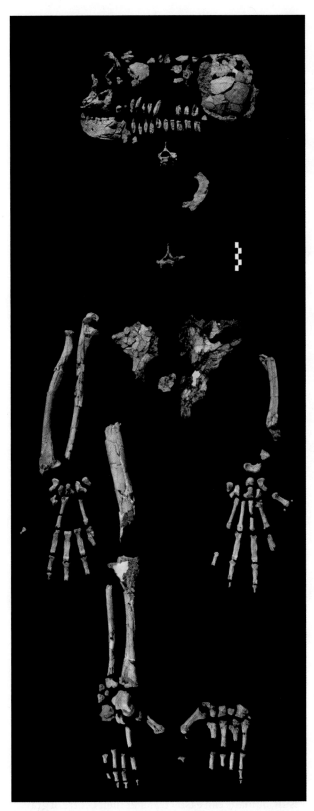

**FIGURE 6.2** | The fossils of *Ardipithecus ramidus,* pictured above, have been interpreted as belonging to a bipedal hominoid living in a forested environment, which challenges the traditional notion that bipedalism evolved in an open, savannah environment.

**FIGURE 6.3** | The earliest evidence of hominin bipedalism comes from the 3.6-million-year-old fossil footprints preserved in hardened volcanic ash at Laetoli, Tanzania.

interpreted too broadly; it is, in fact, defined so variably in time and space that it is almost useless when examining habitat-specific versus habitat-variability explanations of human evolution" (158).

Other very early fragments of fossil hominins include two lower jaws and an arm bone from Kenya, ranging in age between 5.8 and 4.5 mya. Some fragmentary remains from Ethiopia and Kenya are between 4.5 and 3.8 million years old (Boaz 1995, 35; Foley 1995, 70).

The earliest direct evidence of hominin bipedalism is 3.6 million years old. It comes from a trail of footprints that extends over 70 feet, preserved in a layer of hardened volcanic ash laid down during the middle Pliocene at the site of Laetoli, Tanzania (Figure 6.3). When compared to footprints made by modern apes and human beings, experts agree that the Laetoli prints were definitely produced by hominin bipedal loco-motion (Day 1985, 92; 1986, 191; Feibel et al. 1995/96).

Most early hominin fossils showing skeletal evidence of bipedalism have been placed in the genus *Australopithecus*. The oldest of these is *Australopithecus anamensis*, whose fossils come from Kanapoi and Allia Bay in Kenya. *Au. anamensis* dates from 4.2 to 3.9 mya. *Au. anamensis* shows that bipedality had evolved at least a few hundred thousand years before the previous date of 3.6 mya provided by the Laetoli footprints (Leakey et al. 1995).

The majority of the remaining early hominin fossils have been assigned to the species *Australopithecus afarensis*. Fossils assigned to this taxon have also been found at Laetoli and in a region of Ethiopia known as the Afar Depression—hence the species name "afarensis" (see the location of Hadar on Map 6.1). These fossils, which are quite numerous, range between 3.9 and 3.0 million years of age (Johanson and Edey 1981; Kimbel et al. 1994; White et al. 1993). The famous *Au. afarensis* fossil "Lucy" (named after the Beatles' song "Lucy in the Sky with Diamonds") (Figure 6.4) was found 40 per cent intact and undisturbed where she had died, which allowed Donald Johanson and his colleagues to reconstruct her postcranial skeleton in great detail (see the "In Their Own Words" box on finding fossils). The first fairly complete adult skull of *Au. afarensis*, found in the early 1990s, confirmed its small-brained, apelike features. The 0.9-million-year age range of these Hadar fossils suggests a period of prolonged evolutionary stasis within *Au. afarensis*.

Some features of the skeleton of *Au. afarensis* reveal its adaptation to habitual bipedalism, especially when we compare it to the skeletons of modern humans and apes. The spinal column of a chimpanzee joins its head at the back of the skull, as is normally the case in quadrupedal animals. This is revealed by the position of a large hole, the *foramen magnum*, through which the spinal cord passes on its way to the brain. The ape pelvis is long and broad, and the knee is almost directly in line with the femur (or thigh bone) and therefore ill-adapted to support the ape's centre of gravity when it tries to move on its hind legs. As a result, when apes walk bipedally, they appear to waddle in an awkward attempt to stay upright. Finally, the great toe of the ape foot diverges like a thumb from the rest of the digits, a feature that allows apes to use their feet for grasping but

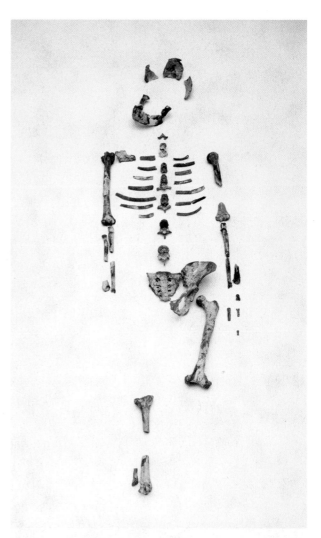

**FIGURE 6.4** | Forty per cent of Lucy's bones were found undisturbed, and her remains included much of her post-cranial skeleton.

inhibits their ability to use this toe for the "push-off" so important for effective bipedalism.

By contrast, the modern human head balances on the top of the spinal column. The foramen magnum in humans is located directly beneath the skull rather than at its back. The basin-shaped human pelvis is the body's centre of gravity, supporting and balancing the torso above it. Finally, the bones of human legs have a knock-kneed appearance, with the femur pointing inward toward the knee joint at the *valgus angle*. As a result, humans can easily transfer their centre of gravity directly over the stepping foot in the course of bipedal walking.

The skeleton of *Au. afarensis* more closely resembles that of modern human beings than that of apes. For example, as Michelle Drapeau (2012) of the

## In Their Own Words

## Finding Fossils

*Searching for remains of the human past is not glamorous work. As he relates the experiences of Alemayehu, one of the most successful fossil hunters on his team, Donald Johanson reveals both the extraordinary discipline required for the search and the near delirium that ensues when the search is successful. (Note that Johanson uses the term* hominid *in place of* hominin *to mean "humans and their immediate ancestors"; this usage is consistent with the common usage of the word in the 1980s.)*

One day Alemayehu found a small piece of a lower jaw with a couple of molars in it. They were bigger than human molars, and he told me that he had a baboon jaw with funny big teeth.

"You think this is a baboon?" I asked him.

"Well, with unusually large molars."

"It's a hominid."

The knee joint of the year before had proved the existence of hominids at Hadar. Everyone had been sanguine about finding more of them in 1974. In fact, the French had been so eager that they had gone rushing out to survey on the very first day, leaving it to the Americans to put up the tents. But after weeks of searching without results, that ardour had dimmed somewhat. Now it flared again, but in no one more than Alemayehu himself.

It is impossible to describe what it feels like to find something like that. It fills you right up. That is what you are there for. You have been working and working, and suddenly you score. When I told Alemayehu that he had a hominid, his face lit up and his chest went way out. Energized to an extraordinary degree, and with nothing better to do in the late afternoons, Alemayehu formed the habit of poking quietly about for an hour or so before dark. He chose areas close to camp because, without the use of a Land Rover, they were easy to get to. He refrained from saying—although I feel sure that this was a factor in his choice of places to survey—that he had begun to realize that he was a more thorough and more observant surveyor than some of the others who were doing that work.

The day after he found the hominid jaw, Alemayehu turned up a complete baboon skull. I had it on the table for a detailed description the next afternoon when Alemayehu burst into camp.

His eyes were popping. He said he had found another of those things. After having seen one, he was sure this was another human jaw. I dropped the baboon skull and ran after Alemayehu, forgetting that I was barefoot. I began to cut my feet so badly on the gravel that I was forced to limp back to my tent to put on shoes. Guillemot and Petter, who were with me, kept going. When I rejoined them, it was in a little depression just a few hundred yards beyond the Afar settlement. Guillemot and Petter were crouching down to look at a beautiful fossil jaw sticking out of the ground. Guillemot ruefully pointed out his own footprints, not ten feet away, where he had gone out surveying that first morning in camp and seen nothing.

A crowd of others arrived and began to hunt around feverishly. One of the French let out a yell—he had a jaw. It turned out to be a hyena, an excellent find because carnivores are always rare. But after that, interest dwindled. It began to get dark. The others drifted back to camp. I stopped surveying and was about to collect Alemayehu's jaw when I spotted Alemayehu struggling up a nearby slope, waving his arms, completely winded.

"I have another," Alemayehu gasped. "I think, two."

I raced over to him. The two turned out to be two halves. When I put them together, they fitted perfectly to make a complete palate (upper jaw) with every one of its teeth in position: a superb find. Within an hour Alemayehu had turned up two of the oldest and finest hominid jaws ever seen. With the addition of the partial jaw of a few days before, he has earned a listing in the *Guinness Book of World Records* as the finder of the most hominid fossils in the shortest time.

Source: Johanson and Edey 1981, 172–3.

University of Montreal has observed, *Au. afarensis's* great toes were generally in line with its other toes. In addition, its femur bent inward toward the knee joint at the valgus angle, and its pelvis was short and basin-like (Figure 6.5). In addition, the skull of *Au. afarensis* balanced on the top of the spinal column, as shown by the position of its foramen magnum. Nevertheless, elements of the postcranial skeleton of *Au. afarensis* clearly recall its recent ape ancestry (Figure 6.6). It has longer arms, in proportion to its legs, than any other hominin. Also, the bones of its fingers and toes are slightly curved, and the toes are much longer, resembling the finger and toe bones of apes. Because these features are related to the typical tree-climbing adaptation of most hominoids, some paleoanthropologists have concluded that *Au. afarensis* must have had significant tree-climbing ability along with bipedalism (Klein 2009, 213; Lewin 1989, 77; Susman et al. 1985).

A final early hominin species of note is *Australopithecus bahrelghazali*, which was contemporaneous with *Au. afarensis*. In 1995, the discovery of 3.5-million-year-old fossil remains from this australopith in Chad extended the known range of australopiths far beyond southern and eastern Africa (Brunet et al. 1995) (Map 6.1).

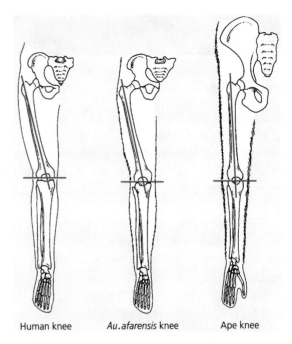

Human knee    *Au. afarensis* knee    Ape knee

**FIGURE 6.5** | The bones of human legs have a somewhat knock-kneed appearance, with the femur pointing inward toward the knee joint at the valgus angle. This allows human beings to easily transfer the centre of gravity directly over the foot in the course of bipedal walking. Ape femurs do not angle inward in this manner, so apes waddle when they try to walk bipedally. Because *Au. afarensis* is humanlike in its valgus angle and in the shape of its pelvis, we conclude that, like us, it walked bipedally.

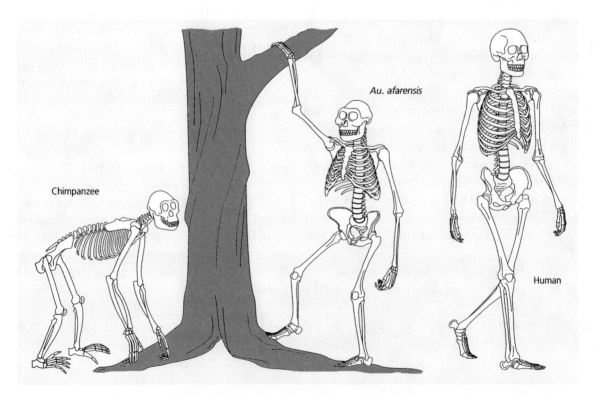

Chimpanzee    *Au. afarensis*    Human

**FIGURE 6.6** | Although *Au. afarensis* was humanlike in some respects, in other respects its skeleton retained adaptations to life in the trees.

## Changes in Hominin Dentition

Once the first australopiths regularly ventured down from the trees and into a variety of new habitats, they presumably began to rely on new food sources. Their new diet appears to have created a set of selective pressures that led to important changes in hominin dentition, first evident in the teeth of *Au. afarensis*. To assess the importance of these changes, it helps to compare the teeth of *Au. afarensis* with those of modern apes and humans.

A striking feature of ape dentition is a *U*-shaped dental arch that is longer front to back than it is side to side. By contrast, the human dental arch is parabolic, or gently rounded in shape and narrower in front than in back. Apes have large, sexually dimorphic canine teeth that project beyond the tooth row. In addition, they possess a *diastema* (plural, *diastemata*), or space in the tooth row for each canine of the opposite jaw to fit into when the jaws are closed. Human canine teeth do not project beyond the tooth row and show little sexual dimorphism, and humans have no diastemata. Ape teeth show functional specialization, with biting incisors, shearing canines, and grinding molars. In addition, the incisors are about the same size as the molars, and the canines are the largest teeth of all. Functional specialization in human teeth is very different. Humans have canines and incisors that are similar in shape and much smaller than their molars.

How does *Au. afarensis* compare? As Figure 6.7 shows, the *Au. afarensis* dental arcade is *U*-shaped, like that of the apes. Its canines, though relatively smaller than those of apes, still project somewhat; and 45 per cent of the *Au. afarensis* specimens examined have diastemata (Lewin 1989, 70). Although *Au. afarensis* canines

were getting smaller, *Au. afarensis* molars were getting larger, marking the beginning of an evolutionary trend toward smaller front teeth and enormous cheek teeth that appears, fully developed, among australopiths that flourished a million years after *Au. afarensis*. The increase in the size of later australopith molars is greater than would be expected if it were merely the result of a larger-bodied hominin having proportionately larger teeth. Thus, paleoanthropologists deduce that the enlarged molars were produced by natural selection (McHenry 1985, 179). Some experts argue that this dental pattern is an effective adaptation to grassland diets consisting of coarse vegetable foods. Because projecting canine teeth prevent the side-to-side jaw movement that grinding tough foods requires, natural selection may have favoured australopiths whose canines did not project beyond the tooth row.

## Who Were the Later Australopiths (3–1.5 mya)?

Fossils of 3-million-year-old australopiths with small front teeth and large cheek teeth were found first in southern Africa and later in eastern Africa, beginning in the 1920s and 1930s. Some of them possessed the typical late-australopith enlargement of the cheek teeth, but their faces were small and lightly built; they were classified together as *Australopithecus africanus* and came to be known as the "gracile australopiths" (Figure 6.8a). *Au. africanus* lived between 3 and 2 mya. Other australopith fossils with more rugged jaws, flatter faces, and enormous molars have been assigned to the species *Paranthropus robustus*, and they are called the "robust australopiths" (Figure 6.8b). *P. robustus* is generally

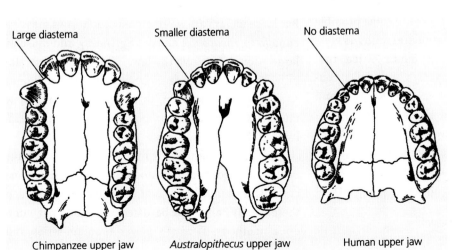

Large diastema    Smaller diastema    No diastema

Chimpanzee upper jaw    *Australopithecus* upper jaw    Human upper jaw

**FIGURE 6.7** | The upper jaw of *Au. afarensis* shows some apelike features, but its dentition shows signs of change in the direction of smaller front teeth and large cheek teeth that would appear fully developed in later australopith species.

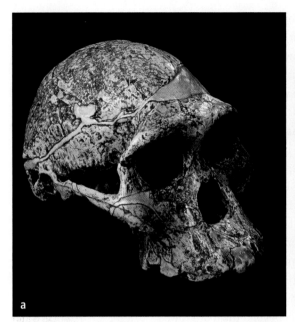
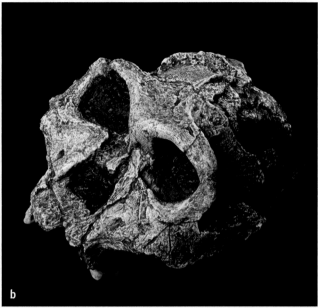

**FIGURE 6.8** | Two-million-year-old bipedal hominins with small front teeth and large cheek teeth fall into two major categories. (a) Gracile australopiths (such as this specimen of *Au. africanus* from Sterkfontein, South Africa) have smaller, more lightly built faces. (b) Robust australopiths (such as this specimen from Swartkrans, South Africa) have more rugged jaws, flatter faces, truly enormous molars, and sagittal crests.

estimated to have lived between 2.5 and 0.7 mya. Recent research using micro-computed tomography (microCT) has revealed how the internal structure of teeth in these later australopiths reflects the timing of tooth eruption and the patterns of surface wear on teeth, giving us clues that suggest their diet consisted mainly of plants (Skinner et al. 2008).

Both gracile and robust australopith fossils show the same adaptation to bipedalism found in *Au. afarensis*. The foramen magnum of both forms is found directly underneath the skull. Also, the size of the braincase (or **cranial capacity**) in both forms increased in size by approximately 25 to 35 per cent, to between 400 and 550 cm³. There are some possible behavioural changes among the australopiths as well. Those discovered in Swartkrans, South Africa, that were living approximately 1.5 mya may have controlled fire and used it to cook meat (C.K. Brain and Sillen 1988). Whether they had hands capable of making stone tools is unclear (Lewin 1989, 83; McHenry and Berger 1998). Robust australopiths in southern Africa may have used fragments of bone and animal horn as digging tools (Tattersall 1998, 125). Current

research by Michelle Drapeau (2012) supports the hypothesis that these and other australopiths had highly dexterous hands that they could have used to shape and manipulate tools. Her work suggests that despite having slightly longer and rounded fingers, *Au. afarensis* had very "human-like" hands that would have allowed for the use and creation of tools, possibly giving this species an adaptive advantage (242).

It turns out that the striking morphological differences between gracile and robust australopiths have to do almost exclusively with their chewing anatomy. To begin with, selection seems to have favoured large molars to grind tough plant foods. But large molars are ineffective without jaws massive enough to absorb the shock of grinding and muscles large enough to move the jaws. The robust australopiths had the flattest faces because their cheekbones had expanded the most, to accommodate huge jaw muscles that attached to bony crests along the midlines of their skulls.

All australopith fossils from southern Africa have been recovered from limestone quarries or limestone caves. Unfortunately, none of the deposits from which these fossils came can be dated by traditional numerical methods, although newer uranium-series and

**cranial capacity** The size of the braincase.

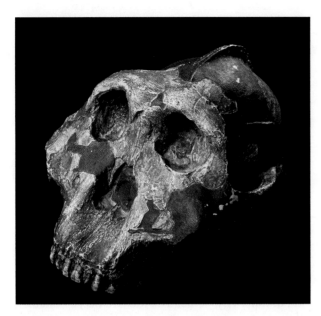

**FIGURE 6.9** | The "Zinjanthropus" skull, classified as *Paranthropus boisei*. When the potassium–argon method was used in 1959 to date the volcanic rock lying above the sediment in which this fossil was found, the date of 1.75 million years stunned the scientific community.

paleomagnetic techniques are more promising. Dating is much easier at eastern African sites like Olduvai Gorge, Tanzania, where volcanic rock layers can be dated using isotopic methods (Figure 6.9). Since 1959, eastern Africa has become the most important source of hominin fossils in the world.

See the Focus on Four Fields on pp. 194–200 for an expanded explanation of dating techniques used in palaeoanthropology.

## How Many Species of Australopith Were There?

How many australopith species (and genera) ought to be recognized continues to be debated. Fleagle (2013, 365) counts six species of *Australopithecus* that are generally recognized, but he also observes that "more are probably waiting to be uncovered" (see Table 6.2). It now appears that robust australopiths go back some 1.75 million years in southern Africa and perhaps 2.5 million years in eastern Africa, becoming extinct between 1.2 and 0.7 mya.

**TABLE 6.2** | Increase in Cranial Capacity in Hominins

| Hominin | Date Range (years ago) | Cranial Capacity (cm³) |
|---|---|---|
| *Sahelanthropus tchadensis* | 7–6 million | 350 |
| *Orrorin tugenensis* | 6 million | [a] |
| *Ardipithecus kadabba* | 5.5–5.2 million | [a] |
| *Ardipithecus ramidus* | 5.8–4.4 million | [a] |
| *Australopithecus anamensis* | 4.2–3.9 million | [a] |
| *Australopithecus afarensis* | 3.9–3.0 million | 375–550 |
| *Australopithecus africanus* | 3–2 million | 420–500 |
| *Australopithecus bahrelgazali* | 3.5–3 million | [a] |
| *Australopithecus sediba* | 1.95–1.78 million | 420 |
| *Australopithecus garhi* | 2.5 million | [a] |
| *Paranthropus aethiopicus* | 2.6–2.3 million | 410 |
| *Paranthropus robustus* | 2.0–1.5 million | 530 |
| *Paranthropus boisei* | 2.1–1.1 million | 530 |
| *Homo habilis* | 2.4–1.5 million | 500–800 |
| *Homo georgicus* | 1.8 million | 600–680 |
| *Homo erectus* | 1.8 million–300,000 | 750–1,225 |
| *Homo ergaster* | 1.8–1.3 million | 910 |
| *Homo antecessor* | 780,000 | [a] |
| *Homo heidelbergensis* | 600,000–200,000 | 1200 |
| *Homo neanderthalensis* | 230,000–27,000 | 1520 |
| *Denisovans* | 400,000–30,000 | [a] |
| *Homo sapiens* | 200,000–present | 1400 |

[a] Unknown at present.

Gracile australopiths apparently flourished between 3 and 2 mya, in both southern and eastern Africa, suggesting an early divergence between the robust and gracile australopith lineages. In 1999, the 2.5-million-year-old fossil of a gracile australopith, called *Australopithecus garhi,* was found in Ethiopia (Asfaw et al. 1999). Not only did *Au. garhi* appear morphologically distinct from other gracile australopiths of roughly the same age, but it was also found in association with primitive stone tools 2.5 to 2.6 million years old (de Heinzelin et al. 1999). The greatest confusion surrounds those gracile fossils dated to about 2 mya. Perhaps most intriguing are the fossils of *Australopithecus sediba,* found at the site of Malapa in South Africa, and dated to between 1.95 and 1.78 mya (Berger et al. 2010). These fossils show a mix of features: their cranial capacity resembles that of *Au. africanus,* whereas their teeth and long thumb bones resemble that of early *Homo.* Fleagle (2013, 368–9) concludes that "Overall, *Au. sediba* seems to be intermediate between fossils currently classified as *Australopithecus* and those attributed to early *Homo,* and researchers differ on which genus is more appropriate."

## How Can Anthropologists Explain the Human Transition?

By 2 mya, bipedal hominins with specialized teeth and expanded brains were walking the open environment of the east African savannah. At least some of them made artifacts out of wood, stone, and bone and used fire. Some observers have concluded that meat eating led to a need for stone tools to kill and butcher animals and that stone-tool manufacture led natural selection to favour hominins with expanded brains. This is the "man the hunter" story about human origins, which purports to explain nearly every physical and behavioural trait that makes humans human as the outcome of our ancestors' devotion to hunting. In 1968, for example, anthropologists Sherwood Washburn and C.S. Lancaster (1968, 299–300) concluded that "the biological bases for killing have been incorporated into human psychology." This story seemed to be supported by early primatological work reporting that savannah baboons lived by a rigid hierarchy in a closed society: large males with huge canines dominated much smaller females and juveniles. As Canadian primatologist Linda Fedigan (1986, 36) remarked, this model

of human origins "can be said to have been traditional and consistent with contemporary role expectations for Western men and women." As a result, the baboon model was quickly accepted by those who considered Western gender-role expectations as natural rather than culturally imposed.

However, the baboon model quickly ran into trouble, both because anthropologists could not agree about how to define "hunting" and because ethnographic fieldwork showed that plant food gathered by women was more important to the survival of foraging peoples than was meat hunted by men (Fedigan 1986, 33–4). For many anthropologists, the Ju/'hoansi people of southern Africa provide helpful insights concerning the social and economic life of the first hominins (see EthnoProfile 11.5: Ju/'hoansi). Richard Lee, a Canadian ethnographer who has worked among the Ju/'hoansi since the 1960s, suggested that several "core features" of Ju/'hoansi society may have characterized the first hominin societies: a flexible form of kinship organization that recognized both the male and the female lines, group mobility and a lack of permanent attachment to territory, small group size (25 to 50 members) with fluctuating group membership, equitable food distribution that leads to highly egalitarian social relations, and a division of labour that leads to sharing (Lee 1974; Lee and DeVore 1968). In addition, women in foraging societies appear to arrange their reproductive lives around their productive activities, giving birth on average to one child every 3 to 4 years (Fedigan 1986, 49).

↺ For further discussion of Fedigan's comparative studies of female primates and humans, see Chapter 5, pp. 107–8.

In sum, ethnographic evidence suggested that females played active roles in the adaptations of our early hominin ancestors. Some feminist anthropologists used this evidence to construct stories of human evolution that stressed the importance of "woman the gatherer," in which the key tools for human adaptation were digging sticks, slings to carry infants, and containers for gathered foods, all of which, they suggest, were probably invented by women. Rather than use an Old World monkey as a primate model, they used the chimpanzee. Jane Goodall's early reports from Gombe, in Tanzania, suggested that chimpanzee females were not constrained within a rigid hierarchy or dominated by aggressive males; they were active and mobile, feeding themselves and their young, and spending most of their lives apart from their mates. Their closest bonds were with their offspring, and the mother–infant group was the most stable feature of chimpanzee society. Perhaps the first human food sharing was between women and their children; perhaps even hunters would have most likely shared food with their mothers and siblings rather than with their mates. This "woman the gatherer" account—no less extremist than the "man the hunter" scenario—tested earlier assumptions about the foundations of human society and found them wanting.

All reconstructions of the lives of ancestral hominins, however, are tempered with the realization that the key features of human behaviour did not all appear at the same time. As such, identifying how and when hominins developed "culture" is not an easy thing to do, especially when we have limited material evidence. Many theories are being developed regarding this idea, and each of these must be considered and tested on its own merits and evidence. As in the case of our skeletal morphology, human behaviour also appears to be the product of mosaic evolution.

## What Do We Know about Early *Homo* (2.4–1.5 mya)?

About 2.5 to 2 mya, the drying trend that had begun in Africa in the Late Miocene became more pronounced, possibly causing a wave of extinction as well as the appearance of new species. During this period, the gracile australopiths disappeared, either by evolving into or being replaced by a new kind of hominin.

### Expansion of the Australopith Brain

Whereas the brains of all australopith species varied within the range of 350 to 550 cm³, the new hominins had larger relative brain sizes. Were these merely advanced gracile australopiths, or did they belong to a new species or even a new genus? For Louis Leakey, who discovered at Olduvai in 1963 a skull with a cranial capacity of 680 cm³, the answer was clear. He asserted that the skull belonged to the genus *Homo* and named it *Homo habilis*—"handy man." Eventually, Leakey and his allies discovered more fossils that were assigned to *H. habilis*. But some paleoanthropologists believed that these fossils showed too much internal variation for a single species, and they proceeded to sort the fossils into new categories.

### How Many Species of Early *Homo* Were There?

How do paleoanthropologists decide if a gracile fossil younger than 2 million years should be placed in the genus *Homo*? The key criterion is still cranial capacity. In general, the cranial capacities of these early *Homo* fossils range from 510 to 750 cm³. Larger brains resided in larger, differently shaped skulls. Compared to the more elongated australopith cranium, the cranium of early *Homo* has thinner bone and is more rounded; the face is flatter and smaller in relation to the size of the cranium; and the teeth and jaws are less rugged, with a more parabolic arch. Most significantly, early *Homo*'s expansion in brain size was not accompanied by a marked increase in body size, meaning that the enlarged brain was a product of natural selection (Figure 6.10). But what advantages did having a bigger brain offer to early *Homo* species? Many researchers have sought to answer this question. For example, Carol MacLeod,

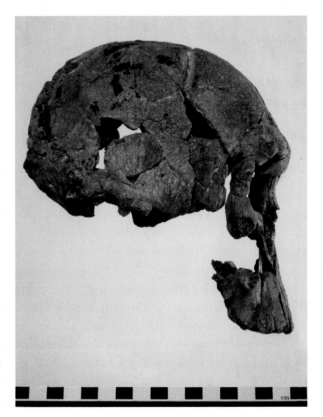

**FIGURE 6.10** | Perhaps the best-known fossil of an early *Homo* is KNM-ER 1470, found by Richard Leakey and his team near Lake Turkana in northern Kenya.

*Homo* The genus to which taxonomists assign large-brained hominins approximately 2 million years old and younger.

from Langara College in Vancouver, has analyzed the differences between ape and human brains, and she has concluded that the most significant changes occurred in our lateral cerebellum (located below the larger cerebral cortex), which allowed us to improve our memory and learning abilities (MacLeod et al. 2003). However, we know little about the actual postcranial morphology of any early *Homo* species.

Today, it is widely believed that several species belonging to the genus *Homo* coexisted in eastern Africa in the early Pleistocene (Fleagle 2013, 376; Tattersall 2012, 88–9). The species of early *Homo* listed in Figure 6.23 are gaining increasing acceptance. And since these coexisting species of *Homo* flourished at the same time as the robust australopiths of eastern Africa (which became extinct only around 1 mya), it appears that more than one hominin genus also coexisted. This situation challenges the suppositions of phyletic gradualism but is understandable from the point of view of punctuated equilibria. Which of these early species of *Homo* might be ancestral to later humans, however, is still being debated.

↻ For an in-depth discussion of the differences between phyletic gradualism and punctuated equilibria theories of evolution, see Chapter 4, pp. 90–1.

### Earliest Evidence of Culture: Stone Tools of the Oldowan Tradition

Stone tools are the most enduring evidence we have of human-created artifacts. Ian Tattersall (1998) emphasizes that the earliest hominins who made identifiable stone tools "*invented* efficient toolmaking from materials they consciously chose" (57), something different from what any living apes have ever been observed to do. The oldest undisputed stone tools, found at Hadar in Ethiopia, are at least 2.5 million years old (Semaw et al. 1997; de Heinzelin et al. 1999). The oldest stone tools found in association with a fossil human ancestor also come from Ethiopia, and they date to 2.33 mya (Kimbel et al. 1994). Other similar tools, dating from 2.5 to 2 mya, have been found elsewhere in eastern and southern Africa. For the most part, these tools consist of *cores* (tennis ball–sized rocks with a few flakes knocked off to produce cutting edges) and *flakes* (chipped-off pieces of rocks that may or may not have been used as small cutting tools). This style of stone-toolmaking is called the Oldowan tradition after the Olduvai Gorge, where the first specimens were found (Figure 6.11).

Oldowan tools are extremely simple and seem indistinguishable from stones that have lost a few flakes through perfectly natural means. Given this simplicity, how can paleoanthropologists conclude that they are dealing with deliberately fashioned artifacts rather than objects modified by natural processes? Answers to such questions come from paleoanthropologists who specialize in taphonomy, the study of the various processes that bones and stones undergo in the course of becoming part of the fossil and archaeological records (Brain 1985). Taphonomists using a scanning electron microscope (SEM) can examine stones and bones for evidence of human activity. Stones used as tools, for example, have characteristic wear patterns along their flaked edges. Flaked rocks that lack wear patterns are not usually considered to be tools unless they are unmistakably associated with other evidence of human activity.

**Oldowan tradition** A stone-tool tradition named after the Olduvai Gorge (Tanzania), where the first specimens of the oldest human tools were found.

**taphonomy** The study of the various processes that objects undergo in the course of becoming part of the fossil and archaeological records.

**FIGURE 6.11 |** An Oldowan chopper with flakes removed from one side (or face).

Paleoanthropologists Pat Shipman, Rick Potts, and Henry Bunn have examined bones for marks of butchery by early hominins. Shipman learned how modern hunters butcher animals and discovered that carnivore tooth marks and stone cut marks on fresh bone look very different under the SEM (Figure 6.12). Shipman and an assistant used the SEM to examine over 2500 fossil bones that had been found at Olduvai and dated at 2 million years old. They found that (1) fewer than half the cut marks seemed to be associated with meat removal; (2) the stone-tool cut marks and carnivore tooth marks showed basically the same pattern of distribution; (3) nearly three-quarters of the cut marks occurred on bones with little meat, suggesting they resulted from skinning; and (4) in 8 out of 13 cases where cut marks and tooth marks overlapped, the cut marks were on top of the tooth marks. Taken together, these patterns suggested to her and her colleagues that, rather than hunting for meat, the Olduvai hominins regularly scavenged carcasses killed by carnivores, taking what they could get (Shipman 1984). It is now widely accepted that scavenging for meat was more likely than hunting among early hominins.

Taphonomists have also re-examined data from eastern African sites once thought to have been home bases, where tools were kept and to which early hominins returned to share meat. They found no convincing evidence of hearths or shelters or other structures that are found at the campsites of later human groups. In some cases, they concluded that the site in question was a carnivore lair or simply a location beside a body of water that attracted many different kinds of animals, some of whose remains ended up buried there. Modern human foragers who hunt for meat never use the same kill site for a long time, leading taphonomists to conclude that their hominin ancestors probably did not do so either. In some cases, both hominins and carnivores may have used a site, and the problem lies in determining which group was responsible for which bones.

The home-base hypothesis for ancient collections of tools and bones has thus been called into question. Rick Potts, however, has offered his "stone cache hypothesis" to explain how stones and bones might

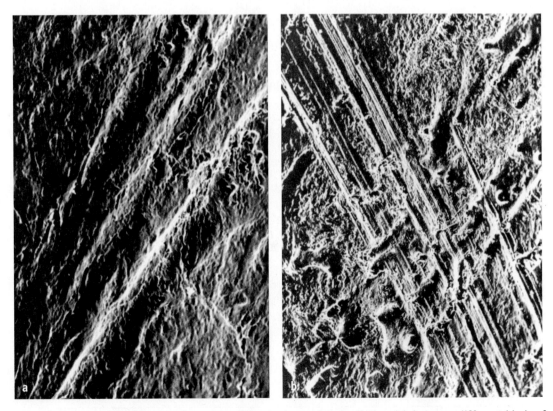

**FIGURE 6.12** | The scanning electron microscope allows taphonomists to distinguish between different kinds of marks on bones. (a) Hyena tooth marks on modern bones. (b) *V*-shaped stone-tool cut marks on modern bones.

have accumulated at Olduvai 2 mya. Using a computer simulation, he found that the most efficient way for early hominins to get stones and animal carcasses together would be to cache (or hide) stones at various spots in areas where they hunted and bring carcasses to the nearest cache for processing. Early hominins might have created the first stone caches accidentally but would have returned to them regularly whenever stone tools were needed, thus reconstructing their niche by creating a collection of stones and animal parts. In Potts's view, stone cache sites could turn into home bases once hominins could defend these sites against carnivores. He hypothesizes that this new way of using the landscape could have created the conditions favouring selection for "a large bodied, diurnal, sweaty, long-distance walking hominin" like *Homo erectus* (Potts 1993, 65).

*Homo erectus* The species of large-brained, robust hominins that lived between 1.8 and 0.3 mya.

## Who Was *Homo Erectus* (1.8–0.3 mya)?

Fossils of early *Homo* species disappear around the beginning of the Pleistocene, or about 1.8 mya. It is assumed that these species either evolved into the large-brained, robust hominins called *Homo erectus* or were replaced by them (Map 6.2). *H. erectus* seems to have coexisted in eastern Africa with the robust australopithecines until between 1.2 and 0.7 mya, when the australopiths became extinct, and was the first hominin species to migrate out of Africa, apparently shortly after it first appeared. A collection of cranial and postcranial hominin fossils found in the Republic of Georgia (located northwest of Turkey) date to 1.8 mya and appear to represent an early *Homo erectus* population of this kind. Five adult crania from this population showed a range of phenotypic variation that may have characterized early populations of *Homo erectus* in general (Lordkipanidze et al. 2013). One of

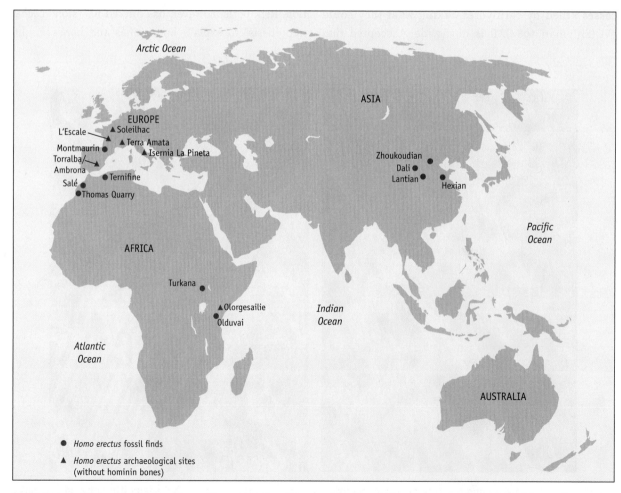

**MAP 6.2 |** The major sites where *H. erectus* fossils or evidence of *H. erectus* settlement (without *H. erectus* fossils) have been found.

these crania belonged to an individual who had lost all his teeth long before he died. Tattersall (2012, 123) interprets this individual's survival as evidence of support from other members of his social group. Rocks yielding *H. erectus* fossils from Java have been dated to 1.8 and 1.7 mya; and Chinese fossils, including the famous specimens from Zhoukoudian, near Beijing, are from 900,000 to 250,000 years old. No agreed-upon *H. erectus* fossils have been found in Western Europe, though artifacts have been found at European sites that date from the time when *H. erectus* was living in Africa and Asia (Klein 2009, 367; Boaz 1995, 33; Browne 1994).

The earliest known African *H. erectus* fossil (sometimes called *H. ergaster*) is of a boy found on the west side of Lake Turkana, Kenya, in 1984 (Figure 6.13). Dated to 1.7 mya, the Turkana boy is the most complete early hominin skeleton ever found and different from other *H. erectus* specimens in several ways. First, the boy was taller: it has been estimated that he would have been more than six feet tall had he reached adulthood. Such a tall, slim body build, found in some Indigenous eastern African peoples today, is interpreted as an adaptation to tropical heat. From this, it has been argued that the Turkana boy's body was cooled by sweating and "may thus have been the first hominin species to possess a largely hairless, naked skin" (Klein 2009, 326). Second, the size and shape of the Turkana boy's thoracic canal is less developed than our own. Nerves passing through this bony canal control muscles used for breathing, and modern human speech makes special demands on these muscles. It appears that neural control over breathing was less developed in *H. erectus*, casting doubt on their ability to communicate using a spoken language (Walker 1993). Third, the Turkana boy looks very different from Javanese *H. erectus* specimens. Some argue that if *H. erectus* was living in Java at the same time that the Turkana boy was living in eastern Africa, they probably belonged to separate species. Thus, paleoanthropologists have reconsidered the possible taxonomic relationships among the various fossils traditionally assigned to *H. erectus*, and they have devised new evolutionary trees (see Figure 6.23).

## Morphological Traits of *H. Erectus*

Morphological traits traditionally used to assign fossils to *H. erectus* involve its cranium, its dentition, and its postcranial skeleton. The cranial capacity of *H. erectus*

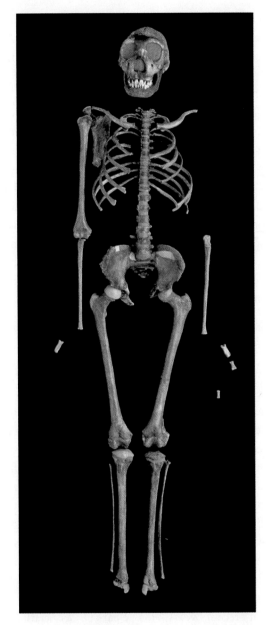

**FIGURE 6.13** | The most complete *H. erectus* skeleton ever discovered is KNM-WT 15000 from Kenya. Believed to have been a 12-year-old boy, this fossil includes a nearly complete postcranial skeleton.

averages around 1000 cm³, a significant advance over early *Homo*, for whom cranial capacity ranged from approximately 500 to 700 cm³. In addition, the skull of *H. erectus* possesses a number of distinctive morphological features, including heavy brow ridges, a five-sided cranial profile (when viewed from the rear), and a bony protuberance at the rear of the skull called a "nuchal crest." The molars of *H. erectus* are reduced in size and the jawbones less robust than those of early *Homo*. In addition, the wear patterns on teeth are different from those found on the molars of early *Homo*. The enamel of *H. erectus* is heavily pitted and scratched, suggesting that its diet was significantly different from that of previous hominins, whose tooth enamel was much smoother.

The postcranial skeleton of *H. erectus* is somewhat more robust than modern human skeletons but is otherwise like our own (see Figure 6.13). In addition, there is only minor sexual dimorphism in *H. erectus*; males are only 20 to 30 per cent larger than females. Reduced sexual dimorphism in primates is often thought to indicate reduced competition for mates among males and to be associated with monogamy and male contributions to the care of offspring. What reduced sexual dimorphism may have meant for *H. erectus*, however, is still an open question.

## Stone Tools Used by *H. Erectus*

Traditionally, the appearance of *H. erectus* in the fossil record has been linked to the appearance of a new stone-tool tradition in the archaeological record: the Acheulean tradition. Acheulean stone tools come in a variety of forms, but the Acheulean biface, or "hand ax," is the most characteristic (Figure 6.14). Acheulean bifaces are shaped from stone cores perhaps twice the size of Oldowan cores. Acheulean tools replaced Oldowan tools in the archaeological record shortly after the appearance of *H. erectus*. Archaeologists traditionally assign the Acheulean tradition and the Oldowan tradition to a single period known as the Lower Paleolithic in Europe and the Early Stone Age (ESA) in Africa.

In recent years, the clear-cut association of Acheulean tools with *H. erectus* has been questioned. First, researchers have found African stone-tool assemblages between 1.5 and 1.4 million years old that contain both Oldowan and larger biface tools, but it is not known which hominins made and used these tools. Second, typical Acheulean tools continue to appear in African sites containing fossils of early *H. sapiens* over a million years later. The conclusion seems to be that there is no

one-to-one correspondence between a particular stone-tool tradition and a particular hominin species. Put another way, more than one hominin species may have made and used similar tools. Thus, researchers must be aware of the challenges that exist when attempting to align one species with one stone-tool tradition.

The Acheulean stone-tool tradition was very well adapted to life in the Pleistocene environments of Europe and Africa, changing little over a period of slightly more than a million years. However, stone tools in eastern Asia were quite unique, reflecting adaptations to the very different environments invaded by *H. erectus* and its descendants (Klein 2009, 256). The best-known stone-tool assemblages associated with *H. erectus* in China lack large bifaces and consist mostly of flakes. Although bifaces have been found in other east Asian early Paleolithic sites, they are few in number, more crudely made than Acheulean bifaces, and more recent in date (around 200,000 years old) (Klein 2009, 386–7). Brian Fagan (1990, 119) pointed out that areas in which large bifaces are rare coincide roughly with the distribution of bamboo and other forest materials in Asia. He argued that bamboo would have made excellent tools capable of doing the work performed elsewhere by stone bifaces.

*H. erectus* also used and controlled fire, a very important and useful tool that likely influenced diet, lifestyle, and living conditions. Not only would fire have allow *H. erectus* to cook food, making its food easier to digest, but it also would have provided a source of heat and a gathering focal point for these hominins. In essence, fire creates a hearth, a central space for socialization and interaction. Fire was likely also a contributing factor that allowed *H. erectus* to disperse into Europe and other temperate zones. The best evidence of fire use by *H. erectus* is found at the site of Gesher Benot Ya'akov in Israel (780,000 years ago) and in Zhoukoudian, China, and Europe (between 670,000 and 400,000 years ago) (Klein 2009, 412–13). And burned cobbles and bones from a southern African site suggest that African *H. erectus* (*H. ergaster*) may have had intermittent control of fire a million years earlier than this (Tattersall 2012, 111–12).

Biological anthropologist Richard Wrangham (2009) suggests that the transition to *H. erectus* was pushed by the control of fire, which led to an increasing reliance on cooked food. In his view, cooking was of major importance in human evolution: "The newly

**Acheulean tradition**   A Lower Paleolithic stone-tool tradition associated with *Homo erectus* and characterized by stone bifaces, or "hand axes."

**Early Stone Age (ESA)**   The name given to the period of Oldowan and Acheulean stone-tool traditions in Africa.

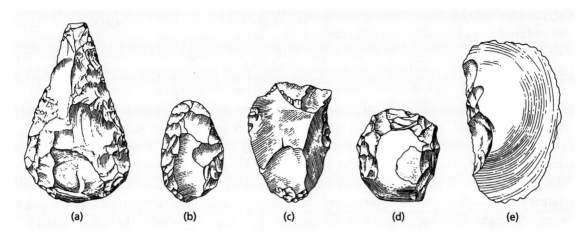

**FIGURE 6.14** | Although the biface, or "hand ax" (a), is the best-known tool from the Acheulean tradition, other core tools, such as scrapers (b), choppers (c and d), and cleavers (e), have also been found.

delicious cooked diet led to their evolving smaller guts, bigger brains, bigger bodies, and reduced body hair" (Wrangham 2009, 194). It also led to smaller teeth, since cooked foods are softer than raw foods. For Wrangham, the things that separate humans from the other primates are the consequences of cooking.

### H. Erectus the Hunter?

Some paleoanthropologists claimed that *H. erectus* was primarily a hunter of big game, based on the fact that the bones of animals such as elephants and giant baboons were found in association with Acheulean tools in such important sites as Zhoukoudian. However, taphonomists question the assumption that *H. erectus* hunters killed the animals whose bones have been found together with Acheulean tools. As Lewis Binford and Chuan Kun Ho (1985) have shown, doubts about how to interpret the bone assemblages from Zhoukoudian were raised almost as soon as the site was excavated. It is extremely difficult to determine whether elephant or baboon bones got into the caves as the result of carnivore or of human activity. Although evidence of fire was found at Zhoukoudian, Binford and Ho called for a thorough re-examination of claims connecting fire to human activities in the caves; and they found no evidence to support the idea that *H. erectus* used fire to cook meat at this particular site.

Earlier in the chapter, we discussed the hypothesis that bipedal locomotion enabled endurance walking and daylight hunting among the australopiths. Recent research has suggested that *endurance running* may also have played a crucial role in the evolution of later hominins, linking the emergence of new forms of hunting with the appearance of *H. erectus*. Biological anthropologist Daniel Lieberman and human biologist Dennis Bramble point out that endurance running is not found among primates other than humans and that the distinctive characteristics of human endurance running are unusual among mammals in general. For example, many people are aware that most mammals can out-sprint human beings, but they may not realize that humans can outrun almost all other mammals (sometimes even horses) for marathon-length distances (Lieberman and Bramble 2007, 289). Lieberman and Bramble argue that endurance running could have been a very powerful adaptation to the environments in which later hominins such as *H. erectus* were living.

Three sets of adaptations make human endurance running possible: *energetics* (the flow and transformation of energy), *stabilization* (how the body keeps from falling), and *temperature regulation* (maintaining body temperature within limits). Human energetic adaptations include tendons and ligaments in the legs and feet that are absent or very much smaller in other primates. These anatomical structures store energy and then push the body forward in a gait that is fundamentally different from the mechanics of walking. Human stabilization adaptations affect the centre of mass and balance during running. These adaptations include a ligament that helps keep the head stable during running and an enlarged *gluteus maximus* (the muscle that makes up the distinctively large human buttocks). The *gluteus maximus*, which hardly contracts during level walking, contracts strongly during running, stiffening the torso and providing a counterbalance to the forward tilt of the trunk.

Human temperature regulation adaptations address what Lieberman and Bramble (2007, 289) consider to be the biggest physiological challenge that runners face: muscle activity generated by running generates as much as ten times more heat than does walking. Most mammals stop galloping after short distances because they cannot cool their body temperature fast enough to prevent *hyperthermia*, or overheating. "Humans, uniquely, can run long distances in hot, arid conditions that cause hyperthermia in other mammals, largely because we have become specialized sweaters" (Lieberman and Bramble 2007, 289). Humans have less body hair and many more sweat glands than do other mammals, which allows for effective body cooling through evapotranspiration.

Exactly how these hominins regulated (and how present-day humans regulate) their body temperatures during exercise was analyzed by Alan Cross at Simon Fraser University. His work supports the suggestion that *H. erectus* was able to run long distances effectively. It also reveals how different lengths of limbs, both arms and legs, can influence thermoregulation of the body in both hot and cold temperatures (Cross et al. 2008; Cross and Collard 2011). Specifically, longer limbs tend to be better at releasing excess heat and are thus advantageous in warmer climates, while shorter limbs tend to be better at retaining heat and are thus advantageous in cooler climates. Thus, it is not surprising that we find evidence of relatively long limbs in *H. erectus* living in warmer regions.

When and why did hominins become good at running long distances? Lieberman and Bramble (2007) argue that running emerged long after bipedal walking evolved—about 2 million years ago, at the time of the transition to *H. erectus*. They argue that endurance running made scavenging meat and especially hunting of medium- to large-sized mammals increasingly successful. They also argue that it made persistence hunting possible: long-distance hominin runners forced prey animals to run at speeds that these animals could not endure for long, driving them to hyperthermia. The animals could then be killed by the only weapons available to hominins such as *H. erectus*—simple stone tools and sharpened, untipped, thrusting spears.

## What Happened to *Homo Erectus*?

*H. erectus* has long been seen as a logical link between more primitive hominins and our own species, *H. sapiens*. When paleoanthropologists assumed that evolution proceeded in a gradual manner, getting from *H. erectus* to *H. sapiens* seemed unproblematic. But thinking of speciation in terms of punctuated equilibria changes things. On the one hand, Richard Klein (2009, 329) concludes that "*H. ergaster* and *H. erectus* resembled each other closely, and reasonable specialists can disagree on whether they can be separated." On the other hand, Ian Tattersall contrasts the fossil record in Asia with the fossil record in Africa during the crucial period between 2 and 1.5 million years ago. During this period, he says, Africa "seems to have been a hotbed of evolutionary experimentation," producing a variety of species of early *Homo*, one of which was *H. ergaster*, whereas Asian fossils assigned to *Homo erectus* show much greater morphological similarity, suggesting little or no evolutionary experimentation (2009, 240). Phyletic gradualists could argue that very little change in *H. erectus* morphology is still more than no change at all; some trends, such as a slight increase in cranial capacity from earlier to later *H. erectus* skulls, support their argument. If, however, regional populations of *H. erectus* are better understood as separate species, this argument requires revision.

Still, the scope of evolutionary adaptation attained by *H. erectus* surpassed that of earlier *Homo* species such as *H. habilis*. The postcranial skeleton of *H. erectus* was essentially modern in form, and its brain was considerably larger than that of its precursors. These features apparently allowed populations of *H. erectus* to make more elaborate tools and to move successfully into arid, seasonal environments in Africa and cooler climates in Eurasia. As best we can tell now, it was from among these populations that the first members of our own species, *H. sapiens*, issued forth.

## How Did *Homo Sapiens* Evolve?

### What Is the Fossil Evidence for the Transition to Modern *H. Sapiens*

The relatively rich and reasonably uniform fossil record associated with *H. erectus* disappears after about 500,000 years ago, to be replaced by a far patchier and

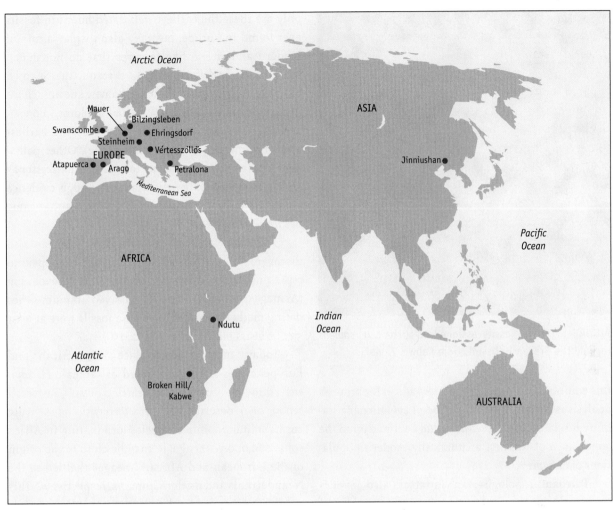

MAP 6.3 | The major sites providing fossils assigned to archaic *H. sapiens*.

more varied fossil record. Some thirty sites in Africa, Europe, and Asia have yielded a collection of fossils sometimes called early or archaic *Homo sapiens* (Map 6.3 and Figure 6.15). Most of these fossils consist of fragmented crania, jaws, and teeth. Postcranial bones thought to belong to archaic *H. sapiens* are robust, like those of *H. erectus*, but they are difficult to interpret because they are few in number and poorly dated and show considerable variation. Interpreting variation is particularly problematic when only a few specimens are available for analysis (Hager 1997). Arguments about interpretations of these fossils have grown heated at times, precisely because their resolution has implications for the way we understand not just the fate of *H. erectus* but also the birth of our own species.

Paleoanthropologist Günter Bräuer used cladistic methods to compare all the skulls from Africa that had been assigned to archaic *H. sapiens*. Bräuer (1989, 132)

argued that his morphological analysis showed that modern *H. sapiens* evolved from *H. erectus* only once, in Africa, and that the period of transition from archaic *H. sapiens* to modern *H. sapiens* was slow, taking some tens of thousands of years. Such a conclusion might be interpreted as an argument for the evolution of modern *H. sapiens* as a result of phyletic gradualism. But is a period of tens of thousands of years relatively long or relatively short, geologically speaking? G. Philip Rightmire (1995) favours a punctuationist analysis of the evolution of modern *H. sapiens*. That is, he regards *H. erectus* "as a real species, stable during a long time period" (1995, 487; see also Rightmire 1990). The appearance of modern *H. sapiens* would have followed the punctuation of

archaic *Homo sapiens* Hominins dating from 500,000 to 200,000 years ago that possessed morphological features found in both *Homo erectus* and *Homo sapiens*.

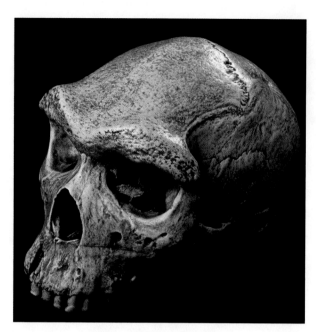

**FIGURE 6.15 | Fossils assigned to archaic *H. sapiens* include the Broken Hill skull, from Kabwe, Zambia.**

this equilibrium some 200,000 years ago. If Rightmire's analysis is correct, then the period of evolutionary stability he claims for *H. erectus* would continue up to the appearance of the first anatomically modern populations of *H. sapiens*.

Paleoanthropologist Ian Tattersall also favours a punctuationist explanation for the origins of *H. sapiens*, but he does not agree that all regional populations assigned to *H. erectus* belonged to a single species. Tattersall includes all archaic *H. sapiens* fossils between 600,000 and 200,000 years of age, from Europe, Africa, and China, in the fossil species *Homo heidelbergensis*; he describes *H. heidelbergensis* as the first "cosmopolitan" hominin species, and he locates its origin somewhere within early African *Homo* (Tattersall 2012, 135–6). Tattersall also believes that *H. heidelbergensis* was responsible for a number of cultural innovations dated to this time period: shelter construction, domestication of fire, fabrication of spears, and the prepared-core technique of stone-tool manufacture (Tattersall 2012, 138–41). In the mid-1990s, moreover, paleoanthropologists working in limestone caves in the Sierra de Atapuerca, Spain, discovered fragments of hominin bones and teeth that are nearly 800,000 years old (Bermúdez de Castro et al. 1997). They argue that these are the remains of an offshoot of *H. ergaster* (African *H. erectus*) and may be ancestral to both *H. heidelbergensis* and *H. sapiens*. Not

only are these the earliest well-dated hominin fossils ever found in Europe, but they also display a mix of modern and *erectus*-like features that do not match those of *H. heidelbergensis*. As a result, the Spanish scholars assigned these fossils to a new species, *Homo antecessor* (*antecessor* is Latin for "explorer, pioneer, early settler," an appropriate name for the earliest known hominin population in Europe). Other paleoanthropologists seem willing to accept *H. antecessor* as a valid species but believe that not enough evidence yet exists to link it firmly to other species that came before or after it.

The same team of Spanish paleontologists also discovered hominin fossils at Atapuerca that appear to represent a very early stage in Neanderthal evolution (Arsuaga et al. 1993). In 2007, improved uranium-series dating methods showed that these fossils were at least 53,000 years old (Tattersall 2012, 156).

Today, most experts place the African and European fossils once classified as "archaic *H. sapiens*" into the species *H. heidelbergensis*. Tattersall (2009, 281) describes *H. heidelbergensis* as a "truly cosmopolitan" hominin species: originating in Africa some 600,000 years ago, it "may lie close to the origin of the European and African lineages that led to the Neanderthals and modern humans, respectively." This conclusion is based on the judgment that these fossils all show derived morphological features not present in *H. erectus*, but none show any of the derived features that are distinctive of either Neanderthals or modern humans (Stringer and Andrews 2005, 150–1). *H. heidelbergensis* "could have emerged in the same kind of rapid burst that may have produced *H. ergaster* a million years earlier" (Klein 2009, 433).

## Where Did Modern *H. Sapiens* Come From?

As noted above, the fossils of archaic *H. sapiens* play a crucial role in a test case for the proponents of speciation by punctuated equilibria. Punctuationists, as we saw, view *H. erectus* as a single, long-lived, geographically dispersed species. They hypothesize that only one subpopulation of this species, probably located in Africa, underwent a rapid spurt of evolution to produce *H. sapiens* 200,000 to 100,000 years ago. After that, *H. sapiens* itself multiplied and moved out of Africa, gradually populating the globe and eventually replacing any remaining populations of *H. erectus* or their descendants. This scenario is usually called the "out of Africa" or replacement model.

The factor triggering this evolutionary spurt is usually thought to be the pattern of fluctuating climate and environmental change caused by the repeated advance and retreat of ice sheets during the Late Pleistocene. In Europe, the last such warm period began about 128,000 years ago followed by a cooling trend that began about 118,000 years ago. The coldest and most intensive Ice Age temperatures peaked about 20,000 years ago, and then the earth's climate warmed up again and the large continental glaciers in northern Europe and North America retreated. In Africa, by contrast, hominin populations experienced strong arid–moist fluctuations called "megadroughts" between about 135,000 and 75,000 years ago (Potts 2012, 161). By about 12,000 years ago, the climatic pattern we know today had been established.

However, some gradualists reject this scenario (Frayer et al. 1993; Thorne and Wolpoff 1992; Wolpoff 1985, 1989). Milford Wolpoff argued that evolution from *H. erectus* to *H. sapiens* occurred gradually throughout the traditional range of *H. erectus*. According to Wolpoff, as each regional population evolved from *H. erectus* to *H. sapiens*, it retained its distinct physical appearance, which was the result of adaptation to regional selection pressures. Wolpoff finds morphological similarities between European *H. erectus* and later European Neanderthals, between *H. erectus* from Java and later Australian *H. sapiens*, and between Chinese *H. erectus* and later Chinese *H. sapiens*. This model assumes a complex pattern of gene flow that would have spread any new genetic mutations arising in one regional population to all the others while at the same time preventing those populations from evolving into separate species. Wolpoff's view is usually called the regional continuity model.

A debate has persisted between proponents of these two models, but as paleoanthropologist Leslie Aiello (1993, 73) points out, "neither of these hypotheses, in their extreme forms, are fully consistent with the known fossil record for human evolution in the Middle and Late Pleistocene." Marta Lahr and Robert Foley (1994) proposed that regional patterns of morphological variation in anatomically modern *H. sapiens* may be the consequence of several different migrations out of Africa by phenotypically different African populations at different times and using different routes.

Taking into account these complications, biological anthropologist John Relethford (2001) proposed what has been called the "mostly out of Africa" model. Relethford agreed with advocates of the replacement model that the fossil evidence suggested an African origin for modern human *anatomy*. However, Relethford argued that this did not necessarily mean that the entire contents of the modern human *gene pool* were exclusively from Africa as well. Chris Stringer (2012, 25), the most prominent paleoanthropologist to defend a recent African origin for modern *H. sapiens*, also states that dispersal events back "into Africa" surely played a role in our species' early history. Current genetic evidence suggests that there was some, albeit limited, gene flow between modern humans and other hominins (Collard and Dembo 2013). This evidence tends to support a third model of modern human evolution, known as the "African hybridization and replacement model." This third model is essentially a combination of the replacement and regional continuity models in which anatomically modern humans evolved in Africa between 200,000 and 100,000 years ago and then moved out into Europe, Asia, and Australasia, interbreeding to some extent with the hominin populations in those areas.

## Who Were the Neanderthals (230,000–27,000 Years Ago)?

Neanderthals get their name from the Neander Tal ("Neander Valley") in Germany, where a fossil skullcap and some postcranial bones were discovered in 1856. Thereafter, paleoanthropologists used the name Neanderthal to refer to other fossils from Europe and western Asia that appeared to belong to populations of the same kind (Map 6.4). The first Neanderthals appeared about 230,000 years ago, during a period of

replacement model The hypothesis that only one subpopulation of *Homo erectus*, probably located in Africa, underwent a rapid spurt of evolution to produce *Homo sapiens* 200,000 to 100,000 years ago. After that time, *H. sapiens* would itself have multiplied and dispersed, gradually populating the globe and eventually replacing any remaining populations of *H. erectus* or their descendants.

regional continuity model The hypothesis that evolution from *Homo erectus* to *Homo sapiens* occurred gradually throughout the traditional range of *H. erectus*.

Neanderthals An archaic species of *Homo* that lived in Europe and western Asia 230,000 to 27,000 years ago.

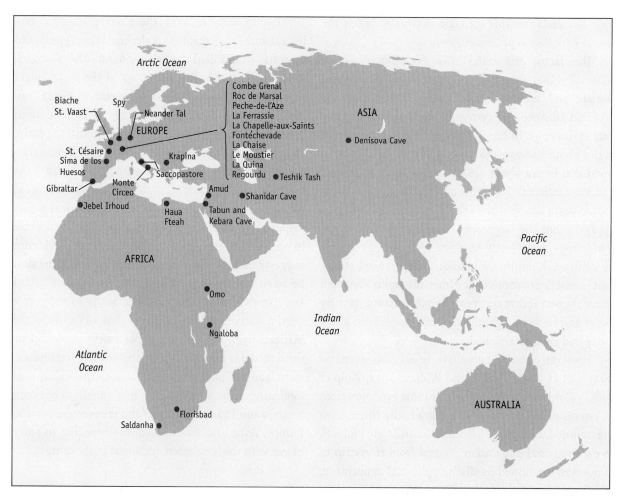

MAP 6.4 | Major Neanderthal sites, indicating the concentration of these hominins in Europe and south-western Asia.

global cooling. The most recently dated Neanderthal fossil, from France, is about 35,000 years old; and another, from Spain, may be even younger, at 27,000 years of age (Hublin et al. 1996). After this date, Neanderthals disappear from the fossil record.

Because numerous cranial and postcranial bones have been recovered, paleoanthropologists have been able to reconstruct Neanderthal morphology with some confidence. Neanderthals were shorter and more robust than modern *H. sapiens*, with massive skulls, continuous brow ridges, and protruding, chinless faces. Neanderthal teeth are larger than those of modern humans and have enlarged pulp cavities and fused roots, a condition known as *taurodontism*. Unlike the jaws of modern human beings, Neanderthal lower jaws possess a gap behind the third molar called a *retromolar space*, which results from the extreme forward placement of teeth in the jaw. This forward placement and the characteristic wear patterns on Neanderthal incisors suggest that Neanderthals regularly used their front

teeth as a clamp (Klein 2009, 461; Stringer and Andrews 2005, 155).

The average Neanderthal cranial capacity (1520 cm³) is actually larger than that of modern human populations (1400 cm³); however, the braincase is elongated, with a receding forehead, unlike the rounded crania and domed foreheads of modern humans. Fossilized impressions of Neanderthal brains appear to show the same pattern of difference between the left and right halves (*brain asymmetry*) that is found in modern human brains. Among other things, this suggests that Neanderthals were usually right-handed. Brain asymmetries are not unique to modern human beings—or even to primates. H.L. Dibble (1989) argues that we cannot conclude that Neanderthal brains functioned like ours simply because we share the same pattern of brain asymmetries. However, if Neanderthal and anatomically modern human populations descended from the same ancestral group (i.e., some form of archaic *H. sapiens*), then it is likely that both groups inherited similarly functioning brains.

Neanderthal postcranial skeletons are not significantly different from those of modern human beings, except for shape of the pelvis and the femur (Aiello 1993, 82). Neanderthal were extremely muscular, as indicated by the markings for muscle attachment on the bones of their limbs. Differences in the Neanderthal hand suggest to paleoanthropologists that it had an unusually powerful grip. Some paleoanthropologists explain Neanderthal robusticity as an adaptation to the stress of colder, glacial conditions in Europe; however, because Neanderthals who lived in the far milder climate of Israel were equally robust, there is little support for this explanation.

The morphological differences that distinguish modern human beings from the Neanderthals are not considered greater than the differences that distinguish two subspecies within some species of mammals. Moreover, genetic information from ancient DNA suggests that Neanderthals may have been genetically similar enough to our direct human ancestors to have interbred with them. Paleoanthropologists these days are recognizing that mobility and processes of reticulation among ancient hominin populations was much greater than suspected, and they are reconsidering how boundaries between fossil species ought to be understood.

## In Their Own Words

### Growing Up Fast: Young Neanderthals Had No Time for Imaginary "What If?" Games

*April Nowell, of the University of Victoria, describes her recent work on Neanderthals, culture, and the importance of childhood games for creative activity.*

As a Paleolithic archaeologist, I study the archaeological record of our earliest human ancestors, from 2.5 million years ago when we have the first stone tools to 10,000 years ago when the last Ice Age ended. My research focuses on the evolution of language, art, and symbol use and the emergence of modern cognition. In particular, I specialize in Neanderthals and what we can learn about their lifeways from studying the remains they left behind and how they used the landscape around them. Because of these research interests, I currently direct an international team of scientists in the excavation and analysis of Lower and Middle Paleolithic sites in Jordan. We have found many stone tools, including some that have blood residue on them from animals that went extinct thousands of years ago.

Over the past few years, I have become interested in the archaeology of children. In prehistoric societies, children likely made up 40 to 60 per cent of the population, but archaeologists have largely been silent about the lives they led and the contributions they made; however, through the work of many dedicated people, this is beginning to change. My own research in this area focuses on how Neanderthal children grew and developed and what this can tell us about the adults they became. The following is an excerpt from an article I wrote for *New Scientist* in 2013:

Humans today live in what we call a symbolic culture. All the objects around us have a symbolic dimension. The clothes we wear, for instance, send out signals about us that are unrelated to their practical function. We form symbolic relationships where no biological relationship exists, with a husband, sister-in-law, godchild, blood-brother, for example. Language, of course, is another key example, the relationship between the words and the objects and concepts to which they refer is completely arbitrary and that is the essence of a symbol.

Neanderthals created few symbolic artifacts. Before about 50,000 years ago there is very little evidence of any that stand up to scientific scrutiny. A few Neanderthal sites dating from 50,000 to 30,000 years ago contain some beads, pigments, raptor talons, and indirect evidence for feathers—all presumably for some kind of body decoration. . . .

The ability to reproduce a three-dimensional form on a two-dimensional surface, or to "see" a figure in ivory, requires a completely different way of imagining the world. Neanderthals created nothing like these artefacts, and I believe this can be explained by the games they played, or more correctly did not play, as children.

Neanderthals matured more slowly than earlier hominins such as *Homo erectus*, but more quickly than modern humans. As a result, they had a shorter childhood than us. We know this because Neanderthals occasionally

Continued

buried their dead, so we have a relatively large collection of Neanderthal infants and children from which to measure their development. One study in particular was a game changer. In 2010, Tanya Smith from Harvard University and colleagues studied Neanderthal and early human teeth, counting daily growth lines to calculate the exact age. By comparing this to the individual's patterns of growth, Smith concluded that Neanderthals grew relatively rapidly and spent less time dependent on their parents.

Why should this make a difference to the minds of Neanderthals compared to modern humans? To understand this, we need to take a closer look at childhood. In general, species like us, with longer dependency periods, tend to play more and engage in many more types of play. This influences our minds, because play is an important part of the healthy cognitive development of many animals, not just humans, and being deprived of opportunities to play can be detrimental. For example, a study on rats demonstrated that those raised normally but without access to playmates suffered from the same kinds of problems as rats with damage to their prefrontal cortex, a region of the brain involved in social behaviour, abstract thinking, and reasoning. In other words, play shapes the brain. But the kind of brain we have also shapes the type of play we engage in.

Humans are unique in that we engage in fantasy play, part of a package of symbol-based cognitive abilities that

Canadian Archaeologist April Nowell excavating Neanderthal sites in Jordan.

includes self-awareness, language, and theory of mind. Its benefits include creativity, behavioural plasticity, imagination, and the ability to plan. Being able to imagine novel solutions to problems and to work out their consequences before implementing them would have been an enormous advantage for our early human ancestors—this is exactly what we are practising when we play "what if" games. From what we can tell, it is unlikely that Neanderthals were able to engage in fantasy play, and it is this level of imagination that underlies the differences in material culture between Neanderthals and early humans.

Source: Nowell 2013, 28–9.

## What Do We Know about the Tool Tradition and Culture of the Middle Paleolithic/Middle Stone Age?

Late archaic human populations in Europe, Africa, and southwestern Asia are associated with a new stone-tool

> **Mousterian tradition** A Middle Paleolithic stone-tool tradition associated with Neanderthals in Europe and southwestern Asia and with anatomically modern human beings in Africa.
>
> **Middle Stone Age (MSA)** The name given to the period of Mousterian stone-tool tradition in Africa, 200,000 to 40,000 years ago.

tradition, the Mousterian tradition, named after the cave in Le Moustier, France, where the first samples of these tools were discovered. Mousterian tools are assigned to the Middle Paleolithic, whereas similar tools from Africa are assigned to the Middle Stone Age (MSA). They differ from the Lower Paleolithic/ESA tools in that they consist primarily of flakes, not cores. Many Mousterian flakes, moreover, were produced by a new method of tool production known as the Levallois technique of core preparation. The earliest MSA tool industries in Africa are probably about 200,000 years old. The earliest Mousterian industries of Europe may be equally old, but dating is far less certain because radiometric techniques cannot provide reliable dates for this period. Although Neanderthals were responsible for Mousterian tools in western Europe, similar tools were made by non-Neanderthal populations elsewhere (Mellars 1996, 5).

Despite differing names and a distribution that covers more than one continent, most Mousterian/MSA stone-tool assemblages are surprisingly similar, consisting of flake tools that were retouched to make scrapers and points (Figure 6.16). Flint was the stone of choice in Europe and southwestern Asia, but quartzite and some volcanic rock types were widely used in Africa, where flint is absent. Most Mousterian/MSA sites are rock shelters located near what were once sources of fresh water. The rock shelters were probably living sites because many contained hearths as well as stone tools. Interestingly, Mousterian sites found in the European part of the former Soviet Union appear to be the earliest hominin sites that exist in these areas. This might mean that Neanderthals were the first hominins capable of settling areas with such a cold, harsh climate.

Mousterian/MSA tools are more varied than the Lower Paleolithic/ESA tools that preceded them. Archaeologists have offered three different explanations for the variation found in western Europe. François Bordes identified five major Mousterian variants and thought they represented five different cultural traditions. Lewis and Sally Binford countered that what Bordes had identified were actually varied tool kits that a single group of people might have used to perform different functions or to carry out different tasks at different times of the year. Both

these interpretations were rejected by H.L. Dibble and Nicolas Rolland, who saw the "variety" of Mousterian assemblages as a by-product of other factors, such as periodic resharpening (which changed the shapes of tools and reduced their size until they were discarded) or the different kinds of stone the tookmakers had used (see Mellars 1996). Archaeologist Paul Mellars reviewed the evidence for each of these arguments, and he concluded that Bordes's original interpretation is the most plausible. Each Mousterian variant has a distinct pattern of spatial and chronological distribution, and some industries are characterized by specific tools that do not occur in the other variants. For Mellars (1996, 355), this shows "a real element of cultural patterning."

What other cultural remains are there from the Middle Paleolithic? In western Europe, Neanderthals left traces of hearths, although their sites were not centred around hearths, as is typical of the Upper Paleolithic. The evidence for stone walls is ambiguous, but there is good evidence for pits and even a post hole, especially at Combe-Grenal in France, where Bordes excavated (Mellars 1996, 295). Moreover, we know that Neanderthals deliberately buried their dead, often with arms and legs folded against their upper bodies. A number of the most famous Neanderthal finds, such as La Ferrassie in France and Shanidar Cave in Iraq, are grave sites. Many paleoanthropologists interpret deliberate burials as evidence for the beginnings of human religion. Accumulations of bear skulls found at some European sites have been interpreted as

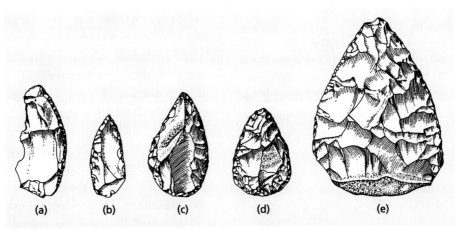

(a)    (b)    (c)    (d)    (e)

**FIGURE 6.16** | Mousterian tools were primarily flake tools, commonly produced by the Levallois technique of core preparation.

collections Neanderthals made for use in a "cave bear cult." Flower pollen scattered over the Shanidar burial was interpreted as the remains of flowers mourners had placed on the grave. Fragments of natural red or black pigments were interpreted as possible ritual cosmetics. However, taphonomic analyses question these interpretations. For example, the cave bear skulls may simply have accumulated where cave bears died; flower pollen was found throughout the Shanidar site and may have been introduced by burrowing rodents; red and black pigments may have been used to tan hides or change the colour of objects. Klein points out that Neanderthals made no formal bone artifacts, and he believes some so-called Neanderthal art objects may be intrusions from later deposits; that is, they may be artifacts made by more recent populations that accidentally found their way into Neanderthal strata as the result of natural forces (Klein 2009, 528). The anatomically modern peoples who came after the Neanderthals, by contrast, left a profusion of decorative objects made of bone, ivory, antler, and shell (Klein 2009, 660ff.; Stringer and Andrews 2005, 212ff.; Mellars 1996).

Many cultural differences exist between the hominins of the Middle Paleolithic and later humans. Tattersall (2012, 207) proposes that "the physical origin of our species lay in a short-term event of major developmental reorganization, even if that event was likely driven by a rather minor structural innovation at the DNA level." Tattersall thinks that this reorganization event probably occurred within a small, isolated African Pleistocene population and that it took a while for subsequent generations to gain awareness of the new potentials for language and symbolic thought that it made possible. That is, for Tattersall (2012, 211), language and symbolic thought are best understood as exaptations: "In the case of *Homo sapiens* the potential for symbolic thought evidently just lurked there, undetected, until it was released by a stimulus that must necessarily have been a cultural one—the biology, after all, was already in place."

A very different kind of evidence may illustrate the culture of the Neanderthals. All the data indicate

**intrusions** Artifacts made by more recent populations that find their way into more ancient strata as the result of natural forces.

that Neanderthals lived hard lives in a difficult habitat, and many Neanderthal bones show evidence of injuries, disease, and premature aging. To survive as long as they did, the individuals to whom these bones belonged would have needed to rely on others to care for them (Chase 1989, 330). As Klein (2009, 585) observes, "group concern for the old and sick may have permitted Neanderthals to live longer than any of their predecessors, and it is the most recognizably human, non-material aspect of their behaviour that can be directly inferred from the archaeological record."

## Did Neanderthals Hunt?

Archaeologists in Germany and Britain have discovered wooden spears that date to the period when Neanderthals were the only hominins in Europe (Klein 2009, 404–5). In addition, several Mousterian stone points show what appears to be impact damage, suggesting use as a weapon. Animal remains at some sites in France and on the island of Jersey suggest that Neanderthals collectively drove the animals over cliffs or engaged in other kinds of mass-killing strategies (Mellars 1996, 227–9). Archaeologists have also found the bones of hoofed mammals such as deer, bison, and wild species of oxen, sheep, goats, and horses at Eurasian Mousterian sites.

P.G. Chase has argued that Neanderthals were skilled hunters of large game and that their diet does not seem to have differed much from that of the modern people who eventually replaced them. He describes the changes that set anatomically modern people apart from Neanderthals in terms that highlight the particular way in which they constructed their niches; that is, he emphasizes the way moderns used symbolic thought and language to transform "the intellectual and social contexts in which food was obtained" (Chase 1989, 334). Recent research done by Eugene Morin of Trent University concurs with Chase regarding Neanderthals' capacity to hunt. Morin (2008) analyzed the mammal remains from various Neanderthal sites, identifying a high percentage of reindeer. Reindeer are migratory mammals, and their herd numbers are not stable. Thus, as Morin has noted, the Neanderthals put themselves at risk as their reliance on reindeer intensified, and they likely experienced years of feast and famine as a result.

What about the flesh of other Neanderthals? Persuasive evidence of cannibalism in association with Neanderthals has been reported from the 100,000-year-old site of Moula-Guercy, in France (Defleur et al. 1993, 1999) and from the 49,000-year-old site of El Sidron, in Spain (Lalueza-Fox et al. 2010, 2005; Rosas et al. 2006). In both sites, the bones of a number of Neanderthal individuals show unmistakable signs of cut marks that indicate some or all of the following: the deliberate cutting apart of bodies, the cutting away of muscles, or the splitting of bones to extract marrow. The question is how to interpret these findings. Middle Paleolithic archaeologist Richard Klein suggests that these remains might reflect a response to nutritional stress rather than a regular dietary practice. He also suggests that in some cases the damage to these bones may have been the work of carnivores that feasted on bodies they had dug out of graves, which still happens in Africa today (Klein 2009, 574–5). Biological anthropologist Jonathan Marks (2009) reminds us that numerous contemporary human groups remove flesh from the bones of the dead, not to consume it but as part of a mortuary ritual. Making sense of these remains is complex because what it means to be human seems to ride in the balance: if Neanderthals ate one another, they would appear "behaviourally non-human (since the consumption of human flesh lies on the symbolic boundary of human behaviour)," whereas mortuary defleshing of the dead "symbolically renders them as more human, since it invokes thought and ritual" (Marks 2009, 225).

## What Do We Know about Anatomically Modern Humans (200,000 Years Ago to Present)?

During the period when classic Neanderthal populations appeared in Europe and western Asia, a different kind of hominin appeared to the south—one that possessed an anatomy like that of modern human beings. These hominins had an average cranial capacity of more than 1350 cm³, domed foreheads, and round braincases. These early modern people also had flatter faces than Neanderthals, usually with distinct chins. Their teeth were not crowded into the front of their jaws, and they lacked retromolar spaces. The postcranial skeleton of these anatomically modern human beings was much more lightly built than that of the Neanderthals, and over time it gradually became smaller and less robust; this trend is most evident in the fossil record of Europe. Many paleoanthropologists believe that these changes were a by-product of niche construction as anatomically modern human beings increasingly dependent on culture buffered themselves from selection pressures that favoured physical strength.

Experts long thought that anatomically modern human beings first appeared about 40,000 years ago in Europe. However, discoveries in recent years have profoundly altered our understanding of modern human origins. It is now accepted that the earliest evidence for anatomically modern humans comes from the sites of Omo Kibish and Herto in Ethiopia (Stringer and Andrews 2005, 160). The oldest are the Omo fossils, dated to 195,000 years ago (McDougall et al. 2005). The Herto fossils are dated to between 154,000 and 160,000 years ago (White et al. 2003). Other fossils attributed to early anatomically modern *Homo sapiens* have been found elsewhere in Africa and elsewhere (see Map 6.5).

Until recently, dating fossils as old as those found in Omo Kibish had been problematic, as traditional radiocarbon methods tend to be ineffective for dating fossils that are more than 60,000 or so years old. As a result, scientists have had to develop new methods that can more accurately date older fossils. Some examples include uranium-series dating, thermoluminescence dating, and methods that measure electron spin resonance. As these methods are being refined, they are providing firmer and firmer dates for the earliest fossils of anatomically modern humans. For example, until recently, archaeologists could assign only relative dates to Middle Paleolithic archaeological sites in southwestern Asia, based on changes in the stone-tool assemblages these sites contained. Especially tricky were sites in Israel where Mousterian tools were found in association both with Neanderthal bones at Kebara and Tabun and with anatomically modern human bones at Qafzeh (Bar-Yosef 1989, 604; Mellars

> **anatomically modern human beings** Hominins assigned to the species *H. sapiens* with anatomical features similar to those of living human populations: short and round skulls, small brow ridges and faces, prominent chins, and gracile skeletal build.

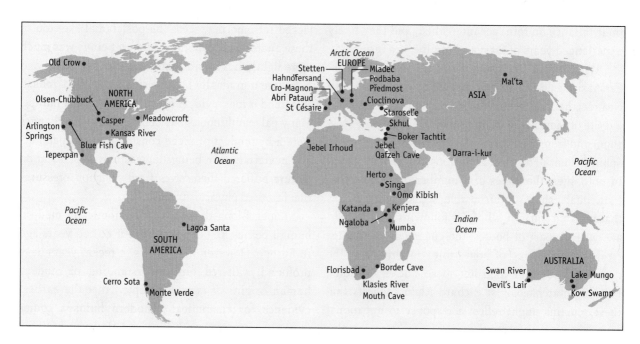

**MAP 6.5** | Fossils of anatomically modern human beings and/or their archaeological remains have been recovered from these Old World and New World sites.

and Stringer 1989, 7). In the 1990s, thermoluminescence, uranium-series dating, and electron spin resonance were added to rodent biostratigraphy and sedimentary data to date both the Neanderthal remains and the modern human remains. This effort yielded dates of 90,000 years and older for both sets of fossils (Figure 6.17). Chris Stringer (2012, 47), who has been closely involved with this work over the years, reports that "Continuing dating work using all the available techniques now suggests that the Skhul and Qafzeh people actually range from about 90,000 to 120,000 years old, while the Tabun Neanderthal is most likely about 120,000 years old. So the emerging scenario is one where populations apparently ebbed and flowed in the region."

Klein (2009, 606) hypothesizes that "the Skhul/Qafzeh people were simply near modern Africans who extended their range slightly to the northeast during the relatively mild and moist conditions of the Last Interglacial, between 127 and 71 [thousand years] ago." In any case, for at least 45,000 years, Neanderthals and moderns apparently lived side by side or took turns occupying southwestern Asia. These sites in southwestern Asia are important discoveries in our evolutionary past. There is now overwhelming evidence of Neanderthals and anatomically modern human beings living at the same time, thereby disputing theories that claim that modern humans descended from Neanderthals.

## What Can Genetics Tell Us about Modern Human Origins?

Based on the assumption that genetic mutations accumulate in DNA at a constant rate, geneticists have been able to construct a "molecular clock" that reveals approximate timespans between crucial genetic developments in our evolutionary past. These timespans are most accurately measured using mitochondrial DNA (mtDNA), which is found in the mitochondria of cells, outside the nucleus, and is transmitted only along the female line (unlike eggs, sperm carry only nuclear DNA). The results of such analyses suggest that the ancestors of modern humans originated in Africa some 100,000 to 200,000 years ago (Cann et. al. 1987; Wilson and Cann 1992). Other analyses of variation in the Y (i.e., the male) chromosome of different regional human populations have also suggested an African origin for modern *H. sapiens* (e.g., Rouhani 1989). Over the past few decades, information about the DNA of many living species, not just our own, has grown at an impressive rate (see Chapter 3).

But most exciting of all has been the invention of techniques that can successfully extract ancient DNA from bones that are tens of thousands of years old. These operations have been performed on the bones of many extinct species, but the successes achieved using bone

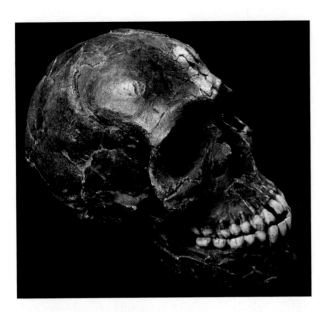

**FIGURE 6.17** | Using thermoluminescence, uranium-series dating, and electron spin resonance, researchers have been able to date this skull of an anatomically modern human, found in Qafzeh Cave, Israel, to about 92,000 years ago.

from Neanderthals and their contemporaries has been dazzling. In 1997, molecular geneticists working in the laboratory directed by Svante Pääbo at the Max Planck Institute for Evolutionary Anthropology in Leipzig, Germany, extracted a sequence of mtDNA with 378 base pairs from the original 1856 Neanderthal-type specimen and compared the Neanderthal sequence with 994 human mtDNA lineages taken from a worldwide sample of living human populations. They concluded that Neanderthal females contributed no mtDNA to modern human populations and reaffirmed that the ancestor of the mtDNA pool of contemporary humans lived in Africa (Krings et al. 1997). Shortly thereafter, they concluded that the last common mtDNA ancestor of Neanderthals and modern humans lived approximately half a million years ago (Krings et al. 1999).

However, Krings and his colleagues have noted that these results tell us nothing about whether Neanderthals contributed *nuclear* genes (i.e., genes located in our cell nuclei) to modern populations. Thus, this research neither supports nor refutes whether modern humans and Neanderthals interbred.

More recent work has begun to answer this question. A major breakthrough was the publication of a draft Neanderthal nuclear genome (Green et al. 2010). Green and his colleagues in the Leipzig lab extracted nuclear DNA from 21 Neanderthal bones from Vindija, Croatia,

and found that 1 to 4 per cent of the genomes of modern non-Africans contained Neanderthal sequences, but that no sequences from modern humans appeared in the Neanderthal genome. They concluded, therefore, that most genetic variation in modern humans outside Africa originated with our anatomically modern ancestors. Finally, because they thought the Neanderthal genome was equally distant from the genomes of modern individuals from around the world, they concluded that the interbreeding between modern humans and Neanderthals probably took place in southwestern Asia, before modern humans spread out and diversified throughout the Old World. These results do not support the regional continuity model but would be consistent with the African hybridization/replacement model.

At the same time, new evidence of our modern human ancestors having interbred with another extinct hominin species, the Denisovans, has come to light from northeast Asia. In 2010, Svante Pääbo and his colleagues extracted both mtDNA and nuclear DNA from two tiny fossils found at Denisova Cave in Siberia. When the Denisova sequences were compared with those of Neanderthals and modern human populations, three key findings emerged: (1) although they lived between 400,000 and 30,000 years ago, the Denisovans were genetically distinct from Neanderthals; (2) the Denisovans and Neanderthals shared a common ancestor who had left Africa nearly 500,000 years ago; and (3) the Denisovan genome was very similar to the genome of modern humans from New Guinea. Pääbo and his colleagues concluded that the Denisovan and Neanderthal populations must have split apart after leaving Africa, but that about 50,000 years ago, the Denisovans interbred with anatomically modern humans, who took some Denisovan DNA with them when they moved into South Asia.

The collection and analysis of ancient DNA has become increasingly detailed and sophisticated. When such data are compared with genome data collected from living human populations all over the world, it is sometimes possible to tell whether genetic variants found in living human populations were part of the gene pool of these ancient populations. For example, the *FOXP2* gene found in living

**Denisovans** A population of Pleistocene hominins known only from ancient DNA recovered from two tiny, 41,000-year-old fossils deposited in Denisova Cave in Siberia.

human populations has been implicated in our ability to speak and use language. A variant of this gene has been recovered from Neanderthal bones in Spain, suggesting that limits on Neanderthal language ability may have been less severe than once thought (Krause et al. 2007). In addition, a variant of the *MC1R* gene, which affects skin pigmentation in modern human populations, has been recovered from Neanderthal bones in Spain and Italy; tests on its functioning suggest that Neanderthals had light skin and red hair (Lalueza-Fox et al. 2007).

Although there is lingering concern that modern DNA might have contaminated some ancient fossil samples, this new genetic evidence is exciting and accumulating at an impressive rate. Still, some perspective is called for. Jonathan Marks (2011, 139) reminds us that "while our DNA matches that of a chimpanzee at over the 98 per cent level, it matches the DNA of the banana the chimpanzee is eating at over the 25 per cent level. Yet there is hardly any way we can imagine ourselves to be over one-quarter banana—except in our DNA." So what does it mean to share 1 to 4 per cent of our genome with Neanderthals? Many paleontologists and archaeologists are likely to be cautious about endorsing the DNA evidence until it is backed up by additional fossil evidence; as Klein (2009, 631) observes, studies of genetic diversity are "a useful and independent means of assessment" of proposed models of human evolution, but "[t]he fossil record must be the final arbiter" when it comes to evaluating such models.

## What Do We Know about the Upper Paleolithic/Late Stone Age (40,000?–10,000 Years Ago)?

Middle Paleolithic/MSA tools disappear in Africa and southwestern Asia by approximately 40,000 years ago and in Europe after about 35,000 years ago. What

---

**Late Stone Age (LSA)** The name given to the period of highly elaborate stone-tool traditions in Africa in which blades were important, 40,000 to 10,000 years ago.

**blades** Sharp-edged stone tools that are at least twice as long as they are wide.

**composite tools** Tools such as bows and arrows in which several different materials are combined (e.g., stone, wood, bone, ivory, antler) to produce the final working implement.

---

replace them are far more elaborate artifacts that signal the beginning of the Upper Paleolithic in Europe and southwestern Asia and the Late Stone Age (LSA) in Africa.

The stone-tool industries of the Upper Paleolithic/LSA are traditionally identified by the high proportion of blades they contain when compared with the Middle Paleolithic/MSA assemblages that preceded them. A blade is defined as any flake that is at least twice as long as it is wide. Blades have traditionally been associated with the anatomically modern humans of the Upper Paleolithic. However, Ofer Bar-Yosef and Steven L. Kuhn (1999) have challenged this understanding of blades. Bar-Yosef and Kuhn (1999) identify over a dozen sites in western Eurasia and Africa that contain Middle Paleolithic or MSA stone-tool assemblages rich in blades (Figure 6.18). Drawing on their expertise in stone-tool manufacture, they point out that blades are not necessarily more difficult to make than Acheulean bifaces, nor are they necessarily superior to flakes for all purposes. In all likelihood, blade technologies were re-invented again and again. Further, new evidence from Tanzania uncovered by Pam Willoughby, of the University of Alberta, suggests that there is a gradual transition in Africa beginning approximately 500,000 years ago and leading up to the LSA (Willoughby and Collins 2010). There is no reason to suppose that Neanderthals or Denisovans or *H. heidelbergensis* were incapable of making blades and, therefore, one cannot assume that the presence of blades indicates the presence of anatomically modern humans. Rather, it is more important to recognize the high proportion and rapid spread of blades, along with many other artifacts, found at archaeological sites as an indication of the LSA.

During the Upper Paleolithic, blades were regularly attached to wood, bone, antler, or ivory in order to form composite tools such as bows and arrows. Bar-Yosef and Kuhn (1999) note that composite tools require interchangeable parts, so the efficient production of standardized blades would have been advantageous and would have encouraged the spread of blade-production techniques that allowed toolmakers better control over the sizes and shapes of the blades they produced. Bar-Yosef and Kuhn conclude that Upper Paleolithic reliance on blades might ultimately have been a historical accident, but "if proliferation of blade and bladelet technologies during the Upper Paleolithic

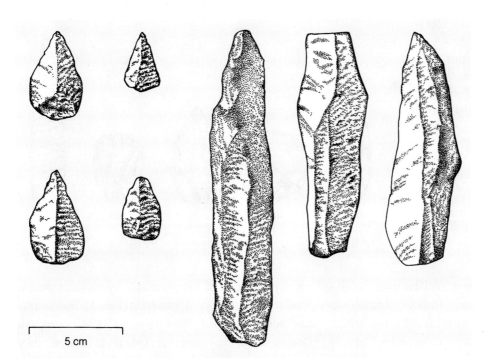

5 cm

**FIGURE 6.18** | Blade tools dating as far back as 90,000 years (during the Middle Stone Age) have been found in the Klasies River Mouth Cave in South Africa.

is in fact linked to composite tool manufacture, it may also reflect the emergence of novel and highly significant patterns of social and economic co-operation within human groups" (323).

Indeed, Upper Paleolithic/LSA people clearly had a new capacity for cultural innovation. Although Mousterian/MSA tool types persist with little change for over 100,000 years, several different Upper Paleolithic/LSA tool traditions replace one another over the 30,000 years or so of the Upper Paleolithic/LSA. Each industry was stylistically distinct and possessed artifact types not found in the others (Figure 6.19). For the earliest anatomically modern people to abandon the Mousterian/MSA culture that had served them well for so long, something important must have happened. Many experts believe this something was a reorganization of the brain, producing the modern capacity for culture. This anatomical change, if it occurred, has left no fossil evidence. However, as knowledge about the genomes of living humans, other primates, and fossil hominins accumulates, it may become increasingly possible to find and date key mutations associated with brain expansion or language ability (Klein 2009, 638ff.; Tattersall 2009, 243–4). For the present, such a change must be inferred from the cultural evidence produced by anatomically modern humans after about 40,000 years ago.

## What Happened to the Neanderthals?

The first appearance of the Upper Paleolithic tool tradition in Europe is important because of what it can tell us about the fate of the Neanderthals. If Neanderthals gradually evolved into modern human beings, it is argued, then this gradual evolution should be documented in archaeological assemblages. In the search for evidence to support this position, the Châtelperronian and Aurignacian stone-tool industries have attracted the most attention.

Châtelperronian assemblages from France are 35,000 to 30,000 years old and contain a mixture of typical Mousterian backed knives and more advanced pointed cutting tools called "burins." They also contain bone tools and pierced animal teeth. Other mixed assemblages similar to the Châtelperronian have been found in Italy, central and northern Europe, and southern Russia (Mellars 1996, 417–18). Aurignacian assemblages, which are roughly 34,000 to 30,000 years old, are Upper Paleolithic blade assemblages. We know that Neanderthals were capable of making Châtelperronian tools because two Neanderthal skeletons were found in 32,000-year-old Châtelperronian

**FIGURE 6.19** | Upper Paleolithic stone-tool industries in Europe were fully developed blade technologies that show considerable stylistic variation over time. Tools *a, b,* and *c* are from the Perigordian culture, a variety of the Gravettian; tool *d* is from the Aurignacian; and tool *e* is from the Solutrean.

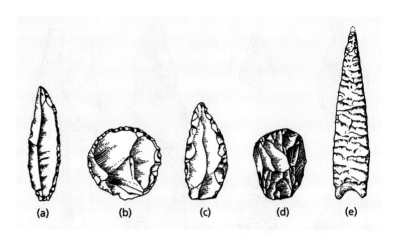

(a)        (b)        (c)        (d)        (e)

deposits at St Césaire, France (Mellars 1996, 412ff.). If Neanderthals invented Aurignacian technology as they evolved into anatomically modern human beings, then the Châtelperronian and other mixed assemblages might be transitional between the Mousterian and the Aurignacian.

Some archaeologists argue, however, that Neanderthals may have borrowed elements of Upper Paleolithic technology from a culturally more advanced population of outsiders. For example, deposits found in some cave sites in southwestern France and northern Spain show Châtelperronian layers on top of some Aurignacian layers, suggesting that two different cultural groups coexisted and occupied the same caves at different times (Mellars 1996, 414). These archaeologists believe that anatomically modern people invented the Aurignacian industry in southwestern Asia and brought it with them when they migrated into central and western Europe 40,000 to 35,000 years ago. The skeletons of anatomically modern human beings begin to appear at European sites around this time, when the ice sheets had begun to melt and the climate was improving. For many archaeologists, the arrival in Europe of both modern human beings and Aurignacian culture during the same time period seems too well correlated to be an accident. No Aurignacian assemblages have been found in eastern Europe, which suggests that the Upper Paleolithic developed differently there (Klein 2009, 586–8, 605).

Even if European Neanderthals borrowed Upper Paleolithic technology from southwestern Asian immigrants, they were gone a few thousand years later. What happened to them? There is no evidence that

the replacement of Neanderthals by modern people involved conquest and extermination, although this has been proposed from time to time. European Neanderthals may have disappeared because they evolved into anatomically modern people, developing Aurignacian tools as they did so, in line with the regional continuity model. This hypothesis, however, runs afoul of the fact that Neanderthals and moderns apparently originated on different continents and coexisted in southwestern Asia for 45,000 years, both of them making and using Mousterian tools. European Neanderthals may have disappeared as they interbred with the in-migrating modern people and as their descendants adopted Aurignacian tools. If this happened, then contemporary European populations might be expected to share morphological traits with their alleged Neanderthal ancestors. As we saw earlier, morphological evidence for such interbreeding during the Pleistocene is stronger for populations in eastern Europe and western Asia than for the classic Neanderthals of western Europe, and Neanderthal genes make up 1 to 4 per cent of our modern nuclear genome. Klein (2009, 586) concludes that "virtually every detectable aspect" of the archaeological record suggests that Neanderthals "lagged behind their modern successors, and their more primitive behaviour limited their ability to compete for game and other shared resources." Neanderthals may have retreated as modern people spread throughout Europe, decreasing in number until, around 27,000 years ago, they simply died out. In sum, at this time, the archaeological evidence is no more able than the fossil or genetic evidence to resolve disputes about the fate of the Neanderthals.

## How Many Kinds of Upper Paleolithic/Late Stone Age Cultures Were There?

Although blades and composite tools are the classic tools of Upper Paleolithic/LSA industry, other tool types appear that are not found in Mousterian/ MSA assemblages, such as endscrapers, burins, and numerous artifacts of bone, ivory, and antler (Figure 6.20). Brian Fagan (1990, 157) calls this technological explosion the "Swiss army knife effect": "like its modern multipurpose counterpart, the core and blade technique was a flexible artifact system, allowing Upper Paleolithic stoneworkers to develop a variety of subsidiary crafts, notably bone and antler working, which likewise gave rise to new weapons systems and tailored clothing."

As we saw earlier, the most distinctive Upper Paleolithic artifacts are composite tools, such as spears and arrows, made of several different materials. The oldest undisputed evidence of wooden bows and arrows in Europe dates from 12,000 to 11,000 years ago; however, bows and arrows may have been used as long as 20,000 years ago in Africa and Eurasia, where researchers have found indirect evidence in the form of stone points, backed bladelets, and bone

**FIGURE 6.20 |** Upper Paleolithic stoneworkers developed bone-, antler-, and ivory-working techniques to a high degree, as is shown by these objects from Europe.

rods resembling arrow shafts (Klein 2009, 679–80). Archaeologists have also found the skeletons of fur-bearing animals whose remains suggest they were captured for their skins, not for food; pointed bone tools that were probably used to sew skins together (the oldest eyed needles appeared between 35,000 and 28,000 years ago); and the remains of tailored clothing in Upper Paleolithic burials dating from between 26,000 and 19,000 (Klein 2009, 673).

Evidence for regular hunting of large game is better at Upper Paleolithic sites than at sites from earlier periods, especially in Europe and Asia. Researchers have found hunting tools as well as the bones of mammoths, reindeer, bison, horses, and antelope, animals that provided not only meat but also ivory, antler, and bone. The mammoth, for instance, supplied bones used for building shelters. Fresh bones and animal droppings were also probably burned as fuel. The Upper Paleolithic way of life probably resembled that of contemporary foragers. Consequently, plant foods probably formed a larger part of the diet than did meat. Reliance on plant foods was probably greater among those living in warmer areas of Africa and southwestern Asia, whereas those living in the cooler climates of eastern Europe and northern Asia may have relied more on animals for food.

The richness and sophistication of Upper Paleolithic culture is documented in many other ways. Upper Paleolithic burials are more elaborate than Mousterian/MSA burials, and some burial sites contain several bodies (Klein 2009, 690–1). Some Upper Paleolithic sites have yielded human bones that have been shaped, perforated, or burned or that show cut marks suggesting defleshing. Some paleoanthropologists conclude that Upper Paleolithic peoples may have been cannibals. However, the shaped or perforated bones may have been trophies or mementos of individuals who had died for other reasons; the burned bones may be the remains of deliberate cremation or accidental charring under a hearth; and the flesh may have been removed from human bones after death for ritual purposes, a practice documented in modern ethnographic literature.

The most striking evidence of modern human culture and creativity is represented in the multitude of unique art forms from the Upper Paleolithic/LSA. In Africa, ostrich-eggshell beads date to 38,000 years ago,

while animal paintings on rocks date to at least 19,000 and possibly 27,500 years ago. Fire-hardened clay objects shaped like animals or human beings, dating to about 28,000 to 27,000 years ago, have been recovered at a Gravettian site in the former Czechoslovakia. This and other Gravettian sites in western and central Europe have yielded human figurines, some of which depict females with exaggerated breasts and bellies, thought to have been made between 27,000 and 20,000 years ago (see Figure 6.20 and the "In Their Own Words" box on women's art in the Upper Paleolithic). Over two hundred caves in southern France and northern Spain, including Lascaux and Altamira, contain spectacular wall paintings or engravings (Figure 6.21). Other painted caves exist in Italy, Portugal, and the former Yugoslavia, and spectacular wall art from rock shelters in northern Australia may be especially old (Renfrew and Bahn 2004, 523). The European paintings portray a number of animal species now extinct and were probably painted between 15,000 and 11,000 years ago, during Magdalenian times. Recently, new techniques have permitted archaeologists to analyze the recipes of pigments used to make these wall images, while accelerator mass spectrometry can be used to date the charcoal used to make other drawings. As a result, archaeologists are increasingly able to determine when images were painted and whether all the images in a particular cave were painted at the same time.

**FIGURE 6.21 |** Upper Paleolithic cave paintings, like this one from Lascaux, France, have been dated to between 15,000 and 11,000 years ago.

## Women's Art in the Upper Paleolithic?

*In a 1996 article in American Anthropologist, Catherine Hodge McCoid and LeRoy D. McDermott proposed that the so-called Venus figures of the early Upper Paleolithic might be more productively understood as women's art rather than as sex objects made from a male point of view.*

Since Édouard Piette (1895) and Salomon Reinach (1898) first described the distinctive small-scale sculptures and engravings of human figures found in the rock shelters and caves of southern France, several hundred more European Upper Paleolithic figures have been identified. The earliest of these, the so-called Stone Age Venuses or Venus figurines, constitute a distinctive class and are among the most widely known of all Paleolithic art objects. As a group they have frequently been described in the professional and popular literature. Most of the figures are about 150 millimetres in height and depict nude women usually described as obese.

In spite of many difficulties in dating, there is a growing belief that most of these early sculptures were created during the opening millennia of the Upper Paleolithic (circa 27,000 to 21,000 BCE) and are stylistically distinct from those of the later Magdalenian. These first representations of the human figure are centred in the Gravettian or Upper Perigordian assemblages in France and in related Eastern Gravettian variants, especially the Pavlovian in the former Czechoslovakia, and the Kostenkian in the former Soviet Union.

Most Pavlovian-Kostenkian-Gravettian (PKG) statuettes are carved in stone, bone, and ivory, with a few early examples modelled in a form of fired loess (Vandiver et al. 1989). Carved reliefs are also known from four French Gravettian sites: Laussel, La Mouthe, Abri Pataud, and Terme Pialet. These images show a formal concern with three-dimensional sculpted masses and have the most widespread geographical distribution of any form of prehistoric art. . . . While considerable variation occurs among PKG figurines, claims of true diversity ignore a central tendency that defines the group as a whole. The overwhelming majority of these images reflect a most unusual anatomical structure, which André Leroi-Gourhan (1968) has labelled the "lozenge composition." What makes this structural formula so striking is that it consists of a recurring set of apparent departures from anatomical accuracy [see illustrations]. The characteristic features include a faceless, usually downturned head; thin arms that either disappear under the breasts or cross over them; an abnormally thin upper torso; voluminous, pendulous breasts; large fatty buttocks and/or thighs; a prominent, presumably pregnant abdomen, sometimes with a large elliptical navel coinciding with the greatest physical width of the figure; and often oddly bent, unnaturally short legs that taper to a rounded point or disproportionately small feet. These deviations produce what M.D. Gvozdover (1989, 79) has called "the stylistic deformation of the natural body." Yet these apparent distortions of the anatomy become apt renderings if we consider the body as seen by a woman looking down on herself. Comparison of the figurines with photographs simulating what a modern woman sees of herself from this perspective reveals striking correspondences. It is possible that since these images were discovered, we have simply been looking at them from the wrong angle of view.

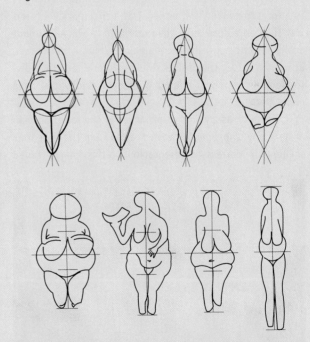

The PKG "lozenge composition." PKG images routinely elevate both the vertical midpoint and greatest width of the female body, and most make what should be one-half of the body closer to one-third. (Figures redrawn and simplified based on information in Leroi-Gourhan 1968.)

Continued

Although it is the centre of visual self-awareness, a woman's face and head are not visible to her without a reflecting surface. This may explain why—although there are variations in shape, size, and position in the heads of these pieces—virtually all are rendered without facial features and most seem to be turned down, as is necessary to bring the body into view. A woman looking down at herself sees a strongly foreshortened view of the upper frontal surface of the thorax and abdomen, with her breasts looming large. Such a perspective helps to explain the apparently voluminous size and distinctive pendulous elongation routinely observed in the breasts of the figurines. Viewed in this way, the breasts of the figurines possess the natural proportions of the average modern woman of childbearing age [see photographs]. Even pieces such as the one from Lespugue, in which the breasts seem unnaturally large, appear naturalistic when viewed from above.

Other apparent distortions of the upper body undergo similar optical transformations from this perspective. For example, the inability to experience the true thickness of the upper body may account for the apparently abnormal thinness seen in the torsos of many figurines. Several figurines also have what seem to be unnaturally large, elliptical navels located too close to the pubic triangle. In a foreshortened view, however, the circular navel forms just such an ellipse, and when pregnant, a woman cannot easily see the space below the navel. Thus, when viewed as women survey themselves, the apparent anatomical distortions of the upper body in these figurines vanish [see photographs].

Similarly, as a woman looks down at the lower portion of her body, those parts farthest away from the eyes look smallest. A correct representation of the foreshortened lower body would narrow toward the feet, thus explaining the small size of the feet in these figurines. It is also true that, for a pregnant woman, inspection of the upper body terminates at the navel with the curving silhouette of the distended abdomen [see photo on left]. Without bending forward, she cannot see her lower body. Thus for a gravid female, the visual experience of her body involves two separate views whose shared boundary is the abdomen at the level of the navel, which is also the widest part of the body in the visual field. The apparent misrepresentation of height and width in the figurines results from the visual experience of this anatomical necessity. The location of the eyes means that for an expectant mother the upper half of the body visually expands toward the abdomen, whereas the lower half presents a narrow, tapering form. Efforts to represent the information contained in these two views naturally resulted in the lozenge compositional formulation, which others have seen as anatomically "incorrect" proportions [see illustrations].

The idea that women sought to gain and preserve knowledge about their own bodies provides a direct and parsimonious interpretation for general as well as idiosyncratic features found among female representations from the middle European Upper Paleolithic. The needs of health and hygiene, not to mention coitus and childbirth, ensure that feminine self-inspection actually occurred during the early Upper Paleolithic. Puberty, menses, copulation, conception, pregnancy, childbirth, and lactation are regular events in the female cycle and involve perceptible alterations in bodily function and configuration (Marshack 1972). Mastery and control of these processes continues to be of fundamental importance to women today. It is possible that the emergence and subsequent propagation

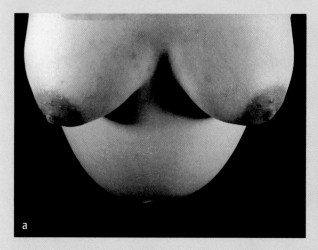 

(a) View of her own upper body by a 26-year-old female who is five months pregnant and of average weight. (b) View of the upper body of the Willendorf figurine from same perspective used at left.

of these images across Europe occurred precisely because they played a didactic function with actual adaptive consequences for women. . . .

. . . These Upper Paleolithic figurines were probably made at a time when there was similarly significant population increase along with cultural and economic restructuring. The early to middle Upper Paleolithic was characterized by productive changes that harnessed energy and by reproductive changes that helped make possible the population expansion and technological changes that followed in the later European Upper Paleolithic. Could women have made a recognizable contribution to the fluorescence of art and technology seen in the opening millennia of this era? Anything they did to improve their understanding of reproduction and thereby reduce infant and maternal mortality would clearly have contributed to this productive and reproductive change. Perhaps the figurines served as obstetrical aids, the relative sizes of the abdomens helping women to calculate the progress of their pregnancies. . . .

Theoretically, if these figurines were used to improve reproductive success, keep more women alive and healthy, and produce healthier children, then natural selection would have been acting directly on the women who made and/or used them. If these Upper Paleolithic figures are naturalistic, accurate self-representations made by women, then it is reasonable to speculate that they might have had such direct, pragmatic purposes.

Source: McCoid and McDermott 1996, 319–24. Reproduced by permission of the American Anthropological Association from *American Anthropologist*, Volume 98, Issue 2, Pages 319–26, June 1996. Not for sale or further reproduction.

## Where Did Modern *Homo Sapiens* Migrate in Late Pleistocene Times?

Upper Paleolithic peoples were more numerous and more widespread than previous hominins. In Europe, according to Richard Klein (2009), Upper Paleolithic sites are more numerous and have richer material remains than do Mousterian sites. Skeletons dating from this period show few injuries and little evidence of disease or violence, and they possess relatively healthy teeth. The presence of skeletons belonging to older or incapacitated individuals at Upper Paleolithic sites suggests that these people, like the Neanderthals, cared for the old and the sick. Analysis indicates that the life expectancy of Upper Paleolithic people was greater than that of the Neanderthals and little different from that of contemporary foragers (Klein 2009, 695ff.).

Archaeologists have found amber, seashells, and even flint in Upper Paleolithic/LSA sites located tens to hundreds of kilometres away from the regions where these items occur naturally. They must have been deliberately transported to these sites, suggesting that Upper Paleolithic peoples, like contemporary foragers, participated in trading networks, or that they migrated over long distances. However, no evidence of trade-based social contacts exists for earlier times. Perhaps the linguistic and cultural capacities of fully modern humans were necessary before such contacts could develop.

### Eastern Asia and Siberia

Physically and culturally modern human beings were the first hominins to occupy the coldest, harshest climates in Asia. Upper Paleolithic blade industries developed in central Asia about 40,000 to 30,000 years ago (Fagan 1990, 195). The oldest reliable dates for human occupation in Siberia are between 35,000 and 20,000 years ago (Klein 2009, 673). During this glacial time, a land bridge known as the Bering land bridge connected eastern Siberia to Alaska. Ice Age animals and Upper Paleolithic peoples ranged across this area, establishing sites in Alaska and Canada; these sites have been found to contain artifacts similar to those of northeast Siberia that date to between 15,000 and 12,000 years ago. Artifacts from one of these sites, Bluefish Caves in the Yukon, may even be more than 20,000 years old. Between 25,000 and 14,000 years ago, passage over land into southern areas of the United States and Mexico would likely have been blocked by continuous ice. Alternatively, as suggested by recent archaeological finds, a migration route southward may have existed along the northwestern coast of North America. Either way, the continental glaciers melted sometime after 15,000 years ago, facilitating both land and water migration into uninhabited regions to the south.

## The Americas

Genetic studies strongly support an Asian origin for Native American populations (Klein 2009, 707; Stringer and Andrews 2005, 198). The earliest known skeletal remains found in the Americas have recently been dated between 13,000 and 11,000 years old, and their morphological variation suggests that the Americas were colonized more than once (Map 6.6) (Raff and Bolnick 2014; Klein 2009, 707; Stringer and Andrews 2005, 198–9). New evidence that provides both morphological and genetic information about the earliest inhabitants of the Americas is being recovered in unusual places (Chatters et al. 2014). In underground caves along Mexico's Yucatan peninsula, researchers have found the skeleton of a juvenile female, whom they have named Naia, estimated to be more than 12,000 years old. Eduard Reinhardt of McMaster University is part of the international team working to recover Naia's remains from their watery grave as well as reconstruct the environmental conditions that existed in central America when humans were first settling in it.

Naia's skeleton represents the earliest human remains recovered in the Americas so far. The youth's morphology supports an early migration out of Beringia, likely along the west coast, and her genetic signature identifies a population continuity model that began in eastern Asia and moved into the Americas.

Research in other regions of the Americas has suggested that the first anatomically modern human beings to inhabit these continents, called "Paleoindians" or "Paleoamericans," were successful hunting peoples. Reliable evidence of their presence comes from sites dated between 11,500 and 11,000 years ago, which contain stone tools called Clovis points (Figure 6.22). Meadowcroft Rockshelter in Pennsylvania may represent an early Clovis site (Stringer and Andrews 2005, 197; Adovasio et al. 1978). Clovis points were finely made and probably attached to shafts to make spears. Rapidly following the Clovis culture were a series of different stone-tool cultures, all of which were confined to North America. Some experts believe that Paleoindian hunting coupled with postglacial climatic changes may

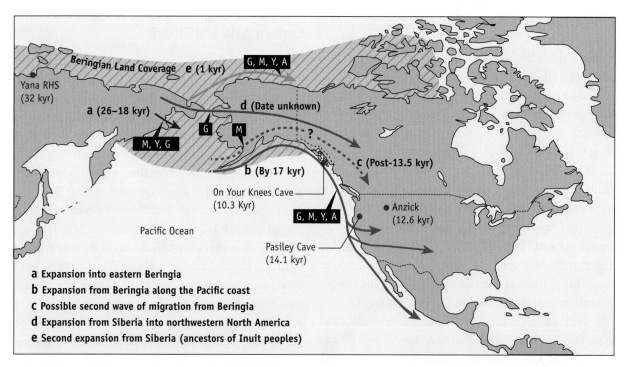

a Expansion into eastern Beringia
b Expansion from Beringia along the Pacific coast
c Possible second wave of migration from Beringia
d Expansion from Siberia into northwestern North America
e Second expansion from Siberia (ancestors of Inuit peoples)

MAP 6.6 | Map of hypothesized migration routes of humans from Asia into North America, with several significant archaeological sites (indicated by black dots). The blue arrows represent possible routes of people from Beringia, while the purple arrows represent possible routes of people from Siberia. The letters G (for genomic), Y (for Y-chromosome), M (for mitochondrial), and A (for archaeological) indicate the type of evidence that supports each hypothesized route. The shading around Asia and northwestern North America represents the estimated extent of Beringia during the last glacial maximum. Note that kya stands for "thousand years ago." (Raff and Bolnick 2014)

**FIGURE 6.22** | Stone tools made by Paleoindian peoples have been found at sites that provide some of the oldest reliable dates for human occupation in North America. The Clovis points pictured here were probably attached to shafts to make spears.

have brought about the extinction of mammoth, camel, horse, and other big-game species in North America; but evidence is inconclusive.

For many years, researchers believed that the people who made these exquisite Clovis points represented the earliest human culture to have existed in the Americas. In 1997, however, the "Clovis barrier" of approximately 11,500 years ago was finally broken when a group of archaeologists and other scientists formally announced that the South American site of Monte Verde, Chile, was 12,500 years old (Dillehay 2000; Suplee 1997). Because it was covered by a peat bog shortly after it was inhabited, Monte Verde contained many well-preserved organic remains, including stakes lashed with knotted twine, dwellings with wooden frames, and hundreds of tools made of wood and bone. Thomas Dillehay (2000) argues that evidence from Monte Verde shows that the people who lived there were not big-game hunters but, rather, generalized gatherers and hunters. A lower level at the same site, dated to 33,000 years ago, is said to contain crude stone tools. If the 33,000-year-old Monte Verde artifacts are genuine, they remain puzzling. First, these artifacts are few and extremely crude. Second, the dearth of sites of such great age in the Americas suggests that if human beings were in the Americas 30,000 years ago, they were very thinly scattered compared to populations in Eurasia and Africa during the same period. Finally, blood-group and tooth-shape evidence supports the idea that the ancestors of Indigenous peoples of the Americas migrated into North America from Asia. If the makers of 33,000-year-old Monte Verde artifacts also came from Asia, archaeologists must explain how these people could have reached South America from Siberia

by that date. Possibly, they travelled over water and ice, but how they got to South America remains a mystery.

In 2011, evidence for pre-Clovis occupations in North America was found at the Debra L. Friedkin site near Austin, Texas: more than 15,000 artifacts assigned to the Buttermilk Creek Complex, dating between 13,200 and 15,000 years ago, were discovered in soil beneath a Clovis assemblage (Waters et al. 2011). The archaeologists who discovered the tools view them as potentially representing the technology from which Clovis was developed; other archaeologists remain unconvinced.

Perhaps ancient DNA analysis may help resolve some of these questions, even as it opens up entirely new sets of questions. Ancient mitochondrial DNA and Y-chromosome DNA were extracted from the skeleton of a male infant found in western Montana (see the "Anzick" location on Map 6.6); the remains were discovered in association with Clovis artifacts and buried around 12,600 years ago, leading to the conclusion that the population to which this individual belonged is more closely related to populations from Central and South America than to populations from anywhere else (Rasmussen et al. 2014). This connection suggests that the child belonged to a population "from which many contemporary Native Americans are descended and is closely related to all indigenous American populations" (Rasmussen 2014, 227–8). Ancient DNA studies are bound to be controversial, but there is no question that they are forming an important component of scientific efforts to answer questions about ancient human migrations all over the world.

## Australasia

Anatomically modern human beings first arrived in Australia between 60,000 and 40,000 years ago, at a time when lower sea levels had transformed the Malayan Archipelago into a land mass called Sunda and when Australia was linked to New Guinea in a second land mass called Sahul. Nevertheless, the migrants would still have had to cross 30 to 90 kilometres of open water. Presumably, they used watercraft, but finding the remains of their boats or the sites where they landed along the now sunken continental shelf is unlikely. Modern people spread throughout the Australian interior by 25,000 to 20,000 years ago. They may have been connected to widespread extinctions of grass-eating marsupials in Australia between 40,000 and 15,000 years ago (Klein 2009, 714ff.).

## Two Million Years of Human Evolution

By 12,000 years ago, modern human beings had spread to every continent except Antarctica, a fact that we take for granted today but that could not have been predicted 2 mya in Africa, when the first members of the genus *Homo* walked the earth. In fact, the more we learn about hominins and their primate ancestors, the more zigs and zags we perceive in our own past. Our species' origin must be regarded as "an unrepeatable particular, not an expected consequence" (Gould 1996, 4). Some paleoecologists have concluded that "human features may not be adaptations to some past environment, but exaptations . . . accidental byproducts of history, functionally disconnected from their origins" (R. Foley 1995, 47). For example, Rick Potts argues that, rather than "survival of the fittest" (i.e., survival of a species narrowly adapted to a specific environment), modern *H. sapiens* better illustrates "survival of the generalist" (i.e., survival of a species that had the plasticity, the "weedlike resilience," to survive the extremes of the rapidly fluctuating climate of the Ice Ages). In other words, our ancestors' biological capacity to cope with small environmental fluctuations was exapted to cope with larger and larger fluctuations. In Potts's view, selection for genes favouring open programs of behaviour "improve an organism's versatility and response to novel conditions" (1996, 239).

Archaeologist Clive Gamble (1994, 182) believes that the human social and cognitive skills that allowed our ancestors to survive in novel habitats were adapted by *H. sapiens* to colonize the world: "We were not adapted for filling up the world. It was instead a consequence of changes in behaviour, and exaptive radiation produced by the cooption of existing elements in a new framework of action." Gamble is sensitive to the ways human-constructed niches modified the selection pressures our ancestors faced: he argues that all the environments of Australia

could never have been colonized so rapidly without far-flung social networks that enabled colonizers to depend on one another in times of need. He sees the colonization of the Pacific as a deliberate undertaking, showing planning and care (1994, 241; see also Dillehay 2000).

The role of niche construction is also implicated in the approach of Richard Klein (2009, 72), who lists a series of "related outcomes of the innovative burst behind the out of Africa expansion" that are detectable in the archaeological record after 50,000 years ago, ranging from standardization and elaboration of artifacts to evidence for increasing elaboration of a built environment (with campsites, hearths, dwellings, and graves) to evidence of elaborate trading networks, ritual activity, and successful colonization of challenging cold climates.

Paleoanthropologists, geneticists, and archaeologists have assembled many of the pieces of the human

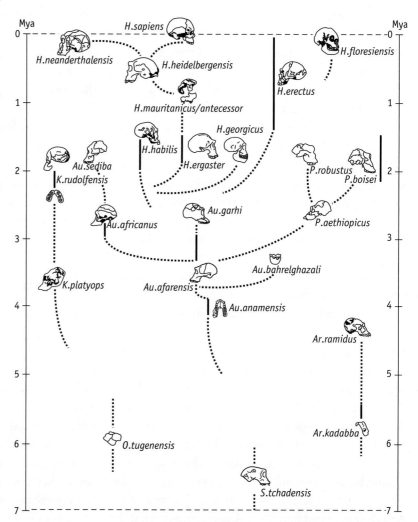

**FIGURE 6.23** | This summary of what is currently known about hominin evolution is open to modification by new data and new interpretation. (Klein 2009, 244)

evolutionary puzzle, but many questions remain. Experts differ, for example, on how to reconstruct the human family tree. Figure 6.23 shows one recent attempt to summarize what is known (and what remains to be established) about the evolution of human beings. Because new data and interpretations appear in the news almost daily, you may want to find out how much this summary has been modified by the time you read this book! Another knotty problem concerns how we interpret mounting evidence that human biology and human culture evolved at different rates. Finally, within a few thousand years after the glaciers retreated, human groups in Asia and the Americas were settling in villages and domesticating plants and animals. Why they should have done so at this particular time is addressed in Chapter 8.

## Chapter Summary

1. Bipedal hominoids that appeared in Africa at the end of the Miocene are known as hominins and are placed in the same lineage as living human beings. Bipedalism may have been favoured by natural selection in hominoids exploiting food resources on the ground, outside the protection of forests. Their diet was probably omnivorous, and they could carry infants, food, and tools in their newly freed hands. The earliest hominin skeletal fossils are 6 to 7 million years old. The best-known early hominin fossils are 2 to 3 million years younger and have been placed in the genus *Australopithecus*. The earliest direct evidence of hominin bipedalism is a 3.6-million-year-old trail of fossilized footprints found in Laetoli, Tanzania.

2. Hominin adaptations apparently led to changes in dentition. The teeth of australopiths show an evolutionary trend toward smaller front teeth and enormous cheek teeth. This dental pattern is interpreted as an adaptation to diets of coarse vegetable foods that required grinding. Fossils of hominins between 3 and 2 million years old with this dental pattern have been found at southern and eastern African sites and have been classified into two groups: the gracile australopiths and the robust australopiths. Robust australopiths had more rugged jaws, flatter faces, and larger molars than did the gracile australopiths. Apart from these differences, the gracile and robust australopiths had similar postcranial skeletons and chimpanzee-sized cranial capacities.

3. The first members of the genus *Homo* appeared about 2.4 mya. Many paleontologists believe that more than one species belonging to *Homo* may have coexisted in eastern Africa in the early Pleistocene alongside the eastern African robust australopiths.

4. Fossils of early *Homo* disappear about 1.8 mya, either by evolving into or being replaced by *Homo ergaster* or *Homo erectus*, the first *Homo* species to spread out of Africa. The cranium of *H. erectus* averages around 1000 cm³, within the lower range of modern human beings. *H. erectus* may have been, to some extent, capable of speech. Wear patterns on teeth suggest that *H. erectus* had a diet different from that of previous hominins. The postcranial skeleton of *H. erectus* is more robust than that of modern humans and shows a marked reduction in sexual dimorphism compared to earlier hominins. *H. erectus* probably did not hunt big-game animals as a major source of food.

5. The oldest undisputed stone tools, classified in the Oldowan tradition, were found in Ethiopia, date to at least 2.5 mya, and may have been made by early *Homo*. Acheulean bifaces are associated with *H. erectus*. In recent years, however, archaeologists have concluded that it is misleading to associate individual stone-tool traditions with only one hominin species. Some archaeologists have suggested that bamboo was available for toolmaking in those areas in Asia where Acheulean bifaces are lacking. Oldowan and Acheulean traditions are usually grouped together in a single period known as the Lower Paleolithic in Europe and the Early Stone Age in Africa.

6. Around 500,000 years ago, *H. erectus* fossils disappear from the fossil record, to be replaced by fossils that show a mosaic of features found in *H. erectus* and *H. sapiens*. Many paleoanthropologists classify these fossils as *Homo heidelbergensis*. A lively debate continues between punctuationists and gradualists about the fate of *H. erectus* and the origin of *H. sapiens*. Punctuationists and cladists favour the replacement model; gradualists favour the regional continuity model.

7. Neanderthals flourished between 230,000 and 27,000 years ago. They were shorter and more robust than anatomically modern *H. sapiens*. Their molars showed taurodontism, their jaws possessed retromolar spaces, and they may have habitually used their incisors as a clamp. Their average cranial capacity was larger than that of modern human populations, although their skull was shaped differently. Neanderthal fossils found in Europe are typically associated with the Mousterian stone-tool tradition. Similar tools found in southwestern Asia and Africa have been assigned to the Middle Paleolithic/Middle Stone Age, which probably began at least 200,000 years ago.

8. Anatomically modern human beings began to appear around 200,000 years ago. Fossil evidence suggests that Neanderthals and moderns likely lived side by side or

took turns occupying the same areas in southwestern Asia for at least 45,000 years, and both populations used the same kinds of Mousterian tools. Studies of ancient DNA have shown that modern humans share 1 to 4 per cent of their nuclear genome with Neanderthals; what this means is still under discussion.

9. By 40,000 years ago in southwestern Asia and 35,000 years ago in Europe, Mousterian/Middle Stone Age tools are replaced by far more elaborate artifacts that signal the beginning of the Upper Paleolithic/Late Stone Age. Upper Paleolithic people made many different stone tools as well as tools and ornaments out of bone, ivory, and antler; composite tools, such as spears and arrows; and clothing from animal fur. They regularly hunted large game and used bones from animals such as mammoths to construct dwellings and to burn as fuel. Upper Paleolithic burials were far more elaborate than Middle Paleolithic burials. Cave paintings and personal ornaments offer the most striking evidence in the Upper Paleolithic for the modern human capacity for culture.

10. Some Upper Paleolithic assemblages, like the Châtelperronian industry from France, contain a mixture of typical Mousterian tools and more elaborate cutting tools, bone tools, and pierced animal teeth. Paleoanthropologists disagree about what these mixed assemblages represent. Some interpret the Châtelperronian industry as evidence that Neanderthals gradually invented Upper Paleolithic tools on their own, which would support the regional continuity model. Others argue that Châtelperronian Neanderthals borrowed Upper Paleolithic techniques from in-migrating modern people who already possessed such techniques under their Aurignacian tradition. This view is compatible with the replacement model. If Aurignacian moderns did replace Neanderthals in Europe, there is no evidence that this was the result of conquest or extermination.

11. Upper Paleolithic peoples show few signs of injury or disease, and their life expectancy was longer than that of Neanderthals. Upper Paleolithic peoples apparently constructed niches that allowed them to participate in widespread trading networks. Anatomically modern people with Upper Paleolithic cultures were the first humans to migrate into the northernmost regions of Asia and into the New World, arriving at least 12,000 years ago, probably earlier. Further, DNA research provides evidence that the New World was populated by more than one wave of immigrants from Siberia. Anatomically modern people first arrived in Australia between 60,000 and 40,000 years ago, probably by boat.

## For Review

1. What is the evolutionary importance of bipedalism and its effects on human mobility?

2. Outline the distinctive characteristics of hominin dentition. What can our teeth tell us about our diet?

3. Explain the differences between robust and gracile australopiths.

4. There is more than one explanation for the evolutionary transition from early hominins to the genus *Homo*. Choose one and write a paragraph defending it by using what you have learned about hominin evolution.

5. Describe how time, soil, and weather conditions might affect the evidence that paleoanthropologists (and archaeologists) study. What methods and tools might researchers use to understand these natural processes?

6. Summarize what is known about *Homo erectus*, morphologically and culturally.

7. Clearly describe the fossil evidence for the evolutionary transition to modern *Homo sapiens*. In what ways does this species differ from Neanderthals?

8. Explain how the origins of *Homo sapiens* might be accounted for by proponents of evolution by punctuated equilibria.

9. Outline the hypothesis for the "mostly out of Africa" model of the origin of modern *Homo sapiens*. What evidence do biological anthropologists use to defend this model? How does this model contrast with the earlier "replacement" model and the "regional continuity" model?

10. Biological anthropologists have been studying Neanderthals for hundreds of years. What do we know about them, and how does this knowledge influence how we think about of human society and culture?

11. Summarize the features anthropologists emphasize in distinguishing anatomically modern humans from other archaic populations of *Homo*. Why are these features important?

12. Choose and defend one of the proposed explanations for the extinction of Neanderthals. Explain why you chose this hypothesis. Refer to April Nowell's hypothesis regarding play in your answer.

13. How do archaeology and biological anthropology contribute to our understanding of the evolution of a modern human capacity for culture?

14. Describe the evidence that archaeologists, biological anthropologists, and others use to identify when the first people arrived in the Americas and who these people were. Are there any contradictions between different sets of data? Explain.

## Key Terms

Acheulean tradition  134
anatomically modern human beings  145
archaic *Homo sapiens*  137
australopiths  118
bipedalism  118
blades  148
composite tools  148

cranial capacity  126
Denisovans  147
Early Stone Age (ESA)  134
*Homo*  129
*Homo erectus*  132
intrusions  144
Late Stone Age (LSA)  148
Middle Stone Age (MSA)  142

mosaic evolution  118
Mousterian tradition  142
Neanderthals  139
Oldowan tradition  130
omnivorous  119
regional continuity model  139
replacement model  139
taphonomy  130

## Suggested Readings

Begun, David R., ed. 2013. *A Companion to Paleoanthropology*. Malden, MA: Blackwell. *A fascinating collection of readings that explore our current knowledge of human evolution. In particular, the chapter by Mark Collard and Mana Dembo, from Simon Fraser University, provides an excellent, up-to-date overview of the various theories of modern human origins.*

Dahlberg, Frances, ed. 1981. *Woman the Gatherer*. New Haven: Yale University Press. *A classic collection of essays challenging the "man the hunter" scenario using bioanthropological data and ethnographic evidence from four different foraging societies.*

Gamble, Clive. 1994. *Timewalkers: The Prehistory of Global Colonization*. Cambridge, MA: Harvard University Press. *Gamble argues that our species' ability to colonize the world was the result of exaptation of attributes we evolved for other purposes. Usefully read in conjunction with the Potts volume below.*

Lee, Richard B., and Irven DeVore, eds. 1968. *Man the Hunter*. New York: Aldine. *The classic collection of articles that undergirded the "man the hunter" scenario of human origins—and paradoxically offered evidence for its critique.*

Lewin, Roger. 2005. *Human Evolution: An Illustrated Introduction*. 5th ed. Boston: Blackwell. *A highly readable introduction to human evolution. Lewin, a science journalist, has worked closely with Richard Leakey and cowritten three books about human origins with him.*

Morell, Virginia. 1996. *Ancestral Passions: The Leakey Family and the Quest for Humankind's Beginnings*. New York: Simon & Schuster. *A biography of the Leakey family over several generations that brilliantly contextualizes their contributions to paleoanthropology.*

Pääbo, Svante. 2014. *Neanderthal Man: In Search of Lost Genomes*. New York: Basic Books. *Svante Pääbo is the director of the Department of Genetics at the Max Planck Institute for Evolutionary Anthropology in Leipzig, Germany. This volume is an engaging account of his personal and professional life, centring on how he and his team of scientists succeeded in sequencing Neanderthal mtDNA, the first-draft Neanderthal genome, and the Denisovan genome, thereby revolutionizing the study of extinct human populations.*

Potts, Rick. 1996. *Humanity's Descent: The Consequences of Ecological Instability*. New York: William Morrow. *A survey of human evolution, in which evidence is presented that the great flexibility of modern Homo sapiens resulted from selection for the ability to survive wide fluctuations in environments, rather than adaptation to any single environment. Usefully read in conjunction with the Gamble volume above.*

Shreeve, James. 1995. *The Neandertal Enigma: Solving the Mystery of Modern Human Origins*. New York: Avon Books. *A science journalist's account of the controversy between replacement and regional continuity theorists.*

Stringer, Chris. 2012. *Lone Survivors: How We Came to Be the Only Humans on Earth*. New York: Holt. *Stringer is best known for proposing that our species had a recent origin in Africa some 200,000 years ago, after which we moved out of Africa and eventually replaced earlier populations of hominins. This volume contains his current views about the evolution of Homo sapiens—the "lone survivors" of millions of years of hominin evolution—and also discusses his involvement with scientists who have developed new and reliable dating methods for the earliest fossils of modern humans.*

Tattersall, Ian. 2012. *Masters of the Planet: The Search for Our Human Origins*. New York: Palgrave-Macmillan. *An up-to-date account of human evolutionary history, anchored in the hominin fossil record, as interpreted by a distinguished paleoanthropologist.*

Willoughby, Pamela R. 2007. *The Evolution of Modern Humans in Africa: A Comprehensive Guide*. Lanham, MD: Rowman Altamira. *Willoughby, an archaeologist at the University of Alberta, provides a thorough examination of what is known about the evolution of modern humans in Africa during the Middle Paleolithic/Middle Stone Age.*

Wolpoff, Milford, and Rachel Caspari. 1996. *Race and Human Evolution: A Fatal Attraction*. New York: Simon & Schuster. *A detailed defence of the regional continuity model by two of its most committed exponents.*

Wrangham, Richard. 2009. *Catching Fire: How Cooking Made Us Human*. New York: Basic Books. *Wrangham, a biological anthropologist, makes a provocative case for the key role played by cooked food in the evolutionary success of humans.*

# Biological Anthropology: Bioarchaeology and the Analysis of Human Remains

## What Secrets Do Our Skeletons Hold?

The study of human remains can be traced back to the development of anthropology as an academic discipline in the nineteenth century. Today, this study typically falls under the umbrella of biological anthropology, a major component of which is bioarchaeology. However, the lines that separate different anthropological specialties are often flexible, and paleoanthropologists, archaeologists, and other types of scientists are also often involved in the analysis of human remains. In this section, we will focus on the methods and techniques typically used by bioarchaeologists.

Bioarchaeology can be thought of as the archaeology of human death, since it relies on the remains left behind by individuals long after they have died. Death is a fact of life and an unavoidable topic for anthropologists who study humans both past and present (Rubertone 2007). The topic intersects with questions about social issues and population dynamics, such as inequalities in wealth, health status, and the occurrence of disease. The analysis and interpretation of mortuary remains reminds us that humans are biocultural organisms. After all, this analysis can reveal a great deal about not only an individual's physical characteristics (e.g., height, weight, sex) but also the cultural practices of the society in which she or he lived (e.g., religious or spiritual practices and the structure of rituals) (ibid., 256).

The excavation and analysis of human remains often involves a systematic set of procedures that begins with surveying, both on foot and with non-invasive techniques like ground-penetrating radar, to locate graves. Once a grave has been located and prior to any excavation, researchers must apply for permission from local governments and request the consent of any known relatives who are still living. In Canada, this latter requirement often involves cooperating with local First Nations or Inuit groups. The highly sensitive nature of burials requires bioarchaeologists to be extremely respectful of those who are buried as well as their living relatives. Each country has different requirements for obtaining permission to excavate and study human remains. In the United States, these requirements are established by federal laws; in Canada, they are generally set out by the province or territory within which the remains are located. (For more on this topic, see Chapter 7, p. 182.)

If and when permission has been granted, the excavation can begin. In most cases, excavation involves retrieving biological remains as well as cultural artifacts associated with the graves. Numerous cultural practices and beliefs influence how humans are buried, where they are buried, and what objects are included in their burials. Bioarchaeologists document evidence of these practices by recording as much as they can about what they uncover. What is the position of the body? Is it on its side, back, or front? Is it "flexed" (i.e., curled up in a fetal position) or laid out flat? Does the site contain the remains of only one individual, or is it a group burial site? Are the graves oriented along an east–west or a north–south axis? Are the remains in any type of container (e.g., jars or coffins)? What types of artifacts are included in the graves? Is there any jewellery? Are there any weapons or tools? The combined interpretation of these multiple sources of data can provide an abundance of information about the individual and her or his society.

## Excavating Burial Sites

What sorts of conflicts might arise before, during, or after the excavation of a grave? Why and in what circumstances might living relatives require a researcher to observe religious or spiritual rituals when examining the remains? When might ownership of the remains become an issue? If artifacts have been uncovered, to whom do they belong?

bioarchaeology The study of human remains from prehistory to provide information about the human past.

## Analysis of Skeletal Remains

Bioarchaeologists often use skeletal remains to look at patterns of age and sex, genetic markers, health status, evidence of disease, and even the types of food the individual consumed while he or she was alive. But where do they begin?

The first step is to look at the skeletal remains and any other biological indicators that are present in the grave. The individual's age at death is usually one of the first characteristics that a researcher identifies. Skeletal size is typically a reliable indicator of age at death for youths up to approximately 12 years of age. For older individuals, analysis of the long bones of the skeleton can provide useful clues. All long bones are composed of a diaphysis (i.e., a shaft) and two epiphyses (i.e., ends). In children and adolescents, the area between the diaphysis and the epiphyses consists of a layer of cartilage known as a "growth plate" or an epiphyseal plate. The epiphyseal plates of different long bones fuse to their diaphysis at different ages. In females, the epiphyseal plates begin to fuse from 12 to 17 years of age; in males, they begin to fuse from 15 to 21 years of age (Bass 1995, 17). As a general guide, the stages of fusion can be used to determine the approximate age of adolescents. If all epiphyses are fused, the individual is likely an adult. Because the aging process beyond early adulthood causes the internal structures of bones to thin and become brittle, researchers can use bone density to estimate the age at death for adults.

Dentition is another key indicator of age at death. The presence of baby (or "milk") teeth indicates a young child, generally under the age of 6 or 7. As a general rule, the first permanent molars erupt at age 6, the second at age 12, and the third (better known as "wisdom teeth") between the ages of 18 and 21. Estimations of older individuals are generally based on the loss of and wear patterns on teeth, and on evidence of dental disease. Different rates of dental disease typically appear in different age groups, with the oldest members of a population generally being most affected by dental disease (such as cavities and abscess) and tooth loss. Teeth can also be used to identify family and relations. For example, the absence of teeth (e.g., no wisdom teeth) or the presence of more teeth than is typical is often associated with genetic markers.

In addition to discovering an individual's age at death, bioarchaeologists also try to determine the sex of the skeleton. Although it is almost impossible to determine the sex of pre-adolescent skeletons based on their physical characteristics, the sex of adult skeletons is generally apparent by looking at the shape of the pelvis (Figure F1.1). Females tend to have larger and more *U*-shaped hips, which facilitates childbirth, while males' hips tend to be narrower.

The structure of the skull also differs between males and females (Figure F1.2). Most notably, eye sockets tend to be more squared in males and more rounded in females. In addition, the chin is more *U*-shaped in males and more *V*-shaped in females. Finally, the occipital condyle (the bump at the rear base of the skull) is much more pronounced in males than in females.

Bioarchaeologists also often look at the skeleton for evidence of health and disease. Children who have been subject to times of stress, like severe fever or malnutrition, often have linear features on their bones indicating that the bones stopped growing. These are known as Harris lines. Children who lack sufficient vitamin D can develop a bone disease known as rickets, which causes

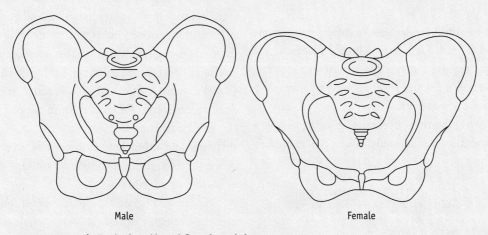

Male                    Female

**FIGURE F1.1** | Typical male and female pelvises.

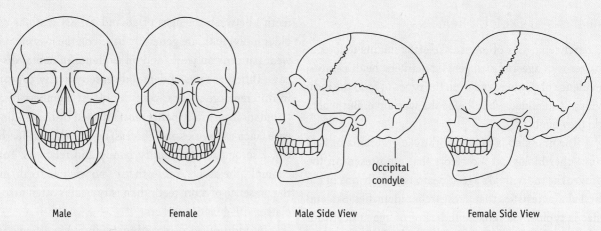

| Male | Female | Male Side View | Female Side View |

Occipital condyle

**FIGURE F1.2** | Typical male and female skulls.

## Estimating Height

Archaeologists can use the long bones of the leg to estimate the living height or stature of an individual. To see how, try the following exercise on yourself:

1. Estimate your height using one of the two formulas below (note that your femur is the long bone that connects your hip to your knee):

   For genetic males: 2.32 x length of femur in cm + 65.53 = _____ (± 3.94 cm)

   For genetic females: 2.47 x length of femur in cm + 54.10 = _____ (± 3.72 cm)

2. Measure your height using a tape measure.

Was your original estimate accurate? What factors might have influenced your results? Are your legs shorter or longer, relative to your overall height, than the formula projects?

long bones, generally in the legs, to soften and become bow shaped (Figure F1.3). Some chronic diseases, like tuberculosis, leprosy, and syphilis, tend to erode or create holes in bones (Figure F1.4). However, most infectious diseases do not affect bones.

Study of the teeth is useful in showing changes in health and diet. Dental analysis involves recording the physical appearance of each tooth in the mouth as well as tooth loss. Abnormally thin enamel can suggest the individual experienced a period of illness or poor nutrition. Tooth loss can indicate prolonged periods of illness or inadequate nutrition. High rates of cavities (also known as "caries") can point to a diet rich in carbohydrates, as the bacteria that cause cavities feed on the sugars in carbohydrates. In addition, excessive wear on teeth can suggest a diet full of tough, fibrous foods.

Stresses of everyday life are also sometimes apparent on skeletal remains. For example, the size and density of the long bones—large and robust, or small and gracile—can suggest the types of activities in which an individual was involved. According to Wolff's law, bones that have been under greater stress or have had to carry greater loads will be larger and denser than bones under less stress or subject to less of a load. Thus, if we spend a lot of time walking or running, or if we regularly carry heavy objects or engage in challenging manual labour, our bones will become denser; however, if we live highly sedentary lives or spend a great amount of time in water or on boats, or if we do little carrying or manual labour, our bones will become less dense. This law is supported, for example, by Stock and Pfeiffer's (2001) discovery of a higher lower-limb robusticity in African terrestrial foragers than in marine foragers of the Andaman Islands. Wear patterns are also apparent in joints and other bones. Repetitive work will wear down joints and often contribute to degenerative diseases like osteoarthritis.

Bioarchaeologists also look at other, more specific musculoskeletal markers (MSMs) to provide evidence of various day-to-day activities. For example, a study of the

**Woloff's law** The principle that a living person's bones adapt to the stress or load to which they are subjected, such that greater stress or load will lead to denser bones and less stress or load will lead to less dense bones.

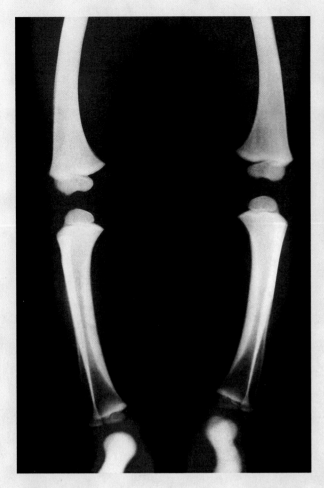

**FIGURE F1.3 |** Long bones of the legs affected by rickets.

**FIGURE F1.4 |** Syphilis lesions on the skull.

of Canada reveal strong evidence of teeth being used as tools. More specifically, it was common for women to soften hides by chewing on them, which resulted in extremely worn front teeth and MSMs on the joint of their jaw. These examples reveal how our skeletons can provide evidence of our life history, including our work habits, our health, and our relations.

## Thinking like a Bioarchaeologist

Imagine that a bioarchaeologist finds your remains 500 years in the future. What assumptions might she or he make about your life? What might the jewellery you are wearing or the items in your possession say about you? What would your bones and teeth reveal about the types of activities you regularly engage in, your past health, or your diet? Do you have any injuries or dental work that would allow a bioarchaeologist to understand your day-to-day life? What aspects of your life would a bioarchaeologist not be able to interpret based on this evidence?

skeletal remains of nineteenth-century Canadian fur traders revealed evidence of excessive use of and strain on these traders' shoulders and back regions that would have been associated with paddling, rowing, lifting, and carrying heavy items (Lovell and Dublenko 1999). Also, there were arthritic lesions (scars) on the ends of their right leg bones that may have been caused by the habitual "kicking" of the leg while driving dog sleds (ibid., 254). Skeletal remains from the Arctic regions

## Key Terms

# 7 How Do We Know about the Human Past?

▲ Wandjina rock paintings at a site in the Caroline Ranges, Kimberley Region, Western Australia, Australia. This form of rock art is thought to be at least 4000 years old. Photo: William D. Bachman/Science Photo Library

## Chapter Outline

In this chapter, you will learn about what archaeologists do: how they excavate the remains of past human societies and then interpret what they find. We will discuss important issues about the past, including laws that protect historic sites and how in some cases these laws are being disregarded through the illegal destruction of precious sites and illegal sales of artifacts by looters. We will also explore new approaches to archaeological research, and we will consider questions such as "Who owns the past?" and "Why is understanding the past important to understanding humanity in its entirety?"

There are essentially two types of anthropologists who study human prehistory: paleoanthropologists and archaeologists. Paleoanthropologists focus on hominin skeletal fossils and genetic remains from the distant past, analyzing our biological evolution from our earliest ancestors through to the appearance of our own species. Archaeologists, on the other hand, focus primarily on reconstructing changes in past human societies using the archaeological record—material evidence of human modification of the physical environment. Beginning with humble stone tools, the archaeological record encompasses many types of artifacts (pottery, metalwork, textiles, and other technological developments) as well as large-scale cultural remnants (architecture, irrigation canals, and ancient farm fields). Archaeology, however, is more than digging up things and looking at old buildings. It provides a long-term perspective on humanity and reveals evidence about how human cultures have changed and adapted to their environments in the past. This is why archaeology is sometimes called "the past tense of cultural anthropology" (Renfrew and Bahn 2008, 12).

## What Is Archaeology?

Archaeologists study human prehistory by analyzing the material remains created by our ancestors. These remains include everything from the simplest stone tools to the impressive Mayan cities of Central America. The main goals of archaeology are to reconstruct how humans lived in the past, to identify how cultures have changed through time, and to understand what influenced these changes. But how do archaeologists

> **archaeological record**  All material objects and structures created by humans and our hominin ancestors.

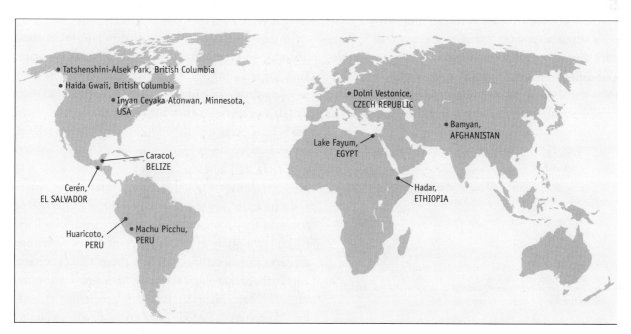

MAP 7.1 | Major locations discussed in Chapter 7.

do this? What kinds of analytical tools do they use? Essentially, archaeologists use a combination of scientific methods similar to those used by environmental biologists and geologists (e.g., analysis of soils and plants) as well as interpretative frameworks that rely on social science perspectives. The former are central to surveying and excavating archaeological **sites** as well as analyzing material remains found at those sites. Surveying involves carefully examining geographical regions to identify potential sites of interest and collecting preliminary data about those sites. Excavations require taking precise measurements, from which 3-D reconstructions of houses and other structures can be made. Lab analysis involves using a variety of methods, including palynology (the study of plant pollen) and trace element analysis to understand past physical environments. Throughout the process, archaeologists apply well-thought-out research questions and hypotheses about human behaviour to frame interpretations of the material remains. In this way, archaeologists combine systematic techniques from both the physical and the social sciences to provide the fullest possible understanding of human prehistory.

The first step in archaeological research involves identifying the precise geographical locations of the remains of past human activity. Once archaeologists have found such a location, they may do small-scale excavations, using a shovel to dig small pits over a large area, or large-scale excavations of entire sites or large portions of sites. In some cases, anthropologists focus on a single site; more commonly, they work to compare several sites in a given region, noting similarities and differences. Archaeologists pay attention not only to portable **artifacts** of human manufacture but also to non-portable remnants of material culture, such as

house walls or ditches, which are called **features**. They also note the presence of **ecofacts**—remains that are not themselves artifacts but that are likely the by-products of human activity (e.g., plant seeds or animal bones connected with food consumption).

When archaeologists study sites through survey or excavation, they carefully record the immediate *matrix* (e.g., soil, gravel, sand, or clay) in which an object is found and its **provenance** (sometimes spelled *provenience*), which is the precise three-dimensional position of the find within the matrix. For each object, they also record any other remains that they find near it, in order to identify associations and relationships between objects (known as their *context* within an archaeological site), which can lead to greater understanding of how the objects may have been used in the past. For example, finding a bowl and a spoon together may suggest that these artifacts were used for food preparation or consumption. Archaeologists also note disturbances to the site made by other humans or small animals, as these sorts of disturbances can cause artifacts to move from where they were originally deposited. This strong emphasis on the *context* in which artifacts are found makes archaeology a holistic undertaking. Undisturbed archaeological sites are important because they contain evidence that may answer key questions about human lifestyles or settlement in certain places at particular times, even when the sites themselves yield none of the elaborate artifacts valued by museums and private collectors.

Archeologists must know what to look for to identify sites and the remains that can serve as evidence. They have to think about the kinds of human behaviour past populations are likely to have engaged in and what telltale evidence for that behaviour might have been left behind. Sometimes the artifacts themselves tell the story: a collection of blank flint pieces, partly worked flint tools, and a heap of flakes suggest that a site was used for flint-tool manufacture. Other times, when archaeologists are unclear about the significance of remains, they use a method called **ethnoarchaeology**, which is the study of the way present-day societies use artifacts and structures and how these objects become part of the archaeological record. Archaeologists studying how contemporary foraging people build traditional shelters—what kinds of materials are employed and how they are used in construction—can predict which materials would be most likely to survive in a

**site**   A precise geographical location of the remains of past human activity.

**artifacts**   Objects that have been deliberately and intelligently shaped by humans or our hominin ancestors.

**features**   Non-portable items created by humans, such as house walls or ditches.

**ecofacts**   Biological remains that are likely associated with food consumption or other human activities.

**provenance**   The three-dimensional position of an artifact within the matrix of an archaeological site.

**ethnoarchaeology**   The study of the way present-day societies use artifacts and structures and how these objects become part of the archaeological record.

buried site and the patterns they would reveal if they were excavated. If such patterns turn up in sites used by prehistoric foragers, archaeologists will already have important clues to their interpretation.

However, archaeologists must not overlook the possibility that a variety of natural and human forces may have interfered with remains once they are left behind at a site. An important source of information about past human diets may be obtained from animal bones found in association with other human artifacts; but just because hyena bones, stone tools, and human bones are found together does not in itself mean that the humans ate hyenas. Careful study of the site may show that all these remains came together accidentally after having been washed out of their original resting places by flash flooding. This is known as taphonomy, or the study of the various processes that may have affected the formation of a particular site. Human activity can have particularly damaging effects on anthropological sites. Modern industrial agricultural practices are one of the most widespread and destructive taphonomic processes; thousands of sites and artifacts across North America have been accidentally destroyed through the mechanized plowing of millions of acres of land. Another highly destructive human activity is the pillaging and looting of archaeological sites, which will be discussed more thoroughly later in this chapter.

> For more on the effect of natural taphonomic processes on hominin sites, see Chapter 6, pp. 130–2.

Even in ideal situations, where a site has lain relatively undisturbed for hundreds, thousands, or millions of years, some kinds of important human activity may not be represented by preserved remains. Wood and plant fibres decay rapidly, and their absence at a site does not mean that its human occupants did not use wooden tools. The earliest classification of ancient human cultural traditions in Europe was based on stone, bronze, and iron tools, all of which can survive for long periods. Baked clay, whether in the form of human-made pottery and figurines or naturally occurring deposits that were accidentally burned in a fire, is also quite durable. Fire can also create charred plant seeds that are virtually indestructible, allowing important dietary clues to survive.

Extreme climates can enhance artifact preservation. Hot, dry climates, such as those in Egypt or northern Chile, hinder decay. Sites in these regions contain not only preserved human bodies but also other organic remains such as plant seeds, baskets, cordage, textiles, and artifacts made of wood, leather, and feathers. Cold climates provide natural refrigeration, which also slows decay. Burial sites in northern or high-mountain regions with extremely low winter temperatures may never thaw out once they have been sealed, preserving even better than dry climates the flesh of humans and animals, plant remains, and artifacts made of leather and wood. This spectacular form of preservation is illustrated by the Kwädąy Dän Ts'ìnchį ("long ago person found") discovery, in which well-preserved human remains were recovered from a retreating glacier in the Tatshenshini-Alsek Park, British Columbia, in August 1999. A range of artifacts were discovered in association with this roughly 500-year-old frozen body, including a robe-style fur garment, a plant-fibre hat, and various wooden artifacts (Beattie et al. 2000).

Occasionally, archaeological sites are well preserved as a result of natural disasters, such as volcanic eruptions (Figure 7.1). Similarly, mudslides may cover sites and protect their contents from erosion, whereas waterlogged sites free of oxygen can preserve a range of organic materials that would otherwise decay. Peat bogs are exemplary airless, waterlogged sites that have yielded many plant and animal remains, including artifacts made of wood, leather, and basketry, as well as the occasional human body. Log pilings recovered from Swiss lakes have been useful both for reconstructing ancient sunken dwellings and for establishing tree-ring sequences in European dendrochronology.

## Surveys

Often, a research problem requires a trip to the field. Traditionally, this meant surveying the region in which promising sites were likely to be found and then excavating the most promising of them. As archaeologists have increasingly come to recognize, however, excavations cost a lot of money and are inevitably destructive. Fortunately, non-destructive remote-sensing technologies have improved significantly in recent years. Survey archaeology can now provide highly sophisticated information about site types, their distribution, and their layouts, all without a spadeful of earth being turned. Surveys have other advantages as well, as archaeologists

**survey** The physical examination of a geographical region in which promising sites are most likely to be found.

**FIGURE 7.1** | Some archaeological sites are well preserved as a result of natural disasters. This adobe house in Cerén, El Salvador (a), was buried under several layers of lava following a series of volcanic eruptions. Sometimes, organic remains leave impressions in the soil where they decayed. These remains of a corn crib and ears of corn from Cerén (b) are actually casts made by pouring dental plaster into a soil cavity.

Colin Renfrew and Paul Bahn (2008, 79) remind us: "Excavation tells us a lot about a little of a site, and can only be done once, whereas survey tells us a little about a lot of sites, and can be repeated." As the kinds of questions archaeologists ask have changed, larger regions—entire landscapes, contrasting ecological zones, trading zones, and the like—are increasingly of interest. And for this kind of research, surveys are crucial.

Surveys can be as simple as walking slowly over a field with eyes trained on the ground. They are as important to paleontologists as to archaeologists. For example, paleontologist Donald Johanson and his colleagues discovered the bones of "Lucy" when they resurveyed a locality in the Hadar region of Ethiopia that had yielded nothing on previous visits (see Chapter 6). Between their previous visits and the one during which they found Lucy's bones, the rainy season had come and gone, washing away soil and exposing the bones. Had Johanson or his colleagues not noticed those bones at that time, another rainy season probably would have washed away Lucy's remains (Johanson and Edey 1981).

Of course, Johanson and his team were not in Hadar accidentally; they had decided to look for sites in areas that seemed promising for good scientific reasons. Archaeologists ordinarily decide where to do their field surveys based on previous work, which can give them clues about where they will most likely find suitable sites. Local citizens who may know of possible sites are also important sources of information. For instance, the Kwädąy Dän Ts'ìnchį discovery mentioned above was made by a group of First Nations hunters who stumbled

upon a body that was melting out of the retreating glaciers. Government archaeologists and members of the nearby Champagne and Aishihik First Nations (CAFN; see EthnoProfile 7.1) collaborated closely to excavate and examine the body. When DNA analysis of the body was conducted, 17 living members of the CAFN discovered that they were related to the "long ago person found" directly through their mother's lineage (Pringle 2008). After scientific analysis had been completed, the body was respectfully laid to rest in a traditional CAFN ceremony.

Aerial surveys can be used for mapping purposes or to photograph large areas whose attributes may suggest the presence of otherwise invisible sites. For example, when contemporary crops are planted in fields that were once used for other purposes, seeds sown over features such as buried walls or embankments will show growth patterns different from those of the plants around them, casting a shadow that is easily seen in aerial photographs. Black-and-white aerial photography is the oldest form of aerial reconnaissance and can provide fairly good image resolution. However, infrared and digital photography, as well as remote-sensing techniques using false-colour, heat-sensitive, or radar imaging, generally produce better results. Recent advances in remote-sensing techniques that are being used to detect archaeological sites include unmanned aerial vehicles (UAVs or drones) and LIDAR systems. UAVs are a low-cost option whereby small remote-controlled planes are fitted with imaging equipment that can take aerial photos from hundreds to thousands of metres in the air. LIDAR uses laser technology that can penetrate dense forest cover to detect archaeological features and sites on the ground. The lasers are attached to low-flying planes and generally used in places covered by rainforests—for example, in Central America and Asia. An impressive example of the benefits of LIDAR is provided by a study of the Mayan Caracol site in Belize, where not only the topography of the site but also causeways and agricultural terraces from 2000 years ago were detected (Chase et al. 2012) (Figure 7.2).

Thanks to modern technology, archaeologists can also learn a lot about what is beneath a site's surface without actually digging. Some machines can detect

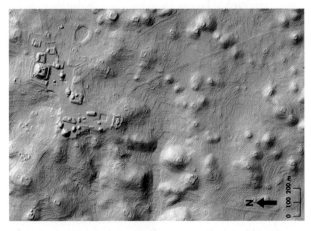

**FIGURE 7.2** | In this LIDAR image of the Caracol site in Belize, the jungle cover has been removed, revealing the linear patterns on the hillsides that represent the agricultural terraces ancient Mayans used to grow food.

buried features and gravitational anomalies using echo sounding or by measuring the electrical resistivity of the soil. Magnetic methods can detect objects made of iron or baked clay, and metal detectors can locate buried metal artifacts. In recent years, ground-penetrating radar (GPR) has become more readily available for archaeological use. GPR reflects pulsed radar waves off features below the surface. Because the radar waves pass through different kinds of materials at different rates, the echoes that are picked up reflect back changes in the soil and sediment encountered as well as the depth at which those changes are found. Advances in data processing and computer power make it possible to produce large three-dimensional sets of GPR data that can be used effectively to produce three-dimensional maps of buried archaeological remains. GPR is very useful when the site to be studied is associated with people who forbid the excavation of human remains.

Geographic information systems (GIS) are also becoming increasingly important in archaeological research. A GIS is a "computer-aided system for the collection, storage, retrieval, analysis, and presentation of spatial data of all kinds" (Fagan and DeCorse 2005, 188). In essence, a GIS is a database with a map-based interface. Anything that can be given a location in space—information about topography, soil, elevation, geology, climate, vegetation, water resources, site location, and field boundaries, as well as aerial photos and satellite images—may be entered into the database, and then maps can be generated with the selected information that the researcher requires. At the same time, statistical analysis can be done on the database, allowing archaeologists to generate new information and to study complex problems of site distribution and settlement patterns over a landscape. GIS is being used to construct predictive models, as well. That is, if certain kinds of settlement sites are found in similar places (close to water, sheltered, near specific food sources), then a GIS model for an area can be used to predict the likelihood of finding a site at a particular location (see Figure 7.3). For archaeologists, the drawback to this kind of predictive modelling is a tendency to overemphasize environmental features as the determining factors in past human settlement patterns. It is easy to measure, map, and digitize features of the natural environment. Social and cultural modifications of the environment, however, are equally important but more difficult to measure using GIS methods.

**FIGURE 7.3** | The layers of landscape information produced by a geographic information system.

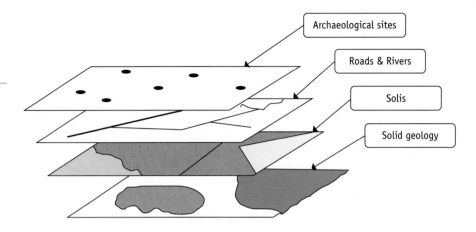

Archaeological sites

Roads & Rivers

Solis

Solid geology

## Archaeological Excavation

Excavation is necessary when archaeologists need to know "a lot about a little of a site" (Renfrew and Bahn 2008). In other words, if an archaeologist is focusing on a specific culture at a specific time, then excavation becomes a necessary component of archaeological research. Excavation is the systematic uncovering of archaeological remains through removal of the deposits of soil and other material covering and accompanying them (Renfrew and Bahn 2008, 580). It is important to remember that excavation is a form of destruction and a site, once excavated, is gone forever. Archaeologists today will excavate only a small part of a site on the assumption that future archaeologists will have better techniques and different questions if they return to the same site. Some sites are shallow, with only one or a few occupation events, while other sites, such as caves that were used for centuries by successive human groups or urban sites that were used for hundreds or thousands of years, are far more complex. In either case, however, excavators keep track of what they find by establishing a rigorous three-dimensional grid system that allows them to record accurate positions of all aspects of the site.

As Renfrew and Bahn (2008, 107) point out, a multi-layered site contains two kinds of information about human activities: contemporary activities that take place horizontally in space, and changes in those activities that take place vertically over time. Artifacts and features associated with one another in an undisturbed context provide evidence for contemporary activities. As excavators uncover one stratum after another in sequence, they gradually reveal evidence

for changes in human activities over time. The more levels of occupation at a site, the more likely it is that some of the levels will have been disturbed by subsequent humans, other animals, or natural forces. It then becomes the excavator's job to determine the degree of disturbance that has occurred and its effect on the site.

Only in shallow sites, like those of the Canadian Arctic, are archaeologists likely to expose an entire occupation level. However, this procedure is prohibitively expensive and destructive on large, multi-levelled sites, especially those found in caves and rock shelters. Archaeologists often use statistical sampling techniques to choose which portions of large, complex sites to excavate, aiming for a balance between major features and outlying areas.

As the excavation proceeds, researchers document the artifacts and site details by taking photographs, writing descriptive field notes, and drawing profiles of the stratigraphic layers exposed during digging. Such record keeping is especially important for structures that will be destroyed as digging continues. Excavated soil is sifted through screens to recover tiny artifacts such as stone flakes or remains of plants or animals. Flotation methods allow archaeologists to separate light plant matter that floats (e.g., bits of wood, leaves, fibres, some seeds, stems, and charcoal) from heavier items that sink (e.g., rocks, sand, bones, pottery, and chipped stone). Everything is labelled and bagged for more detailed analysis in the laboratory.

Work on an archaeological dig ranges from the backbreaking shifting of dirt to the delicate brushing away of soil from a key fossil or artifact. Each dig brings special challenges. Archaeologist Robert Wenke (1999, 84) describes his team's daily routine during the first three months of a six-month field season as they searched for evidence for the emergence of agriculture

> **excavation**  The systematic uncovering of archaeological remains through removal of the deposits of soil and other material covering them and accompanying them.

## In Their Own Words

### GIS and Métis Settlement

*One of the central questions in anthropology is how new identities, new peoples, and new cultures emerge and take hold. What tools can help archaeologists investigate how peoples and cultures changed in the recent past? Kisha Supernant, a Métis archaeologist from the University of Alberta, offers some insight as she discusses how she studies the emergence of the Métis Nation using archaeology and geographic information systems (GIS) in collaboration with contemporary Métis people.*

The Métis of Canada are an Aboriginal people who arose as a new Nation out of the history of the fur trade and contact between Indigenous and European peoples in Canada. The history of the Métis Nation is embedded within the history of nation-building in Canada, evoking images of Louis Riel, Red River, and rebellion, but their history is too often told from the outside. Archaeology has the potential to explore the daily lives and identities of Métis people during a time when they were not writing their own history. Much of the written history of the Métis focuses on the activities at and around Red River, located in what is today Winnipeg, Manitoba. However, the Métis were a highly mobile people who moved extensively throughout the prairie, parkland, and boreal forest of western Canada. During the mid-1800s, Métis families began building cabins and spending winters out on the prairie and parkland. This practice, known as an overwintering or *hivernant* way of life, left archaeological traces at locations where Métis people would live for six to seven months of the year.

I have been exploring Métis overwintering sites by combining archaeological analysis of past material culture and extensive site mapping using GIS. Archaeological excavations reveal patterns of Métis daily life, including diet, social activities, technologies, and the importance of social practices such as Métis beading. Using high-precision mapping techniques, I am able to identify tiny traces of human activity and place these into a spatial context. Using this data, I can draw conclusions about how Métis people used space at different scales, from the insides of cabins to site layouts to comparison between different sites.

One of the key wintering sites I have worked on is the Buffalo Lake Métis wintering site, located on the northeast corner of Buffalo Lake, Alberta. This site was occupied from 1872 to 1878 and may have had 400 cabins of Métis families during the winter of 1875 (Doll et al. 1988). Many of the cabin locations have been subject to disturbance, but my students and I are using GIS mapping, remote sensing, and targeted excavation to explore the full extent of the site. If 400 cabins were present in 1875, the Buffalo Lake site would have been the largest concentration of people between Red River, Manitoba, and the Pacific Ocean, with potentially 1000 to 2000 people overwintering there.

Once identified, the archaeological record of overwintering sites can then be used to test how Métis patterns can be distinguished from settler or First Nations material culture and use of space, highlighting the importance of geographic mobility during the fur trade as a defining characteristic of a Métis cultural landscape. Working in collaboration with contemporary Métis communities allows modern people to connect to a history of Métis daily life that is often untold or forgotten in the story of Canada. Traces of the Métis past also tell us whether or not we can see the emergence of new cultures and new identities in the archaeological record, contributing to the central anthropological question: how do we belong?

Source: Courtesy of Kisha Supernant, of the University of Alberta, 2015.

---

after 7000 BCE at a site on the southern shore of Lake Fayum in Egypt:

> We began by making a topological map of the area we intended to work in. We then devised a sampling program and collected every artifact in the sampling units defined, that is, in the hundreds of 5 × 5 meter squares in our study area. The average temperature during much of this work was over 40°C (104°F), and by mid-day the stone tools were often so hot we would have to juggle them as we bagged them. Afternoons were spent sorting, drawing, and photographing artifacts, drinking warm water, and drawing each other's attention to the heat.

Most of the labour of cleaning, classifying, and analyzing artifacts and ecofacts usually takes place in laboratories after the dig is over and frequently requires several years to complete. Researchers clean the artifacts well enough for close examination—but not so well that possible organic residues (grain kernels inside pots, traces of blood on cutting edges) are lost. They then classify the artifacts according to the materials out of which they are made, their shapes, and their surface decoration, if any, and arrange them in typologies, using ordering principles similar to those employed for fossil taxonomies. Once the artifacts are classified, researchers analyze records from the dig for the context or patterns of distribution in space or time. It is important to emphasize that all sources of information collected during the excavation—notebooks, drawings, plots of artifact distributions, photographs, and computer data—are as much part of the results of the excavation as the materials excavated are.

As you will recall from Chapter 6, the artifacts and structures from a particular time and place in a site are called an **assemblage**. Cultural change at a particular site may be traced by comparing assemblages from lower levels with those found in more recent levels. When surveys or excavations at several sites turn up the same assemblages, archaeologists refer to them as an "archaeological culture." Such groupings can be very helpful in mapping cultural similarities and differences over wide areas during past ages.

One pitfall, however, which earlier generations of archaeologists did not always avoid, is assuming that archaeological cultures necessarily represent real social groups as they actually existed. As archaeologist Ian Hodder (1982) has reminded us, archaeological cultures are the product of scientific analysis and may not represent all aspects of past human behaviour. Hodder's ethnoarchaeological research among several contemporary ethnic groups in eastern Africa showed that artifact distributions do sometimes coincide with ethnic boundaries when the items in question are used as symbols of group identity. He found, for example, that the ear ornaments worn by women of the Tugen, Njemps, and Pokot groups were distinct from one another and that women from one group would never wear ear ornaments typical of another. However, other items of material culture, such as pots or tools, which were not used as symbols of group identity, were distributed in patterns very different from those typical of ear ornaments. Such artifact distribution patterns could be misinterpreted by future researchers and result in a misleading archaeological culture.

**assemblage**  Artifacts and structures from a particular time and place in an archaeological site.

Correlations between archaeological cultures and present-day cultures are important because they can help archaeologists explain cultural variation and reconstruct cultural change through time. Anthropologists seek to answer a variety of questions regarding how humans lived in the past and the reasons new technologies and ways of life developed. One of the major cultural changes in human prehistory involves small bands of foragers who decided to settle down and farm for a living. When, where, and why did this happen? Further, why did some of these settlements then grow into large and complex urban centres? Patterned distributions of artifacts offer clues about groups of people who might have been responsible for these developments; however, we need to remember the risks of associating these distributions too rigidly with real past societies.

For more on the process of plant and animal domestication, see Chapter 8, pp. 208–12.

# How Do Archaeologists Interpret the Past?

## Archaeological Objectives and Approaches

Renfrew and Bahn (2008, 17) outline four objectives that have guided archaeology since it developed as a discipline in the early to mid-1900s. Initially, archaeologists used traditional approaches that focused only on *reconstructing the material remains* of the past by putting together pots, reassembling statues, and restoring houses. This was followed by a focus on *reconstructing the lifeways*—the culture—of the people who left those material remains. Since the 1960s, however, a third objective has been *explaining the cultural processes* that led to ways of life and material cultures of particular kinds. This has been the focus of what came to be known as *processual archaeology*.

Processual archaeologists "sought to make archaeology an objective, empirical science in which hypotheses about all forms of cultural variation could be tested" (Wenke 1999, 33). They integrated mathematics into their work, using statistics to analyze the distribution of artifacts at a site, the transformations of artifact usage over time, or the dimensions of trade networks. Their interest in human adaptations to various environments in the course of cultural evolution led to an interest in the field of cultural ecology, in which cultural processes must be understood in the context of climate change, the variability of economic productivity in different environments, demographic factors, and technological change. As a general rule, processual archaeologists downplayed explanations in which people play an active role as agents who are conscious, to a greater or lesser degree, of what is happening around them and whose activities contribute to cultural maintenance or change.

In recent years, however, archaeologists have begun to ask new questions—leading to a fourth objective. Many have concluded that processual archaeology neglected human agency and the power of ideas and values in the construction of ancient cultures. A variety of new approaches, which are sometimes called *post-processual* or *interpretive archaeology*, stress the *symbolic and cognitive aspects of social structures and social relations*. Some post-processual archaeologists focus on power and domination in their explanations of certain aspects of the archaeological record; they draw attention to the ways that archaeological evidence may reflect individual human agency and internal contradictions within a society. Other post-processual archaeologists point out that similar-looking features can mean different things to different people at different sites, which is why it can be seriously misleading to assume that all cultural variation can be explained in terms of universal processes like population growth or ecological adaptation. (We will look at varieties of post-processual archaeology at the end of this chapter.)

However, while objectives such as these can lead to better understandings of past societies, we must always remember that increasingly precise archaeological methods and subtle archeological theorizing are worthless if there is nothing left to study. By the twenty-first century, the looting and destruction of archaeological sites had reached crisis proportions. Michael Bisson provides a salient example of this when he describes finding a prehistoric artifact for sale in a Canadian pawn shop (Bisson and Bolduc 1994). Thus, archaeologists have come to recognize that stewardship of the remains of the human past may be their most pressing responsibility (Fagan and DeCorse 2005, 25).

## Subsistence Strategies

One of the most important aspects that anthropologists seek to understand about the human past is how we lived and survived. All organisms, including human beings, construct their own ecological niches by inventing ways of using their relationships with one another and with the physical environment to make a living. *Subsistence* is the term often used to refer to the satisfaction of the most basic material survival needs: food, clothing, and shelter. The different ways that people in different societies go about meeting subsistence needs are called **subsistence strategies**.

Connections between subsistence strategies and economic practices are fully outlined in Chapter 11.

Anthropologists have devised a typology of subsistence strategies that has gained wide acceptance (Figure 7.4). The basic division is between food collectors, or *foragers* (those who gather, fish, or hunt), and food producers (those who depend on domesticated plants or animals or both). The strategies followed by food collectors depend on the richness of the environments in which they live. Small-scale food collectors live in harsher environments and are likely to change residence often in search of resources, as the Ju/'hoansi traditionally did. By contrast, complex food collectors live in environments richly endowed with dependable food sources and may even, like the Indigenous peoples of the northwest coast of North America, build settlements with permanent architecture. As we shall see, archaeological evidence shows that some of the first food producers in the world continued food collection for many generations, raising a few crops on the side and occasionally abandoning food production to return to full-time foraging.

For more on the Ju/'hoansi, see EthnoProfile 11.5, on p. 314.

Food producers may farm exclusively or herd exclusively or do a little of both. Those who depend on herds are called *pastoralists*. Among those who farm, there are further distinctions. Some farmers depend primarily on human muscle power plus a few simple tools such as digging sticks or hoes or machetes. They clear plots of uncultivated land, burn the brush, and plant their crops in the ash-enriched soil that remains. Because this technique exhausts the soil after two or three seasons, the plot must then lie fallow for several years as a new plot is cleared and the process is repeated. This form of cultivation is called *extensive agriculture*, emphasizing the extensive use of land as farm plots are moved every few years (see Figure 7.5). Other farmers use plows, draft animals, irrigation, fertilizer, and the

**subsistence strategy** The ways that people in a particular society go about meeting their basic material survival needs.

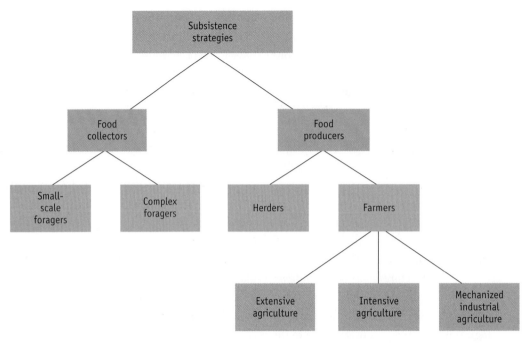

**FIGURE 7.4** | Subsistence strategies.

like. Their method of farming—known as *intensive agriculture*—brings much more land under cultivation at any one time and produces significant crop surpluses. Finally, *mechanized industrial agriculture* is found in societies in which farming or animal husbandry has become organized along industrial lines. Agribusiness "factories in the field" or animal feedlots transform food production into a large-scale, technology-dependent industry of its own.

## Bands, Tribes, Chiefdoms, and States

A key task facing anthropologists and archaeologists in the nineteenth- century was to measure and classify the range of variation in forms of human society over time and across space, as well as to explain cultural and social change over time. In particular, developing explanations for the origin of the state was a key preoccupation, as seen in the work of American anthropologist Lewis Henry Morgan. Morgan was struck by certain patterns

**FIGURE 7.5** | Extensive agriculture, sometimes known as *swidden* or *slash-and-burn horticulture*, requires a substantial amount of land, since soils are exhausted within a couple of years and may require as many as twenty years to lie fallow before they can be used again.

**TABLE 7.1** | Formal Categories Used by Anthropologists to Classify the Forms of Human Society

| Category | Description |
|----------|-------------|
| Band | A small, predominantly foraging society of 50 or fewer members that divides labour by age and sex only and provides relatively equal access for all adults to wealth, power, and prestige. |
| Tribe | A farming or herding society, usually larger than a band, that relies on kinship as the framework for social and political life; provides relatively egalitarian social relations but may have a chief who has more prestige (but not more power or wealth) than others. Sometimes called a *rank society*. |
| Chiefdom | A socially stratified society, generally larger than a tribe, in which a chief and close relatives enjoy privileged access to wealth, power, and prestige and which has greater craft production but few full-time specialists. |
| State | An economic, political, and ideological entity invented by stratified societies; possesses specialized government institutions to administer services and collect taxes and tributes; monopolizes use of force with armies and police; possesses high level and quality of craft production. Often developed writing (particularly in early states). |
| Empire | Forms when one state conquers another. |

he found, in which particular forms of social and political organization seemed regularly to correlate with particular forms of economic and technological organization, which he called "the arts of subsistence." Morgan's book *Ancient Society*, published in 1877, summarized the basic orientation of what became known as *unilineal cultural evolutionism*: "The latest investigations respecting the early condition of the human race are tending to the conclusion that man-kind commenced their career at the bottom of the scale and worked their way up from savagery to civilization through the slow accumulations of experimental knowledge" ([1877] 1963, 3).

By the early twentieth century, the extravagant claims of some unilineal schemes of cultural evolutionism led most anthropologists to abandon such theorizing. Key critics in Britain were social anthropologists A.R. Radcliffe-Brown and Bronislaw Malinowski. Radcliffe-Brown argued that the evidence about social forms in past periods of human history was so incomplete that all such schemes amounted to little more than guesswork. Malinowski and his students used detailed ethnographic information to explode popular stereotypes about so-called savage peoples. In the United States, Franz Boas was highly critical of the racist assumptions in unilineal evolutionary schemes. He and his students worked to reconstruct the histories of Indigenous North American societies, and they were struck by the links among neighbouring societies, especially by the ways in which people, ideas, rituals, and material artifacts regularly flowed across porous social boundaries. Boas was quick to note that if borrowing, rather than independent invention, played an important role in cultural change, then any unilineal evolutionary scheme was doomed.

After World War II, archaeologists and cultural anthropologists in North America worked to combine archaeological and ethnographic information from a range of human societies in order to construct models of cultural evolution that would capture key turning points in social change while avoiding the assumptions about race and progress that had marred earlier attempts. By the 1960s, they had produced economic and political classifications of human social forms that mapped onto each other in interesting ways. As archaeologist Matthew Johnson (1999, 141) summarizes,

> cultural anthropologists Elman Service and Morton Fried ... have been particularly influential on archaeologists. Service gives us a fourfold typology ranging along the scale of simple to complex of band, tribe, chiefdom, and state. Fried offers an alternative [political] scheme of egalitarian, ranked, stratified, and state [societies]. ... Both start and stop at the same point (they start with "simple" gatherer–hunter societies, though their definitions of such societies differ, and end with the modern state). They both also share a similar methodology.

(See also Wenke 1999, 340–4 and Table 7.1 above).

The **band** is the characteristic form of social organization found among foragers. Foraging groups are small, usually numbering no more than

> **band**   The characteristic form of social organization found among foragers. Bands are small, usually no more than 50 people, and labour is divided ordinarily on the basis of age and sex. All adults in band societies have roughly equal access to whatever material or social valuables are locally available.

50 people, and labour is divided ordinarily on the basis of age and sex. All adults in band societies have roughly equal access to whatever material or social valuables are locally available, which is why anthropologists call bands "egalitarian" forms of society. A society identified as a tribe is generally larger than a band, and its members usually farm or herd for a living. Social relations in a tribe are still relatively egalitarian, although there may be a chief who speaks for the group or organizes certain group activities. The chief often enjoys greater prestige than other individuals do, but this prestige does not ordinarily translate into greater power or wealth. Social organization and subsistence activities are usually carried out according to rules of kinship. However, many societies of foragers, farmers, and herders have developed what Elman Service called "pantribal sodalities" (1962, 113). Sodalities are "special-purpose groupings" that may be organized on the basis of age, sex, economic role, or personal interest. "[Sodalities] serve very different functions—among them police, military, medical, initiation, religious, and recreation. Some sodalities conduct their business in secret, others in public. Membership may be ascribed or it may be obtained via inheritance, purchase, attainment, performance, or contract. Men's sodalities are more numerous and highly organized than women's and, generally, are also more secretive and seclusive in their activities" (Hunter and Whitten 1976, 362).

For more on how social organization and subsistence activities follow rules of kinship and other social groupings, see Chapter 12, pp. 335–7.

---

tribe   A society that is generally larger than a band, whose members usually farm or herd for a living. Social relations in a tribe are still relatively egalitarian, although there may be a chief who speaks for the group or organizes certain group activities.

sodalities   Special-purpose groupings that may be organized on the basis of age, sex, economic role, or personal interest.

chiefdom   A form of social organization in which a leader (the chief) and close relatives are set apart from the rest of the society and allowed privileged access to wealth, power, and prestige.

status   A particular social position in a group.

state   A stratified society that possesses a territory that is defended from outside enemies with an army and from internal disorder with police. A state, which has a separate set of governmental institutions designed to enforce laws and to collect taxes and tribute, is run by an elite that possesses a monopoly on the use of force.

---

Sodalities create enduring diffuse solidarity among members of a large society, in part because they draw their personnel from a number of "primary" forms of social organization, such as lineages (Figure 7.6).

The chiefdom is the first human social form to show evidence of permanent inequalities of wealth and power, in addition to inequality of status. Ordinarily, only the chief and close relatives are set apart from the rest of society; other members continue to share roughly similar social status. Chiefdoms are generally larger than tribes and show a greater degree of craft production, although such production is not yet in the hands of full-time specialists. Chiefdoms also exhibit a greater degree of hierarchical political control, centred on the chief and relatives of the chief, based on their great deeds. Archaeologically, chiefdoms are interesting because some, such as the southern Natufians, who lived east of the Mediterranean Sea and were one of the first cultures in the world to domesticate plants and animals, apparently remained as they were and then disappeared, whereas others went on to develop into states. The state is a stratified society that possesses a territory that is defended from outside enemies with an army and from internal disorder with police. States, which have separate governmental institutions to enforce laws and to collect taxes and tribute, are run by an elite who possesses a monopoly on the use of force.

Most archaeologists who use this general evolutionary scheme to help them interpret their findings reject the unilineal determinism that gave nineteenth-century cultural evolutionism such a bad name. Indeed, to the extent that the term *evolution* has come to refer to goal-directed, deterministic cultural processes, many archaeologists might prefer to describe what they do as cultural *history* or *prehistory* since these terms leave room for openness and contingency in human affairs, explicitly acknowledging that human cultural development does not move on rails toward a predestined outcome.

Given these qualifications, can knowledge about bands, tribes, and chiefdoms continue to be of value to anthropologists? For one thing, most archaeologists who use these categories do not think of them as sharply divided or mutually exclusive categories but, rather, as points on a continuum. Indeed, a single social group may move back and forth between more than one of these forms over time, as was the

**FIGURE 7.6** | Members of the Oruro, Bolivia, devil sodality dance.

case with the Natufians. Most anthropologists would probably agree that knowledge about human cultural prehistory is important in helping us understand what it means to be human, even if our more immediate research interests do not focus on prehistory itself. For example, knowledge that gender relations in band societies tend to be egalitarian and that human beings and their ancestors lived in bands for most of evolutionary history has been important to feminist anthropologists; knowledge that nation-states and empires are recent developments in human history that came about as a result of political, technological, and other sociocultural processes undermines the assumptions of scientific racism.

At the same time, archaeologists are interested in why certain kinds of developments came about in one place and time rather than another. Prehistorians note that there were numerous settled villages in southwest Asia 10,000 years ago, but only a few of them became cities or city-states. Some foragers settled down to become farmers or animal herders in some times and places while some of their neighbours managed to find a way to continue to survive by gathering and hunting in bands right up until the end of the twentieth century. Indeed, in parts of the world, like Afghanistan, tribal organizations continue to thrive and attempts to establish centralized states regularly fail. Archaeology, history, and ethnography can help explain why these developments have

(or have not) occurred by seeking to identify social structural elements and cultural practices that may enhance, or impede, the transformation of one kind of social form into another. However, one must be aware that classification is not an end in itself. Today's archaeologists do not see the categories of band, tribe, chiefdom, and state as eternal forms through which all societies are fated to pass. Instead, these are understood as theoretical constructs based on available evidence and subject to critique. Their main value comes from the way in which they give structure to our ignorance.

Intensified processes of globalization in the late twentieth and early twenty-first centuries have revitalized the interest of many anthropologists in cultural borrowing, vindicating the Boasians' claims about the porous nature of social boundaries and the cultural adaptability of which all human societies are capable. At the same time, it has become clear that not all kinds of movements across social and cultural boundaries are equally easy or equally welcome everywhere. Anthropologists continue to pay attention to those structural features of contemporary societies—such as political boundaries between nation-states and international economic structures—that continue to modulate the tempo and mode of cultural, political, and economic change.

For more on the processes of globalization and the movement of ideas and peoples around the world, see Chapter 15.

## Whose Past Is It?

As a social science discipline, archaeology has its own theoretical questions, methodological approaches, and history. In recent years, archaeologists have explicitly had to come to terms with the fact that they are not the only people interested in what is buried in the ground, how it got there, how it should be interpreted, and to whom it belongs. In some cases, archaeological sites have come to play an important role in identity formation for people who see themselves as the descendants of the builders of the site. Machu Picchu in Andean Peru, the Pyramids in Egypt, the Acropolis of Athens in Greece, Great Zimbabwe in Zimbabwe, and Masada in Israel are just a few examples of ancient monuments that have great significance for people living in modern states today. The meanings people take from them do not always coincide with the findings of current archaeological research. At the same time, these sites, and a great many others, have become major tourist destinations. Geographically remote Machu Picchu, for example, now receives about 300,000 tourists per year, a number that is both impressive and worrisome, since the constant movement of tourists may be doing permanent damage to the site (Figure 7.7). Nations, regions, and local communities have discovered that the past attracts tourists and their money, which can provide significant income in some parts of the world. The past may even be mobilized by the entertainment industry: for example, increasingly popular "time capsule" sites invite tourists to visit places where local people wear costumes and carry out the occupations associated with a "re-created" past way of life.

Nevertheless, not all peoples welcome either archaeologists or tourists. For example, as former colonies became independent states, their citizens became interested in uncovering their own past and gaining control over their heritage. This has often meant that the artifacts discovered during archaeological research must stay in the country in which they were found. Ownership of a peoples' heritage and antiquities is an important form of control over that peoples' history, and citizens of places like Greece and Egypt are now asking museums in Western countries to return cultural property—substantial quantities of material artifacts—that were removed long ago by colonizers. Still, many of the artifacts and relics acquired by European colonial

**FIGURE 7.7** | Although Machu Picchu is a spectacular example of human ingenuity and achievement, it has had to endure increasing pressure from visitors who come to admire it. The Peruvian government has proposed closing the Inca trail during the rainy season to protect the sites.

powers during the eighteenth and nineteenth centuries, often illegally or by force, have yet to be returned to their rightful owners. These items include Nefertiti's bust, which was crafted in Egypt in the fourteenth century BCE and is currently held in a German museum; the Rosetta stone, which was inscribed in Egypt in the second century BCE and is currently held in the British Museum; and the Parthenon Marbles, which were sculpted in Greece in the fifth century BCE and are also currently held in the British Museum. These and other objects, some of which are considered sacred by their makers and were not intended for public view, have been openly displayed in Western museums for many years. Is displaying sacred objects in public, even among people who do not believe in their sacredness, disrespectful to their makers? Is it just another way of representing the political power of the current owners? Renfrew and Bahn (2004, 552) suggest that the matter may be more complex:

> [One can] ask whether the interest of the great products of human endeavor does not in fact transcend the geographical boundaries of modern-day nationalism. Does it make sense that all the Paleolithic hand axes and other artifacts from Olduvai Gorge or Olorgesaillie in East Africa should remain confined within the bounds of the modern nations where they have been found? Should we not all be able to benefit from the insights they offer? And is it not a profound and important experience to be able, in the course of one day in one of the world's great museums, to be able to walk from room to room, from civilization to civilization, and see unfolded a sample of the whole variety of human experience?

But artifacts are not all that have come out of the ground over the course of a century and a half of archaeological research. Human skeletal material has also been found and excavated, often from intentional burial sites. For archaeologists and biological anthropologists, this skeletal material offers important data on past patterns of migration, disease, violence, family connections, social organization and complexity, technology, cultural beliefs, and many other phenomena. Constantly improving analytical techniques are increasing the quality of data that can be extracted from skeletal remains, making this material even more valuable to understand human prehistory and evolution. Yet, these may be the remains of ancestors of peoples now living in the area from which the bones were removed, and many of these peoples believe that the dead should not be disturbed and that it is disrespectful to have their ancestor's bones analyzed.

This has been a particularly important issue for archaeology in the United States and Canada because most of the collections of skeletal materials (and sacred objects) came from First Nations populations. Most First Nations and Inuit groups are deeply upset by the excavation of Indigenous burials, and by the subsequent scientific analysis and public display of the bones of their ancestors (Figure 7.8). For these groups, excavation,

analysis, and display of their ancestors represents a continued disrespect and colonial domination that has been commonplace for Indigenous peoples in North America since Europeans first arrived. Thus, their objections have both spiritual and political dimensions. In the United States, these objections were recognized in the Native American Graves Protection and Repatriation Act (NAGPRA), passed by the US Congress in 1990. In Canada, the heritage protection laws are quite different.

In Canada, there is no single legal framework that protects all archaeological sites on lands and waters controlled by the federal and provincial governments. Rather, individual provinces and territories enact their own heritage protection and repatriation legislation, which they enforce on all sites within their boundaries except for national historic sites that are protected and controlled by Parks Canada. Generally, the regulations regarding site protection and cultural resource management (CRM) are similar across Canada, but the implementation and enforcement of these regulations may differ. In addition, archaeologists working in Canada

**FIGURE 7.8** | Deeply concerned that the remains of Haida ancestors had been stored in museums and moved to distant locations, the Haida Repatriation Committee (HRC) has undertaken extensive work on behalf of the Haida Nation to bring ancestral remains housed in museums home to Haida Gwaii (an archipelago off the northern coast of British Columbia). Once returned, the remains are respectfully buried according to traditional Haida ceremonies. Here, one of the founding members of the HRC, Andy Wilson, stands in front of the Royal British Columbia Museum holding a hand-crafted burial box designed to hold the remains of an ancestor.

are encouraged to follow the Principles of Ethical Conduct created by the Canadian Archaeological Association (CAA), which requires them to "exercise respect for archaeological remains and for those who share an interest in these irreplaceable and non-renewable resources" and to work respectfully with Indigenous peoples of Canada (CAA 2015).

Because of their training and expertise, archaeologists are frequently involved in protecting and managing cultural resources in Canada. In fact, CRM constitutes approximately 90 per cent of all archaeological investigations in this country. In northern Alberta, for example, rapid development of the oil and gas industry has called for an exponential number of CRM regional surveys and site discoveries. In addition, in regions such as northern Quebec and Labrador, First Nations and Inuit peoples play a large role in managing archaeological sites and cultural heritage. In all cases, however, CRM archaeological investigations require that only qualified individuals (i.e., those with a Master's degree in archaeology and field experience) are issued permits to work in the area (Thomas et al. 2009, 479–84).

With respect to human remains and burial goods, questions of repatriation are often negotiated between the province or territory and local First Nations or Inuit groups on a case-by-case basis. In British Columbia, human remains are considered "archaeological objects" and, as such, are subject to the province's heritage conservation legislation, while in Saskatchewan, burials not found in a cemetery are considered property of the federal government. In some cases, human remains may be studied for scientific analysis if permission to do so is granted by the local First Nations community. In Alberta, the First Nations Sacred Ceremonial Objects Repatriation Act gives Indigenous peoples the right to apply for the return of sacred ceremonial objects that are currently in the possession of government entities. Recently in Ontario, the University of Toronto returned over 1700 Huron-Wendat skeletons to their local First Nations groups in Ontario and Quebec. This unique and successful repatriation event led to the establishment of alliances between the university and local First Nations communities (Pfeiffer and Lesage 2014).

In most cases, Canadian institutions are working proactively with First Nations communities to develop repatriation policies and procedures. The Canadian Museum of Civilization (2011), for example, has developed detailed policies on repatriation. Thomas, Kelly, and Dawson (2009, 484) describe an example of a working relationship between Manitoba's provincial museum and the Nisichawayasihk Cree First Nation:

A partnership between Nisichawayasihk (Nelson House) Cree First Nation and the Manitoba Museum was formed as part of the 1977 Northern Flood Agreement with the Province of Manitoba. The partnership was defined to work out the recovery, analysis, and display of artifacts found within the Churchill diversion basin in northern Manitoba. Under this agreement, burials are excavated in cooperation with Elders from Nelson House and the Manitoba Museum. Elders view the excavations as ethical because they believe that the ancestors are allowing themselves to be discovered, so that adults and children in their community can learn about the past. Scientific analysis has been allowed by the Cree First Nation, with the understanding that the burials and grave goods will be eventually returned to Nelson House for re-internment.

The Kwäday Dän Ts'ìnchį ("long ago person found") discovery in 1999, discussed earlier in this chapter, provides another example of a successful partnership between researchers and members of a First Nation. Following the initial discovery of the human remains, a collaborative research committee was formed that included representatives from the Champagne and Aishihik First Nations, on whose land the body was found, as well as biological anthropologists and archaeologists. This group worked together to oversee the sampling procedures and the analysis of results, which was followed by the cremation of the body and the ceremonial distribution of the ashes. As the above examples suggest, the negotiation-based repatriation process in Canada can be highly productive, and it has great potential to be able to meet the diverse needs of First Nations peoples across the country (see Koehler 2007).

Indigenous peoples in Canada and the United States are not the only ones concerned with the treatment of human remains unearthed by archaeologists and others. In Australia, Aboriginal people have successfully pressed for the return of the remains of their ancestors, remains that were often collected unethically, sometimes through grave robbing and even murder. In recent years, the Australian government has established programs for the repatriation of cultural material and human remains that are held in Australian museums or other institutions, and it has worked to secure the repatriation of Aboriginal remains from outside Australia. According to the Australian government:

> The aim of the program is to repatriate all ancestral remains and secret sacred objects from the eligible museums to their communities of origin. The four specific objectives are to: identify the origins of all ancestral remains and secret sacred objects held in the museums where possible; notify all communities who have ancestral remains and secret sacred objects held in the museums; arrange for repatriation where and when it is requested; appropriately store ancestral remains and secret sacred objects held in the museums at the request of the relevant community. (Department of Communications, Information Technology, and the Arts 2005)

The Australian Archaeological Association has supported these initiatives.

## Plundering the Past

Many people in the world were shocked and appalled in March 2001 when the extremist Taliban government of Afghanistan decided to destroy the Bamiyan Buddhas, two giant sculptures carved into the face of a cliff about 1500 years ago (Figure 7.9). Even though almost no Buddhists live in Afghanistan today, these sculptures had long been part of the cultural heritage of the Afghan people. Despite world condemnation of this decision—including fierce objection from representatives of the Islamic Conference, which represented 55 Muslim nations—the Taliban insisted that these human images were impious and destroyed them along with even older objects in the national museum. This act distressed many people, perhaps not only because it seemed so narrow-minded and thoughtless but also because the statues were irreplaceable examples of human creative power.

Nevertheless, destruction of the human past on a much greater scale goes on every day as a consequence of land development, agriculture, and looting for sale to collectors. The construction of roads, dams, office buildings, housing developments, libraries, subways, and so on has enormous potential to damage or destroy evidence of the past. As mechanized agriculture has spread across the world, tractors and deep plows tear across settlement sites and field monuments. While construction, development, and agriculture cannot be stopped, they can be made more sensitive to the potential damage they can do.

Unfortunately, such cannot be said for looting and the market in stolen antiquities. There is nothing really new about looting—the tombs of the pharaohs of Egypt were looted in their own day—but the scale today surpasses anything that has come before. It is safe to say that any region of the world with archaeological sites also has organized looting, and the devastation looters leave behind makes any scientific analysis of a site impossible. We have seen how important it is for archaeologists to record the precise placement (i.e., provenance) of every object they excavate. When that context is destroyed, so is the archaeological value of a site. "In the American Southwest, 90 per cent of the Classic Mimbres sites (c. 1000 CE) have now been looted or destroyed. In southwestern Colorado, 60 per cent of prehistoric Anasazi sites have been vandalized. Pothunters work at night, equipped with two-way radios, scanners, and lookouts. They can be prosecuted under the present legislation only if caught red-handed, which is almost impossible" (Renfrew and Bahn 2008, 563). Looters steal to make money. Buyers, including museums and private collectors, have been willing to overlook the details of the process by which ancient objects come into their hands. While museum owners have taken some steps to make sure that they purchase (or accept as gifts) only objects that have been exported legally from their countries of origin, private collectors remain free to feed on the illegal destruction of the heritage of the world's people.

A shocking example of the illegal artifact trade came to light in 1993 when Michael Bisson, of McGill

**FIGURE 7.9** | Many people in the world were shocked when the Taliban leaders of Afghanistan blew up two 1500-year-old statues of the Buddha, which were located in the province of Bamyan, Afghanistan. The photos above show (a) one of the statues before its destruction and (b) the empty cutout left behind following the destruction of the statues.

University, walked into an antiquities store in Montreal and was handed a small sculpture of an unclothed pregnant woman, carved in ivory and obviously extremely old. The piece was similar to European Upper Paleolithic figurines generally considered to be around 20,000 years old. In total, the antiquities dealer had seven of these figurines, which had been stolen from the Grimaldi Caves site in Italy during a dig in the late nineteenth century. The significance of the statues Bisson happened upon is huge, as they displayed previously unknown variations in the style of the representations and in the details they depicted (e.g., some of the figurines depicted women in the process of giving birth). The fact that these figurines had been stolen and hidden away in private collections before they could be scientifically examined within the context in which they were originally discovered demonstrates the irreparable harm that can be caused by the commercial artifact trade (Bisson and Bolduc 1994, 459–62).

To combat these sorts of destructive actions, historic protection laws were developed in the 1960s and 1970s in Canada. To meet the requirements of these laws, the archaeological specialty of cultural resource management (CRM) was developed. CRM is an attempt to ensure that cultural resources threatened by development projects are properly managed—"recorded, evaluated, protected, or, if necessary, salvaged" (Fagan and DeCorse 2005, 483). CRM is a multi-million-dollar undertaking and the major source of employment for archaeologists in Canada; it is practised by private companies, federal agencies, universities, and individuals. For example, CRM surveys must often be conducted prior to the start of large-scale development projects involving pipelines, bridges, roadways, and other structures that reshape the natural landscape. This type of work typically requires archaeologists to collaborate with provincial (or in some cases federal) administrative offices that issue permits and require comprehensive reporting of archaeological finds (Lea and Frost 2012). In addition, CRM projects often require establishing partnerships with First Nations communities when development occurs on reserve land. Originally, the legal grounds for CRM developed out of a concern for conservation rather than research. Over time, however, it has become clear that CRM archaeology contributes in a very significant way not just to the preservation of the past but also to basic archaeological research and theory. In this way, we see again how archaeologists have become the stewards of the past, a role that requires great energy and skill.

## Contemporary Trends in Archaeology

As we have seen, contemporary social issues lead archaeologists to rethink how they study the human past. We now consider three examples of contemporary archaeology that illustrate these developments.

### Archaeology and Gender

By the 1980s, awareness of the unequal treatment of women in modern European and American societies had led archaeologists (both women and men) to examine why women's contributions had been systematically written out of the archaeological record. Building on anthropological studies of living people, feminist archaeology rejected biological determinism of sex roles, arguing that cultural and historical factors were responsible for how a society allocated tasks and that this allocation could change over time. The goal was to develop a view of the past that "replaces focus on remains with a focus on people as active social agents" (Conkey and Gero 1991, 15).

Feminist archaeology did not depend on new technological breakthroughs in excavation methods to pursue this goal. Rather, by using what they already knew about living human societies, together with available historical documents, feminist archaeologists asked new kinds of questions. For example, Joan Gero (1991) drew attention to male bias in discussions of the oldest, best-known collections of human artifacts: stone tools. Gero showed how traditional archaeological discussion of stone-tool technologies focused on highly formalized, elaborately retouched, standardized core

tools. This focus, together with the assumption that such tools were made by men to hunt with, turns men and their activities into the driving force of cultural evolution. It simultaneously downplays or ignores the far more numerous flake tools that were probably made and used by women in such tasks as processing food or working wood and leather. Gero cited ethnographic and historical reports that describe women as active makers of stone tools, including more elaborate core tools, exposing as false the supposition that women are not strong or smart enough to produce these tools.

Gero then applied her findings to her analysis of a multi-layered site at Huaricoto in highland Peru. The lowest occupation level at Huaricoto dates from a period in which the site was a ceremonial centre visited by foragers who apparently made elaborate biface (two-sided) core tools out of imported stone in a workshop on the site. The most recent occupation level dates from a later period, when the site was no longer a ritual centre but had become a residential settlement whose inhabitants used many flake tools made of local stone for a variety of subsistence tasks. Gero (1991, 184) pointed out that "the flake tool performs many of the same actions unceremoniously that bifaces perform in a ritualistic setting." She suggests that the change from ceremonial centre to village settlement probably involved a shift not in the use of stone tools but rather in their social significance: male status may have been connected with stone-tool production during the early period but had probably become connected with some other kind of prestige goods instead (perhaps ceramics or textiles) by the later period. Stone tools continued to be made and used, but they were utilitarian flake tools, and their makers and users were most likely women.

Insights from feminist archaeology inform more recent work in gender archaeology, which "addresses the needs of contemporary gender studies for an understanding of how people come to understand themselves as different from others; how people represent

**feminist archaeology** A research approach that explores why women's contributions have been systematically written out of the archaeological record and suggests new approaches to the human past that include such contributions.

**gender archaeology** Archaeological research that draws on insights from contemporary gender studies to investigate how people come to recognize themselves as different from others, how people represent these differences, and how others react to such claims.

these differences; and how others react to such claims" (Joyce 2008, 17). Contemporary gender studies asks, for example, why archaeologists often assume that the meanings of artifacts from all societies across space and over time should be interpreted in terms of a universal male–female division. As Rosemary Joyce observes, "The experiences of people in the contemporary world are actually a good deal more varied than those expected under the normative two-sex/two-gender model" (18). Gender archaeologists have found that new questions can be asked about variation in sex, gender, and other kinds of human difference in past societies if attention shifts away from the universals and focuses instead on detailed contextual features of specific archaeological sites.

Focusing on site-specific details affects the kinds of interpretations that archaeologists make. First, the meaning of a common artifact, whether found in a household rubbish dump or in a burial site, cannot be assumed to remain unchanged over time. This insight was central to Gero's reinterpretation of stone tools and their use at Huaricoto. Gero's approach also illustrates a second point: archaeological analyses that focus on the highly elaborated artifact can downplay or ignore patterns that would be visible if all relevant artifacts, ordinary and extraordinary, are considered. Joyce argues that Paleolithic figurines depicting females with exaggerated breasts and bellies have been misunderstood. Because of a widely shared assumption that *all* figurines depicting human females had to be "fertility symbols," archaeologists have tended to ignore other contemporary figurines that did not easily fit such an interpretation. For example, the 30,000-year-old central European

For a reinterpretation of these "fertility symbols," see Chapter 6, pp. 153–5.

Paleolithic site of Dolní Vestonice yielded figurines representing animals and human males as well as human females; moreover, the only figurines that depicted the wearing of woven clothing were some of the female figurines (Figure 7.10). Since most female and all male figurines lacked any representation of clothing, archaeologists now suggest that the female figurines with clothing represent a few women at this time and place who "gained individual status from their skill at producing textiles" (Joyce 2008, 15). This interpretation is strengthened by evidence from contemporary burials that clothing of men and women was not differentiated

**FIGURE 7.10** | Sculpture head of woman, Dolní Vestonice. The Dolní Vestonice site in the Czech Republic has yielded an extensive number of figures, some of which seem to represent women of status.

by gender and did not resemble the images of clothing portrayed on figurines (2008, 15).

Third, Joyce stresses the need for archaeologists to think of material artifacts "as having had lives of their own . . . made, used, and discarded, and during which people's experiences and associations with them would have varied" (2008, 28). Focusing on the social lives of individual artifacts shifts attention away from artifacts to the individuals who made those artifacts and highlights the variety of motivations they may have had for making those artifacts the way they did. It also draws attention to the likelihood that all images were not accepted at face value but instead offered "a means for the circulation of propositions that might be contested" (2008, 16). As a result, the same images might well have meant different things to different members of the social group that produced or used them. This approach provides "a critical basis for challenges to orthodox interpretations that might otherwise ignore complexities in human societies now as much as in the past" (2008, 16, 17).

The value of such an approach is displayed in the work of bioarchaeologist Sandra Hollimon, who was faced with interpreting remains of Chumash burials in California. As Joyce explains, contemporary Chumash culture traditionally recognized a third gender—"two-spirited" men whose status is neither male nor female. Moreover, as is the case in a number of Native North American societies, such two-spirited individuals were often skilled craftspeople, who were given baskets in exchange for their work. Hollimon first expected that the graves of two-spirited individuals would stand out from the graves of women or other men because they would contain male skeletons accompanied by baskets. It turned out, however, that baskets were found together with the skeletal remains of both women and men. This prompted Hollimon to wonder if gender distinctions were not important in Chumash mortuary practices. She looked for other patterns of difference in the remains and discovered a typically female form of spinal arthritis in the skeletons of two young males. This form of arthritis was associated with regular use of digging sticks, typically women's work but also the work of two-spirited men.

These two particular male skeletons had been buried both with digging stick weights and with baskets, which strengthened the conclusion that they belonged to two-spirited males. However, digging sticks and baskets were tools traditionally associated with Chumash *undertakers*, who could be either two-spirited men or postmenopausal women. Hollimon concluded that the *status* of undertaker apparently was more significant in Chumash burial practices than was the *gender* of the individual being buried. "In Chumash society, these people helped the spirits of the dead make the transition to their next stage of life. To be able to do this, they needed a special spiritual status. This special status was limited to those whose sexual activity could not lead to childbirth" (Joyce 2008, 60). The lesson is clear: "not finding three burial patterns led to a realization that sex may not have been the most significant basis for the identity of these people.... Genders were not permanent categorical identities, but rather distinctive performances related to sexuality that could change over a person's life" (2008, 61).

## Collaborative Approaches to Studying the Past

Janet Spector was one of the first archaeologists in North America to initiate a collaborative research project with the descendants of the people who once occupied the sites she excavated. Her work in Minnesota is an example of historical archaeology (Figure 7.11)—the study (in this case) of post-European contact sites in North America. Like other feminist archaeologists, Spector wanted to shift attention from the artifacts to the people who made them, from a preoccupation with active men and passive women to a more realistic assessment of active women and men, and from a focus on the remains as evidence of European contact to what these remains suggested about "Indian responses or resistance to European expansion and domination" (Spector 1993, 6).

In 1980, Spector and her team began to dig at a site near Jordan, Minnesota, known by the Dakota as *Inyan Ceyaka Atonwan*, or "Village at the Rapids." She examined historical documents that referred to the site for clues about what tasks were carried out by men and women at the site, as a guide to what kinds of material remains to look for. After several seasons, concerned that her work might be meaningless or offensive to the Dakota, Spector met a Dakota man who was a descendant of a man named Mazomani, one of the original inhabitants of the Village at the Rapids. Eventually, other descendants of Mazomani visited the site. By the 1985–1986 season, Dakota and non-Dakota were collaborating in teaching Dakota language, oral history, ethnobotany, ecology, and history at the site while digging continued. A Dakota elder conducted a pipe ceremony at the site shortly before the field season began, which symbolized for Spector the Dakota people's permission to work there.

Since the early 1980s, collaborative archaeological research of this kind has become increasingly common. In Canada, there are a number of projects in which archaeologists work with Aboriginal peoples to include their world views and traditional perspectives. In these projects, researchers interpret artifacts and sites using combined ideas about history, which they form by taking into account oral stories, songs, place names, and landscape use. A great example of this is the work done by Gerry Oetelaar, from the University of Calgary, in association with Blackfoot (Niitsitapi) elders in the Northern Plains region. In this project, the elders assist Oetelaar in the interpretation of patterns of stone

**historical archaeology** The study of archaeological sites associated with written records; frequently, the study of post-European contact sites.

**FIGURE 7.11** | Historical archaeologists, shown working on an archaeological dig at the Colony of Avalon in Newfoundland, supplement written documents with records of settlement patterns, structures, and artifacts, which reveal valuable information about the past that was never written down.

circles (i.e., tipi rings) to reconstruct patterns of how people arranged space and socialized within past settlements. Other projects that involve collaboration with First Nations peoples include the stewardship program led by Dana Lepofsky of Simon Fraser University (see the "Anthropology in the Contemporary World" box) and the Aboriginal internship program established at the Manitoba Museum by E. Leigh Syms. Through his program, Syms created positive relationships with First Nations groups in Manitoba, initiating and guiding the process of co-operative education regarding First Nations heritage. Training Indigenous peoples to become professional archaeologists is an outcome of Syms's program. One of the most accomplished graduates of this program is Kevin Brownlee, who is currently the curator of archaeology at the Manitoba Museum.

## Cosmopolitan Archaeologies

A variety of far-reaching changes associated with globalization have swept the world in recent decades.

These changes have affected the way all anthropologists do research, and archaeologists are no exception. A major change that has impacted archaeological work in the field is the rapid expansion of global tourism. Today, huge numbers of tourists from all over the world want to visit archaeological sites such as Machu Picchu or Kakadu National Park, both of which have been named UNESCO World Heritage Sites.

As we discussed earlier in this chapter, nations, regions, and local communities can make a lot of money managing flows of wealthy tourists to well-known cultural heritage sites. When tourist traffic threatens to destroy such sites, therefore, it is not merely the ruins themselves that are at stake; the livelihoods of local people and governments are also threatened. Moreover, powerless minorities with traditional connections to these sites frequently find themselves shoved aside as national and international institutions step in and take over. In the past, most archaeologists tried to do their research while avoiding local legal and political

## Anthropology in the Contemporary World

### Archaeology as a Tool of Civic Engagement

Barbara J. Little and Paul A. Shackel (2007) use the term *civic engagement* to refer to an important direction in contemporary archaeology. Civic engagement in archaeology refers to involvement and participation in public life, especially in directing people's attention to "the historical roots and present-day manifestations of contemporary social justice issues" (Little and Shackel 2007, 2). Civic engagement also refers to connecting archaeologists and the work they do to the communities that are connected in one way or another to archaeological sites and the history they embody.

An excellent example of civic engagement comes from a community-based stewardship program being run out of out of Simon Fraser University. Led by Dana Lepofsky, the Tla'amin–Simon Fraser University Archaeology and Stewardship Program is a combined field school and research project as well as a useful venue for spreading knowledge about a community's cultural heritage. Its guiding principles and goals include collaboration with the Tla'amin First Nation and training of Tla'amin youth and university students. The research crews work together with Tla'amin elders to facilitate exchanges of knowledge and history between the Indigenous peoples and the researchers. Through its work, the field school has formed bridges between groups that in other instances may be at odds. As Lepofsky (2011, 17) states: "Discussions of land claims are put aside to hold a projectile point and marvel at the fact that someone held this same point several millennia before. The artifact in these instances becomes more than just a stone tool; it is the medium by which intercommunity communication begins."

Involving local Tla'amin youth is an important part of this community-based project. Digging at the site, touching artifacts, and listening to the elders' accounts of their peoples' history encourages the youth of today to actively form connections between the past and the present. The outcome is a richer experience for all; the young people acquire a more in-depth understanding of the cultural heritage of the Tla'amin, while older members of the Tla'amin First Nation are able to use information garnered from this work to advance their goals of self-governance and self-representation.

The following are but a few of the ways that Lepofsky (2011, 19) suggests to engage the community in local archaeological research projects and to communicate to community members the importance of the past:

1. Host a community potluck at which issues related to the research project can be discussed.
2. Create an artifact kit and make it available to the public so people can touch the artifacts that have been found.
3. Make an engaging pamphlet about the research project and pass it out at public events.
4. Go to local schools or community centres and educate students about the heritage of the sites.
5. Create an engaging website that discusses the project's progress and disseminates its findings.

For more on the goals and achievements of the Tla'amin–Simon Fraser University Archaeology and Stewardship Program, see the project's website: www.sliammonfirstnation.com/archaeology.

involvements, hoping to achieve "a 'do no harm' model of coexistence" (Meskell 2009, 5). Today, many archaeologists have adopted the view that their first obligation should be to those local (and often marginalized) people with traditional connections to the archaeological sites where they work. This is the view taken, for example, by many archaeologists who advocate for the protection of sites located in Canada's fragile North, such as the Dorset site on Qajartalik Island, Nunavut (Figure 7.12). But more and more archaeologists are finding that this kind of single-minded commitment is increasingly problematic, as they and their local allies must find a way to deal with a range of other local and global stakeholders who have their own, often conflicting, ideas about how cultural heritage should be managed.

Like many contemporary cultural anthropologists, some archaeologists have been moved by these struggles to question a view of the world that divides it up into a patchwork quilt of distinct, neatly bounded "cultures," each of which embodies a unique heritage that

**FIGURE 7.12** | Fragile sites such as this Dorset petroglyph site on Qajartalik Island, Nunavut, which dates to sometime between 2200 and 1000 BCE, require careful monitoring to ensure they are not damaged by careless visitors. Archaeologists of the Avataq Cultural Institute have realized for decades the importance of taking into account the perspectives of local inhabitants as they work to monitor and protect this site.

must be protected from change at all costs. Again, like many of their cultural anthropologist colleagues, these archaeologists have concluded that the only way forward is to cultivate a "cosmopolitan" point of view. For many cultural anthropologists, *cosmopolitanism* means being able to move with ease from one cultural setting to another. Cultural anthropologists regularly develop cosmopolitan skills and awareness as they move in and out of fieldwork situations. Moreover, people everywhere—tourists, immigrants, and refugees, for example—have crafted a variety of different kinds of cosmopolitan skills in order to cope successfully with movement from one cultural setting to another.

For a broader discussion of cosmopolitanism and its links to the globalization process, see Chapter 15, p. 452.

For archaeologists, adopting a cosmopolitan orientation means giving up Western/colonial assumptions about the meaning of the past. It means acknowledging, for example, that preservation of material artifacts may in fact sometimes go against the wishes of local groups with close connections to those artifacts. Dealing with such challenges means that cosmopolitan archaeologists will no longer be able to avoid involvement in legal and political debates about the future of cultural heritage, even as they come to recognize that their views may carry less weight than the views of other stakeholders. "Cosmopolitans suppose...that all cultures have enough overlap in their vocabulary of values to begin a conversation. Yet counter to some universalists, they do not presume they can craft a consensus" (Meskell 2009, 7).

Archaeologist Chip Colwell-Chanthaphonh (2009, 143), for example, asks, "Can the destruction of heritage ever be ethically justified? If so, by what principle, why, and under what conditions?" He speaks of "the preservation paradox"—that is, the idea that "the concept of preservation is itself culturally conceived," with the result that "one group's notion of cultural preservation can be another group's notion of cultural destruction." Colwell-Chanthaphonh describes disagreements about the ethics of preservation of artifacts valued in different ways by different groups in the American southwest. Commitment to a "salvage ethic" led nineteenth-century collectors to "rescue" sculptures that the Zuni purposefully left to deteriorate in sacred shrines. "This is the core of the salvage ethic, the urge to 'preserve' objects by physically protecting them. But for the Zunis, such acts that aspired to cultural preservation were in fact acts of cultural destruction" (Colwell-Chanthaphonh 2009, 146).

Conflict over whether to preserve or to destroy ancient rock carvings is an issue that divides the Navajo people and the Hopi people, both of whom have lived in the American southwest for a very long time. Hopi people wish to preserve these rock carvings, which they regard as "monuments to Hopi history, proof of ancestral homelands and clan migrations" (Colwell-Chanthaphonh 2009, 149). Navajo people, however, regard all ruins from the past, including these rock carvings, as products of human evil or the activity of witches. Contact with the rock carvings is believed to cause sickness or other misfortunes, and curing ceremonies involve the destruction of the carvings. These days, moreover, the Hopi and Navajo peoples are far from being the only groups who assign meaning to carvings and ancient ruins in the American southwest As Colwell-Chanthaphonh points out,

> the ancient ruins of Chaco Canyon in New Mexico are at once a Hopi ancestral site, a locus of Navajo spiritual power, a ritual space for New Agers, an archaeological and scientific resource, a National Historical Park of the United States, and a UNESCO World Heritage Site.... Clearly, in anthropological as much as ethical terms, such a complex convergence of people, communities, and institutions cannot be reduced to just intranationalist, nationalist, or internationalist claims. The key ethical problem . . . is not so much categorizing rights but trying to illuminate the relationships. (151)

This is the reason a cosmopolitan approach appeals to him: "we must develop a sophisticated understanding of how heritage works from the individual level, to the community, to the nation and beyond it. . . . A just solution cannot simply pick out the rights of one group but must instead interweave these multiple values" (152). Colwell-Chanthaphonh recommends what he calls "the principle of complex stewardship": that is, "we should maximize the integrity of heritage objects for the good of the greatest number of people, but not absolutely" (160). To maximize the integrity of heritage objects would support those who want objects preserved. Concern for the good of the greatest number, however, would mean that the positions of other stakeholders with different views would also be included and might carry great weight, especially if they outnumbered the preservationists. Even then, however, the majority position might not necessarily carry the day because special consideration would need to be given to those whose ancestors made the objects or who are closely connected to them in other ways. The principle of complex stewardship is not a ready-made solution to disputes about the management of cultural heritage; rather, it is "a frame archaeologists can use to begin deliberations on ethical predicaments" (161). Finding solutions, for cosmopolitans, involves negotiations whose outcome cannot be predicted in advance.

## Chapter Summary

1. By the end of the last Ice Age, cultural variation, not biological species differences, distinguished human populations from one another. Archaeologists interpret cultural variation and cultural change in the human past.

2. Archaeologists trace patterns in past human cultures by identifying sites and regions of human occupation and by recovering artifacts, features, and other remains of human activity from these sites. In all cases, they are concerned with recording information about the context in which these remains are found.

3. The survival of archaeological remains depends on what they are made of and the conditions they experienced over time. Very dry and very cold climates and oxygen-free, waterlogged settings preserve many organic remains that would decay under other circumstances. Natural catastrophes, such as mudslides and lava flows, sometimes bury sites and preserve their contents remarkably well. Ethnoarchaeology and taphonomy are two methods archaeologists use to help them interpret the meaning of the remains they find.

4. Before archaeologists begin their work, they survey the region they are interested in. Surveys, whether on the ground or from the air, can yield important information that cannot be gained from excavations. Excavations are done when archaeologists want to know a lot about a small portion of a site. The style of excavation depends on the kind of site being excavated. As the excavation proceeds, archaeologists keep careful records to preserve contextual information. Much of the final analysis of the remains is carried out in laboratories.

5. Artifacts and structures from a particular time and place in a site are grouped together in assemblages; similar assemblages from many sites are grouped together in archaeological cultures. Archaeological cultures are constructed by archaeologists to reflect patterns in their data, so these cultures cannot be assumed to represent specific ethnic groups that existed in the past.

6. Archaeology has changed focus over time, from reconstructing material remains or lifeways of past human groups to explaining the cultural processes that led to

particular kinds of material culture to emphasizing the role of human agency and the power of ideas and values in the construction of past cultures. Contemporary archaeologists also recognize that stewardship of the remains of the human past is one of their most important responsibilities.

7. Material remains indicating a past culture's subsistence strategy can tell archaeologists a lot about how members of that culture lived and survived. Traditionally, archaeologists distinguish between food collectors and food producers, although they also recognize that many societies across history have depended on features of both of these strategies to meet their basic material survival needs.

8. Archaeologically reconstructed societies are classified using a taxonomy of forms of human society that was developed in conjunction with cultural anthropologists in the middle of the twentieth century. Its major categories are *bands*, *tribes*, *chiefdoms*, and *states*.

9. In recent years, many archaeologists have rethought their traditional methods. Feminist archaeologists have explored why women's contributions have been systematically written out of the archaeological record. Gender archaeologists have questioned the assumption that a male–female gender division is universal and have asked instead how variation in sex, gender, and other kinds of difference can be inferred from archaeological remains of past societies. Collaborative forms of archaeological research have increasingly involved co-operation between scientists and members of groups with past or current connections to the sites under investigation. In recent years, however, archaeological sites and artifacts have become the target of claims by a number of additional groups, including local and national governments, international institutions such as UNESCO, and tourists. These groups do not always agree about the value of cultural heritage preservation or about who has the right to decide the fate of remains from the past. Many archaeologists have concluded that it is vital to develop a cosmopolitan understanding of the claims of these varied stakeholders and to promote conversations among them, even if achieving consensus may not be possible.

## For Review

1. What do archaeologists do? Consider popular cultural representations of archaeologists (e.g., Indiana Jones). Do these representations align with what you have learned in this chapter?

2. Compare and contrast survey archaeology and excavation.

3. What kinds of questions do archaeologists ask about the human past? What kinds of evidence do they look for in order to answer these questions?

4. List the different human subsistence strategies presented in this chapter. How have cultural anthropologists and archaeologists contributed to the identification of these strategies?

5. How have cultural anthropologists and archaeologists used the categories of *band*, *tribe*, *chiefdom*, and *state* in their work? In what ways are these categories useful? What are their drawbacks?

6. Who owns the past? In your answer, draw on examples presented in this chapter.

7. Research some of the provincial repatriation laws that are used in Canada. What are some similarities and differences between the different laws? How do these laws compare with repatriation laws used in other countries?

8. Explain why the looting of archaeological sites is so problematic for archaeological attempts to reconstruct the human past.

9. Using case studies in which gender considerations inform archaeological work, describe feminist archaeology.

10. What sorts of collaborative approaches do archaeologists take to studying the past? Describe some of the methods that Dana Lepofsky has used to engage local communities with her field school.

11. In what ways can archaeologists strike a balance between ensuring the protection of archaeological sites and promoting cultural knowledge through tourism?

12. What does it mean to speak of a "cosmopolitan" orientation in archaeology? Refer in your answer to the examples given in this chapter.

## Key Terms

archaeological record   167
artifacts   168
assemblage   174
band   177
chiefdom   178
ecofacts   168
ethnoarchaeology   168

excavation   173
features   168
feminist archaeology   185
gender archaeology   185
historical archaeology   187
provenance   168
site   168

sodalities   178
state   179
status   178
subsistence strategy   175
survey   169
tribe   178

## Suggested Readings

Feder, Kenneth. 2013. *Frauds, Myths, and Mysteries: Science and Pseudoscience in Archaeology.* 8th ed. New York: McGraw-Hill. *Feder shows how scientific archaeological methods can be used to expose dubious claims about the past.*

Joyce, Rosemary A. 2008. *Ancient Bodies, Ancient Lives: Sex, Gender, and Archaeology.* New York: Thames and Hudson. *A sophisticated yet accessible introduction to gender archaeology. Highly recommended.*

Price, T. Douglas, and Anne Birgitte Gebauer. 2002. *Adventures in Fugawiland: A Computer Simulation in Archaeology.* 3rd ed. New York: McGraw-Hill. *This simulation, for Windows PC only, gives users "hands-on" experience in basic archaeological field techniques.*

Renfrew, Colin, and Paul Bahn. 2012. *Archaeology: Theories, Methods, and Practice.* 6th ed. New York: Thames and Hudson. *A voluminous, profusely illustrated, up-to-date introduction to all facets of modern archaeology.*

Thomas, David, Robert Kelly, and Peter Dawson. 2009. *Archaeology.* First Canadian edition. Toronto: Nelson Education. *An introductory archaeology text with important information on* CRM *and other work taking place in Canada.*

Trigger, Bruce G. 2006. *A History of Archaeological Thought.* 2nd ed. Cambridge: Cambridge University Press. *The most in-depth and seminal introduction to archaeological theory available. A must for archaeology students.*

# Archaeology: Dating Methods in Archaeology and Paleoanthropology

## Dating Archaeological and Paleoanthropological Remains

Anthropologists who study the human and prehuman past—paleoanthropologists and archaeologists—are vitally concerned with accurately determining when the organisms whose fossils they find actually lived and at what point in time the artifacts they find were made and used. Without firm dates, paleoanthropologists cannot accurately reconstruct such things as the path of extinction and evolution that led to modern humans, and archaeologists cannot accurately trace such things as cultural development. Numerous scientific methods have been developed to date hominin fossils and artifacts, and some of these will be described below.

Exact dates are often difficult to establish, since many factors can affect how successfully artifacts and fossils are preserved over time. The type of dating method used depends on the type of material to be dated, as well as the environmental and geological setting of the deposits. Two major dating methods are in use today: relative dating methods and chronometric (or "absolute") dating methods. *Relative dating methods* are used to determine whether an object is older or younger than another object. By formulating a chronological sequence of artifacts or fossils, researchers can begin to compare and contrast these items and establish the relationships between them. In essence, relative dating allows anthropologists to identify the approximate age of an item but not its exact age. In order to establish

---

**relative dating methods**  Dating methods that arrange material evidence in a linear sequence, each object in the sequence being identified as older or younger than other objects.

**chronometric (or "absolute") dating methods**  Dating methods based on laboratory techniques that assign age in years to material evidence.

**strata**  Layers; in geological terms, a stratum is a layer of rock and soil.

**stratigraphic superposition**  A relative dating method that relies on the depth of strata and associated artifacts and fossils.

---

more exact dates, archaeologists and paleoanthropologists use *chronometric dating methods*, which rely on scientific techniques performed in laboratory settings.

It is important to note that although chronometric dating is more accurate than relative dating, it should not be taken as providing an "absolute date," as there is always a margin of error that must be considered. As with any other scientific procedure, it is essential to document the uncontrolled variables that may affect the outcome of the procedure. In addition, the quality of the object must be considered, as this can affect the reliability of the date that either relative or chronometric dating methods indicate. In order to generate a reliable argument for a date, archaeologists and paleoanthropologists tend to combine multiple dating methods and techniques whenever possible. This sort of multi-pronged approach typically results in a number of dates that will, when taken together, provide a more reliable date.

## Relative Dating Methods

Relative dating methods are useful to begin to create a timeline for different objects. While these methods are not as exact as chronometric dating methods are, they allow archaeologists and paleoanthropologists to understand whether certain fossils or artifacts are older or younger than others.

### Stratigraphic Methods

Over time, fossils and artifacts become integrated into the natural environment, forming part of geological deposits. Thus, archaeological and paleoanthropological investigations often involve meticulous excavation of rock or soil layers, known as strata, and their associated artifacts and fossils in order to calculate relative dates. Stratigraphic superposition is a form of relative dating that is based on the idea that older strata will generally be deeper underground, with more recent

FIGURE F2.1 | Stratigraphic superposition is dramatically on display in the Grand Canyon, where layers of rock and soil, laid down sequentially over millions of years, have been exposed by erosion.

strata found above (Figure F2.1). Researchers document the relative depth of these layers to create a timeline according to the law of superposition.

However, it is important to realize that many natural and human influences can alter these geological and archaeological deposits. For example, strata can be dug up, eroded, and washed or blown away. Molten lava can also disturb strata as it forces its way through fractures in the rock on its way to the surface. As you might expect, such disturbances can make dating through stratigraphic superposition more challenging. Even when researchers are aware that these sorts of disturbances have occurred, they cannot always place fossils and artifacts back into their original strata within the stratigraphic record. Sometimes, however, researchers can look at nearby sites that have not been disturbed to create a local relative dating sequence. This sequence can then be used to date fossils and artifacts from disturbed sites through comparison.

By associating the relative age of certain fossils with the distribution of groups of these fossils, archaeologists are able to identify patterns of fossil distribution in different rock layers. This approach is known as biostratigraphic dating. Two kinds of fossil species are most useful for this type of dating: those that spread out quickly over a large area following the widespread extinction of their parent species, and those that evolved so rapidly that a fossil representing any evolutionary stage is a good indicator of the relative age of other fossils found in association with it.

## Typological Sequences (Archaeology)

After artifacts have been recovered from a site, they are typically classified into groups (or types) based on similarities and differences. When classifying artifacts, researchers must choose the attributes on which they will base their comparisons very carefully, as different qualities will lead to different typological categories. For example, grouping artifacts based on the materials of which they were made would result in all ceramics being grouped into the same category, regardless of their function. This sort of approach represents a *characteristic* typology. Conversely, grouping ceramics based how or why they were used would result in bowls being grouped separately from cups or plates. This sort of approach represents a *functional* typology. Once groups of similar objects have been formed, they can be organized into a sequence based on how their appearance changed over time.

As you can see, artifacts can be grouped and organized in various ways and based on different characteristics. The specific typology a researcher chooses to create generally depends on the questions that he or she wants to answer. Recognizing the benefits and limitations of each possible approach helps the researcher choose the typology most appropriate to her or his study.

law of superposition A principle of geological interpretation stating that layers lower down in a sequence of strata must be older than the layers above them and, therefore, that objects embedded in lower layers must be older than objects embedded in upper layers.

biostratigraphic dating A relative dating method that relies on patterns of fossil distribution in different rock layers.

## Grouping Artifacts

Most Canadians have an assortment of jackets and coats that have specific uses—thick coats that keep them warm in winter, waterproof coats that keep them dry in the rain, dressy jackets that make them look sharp on formal occasions, and so on. Think about the collection of jackets and coats that you own, and identify the various ways you could organize them into types (e.g., by colour, material, or function). Once you have identified a few approaches, choose the one that you think would be most useful for categorizing your jackets and coats, and create a typological sequence. Why did you choose the categories that you did? Why was this approach effective? What would be an ineffective approach? Why? What assumptions did you make when organizing your groups, and how could these assumptions misrepresent your collection?

## Thinking like an Archaeologist

Consider how the popularity of different types of family cars has changed over the past fifty years.

| Period | Most Popular Family Vehicle |
| --- | --- |
| 1960s–early 1970s | Station wagon |
| mid 1970s–early 1990s | Minivan |
| mid 1990s–present | SUV |

With is progression in mind, imagine that you are an archaeologist working in the twenty-third century and you are digging up an auto-wrecking yard that has been buried since 2050. Using the information listed above, assign approximate dates to the following strata.

1. Strata "O," which contains many minivans, few station wagons, and no SUVs
2. Strata "L," which contains station wagons but no minivans or SUVs
3. Strata "T," which contains many SUVs, a few minivans, and hardly any station wagons

Now put these strata in relative order, from oldest to most recent. (You should find that your ordering spells "LOT.") If you were not already aware of the decades in which these vehicles were popular, how might you have decided which strata was oldest and which was most recent?

When sequencing artifacts, archaeologists often assume that artifacts that look alike were made at the same time. Based on such assumptions, archaeologists can arrange groups of similar artifacts into a linear sequence; this technique is referred to as seriation. Specific changes in artifact types can be seen as a trajectory of style changes that is most commonly apparent in artifacts like pottery and stone tools. Organization based on changes in styles is referred to as *contextual seriation*. Organizing types based on style changes can be challenging, as the changes that are detectable may be very subtle. Moreover, it is difficult to get the order of artifacts exact using this method. However, this type of seriation can be very useful when one or more objects can be dated, as estimates for the dates of the rest of the artifacts in the series can then be established with greater accuracy.

A slightly different approach to seriation, known as *frequency seriation*, takes into account the frequency with which certain artifacts appear at certain points in the archaeological record. This method assumes that the proportion of artifact styles in an assemblage represents the popularity of those styles at the time the assemblage was formed. When the frequencies of different artifacts from a series of assemblages are plotted on a graph and sites containing similar frequencies are kept together, the result is a relative chronology of assemblages based on the rising and falling frequencies of the different styles. As with contextual seriation, frequency seriation is most useful when a date for one or more artifacts within the series can be determined, as this creates a fixed point around which all other artifacts in the series can be arranged.

## Chronometric (or Absolute) Dating Methods

Compared to relative dating methods, chronometric dating methods provide more precise dates. They do this by using two different approaches: isotopic dating and non-isotopic dating. Isotopic dating methods are

**seriation** A relative dating method based on the assumption that artifacts that look alike must have been made at the same time.

**isotopic dating** Chronometric dating methods based on scientific knowledge about the rate at which various radioactive isotopes of naturally occurring elements transform themselves into other elements by losing subatomic particles.

**non-isotopic dating** Chronometric dating methods that assign age in years to material evidence but not by using rates of nuclear decay.

typically used to determine dates for objects that are billions of years old. Non-isotopic dating methods, on the other hand, are most useful for determining dates for objects that were created or deposited more recently.

## Isotopic Methods

Isotopic dating methods rely on changes through time that occur in the chemistry of artifacts, ecofacts, and fossils. Various radioactive isotopes exist naturally in rocks and living organisms, and these isotopes transform into other elements by losing subatomic particles. When this *decay* occurs in a radioactive isotope, it is measured in terms of its *half-life*—the time it takes for half of the original radioactive sample to decay into the

non-radioactive end product. Rates of decay make useful atomic clocks because they are typically unaffected by other physical or chemical processes.

Geologists using isotopic dating methods to determine the ages of rocks generally agree that the earth is about 4.6 billion years old. Paleoanthropologists are most interested in only a tiny fraction of all that geological time, perhaps the last 65 million years, the period during which non-human primates and then human beings evolved. Archaeologists focus on an even narrower slice: the last 2.5 million years.

Described below are several reliable isotopic dating methods. A more complete list of numerical dating methods, with the periods for which dates are the most accurate, appears in Figure F2.2.

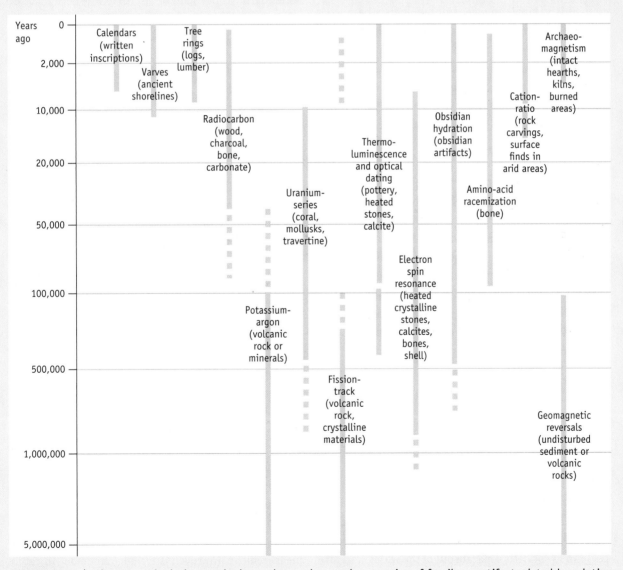

**FIGURE F2.2** | Chronometric dating methods can be used to anchor a series of fossils or artifacts dated by relative methods to a fixed point in time. This chart summarizes some of the most important chronometric methods, showing the spans of time and materials for which each is applicable. (Adapted from Renfrew and Bahn 2008, 133.)

## Potassium–Argon Dating

Potassium is one of the most commonly occurring elements in the earth's crust. One isotope of potassium that occurs in relatively small quantities is radioactive potassium 40, which decays at a known rate into argon 40. During volcanic activity, very nearly all of the argon 40 in molten lava escapes, resetting the atomic clock to zero. Potassium, however, does not escape. As lava cools and crystallizes, any argon 40 that collects in the rock can only have been produced by the decay of potassium 40. The date of the formation of the volcanic rock can then be calculated, based on the half-life of potassium 40, which is 1.3 billion years.

The potassium–argon method is accurate for dates from 4.6 billion to about 100,000 years ago. This method is valuable to paleoanthropologists because it can date volcanic rock formed early in the evolutionary history of non-human primates and human beings and thus any fossils found in or under volcanic rock layers themselves. Fortunately, volcanic activity was common during these periods in areas like eastern Africa, where many important fossils of early human ancestors have been found.

Potassium–argon dating has two main limitations. First, it can be used only on volcanic rock. Second, its margin of error is about ±10 per cent. A volcanic rock dated by the potassium–argon technique to 200,000 years ago ±10 per cent could have been formed anywhere from 220,000 to 180,000 years ago. Nevertheless, no other technique yet provides more accurate dates for the periods in which early hominin evolution occurred. Since the late 1980s, a variant called the $^{40}Ar/^{39}Ar$ method has been developed, which produces more precise dates using samples as small as a single grain of volcanic rock.

## Uranium-Series Dating

This dating method is based on two processes. First, when uranium 238, uranium 235, and thorium 232 decay, they produce intermediate radioactive isotopes until eventually they transform into stable isotopes of lead. Second, uranium is easily dissolved in water; as it decays, the intermediate isotopes it produces tend to solidify, separate out of the water, and mix with salts that collect on the bottom of a lake or a sea. Using their knowledge of the half-lives of uranium isotopes and their intermediate products, scientists

can date soil deposits that formed in ancient lake or sea beds.

Uranium-series evidence can be used to date broad climatic events, such as glaciations, that may have affected the course of human evolution. But it also allows paleoanthropologists to date inorganic carbonates, such as limestone, that accumulate in cave, spring, and lake deposits where hominin fossils are sometimes found. Uranium-series dating is significant because it is useful for dating many important archaeological sites that contain inorganic carbonates and because it provides dates for periods of time not covered well by other dating methods, particularly the period between 150,000 and 350,000 years ago, when *Homo sapiens* first appeared (Klein 2009, 38–41). At present, uranium-series dating is particularly useful for the period 50,000 to 500,000 years ago.

## Radiocarbon Dating

Radiocarbon dating may be the method of absolute dating best known to non-anthropologists, and it is the most common dating technique used by archaeologists. It measures the ratio of stable carbon (carbon-12) to radioactive carbon (carbon-14) in once-living organisms. The method is based on four assumptions: (1) that the amount of radioactive carbon-14 in the atmosphere has remained constant over time, (2) that radioactive and non-radioactive carbon mix rapidly so that the ratio of one to the other in the atmosphere is likely to be the same everywhere, (3) that radioactive carbon is just as likely as non-radioactive carbon to enter into chemical compounds, and (4) that living organisms are equally likely to take radioactive carbon and non-radioactive carbon into their bodies.

If these assumptions hold, then we can deduce that equal amounts of radioactive and non-radioactive carbon are present in all living tissues. Once an organism dies, however, it stops taking carbon into its system and the radioactive carbon-14 in its remains begins to decay at a known rate. The half-life of carbon-14 is 5730 years, making radiocarbon dating extremely useful for dating the remains of organisms that died as long ago as 30,000 to 40,000 years. Samples older than about 40,000 years usually contain too little carbon-14 for accurate measurement. However, a recent refinement in radiocarbon technology called *accelerator mass spectrometry* (or AMS) solves that problem in part for smaller samples. AMS counts the actual atoms of carbon-14 in a sample.

Charcoal, for example, can be reliably dated to 55,000 years ago using AMS (Klein 2009, 46).

Radiocarbon dating is not flawless. Evidence shows that the amount of carbon-14 in the earth's atmosphere fluctuates periodically as a result of such factors as solar activity, changes in the strength of the earth's magnetic field, and changes in the amount of carbon dioxide dissolved in the world's oceans. Scientists are also concerned that an organism's tissues can become contaminated by carbon from outside sources either before or after death; this problem is particularly acute in very old samples analyzed by AMS. If undetected, any of these factors could yield inaccurate radiocarbon dates.

Scientists have discovered that radiocarbon dates for samples less than about 7500 years old differ from their true ages anywhere from 1 to 10 per cent. Fortunately, radiocarbon dates can be corrected by dendrochronology (see below) over roughly the same 7000-year time span. Most archaeologists use radiocarbon dates corrected by dendrochronology to convert radiocarbon years into calendar years, assigning dates in "radiocarbon years" rather than in calendar solar years. Radiocarbon years are indicated when they are followed by the letters BP, meaning "before present"; for purposes of calibration, "present" was established as 1950. In addition, radiocarbon ages are always given with a plus-or-minus range, reflecting the statistical uncertainties of the method (e.g., 14,000 + 120 years ago [Klein 2009, 45]).

### Thermoluminescence

Rocks and clay are often exposed to radiation emitted by naturally occurring radioactive isotopes of uranium, thorium, and potassium that occur in the atmosphere. Electrons can then become trapped in the crystal structure of the irradiated substance. If the irradiated substance is subsequently heated, however, the trapped electrons will be released together with a quantity of light directly in proportion to their number. The light released in this process is called *thermoluminescence*.

If we know the amount of radiation our sample receives per year, heat it up, and measure the amount of thermoluminescence released, then we can calculate the number of years since the sample was last heated. This is a handy way of determining the date when ancient pottery fragments were last fired, when burnt-flint artifacts were last heated, or even when naturally occurring clays were heated accidentally by a fire burning above them. The accuracy of this method may be questioned if it can be determined either that trapped electrons sometimes escape without being heated or that radiation doses are not constant. Nevertheless, thermoluminescence is valuable because, like the uranium-series method, it uses an alternative set of materials to yield reliable dates for the troublesome gap between the upper limits of the radiocarbon method and the lower limits of the potassium–argon method—between 40,000 and 100,000 to 300,000 years ago (Fagan 1991, 64; Klein 2009, 35).

## Non-isotopic Methods

Unlike isotopic techniques, non-isotopic dating methods do not use rates of elemental decay to provide numerical dates of materials recovered from excavations.

### Dendrochronology

Dendrochronology yields numerical dates for trees and objects made of wood. A crosscut section of a mature tree exposes a series of concentric rings, which normally accumulate one per year over the tree's life. (Old trees do not need to be cut down to recover the tree-ring chronology they contain; instead, scientists bore long, thin holes into their trunks and remove samples that preserve the sequence.) Tree rings are thicker in wet years and thinner in dry years. The pattern of thick and thin rings is similar for all trees growing in the same habitat over many years. The older the tree, the more growth rings it has and the more complete is its record of the growth pattern for the locality. Clearly, only trees with seasonal growth patterns can be used successfully in dendrochronology—those that grow all year round, such as those in tropical rainforests, do not produce variable ring patterns.

Tree rings are similar to rock layers because scientists can use their distinctive sequences to correlate different sites with one another. Figure F2.3 shows how the tree-ring sequences from three old trees cut down at different times can be cross-correlated to yield an uninterrupted chronology that covers 100 years. Scientists use this master chronology to match wood recovered from archaeological sites against the appropriate sequence to determine when a tree lived and when it was cut down. Tree-ring chronologies based on the California bristlecone pine extend more than 8000 years into the past. In Europe, chronologies based on oak trees go back to about 6000 years ago (Renfrew and Bahn 2008, 139).

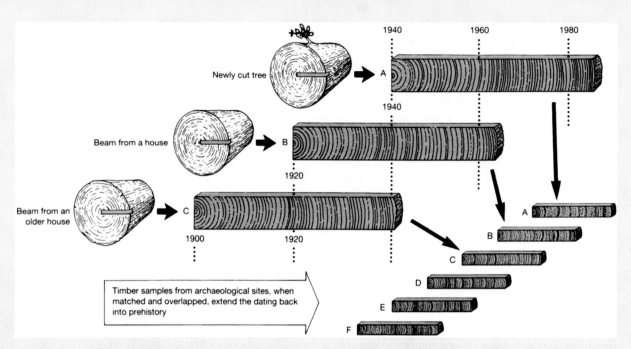

**FIGURE F2.3** | Trees with annual growth rings are similar to rock layers in that their distinctive sequences can be correlated across sites to yield an uninterrupted chronology that may go back hundreds or thousands of years. Researchers use this master chronology to assign chronometric dates to wood recovered from archaeological sites. (Original drawn by Simon S.S. Driver, based on other sources [Renfrew and Bahn 2008, 139].)

## Amino Acid Racemization (AAR)

The method known as amino acid racemization (AAR) is based on the fact that amino acids in proteins can exist in two mirror-image forms, left-handed (L-amino acids) and right-handed (D-amino acids). Usually, only L-amino acids are found in living organisms, but after the organism dies, they are converted into D-amino acids. The rate of conversion is different for each amino acid and depends on a variety of factors, including the surrounding temperature, moisture, and acidity level. If those levels can be determined since the time the specimen died, the ratio of D to L forms can be used to calculate how long ago death occurred. AAR has proved most accurate when dating fossilized shells (Klein 2009, 50).

## Choosing the Right Dating Method

Of the dating methods described above, which one would you use to date each of the following objects? In each case, explain why you chose the dating method that you did.

1. Wood beams from a colonial site in Ontario
2. Shells found in a midden (i.e., garbage heap) deposit from a Mi'kmaq site in Nova Scotia
3. Pottery from an Inka site in Peru
4. Volcanic deposit associated with an *H. erectus* skeleton from southeastern Asia
5. Caribou bones from an Inuit site in Arctic Canada
6. *H. sapiens* burial remains found among limestone cave deposits in southern Africa

# Key Terms

| | | |
|---|---|---|
| biostratigraphic dating   195 | law of superposition   195 | strata   194 |
| chronometric (or "absolute") dating methods   194 | non-isotopic dating   196 | stratigraphic superposition   194 |
| isotopic dating   196 | relative dating methods   194 | |
| | seriation   196 | |

# 8

# Why Did Humans Settle Down, Build Cities, and Establish States?

▲ Modern cityscape and ancient Pyramids of Giza, Cairo, Egypt. Photo: Alex Saberi/Getty Images

## Chapter Outline

- How Is the Human Imagination Entangled with the Material World?

- Is Plant Cultivation a Form of Niche Construction?

- How Do Anthropologists Explain the Origins of Animal Domestication?

- How Do Anthropologists Explain the Development of Domestication?

- How Did Domestication, Cultivation, and Sedentism Begin in Southwestern Asia?

- What Were the Consequences of Domestication and Sedentism?

- How Do Anthropologists Define Social Complexity?

- What Is the Archaeological Evidence for Social Complexity?

- How Can Anthropologists Explain the Rise of Complex Societies?

- Chapter Summary

- For Review

- Key Terms

- Suggested Readings

Modern human beings took what appear in retrospect to have been three major steps that profoundly transformed the lives of their descendants: some of them settled in one place for extended periods of time; some of them later began to intervene in the reproductive cycle of plants and animals; and about 7500 years ago, a number of cultures independently developed social systems characterized by structural complexity and status inequality. In this chapter we survey what anthropological research can tell us about the causes and consequences of these developments.

Today, many of us take settled life and dependence on agriculture for granted, but anthropologists argue that this was neither an easy nor an inevitable outcome of human history. In this chapter, we provide an overview of what anthropologists are able to say about the changes in human subsistence patterns, especially the factors responsible for the domestication of plants and animals. We then consider the impact of human dependence on culturally constructed agricultural niches for subsequent developments in human prehistory.

## How Is the Human Imagination Entangled with the Material World?

Human dependence on culture is as much a requirement for survival as it is a source of freedom. Human imagination and cultural experimentation can suggest which aspects of the material world to pay attention to, and these suggestions can become part of a cultural tradition. At the same time, once a group commits itself to paying attention to some parts of the material world rather than others, it entangles itself in a set of relationships that it may not be able to abandon freely. These relationships become entrenched: they exert a determinant pressure on future choices. As we shall see, when people began to rely on cultivated plants and domesticated animals, not only did their use of the same landscape change, but also they found that they could not easily go back to their previous ways of using the environment to gather wild plants and hunt animals.

A good place to begin to study the relationship between human imagination and the material world

**domestication** Human interference with the reproduction of another species, with the result that specific plants and animals become more useful to and dependent on people.

is to consider how the need to make a living has led human beings to develop different forms of social organization in different natural environments. It turns out, however, that people can make a living in much the same way in different environments or in different ways in the same environment. People work in factories in the tropical coastlands of Nigeria and in the bitter cold of Siberia in Russia; in Papua New Guinea, similar environments are used for gardening by some people, whereas others have established huge plantations. Our study therefore requires us to pay attention to factors that do not depend on the natural environment alone: features of a group's cultural tradition, for example, or external influences due to unpredictable historical encounters with other human groups. In sum, documenting and accounting for major transformations in human material adaptations requires attention to ecological, economic, and socio-cultural factors.

Paleoanthropologists and archaeologists combine their knowledge with that of other scientific specialists in order to reconstruct earlier modes of human life. Based on these reconstructions, we know that our ancestors lived by gathering and hunting, at a band level of social organization, for most of human prehistory. But about 10,000 years ago, at the end of the Pleistocene, the last ice sheets retreated, sea levels rose, and environments changed. In some places around the globe, human beings responded to these changes by systematically interfering with the reproduction of other species, in order to modify those species to better suit human purposes. This process is called domestication, and it occurred independently in seven different areas of the world between 10,000 and 4000 years ago (B. Smith 1995a, 12–13).

Anthropologists have used concepts from the discipline of ecology to better understand the ways in which human beings responded to these environmental

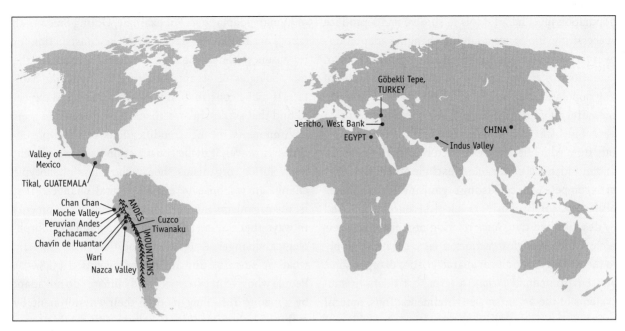

**MAP 8.1 |** Major locations discussed in Chapter 8. (See Map 8.3 for the locations of major Natufian sites discussed in this chapter.)

changes. In general, ecologists are not content to speak vaguely of "the environment" when they discuss the relationships that species develop with each other and with the material world in which they live. Rather, they look for patterns in these relations in specific geographic settings. Traditionally, a population of a species is said to have adapted to a particular local physical environment, or *habitat*, when it has found a place, or *ecological niche*, for itself in the local community of organisms within that habitat (Figure 8.1). Many contemporary ecologists would argue that ecological niches are best defined in terms of the activities of a particular species, including the space, time, and resources that a population utilizes on a daily or seasonal basis (Odling-Smee et al. 2003, 39).

Traditional ecological studies of animal populations in particular habitats have explained the social organization of that population's members—a troop of baboons, for example—by conceiving of space, time, and resources as limiting factors to which that

**FIGURE 8.1 |** A population is said to have adapted to a particular habitat when it has found its ecological niche within the larger community of organisms living in that habitat.

population must adapt if it is to survive and reproduce successfully. Biologists studying changing adaptations over time convert this ecological niche concept into an **evolutionary niche** concept by treating "the niche of any population as the sum of all the natural selection pressures to which the population is exposed . . . that part of its niche from which it is actually earning its living, from which it is not excluded by other organisms, and in which it is either able to exclude other organisms or to compete with coexisting organisms" (Odling-Smee et al. 2003, 40). Two further ecological concepts are used to describe the dynamics relating organisms to their niches: morphological *features*, a term ecologists apply to the phenotypic traits or characteristics of organisms, and environmental *factors*, a term that refers to subsystems of the organism's environment. "Thus, natural selection can be described as promoting a matching of features and factors" (Odling-Smee et al. 2003, 41).

Ordinarily, ecologists and evolutionary biologists assume that environmental factors are more powerful than morphological features of organisms: that is, natural selection involves an organism's adaptation *to* the environment. Ever since Darwin, it has been clear that this process of adaptation has played a powerful role in the evolution of life on earth. However, as we noted in earlier chapters and as the notion of ecological niche implies, organisms are not passive occupants of rigid environmental slots. Their activities regularly modify the factors in their habitats, as when birds build nests, gophers dig burrows, or beavers build dams. Organisms can pass these sorts of modification processes, known as *niche construction*, on to their descendants (or to other organisms living in their local communities). To qualify as niche construction, the modifications made by organisms to their environments must persist and/or accumulate over time, in order to affect selection pressures. The legacy of altered environments with modified selection pressures is what Odling-Smee et al. (2003, 42) call an "ecological inheritance."

How widely the process of niche construction can be successfully applied throughout the living world is controversial. But it makes excellent sense of the history

For additional discussion of niche construction and selection pressures in an evolutionary context, see Chapter 3, pp. 62–3.

of human adaptations. For example, Odling-Smee et al. (2003) argue that the effects of niche construction (or its absence) should be visible when we consider the morphologies of organisms living in particular habitats. If niche construction is absent, we should expect to find that successful organisms have adapted to their environments through modifications of their phenotypes. However, if niche construction has been present in evolution, organisms should show less phenotypic change in response to environmental changes. That is, the organisms modify their selective environments in ways that buffer them against selection for morphological changes. And they argue that this is exactly what we seem to find in human evolution (348–50). People who live in extremely cold climates do not adapt by growing fur—they modify their environment by making clothing, building shelters, and heating those shelters.

As we saw in chapters 6 and 7, the archaeological record documents a changing legacy of human modifications to environments that, at certain points, also allowed our ancestors to make a successful living in geographical regions of the world that previously had been impenetrable to them. Particularly in the past 200,000 years, we see minor physical changes in humans alongside dramatic expressions of human cultural changes and environmental modification. It is within this context that questions about transitions in human adaptive patterns are most fruitfully addressed.

## Is Plant Cultivation a Form of Niche Construction?

For many years, scholars have argued about the extent to which plant domestication was accidental or intentional. Biologist David Rindos, for example, suggests that domestication could have occurred without people's full awareness of what they were doing. Reminding us that human beings are just another animal species that eats plants, Rindos argues that the relationship between humans and plants is no different in principle from the relationship between a species of ant and a species of acacia. The ants live inside enlarged thorns on acacia trees. They consume a sugary substance produced at the base of the acacia leaves, and they feed modified leaf tips to their larvae. But the ants also eat other insects that would otherwise attack acacia leaves. Ant activity is so

**evolutionary niche** Sum of all the natural selection pressures to which a population is exposed.

beneficial to the acacia trees that "when ants were experimentally removed from acacias, the plants were severely attacked and all died within a year" (Rindos 1984, 102).

The unintended, mutually beneficial effects of acacia trees and ants on each other modify the natural selection pressures each species experiences; this is what biologists call *mutualism*. Examples of multispecies mutualism illustrate the important fact that species need not be related to one another only as predators and prey. Together, mutualistic species achieve higher biological fitness than either could have achieved on its own. At the same time, to focus narrowly on the mutualistic *species* themselves neglects the wider environmental context within which both species must make a living. Rindos's example needs to invoke that context in order to explain why acacia trees did so poorly when the ants were removed. It is not simply that these two species lived together in a non-predatory manner; rather, each species served to modify significantly the ecological niche of the other species, buffering it from selective pressures that it would otherwise have been exposed to.

Clearly, ants and acacia trees were able to develop this relationship without conscious planning. But does this mean, as Robert Wenke quipped (1999, 271), that "people have proved to be excellent devices for cereals to conquer the world"? Not likely. And many archaeologists are wary of this way of approaching plant domestication by humans. First, to argue that domestication was an unconscious process overlooks the fact that human beings of the late Pleistocene were fully modern and highly aware of their environment. Thus, they likely deliberately selected those plants that were easier to harvest, more nourishing, and tastier. In this view, humans actively intervened in the gene pool of the wild plants; domestication involved conscious decisions. Second, paying attention only to the plants and the people involved in domestication ignores the kinds of *environmental modifications* needed to make plant domestication successful, which clearly depended on conscious, active human intervention.

An alternative way to look at this process is to consider the intensity of human interactions with plants. T. Douglas Price and Anne Birgitte Gebauer (1995), for example, distinguish between domestication and cultivation. *Domestication* is human interference with the reproduction of another species, with the result that specific plants and animals become both more useful

to and dependent on people. It modifies the genotypes and phenotypes of plants and animals as they become dependent upon humans. *Cultivation*, by contrast, is a concentrated process involving the activities of preparing fields, sowing, weeding, harvesting, and storing products, which requires a new way of thinking about subsistence and new technology to bring it about (Price and Gebauer 1995, 6). That is, habitats suitable for domesticated species must be carefully constructed and maintained in order for the domesticated species to mature and be harvested successfully. Indeed, the same process is required for successful animal domestication.

From this perspective, agriculture is best understood as the systematic modification of "the environments of plants and animals to increase their productivity and usefulness" (Wenke 1999, 270). Price and Gebauer call this systematically modified environment (or constructed niche) the agroecology, which becomes the only environment within which the plants (or animals) can flourish (Figure 8.2). Bruce Smith (1995a) emphasizes that activities that led to domestication were conscious, deliberate, active attempts by foraging peoples to "increase both the economic contribution and the reliability of one or more of the wild species they depended on for survival, and thus reduce risk and uncertainty" (16). Such activities include burning off vegetation to encourage the growth of preferred plants that thrive in burned-over landscapes or to attract wild animals that feed on such plants (Figure 8.3). These are clear examples of niche construction. The ancestors of domesticated seed plants like wheat were weedy generalists that, in addition to their dietary appeal, thrived in disturbed environments. Such attributes made them prime candidates for domestication.

To better understand how domestication and agriculture developed, both must be distinguished from sedentism, which is the process of increasingly permanent human habitation in one place and contrasts with the less permanent, more nomadic

**agriculture**  The systematic modification of the environments of plants and animals to increase their productivity and usefulness.

**agroecology**  The systematically modified environment (or constructed niche) that becomes the only environment within which domesticated plants can flourish.

**sedentism**  The process of increasingly permanent human habitation in one place.

**FIGURE 8.2 |** Industrial agriculture converts acres of habitat into a uniform agroecology for growing commercial crops. These constructed niches offer protection from disease, drought, and insect infestations that the plants would be highly susceptible to in other environments. Canola, one of Canada's most economically valuable crops, is planted and harvested on more than 5 million hectares of land across the country.

patterns of habitation experienced by earlier hominins. It is important to recognize that people do not have to become farmers to become sedentary. The sedentary adaptations of the Indigenous peoples of the northwest coast of Canada (e.g., the Haida people of Haida Gwaii) depended not on agriculture but on seasonally re-occurring salmon runs. These reliable sources of food were "harvested" as regularly as crops but involved minimal ecological interference and no processes of domestication.

Sedentism is probably more usefully understood as a consequence of humans choosing to depend on resources in particular kinds of constructed niches. Sedentism is a key element that modifies the selection pressures of those who come to depend on subsistence resources in a fixed location, be it a riverbank or a cultivated field or a pasture. Human beings who farm for a living are often able to support larger populations as they buffer themselves against periodic famine. At the same time, they are vulnerable to a variety of new selection pressures brought about by

> For a discussion of how sedentism and agricultural practices contributed to the spread of malaria-carrying mosquitoes in tropical regions, see Chapter 4, pp. 75–6.

**FIGURE 8.3 |** In Australia, hunter-gatherers burn vegetation to encourage the growth of certain types of plants.

sedentary life: exposure to threats from disease organisms that breed and spread more successfully among settled people than among nomads.

What other challenges faced those who first interfered in the life cycles of wild plants? If the plant was a grass, like wheat, they had to cope with that plant's reproductive pattern. The wheat kernel, both domesticated and wild, is encased in a spikelet and attached to the cereal shaft by a structure called the "rachis" (Figure 8.4). In wild wheat, the rachis becomes extremely brittle as the kernel ripens, and the kernels on any stem ripen from bottom to top over a week or two. As each kernel ripens, the rachis can be broken by an animal walking through the stand of wheat or even by a gust of wind, dispersing the kernel into the air and eventually onto the ground. Wild wheat has two rows of kernels on each stalk. Because the kernels ripen at different times, the seeds have a greater chance of scattering in different directions and not all landing at the foot of the parent plant in a clump. The kernel of wild wheat is enclosed in a tough outer husk called a "glume," which protects the kernel from frost and dehydration and allows it to remain viable for as long as twenty years in the ground.

To be useful to human beings, wild wheat would require a much less brittle rachis, seed heads that mature at the same time, and a softer glume. It would also require a larger, more easily visible seed head (in terms of both kernel size and number of kernel rows on a stalk). Plants with these variations would have been selected by humans, which would have led to the genes responsible for these traits becoming increasingly prevalent in the wheat-plant population. Given the rapid changes that occur in plant genetics, these changes may have taken only a few generations, during which time the plants would have contributed more and more to the human diet. The earliest domesticated wheat shows precisely these evolutionary trends, including six rows of kernels on a stalk rather than two.

The constructed niches favourable for cultivation have also varied over time and space in several important ways, and they did not appear overnight. David Harris (1989, 17) provides a useful overview of these patterns and classifies the relationships between plants and people into four major food-yielding systems: (1) wild-plant-food procurement, (2) wild-plant-food production, (3) cultivation, and (4) agriculture (Figure 8.5). Harris notes that there are three points at which the amount of energy people put into plant-food activities increases

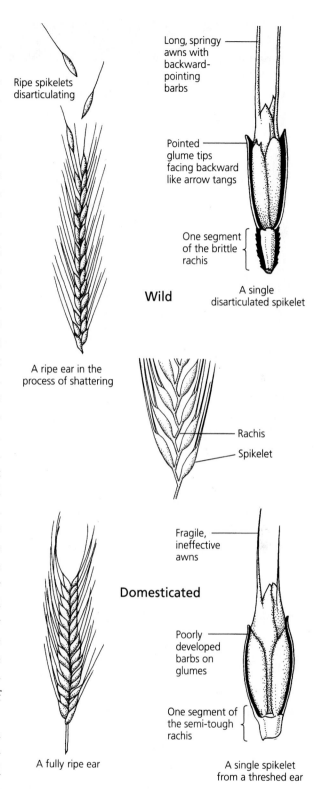

Ripe spikelets disarticulating

Long, springy awns with backward-pointing barbs

Pointed glume tips facing backward like arrow tangs

One segment of the brittle rachis

**Wild**

A single disarticulated spikelet

A ripe ear in the process of shattering

Rachis

Spikelet

Fragile, ineffective awns

**Domesticated**

Poorly developed barbs on glumes

One segment of the semi-tough rachis

A fully ripe ear

A single spikelet from a threshed ear

**FIGURE 8.4** | Wheat kernels form within spikelets that attach to the plant by a structure called the "rachis." The rachis of wild wheat is brittle, which aids the dispersal of seeds. The rachis of domesticated wheat is not brittle, and spikelets remain attached to the ear during harvest.

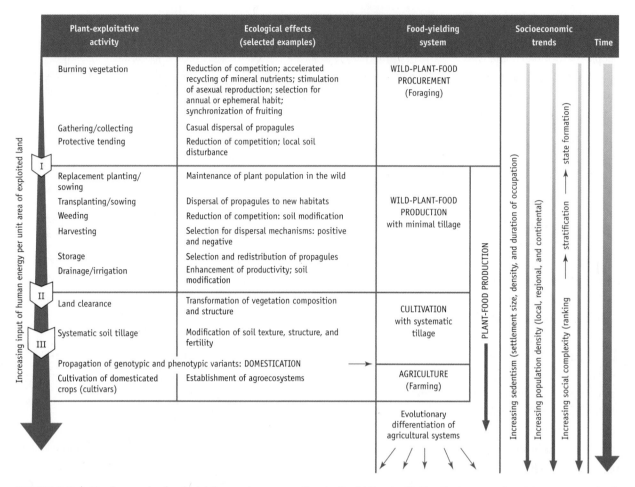

**FIGURE 8.5** | The four major food-yielding systems according to David Harris. Notice that energy-input to energy-output ratios jump sharply where wild plant-food production begins, where cultivation begins, and where agriculture begins. (The *propagules* referred to in the second column are the forms by which plants are reproduced—seeds, shoots, and so on).

sharply: (1) when wild plant-food production begins, (2) when cultivation begins, and (3) when agriculture begins.

## How Do Anthropologists Explain the Origins of Animal Domestication?

*Animal domestication* can be defined as "the capture and taming by human beings of animals of a species with particular behavioural characteristics, their removal from their natural living area and breeding community, and their maintenance under controlled breeding conditions for mutual benefits" (Bökönyi 1989, 22). This definition views animal domestication as a consequence of people's attempts to control the animals they were hunting, which assumes active human intervention in selecting which animals to domesticate and how

to domesticate them. Animals are more mobile than plants, and although culling wild herds can induce some changes in the gene pool, it is only by confining animals or maintaining them in captivity that human beings can intervene in their breeding patterns.

Of course, the innocent phrase "maintaining them in captivity" covers a range of different modifications to the environments of domesticated animals. Captive animals, especially those successfully domesticated, become dependent on the modified niche supplied to them by human beings. As we will see, these modifications may range from protecting selected animals from other predators to supplying them with food and water to close monitoring of their life cycles, from birth to slaughter, under highly artificial conditions. And again, human commitment to the construction of niches favourable to domesticated animals simultaneously modifies the selection pressures humans experience: dependence on a reliable supply of meat and skins may mean that a human group is obliged to follow a herd wherever it chooses to go or to modify their own adaptations seasonally to move herds to reliable supplies of water and forage. Such movements will make humans vulnerable to negative as well as positive encounters with other habitats and other living organisms, including other human beings, with whom they will have to come to terms if their pastoral adaptation is to succeed. Not all people are pleased when herders pasture their animals in areas where cultivated plants are growing.

Animal domestication is difficult to identify with precision in the archaeological record. However, Wenke (1999) provides four main types of evidence that may be used by archaeologists to assess this process. First, the presence of an animal species outside its natural range may indicate herding. For example, because the southern Levant (the coastal area at the eastern end of the Mediterranean Sea; see Map 8.2) is outside the area in which wild sheep evolved, scholars say that sheep remains found there constitute evidence of herding: the sheep must have been brought into the area by people. But it is important to recognize that for this argument to be effective, we must be sure we know precisely what the natural range of the wild species was.

Second, morphological changes occur in most animals as domestication progresses. Wenke and Olszewski (2007, 253) point out that the shape and size of sheep horns reflect the process of domestication. Wild sheep have larger, stronger horns than do domesticated sheep, since large horns are connected with the breeding hierarchies that males establish through fighting. The selective pressure for these horns was reduced as sheep were domesticated, so horn size and shape changed.

Third, an abrupt population increase of some species relative to others at a site is often taken as evidence of domestication. About 9000 years ago in southwestern Asia, archaeological sites were dominated by large numbers of gazelle bones that decrease rapidly to be replaced by high percentages of bones from sheep and goats.

Fourth, the age and sex of the animals from archaeological sites can be used to infer the existence of domesticated animals. Abundant remains of immature or juvenile herd animals, especially males, represents human involvement with the herd. Why? In the wild, animals killed for meat come from a much wider age range; there is no emphasis on younger, especially younger male, animals. Also, human beings who manage herds kill immature males more readily

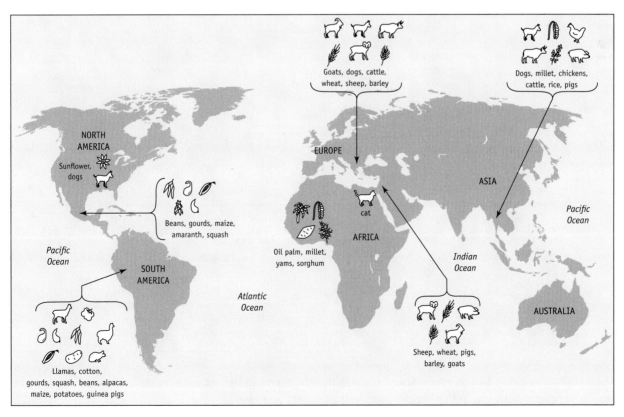

**MAP 8.2** | A map of probable locations where various plants and animals were domesticated.

than females because only a small number of males are required for reproduction, while larger numbers of females provide more offspring, more milk, and other products such as dung, wool, and hair. Therefore, differences in age and sex indicated by animal remains can help to identify the presence of a domesticated herd and establish its function: for example, a meat herd contains a lot of adolescent and young adult animals, while a dairy herd consists mostly of adult females.

When and why did animal domestication begin? Dogs were the first domesticated animals; the earliest evidence for their domestication dates to around 16,000 years ago and was found in a Magdalenian cave site in northern Spain. Clearly, there were significant mutual advantages for both dogs and human beings to team up in the hunt. The earliest domesticated wolves must have been fearsome hunting companions in the Paleolithic, but over time human–dog relationships became very close. A human grave at Mallaha, in modern Israel, dating to about 12,000 years ago, contains the remains of a puppy buried under the arm of a human corpse. Other sites in the area also have remains of dogs, which are quite distinct from the remains of wolves (Figure 8.6).

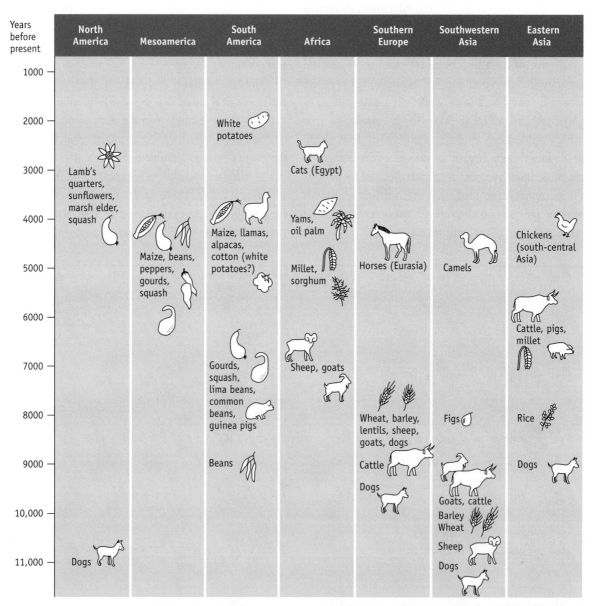

**FIGURE 8.6 |** A chronology of probable dates when various plants and animals were domesticated in different regions. Also note that evidence from northern Spain indicates that dogs were likely first domesticated, to some degree, to be used as hunting companions in that region approximately 16,000 years ago.

It seems that other animals were domesticated to provide food rather than to help get food. It seems likely that people in different areas experimented with animals found around them to determine which ones were both desirable as food and amenable to human control. Both sheep and goats were relatively harmless, gregarious herd animals that had multiple uses for human beings and were found seasonally in the same locales as the ripening plants that people wanted to harvest.

However, the evidence suggests that the natural ecological zones of wild sheep and goats in southwestern Asia were distinct, and it is likely that their distribution did not overlap much, if at all (Map 8.2 and Figure 8.6). In other words, sheep and goats were likely domesticated in different places and at different times. The earliest evidence for goat herding is about 11,000 to 10,000 years before the present, in a narrow zone along the Zagros Mountains (in modern-day southern Iran). The earliest sites for domesticated sheep were perhaps in central Anatolia (the Asian part of modern Turkey). The evidence for two other major animal domesticates, cattle and pigs, is much more difficult to assess but seems to point to multiple domestication sites for cattle from China to western Europe after 11,000 years ago. Domesticated pig bones have been found throughout southwestern Asia as far back as 8000 years.

Jarman and his associates (1982, 51–4) outline six stages on a continuum of relationships between domesticated animals, humans, and the environment. The first is *random hunting*, in which hunters make no attempt to control herds but hunt animals as they find them. The second stage, *controlled hunting*, involves the selective hunting of herds—killing young males, for example. This is the beginning of regular human intervention in the herd species' gene pool. In the third stage, *herd following*, specific herds and specific groups of people begin to interact regularly; as the herd moves from place to place, the people also move. The fourth stage, *loose herding*, is when people begin to control the movements of the herd. They move the herd at various times of the year, ensuring that all of the animals move safely at the same time. They also actively intervene in the herd's gene pool through selective breeding and culling. The fifth stage, *close herding*, is the most familiar practice in much of Canada, the United States, and western Europe. The animals' mobility is limited, and their gene pool is actively managed. In the sixth stage, *factory farming*, there is very intensive human intervention in all aspects

of the animals' lives, and in most cases animals never leave the building or feedlot in which they are raised.

Not all animals that were hunted, even in a controlled way, were domesticated. The bison/buffalo is a good example: there is evidence of controlled hunting using buffalo jumps and paddocks in the Canadian Prairies and elsewhere in North America as early as 4000 years ago, and selective hunting may have led to significant changes in the bison/buffalo gene pool, but there is no evidence of domestication. Clearly, culling herds of certain kinds of animals—male rather than female, less woolly rather than more woolly, thinner rather than fatter—affects the gene pool in ways that demonstrate that people have an influence on animals even if the animals are not fully domesticated. Thus, *herd following* blends almost imperceptibly into *loose herding*.

## How Do Anthropologists Explain the Development of Domestication?

About 10,000 years ago, after more than 4 million years of hominin evolution and more than 100,000 years of successful foraging by *H. sapiens*, human beings living in distant and unconnected parts of the world nearly simultaneously developed subsistence strategies that involved domesticated plants and animals. Why? Although some scholars have argued for a single, universal explanation that would explain all cases of domestication, such as dramatic population increases or intense climatic change, there is little evidence to support any single model of causation. Rather, most scholars agree that explanations for the beginnings of domestication must take into account multiple factors.

One such multifaceted explanation is called broad-spectrum foraging. This explanation is based on the reconstruction of the environmental conditions around 12,000 years ago, when the land glaciers in Europe, Asia, and North America melted and the very large Ice Age animals (e.g., mammoths, giant sloths) began to die out and were replaced by increased numbers of smaller animals (e.g., deer). Sea levels rose and

**broad-spectrum foraging** A subsistence strategy based on collecting a wide range of plants and animals by hunting, fishing, and gathering.

lakes became abundant, while fish and shellfish became more plentiful in the warmer, shallower waters.

The effects on plants were equally dramatic as forests and woodlands expanded into new areas. Consequently, many scholars argue, people had to change their diets from ones based on large ice age mammals to ones based on a broader spectrum of foods, including foraged plants, smaller animals, and fish. This broadening of the economy is said to have led to a more secure subsistence base, the emergence of sedentary communities, and a growth in population. In turn, population growth pressured the resource base of the area, and people were forced to eat "third-choice" foods, particularly wild grain, which was difficult to harvest and process but which responded to human efforts to increase yields. The broad-spectrum foraging argument appears to account for plant domestication in the Americas and to some extent in southwestern Asia. However, in Europe, broad-spectrum foraging was so successful that domestication involved other processes (e.g., the transfer of domesticated crops into Europe from southwestern Asia).

A very different theory for the development of domestication was introduced by Barbara Bender (1977), who suggested that before farming began there was competition between local groups to achieve dominance over each other through feasting. According to this theory, there was an increasing expenditure of resources on ritual and exchange, engaging neighbours in a kind of prehistoric feasting extravaganza. To meet the demands for food and other resources, land use was intensified, and the development of food production followed. This argument emphasizes social factors, rather than environmental or technical factors, and takes a localized, regional approach. It is supported by ethnographic accounts concerning competitive exchange activities, such as the traditional *potlatch* ceremonies of the Haida and other Aboriginal peoples from the northwest coast of Canada. These peoples were foragers in a rich environment that enabled them to settle in relatively permanent villages without farming or herding. Competition among neighbouring groups led to ever more elaborate forms of competitive exchange, with increasingly large amounts of food and other goods being given away at each subsequent potlatch. Recently, archaeologists have found increasing evidence of feasting among early farmers. Brian Hayden (et al. 2013), of Simon Fraser University, and others have suggested that plant domestication in both the Americas and in southwestern Asia

was linked to brewing alcoholic drinks (from various plants including maize, grains, and cocoa) for feasts. Analysis of pottery and other vessels from these times reveals plant residues that include chemical signatures indicating alcoholic content. Although this evidence is not definitive, it does support Bender's argument.

Today, archaeologists tend to avoid grand theories that assume domestication occurred in the same way and for the same reasons in all times and places. Many prefer to take a regional approach, searching for causes particular to one area that may or may not apply to other areas. Currently, the most powerful explanations seem to be *multiple-strand theories* that consider the combined local effect of climate, environment, population, technology, social organization, and diet on the emergence of domestication. The multiple-strand approach is well illustrated in an article by McCorriston and Hole (1991), and their work forms the basis for the following case study of domestication in ancient southwestern Asia.

## How Did Domestication, Cultivation, and Sedentism Begin in Southwestern Asia?

Natufian foragers from southwestern Asian are considered to be the first people to have begun domesticating plants and animals for food, about 12,500 years ago. Preceded by the Kebaran, who were a highly mobile group of foragers that relied on the intensive exploitation of wild cereals (notably wild wheat and barley), nuts (especially acorns, pistachios, and almonds), and wild game (especially gazelle and red deer) (Chazan 2014), the Natufians began to establish more permanent settlements and were able to exploit what were, at first, increasingly rich supplies of reliable, year-round resources such as wild cereals, fish, and large herds of gazelle. Although many Natufian sites were small hunting camps, some Natufian villages, or base camps, reached a size of 1000 square metres (about a quarter of an acre) and beyond (Belfer-Cohen 1991, 176–7). Henry (1989, 218) estimates that the Natufian hamlets ranged from 40 to 150 people; they were five to ten times larger than the Kebaran mobile foraging camps that preceded them.

Natufian housing architecture supports the hypotheses that Natufian villages were permanent settlements and not mobile campsites (Map 8.3).

regularly with others who are not closely related to them. In these situations, the production of such objects as personal ornaments helps to create a sense of identity among smaller groups while allowing members of those groups to participate in a larger society (Belfer-Cohen 1988, 1991; Lewis-Williams 1984). Elaborate ritual and ceremonial activities, with the consumption of food and brewed beverages, would also have soothed interactions and reduced tensions in increasingly large communities where co-operation was essential (Hayden et al. 2013, 145).

## Natufian Social Organization

Information about social organization from the archaeological record is indirect, often interpreted from burials and grave goods. However, Donald Henry (1989) believes that over time Natufian society developed social divisions with unequal access to wealth, power, and prestige. That is, Natufian society showed social stratification, an important sign of social complexity. His evidence comes from Natufian burials.

In early Natufian times, the dead were buried together in small groups, which Henry believes corresponded to subgroups of a larger community (e.g., extended family burials). There is skeletal evidence from the Hayonim Cave site that relatives lived in the same area for several generations. Almost half the skeletons recovered from this site showed evidence of the genetically recessive trait *third-molar agenesis* (failure of the third molars, or wisdom teeth, to develop). This trait occurs at much lower frequencies—on the order of 0 to 20 per cent—in other human populations. Evidence from six other Natufian sites revealed the normal frequency of third-molar agenesis, suggesting that the group that lived at Hayonim Cave mated with other members of their own group rather than with outsiders. It seems this mating pattern continued at Hayonim Cave for about 1000 years (Henry 1989, 208). These group burials sometimes included decorative shell headdresses and collars, which were valuable objects with no identifiable practical use (Figure 8.7). In other cases, elaborate grave goods and even dogs were buried

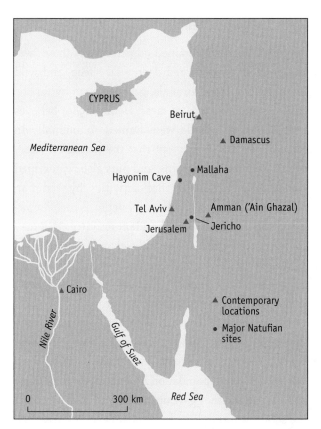

**MAP 8.3 |** Major Natufian sites in the southern Levant in relation to other contemporary features.

Natufian houses were dug partially into the ground and had walls of stone and mud with timber posts and probably roof beams. At the Mallaha site, archaeologists have found houses with plaster-lined storage pits and burials beneath the floors. Archaeologists infer that such buildings, which required a considerable amount of labour and materials to build, were not constructed for brief residence only. Archaeologists have also found massive stone mortars used to grind seeds, which people would not have transported nor invested the time and effort to make if they were going to abandon them after one season's use. In addition, the remains of migratory birds and a great number of young gazelle bones indicate year-round hunting from the hamlets because migratory birds fly over the area during different seasons and young gazelles are born at one time only during the year.

In addition, there was significant artistic production of personal ornaments and headdresses among the Natufians. Anna Belfer-Cohen and others suggest that artistic activity may be viewed as indirect evidence for a sedentary way of life that forces people to interact

**grave goods**  Objects buried with a corpse.

**social stratification**  A form of social organization in which people have unequal access to wealth, power, and prestige.

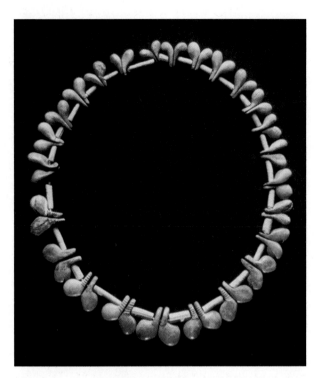

**FIGURE 8.7** | A Natufian collar with 25 fragments of dentalia (a type of shell) separating bone beads. This collar was found in a male burial site.

## Natufian Subsistence

Initially, Natufians obtained 98 per cent of their meat protein from gazelles, red deer, wild sheep, and wild goats. Among these animals, gazelles were by far the most common sources of meat. Henry (1989) believes entire herds of gazelle were hunted communally in game drives and points out that the increased attention to gazelles, wild grains, and nuts also represented specialization of subsistence activities by Natufian foragers (91). They were what we refer to as *complex foragers*, who live in areas of abundant resources that may appear inexhaustible (Price and Gebauer 1995, 7), making them different from *generalized foragers*, who live in less generous environments and cope with shortages by diversifying their subsistence activities.

Unfortunately for the Natufians, because they focused on a few abundant resources, their economy was subject to environmental fluctuations. They fed an increasingly large population by intensively exploiting small areas, and they gave up mobility by settling down. The short-term stability of sedentism and intensive collection made their society less flexible in its ability to respond to environmental change. Around 10,500 years ago, the shallow interior lakes of the southern Levant began drying up, and the Mediterranean woodlands on which the Natufians depended for nuts and other foods was reduced by 50 per cent. As a result, some Natufians returned to simple foraging, developing what archaeologists refer to as the "Harifian culture," while those in the central core of the Natufian area began the process of encouraging cereal plants to grow in areas that were no longer ideal.

The first evidence for domesticated cereals—specifically, wheat and barley—in this core Natufian area dates to approximately 10,300 years ago. For archaeologists, the appearance of domesticated plants signals the beginning of the Neolithic; in the southern Levant, it also signals the appearance of a new culture called the Pre-Pottery Neolithic A (PPNA), whose members cultivated plants but did not use pottery. PPNA sites were much larger than the preceding Natufian settlements, with a surface area of about 2.5 hectares (about 6 acres) and perhaps 300 or more inhabitants (B. Smith 1995a, 3). Henry (1989) suggests that this was due to the concentration of populations from smaller, more numerous hamlets in a setting where "large tracts of arable

with children. Both these burial practices indicate the differentiation of subgroups and inherited status differences. These group burials suggest that in early Natufian times social position depended on which group a person belonged to, rather than on a community-wide set of social standards.

In later times, there were still differences in grave goods from one burial to the next, but the dead were buried individually in cemeteries. This new pattern suggests that the old social organization structures that aligned with extended family groups had been destroyed and replaced by a new pattern in which resources were controlled by an entire community and stratification was community wide. Some people now coordinated activities for the group as a whole and had come to occupy high-status positions that cross-cut subgroup boundaries. For these reasons, Henry suggests that Natufian social organization had come to resemble what is called a "chiefdom" in anthropological literature.

↻ For a discussion of chiefdoms in relation to other forms of social organization, see Chapter 7, p. 178.

Neolithic The "New Stone Age," which began with the domestication of plants 10,300 years ago.

land, suitable for hoe cultivation, adjoined year-round water sources" (53–4).

Jericho, a PPNA site, was located on the edge of an *alluvial fan* (a fan-shaped accumulation of sediment from flowing water at the mouth of a ravine) on a permanent stream, near hills rich in gazelle, wild grains, and nuts. The stream provided clear drinking water, while the alluvial fan provided mud for bricks and its regular floods provided rich soil for plants. By about 9300 years ago, the inhabitants of Jericho had built a stone wall 3 metres thick, 4 metres high, and perhaps 700 metres in circumference (Figure 8.8). The wall was likely erected as protection from the floods, since similar protections from flooding are found at other PPNA sites (Bar-Yosef and Kislev 1989, 635).

Trade was also significant in PPNA Jericho. Obsidian is an extremely sharp and highly prized volcanic glass that is found in relatively few places worldwide (Map 8.4). Anatolia, in modern Turkey, contained the major sites for obsidian in Neolithic southwestern Asia. Archaeologists have found Anatolian obsidian in Jericho, some 700 kilometres from Anatolia; it is unlikely that residents travelled that distance to get it themselves. Jericho also contained marine shells from the Mediterranean Sea and the Black Sea as well as *amulets* (charms against evil or injury) and greenstone beads. These objects suggest not just trade from village to village but also trade between the settled farmers

**FIGURE 8.8** | By about 9300 years ago, the inhabitants of Jericho had built a stone wall, probably to protect the settlement from yearly flooding.

and the foraging peoples living in the semi-arid regions or higher areas.

Beginning about 9500 years ago, the PPNA culture was replaced by the Pre-Pottery Neolithic B (PPNB) culture, which represents the rapid expansion of cultivation. Although there are but a handful of PPNA sites, all

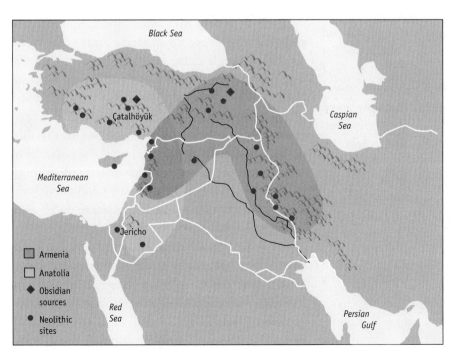

**MAP 8.4** | The distribution of obsidian in Neolithic southwestern Asia from sources in Anatolia (west) and Armenia (east). Obsidian is an extremely sharp and highly prized volcanic glass. It was traded widely in Neolithic times and has been found as far as 800 kilometres away from its source.

in a small area around Jericho, there are more than 140 PPNB sites, many of which are very large and some of which are found in Anatolia and the Zagros Mountains. As the new farming technology moved north and east, it was adapted to fit local circumstances. At some point, farmers met herders from the Zagros Mountains and north Mesopotamia who had domesticated sheep and goats, animals that were well known in their wild state throughout the area. The agriculturalists adopted these herding techniques, which spread quickly and were incorporated into the agricultural life of the entire region. By 8000 years ago, the farmers in southwestern Asia practised a mixed agricultural strategy, incorporating grains and livestock.

Architecture became more sophisticated during the PPNB times, with the construction of buildings that may have been used as temples. At Göbekli Tepe, a site located in modern-day Turkey, structures with impressive carved stone pillars suggest that specialized ritual spaces were becoming part of PPNB people's social practices. Edward Banning (2011), from the University of Toronto, has closely analyzed these structures to determine if they were in fact specialized temples or elaborate houses. His results suggest that they were in fact both—domestic houses with richly symbolic contents and uses.

## Domestication Elsewhere in the World

The conditions under which domestication began, and the times at which it began, varied around the world. In highland Mexico, for example, the pre-domestication population was relatively stable and sedentism had not yet occurred. There are no indications of the kinds of long-term shifts in resource density in Mexico that were characteristic of the eastern Mediterranean. As noted earlier, many scholars agree that broad-spectrum foraging was practised prior to the transition to domestication in the Americas, including Mexico. The mix of crops characteristic of domestication in the Americas also differs from that of the eastern Mediterranean. In Mesoamerica, maize and squash appeared around 6000 years ago, with beans about 2000 years ago. In eastern

Canada, maize appeared around 1500 years ago, while it appeared around 1000 years ago at Head-Smashed-In Buffalo Jump in Alberta. Goosefoot, marsh elder, sunflowers, and squash were also domesticated in eastern North America (B. Smith 1995a, 189–90). In South America, maize appears between 4000 and 3000 years ago but was only one of several domesticates. In other areas of South America, soil conditions, altitude, and climate favoured root crops—manioc or potatoes—as well as beans and quinoa (a high-altitude grain), which were of greater importance. Cocoa and chili, which were domesticated around 4000 years ago, were also important in this region (Powis et al. 2008). Animal domestication was far less important in the Americas than it was in Mesopotamia, largely due to the absence of large, domesticable animals. The Andean llama is the largest animal domesticated in the Americas. Although much smaller, the turkey was domesticated and became a valuable food source in various places across the Americas. Other plants and animals were domesticated outside of the Americas. A variety of crops, including coffee, millet, okra, and sorghum, were domesticated in different parts of Africa. And a large number of important plant domesticates came from eastern Asia, including rice, yam, tea, sugarcane, garlic, onion, apple, and carrot (Map 8.2 and Figure 8.6).

Archaeologists are coming to agree that complex foragers living in areas of relatively abundant resources were probably responsible for domestication wherever it developed (Price and Gebauer 1995, 7; B. Smith 1995a, 213). Rich and complex archaeological and genetic evidence from specific areas of the world downplays single-cause explanations of domestication and stresses the need to consider each domestication event on its own terms. Melinda A. Zeder and Bruce D. Smith (2009) are impressed by abundant and varied data from southwestern Asia showing that during several thousand years prior to the appearance of agriculture, "people appear to have been auditioning a wide variety of region-specific plants and animals for leading roles as domesticated resources in the absence of population increase or resource imbalance" (683).

In the face of such evidence, Zeder and Smith (2009) conclude that "the concept of niche construction provides a useful alternative perspective," emphasizing as it does "the engineering of local ecosystems and the manipulation of targeted resources within local biotic communities" (687). Zeder and Smith insist that humans "were

Mesopotamia    The area made up of the Tigris–Euphrates river system, corresponding to modern-day Iraq, Kuwait, the northeastern section of Syria, and parts of Turkey and Iran. Often referred to as the "cradle of civilization" where early complex societies developed.

actively, and with deliberate intent, shaping adaptive niches with the conscious goal of enhancing the density and productivity of desired resources" (688). Related concerns appear in the work of archaeologists who have adopted from cultural anthropology *theories of practice* that, like niche construction, "examine how humans create macroscale features such as traditions or sociopolitical institutions (structures) through their own daily actions" (Bruno 2009, 703). Bruno (2009) also emphasizes the importance for archaeologists of *historical ecology*, which also "focuses on how long-term, accumulative human activities cause observable changes in the natural environment thus creating a 'landscape'" (704). To the extent that the process of niche construction is understood as a form of practical activity and that engineered environments are understood as the outcomes of such practical activity, both approaches point in the same direction (Schultz 2009). Their incorporation into anthropological theories of cultural transitions such as the origins of agriculture or social complexity promises to shed important new light on these developments.

## What Were the Consequences of Domestication and Sedentism?

Constructed agricultural niches, within which domesticated plants and animals could thrive, promoted sedentism and transformed human life in ways that still have repercussions today. First, land was no longer free, available to anyone; instead, it was transformed into particular territories, collectively or individually owned, on which people raised crops and animals. Thus, sedentism and a high level of resource extraction (whether by complex foraging or farming) resulted in concepts of property ownership and entitlement that were rare in previous foraging societies. Graves, grave goods, permanent housing, grain-processing equipment, and the fields and herds connected people to specific places. The human footprint on the environment became more obvious following sedentization and the rise of farming: people built terraces or walls to hold back floods, transforming the landscape in more dramatic ways. Second, settling down affected female fertility and contributed to a rise in population. In foraging societies, a woman's pregnancies tend to be spaced three to four years apart because of an extended period of breastfeeding. That is, children in foraging societies

are weaned at three or four years of age but still nurse whenever they feel like it, as frequently as several times an hour (Shostak 1981, 67) (Figure 8.9). This nursing stimulus triggers the secretion of a hormone that suppresses ovulation (Henry 1989, 41). Henry (1989, 43) summarizes the effects of foraging on female fertility:

> It would appear then that a number of interrelated factors associated with a mobile foraging strategy are likely to have provided natural controls on fertility and perhaps explain the low population densities of the Paleolithic. In mobile foraging societies, women are likely to have experienced both long intervals of breastfeeding by carried

**FIGURE 8.9** | The Ju/'hoansi's foraging diet lacks soft foods that can be easily digested by infants. Women therefore breastfeed their children for several years, until these children are old enough to chew and digest solids. This practice reduces a woman's chances of getting pregnant again for several years, while at the same time freeing her from having to find and prepare food for her child.

children as well as the high energy drain associated with subsistence activities and periodic camp moves. Additionally, their diets, being relatively rich in proteins, would have contributed to maintaining low fat levels, thus further dampening fecundity.

With complex foraging and increasing sedentism, these brakes on female fecundity would have been eased. This is not to say that a sedentary life is less physically demanding. Farming requires its own heavy labour, from both men and women. The difference seems to be in the kind of physical activity involved. For instance, walking long distances while carrying heavy loads and children was replaced by sowing, hoeing, harvesting, storing, and processing grain. A diet increasingly rich in cereals would have significantly changed the ratio of protein to carbohydrate in the diet. This would have changed the levels of prolactin, increased the positive energy balance, and led to more rapid growth in the young and an earlier age for first menstruation. The ready availability of ground cereals would have enabled mothers to feed their infants soft, high-carbohydrate porridges and gruels. The analysis of infant fecal material recovered from the Wadi Kubbaniya site in Egypt seems to demonstrate that a similar practice was in use with root crops along the Nile at what may have been a year-round site by 19,000 years before the present (Hillman 1989, 230).

The influence of cereals on fertility has been observed by Richard Lee (1992) among settled Ju/'hoansi, who somewhat recently began to eat cereals and experienced a marked rise in fertility. Renee Pennington (1992) notes that the increase in Ju/'hoansi reproductive success also seems to be related to a reduction in infant and child mortality rates. But diets based on high-carbohydrate grains are less nutritious than the diets of hunters and gatherers. Skeletons from Greece and Turkey in late Paleolithic times indicate an average height of 5 feet 9 inches (1.75 metres) for men and 5 feet 5 inches (1.65 metres) for women. With the adoption of agriculture, the average height declined sharply; by about 5000 years ago, the average man was about 5 feet 3 inches (1.60 metres) tall, and the average woman was about 5 feet (1.52 metres) tall. Even modern Greeks and Turks

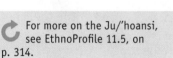

For more on the Ju/'hoansi, see EthnoProfile 11.5, on p. 314.

are still not, on average, as tall as the late Paleolithic people of the same region.

In the short term, agriculture was probably developed in ancient southwestern Asia, and perhaps elsewhere, to increase food supplies to support an increasing population at a time of serious resource stress. Because the agroecology created an environment favourable to the domesticated plants, farmers were able to cultivate previously unusable land. When such vital necessities as water could be brought to the land between the Tigris and Euphrates rivers in Mesopotamia, for example, land on which wheat and barley were not native could support dense stands of the domesticated grains. The greater yield of domesticated plants per unit of ground also led to a greater proportion of cultivated plants in the diet, even when wild plants were still being eaten and were as plentiful as before. But as cultivated plants took on an increasingly large role in prehistoric diets, people became dependent on plants and the plants in turn became completely dependent on the agroecology created by the people. According to Richard Lee (1992, 48), the Ju/'hoansi, who live in the Kalahari Desert, use more than 100 plants (14 fruits and nuts, 15 berries, 18 species of edible gum, 41 edible roots and bulbs, and 17 leafy greens, beans, melons, and other foods). By contrast, modern farmers rely on far fewer plants, and of those, only three—wheat, maize, and rice—feed most of the world's people. Historically, only one or two grain crops were staples for a specific group of people. If hail, floods, droughts, infestations, frost, heat, weeds, erosion, or other factors destroyed the crop or reduced the harvest, the risk of starvation increased. Deforestation, soil loss, silted streams, and the loss of many native species followed domestication. In the lower Tigris–Euphrates Valley, irrigation water used by early farmers carried high levels of soluble salts, poisoning the soil and making it unusable to this day (Figure 8.10).

New features of the agroecology also created new opportunities for the spread of diseases like malaria and tuberculosis. As increasing numbers of people began to live near each other in relatively permanent settlements, the disposal of human (and eventually animal) waste also became increasingly problematic. Food storage was a key element in agroecological niches, but stored grains attracted pests, like rats and mice, which coevolved with the domesticated crops that attracted them (Figure 8.11). Some of these pests also spread disease-causing microorganisms that thrived in human, animal, and plant

**FIGURE 8.10** | The lower Tigris-Euphrates Valley; irrigation water used by early farmers carried high levels of soluble salts, poisoning the soil and making it unusable to this day.

people's resistance to disease. Foragers could just walk away from disease, reducing the likelihood that it would spread; but this option is closed for settled people. Thus, increased exposure to epidemic disease was a major consequence of the modified selection pressures to which human populations became vulnerable as a consequence of their ancestors' construction of agroecological niches.

Maintaining an agroecology that supported domesticated plants and animals required much more labour than did foraging. People had to clear the land, plant the seeds, tend the young plants, protect them from predators, harvest them, process the seeds, store them, and select the seeds for planting the next year; similarly, people had to tend and protect domesticated animals, cull the herds, shear the sheep, milk the goats, and so on. This heavy workload was not divided up equally among members of the population. Increasing dependence on agriculture produced an increasingly complex division of labour, which set the stage for the emergence of complex hierarchical societies with different forms of social inequality.

Insight into the processes producing these changes is offered by economic anthropologist Rhoda Halperin (1994). Borrowing concepts from economic historian Karl Polanyi, Halperin argues that every economic system can be analyzed in terms of two kinds of movements: *locational movements*, or "changes of place," and *appropriational movements*, or "changes of hands." In her view, ecological relationships that affect the economy are properly understood as changes of place, as when people must move into the grasslands, gather mongongo nuts, and transport them back to camp. Economic relationships, by contrast, are more properly understood as

wastes. The larger the number of people living very near each other, the greater the likelihood of communicable disease transmission: by the time one person recovers from the disease, someone else reaches the infectious stage and can re-infect the first; as a result, the disease never leaves the population. Finally, the nutritional deficiencies of an agricultural diet may have reduced

**FIGURE 8.11** | A major challenge for societies that rely on food storage is preventing the stored food from attracting pests such as rats and mice. A common solution to this problem—illustrated by the design of this *stabbur*, or food-storage cabin, in Norway—has been to raise food-storage facilities high off the ground, where rodents cannot easily access them.

changes of hands, as when mongongo nuts are distributed to all members of the camp, whether or not they helped to gather them. Thus, ecological (locational) movements involve transfers of energy; economic (appropriational) movements, by contrast, involve transfers of rights (Halperin 1994, 59). Analyzed in this way, people's rights to consume mongongo nuts cannot be derived from the labour they expended to gather them.

Another way of seeing the difference is to pay attention to the connection between food storage and food sharing. An ecologist might argue that those who gather mongongo nuts have no choice but to share them and consume them immediately because they have no way to store this food if it is not eaten. Anthropologist Tim Ingold (1983) agreed that the obligation to share would make storage unnecessary, but he also pointed out that sharing with others today ordinarily obligates them to share with you tomorrow. Put another way, sharing food can be seen not only as a way of avoiding spoilage but also as a way of storing up IOUs for the future.

Once societies develop ways to preserve and store food and other material goods, however, new possibilities open up. Archaeological evidence indicates that the more food there is to store, the more people invest in storage facilities (e.g., pits, pottery vessels) and the more quickly they become sedentary. Large-scale food-storage techniques involve a series of "changes of place" that buffer a population from ecological fluctuations for long periods of time. But techniques of food storage alone predict nothing about the "changes of hands" that food will undergo once it has been stored. Food-storage techniques have been associated with all subsistence strategies, including that of complex food collectors. This suggests that economic relations of consumption, involving the transfer of rights in stored food, have long been open to considerable cultural elaboration and manipulation (Halperin 1994, 178).

When people initially cultivated plants, they could not have anticipated all of the challenges that this process would create. Initially, agriculture had several apparent advantages, the foremost of which was that farmers could extract far more food from the same amount of land than could foragers. Put another way, to feed the same number of people, a dry farmer needs

20 times less land than a forager and an irrigation farmer needs 100 times less land (Figure 8.12). Foragers know that they will find enough food to eat, but they never know how much of any given food resource they will find or exactly when or where they will find it. By contrast, farmers can predict, with a given amount of seed—and favourable conditions—the approximate size of a harvest. Herders can predict how many lambs they will have in the spring based on the number of rams and ewes in their herds. Sedentism and a fairly reliable and predictable domesticated food supply provided new opportunities for social complexity.

## How Do Anthropologists Define Social Complexity?

Early Neolithic farming and herding societies differed little from the foraging societies they replaced. For the Natufians, foraging continued to be important alongside cultivation for many generations. In the same way, the social organization of these societies differed little from that of foraging societies; although people began to settle in permanent villages, archaeological evidence suggests that no great differences in wealth, power, or prestige divided villagers initially. Put another way, these early farming villages continued to practice egalitarian social relations. Things began to change, however, beginning about 5000 years ago in southwestern Asia and shortly thereafter in Egypt, the Indus Valley (India), China, Mesoamerica (the Valley of Mexico), and the Andes (Peru) (see Map 8.1). These six regions of the globe were the first

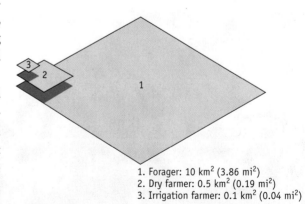

1. Forager: 10 km² (3.86 mi²)
2. Dry farmer: 0.5 km² (0.19 mi²)
3. Irrigation farmer: 0.1 km² (0.04 mi²)

**FIGURE 8.12** | Each square shows the proportionate amount of land needed to feed a single individual using three different food-getting strategies: foraging, dry farming, and irrigation farming.

egalitarian social relations  Social relations in which no great differences in wealth, power, or prestige divide members from one another.

## *In Their Own Words*

## The Food Revolution

*Although dietary quality declined for the earliest full-time farmers, later contact and trade among different farming societies enriched diets everywhere. Over the past 500 years, as Jack Weatherford emphasizes, foods domesticated in the New World have played a particularly important role in the "food revolution."*

On Thanksgiving Day North Americans sometimes remember the Indians who gave them their cuisine by dining upon turkey with cornbread stuffing, cranberry sauce, succotash, corn on the cob, sweet potato casserole, stewed squash and tomatoes, baked beans with maple syrup, and pecan pie. Few cooks or gourmets, however, recognize the much broader extent to which American Indian cuisine radically changed cooking and dining in every part of the globe from Timbuktu to Tibet. Sichuan beef with chilies, German chocolate cake, curried potatoes, vanilla ice cream, Hungarian goulash, peanut brittle, and pizza all owe their primary flavourings to the American Indians.

The discovery of America sparked a revolution in food and cuisine that has not yet shown any signs of abating.

Tomatoes, chilies, and green peppers formed the first wave of American flavourings to circle the globe, but the American Indian garden still grows a host of plants that the world may yet learn to use and enjoy. These plants may have practical uses, such as providing food in otherwise unusable land or producing more food in underused land. They also vary the daily diets of people throughout the world and thereby increase nutrition. Even in this high-tech age, the low-tech plant continues to be the key to nutrition and health. Despite all the plant improvements brought about by modern science, the American Indians remain the developers of the world's largest array of nutritious foods and the primary contributors to the world's varied cuisines.

Source: Weatherford 1988, 115.

---

to independently develop a new way of organizing society called *social stratification*, based on the assumption that different groups in society were entitled to different amounts of wealth, power, and prestige.

A move from egalitarian forms of social organization to social stratification involves the development of social complexity. Social stratification was made possible when societies produced amounts of food that exceeded the basic subsistence needs of the population. Storage of excess food resulting from surplus production and control over its distribution made it possible for some members of a society to stop producing food altogether and to specialize in various occupations (e.g., weaving, pot making) or in new social roles (e.g., warrior, priest). In some cases, occupational specialization also created a wide gulf between most members of a society and members of a more prestigious social class of rulers who successfully claimed the bulk of this new surplus as their own. Societies organized in this way could support many more people than could the egalitarian societies that preceded them, not only because they successfully produced, stored, and distributed more food

but also because they invented new ways of compelling people to carry out many new tasks. As a result, anthropologists refer to these as the first complex societies to appear in the archaeological record.

## Why Is It Incorrect to Describe Foraging Societies as "Simple?"?

Although the concept of a complex society seems straightforward enough, anthropologists must define this expression carefully to avoid misunderstanding.

**surplus production** The production of amounts of food that exceed the basic subsistence needs of the population.

**occupational specialization** Specialization in various occupations (e.g., weaving or pot making) or in new social roles (e.g., king or priest) that is found in socially complex societies.

**class** A ranked group within a hierarchically stratified society whose membership is defined primarily in terms of wealth, occupation, or other economic criteria.

**complex societies** Societies with large populations, an extensive division of labour, and occupational specialization.

It is common to assume that the opposite of *complex* is *simple*, yet foraging and farming societies are not "simple" societies. In order to survive, foragers had to file away in their minds an enormously complex amount of information about different varieties of plants, seasonal habits of animals, details of kinship, and nuances of their religion and art. It was the comparatively simple technology of foragers—based on wood, stone, and bone tools that could be easily made by everyone—that was very different from the more complex technology that had to be developed and mastered in order to build massive pyramids, weave cloth, or smelt and mold metals such as copper, tin, and iron. These activities not only required highly specialized knowledge of architecture, textiles, and metallurgy but also presupposed a form of social organization that permitted some members of society to become highly specialized in certain activities while other members carried out different tasks.

Differences in technology and social organization say nothing about the complexity of the minds of the people involved. However, such differences strongly shaped the scale and texture of life in the two kinds of society. Setting up camp in a foraging society involved fewer decisions, in terms of technology and social organization, than did the construction of a pyramid. Pyramid building required more than architectural skill; suitable materials had to be found, quarried, or produced and transported to the site. Additionally, suitable workers had to be found, trained, supervised, fed, and lodged for the duration of construction, which may have taken decades. Finally, all these specialized activities had to occur in the right order for the project to be successfully completed. Not only would a foraging band—some fifty individuals of all ages—have been too small to carry out such a project, but their traditional egalitarian social relations also would have made the giving and taking of orders impossible. Indeed, the whole idea of building massive pyramids would have probably seemed pointless to them.

A society that not only wants to build pyramids but also has the material, political, and social means to do so is clearly different from a foraging band or a Neolithic farming village. For archaeologist T. Douglas Price (1995, 140), a complex society has "more parts

monumental architecture   Architectural constructions of a greater-than-human scale, such as pyramids, temples, and tombs.

and more connections between parts." Anthropologist Leslie White (1949) spoke in terms of a major change in the amount of energy a society can capture from nature and use to remodel the natural world to suit its own purposes. The members of foraging bands also depended on energy captured from the natural world but on a scale vastly smaller than that required to build pyramids. Archaeologist Robert Wenke (1999, 348) emphasizes that, in complex societies, "the important thing is that the ability and incentive to make these investments are radically different from the capacities of Pleistocene bands, in that they imply the ability of some members of society to control and organize others."

## What Is the Archaeological Evidence for Social Complexity?

How do archaeologists recognize social and cultural complexity when they see it? Important clues are certain kinds of remains that begin to appear in the archaeological record after about 5000 years ago. Among the most widespread indicators of social complexity are the remains of monumental architecture. Contemporary monumental architecture includes such structures as the Eiffel Tower in Paris, France; West Edmonton Mall in Alberta; and the Petronas Towers in Kuala Lumpur, Malaysia (Figure 8.13). Ancient monumental architecture included public buildings, private residences, tombs, settlement walls, irrigation canals, and so on. Together with monumental architecture, however, archaeologists usually find evidence of technologically simpler constructions. Assemblages that demonstrate such architectural variability contrast with those from earlier periods, when dwellings were simpler and more uniform and monumental structures were absent.

Most of the earliest monumental architecture consisted of raised platforms, temples, pyramids, or pyramid-like structures (Figure 8.14). Different building techniques were used to construct these monuments in different areas, and the structures did not all serve the same purposes. In all cases, builders were limited by the types of materials and technologies to which they had access. In places like the Maya lowlands in modern Central America, builders had to work without metal, winches, hoists, or wheeled carts. Under these circumstances, the only tall structures they could have built were such basic geometric forms as squares, rectangles, and pyramids (Wenke 1999, 577).

Among the monumental structures built in the earliest complex societies were tombs. Differences in the size and construction of burials closely align with differences in the size and construction of residences, and both suggest the emergence of a stratified society. Graves that are larger and built of more costly materials often contain a variety of grave goods that were buried with the corpse. The occurrence of smaller, more modest graves, often with few or no grave goods, in the same place and time provides evidence for social stratification. The number and quality of grave goods found with a corpse give clues regarding the wealth and status of the buried individual. Many of the grave goods recovered from rich tombs are masterpieces of ceramics, metallurgy, weaving, and other crafts, indicating that the society had achieved a high degree of technological skill and, thus, a complex division of labour. In some cases, ritual burials of animals, either alongside people or on their own, offer evidence of the highly stratified nature of a society. For example, Haskel Greenfield, of the University of Manitoba, and his colleagues (2012) have found evidence connecting the ritual burial of a domesticated ass—an animal that likely played an important role in manual labour and trade—to the existence of a "commoner neighbourhood" on the outskirts of a city in the Levant.

Evidence of complex occupational specializations is found when there are **concentrations of particular artifacts** in specific areas of a site. For example, broken

FIGURE 8.13 | Monumental modern architecture: the Petronas Towers dwarf the surrounding city of Kuala Lumpur, Malaysia.

**concentrations of particular artifacts** Sets of artifacts indicating that particular social activities took place at a particular area in an archaeological site when that site was inhabited in the past.

FIGURE 8.14 | Among the most widespread indicators of early social complexity are the remains of monumental architecture, such as the Temple of the Great Jaguar at the Mayan site of Tikal, Guatemala.

pots or kilns found evenly distributed throughout a settlement might suggest that pottery was made by individual families. However, considerable evidence of pottery manufacture concentrated within a particular area strongly suggests the existence of a potter's workshop and, thus, occupational specialization. Remains of the tools and materials used to make artifacts—potter's wheels, spindle whorls, or iron slag, for example—often provide important information about the degree to which craft technology developed at a particular time and place.

The emergence of complex societies seems connected with a phenomenal explosion of architectural and artistic creativity. Although anthropologists admire the material achievements of these ancient societies, many are struck by the "wasteful" expenditure of resources by a tiny ruling elite. Why, for example, did virtually every original complex society build monumental architecture? Why did they not invest their increasing technological and organizational power in less elaborate projects that might have benefitted the ordinary members of society? Why were masterpieces of pottery, metallurgy, and weaving often hoarded and buried in the tombs of dead rulers instead of being more widely available? Archaeologist Michael Hoffman, an expert on prehistoric Egypt, proposed that the key to understanding the first complex societies lies in their social organization. For the first time in human history, tremendous power was concentrated in the hands of a tiny elite—who undoubtedly found their privileges challenged by their new subjects. Under such circumstances, the production of monumental architecture and quantities of luxury goods served as evidence of the elite's fitness to rule. Hoffman (1991, 294) prefers to call these objects "powerfacts" rather than "artifacts" because their role was to demonstrate the superior power of the rulers (see also Hayden 1995, 67) (Figure 8.15).

So far, we have described the kinds of archaeological remains that suggest that a site was once part of a complex society. But complex societies ordinarily consisted of a number of settlements organized in a hierarchy, usually based on the size of the settlement and/or the presence of monumental architecture. For example, today this hierarchy would be represented in ascending order by hamlets, villages, towns, and cities. To establish the presence of different types of

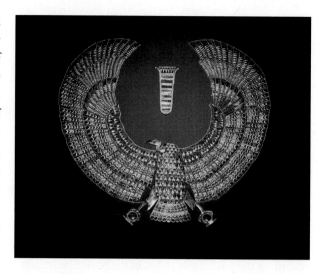

**FIGURE 8.15** | A "powerfact" from the tomb of Tutankhamun, a fourteenth-century BCE Egyptian pharaoh. A collar found around the neck of Tutankhamun's mummy is composed of gold, coloured glass, and obsidian. There are 250 inlaid segments, and each claw is grasping a *shen*, a symbol of totality.

sites, archaeologists must survey the region to determine how any given site compares to other settlements occupied at the same time in the same area. When the survey is completed, archaeologists tabulate and map the different kinds of sites in an area and create a series of maps showing the changes in settlement size and population over time. Systematic survey and mapping work in southern Iraq permitted Robert Adams and Hans Nissen to show how the small, scattered settlements that prevailed in the countryside of ancient Mesopotamia around 8000 years ago were gradually abandoned over the centuries, such that by about 5200 years ago virtually everyone was living in a handful of large settlements, which Adams and Nissen (1972) call "cities."

## Why Did Stratification Begin?

Until approximately 10,000 years ago, when the last ice sheets retreated, all of our ancestors lived as foragers in *band*-type social organizations. Following this, those who came to farm or herd for a living were able to support larger populations and are classified as *tribes* or, as some archaeologists refer to them, *transegalitarian societies* (Hayden 1995, 18). Seemingly poised between equality and hierarchy, transegalitarian societies have flourished at various times and places up to the present day. The *chiefdom* is an example—indeed, the earliest clear example—of a socially stratified society, beginning with the Natufians. Ordinarily in a chiefdom, only the chief and close relatives are set apart and allowed privileged access to wealth, power, and prestige; other members of the society continue to share roughly similar social status. Chiefdoms are generally larger than tribes and show a greater degree of craft production, although such production is not yet in the hands of full-time specialists. Chiefdoms also exhibit a greater degree of hierarchical political control, centred on the chief, relatives of the chief, and their great deeds. Archaeologically, chiefdoms are interesting because some, such as the southern Natufians, apparently remained as they were and then disappeared, whereas others went on to develop into states.

Descriptions of the categories anthropologists use to classify forms of human societies can be found in Chapter 7, on pp. 176–9.

The *state* is a stratified society that possesses a territory that is defended from outside enemies with an army and from internal disorder with police. States, which have separate governmental institutions to enforce laws and to collect taxes and tribute, are run by an elite that possesses a monopoly on the use of force. In early states, government and religion were mutually reinforcing: rulers were often priests or were thought to be gods. State societies are supported by sophisticated food-production and food-storage techniques. Craft production is normally specialized and yields a dazzling variety of goods, many of which are refined specialty items destined for the ruling elite. Art and architecture also flourish, and writing frequently has developed in state societies. Shortly after the appearance of the first state in an area, other states usually develop nearby. From time to time, one might conquer its neighbours, organizing them into a vaster political network called an *empire*.

Monumental public buildings of a religious or governmental nature, highly developed crafts (e.g., pottery, weaving, and metallurgy), and regional settlement patterns that show at least three levels in a hierarchy of social complexity are all archaeological evidence of a state. Interstate conflict is suspected when towns and cities are surrounded by high walls and confirmed by artifacts that served as weapons, by art depicting battle, and by written documents that record military triumphs. Because writing developed in most of the early states, various inscriptions often provide valuable information on social organization that supplements the archaeologist's reconstructions.

Archaeologists assume regional integration when they find unique styles in architecture, pottery, textiles, and other artifacts distributed uniformly over a wide area; such evidence is called a *cultural horizon*. For archaeologists, the term *civilization* usually refers to the flowering of cultural creativity that accompanies the rise of state societies and persists for a long time. Widespread uniformity in material culture, however, need not imply a single set of political institutions. Archaeologists who wish to speak of a state or an empire, therefore, require additional evidence, such as a hierarchy of settlement patterns or written records that spell out centralized governmental policies. Cultural change in all early complex societies tended to alternate between periods of relative cultural uniformity and political unity and periods of regional differentiation and lack of political integration.

We should note that the preceding categories and the framework for cross-cultural comparison that they provide have been critiqued in recent decades. Post-processual archaeologists like Shanks and Tilley (1987), for example, argue that traditional comparisons of ancient "state" societies pay too much attention to environmental and technological similarities while ignoring or dismissing the significance of the distinct cultural patterns of meanings and values that made each of these ancient civilizations unique. Other archaeologists, however, maintain that the similarities among ancient civilizations are just as striking as the cultural differences among those civilizations and require explanation (Trigger 1993). While this debate continues, many archaeologists have tried to strike a balance, acknowledging the overall descriptive value of a formal category like "state" but carrying out research projects that highlight the cultural variation to be found among societies grouped together as "states" (Wenke 1999, 346).

## How Can Anthropologists Explain the Rise of Complex Societies?

Given that humans lived in foraging bands for most of their history and that, in some parts of the world, village farming remained a stable, viable way of life for hundreds or thousands of years, it is not obvious why complex societies should ever have developed at all. Over the years, anthropologists have proposed a number of explanations. Some of their hypotheses (like some designed to explain our ancestors' turn to domestication or sedentism) argue for a single, uniform cause, or prime mover, that triggered the evolution of complex society worldwide. Indeed, as we will see, many of these prime movers are the same factors suggested to explain the development of domestication and sedentism.

For a long time, scholars thought that the domestication of plants and sedentary life in farming villages offered people the leisure time to invent social and technological complexity. This explanation is questionable, however, because many farming societies never developed beyond the village level of organization. In addition, social complexity apparently can develop without the support of a fully agricultural economy, as among the Natufians. Finally, ethnographic research has shown that foraging people actually have more leisure time than most village farmers do.

Other scholars suggest that social complexity depended on arid or semiarid environments (Figure 8.16). The first complex societies in Egypt, Mesopotamia, and the Indus Valley were located in dry regions crossed by a major river, which provided water for intensified agricultural production following the construction of irrigation canals. The apparent connection between farming in an arid environment, the need for irrigation

water, and the rise of complex societies led Karl Wittfogel (1957) to hypothesize that complex societies first developed in order to construct and maintain large irrigation systems. Wittfogel argued that these irrigation systems could not have functioned without a ruling elite to direct operations. Thus, he sees the development of what he calls *hydraulic agriculture* as the key to the evolution of complex society. This hypothesis, although suggestive, has also been called into question. First, societies such as the Hohokam of the American southwest apparently operated an extensive irrigation system without developing social stratification or cultural complexity (Wenke 1999, 356). Second, the sorts of complex irrigation systems Wittfogel had in mind—those requiring a bureaucracy—appear late in the archaeological record of several early civilizations, long after the first appearance of monumental architecture, cities, and other signs of social complexity (see, e.g., Adams 1981, 53). Irrigation may have played a role in the development of complex societies, but it was apparently not the single prime mover that brought them into existence.

Because many early groups of village farmers never developed a high degree of social complexity, archaeologists see its appearance more as the exception, not the rule. Some suggest that population pressure was the decisive force: if the food supply could not keep up with a growing population, social chaos would have resulted unless someone were able to exercise power to allocate resources and keep the peace. This scenario is rejected,

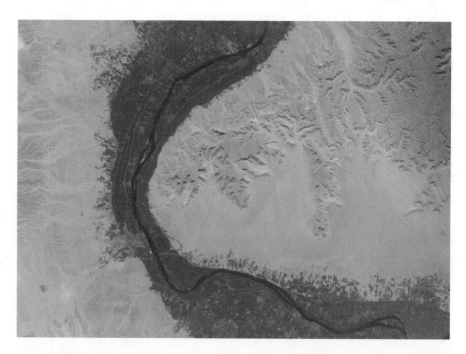

**FIGURE 8.16** | The civilization of ancient Egypt was supported by agricultural practices that relied on the regular flooding pattern of the Nile River. In this photograph taken from a space shuttle, the wide, dark band crossing the light desert region is the cultivated floodplain of the Nile. The river itself is the very dark, narrow line snaking its way through this cultivated area.

however, by those who argue that social inequality developed in societies where resources were abundant and opportunistic individuals could gain power by using surpluses to indebt others to them through competitive feasting or control of labour (Arnold 1995; Hayden et al. 2013). Also, archaeological evidence from more than one part of the world shows that population pressure was not a problem when social complexity first appeared. Some archaeologists now suggest that human societies were able to limit population growth if they chose to do so, whether by migration, infanticide, abortion, contraception, or late marriage. Finally, the greatest decline in fertility in the modern Western world did not occur among the hungry, nor was it triggered by the invention of new birth-control technology: it was the well-fed, middle-class families, not the poverty-stricken workers, who began to have fewer children in capitalist societies. The forces that change reproductive rates are far more complex than a simple population-pressure model would allow.

If population pressure did not undermine the egalitarian social relations of village farmers, perhaps conflict with other villagers was to blame. If all available farmland were settled, for example, making it impossible for people to move away at times of conflict, the only solution, apart from chaos, would have been to establish rules to resolve conflicts, thus leading to the development of more complex political structures (Nissen 1988, 60–1). Sooner or later, however, if chaos could not be contained, warfare might have broken out between neighbouring villages. Indeed, Brian Hayden (1995) suggests that power-seeking individuals might well have manipulated such tensions, using economic surpluses to settle conflicts and amassing personal wealth and power in the process. This could not occur, in his view, until people became willing to accept **bloodwealth**, a crucial innovation not found in egalitarian societies (Hayden 1995, 32). Bloodwealth is economic surplus paid by perpetrators to compensate their victims for their loss. If bloodwealth payments disproportionately favoured some individuals or groups over others, their social relations would no longer be egalitarian.

Warfare, population pressure, and arid environments all play roles in Robert Carneiro's (1970) theory of the rise of the first states in Peru, Mesopotamia, and Egypt and of later, secondary states elsewhere. In Carneiro's scheme, population pressure would have led to increasing conflict between neighbouring villages once it was no longer possible for villagers to cultivate

new lands. This situation, which he calls *environmental circumscription*, might have been especially likely in early farming societies that grew up along river valleys running through deserts, such as those in Mesopotamia, Egypt, and coastal Peru. When the desert barrier halted village expansion, new farmlands could be obtained only by taking them away from other villages by force. Carneiro's theory has stimulated much discussion. However, the role he assigns to population pressure is open to the criticism raised earlier, and many archaeologists still have not found evidence that would confirm or refute Carneiro's hypotheses.

Clearly, any force that could destroy the egalitarian relations that prevailed in farming societies for hundreds or thousands of years would have had to be very powerful. In this connection, David Webster (1975) suggested that the turning point came in farming societies that were chiefdoms. You will recall that chiefdoms possess a limited form of social stratification that sets the chiefly line above other members of society, who continue to enjoy social equality reinforced by kinship. If warfare in such a society undermined the old relations of kinship, people might eventually be desperate for social order and accept social stratification if that restored stability.

All the prime movers discussed so far involve technological, economic, environmental, or biological factors that would have forced societies into complexity no matter what their previous cultural traditions might have been. Realizing that these external factors were less powerful than once believed, many anthropologists turned their attention to internal, sociocultural factors that might have led to the rise of social complexity: recall Barbara Bender's theory about the origin of domestication, which has inspired Brian Hayden (1981), among others. During the 1960s and 1970s, some anthropologists were influenced by the work of Karl Marx and his followers, who argued that attempts to resolve contradictions that develop within a particular form of social organization can lead to profound social change. Marxian analysis might suggest, for example, that external trade in luxury items by the leaders of early chiefdoms may have generated conflict between the chief's family (whose interests were served by trade)

**bloodwealth** Material goods paid by perpetrators to compensate their victims for their loss.

and the common people (whose interests were undermined by it) (Kipp and Schortman 1989). Such a conflict of interests might eventually have thrown a chiefdom completely out of equilibrium, leading to the kind of social transformation suggested by Webster (1975).

Written documents, when available, can sometimes provide enough detailed insight into social organization to identify social hierarchies and trace their development over time. But for ancient complex societies that lacked writing—and this includes all six of the first such societies—the Marxian approach is exceedingly difficult to apply to archaeological materials. Many of the remains of the earliest complex societies are incomplete and could be compatible with more than one form of social organization. Indeed, any theory, Marxian or not, that seeks to explain the rise of a complex society in terms of social relations, political culture, or religious beliefs faces the same problem. However important they may have been, such phenomena do not fossilize and cannot be reliably inferred on the basis of archaeological data alone, an uncomfortable fact that continues to frustrate archaeologists trying to reconstruct prehistory.

Anthropologists cannot offer a single, sweeping explanation of cultural evolution, although this was their hope at the end of the nineteenth century. But their attempts to test various hypotheses that promise such explanations have led to a far richer appreciation of the complexities of social and cultural change. Archaeologist Robert Wenke observes that "cultural evolution is not a continuous, cumulative, gradual change in most places. 'Fits and starts' better

describes it" (1999, 336). He further emphasizes the remarkable adaptability of cultural systems, noting in a discussion of Mesoamerica that environmental and ecological analyses can only explain so much: "once we get beyond this simple ecological level of analysis, we encounter a welter of variability in sociopolitical forms, economic histories, settlement patterns, and the other elaborations of these complex societies" (609). The rest of this chapter offers a sample of some of this variability, examining evidence bearing on the rise of the first complex societies in South America.

## Andean Civilization

The Andean region of South America gave birth to a rich, complex, and varied civilization that culminated in the Inka Empire, the largest political system to develop in the New World before the arrival of Europeans. The very richness and complexity of this civilization, however, coupled with insufficient funding for archaeological research, has meant that only the barest outlines of its development can be traced (Table 8.1).

The geography of the Andes is distinctive and had an important influence on the development of local complex societies. This is a region of young, steep-sided mountains and volcanoes. Along the Pacific can be found deserts on which rain has not fallen for centuries as well as a narrow, lowland coastal strip covered with lush greenery that is supported not by rain but by fog rising from the ocean. This is the zone of the *lomas*, or fog meadows, which is crossed by over two dozen short

**TABLE 8.1** | Cultural Periods of Andean Civilization

| Time Scale | Selected Culture | | | Period/Horizon |
|---|---|---|---|---|
| 1500 CE | Inka | | | Late Horizon |
| 1250 CE | Chimú | | | Late Intermediate period |
| 1000 CE | | | | |
| 750 CE | | Wari | Tiwanaku | Middle Horizon |
| 500 CE | | | | |
| 500 BCE | Moche | | | Early Intermediate period |
| 1000 BCE | | Chavín | | Early Horizon |
| 2000 BCE | | | | Initial period |
| 4000 BCE | | | | Preceramic period |
| 6000 BCE | | | | |
| 8000 BCE | Paijan | | | |
| 10,000 BCE | | Luz | | Lithic Period |

rivers flowing from the highlands. The western edge of the loma lowlands rises abruptly through several climatic zones to the highlands, or *sierra*, of the Andes Mountains. Rolling grassland areas at an elevation of between 3900 and 5000 metres form a zone called the *puna*, the highest level suitable for human habitation. Finally, the eastern slopes of the Andes descend into the humid tropical forests of the Amazon headwaters, a zone called the *selva*. In recent years, mounting evidence suggests that farming cultures in the tropical forest contributed many of the domesticated plants that later became indispensable to Andean agriculture (Chauchat 1988; Raymond 1988; Rick 1988).

The presence of humans in South America before 15,000 years ago is still being debated, but bands of foragers were definitely living along the Peruvian coast between 14,000 and 8000 years ago and in the sierra between 11,000 and 10,000 years ago. Lowland groups took advantage of the unique upswelling of the cold coastal current—which kept nutrients for ocean-dwelling organisms close to the surface—to exploit a bounty of marine food resources. Between about 5000 and 4000 years ago, quinoa, guinea pigs, potatoes, and camelids (llamas and alpacas) were domesticated in the highlands. Neither the coastal foragers nor the earliest highland farmers made pottery, however. By 3200 years ago, the first maize appears on the Ecuadorian coast (B. Smith 1995a, 157, 181).

On the Peruvian coast, between 5000 and 4500 years ago, villagers began to construct multi-roomed buildings, which were later filled in to form pyramid-shaped mounds. Complexes of platforms, pyramids, and raised enclosures first appeared after 4000 years ago at sites like El Paraiso on the coast and Kotosh in the highlands. There is evidence that the early coastal mound builders were not farmers but villagers who relied on food from the sea. Possibly the first mound builders in the highlands were not farmers either, but highland settlements soon became dependent on the cultivation of maize and other crops. Between 3800 and 2900 years ago, the number of sites with monumental architecture increased in the coastal valleys, as did the proportion of cultivated plants in the coastal diet, which suggests that irrigation agriculture had become important in coastal economies. There is also evidence of increasing contact between coastal and highland settlements during this period: the *U*-shaped plan of coastal ceremonial sites began to appear in the highlands, while llamas became

important, economically and ritually, on the coast (Pineda 1988).

These early developments toward social complexity appeared among peoples with distinct cultural traditions. However, between 2900 and 2200 years ago, a single cultural tradition with its own styles of art, architecture, and pottery spread rapidly throughout central and northern Peru. This phenomenon is called the Chavín Horizon, and the period in which it occurred is usually called the Early Horizon because this was the first time in Andean history that so many local communities had adopted a single cultural tradition (Figure 8.17). Much is obscure about the Chavín period. It does not seem that Chavín culture spread by conquest, nor did it totally replace the local traditions of those who adopted it; but its appearance was accompanied by a new level of social and economic interaction between previously isolated local societies.

**FIGURE 8.17** | Chavín culture spread widely during the Early Horizon in Peru (900–200 BCE). The monumental sculpture shown here is the Lanzón in the Old Temple at the ceremonial complex of Chavín de Huantar.

Most experts agree that the spread of Chavín culture was connected with the spread of a religious ideology, sometimes called the Chavín cult. Richard Berger (1988) suggests that this may have been a regional cult that was voluntarily adopted by a number of different ethnic groups, perhaps a forerunner of the cult of Pachacamac that flourished in sixteenth-century Peru. The Chavín cult got its name from the highland ceremonial centre Chavín de Huantar, which was important toward the end of the Early Horizon. The flowering of pottery, metallurgy, and textile production that marks the Chavín Horizon may have been encouraged by a religious elite eager to enhance its status among its new followers.

The Chavín cult and the regional integration that went with it fell apart after 2200 years ago. Although this development led to the reemergence of village life in some regions, complex society did not collapse everywhere. During the Early Intermediate period (200 BCE–600 CE), separate cultural groups followed their own paths. On the coast, over a dozen new regional states appeared, but only a few are well known archaeologically. The Moche state, for example, encompassed several river valleys on the north coast and continued the earlier pattern connecting religion, monumental architecture, and rich grave goods. The largest structures in ancient Peru that were built of sun-dried bricks (or adobe) were constructed in the Moche Valley during the Early Intermediate period, as was an elaborate system for the distribution of water. The Moche also developed a distinctive art style that appeared in ceramics, textiles, and wall paintings (Figure 8.18).

On the south coast, a complex society centred in the Nazca Valley produced monumental pyramids, terraced hills, burial areas, and walled enclosures, as well as elaborate pottery and textiles. It also produced the famous Nazca lines, monumental markings that were made by brushing away the dark, upper layer of the desert surface to expose the lighter soil beneath (Figure 8.19). The earliest markings are drawings of animals and supernatural figures, also found on textiles, whereas later markings are mostly straight lines. The exact significance of the Nazca lines is unclear. Similar structures are known elsewhere in Peru, and many experts suspect that the lines may have been memorial markers or part of a calendrical system.

In the Andean highlands, many small, independent societies developed during the Early Intermediate period. Of these, perhaps the most significant was the

**FIGURE 8.18** | Ceramics were developed to a high level of sophistication in early states, as shown by this stirrup-spout portrait jar produced by the Moche civilization, which flourished in northern Peru between 250 and 500 CE. It is important to note that pottery was also made and used by people who were not settled, full-time farmers.

tradition that grew up in the basin of Lake Titicaca in the southern highlands. Titicaca-basin culture possessed distinctive traditions in architecture, textiles, and religious art that heavily influenced later complex societies in the region (Conklin and Moseley 1988).

After 600 CE, the cultural fragmentation of the Early Intermediate period was reversed in two regions of Peru. A complex society called Tiwanaku (sometimes spelled *Tiahuanaco*) began to spread the Titicaca-basin culture throughout the southern highlands of the Andes. In the central highlands and central coast, a second complex society known as Wari (sometimes spelled *Huari*) extended its influence. Both these

regional powers were named after large prehistoric cities that presumably served as their capitals. The period during which these two states spread their cultural and political influence (600–1000 CE) is called the Middle Horizon of Andean cultural evolution.

Wari and Tiwanaku share some common cultural attributes, but archaeologists have difficulty deciphering the nature of their relationship with each other. Tiwanaku had a religiously oriented ruling hierarchy; Wari did not. The architecture of Wari administrative centres lacks residences, storehouses, and community kitchens, which were built in Tiwanaku provincial settlements for members of the religious bureaucracy. William Isbell (1988) connects the administrative structure of Wari to an earlier, non-hierarchical form of social organization that had flourished in the Ayacucho Valley during the Early Intermediate period. In that system, highland communities founded colonies in the different ecological zones that ranged between the highlands and the coast, thus providing the highland communities and their various colonies with a full range of products from each zone. This distinctive Andean pattern of niche construction, which integrates economic resources from a variety of environments, is called the *vertical archipelago system*.

Isbell (1988) thinks that the rulers of Wari adopted the form of centralized, hierarchical government from Tiwanaku but not the religious ideas that went with it. Wari then used these centralized political structures to transform the egalitarian vertical archipelago system of the Early Intermediate period into a socially stratified system of wealth collection for the state (182). Archaeological evidence for state-sponsored feasting in return for collective labour on state land may have been found at the Middle Horizon site of Jargampata, located 20 kilometres from Wari. More recent work conducted by Lidio Valdez, from MacEwan University, and his colleagues (2010) also suggests that maize beer associated with feasts may have been an integral part of the Wari political organization, in much the same way as it was for the Inka in later times. Both the vertical archipelago system and facilities for state-sponsored feasts for labourers on state land were later incorporated into the society of the Inkas. Isbell (1988) also thinks that the Inka administrative system, involving regional capitals linked by highways with way stations for runners, may have first developed in Wari.

After about 1000 CE, Wari and Tiwanaku declined, ushering in the Late Intermediate period, which lasted until the rise of the Inkas in 1476 CE. It was during the Late Intermediate period that the pilgrimage centre of Pachacamac, on the central coast, became fully established (Keatinge 1988). Independent regional states with distinct cultures emerged in half a dozen areas of Peru, the best known of which is the Chimú state, Chimor, on the north coast. The capital of the Chimú state, Chan Chan, is located in the Moche Valley.

Chimú administered a complex irrigation system in a number of adjacent river valleys. Most of the farmers of the Chimú state appear to have lived in cities. Although the connection between hydraulic agriculture and state power seems clear in the case of Chimú, other large valleys on the central and south coast were equally well suited to hydraulic agriculture but never produced equally centralized states (Parsons and Hastings 1988).

Both Chan Chan, the Chimú capital, and Cuzco, the Inka capital, were located in areas that lay on the border between spheres of cultural and political influence during the Middle Horizon. The rise of Cuzco began in Late Intermediate times, when kingdoms that descended from Tiwanaku and Wari began to fight with one another. Warfare continued until the 1460s, when the Inkas, whose empire had begun only 20 years earlier, subdued neighbouring states and brought them into their expanding empire (Parsons and Hastings 1988). By 1476, the Inkas put down the last of a series of internal rebellions, firmly establishing their empire of Tawantinsuyu, which means "world of four quarters." When the Spanish arrived in 1525, the Inka Empire stretched from present-day Colombia to central Chile, from the Pacific coast to the rainforests of the eastern Andean slopes (Wenke 1999, 640).

During the period of Inka dominance from 1476 to 1525, known as the Late Horizon, the Inkas built on the achievements of hundreds of years of Andean civilization. They further developed the vertical archipelago system, expanded the road system, and built new monumental palaces, temples, storage facilities, barracks, and way stations on highways. They maintained control of their vast empire through military force, by moving large sections of the population from one region to another for political reasons, and by continuing to recruit labour for state projects in return for state-sponsored feasting. Unlike Chimú, which was largely urban, the Inka Empire was based in rural villages. Society was organized in large kin groups called *ayllu*, which were then grouped together into higher-level units. But the administrative system was not identical in all regions of the empire: in places like Chan Chan, the Inkas made use of pre-existing administrative structures, but in areas where centralized administration did not exist, such as Huánuco Pampa in the central highlands, they built new administrative centres from the ground up (Morris 1988).

The Andes are so ecologically diverse and so much data remain unrecovered that it may seem hazardous to speculate about the causes for the rise of complex society in this region. If the first complex societies on the Peruvian coast were based on a steady supply of food from the sea, rather than agriculture, the notion that village agriculture must precede the rise of social complexity is dealt a blow. Moreover, the fact that these first complex coastal societies were without pottery was no more a barrier to development than was the fact that the early Andean states, up to and including the Inkas, were without a written language (Figure 8.20). Carneiro's environmental circumscription hypothesis seems suggestive when we consider the rise of the first multi-valley states on the coast during the Early Intermediate period, but the constant warfare required for his scheme does not become significant until much later, long after complex states had already emerged. Hydraulic agriculture was clearly important to the rise of the Chimú state, yet it emerged hundreds of years after the first complex societies on the coast. Even if hydraulic agriculture had been important during the Late Intermediate period, as we saw in comparing the Chimú with their neighbours, it cannot explain why people living in similar ecological settings in nearby valleys did not produce similar states. Much work remains to be done, but none of the current gaps in our knowledge detracts from the dazzling achievements of this unique civilization.

FIGURE 8.20 | The Indigenous civilizations of the Andes never developed systems of writing but were able to record important information using the *quipu*, a system of knotted strings. Based on a decimal system, quipu knots were coded by size, location, relative sequence, and colour.

## Chapter Summary

1. About 10,000 years ago, the retreat of the last glaciers marked the end of the Pleistocene. The earth's climate changed significantly, affecting the distribution of plants and animals and transforming the ecological settings in which human beings made their livings. Soon thereafter, human beings began to develop new ways of adapting by intervening in these changed environmental settings in order to create new niches for themselves.

2. Plant and animal domestication are usefully understood as forms of niche construction. Not only did human beings interfere with the reproduction of local species, to make them more useful for human purposes, but they also remodelled the environmental settings in which plants were grown and animals were fed and watered. When the invention of agriculture is viewed as niche construction, there is no question that it involved conscious human choice. Intelligent human beings consciously chose to domesticate wild plants that were easy to harvest, nourishing, and tasty; but they also had to consciously create the tools and plan the activities that would make cultivation of a domestic crop possible and successful.

3. The niches human beings construct to exploit plants are not all the same. Anthropologists have identified four major ways in which humans relate to plant species: wild plant-food procurement, wild plant-food production, cultivation, and agriculture. In each successive form, the amount of energy people apply to get food from plants increases, but the energy they get back from plants increases even more.

4. Animal domestication apparently developed as people consciously attempted to control the animals that they were hunting in order to intervene in their breeding patterns. Archaeological evidence for animal domestication may be indicated in one of four ways: when an animal species is found outside its natural range, when animal remains show morphological changes that distinguish them from wild populations, when the numbers of some species at a site increase abruptly relative to other species, and when remains show certain age and gender characteristics. The earliest animal domesticated, some 16,000 years ago, was the dog. Although archaeologists can pinpoint the regions where goats were domesticated, the earliest sites for domesticated sheep are not clear. It seems that cattle and pigs were domesticated at different sites in the Old World. Domestication of animals seems to have been slower and less important in the New World than it was in the Old World.

5. The niches humans have constructed to make use of animals vary. They include random hunting, controlled hunting, herd following, loose herding, close herding, and factory farming. Once humans domesticated animals, their focus shifted from hunting wild animals to raising and slaughtering domesticated animals, which may have triggered concern for private property.

6. Scholars have suggested different factors responsible for plant and animal domestication; none alone is entirely satisfactory. Today, most archaeologists prefer multiple-strand theories that focus on the particular sets of factors that were responsible for domestication in different places. One good example of a multiple-strand approach to domestication is shown by recent studies of the Natufian cultural tradition in southwestern Asia, which developed about 12,500 years ago. Post-Pleistocene human niches involving sedentism and domestication had both positive and negative consequences for human beings who came to depend on them. By the time farmers became fully aware of agriculture's drawbacks, their societies had probably become so dependent on agriculture that abandoning it for some other subsistence strategy would have been impossible.

7. Neolithic farming villages were basically egalitarian societies, like the foraging societies that had preceded them. However, beginning about 5000 years ago in southwestern Asia and shortly thereafter in Egypt, the Indus Valley (India), China, Mesoamerica (the Valley of Mexico), and the Andes (Peru), humans independently developed social stratification. Social stratification occurred when surplus food production made it possible for some members of society to stop producing food altogether and to specialize in various occupations. A wide gulf developed between most members of a society and members of a new social class of rulers who controlled most of the wealth. The earliest socially stratified societies were chiefdoms in which the chief and close relatives had privileged access to wealth, power, and prestige while other members of the society continued to share roughly similar social status.

8. Archaeological evidence of social complexity includes the remains of monumental architecture, elaborate burials alongside much simpler burials, and concentrations of particular artifacts in specific areas of an archaeological site that might indicate occupational specialization. Complex societies are normally made up of a number of settlements organized in a hierarchy: state organization is suspected when regional settlement

patterns show at least three levels in the settlement hierarchy. Art and written inscriptions may provide further information about ancient social organization. Cultural change in all early complex societies tended to alternate between periods of relative cultural uniformity and political unity and periods of regional differentiation and lack of political integration.

9. Anthropologists have devised a number of different hypotheses to explain why complex societies developed. Frequently, the hypothesis places emphasis on a single cause, or prime mover. Although some of the causes that have been proposed as this prime mover were important in some places, they were not all important everywhere. Nevertheless, attempts to test these hypotheses about prime movers have led to a far richer appreciation of the complexities of social and cultural change in prehistory.

10. Andean civilization developed in a distinctive geographical setting. Foragers were living on the Peruvian coast between 14,000 and 8000 years ago and in the sierra of the Andes Mountains between 11,000 and 10,000 years ago. The first monumental architecture appeared after 4000 years ago. Irrigation agriculture became important along the coast between 3800 and 2900 years ago. Numerous independent states rose and fell on the coast and in the highlands until the rise of the Inka Empire in the late 1400s. During Inka times, the achievements of earlier states were consolidated and expanded. When the Spanish arrived in 1525, the Inka Empire stretched from present-day Colombia to central Chile, from the Pacific coast to the rainforests of the eastern Andean slopes.

11. The Andes are so ecologically diverse and so much information remains uncovered that it seems hazardous to speculate about the causes for the rise of complex societies in this region. Village agriculture was not responsible for the rise of complexity on the Peruvian coast. Environmental circumscription may explain the rise of the first states on the coast in the Early Intermediate period, but warfare and hydraulic agriculture did not become important until long after complex states had emerged. The most puzzling question is why people living in similar ecological settings in nearby valleys did not produce similar states.

## For Review

1. Why do archaeologists use concepts borrowed from ecology to understand how humans have responded their environments? What are these concepts, and how can they help us understand the human past?

2. What differentiates domestication from agriculture? Illustrate your answer with examples from this chapter.

3. Describe the different explanations offered by archaeologists for the domestication of plants and animals by humans. Select the one that you agree with most, and write a paragraph outlining your argument.

4. Summarize the discussion of the beginnings of domestication in southwestern Asia.

5. Who were the Natufians? What does archaeological research tell us about the processes of plant and animal domestication in Natufian society?

6. Summarize the key consequences of domestication and sedentism for human ways of life. In what ways have these consequences shaped modern ways of life in Canada?

7. What is social complexity? What is the archaeological evidence for social complexity?

8. Explain what Michael Hoffman means by the term *powerfacts*. In modern North American societies, what objects might serve a purpose similar to that of powerfacts in early complex civilizations?

9. What were the world's first complex societies, and where were they located? What was unique about these locations?

10. Outline the different hypotheses that archaeologists put forward to explain the beginning of complex societies. How did sedentism affect social complexity?

11. Discuss the rise of social complexity in the Andes by addressing the geographic influences as described in this chapter.

## Key Terms

agriculture   205
agroecology   205
bloodwealth   227
broad-spectrum foraging   211
class   221
complex societies   221

concentrations of particular artifacts   223
domestication   202
egalitarian social relations   220
evolutionary niche   204
grave goods   213
Mesopotamia   216

monumental architecture   222
Neolithic   214
occupational specialization   221
sedentism   205
social stratification   213
surplus production   221

## Suggested Readings

Blake, Michael, Bruce Benz, Nicholas Jakobsen, Ryan Wallace, Sue Formosa, Kisha Supernant, Diana Moreiras, and Alex Wong. 2012. *Ancient Maize Map, Version 1.1: An Online Database and Mapping Program for Studying the Archaeology of Maize in the Americas.* Vancouver: Laboratory of Archaeology, University of British Columbia. http://en.ancientmaize.com. *This interactive online database and map, developed by Michael Blake and colleagues from the University of British Columbia, highlights when maize was first domesticated at different sites throughout the Americas.*

Chang, Kwang-Chih. 1986. *The Archaeology of Ancient China*, 4th ed. New Haven: Yale University Press. *A fascinating account of the rise of social complexity in China by one of the most distinguished interpreters of Chinese civilization in North America.*

Henry, Donald O. 1989. *From Foraging to Agriculture: The Levant at the End of the Ice Age.* Philadelphia: University of Pennsylvania Press. *A detailed, well-illustrated discussion of the archaeology of ancient southwestern Asia at the time of the emergence of agriculture. Particularly good on cultural variation.*

Hoffman, Michael A. 1991. *Egypt before the Pharaohs: The Prehistoric Foundations of Egyptian Civilization.* Revised ed. Austin: University of Texas Press. *A highly readable account of the important developments in prehistoric Egypt that made the civilization of the pharaohs possible.*

Price, T. Douglas, and Anne Birgitte Gebauer, eds. 1995. *Last Hunters, First Farmers: New Perspectives on the Prehistoric Transition to Agriculture.* Santa Fe, NM: SAR Press. *A collection of scholarly articles exploring, among other topics, the importance of complex foraging societies in the process of domestication.*

Price, T. Douglas, and Gary M. Feinman, eds. 1995. *Foundations of Social Inequality.* New York: Plenum. *A fascinating collection of scholarly articles exploring the various factors responsible for institutionalizing social inequality in the first complex societies.*

Smith, Bruce D. 1995. *The Emergence of Agriculture.* New York: Scientific American Library. *An accessible, beautifully illustrated discussion of domestication throughout the world.*

Soustelle, Jacques. 1961. *Daily Life of the Aztecs on the Eve of the Spanish Conquest.* Stanford: Stanford University Press. *A classic text that attempts to reconstruct for modern readers exactly what the title claims.*

Wenke, Robert J., and Deborah I. Olszewski. 2006. *Patterns in Prehistory: Humankind's First Three Million Years.* 5th ed. New York: Oxford University Press. *An excellent, up-to-date, and highly readable account of the rise of social complexity in Mesopotamia, Egypt, the Indus Valley, China, Mesoamerica, and the Andes as well as a chapter on early cultural complexity in pre-European North America.*

# 9 Why Is Understanding Human Language Important?

▲ A teacher instructs students using sign language at a school for deaf, mute, and blind students, Srinagar, Jammu and Kashmir State, India. Photo: Yawar Nazir/Getty Images

## Chapter Outline

Only human beings have symbolic language, and it is so deeply a part of our lives that we rarely even think about how unusual it is. In this chapter, you will learn about what makes human symbolic language different from other forms of animal communication. You will also explore its deep connections to other symbolic dimensions of social and cultural life, including the ways language shapes—and is shaped by—the way we see the world around us.

As we saw in Chapter 5, primates depend on learned behaviour to survive, and some primate species appear to have developed their own cultural traditions. Primates also communicate with one another in a variety of ways, most obviously by relying on vocal calls to alert one another about significant aspects of their environment, from the presence of food to the threat of a predator. In the past, some anthropologists hypothesized that human language was simply an elaboration of the call system of our ancestors, but this hypothesis proved to be incorrect. In fact, the more anthropologists and other scientists studied human language, the more obvious it has become that human languages are very different from primate call systems. Indeed, they have realized that human language is a *second* learned system of communication that evolved in our lineage *alongside* the call system we inherited from our primate ancestors. Humans still possess a simple, species-specific system of calls, but because the languages we speak consist of a complex symbols, our languages are distinct from call systems.

A symbol is something that stands for something else. Human symbolic language is perhaps the clearest illustration of the central role played by symbols in all of human culture. Indeed, it is the dependence of human language on symbols that makes it such a flexible and creative system of communication—and far more powerful than any primate call system could ever be. So when anthropologists talk about human language, they always mean human *symbolic* language. This is why we define language as the system of arbitrary symbols human beings use to encode and communicate about their experience of the world and of one another. The role played by symbols in human language sets it apart from the non-symbolic communication systems of other living species. Symbolic language has made possible many human achievements, but it is a double-edged sword: it allows people to communicate with one another, but it also creates barriers to communication, especially because not

all humans speak the same language. This chapter explores the ambiguity, limitations, and power of human language and its connections to other forms of human symbolic activity.

## How Do We Communicate without Language?

Before we begin to look more closely at humans' use of language, it is important to recognize that there are various ways in which we are able to send messages to one another without using language. For example, we can communicate through gestures, postures, facial expressions, non-verbal vocalizations such as laughing or sobbing, and even our use of the space around us. These sorts of non-verbal communication allow us to inform others about our feelings and even express our social and cultural identity. It is likely that we communicate well over 60 per cent of our messages non-verbally (Ottenheimer 2013, 131), and non-verbal communication can be as effective as language in transmitting simple messages between people. However, many of the non-verbal signals we use are culture specific, learned through living within a specific community; as such, accurate interpretation of these signals requires the receiver of the message to be aware of the non-verbal communication customs of the sender's culture.

When most people think about non-verbal communication, they usually think of body language—movements and postures that communicate attitudes

language The system of arbitrary symbols people use to encode their experience of the world and of others.

non-verbal communication The process of sending and receiving messages without the use of words (e.g., through gestures, facial expressions, or non-verbal vocalizations).

body language Movements and postures that communicate attitudes and feelings non-verbally.

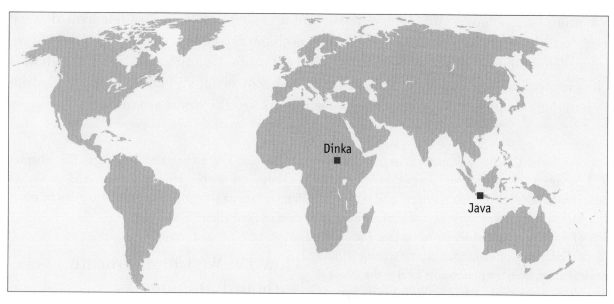

MAP 9.1 | Locations of societies whose EthnoProfiles appear in Chapter 9.

and feelings non-verbally. The study of these sorts of cues is known as kinesics. In everyday interactions, we often use simple body movements—for example, a wave good bye, a tap on the shoulder, a smile, a wink, or an impatient tapping of a foot—to enhance or even stand in for verbal messages. As with most forms of non-verbal communication, however, the meaning attached to these sorts of gestures tends to differ from culture to culture (Figure 9.1). Consider that Nicaraguans point at things with their lips and indicate questions by wrinkling their noses, and that Comorans encourage others to come closer by moving a hand in what North Americans would interpret as a goodbye wave (Ottenheimer 2013, 132). Also consider that putting one's thumb and forefinger together in a circle with the other three fingers pointing upward means "okay" in Canada, while this same gesture conveys that something is worthless in France and may be considered an insult in some parts of Germany (ibid., 142).

In addition to body language, smells, tastes, and non-verbal vocal sounds also communicate feelings and information. The smell of fresh baking can suggest home and comfort: the smell of cigars and perfumes can imply status: and pine or lemon scents can suggest cleanliness. Flavours tend to characterize

certain cultures; for example, spicy foods like salsas and curries are often associated with cultures from warmer climates, while less flavourful foods are typically linked with cultures from northern regions. Non-verbal vocalizations can convey a wide variety of messages, from a forceful declaration of anguish delivered through a sharp cry of pain to a subtle comment of derision delivered through a soft laugh. (See the "In Their Own Words" box on the "Clinton cackle" for a great example of how complex messages can be conveyed through a well-timed laugh.)

Use of space is another way in which we send non-verbal messages. The study of how different societies perceive and use space is known as proxemics. A major focus of proxemics is the space we create around ourselves when interacting with others. Consider what you typically do when you meet someone new. Do you nod, bow, extend your hand, or give kisses on both cheeks? When you are having a conversation, how close do you stand to the other person? For most people, there is a point in space at which a conversation partner can be "too close"; how we define this point depends on both our culturally learned understanding of the space around us and our relationship with the other person. Edward T. Hall (1966), who was one of the first to look at proxemics, proposed the existence of four different kinds of interpersonal space that could be compared cross-culturally: intimate, personal, social, and public (Figure 9.2). The first two categories relate to the space we feel comfortable sharing with people with whom we

kinesics  The study of body movement, gestures, and facial expressions as a form of communication.

proxemics  The study of how different societies perceive and use space.

**FIGURE 9.1 |** The meaning attached to body language differs from culture to culture. A traditional Maori greeting in New Zealand is the *hongi*, in which two people welcome each other by pressing their noses and foreheads together.

## In Their Own Words

### The "Clinton Cackle": Hillary Rodham Clinton's Laughter in News Interviews

*Tanya Romaniuk of York University has recently investigated interviewees' use of laughter in response to an interviewer's questions in the context of broadcast news interviews (BNIs). In her investigation, she looks specifically at how United States politician Hillary Rodham Clinton (HRC) used laughter during interviews while she was campaigning for the Democratic nomination for president in 2007.*

Through an examination of HRC's laughter in news interviews, I have attempted to describe some of the patterned ways in which laughter occurs, . . . and some issues that arise [in the context of BNIs]. Given that the turn-taking system for news interviews is designed for interviewees' answers to be responsive actions relevant only on the completion of a question (Clayman 2001), it is illuminating to consider how HRC negotiates this constraint through her use of laughter. Operating on the interviewer's talk while it is being produced allows HRC to provide implicit commentary on the talk without waiting until question completion, and prior to providing a substantive response. In this way, HRC demonstrates how laughter can be used as an interactional resource for interviewees in the context of news interviews. . . . In the context of BNIs, at least, the practice described [here] is one that other interviewees deploy in similar circumstances. . . .

. . . [I]t seems that there is no doubt that laughter is one interactional resource interviewees make use of in order to mitigate the force of an interviewer's adversarial questioning before providing a substantive response. While further research into this practice in the context of news interviews is certainly warranted, so too is work in other institutional contexts, in which interactional roles are also shaped and constrained by institutional identities. For example, [one researcher] found that in job interviews, applicants laughed more frequently than interviewers, just as [other researchers have] found that patients laughed more often than physicians in medical interviews. While I suspect that it is also more likely that interviewees laugh more often than interviewers in BNIs, this hypothesis, and others concerning the use of laughter in other institutional contexts, is worthy of exploration. Indeed, detailed analyses of laughter and its interplay with other verbal and non-verbal actions lead to a deeper understanding of the range of meanings it can convey in social interaction.

Source: Romaniuk 2009, 42.

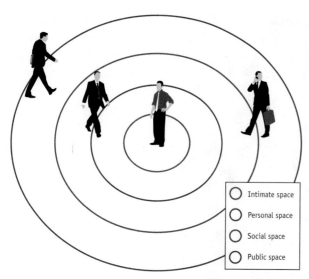

**FIGURE 9.2** | People can be thought to have four spheres of personal space: intimate, personal, social, and public. The amount of space we leave between ourselves and others depends on both our culturally learned understanding of the space around us and our relationship with the other person.

have a close relationship (e.g., when talking to family or friends); the other two relate to the space we feel comfortable sharing with strangers (e.g., when standing in line at the grocery store or sitting in a waiting room). Generally, most Canadians feel uncomfortable standing within a metre of a stranger, while most Europeans feel comfortable standing half that distance from a stranger (Ottenheimer 2013, 136). It is important to be aware of how space is used among different communities and how it communicates important ideas non-verbally, especially when working with people from differing cultures.

## How Are Language and Culture Related?

Human language is perhaps the strongest example of a biocultural phenomenon. Within the last 100,000 years, changes to the human brain, our genetic structure (e.g., the FOXP2 gene), and the anatomy of the human mouth and throat combined to make language a possibility. At the same time, language is clearly cultural in that it is *learned* and *shared* among a group of people. Indeed,

**linguistics** The scientific study of language.

studies of how babies acquire language at specific rates demonstrate how important language is to the enculturation of children. Clearly, human anatomy and development are linked to cultural learning.

It is important to remember that all human language systems involve more than just the sounds that come out of people's mouths. Languages are cultural products with embedded meanings and behavioural patterns that stretch beyond individuals, across space, and over time. Anthropologists have long been particularly attentive to the multiple powerful dimensions of language, especially when ethnographic fieldwork in societies presented them with the challenge of learning unwritten languages without formal instruction. At the same time, anthropologists who transcribed or tape-recorded speech could lift it out of its cultural context to be analyzed on its own. Their analyses revealed grammatical intricacies and complexities suggesting that language might be a good model for the rest of culture. It also became obvious that the way people use language provides important clues to their understanding of the world and of themselves. Indeed, some theories of culture are explicitly based on ideas taken from **linguistics**, the scientific study of language.

Similar to the issues with the use of the term *culture*, the concept of "language" has regularly involved a distinction between *Language* and *languages*. *Language* with a capital *L* (like *Culture* with a capital *C*) has often been viewed as an abstract

> For the debate over the use of the terms *Culture* and *cultures*, see Chapter 2, pp. 37–8.

property belonging to the human species as a whole, not to be confused with the specific *languages* of groups of people. This distinction acknowledges that all human groups possess fully developed *languages*. Today, however, linguistic anthropologists realize that generalized views of "languages" can be as problematic as generalized views of "cultures." There are many difficulties associated with demarcating the boundaries between one language and another, or between dialects and languages, as will see in our discussion of pidgins and creoles later in this chapter. As well, it is important to distinguish *language* from *speech*. Many people often equate language with *spoken* language (speech), but languages can take non-spoken forms such as writing, Morse code, or sign language.

Nevertheless, all human linguistic communication, regardless of the medium, depends on more than words alone. Native speakers of a language share not just vocabulary and grammar but also a number of assumptions about how to speak that may not be shared by speakers of a different language. Students learning a new language discover early on that word-for-word translation from one language to another does not work. Sometimes there are no equivalent words in the second language; but even when there appear to be such words, a word-for-word translation may not mean in language B what it meant in language A. For example, when English speakers have eaten enough, they say "I'm full." This may be translated directly into French as "Je suis plein." To a native speaker of French, this sentence (especially when uttered at the end of a meal) has the nonsensical meaning "I am a pregnant [male] animal." Alternatively, if uttered by a man who has just consumed a lot of wine, it means "I'm drunk."

Learning a second language is often frustrating and even unsettling; someone who once found the world simple to talk about suddenly turns into a babbling fool. Studying a second language, then, is less a matter of learning new labels for old objects than it is of learning how to identify new objects that go with new labels. The student must also learn the appropriate contexts in which different linguistic forms may be used: a person can be "full" after eating in English but not in French. Knowledge about context is cultural knowledge.

## How Do Languages Change over Time?

All languages change over time. The study of this evolution of language is known as historical linguistics, which investigates relationships between words and sounds within a language, as well as connections between different languages. For example, historical linguists may investigate the connections among the Nordic languages (in particular, Icelandic, Norwegian, Danish, and Swedish) by looking at the natural change of these languages over time and how contact with other cultures influenced their evolution. Iceland, for example, is an extremely isolated place in the North Atlantic region where, until relatively recently, the local language (Icelandic) was not heavily influenced by other cultures and changed primarily as a result of internal factors. As a result, Icelandic is most similar to the original Nordic language, Old Norse, which the Vikings would have spoken. The connections among modern Nordic languages indicate a genealogical relationship that historical linguists can use to reconstruct links between Nordic cultures across time. The further historical linguists trace modern languages back in time, the more connections they uncover. For example, tracing English back beyond 6000 years or so reveals its roots in the foundational Proto Indo-European (PIE) language, to which French, Spanish, Russian, and most other modern European languages also trace their roots. The analysis of when and how language groups diverged from one another is an important aspect of historical linguistics, one that is often used to supplement archaeological research. Similar words in discrete languages provide important evidence that archaeologists use to recreate migration patterns and invasions of different groups in the past. When speakers of different languages come into contact, they often borrow words from the unfamiliar language and incorporate them into their own language; this phenomenal is referred to as *external* language change.

Languages continue to change in the present as well, and these changes tend to reflect cultural adaptations on a larger scale. Consider recent words associated with technology—for example, *smartphone*, *blog*, *Instagram*, or even *groupon*. These words did not exist a decade ago, but because they have been adopted by so many people, even on a global scale, we understand what they mean (Figure 9.3). Incorporating new words is not the only way that languages can change. Meanings of existing words and phrases can change as well. How would you define words like *spam* or *twitter*? Until recently, *twitter* was a manner in which birds sing, while *spam* was the name of a luncheon meat (made of SPiced hAM) that was created in 1937. Often these changes to language are generational and reflect *internal* changes to language and culture.

**native speaker** A person who has spoken a particular language since early childhood.

**historical linguistics** The study of relationships between languages and how they change over time.

"Possessive pronouns? Um, iPod, yourPod, theirPod?"

FIGURE 9.3 | As cultures change, new words must be invented and incorporated into the existing language to describe new technologies and experiences. Before the release of the first iPod in 2001, the word *iPod* would have meant little to most English speakers. Today, the term is widely recognized around the world, even by non-English speakers.

## How Do People Talk about Experience?

Each natural human language is adequate for its speakers' needs, given their particular way of life. Speakers of a particular language tend to develop larger vocabularies to discuss those aspects of life that are of importance to them. The Inuit of the Canadian Arctic Archipelago, for example, have long relied on ice and ice floes for subsistence hunting and winter travel. As a result, they have more than one hundred words that describe ice and ice forms, including thick ice, thinning ice, old ice, and new ice. As another example, English speakers have created an elaborate vocabulary for discussing computers and computer-related technologies. However, despite differences in vocabulary and grammar, all natural human languages ever studied by linguists have proven to be equally complex. Just as there is no such thing as a "primitive" human culture, there is no such thing as a "primitive" human language.

Traditionally, languages are associated with concrete groups of people called *speech communities*.

 For more on the Canadian Inuit, see EthnoProfile 13.3, on p. 360.

Nevertheless, because all languages possess alternative ways of speaking, members of particular speech communities do not all possess identical knowledge about the language (or languages) they share, nor do they all speak the same way. Individuals and subgroups within a speech community make use of linguistic resources in different ways. Consequently, there is a tension in language between diversity and commonality. Individuals and subgroups attempt to use the varied resources of a language to create unique, personal voices or ways of speaking. These efforts are countered by pressures to negotiate shared codes for communication within larger social groups. In this way, language patterns are produced, imitated, or modified through the activity of speakers. A particular language that we isolate at any given moment is but a snapshot of a continuing process.

There are many ways to communicate our experiences, and there is no absolute standard favouring one way over another. Some things that are easy to say in language A may be difficult to say in language B, yet other aspects of language B may appear much simpler than equivalent aspects of language A. For example, English ordinarily requires the use of determiners (*a, an, the*) before nouns, but this rule is not found in all languages. Likewise, the verb *to be*, called the "copula" by linguists, is not found in all languages, although the relationships we convey when we use *to be* in English may still be communicated. In English, we might say "There *are* many people in the market." Translating this sentence into Fulfulde, the language of the Fulbe of northern Cameroon, we get "Him'be boi 'don nder luumo," which, word-for-word, reads "people-many-there-in-market" (Figure 9.4). No single Fulfulde word corresponds to the English *are* or *the*.

Differences across languages are not absolute. In Chinese, for example, verbs never change to indicate tense; instead, separate expressions referring to time are used. English speakers may conclude that Chinese speakers cannot distinguish between past, present, and future. This structure seems completely different from English structure. But consider such English sentences as "Have a hard day at the office today?" and "Your interview go well?" These abbreviated questions, used in informal English, are very similar to the formal patterns of Chinese and other languages of southeastern Asia (Akmajian et al. 1997, 194–5).

**FIGURE 9.4** | Him'be boi 'don nder luumo. ("There are many people in the market.")

## In Their Own Words

### Cultural Translation

*Linguistic translation can be complicated and beset with pitfalls. Cultural translation, as David Parkin describes, requires knowledge not only of different grammars but also of the various different cultural contexts in which grammatical forms are put to use.*

Cultural translation, like translation from one language to another, never produces a rendering that is semantically and stylistically an exact replica of the original. That much we accept. What is not often recognized, perhaps not even by the translators themselves, is that the very act of having to decide how to phrase an event, sentiment, or human character engages the translator in an act of creation. The translator does not simply represent a picture made by an author. He or she creates a new version, and perhaps in some respects a new picture—a matter that is often of some great value.

So it is with anthropologists. But while this act of creation in reporting on "the other" may reasonably be regarded as a self-sustaining pleasure, it is also an entry into the pitfalls and traps of language use itself. One of the most interesting new fields in anthropology is the study of the relationship between language and human knowledge, both among ourselves as professional anthropologists and laypeople, and among peoples of other cultures. The study is at once both reflexive and critical.

The hidden influences at work in language use attract the most interest. For example, systems of greetings have many built-in elaborations that differentiate subtly between those who are old and young, male and female, rich and poor, and powerful and powerless. When physicians discuss a patient in his or her presence and refer to the patient in the third-person singular, they are in effect defining the patient as a passive object unable to enter into the discussion. When anthropologists present elegant accounts of "their" people that fit the demands of a convincing theory admirably, do they not also leave out [of] the description any consideration of the informants' own fears and feelings? Or do we go too far in making such claims, and is it often the anthropologist who is indulged by the people, who give him or her the data they think is sought, either in exchange for something they want or simply because it pleases them to do so? If the latter, how did the anthropologist's account miss this critical part of the dialogue?

Source: Parkin 1990, 290–1.

This kind of overlap between two very different languages demonstrates at least four things. First, it shows the kind of cross-linguistic commonality that forms the foundation both for learning new languages and for translation. Second, it highlights the variety of expressive resources to be found in any single language. For example, we learn that English allows us to use either tense markers on verbs (-s, -ed) or unmarked verbs with adverbs of time (have + today). Third, we learn that grammatical patterns can be associated with formal or informal usage. Fourth, it shows that the same structures can have different functions in different languages. As anthropological linguist Elinor Ochs (1986, 10) observes, most cross-cultural differences in language use "turn out to be differences in *context* and/or *frequency of occurrence.*"

## What Makes Human Language Distinctive?

In 1966, the anthropological linguist Charles Hockett listed a number of different *design features* of human language that, in his estimation, set it apart from other forms of animal communication. Six of these design features are regularly used to define what makes human language a distinctive form of communication: *openness, displacement, arbitrariness, duality of patterning, semanticity,* and *prevarication.*

*Openness* indicates that human language is productive. Speakers of any given language not only can create new messages but also can understand new messages created by other speakers. Someone may have never said to you "Put this Babel fish in your ear," but knowing English, you can understand the message. Openness might also be defined as "the ability to understand the same thing from different points of view" (Ortony 1979, 14). In language, this means being able to talk about the same experiences from different perspectives, to paraphrase using different words and various grammatical constructions. Indeed, it means that the experiences themselves can be differently conceived, labelled, and discussed. In this view, no single perspective would necessarily emerge as more correct in every respect than all others.

The importance of openness for human verbal communication is striking when we compare, for example, spoken human language to the vocal communication systems (or *call systems*) of monkeys and apes. Biological anthropologist Terrence Deacon (1977) points out that, in addition to spoken symbolic language, modern human beings possess a set of six calls: laughing, sobbing, screaming with fright, crying with pain, groaning, and sighing. Linguistic anthropologist Robbins Burling (2005, 16) also emphasizes the difference between call systems and symbolic language: "Language . . . is organized in such utterly different ways from primate or mammalian calls and it conveys such utterly different kinds of meanings, that I find it impossible to imagine a realistic sequence by which natural selection could have converted a call system into a language. . . . We will understand more about the origins of language by considering the ways in which language differs from the cries and gestures of human and non-human primates than by looking for ways in which they are alike." In Deacon's view, human calls appear to have *coevolved alongside* symbolic language, together with gestures and the changes in speech rhythm, volume, and tonality that linguists call *speech prosody*. This would explain why calls and speech integrate with one another so smoothly when we communicate vocally with one another.

Non-human primates can communicate in rather subtle ways using channels of transmission other than voice. However, these channels are far less sophisticated than, say, American Sign Language. The number of calls in a call system ranges from 15 to 40, depending on the species; and the calls are produced only when the animal finds itself in a situation including such features as the presence of food or danger, friendly interest and the desire for company, or the desire to mark a location or to signal pain, sexual interest, or the need for maternal care. If the animal is not in the appropriate situation, it does not produce the call. At most, it may refrain from uttering a call in a situation that would normally trigger it. In addition, non-human primates cannot emit a signal that has some features of one call and some of another. For example, if the animal encounters food and danger at the same time, one of the calls takes precedence. For these reasons, the call systems of non-human primates are said to be *closed* when compared to open human languages.

Closed call systems also lack *displacement*, our human ability to talk about absent or non-existent objects and past or future events as easily as we discuss our immediate situations. Although non-human primates clearly have good memories, and some species, such as chimpanzees, seem to be able to plan social action in advance (such as when hunting for meat), they cannot use their call systems to discuss such events.

Closed call systems also lack *arbitrariness*, the fact that there is no universal, necessary link between particular linguistic sounds and particular linguistic meanings. For example, the sound sequence /boi/ refers to a "young male human being" in English but means "more" or "many" in Fulfulde (see Figure 9.4). One aspect of linguistic creativity is the free, creative production of new links between sounds and meanings. Thus, arbitrariness and openness imply each other: if all links between sound and meaning are open, then any particular links between particular sounds and particular meanings in a particular language must be arbitrary. In non-human primate call systems, by contrast, links between the sounds of calls and their meanings appear fixed, and there is no easy slippage between sounds and what they stand for from one population to the next.

Arbitrariness is evident in the design feature of language *duality of patterning*. Human language, Hockett claimed, is patterned on two different levels: sound and meaning. On the first level, the arrangement of the small set of meaningless sounds (or *phonemes*) that characterize any particular language is not random but systematically patterned to create meaning-bearing units (or *morphemes*): in English, the final /ng/ sound in *song*, for example, is never found at the beginning of a sound sequence, although other languages in the world do allow that combination. The result is that from any language's set of phonemes (in English, there are some 36 phonemes) a very large number of correctly formed morphemes can be created. On the second level of patterning, however, the rules of grammar allow for the arrangement and rearrangement of these single morphemes into larger units—utterances or sentences—that can express an infinite number of meanings ("*The boy bit the dog*" uses the same morphemes as "*The dog bit the boy*," but the meaning is completely different). Since Hockett first wrote about the design features of human language, many linguists have suggested that there are more than just two levels of patterning in language—that there are levels of phonemes and morphemes as well as levels of sentence structure (*syntax*), meaning (*semantics*), and use (*pragmatics*). In each case, patterns that characterize one level cannot be reduced to the patterns of any other level but can serve as resources for the construction of more comprehensive levels. For example, units at the level of sound (or phonemes), patterned in one way, can be used to create units of meaning (or morphemes) at a different level, patterned in a different way. Morphemes, in turn, can be used to create units at a different level (sentences) by means of syntactic rules that are different from the rules that create morphemes, and syntactic rules are again different from the rules that combine sentences into discourse. Ape call systems, by contrast, appear to lack multilevel patterning of this kind (Wallmann 1992).

Arbitrariness shows up again in the design feature of *semanticity*—the association of linguistic signals with aspects of the social, cultural, and physical world of a speech community. People use language to refer to and make sense of objects and processes in their world. Nevertheless, any linguistic description of reality is always somewhat arbitrary because all linguistic descriptions are selective, highlighting some features of the world and downplaying others. (Semanticity is not the same thing as *semantics*, which refers to the formal study of linguistic meaning.)

Perhaps the most striking consequence of linguistic openness is the design feature *prevarication*. Hockett's (1966, 10) remarks about this design feature deserve particular attention: "Linguistic messages can be false, and they can be meaningless in the logician's sense." In other words, not only can people use language to lie, but also utterances that seem perfectly well formed grammatically may yield nonsense. An example is the following sentence invented by linguist Noam Chomsky (1957, 15): "Colourless green ideas sleep furiously." This is a grammatical sentence on one level—the right kinds of words are used in the right places—but on another level it contains multiple contradictions. The ability of language users to prevaricate—to make statements or ask questions that violate convention—is a major consequence of open symbolic systems. Apes using their closed call systems can neither lie nor formulate theories.

## What Does It Mean to "Learn" a Language?

Years ago studies of child language amounted to a list of errors that children make when attempting to gain what Chomsky calls linguistic competence, or mastery

---

**grammar**  A set of rules that aim to describe fully the patterns of linguistic usage observed by speakers of a particular language.

**linguistic competence**  A term coined by linguist Noam Chomsky to refer to the mastery of adult grammar.

**FIGURE 9.5** | Social and cultural contexts impact how children learn to communicate. For example, children in Canada often learn that it is appropriate to use formal grammar and polite terms in the context of a family dinner.

of adult grammar. For some time, however, linguists who study children's verbal interactions in social and cultural contexts have drawn attention to what children can do very well. "From an early age they appear to communicate very fluently, producing utterances which are not just remarkably well-formed according to the linguist's standards but also appropriate to the social context in which the speakers find themselves. Children are thus learning far more about language than rules of grammar. [They are] acquiring communicative competence" (Elliot 1981, 13).

Communicative competence, or mastery of adult rules for socially and culturally appropriate speech, is a term introduced by American anthropological linguist Dell Hymes (1972). As an anthropologist, Hymes objected to Chomsky's notion that linguistic competence consisted only of being able to make correct judgments of sentence grammaticality (Chomsky 1965, 4). Hymes observed that competent adult speakers do more than follow grammatical rules when they speak. They are also able to choose words and topics of conversation appropriate to their social position, the social position of the person they are addressing, and the social context of interaction (Figure 9.5).

## How Does Context Affect Language?

Anthropologists are very much aware of the influence of context on how people use language. For example, consider how you communicate on social media or via text in comparison to how you communicate when you are at your job or giving a presentation at school. Most likely,

your use of language is far more formal in the latter contexts than in the former. If you were speaking French you would also have to take into consideration the distinction between *tu* (second-person singular, used when referring to close friends) and *vous* (second-person plural, used when referring to strangers, casual acquaintances, and people in positions of authority), both of which translate into English as *you*. While most native French speakers know almost instinctively which word to use, the choice can be more difficult to non-native speakers. To be safe, most students of French use *vous* for all individuals, to avoid appearing too familiar with native speakers whom they do not know well. But certain difficulties remain. For example, if you are dating a French person, at what point in the relationship does the change from *vous* to *tu* occur, and who decides? Moreover, sometimes—for example, among university students—the normal term of address is *tu* (even among strangers); it is used to indicate social solidarity. English speakers who are learning French wrestle with these sorts of context-related linguistic dilemmas all the time. Rules for the appropriate use of *tu* and *vous* seem to have nothing to do with grammar, yet the choice between one form and the other indicates whether the speaker is someone who does or does not know how to speak French.

But French seems quite straightforward when compared with Javanese, in which all the words in a sentence must be carefully selected to reflect the social relationship between the speaker and the person addressed (see EthnoProfile 9.1: Java). In the 1950s, when Clifford Geertz first did fieldwork in Java, he discovered that it was impossible to say anything in Javanese without also communicating your social position relative to the person to whom you are speaking. Even a simple request—like "Are you going to eat rice and cassava now?"—required that speakers know at least five different varieties of the

**communicative competence**  A term coined by anthropological linguist Dell Hymes to refer to the mastery of adult rules for socially and culturally appropriate speech.

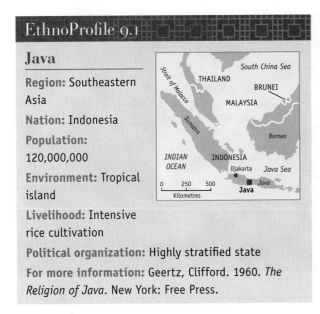

**EthnoProfile 9.1**

## Java

**Region:** Southeastern Asia

**Nation:** Indonesia

**Population:** 120,000,000

**Environment:** Tropical island

**Livelihood:** Intensive rice cultivation

**Political organization:** Highly stratified state

**For more information:** Geertz, Clifford. 1960. *The Religion of Java*. New York: Free Press.

language in order to communicate socially as well as to make the request. This example illustrates the range of diversity present in a single language and how different varieties of a language are related to different subgroups within the speech community.

## How Does Language Affect How We See the World?

During the first half of the twentieth century, two American anthropological linguists, Edward Sapir and Benjamin Whorf, observed that the grammars of different languages often described the same situation in different ways. They concluded that language has the power to shape the way people see the world. This claim has been called the linguistic relativity principle, or the "Sapir–Whorf hypothesis." This principle has been highly controversial because it is a radical proposition that is difficult to test and, when it has been tested, the results have been ambiguous.

The so-called strong version of the linguistic relativity principle is also known as *linguistic determinism*. It is a totalizing view of language that reduces patterns of thought and culture to the grammatical patterns of the language spoken. If a grammar classifies nouns in male and female gender categories, for example, linguistic determinists claim that speakers of that language are forced to think of males and females as radically different kinds of beings. By contrast, a language that makes no grammatical distinctions on the basis of gender supposedly trains its speakers to think of males and females as exactly the same. If linguistic determinism is correct,

then a change in grammar should change thought patterns: if English speakers replaced *he* and *she* with a new, gender-neutral third-person singular pronoun, such as *te*, then, linguistic determinists predict, English speakers would begin to treat men and women as equals.

There are a number of problems with linguistic determinism. In the first place, there are languages such as Fulfulde in which only one third-person pronoun is used for males and females (*o*); however, male-dominant social patterns are quite evident among Fulfulde speakers. In the second place, if language determined thought in this way, it would be impossible to translate from one language to another or even to learn another language with a different grammatical structure. Because human beings *can* learn foreign languages and translate from one language to another, the strong version of the linguistic relativity principle cannot be correct. Third, even if it were possible to draw firm boundaries around speech communities (which it is not), every language provides its native speakers with alternative ways of describing the world. Finally, in many societies, people learn to speak more than one language fluently. Yet people who grow up bilingual do not also grow up unable to reconcile two contradictory views of reality. Indeed, bilingual children ordinarily benefit from knowing two languages, do not confuse them, can switch readily from one to another, and even appear to demonstrate greater cognitive flexibility on psychological tests than do monolinguals (Elliot 1981, 56). Consequently, bilingualism, or even multilingualism, is a highly valued skill, especially in our modern globalized world. In Canada, where students are given the opportunity to learn both of the country's official languages in school, approximately 17.5 per cent of the population is able to conduct a conversation in both French and English (Lepage and Corbeil 2013) (Figure 9.6).

As an alternative to the more problematic "strong" version of the linguistic relativity principle, theorists have proposed a "weak" version that rejects linguistic determinism but continues to claim that language shapes thought and culture. Thus, grammatical gender might not determine a male-dominant social order, but it might facilitate the acceptance of such a social order because the grammatical distinction between *he* and *she* might make separate and unequal gender roles seem

**linguistic relativity principle** A position, associated with Edward Sapir and Benjamin Whorf, that asserts that language has the power to shape the way people see the world.

**FIGURE 9.6** | Canada is officially a bilingual country, and children across the country have the opportunity to learn both English and French in school.

"natural." Because many native speakers of English also are strong promoters of gender equality, however, the shaping power of grammar would seem far too weak to merit any scientific attention.

Neither Sapir nor Whorf favoured linguistic determinism. Sapir argued that language's importance lies in the way it directs attention to some aspects of experience rather than to others. He was impressed by the fact that "it is generally difficult to make a complete divorce between objective reality and our linguistic symbols of reference to it" (Sapir [1933] 1966, 9, 15). Whorf's views have been more sharply criticized by later scholars. His discussions of the linguistic relativity principle are complex and ambiguous. At least part of the problem arises from Whorf's attempt to view grammar as the linguistic pattern that shapes culture and thought. Whorf's contemporaries understood grammar to refer to rules for combining sounds into words and words into sentences. Whorf believed that grammar needed to be thought of in broader terms (Schultz 1990), but he died before working out the theoretical language to describe such a level.

In recent years, interest in the "Whorfian question" has revived, and scholars have recognized that there are several different ways to ask about the relationship of language to thought. Especially exciting is the new perspective that comes from focusing on the influence of language in pragmatic contexts of use. Dan Slobin's "thinking for speaking" hypothesis, for example, suggests that the influence of linguistic forms on thought may be greatest when people prepare to speak to others on a specific topic in a specific setting. "One fits one's thoughts into available linguistic forms. . . . 'Thinking for speaking' involves

picking those characteristics that (a) fit some conceptualization of the event, and (b) are readily encodable in the language" (Slobin 1987, 435). Slobin points out that related challenges are faced by speakers involved in "thinking for writing" or "thinking for translating." Thinking for translating is especially intriguing, particularly when translators must render features that are grammatically encoded in one language into a second language in which they are not encoded, or vice versa (Slobin 2003).

Dedre Gentner and Susan Goldin-Meadow (2003) point out that some researchers still take a traditional Whorfian approach, viewing language as a lens through which people view the world. Others think of language as a tool kit, a set of resources that speakers make use of to build more elaborate conceptual structures. Still others think of language as a category maker, influencing the way people classify experiences and objects in the world. They note that the research that produces the most consistent evidence of the influence of language on thought comes from those who view language as a tool kit—that is, as a set of resources that speakers make use of for conceptual or communicative purposes (Gentner and Goldin-Meadow 2003, 10). Nevertheless, they emphasize that defining the research question in such variable ways means that "we are unlikely to get a yes-or-no answer to the whole of Whorf's thesis. But if we have delineated a set of more specific questions for which the answer is no to some and yes to others, we will have achieved our goal" (12).

## Pragmatics: How Do We Study Language in Contexts of Use?

**Pragmatics** can be defined as the study of language in the context of its use. Each context offers limitations and

**pragmatics** The study of language in the context of its use.

opportunities concerning what we may say and how we may say it. Everyday language use is thus often characterized by a struggle between speakers and listeners over definitions of context and appropriate word use. Linguistic anthropologist Michael Silverstein (1976, 1985) was one of the first to argue that the referential meaning of certain expressions in language cannot be determined unless we go beyond the boundaries of a sentence and place the expressions in a wider context of use. Two kinds of context must be considered. *Linguistic context* refers to the other words, expressions, and sentences that surround the expression whose meaning we are trying to determine. The meaning of *it* in the sentence "I really enjoyed it" cannot be determined if the sentence is considered on its own. However, if we know that the previous sentence was "My aunt gave me this book," we have a linguistic context that allows us to deduce that *it* refers to *this book*. *Non-linguistic context* consists of objects and activities that are present in the situation of speech at the same time we are speaking. Consider the sentence "Who is that standing by the door?" We need to inspect the actual physical context at the moment this sentence is uttered to find the door and the person standing by the door and thus give a referential meaning to the words *who* and *that*. Furthermore, even if we know what a door is in a formal sense, we need the non-linguistic context to clarify what counts as a door in this instance (e.g., it could be a rough opening in the wall) (Figure 9.7).

By going beyond formal grammatical analysis, pragmatics directs our attention to **discourse**, understood as a stretch of speech longer than a sentence united by a common theme. Discourse may be a series of sentences uttered by a single individual or a series of rejoinders in a conversation among two or more speakers. Many linguistic anthropologists accept the arguments of M.M. Bakhtin (1981) and V.N. Voloshinov (see, e.g., Voloshinov [1926] 1987) that the series of verbal exchanges in conversation is the primary form of discourse. In this view, the speech of any single individual, whether a simple *yes* or a book-length dissertation, is only one rejoinder in an ongoing dialogue.

## Ethnopragmatics

Linguistic anthropologists pay attention not only to the immediate context of speech, linguistic and non-linguistic, but also to broader contexts that are shaped by unequal social relationships and rooted in history

**FIGURE 9.7 |** To answer the question "What is that on the door?" requires that we examine the actual physical context at the moment we are asked the question to try to determine what *that* refers to. Is it the locks? Is it the door handles? Is it the studs on the door? Also, what part of the structure is the "door"?

(Brenneis and Macaulay 1996; Hill and Irvine 1992). Alessandro Duranti (1994, 11) calls this **ethnopragmatics**, "a study of language use which relies on ethnography to illuminate the ways in which speech is both constituted by and constitutive of social interaction." Such a

**discourse**  A stretch of speech longer than a sentence united by a common theme.

**ethnopragmatics**  The study of language use that relies on ethnography to illuminate the ways in which speech is both constituted by and constitutive of social interaction.

study focuses on *practice*, human activity in which the rules of grammar, cultural values, and physical action are all conjoined (Hanks 1996, 11). Such a perspective locates the source of meaning in everyday routine social activity, or *habitus*, rather than in grammar. As a result, phonemes, morphemes, syntax, and semantics are viewed as *linguistic resources* people can make use of, rather than rigid forms that determine what people can and cannot think or say.

If mutual understanding is shaped by shared routine activity and not by grammar, then communication is possible even if the people interacting with one another speak mutually unintelligible languages. All they need is a shared sense of "what is going on here" and the ability to negotiate successfully who will do what (Hanks 1996, 234). Such mutually co-engaged people shape *communicative practices* that involve spoken language but also include values and shared habitual knowledge that may never be put into words. Because most people in most societies regularly engage in a wide range of practical activities with different subgroups, each one will also end up knowledgeable about a variety of different communicative practices and the linguistic habits that go with them. For example, a college student might know the linguistic habits appropriate to dinner with her parents, to the classroom, to worship services, to conversations in the dorm with friends, and to her part-time job in a restaurant (Figure 9.8). Each set of linguistic habits she knows is called a *discourse genre*. Because our student simultaneously knows a multiplicity of different discourse genres she can choose among when she speaks, her linguistic knowledge is characterized by what Bakhtin called *heteroglossia* (Bakhtin 1981).

For Bakhtin, heteroglossia is the normal condition of linguistic knowledge in any society with internal divisions. Heteroglossia describes a coexisting multiplicity of linguistic norms and forms, many of which are anchored in more than one social subgroup. Because we all participate in more than one of these subgroups, we inevitably become fluent in many varieties of language, even if we speak only English! Our capacity for

**FIGURE 9.8** | When interacting with friends, young people tend to employ linguistic habits that are much less formal than those they might use when interacting with someone in a position of authority such as a professor or an employer.

heteroglossia is an example of linguistic openness: it means that our thought and speech are not imprisoned in a single set of grammatical forms, as linguistic determinists argued. Indeed, if our college student reflects on the overlap as well as the contrasts between the language habits used in the dorm and those used in the restaurant, she might well find herself raising questions about what words really mean. To the extent that her habitual ways of speaking are deeply rooted in everyday routine activity, however, they may guide the way she typically thinks, perceives, and acts. And so, the linguistic relativity hypothesis may be correct—not on the level of grammatical categories but on the level of discourse (Hanks 1996, 176, 246; Schultz 1990).

## What Happens When Languages Come into Contact?

In local communities where they know each other well, speakers and listeners are able, for the most part, to draw on knowledge of overlapping language habits to converse or argue about moral and political issues. Sometimes, however, potential parties to a verbal exchange find themselves sharing little more than physical proximity to one another. Such situations arise when members of communities with radically different language traditions and no history of previous contact with one another come face to face and are forced to communicate. There is no way to predict the outcome of such enforced contact on either speech community, yet from these new shared

**pidgin** (1) A language with no native speakers that develops in a single generation between members of communities that possess distinct native languages. (2) A shared secondary language in a speech community in which speakers also use some other main language.

experiences, new forms of practice, including a new form of language—pidgin—may develop.

"When the chips are down, meaning is negotiated" (Lakoff and Johnson 1980, 231). The study of pidgin languages is the study of the radical negotiation of new meaning, the production of a new whole (the pidgin language) that is different from and reducible to none of the languages that gave birth to it. The shape of a pidgin reflects the context in which it arises—generally one of colonial conquest or commercial domination. Vocabulary is usually taken from the language of the dominant group, making it easy for that group to learn. The system of pronunciation and sentence structure may be similar to the subordinate language (or languages), however, making it easier for subordinated speakers to learn. Complex grammatical features marking the gender or number of nouns or the tenses of verbs tend to disappear (Holm 1988).

### What Is the Difference between a Pidgin and a Creole?

Pidgins are traditionally defined as reduced languages that have no native speakers. They develop, in a single generation, between groups of speakers that possess distinct native languages. When speakers of a pidgin language pass that language on to a new generation, linguists have traditionally referred to the language as a creole. As linguists studied pidgins and creoles more closely, they discovered that the old distinction between pidgins and creoles did not seem to hold up. In the Pacific, for example, linguists have discovered pidgin dialects, pidgin languages used as main languages of permanently settled groups, and pidgins that have become native languages. Moreover, creolization can take place at any time after a pidgin forms, creoles can exist without having been preceded by pidgins, pidgins can remain pidgins for long periods and undergo linguistic change without acquiring native speakers, and pidgin and creole varieties of the same language can coexist in the same society (Jourdan 1991, 192ff.). In fact, it looks as if heteroglossia is as widespread among speakers of pidgins and creoles as it is among speakers of other languages.

### How Is Meaning Negotiated?

More information has been gathered about the historical and sociocultural contexts within which pidgins first formed. Here, as elsewhere in linguistic anthropology, the focus has turned to communicative practice. From this perspective, creolization is likely when pidgin speakers find themselves in new social contexts requiring a new language for *all* the practical activities of everyday life; without such a context, it is unlikely that creoles will emerge. Accordingly, a pidgin is now defined as a secondary language in a speech community that uses some other main language, and a creole is understood as a main language in a speech community, whether or not it has native speakers (Jourdan 1991, 196).

Viewing pidgin creation as a form of communicative practice means that attention must be paid to the role of pidgin creators as agents in the process. As we negotiate meaning across language barriers, it appears that all humans have intuitions about which parts of our speech carry the most meaning and which parts can be safely dropped. Neither party to the negotiation, moreover, may be trying to learn the other's language; rather, "speakers in the course of negotiating communication use whatever linguistic and sociolinguistic resources they have at their disposal, until the shared meaning is established and conventionalized" (Jourdan 1991, 200).

## What Is Linguistic Inequality?

Pidgins and creoles turn out to be far more complex and the result of far more active human input than we used to think, which is why they are attractive to linguists and linguistic anthropologists as objects of study. Where they coexist, however, alongside the language of the dominant group (e.g., Hawaiian Pidgin English and English), they are ordinarily viewed as defective and inferior languages. Such views can be considered as a result of the situation that led to the formation of most of the pidgins we know about: European colonial domination. In a colonial or postcolonial setting, the language of the colonizer is often viewed as better than pidgin or creole languages, which are frequently thought to be broken, imperfect versions of the colonizer's language. The situation only worsens when formal education, the key to

creole (1) A complex language with native speakers that has developed over one or more generations from two or more distinct languages. (2) A complex language that has developed from two or more distinct languages and that is used as a main language, whether or not it has native speakers.

participation in the European-dominated society, is carried out in the colonial language. Speakers of pidgin who remain illiterate may never be able to master the colonial tongue and may find themselves effectively barred from equal participation in the civic life of their societies.

To take one language variety as the standard against which all other varieties are measured might be described as "linguistic ethnocentrism," and such a standard may be applied to any language, not just pidgins and creoles. This is one kind of linguistic inequality: making value judgments about other people's speech in a context of dominance and subordination. A powerful example of the effects of linguistic inequality is found in the history of Aboriginal children who were forced into the residential school system of Canada (Figure 9.9).

Beginning in the late 1880s, the government of Canada implemented an assimilation policy that required First Nations, Métis, and Inuit children to attend residential boarding schools. With the aim of "civilizing" the children (sometimes referred to as "taking the Indian out of the child"), the Canadian government provided funding for the schools, which were run by Christian churches of various denominations. By the 1930 to 1940s, approximately 50 per cent of all First Nations children were living in these schools, separated from their families and cultures. In total, more than 150,000 Aboriginal children passed through the residential school system before the last federally funded schools closed in the late 1990s (Truth and Reconciliation Commission of Canada 2015, 3). Speaking Aboriginal languages at school was strictly forbidden, and students who disobeyed the rules often faced severe physical and emotional punishments. For example, Celia Haig-Brown (1988, 11) recalls how her father, "who attended the Alberni Indian Residential school for four years in the twenties, was physically tortured by his teachers for speaking Tseshaht: they pushed sewing needles through his tongue, a routine punishment for language offenders." Isolated from their families for months on end, many students lost the ability to speak their own languages and, subsequently, were unable to pass on those languages to their children. Even as adults, many residential-school survivors were too traumatized and ashamed to speak or relearn their original language. Others discouraged their children from learning their ancestral language, believing that fluency in English or French would make their lives easier. As a result, generations of Aboriginal peoples in Canada are still experiencing the repercussions of language loss and cultural genocide. Marie Battiste (1986, xx) suggests that this type of forced assimilation and linguistic dominance can be considered the final stage of a "cognitive imperialism" that essentially "white-wash[ed] the tribal mind and soul."

On 11 June 2008, the Canadian government presented a formal apology to all who had been harmed

**FIGURE 9.9 |** Canada's residential school system provides a powerful and troubling example of how a dominant culture's linguistic ethnocentrism contributed to the loss of Aboriginal languages. First Nations children forced to attend residential schools were prohibited from speaking Aboriginal languages and punished for doing so. Here, Cree students learn English in a classroom at an Anglican Church-run missionary school in Lac La Ronge, Saskatchewan, in 1945.

in the residential school system, and numerous foundations were established to assist those who were in need of healing and reconciliation. Also established in 2008 was the Truth and Reconciliation Commission of Canada (TRC), which was given the task of investigating the full consequences of the Canadian residential school system. After years of conducting interviews and examining historical records, the TRC released its final report in early June 2015. On the topic of language loss, the report concluded that the residential school system had "contributed significantly to the fragile state of Aboriginal languages in Canada today":

> Many of the almost ninety surviving Aboriginal languages in Canada are under serious threat of extinction. In the 2011 census, 14.5 per cent of the Aboriginal population reported that their first language learned was an Aboriginal language. In the previous 2006 census, 18 per cent of those who identified as Aboriginal had reported an Aboriginal language as their first language learned, and a decade earlier, in the 1996 census, the figure was 26 per cent. This indicates nearly a 50 per cent drop in the 15 years since the last residential schools closed.

Despite the establishment of cultural and language revitalization programs on reservations across the country, the statistics on Aboriginal language use appear grim: across Canada, only 25 per cent of the Aboriginal population is able to speak or understand an Aboriginal language with full fluency (Norris 2007). Moreover, the majority of these speakers belong to older generations. Thus, as these speakers age and pass on, the Aboriginal languages they speak will become increasingly endangered. Aboriginal people living in urban areas face the greatest obstacles to learning and speaking their native languages because they are geographically isolated from their communities and may lack cultural support. At the same time, growing numbers of people—young and old, Aboriginal and non-Aboriginal—are recognizing the central importance of language to cultural identity and thus the urgent necessity to revitalize Aboriginal languages (see the "Anthropology in the Contemporary World" box on Aboriginal language revitalization).

## What Is Language Ideology?

Building on earlier work on linguistic inequality, linguistic anthropologists in recent years have developed a focus on the study of language ideology—ways of representing the intersection "between social forms and forms of talk" (Woolard 1998, 3). While the study of language ideology discloses speakers' sense of beauty or morality or basic understandings of the world, it also provides evidence of the ways in which our speech is always embedded in a social world of power differences. Language ideologies are markers of struggles between social groups with different interests, revealed in what people say and how they say it. The way people monitor their speech to bring it into line with a particular language ideology illustrates that language ideologies are "active and effective . . . they transform the material reality they comment on" (Woolard 1998, 11). In settings with a history of colonization, where groups with different power and different languages coexist in tension, the study of language ideologies has long been significant (Woolard 1998, 16). The skills of linguistic anthropologists especially suit them to study language ideologies because their linguistic training allows them to describe precisely the linguistic features (e.g., phonological, morphological, or syntactic) that become the focus of ideological attention, and their training in cultural analysis allows them to explain how those linguistic features come to stand symbolically for a particular social group.

Language ideology in Canada centres on the fact that we are a bilingual country founded by two predominantly white colonizing nations. The Official Languages Act (1969) recognized English and French as our two official languages, which has affected everything from labelling on food products to employment in federal agencies to funding for education. In essence, nation building and belonging in Canada are framed within the ideology of bilingualism and biculturalism. Further, as a bilingual country, Canada has created a positive image of itself as a tolerant and progressive society. However, even English and French are not treated equally in all communities across the country. French speakers living outside of Quebec are

---

**language ideology** A marker of struggles between social groups with different interests, revealed in what people say and how they say it.

## Anthropology in the Contemporary World

### Aboriginal Language Revitalization

*Without the language, we are warm bodies without a spirit.*

—Mary Lou Fox, Ojibwe elder

Many linguists and linguistic anthropologists who specialize in the study of Aboriginal languages in Canada are increasingly involved in collaborating with Aboriginal peoples to preserve and revive Aboriginal languages in the face of threatened decline or extinction. According to the 2011 Census of Population, there exist in Canada over sixty distinct Aboriginal languages, which are generally grouped into 12 language families (Statistics Canada 2012) (Map 9.2; Table 9.1). Each of these languages forms a crucial part of the history and cultural identity of the people who speak it, and of the people whose ancestors spoke it in the past. Thus, language revitalization is an essential component of cultural revitalization. Moreover, it is essential to the revival of Aboriginal knowledge and to efforts toward self-governance and the promotion of Aboriginal rights (Battiste 2012). For many Aboriginal people, speaking their traditional language is not only an expression of identity, it is also an assertion of empowerment.

Despite a lengthy history of language loss, especially as a result of residential schooling, many Aboriginal people today maintain hope for the success of their endeavours to revitalize their traditional languages. Many also refuse to consider those languages that have no fluent speakers as "extinct," instead referring to them as "sleeping

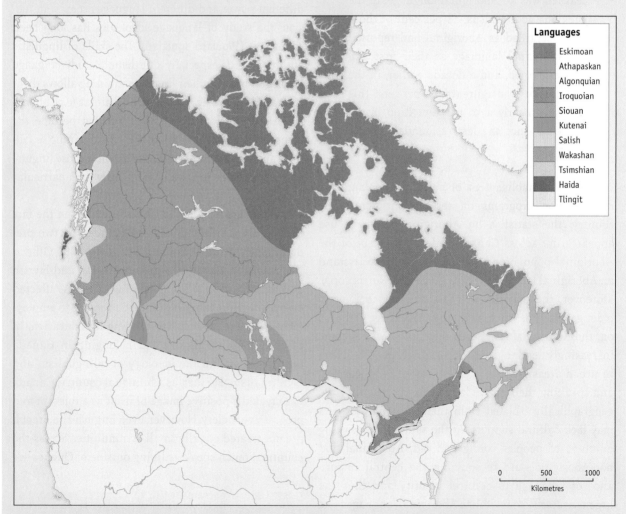

**Languages**
- Eskimoan
- Athapaskan
- Algonquian
- Iroquoian
- Siouan
- Kutenai
- Salish
- Wakashan
- Tsimshian
- Haida
- Tlingit

**MAP 9.2 |** Traditional distribution of Aboriginal language groups, before contact with Europeans.

**TABLE 9.1** | Number and location of native speakers of Aboriginal languages, Canada, 2011

| Aboriginal Language Families and Main Languages | Provincial and Territorial Main Concentrations | Number of Speakers[a] |
|---|---|---|
| **Algonquian Languages** | **Manitoba (24.7%), Quebec (23.0%)** | **144,015** |
| Cree languages | Saskatchewan (28.8%), Manitoba (24.0%), Alberta (21.9%), and Quebec (18.5%) | 83,475 |
| Ojibway | Ontario (46.3%) and Manitoba (44.3%) | 19,275 |
| Innu/Montagnais | Quebec (80.9%) and Newfoundland and Labrador (18.7%) | 10,965 |
| Oji-Cree | Manitoba (69.1%) and Ontario (30.7%) | 10,180 |
| Mi'kmaq | Nova Scotia (60.2%) and New Brunswick (27.5%) | 8,030 |
| Atikamekw | Quebec (99.9%) | 5,915 |
| Blackfoot | Alberta (97.5%) | 3,250 |
| **Inuit (Eskimoan) Languages** | **Nunavut (61.6%) and Quebec (31.3%)** | **35,500** |
| Inuktitut | Nunavut (63.1%) and Quebec (32.3%) | 34,110 |
| **Athapaskan Languages** | **Saskatchewan (40.5%) and Northwest Territories (22.7%)** | **20,700** |
| Dene | Saskatchewan (70.6%) and Alberta (15.2%) | 11,860 |
| Tlicho (Dogrib) | Northwest Territories (96.2%) | 2,080 |
| Slavey[b] | Northwest Territories (85.9%) | 1,595 |
| Carrier | British Columbia (98.0%) | 1,525 |
| **Siouan Languages** | **Alberta (76.9%) and Manitoba (16.6%)** | **4,425** |
| Stoney | Alberta (99.5%) | 3,155 |
| Dakota | Manitoba (62.5%) and Alberta (21.6%) | 1,160 |
| **Salish Languages** | **British Columbia (98.0%)** | **2,950** |
| Shuswap (Secwepemctsin) | British Columbia (97.0%) | 675 |
| Halkomelem | British Columbia (98.2%) | 570 |
| **Tsimshian Languages** | **British Columbia (98.1%)** | **1,815** |
| Gitksan | British Columbia (98.9%) | 925 |
| Nisga'a | British Columbia (96.7%) | 615 |
| **Wakashan Languages** | **British Columbia (95.3%)** | **1,075** |
| Kwakiutl (Kwak'wala) | British Columbia (98.0%) | 495 |
| Nootka (Nuu-chah-nulth) | British Columbia (90.6%) | 320 |
| **Iroquoian Languages** | **Ontario (82.7%) and Quebec (10.6%)** | **1,040** |
| Mohawk | Ontario (73.4%) and Quebec (18.3%) | 545 |
| **Michif[c]** | **Saskatchewan (40.6%), Manitoba (26.6%), and Alberta (11.7%)** | **640** |
| **Tlingit** | **Yukon (84.6%) and British Columbia (11.5%)** | **130** |
| **Kutenai** | **British Columbia (100%)** | **100** |
| **Haida** | **British Columbia (93.3%)** | **75** |
| **Aboriginal Languages[d]** | **British Columbia (43.6%) and Ontario (30.2%)** | **1,010** |
| **Total Aboriginal Mother-Tongue Population** | **Quebec (20.9%), Manitoba (17.7%), and Saskatchewan (16.0%)** | **213,490** |

[a] Counts for languages with a family do not add to the total of the language family because only the main languages are shown.

[b] Not otherwise specified.

[c] Michif is the traditional language of the Métis.

[d] Not included elsewhere.

Source: Statistics Canada 2012.

languages" that can be "awakened" with effort (Huang 2009). In many communities, a major form this effort takes is the establishment of Aboriginal-run language classes for young people. The hope among many Aboriginal people is that by taking back responsibility for educating their children, they may one day be able to undo much of the cultural damage done by the legacy of the residential school system. And, in many communities, these efforts seem to be having a positive effect, as growing numbers of younger Aboriginal Canadians are learning the language

continued

of their ancestors as a second language (Norris 2007). While learning these languages as second rather than first languages is not an ideal solution, it is an essential part of the process of language revitalization in situations where parents are no longer able to teach their children the language of their ancestors because they themselves are not fluent in that language (ibid.).

What role can anthropologists play in these sorts of community-based approaches to language revitalizations? A central goal for many linguistic anthropologists working in this realm is to record and document Aboriginal languages as they are used by native speakers. These recordings can be very useful when working with elders who may have forgotten their native language, as listening to recordings of the language can reignite their memory and help them strengthen their language skills. Anthropological research can also help project leaders identify the most effective approaches, tools, and programs for working with any given group. For example, the Nunavut government has drawn on such research in creating television shows that teach Inuktituk to children and in planning language classes and speaking groups for adults. At the same time, input from anthropologists should never replace the voices of the people of the communities in which the programs are being run. To succeed, language revitalization initiatives must be collaborative, with community members playing a central role in their development and their implementation.

Source: *http://indigenousfoundations.arts.ubc.ca/home/culture/languages.html*

often considered minorities and pressured to adopt English as their primary language. Likewise, English speakers living in Quebec are often considered minorities there and are pressured to adopt French as their primary language.

Canada's binary linguistic ideology has had even greater consequences for all those "others" who speak neither English nor French as their first language. This struggle for identity and belonging by linguistic "others" in Canada is discussed fully in Eva Haque's recent book *Multiculturalism within a Bilingual Framework* (2012). Haque argues that race, culture, and language are inextricably linked to notions of who we are as a nation. In many ways, "belonging" in Canada requires one to identify with one of the two official founding nations (England and France). Haque traces the numerous ways that the use and promotion of our two official languages creates a "convenient alibi for racial ordering" in a country that espouses multiculturalism. Bilingualism functions in a multiculturalist framework in Canada, creating unintended tensions and inequalities that are often contradictory in policy and in practice.

## How Do Issues of Language Use and Gender Intersect?

In many cultures, language habits tend to differ along gender lines. Since the early 1970s, feminists have analyzed the linguistic models that shape how men and women communicate. Deborah Tannen (1990), a sociolinguist, suggests that in Western cultures, men and women use language in opposing ways: men use it in a competitive manner, especially in public, while women use it to form relationships, especially in private settings. Consequently, miscommunication between men and women often occurs when members of one gender assume that members of the other gender are using language in the same way as they are.

The words we use to talk about people of different genders also structure how we ascribe qualities to each gender. In North America, for example, we often use male-gendered words such as *he*, *him*, *his*, and *guys* to describe individuals or groups of people whose gender is unknown. This usage suggests that men have a normative, and sometimes preferentially positive, status. Consider also the wide variety of gendered terms that are commonly used to describe professional or work-related roles. Terms like *mailman*, *policeman*, and *businessman* all describe professional roles traditionally filled by men in past generations, while words like *housewife*, *waitress*, and *hostess* describe roles traditionally filled by women. Although gender-neutral terms that use *person* in place of *man* or *woman* or that drop the *-ess* typically associated with female-gendered words are becoming more common, this type of gendered language use persists. The existence of differences in the ways in which we use gendered words provides insight into distinct social roles and power frameworks that exist between genders cross-culturally. Language use,

## In Their Own Words

### Borrowed Words, Mock Language, and Nationalism in Canada

*Rachelle Vessey looks at how borrowed words are used as boundary markers by French- and English-speaking Canadians.*

In Canada, where languages serve as symbols of the national divide, borrowed words used in discussions of the nation appear to have different meanings from their translation equivalents. They serve as a covert means of signalling group boundaries that are based not only on language, but also on the broader cultural elements that are indexed by languages. . . .

This study showed that *nationale* was used differently to *national* in English. . . . The term *nationale* seems to indirectly index French-speaking nationalism in Quebec, which appears to be marked as different from Canadian nationalism and predominantly negatively evaluated. As a result, the English use of the borrowed form *nationale* arguably constitutes mock language. In a similar way, in the French corpus the terms *Canadian* and *Canadians* were used differently to *Canadien/s* and *Canadienne/s*. . . . In the French data, *Canadian/s* appears to refer to "belonging to or association with Canada," but also indirectly indexes an English-speaking country, which is suggested to be separate from Quebec. Thus, the implicature of English-Canada French-Quebec group difference indicates that the French use of the borrowed form *Canadian/s* also constitutes mock language.

These words not only achieve meaning through their direct context . . . but also gain meaning from the wider context of the Canadian linguistic situation. . . . These examples have demonstrated that borrowed words have especially important meaning in multilingual and multicultural contexts, and they pose particularly interesting challenges to researchers. This case study of only two borrowed words in Canada suggests different understandings of language and nationalism in two cultural communities. . . . [L]ow levels of French–English bilingualism prevent individuals from accessing perspective of the other (largely monolingual) group. Thus, to a large degree, English and French speakers live in relative isolation from one another. . . .

Perhaps ironically, many Canadians are not aware they live in isolation from the other group, because they see and hear speakers of the other official language (e.g., federal politicians and spokespeople) on a daily basis; however what they witness is often in translation. . . . [T]he other official language is rarely encountered in the original. . . . [R]ather than truly engaging the other language, Canadians sometimes use borrowed words to index belonging in specific linguistic and national communities.

Source: Vessey 2014, 186–7. Reprinted by permission of the publisher (Taylor & Francis Ltd, http://www.tandfonline.com).

then, may be considered as a partner in creating cultural models for males and females.

## What Is Lost If a Language Dies?

At the beginning of the twenty-first century, many anthropologists and linguists have become involved in projects to maintain or revive languages with small numbers of native speakers. As touched on earlier in this chapter in relation to Aboriginal languages in Canada, these languages are in danger of disappearing as younger people in the speech community stop using the language or never learn it in the first place. Communities concerned about language revitalization can range from Irish speakers in the United Kingdom to Mi'kmaq speakers in Nova Scotia to users of an Aboriginal sign language in Australia.

And the threats to these languages range widely as well. They include the spread of "world" languages like English and the marginalization of one dialect in favour of a neighbouring dialect. They also include support for a "national" sign language (e.g., in Thailand) in place of local, "Indigenous" sign languages used by small communities, and the spread of technologies that can "save" people from being deaf (Walsh 2005). How seriously different "small languages" are endangered depends on what counts as small and how imminent the threat is perceived to be—and experts can differ in their evaluation of these matters.

## In Their Own Words

### Revitalizing Indigenous Languages in the Urban Amazon

*Sarah Shulist of MacEwan University outlines her research on language loss and revitalization among the Kotiria, Indigenous peoples whose traditional homelands are in the northwest Amazon region of Brazil and Colombia. As Shulist notes, many Kotiria today face loss of their language as they move from rural areas to cities.*

My work in the northwest Amazon of Brazil looks at the relationship between two of the most important social changes happening in the lives of Indigenous people, both in that region and in many others around the world—language shift and urbanization. Even though more and more of the world's Indigenous people are living in cities, language revitalization efforts are mainly being implemented in rural areas or recognized Indigenous territories/reserves. The presence of a larger and more diverse population, the disconnection from the territorial homeland, and the necessity of interaction with fundamentally different social structures and institutions make it very difficult to imagine ways of supporting Indigenous languages and cultures in these contexts.

The Kotiria (Wanano) people living in the city of São Gabriel da Cachoeira, Amazonas, are facing these challenges. In this small city of 13,000 people, 85 per cent of the population is Indigenous, and at least a dozen Indigenous languages are spoken by its inhabitants. The Kotiria's traditional territory is located in a remote part of the upper Uaupés (Vaupés) basin, in both Brazil and Colombia, and although there are only about 1000 speakers of the language left in total, the fact that it is still being learned as a first language by children in the rural areas means that it is in a stronger position than many other endangered languages of the world. The language has further been strengthened by the creation of a Kotiria-medium school within the Kotiria's traditional territory. This school is important both because it has led to an increase in materials available for learning and using the language, and because it has helped prevent the migration of families out of these communities in pursuit of educational opportunities for their children.

About 35 Kotiria families make their permanent homes in the city of São Gabriel, however, and the children born to those families do not formally learn the Kotiria language. In reflecting on their decision to live in an urban area, the parents of these children express less concern over the risk that the Kotiria language could disappear from use entirely—since they are confident that it remains strong in the rural communities—and more over the possibility that their children might become disconnected from their identities as Indigenous Kotiria people. Among the Kotiria, language is important not only to marking one's identity but also to coming to understand what it means to be Kotiria and what one's place in the world is. The Kotiria are one of many peoples in the northwest Amazon region who use language as a marker of kinship. This marker becomes particularly important when it comes to marriage, as individuals are required to marry someone from another language group (a practice known as "linguistic exogamy"). These social rules have meant that, among these groups, households were always made up of a mother who spoke one primary language and a father who

Linguistic anthropologists have paid particular attention to Indigenous languages spoken by small communities who have experienced a history of colonization by outsiders and who are minorities within states where colonial languages dominate. At the same time, as Michael Walsh (2005) explains, Indigenous language situations are not all alike. In Guatemala, for example, "Mayan languages are spoken among a majority of the populations, and the languages are all closely related; so it is possible to have a more unified approach to Mayan language revitalization. Mayas in Guatemala are now using

their languages in schools, and they are taking steps toward gaining official recognition of their languages" (296). Sometimes, however, colonial borders separate members of an Indigenous language community, meaning that speakers on one side of the border may be better supported in their language revitalization efforts than speakers on the other side of the border are. Examples include Ojibwe speakers (who are better supported in Canada than in the United States) and Quichua speakers (who receive different levels of support in Ecuador, Bolivia, and Peru) (Walsh 2005, 296). And sometimes the spoke a different one. While children in the rural territories are usually raised speaking both languages of their parents (and often more), the fact that children use only one (the father's language) both to understand who they are and to determine who they can marry means that each person has a strong motivation to preserve his or her *own* language.

In the case of the Kotiria living in São Gabriel, the pressures created by urbanization include some that are common the world over and others that are unique to the Kotiria situation. Although small by North American standards, the size of São Gabriel means that speakers of Kotiria are dispersed throughout a relatively large population and do not encounter one another on a daily basis. Young people growing up in the city are influenced more by mainstream Brazilian (and global) entertainment than by Kotiria culture, and they prioritize romantic love matches over linguistic exogamy, reducing the importance they place on their linguistic choices. Kotiria adults—primarily the fathers, who are the ones expected to transmit their identities and cultural knowledge to their children—have to work in formal positions in order to earn money to support their family, which takes them away from their children during the bulk of the day. Their children, meanwhile, spend the majority of their days attending Portuguese-language schools. In the rural context, the patterns of subsistence agriculture and fishing incorporate children as they get older, and linguistic and cultural knowledge is transmitted as they accompany their parents in these routines.

The Kotiria demonstrate a central theme of language revitalization for urban Indigenous people—it is very difficult, if not impossible, to recreate the social and family structures that support the transmission of Indigenous languages in more traditional communities. For these people, who feel a very powerful sense of loss in seeing their children unable to speak their language, it is not enough to have documentary work that helps to ensure the continuity of their language in rural areas, when for various reasons they are unable to return to live in those communities. Despite the challenges they face, however, the urban Kotiria are beginning a process of recognizing that the effort needed to support their language is as much about the creation of new social environments for using, transmitting, and discussing the language and cultural knowledge as it is about the development of pedagogical materials for teaching it. During my research visits to São Gabriel, I have helped to form an organization of Kotiria people, led by residents of the urban area, that will work to document and disseminate knowledge of their language and cultural practices in the city as well as in the rural communities. I have worked with members of this group in advocacy efforts to establish a Kotiria-medium school in the urban area, and to identify and understand the legal, ideological, and practical barriers that remain to be overcome in order to achieve this goal. We have also developed a set of strategies for the creation of new contexts in which the Kotiria language can be used, and for reaching young people who need to learn both the language and its importance for identity and cultural practice. Applying my anthropological training in order to better understand the social transformations taking place around language loss and the possibility of revitalization has led me to believe that linguistic anthropologists play a vital role in shaping effective programs and policy efforts.

Source: Courtesy of Sarah Shulist, 2015.

ethnolinguistic practices of speakers can interfere with language retention: Among Ilgar speakers in northern Australia, for example, conversation between opposite-sex siblings is forbidden. This means that a man finds himself "talking his mother tongue to people who don't speak it, and not talking it with the couple of people who do" (Evans 2001, 278; cited in Walsh 2005, 297).

Attempts to implement language revitalization have met with mixed success. Methods that work for literate groups (e.g., French speakers in Quebec) may be inappropriate for programs of language revival among speakers of languages that lack a long tradition of literacy, which is often the case with Indigenous languages in the Americas and Australia. In some cases, where prospects for revitalization are poor, it has been suggested that the functions of the endangered language can be transferred to a different language. This is a well-known phenomenon in the case of colonial languages like Spanish and English, which have all experienced "indigenization" as the communities who adopt them tailor them to fit their own local communicative practices. Other scholars have pointed out that language loss is nothing new. In the ancient world, for example, the spread of Latin led to the extinction of perhaps 50 of the 60 or so languages spoken in the Mediterranean prior to 100 BCE. However, the extension of Latin into ancient Europe also led to the birth of the Romance languages, some of whose native speakers (e.g., the French) express concern that the survival of their mother tongue is also threatened by the spread of global English (Walsh 2005; Sonntag 2003). New languages emerging from the processes of pidginization and creolization also continue to appear. For example,

Copper Island Aleut is a hybrid of Russian and Aleut (Walsh 2005, 297).

Maintaining or reviving endangered languages faces many obstacles, not the least of which is the concern of many parents who care less about preserving their dying language than they do about making sure their children become literate in a world language that will offer them a chance at economic and social mobility. Some Indigenous groups are concerned that loss of language will mean loss of access to traditional sources of religious or

## Anthropology in the Contemporary World

### Language Preservation in Baie Sainte-Marie: *Acadajonne ou Français?*

What is an endangered language? And why should such languages be saved? These questions framed the debates that occurred in the community of Baie Sainte-Marie, Nova Scotia, regarding *Acadajonne*, an endangered language thought by locals to represent an authentic form of French used in the late sixteenth and early seventeenth centuries. As Annette Boudreau and Lise Dubois (2007) discovered, the preservation of a language is often connected to political and symbolic values that are connected to social beliefs. Minority French-speaking communities outside of Quebec define themselves and their French language (sometimes referred to as *francité*) with respect to how they fit into the dominant anglophone society and the larger world of *la Francophonie* (worldwide speakers of French).

Baie Saint-Marie is a small francophone community that exists within an anglophone-dominated region of Nova Scotia. The survival of the community is linked to its members' continued use of *Acadajonne*, which has significant historical meaning to them. Locals feel that their language connects them to their ancestors, French colonists who originally settled the Baie Saint-Marie in 1604, were deported by the British in the late eighteenth century, and returned to reclaim the area by the mid-nineteenth century. This narrative of settlement, deportation, and resettlement creates a collective memory and sense of identity that ties the *Acadajonne* speakers of Baie Saint-Marie together and to the region. Associated with residents' historical connection to place is the fact that *Acadajonne* is the oldest variety of French still spoken in North America. *Acadajonne* has numerous words that have survived since colonization.

However, despite the importance of *Acadajonne* to those who speak it, there are both francophones who would suggest that this form of French is not worthy of being preserved and anglophones who would prefer English to be the only language used in the region.

While questions about the value of preserving *Acadajonne* as a distinct language have endured for generations, the debate intensified in the 1990s when a local community radio station began to use *Acadajonne* in its broadcasts. Today, those who support the use of what has long been a stigmatized form of French see the promotion of *Acadajonne* as a fight for legitimacy. Those who oppose its use suggest that it is not "proper" French and should therefore not be taught in schools or broadcast on airwaves; they suggest that widespread use of *Acadajonne* in the region may create a linguistic ghetto for *Acadajonne* speakers. In the course of their research, it became apparent to Boudreau and Dubois that the use of *Acadajonne* may be identified as a political resistance to the elite francophones in the area.

The power struggle between the two groups of francophones centres on the desire to gain social advantages through the use of language. And in this case, the promotion of tourism and commerce is an important consideration. Yet significant questions remain. Does the authenticity of Baie Sainte-Marie as an early French Acadian colony rest on whether or not *Acadajonne*, the language of the original settlers, continues to be used? Or is *Acadajonne* in fact a ghetto language that should be replaced with "proper" spoken French?

spiritual power, which can only be addressed in the traditional tongue. Yet other Indigenous speakers would not like to see what was once a fully functioning mode of communication reduced to nothing but ceremonial use. Clearly, language endangerment is a very delicate topic of discussion. This is unfortunate, in Walsh's view, since practical solutions require "frank and forthright discussions of the issues . . . and good clear statements of advice" (2005, 308). But Walsh also believes that concerned people who want to save their languages ought to try to do what they can and not wait until scholarly experts arrive at consensus.

## How Are Language and Truth Connected?

For the late Thomas Kuhn (1979), a philosopher of science, metaphor lay at the heart of science. Kuhn argued that changes in scientific theories were "accompanied by a change in some of the relevant metaphors and in corresponding parts of the network of similarities through which terms attach to nature" (416). Kuhn insisted that these changes in the way scientific terms link to nature are not reducible to logic or grammar. "They come about in response to pressures generated by observation or experiment"—that is, by experience and context. And there is no neutral language into which rival theories can be translated and subsequently evaluated as unambiguously right or wrong (ibid.). Kuhn asks the question, "Is what we refer to as 'the world' perhaps a product of mutual accommodation between experience and language?" (ibid.)

If our understanding of reality is the product of a dialectic between experience and language (or, more broadly, culture), then ambiguity will never be permanently removed from any of the symbolic systems that human beings invent. Reflexive consciousness makes humans aware of alternatives. The experience of doubt, of not being sure what to believe, is never far behind.

This is not merely the experience of people in Western societies. When E.E. Evans-Pritchard lived among the Dinka of Africa in the early twentieth century, he found that they experienced a similar form of disorientation (see EthnoProfile 9.2: Dinka). The Dinka

EthnoProfile 9.2

**Dinka**

**Region:** Eastern Africa
**Nation:** South Sudan
**Population:** 2,000,000
**Environment:** Savannah
**Livelihood:** Principally cattle herding, also agriculture
**Political organization:** Traditionally, egalitarian with noble clans and chiefs; today, part of a modern nation-state
**For more information:** Deng, Francis Madeng. 1972. *The Dinka of the Sudan*. New York: Holt, Rinehart, and Winston.

people, he wrote, were well aware of the ambiguity inherent in language, and they exploited it by using metaphor (what they called *sanza*) to disguise speech that might be received badly if uttered directly. For example, "A man says in the presence of his wife to his friend, 'Friend, those swallows, how they flit about in there.' He is speaking about the flightiness of his wife and in case she should understand the allusion, he covers himself by looking up at the swallows as he makes his seemingly innocent remark" (Evans-Pritchard 1963, 211). Evans-Pritchard later observed that *sanza* "adds greatly to the difficulties of anthropological inquiry. Eventually the anthropologist's sense of security is undermined and his confidence shaken. He learns the language, can say what he wants to say in it, and can understand what he hears, but then he begins to wonder whether he has really understood. . . . [H]e cannot be sure, and even they [the Dinka] cannot be sure, whether the words do have a nuance or someone imagines that they do" (228). However much we learn about language, we will never be able to exhaust its meanings or circumscribe its rules once and for all. Human language is an open system, and as long as human history continues, new forms will be created and old forms will continue to be put to new uses.

For more on the use of metaphor among the Dinka, see Chapter 10, p. 287.

## Chapter Summary

1. Symbolic language is a uniquely human faculty that both permits us to communicate with one another and sets up barriers to communication. At the same time, while language is necessary to communicate complex messages, humans frequently send non-verbal cues—for example, through body language, non-verbal vocalizations, and use of space—that can be as effective as language in communicating simple messages.

2. The anthropological study of languages reveals the cultural factors that shape language use. In every language, there are many ways to communicate our experiences, and there is no absolute standard favouring one way over another. Individual efforts to create a unique voice are countered by pressures to negotiate a common code within a larger speech community.

3. Of Charles Hockett's design features of language, six are particularly important: openness, displacement, arbitrariness, duality of patterning, semanticity, and prevarication.

4. Early linguistic anthropologists like Edward Sapir and Benjamin Whorf suggested that language has the power to shape the way people see the world. This concept is called the "linguistic relativity principle." How this shaping process works is still investigated by some linguistic anthropologists, who argue that linguistic relativity should not be confused with linguistic determinism, which they reject.

5. Ethnopragmatics locates linguistic meaning in routine practical activities, which turn grammatical features of language into resources people can use in their interactions with others. It pays attention both to the immediate context of speech and to broader contexts that are shaped by unequal social relationships and rooted in history.

6. Because linguistic meaning is rooted in practical activity, which carries the burden of meaning, different social groups engaged in different activities generate different communicative practices. The linguistic habits that are part of each set of communicative practices constitute discourse genres. People normally command a range of discourse genres, which means that each person's linguistic knowledge is characterized by heteroglossia.

7. When very different languages come into contact, those involved often construct a pidgin language to aid communication. The study of pidgin languages is the study of the radical negotiation of new meaning. Pidgin languages exhibit many of the same linguistic features as non-pidgin languages. In colonial and postcolonial settings, the language of the colonizer is frequently viewed as superior to the language(s) of the colonized. The residential school system established in Canada in the 1880s for the forced assimilation of First Nations children is an example of a dominant group's attempt to gain linguistic and cultural control over less powerful peoples in a postcolonial context.

8. Language ideologies are unwritten rules shared by members of a speech community concerning what kinds of language are valued. Language ideologies develop out of the cultural, social, and political histories of the groups to which they belong. Knowing the language ideology of a particular community can help listeners make sense of speech that otherwise would seem inappropriate or incomprehensible to them.

## For Review

1. Explain why language is a key concept studied by anthropologists. How is it related to culture? How is it related to human biology?

2. Distinguish among language, speech, and communication. Explain the significance of these differences.

3. Summarize the key points for each of the six design features of language discussed in this chapter (openness, displacement, arbitrariness, duality of patterning, semanticity, and prevarication). How does each feature separate human language from the call systems used by monkeys and apes?

4. Describe linguistic competence. How does it differ from communicative competence? Why do anthropologists draw a distinction between these two concepts?

5. Why do linguistic anthropologists emphasize the importance of context in language use?

6. What is the linguistic relativity principle? Summarize the problems with linguistic determinism, and describe the steps that contemporary linguists and linguistic anthropologists have taken to address these problems.

7. What is the traditional distinction between a pidgin and a creole? What is the more recent distinction that anthropologists have found to be more productive? Are there situations in which these terms might be interchangeable?

8. How was language used as a tool of power in residential schools in Canada? Include in your discussion the concept of language ideology.

9. What are some of the difficulties in achieving language revitalization? What are some of the benefits? Use examples from this chapter in your answer.

10. List some words and expressions that we use to refer to men and some that we use to refer to women. What do these words suggest about the qualities we ascribe to men and to women?

## Key Terms

body language  237
communicative competence  246
creole  251
discourse  249
ethnopragmatics  249
grammar  245

historical linguistics  241
kinesics  238
language  237
language ideology  253
linguistic competence  245
linguistic relativity principle  247

linguistics  240
native speaker  241
non-verbal communication  237
pidgin  250
pragmatics  248
proxemics  240

## Suggested Readings

Akmajian, Adrian, Richard A. Demers, Ann K. Farmer, and Robert M. Harnish. 2010. *Linguistics: An Introduction to Language and Communication*. 6th ed. Cambridge, MA: MIT Press. *A fine introduction to the study of language as a formal system.*

Blum, Susan, ed. 2008. *Making Sense of Language: Readings in Culture and Communication*. New York: Oxford University Press. 2nd ed. *An engaging and accessible collection of original essays by a wide range of scholars, inside and outside anthropology, past and present, who explore the many dimensions of human language.*

Brenneis, Donald, and Ronald K.S. Macaulay, eds. 1996. *The Matrix of Language: Contemporary Linguistic Anthropology*. Boulder, CO: Westview Press. *A wide-ranging collection of essays by anthropologists studying linguistic habits in their sociocultural contexts.*

Burling, Robbins. 2005. *The Talking Ape: How Language Evolved*. Oxford: Oxford University Press. *A lively introduction for non-specialists to the nature and evolution of human language, written by a distinguished linguistic anthropologist.*

Danesi, Marcel. 2012. *Linguistic Anthropology: A Brief Introduction*. Toronto: Canadian Scholars' Press. *In this concise text, Canadian linguistic anthropologist Marcel Danesi provides an accessible introduction to the anthropological study of the relations between language and society.*

Duchéne, Alexandre, and Monica Heller. 2007. *Discourses of Endangerment: Interest and Ideology in the Defense of Languages*. New York: Continuum Publishers. *This book, which is co-edited by University of Toronto professor Monica Heller, provides a global representation of papers on the endangerment of languages in the context of multilingualism. It addresses the connections between language, identity, and power.*

Miller, J.R. 1996. *Shingwauk's Vision: A History of Native Residential Schools*. Toronto: University of Toronto Press. *An Aboriginal perspective on the history of the residential school system in Canada.*

Task Force on Aboriginal Languages and Cultures. 2005. *Towards a New Beginning: A Foundational Report for a Strategy to Revitalize First Nation, Inuit, and Métis Languages and Cultures*. Ottawa: Department of Canadian Heritage. Available online at www.afn.ca/uploads/files/education2/towardanewbeginning.pdf. *A highly informative government report documenting the revitalization of Aboriginal languages in Canada.*

# Linguistic Anthropology: Components of Language

## The Anthropological Study of Language and Language Use

Linguistic anthropologists are trained in cultural anthropology but must also master the finer points of language structure, which is the focus of formal linguistics. In this section, we offer a brief introduction to each of the four key areas of specialization in formal linguistics—phonology, morphology, syntax, and semantics—illustrated by examples of how language is used in Canada. We also examine some of the broader concerns that shape the anthropological study of language and its use.

Linguistic anthropologists seek to understand the many ways in which language is learned, expressed, and transformed among groups of people. To do so, they look closely at how people use language in their everyday lives. Thus, their research often involves the use of ethnographic methods (see the "Focus on Four Fields" section on cultural anthropology, on pp. 386–91, for more on these methods). Participant observation—a method of data collection in which the researcher lives and works closely with the people whose way of life she or he is studying while participating in their lives as much as possible—can provide keen insight into the ways in which people use language in everyday encounters. Formal and informal interviews can also reveal key aspects of language use while allowing the researcher to ask questions related to interviewees' perceptions of language use in their communities. When interacting with or observing participants, linguistic anthropologists frequently make field notes and use video cameras and digital recorders to document spoken language; recording speech this way allows researchers to go back and look for fine details they may have missed the first time. A stretch of speech on a particular topic that includes multiple sentences or conversational exchanges is ordinarily called *discourse*. Modern technology allows linguistic anthropologists to analyze discourse in fine detail, enriching their understanding of the nuances of language use within a specific culture.

Discourse analysis can help linguistic anthropologists identify not only what is unique about a particular language but also what may be similar across different languages. To be sure, many differences are apparent across languages, in terms of individual words and sounds as well as patterns of words and sounds. However, just as anthropologists now recognize that all living human populations belong to a single species that emerged between 100,000 and 200,000 years ago, so it is that linguists and anthropologists agree that all languages spoken by modern human populations are equally sophisticated, and that anything that can be said in one language can be said in any other language, even if only in a more round-about way. Linguists and linguistic anthropologists alike take for granted that

- all languages have grammar (i.e., they have organizational rules that aid effective communication);
- all spoken languages have consonant sounds and vowel sounds;
- all languages are complex; there is no such thing as a primitive human language; and
- all languages change over time.

## Learning a New Language

Have you ever tried to learn a language other than the one(s) you learned at home as a child? What did you find challenging about learning a second (or third, or fourth) language? What similarities did you find between the new language and your original language(s)? Did the process of learning a new language affect how you thought about your native language(s)?

## Spoken vs Written Language

Linguistic anthropologists often distinguish between spoken language and written language. Most anthropologists find it likely that spoken language evolved approximately 100,000 years ago as our species, *Homo sapiens*, developed. Written language came much later: there is evidence to support the development of written language around 5000 to 8000 years ago, beginning as a form of symbols used to document various economic transactions.

Spoken language differs from written language in several ways. To begin, spoken language consists of *sounds*, whereas written language consists of *letters* or *characters*. Spoken language tends to come to us more naturally than does written language—after all, as young children, we learn to speak far earlier than we learn to read or to write. Written language is often more difficult to master because it requires closer adherence to the "rules" of grammar, especially when written forms of the language are expected to conform to an explicit standard that is different from everyday speech. Spoken language, on the other hand, often requires less structure because a speaker can rely on gestures and fluctuations in vocal tone to help convey her or his meaning. Linguists and linguistic anthropologists agree that signed languages such as American Sign Language are as fully developed as spoken human languages, even though the rules for signed communication have little in common with the rules of spoken grammar. Both spoken and written forms of any language are closely related, and linguistic anthropologists have often documented the processes by which new written codes have been developed for previously unwritten languages, as a prerequisite to the extension of literacy education by missionaries or colonial authorities, or in the context of national unification.

## Linguistic Change

A fundamental characteristic of language is that it changes over time. Part of this change occurs as we incorporate new words and expressions into a language, and as we adapt the meaning of existing words and expressions. Often, new words are imported into one language from another language; when this happens, the word may be adopted in its original form (e.g., *poutine*, adopted from French, meaning "a dish of fried potatoes covered in cheese curds and gravy"), or it may be adapted to fit more naturally into the new language (e.g., when the French word *cinéma* entered the English language, the accent over the *e* was dropped in its spelling, and the pronunciation shifted to incorporate vowel sounds more typical of English than of French). In other cases, new words are invented or coined to describe new technologies or experiences; recent examples include *crowdfund*, *photobomb*, and *smartphone*. Studying how and why new words enter a particular language can give linguistic anthropologists insight into external influences on that language as well as new concerns arising among speakers of that language.

### Analyzing Discourse

Find a partner and have a short (five- to ten-minute) discussion about the things you enjoy doing when you are not at school or at work. Record your conversation. When you have finished, listen to the recorded conversation and transcribe what you and your partner said. Has any of the meaning you understood from your conversation been lost in the transcription? Why? How does the way you used language in your conversation compare to the way you would use language in a letter or a written assignment for class? What adjustments would you need to make to the written version of your conversation to make the meaning clear to another reader?

### Thinking about Linguistic Change

How have texting and online forms of communication affected our use of language? Does the use of abbreviations such as *LOL*, *bro*, and *totes* have a place outside of the digital world? Does the use of such abbreviations suggest that we have become linguistically lazy, or are they indicative of some other form of cultural change? How do sitcoms, movies, and other forms of popular entertainment reinforce and spread such usages?

# The Formal Study of Language: Phonology, Morphology, Syntax, and Semantics

## Phonology: Sounds

The study of the sounds of language is called phonology. The sounds of human language are special because they are produced by a set of organs—the speech organs (e.g., the lips, the tongue, the teeth, the uvula, the pharynx, and the vocal cords)—that belong only to the human species (Figure F3.1). Also unique to our species is a suspended hyoid bone (a *U*-shaped bone located just below the lower jawbone), which allows for a wider, more complex range of motion of the tongue and certain other speech organs. The various sounds that our vocal systems produce are called *phones*, and the basic units of distinct sound that are characteristic of a language and that come together to form words are known as *phonemes*.

When examining phonology, linguistic anthropologists look closely at the range of phonemes used by humans when speaking a particular language. This

phonology  The study of the sounds of language.

involves identifying phonemes characteristic of the language was well as the patterns into which those sounds are organized. No language makes use of all the many phonemes the human speech organs can produce, and no two languages use exactly the same set. Furthermore, speakers of the same language may differ from one another in the way they pronounce or pattern their phonemes; this differentiation produces *accents*. Speakers of the same language with different accents are usually able to understand one another, but their distinctive articulation is a clue to their regional, ethnic, or social class origins. For example, a native English speaker from Alberta and a native English speaker from Newfoundland would be able to understand each other's speech, but their pronunciation of certain words would reveal their regional origins. A linguistic anthropologist with an ear trained for subtle differences in accents might also be able to narrow down more precisely where each came from (e.g., a major city or a particular rural area), whether either speaker had spent a significant portion of her or his formative years outside of her or his home province (e.g., perhaps the Albertan lived in England for several years as a child), the social class to which each belongs, and/or the highest level of education each likely achieved.

When children first start to learn their native language, they do so by listening to the sounds of the language that is being spoken around them. In time, they come to discern the discreet sounds in the language, and they learn how to reproduce those sounds using their own speech organs. Initially, children tend to learn language sounds from their parents or other caregivers; however, as they develop, they tend to adopt the pronunciation and speech patterns of their peers. The result of this learning process is that a person's speech organs become accustomed to producing the sounds of a specific language, as it is spoken among a particular group of people. For older children and adults, learning to speak a language that makes use of phonemes that are very different from those of their native language can be difficult because producing those phonemes requires their speech organs to move in new ways. An example familiar to many

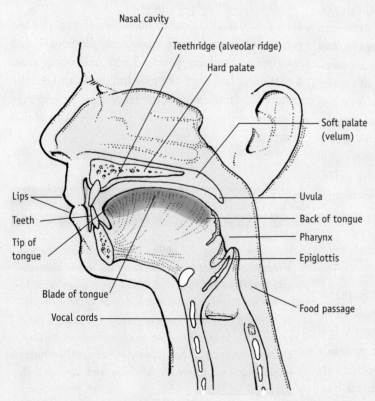

**FIGURE F3.1 | The speech organs.**

Nasal cavity

Teethridge (alveolar ridge)

Hard palate

Soft palate (velum)

Lips

Teeth

Tip of tongue

Uvula

Back of tongue

Pharynx

Epiglottis

Blade of tongue

Food passage

Vocal cords

## Dialects

Note that linguistic anthropologists often use *dialects* to discern the regional, ethnic, or social class origins of the people with whom they interact. Dialects are more complex than accents, as they involve variants in pronunciation as well as distinctive words (e.g., *mang* to mean "a mixture" or "to mix or mangle" in Newfoundland English), word forms (e.g., *y'all* for *you all* in Southern American English), interpretations of words (e.g., *lime* to mean "hang out" in Trinidadian English), and grammatical structures (e.g., *go to the shops for the milk* in Scottish English [Brinton and Arnovick 2011, 462]). To get a sense of how accents and dialects can differ within a language, visit the website of the International Dialects of English Archive (www.dialectsarchive.com) and listen to a few of the audio files available from its collection. Are some accents or dialects more difficult to understand? Why?

English-speaking Canadians is the rolling *r* sound characteristic of French. Another example comes from the Hawaiian language, which relies on only 13 phonemes (compared to English, which has approximately 36) and which contains a number of complex vowel sounds that are not used in English and, thus, that native English speakers find difficult to pronounce.

### Morphology: Word Structure

Morphology is the study of the minimal units of meaning in a language. In English, we typically think of meaningful units of language as *words*. We tend to think of words as the building blocks of sentences and of sentences as strings of words. But words are not all alike: some words (e.g., *book*), cannot be broken down into smaller meaningful elements; others (e.g., *bookworm*) can. The puzzle becomes more complex when we try to translate words from one language into another. Sometimes expressions that require only one word in one language require more than one word in another (e.g., *préciser* in French is *to make precise* in English). Other times, we must deal with

## Studying the Sounds of Language

Why are linguistic anthropologists interested in phonology? What can they learn from mapping out the possible ways that human beings use their speech organs to create the sounds of language? What can they learn from examining the sounds, sound combinations, and sound patterns specific to a particular language?

languages whose utterances cannot easily be broken down into words. Consider the utterance *nikookitepeena* from Shawnee (an Aboriginal language spoken in North America that is part of the Algonquian language family), which translates into English as "I dipped his head in the water" (Whorf 1956, 172) (see Table F3.1). Although the Shawnee utterance is composed of parts, the parts do not possess the characteristics most speakers of English, for example, would attribute to words.

In order to study the morphology of all of the various languages spoken around the world, anthropological linguists need a concept that can refer to both words and the parts of an utterance that cannot be broken down into words. Thus, they rely on the concept of *morphemes*, which are traditionally defined as "the minimal units of meaning in a language." In English, morphemes include units that we would consider to be

## Studying Morphemes

Why are linguistic anthropologists interested in morphology? What is the advantage of focusing on *morphemes* rather than *words*? What can researchers learn by comparing morphemes across different languages? How many morphemes can you find in the following English-language sentence?

Fieldworkers often rely on input from informants when examining local languages and customs.

morphology   In linguistics, the study of the minimal units of meaning in a language.

**TABLE F3.1** | Morphemes of a Shawnee Utterance and Their English Glosses

| *ni* | *kooki* | *tepe* | *en* | *a* |
|------|---------|--------|------|-----|
| I | immersed in water | point of action at head | by hand action | cause to him |

words (e.g., *sing*, *red*, *boy*) as well as units that we would consider to be word affixes (e.g., *anti-*, *pro-*, *-ed*, *-ing*, *-s*). Breaking down meaningful components of language into their smallest meaning-bearing parts raises an important question: What determines a word boundary in the first place? Words, or the morphemes they contain, represent the fundamental point at which the arbitrary pairing of sound and meaning occurs.

## Syntax: Sentence Structure

A third component of language is syntax, or sentence structure. The study of syntax involves looking at how morphemes are meaningfully combined into longer, more complex units of language—phrases, clauses, and complete sentences. Each language has its own rules about how the placement of words in relation to other words affects their meaning. Typically, these rules are based on the conceptualization of words as fitting into different "parts of speech," each of which has a defined relationship to other words. In English, for example, words are typically divided by function into eight parts of speech: nouns, which typically identify people or things that are acting or being acted upon; verbs, which typically indicate action; pronouns, which typically stand in for nouns; adjectives, which typically describe nouns or pronouns; adverbs, which typically describe verbs, adjectives, or other adverbs; prepositions, which typically expresses a relationship between a noun or a pronoun and another word; conjunctions, which typically join other words together; and interjections, which typically function independently of other words to express emotion. Which of these categories a word fits into in a given sentence depends on the function it is fulfilling in relation to the words around it.

Understanding the rules that govern the syntax of a language allows us to understand why certain arrangements of words hold the meaning that they do for speakers of that language. It also helps us to understand why certain arrangements of words result in ambiguity. For example, consider the following sentence: "Smoking grass means trouble." For most speakers of English, this sentence exhibits what linguists call *structural* (or

**syntax**    The arrangement of words (or morphemes) into sentences.

**semantics**    The study of meaning in language.

*syntactic*) *ambiguity*. Based on the structure of this sentence, it is unclear whether the speaker is referring to the use of marijuana (informally referred to as *grass*) or to the warning signs of a prairie fire. In the first reading, *smoking* is a verb functioning as a noun; in the second, it is a verb functioning as an adjective. This example clearly illustrates how the role a world plays in a sentence (and therefore its meaning) depends on sentence structure.

## Identifying Syntactic Ambiguity

Read the sentences below and identify any syntactic ambiguities they contain. Can you think of a way to reword each sentence to avoid ambiguity? How might knowing more about the context surrounding the statements help to clarify their meaning? What does this suggest about the importance of context to the interpretation of language?

Running water causes waste.

I waved at the woman with my gloves.

The father of the girl and the boy fell into the lake.

## Semantics: Meaning

Of the four linguistic resources outlined here, semantics, the study of meaning in language, is perhaps the most difficult for linguists to study. After all, *meaning* is a highly ambiguous term. What do we mean when we say that a sentence *means* something? We may be talking about what each individual word in the sentence means, or what the sentence as a whole means, or what I mean when I utter the sentence, which may differ from what someone else would mean if she or he uttered the same sentence.

Semanticists examine all of the possible meanings that are assigned to words and groups of words. They look at how words are linked to one another within a language, exploring relations such as *synonymy*, or "same meaning" (e.g., *old* and *aged*); *homophony*, or "same sound, different meaning" (e.g., *would* and *wood*); and *antonymy*, or "opposite meaning" (e.g., *tall* and *short*). They also examine words in terms of *denotation* (i.e., what words are commonly understood to refer to in the real world) and *connotation* (i.e., the meaning that words carry based on the contexts in which they are used in everyday speech).

To find a word's standard *denotative* meaning, we might consult a dictionary. According to the *Canadian Oxford Dictionary*, for example, a pig is "a domesticated even-toed ungulate derived from the wild boar *Sus scrofa*, with a large head, a broad flat snout, and a stout, often almost hairless body, raised as a source of bacon, ham, pork, etc." This sort of definition would be widely accepted by English speakers, although its exact meaning would depend on an understanding of all the other English words on which the definition relies—*ungulate, wild boar, large, snout, bacon*, and so on. Finding a word's *connotative* meaning, however, can be more complex. In the context of anti-war demonstrations in the 1960s, for example, a *pig* was a police officer. From a denotative point of view, to call police officers *pigs* is to create ambiguity deliberately, to muddle rather than to clarify. It is an example of metaphor, a form of figurative or non-literal language that violates the formal rules of denotation by linking expressions from unrelated semantic domains. Metaphors are used all the time in everyday speech. Does this mean, therefore, that people who use metaphors are talking nonsense? What can it possibly mean to call police officers *pigs*?

We cannot know until we place the statement into some kind of *context*. If we know, for example, that protesters in the 1960s viewed the police as the paid enforcers of racist elites responsible for violence against the poor and that pigs are domesticated animals that are often viewed as fat, greedy, and dirty, then the metaphor "police are pigs" begins to make sense. This interpretation, however, does not reveal the meaning of the metaphor for all time. Our ability to use the same words in different ways (and different words in the same way) is the hallmark of the *openness* feature of language (Hockett 1966). As this example illustrates, much of the referential meaning of language escapes us if we neglect the context of language use.

## Thinking about Language and Communication

Consider the relationship between society and language. How does our environment (family, school, hobbies, religion, social media, etc.) influence the way we use language to communicate? In what ways does our interpretation of language depend on our understanding of the social and/or cultural context in which it is being used? To what extent does linguistic communication rely on the sender and the receiver of a message sharing a common frame of reference? How would you describe the meaning of the word *red* to someone who has never been able to see? Or the meaning of *hat trick* to someone who has never seen a hockey game? Or the meaning of *double double* to someone who has never tasted coffee?

## Key Terms

morphology   267
phonology   266

semantics   268
syntax   268

# 10   *How Do We Make Meaning?*

▲ A Jewish woman lights Shabbat (Sabbath) candles on a Friday night. Photo: PhotoStock-Israel/Getty Images

## *Chapter Outline*

- What Is Play?
- What Is Art?
- What Is Myth?
- What Is Ritual?
- How Are World View and Symbolic Practice Related?
- What Are Symbols?
- What Is Religion?

- World Views in Operation: Two Case Studies
- How Do People Maintain and Change Their World View?
- How Are World Views Used as Instruments of Power?
- Chapter Summary
- For Review
- Key Terms
- Suggested Readings

Human beings are creative, not just in their use of language but in a variety of symbolic forms. We look at several different kinds of creative symbolic forms in this chapter, including play, art, myth, ritual, and religion. But human cultural creativity is never entirely unconstrained. You will also learn about how symbolic forms are shaped by power relations in different social settings.

Building on the discussion of language and symbolism from the previous chapter, this chapter looks at human play, art, myth, ritual, and religion—dimensions of human experience in which the interplay of openness and creativity encounters rules and constraints, enabling people to produce powerful and moving symbolic practices that transform the character of human life.

## What Is Play?

In Chapter 9, we explored the concept of "openness" in relation to language. *Openness* was defined as the ability to talk or think about the same thing in different ways and different things in the same way. If we expand openness to include all behaviour—that is, the ability not just to talk or think about but also to *do* the same thing in different ways or different things in the same way—we begin to define play. All mammals play, and humans play the most and throughout their lives.

Robert Fagen (1981, 1992, 2005) looks at play as a product of natural selection that may have significant fitness value for individuals in different species. Play gives young animals (including young human beings) the exercise they need to build up the skills necessary for physical survival as adults: fighting, hunting, or running away when pursued. Play may be important for the development of cognitive and motor skills and may be connected with the repair of developmental damage caused by either injury or trauma. It may also communicate the message "all's well," signalling "information about short-term and long-term health, general well-being, and biological fitness to parents, littermates, or other social companions" (Fagen 1992, 51). In species with more complex brains, playful exploration of the environment aids learning and allows for the development of behavioural versatility. Fagen (2005) suggests that play reflects natural selection for unpredictability. That is, to be able to produce unpredictable behaviours can be advantageous for an intelligent species faced with unanticipated adaptive challenges.

Evidence from archaeological sites suggests that play may have been an important aspect of childhood for our *Homo sapiens* ancestors, and that it may in fact define our species' creative evolution and development of symbolic communication. Miniature artifacts that resemble full-size "adult" tools (e.g., bows and arrows, knives, scrapers, sewing needles) are interpreted as toys that children would have played with to learn essential skills necessary to become successful adults in their respective prehistoric cultures. These miniatures have been recovered from a variety of sites around the world, including Icelandic sites (Callow 2006), Mesoamerican sites (Joyce 2000), and Thule sites in the Canadian Arctic (Park 1998) (see the "Anthropology in the Contemporary World" box on the archaeology of childhood). Evidence from various sites also suggests that children were apprentices, learning how to make their own artifacts using flint knapping (Hogberg 2008) and potting techniques (Fewkes 1923; Smith 1998). In contrast, our closest hominin relatives, the Neanderthals, likely matured quickly, were less dependent on adults when they were young, and did not have time to play and be creative with toys, as their childhood was relatively short (Nowell 2013). Consequently, as April Nowell from the University of Victoria suggests, this lack of play time did not allow for Neanderthals to experience "what if" fantasy games, test out artifacts, and experiment with different aspects of their world. It is highly likely that the "fantasy games" played by modern humans allowed for them to be more creative and develop symbolic representations of their world (Nowell 2013, 29).

For a first-hand discussion of Nowell's research on Neanderthals and play, see the "In Their Own Words" box in Chapter 6, on pp. 141–2.

**play** A framing (or orienting context) that is (1) consciously adopted by the players, (2) somehow pleasurable, and (3) systemically related to what is non-play by alluding to the non-play world and by transforming the objects, roles, actions, and relations of ends and means characteristic of the non-play world.

## Anthropology in the Contemporary World

### Archaeology of Childhood

Childhood can be a magical time—carefree days of toys and games. This is as true today as it was in prehistoric times. But as every parent knows, child's play is serious business. It is how children learn to be grown-ups, to use the tools of adults, and to make their own place in society.

Although anthropologists have always been aware that children made up a significant proportion of prehistoric societies, the archaeological focus on children's activities is relatively new. Robert Park (1999) from the University of Waterloo has done some novel work with "miniature" artifacts from Thule archaeological sites across Arctic Canada. His research provides a new perspective on the use of small artifacts and how children learned to become adults in prehistoric cultures. In his research, Park examines smaller versions of various utilitarian items, like bows and arrows, and he suggests that these smaller artifacts were used by children to learn and practise how to be an adult in Thule culture. Ethnographic evidence from Inuit children collected by Diamond Jenness (1922) early in the twentieth century assists in the understanding of how children living in the Arctic played at being adults.

The Thule settled the Arctic Archipelago approximately 1000 years ago and adapted to their harsh surroundings by concocting an impressive array of highly specialized tools. The richness and diversity of their material culture is well represented in the archaeological record. The toys of the Thule children were almost as diverse as the tools and gadgets used by their parents. The remnants of these child-sized artifacts suggest nothing less than an extensive miniature material culture—one that can be plumbed by archaeologists just as surely as the full-sized culture it mimics.

Building on a rich body of ethnographic data drawn from oral traditions, records of casual visitors, and extensive studies by scholars, Park used data on more than 9700 artifacts (369 of which were miniatures) collected from 31 Thule sites in Canada and northern Greenland to explore childhood practices in the prehistoric Arctic. He divided the "miniature" artifacts into three broad categories that would be familiar to many children today: playing house, playing with dolls, and playing at hunting.

According to Jenness, playing house and playing at hunting were common practices among the Inuit children he observed. He noted that in summer the children liked to "set up house in an empty tent" (Jenness 1922, 170). In addition, "both boys and girls learn[ed] to stalk game by accompanying their elders on hunting excursions; their fathers [would] make bows and arrows for them suited to their strength" (Ibid.). One specific kind of play was restricted only to girls: that of making and playing with dolls. For boys, greater focus was placed on hunting activities where they learned how to use miniature harpoons to help pull ashore seals killed by the adults.

What is promising archaeologically about these kinds of findings is that they are clearly associated with a miniature material culture. The children at these sites engaged in a wide range of "play" that mimicked adult behaviour. This suggests that the Inuit practice of treating children as small adults was characteristic of their Thule ancestors as well. In a broader context, treating children as small adults is not unique to the Inuit of the early twentieth century or to the Thule of hundreds of years ago—the practice remains familiar to us today, although the degree to which it is expressed varies from culture to culture.

### What Do We Think about Play?

Moving from everyday reality to the reality of play requires a radical transformation of perspective. To an outside observer, the switch from everyday reality to play reality may go undetected. However, sometimes the

> **metacommunication**   Communication about the process of communication.
>
> **framing**   A cognitive boundary that marks certain behaviours as "play" or as "ordinary life."

switch can have serious consequences for other people and their activities. In this case, play and non-play must be signalled clearly so that one is not mistaken for the other.

According to Gregory Bateson (1972), shifting into or out of play requires metacommunication, or communication about communication. Metacommunication provides information about the relationship between communicative partners. In play there are two kinds of metacommunication. The first, called framing, sends a message that marks certain behaviours either as play or as ordinary life. Dogs, for example, have a *play face*, a signal understood by other dogs (and recognizable by some human beings) indicating a willingness to play. If dogs agree to play, they bare their fangs and one animal attacks the other, but bites become nips. Both dogs have agreed to enter the *play frame*, an imaginative world in which bites do not mean bites. Within the play frame, a basic element of Western logic—that *A* = *A*—does not apply; the same thing is being treated in different ways. Human beings have many ways of marking the play frame: a smile, a particular tone of voice, a referee's whistle, or the words "Let's pretend." The marker says that "everything from now until we end this activity is set apart from everyday life." The second kind of metacommunication involves **reflexivity**. Play offers us the opportunity to think about the social and cultural dimensions of the world in which we live. By suggesting that ordinary life can be understood in more than one way, play can be a way of speculating about what can be rather than about what should be or what is (Handelman 1977, 186). When we say that jokes keep us from taking ourselves too seriously, for example, we are engaging in reflexive metacommunication. Joking allows us to consider alternative, even ridiculous, explanations for our experience.

## What Are Some of the Effects of Play?

Helen Schwartzman (1978, 232–45) has demonstrated how play, through satire and clowning, may allow children to comment on and criticize the world of adults. A powerful example of this kind of commentary is described by anthropologist Elizabeth Chin (1999), who studied African American girls and their dolls in Newhallville, a working-class and poor neighbourhood in New Haven, Connecticut. Although "ethnically correct" dolls are on the market, very few of the girls had them because they cost too much. The poor children Chin knew in Newhallville had white dolls. But in their play these girls transformed their dolls in a powerful way by giving them hairstyles like their own. The original designers gave the dolls smooth, flowing hair to be brushed over and over again and put into a ponytail. But the girls' dolls had beads in their hair, braids held at the end with twists of aluminum foil or barrettes, and braids that were themselves braided together (315). As Chin observes, "In some sense, by doing this, the girls bring their dolls into their own worlds, and whiteness here is not

**FIGURE 10.1** | Play enables this girl in Guider, Cameroon, to incorporate her European doll into the world she knows.

absolutely defined by skin and hair, but by style and way of life. The complexities of racial references and racial politics have been much discussed in the case of black hair simulating the look of whiteness; what these girls are creating is quite the opposite: white hair that looks black" (315). It is not that the girls did not realize that their dolls were white; it is that through their imaginative and material work they were able to integrate the dolls into their own world. The overt physical characteristics of the dolls—skin colour, facial features, hair—did not force the girls into treating the dolls in ways that obeyed the boundaries of racial difference. Their transformative play does not make the realities of poverty, discrimination, and racism disappear from the worlds in which they live; but Chin points out that "in making their white dolls live in black worlds, they . . . reconfigure the boundaries of race" and in so doing "challenge the social construction not only of their own blackness, but of race itself as well" (318) (Figure 10.1).

**reflexivity** Critical thinking about the way one thinks; reflection on one's own experience.

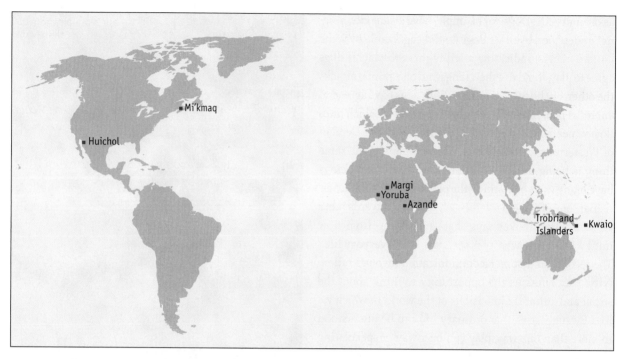

**MAP 10.1** | Locations of societies whose EthnoProfiles appear in Chapter 10.

# What Is Art?

In Western societies, art includes sculpture, drawing, painting, dance, theatre, music, and literature, as well as such similar processes and products as film, photography, mime, mass media production, oral narrative, festivals, and national celebrations. These are the kinds of objects and activities that first caught the attention of anthropologists who wanted to study art in non-Western societies. Whether non-Western peoples referred to such activities or products as "art," however, is a separate question. People everywhere engage in these kinds of playful creativity, yet activities defined as "art" differ from free play because they are circumscribed by rules. Artistic rules direct particular attention to, and provide standards for evaluating, the *form* of the activities or objects that artists produce.

## Is There a Definition of Art?

Anthropologist Alexander Alland (1977, 39) defines art as "play with form producing some aesthetically successful transformation-representation." For Alland, *form* refers to the rules of the art game: the culturally

> **art** Play with form producing some aesthetically successful transformation-representation.

appropriate restrictions on the way this kind of play may be organized in time and space. We can also think about form in terms of style and media. A *style* is a schema (a distinctive patterning of elements) that is recognized within a culture as appropriate to a given medium. The media themselves in which art is created and executed are culturally recognized and characterized (Anderson 1990, 272–5). A painting is a form: it is two-dimensional; it is done with paint; it is intentionally made; it represents or symbolizes something in the world outside the canvas, paper, or wood on which it is created. There are different kinds of paintings as well. There is the painting form called "portrait"—a portrait depicts a person, it resembles the person in some appropriate way, it is done with paint, it can be displayed, and more.

By "aesthetic," Alland (1977, xii) means appreciative of, or responsive to, form in art or nature. "Aesthetically successful" means that the creator of the piece of art (and possibly its audience) responds positively or negatively to it ("I like this," "I hate this"). Indifference is the sign of something that is aesthetically unsuccessful. It is probably the case that the aesthetic response is a universal feature in all human societies.

Aesthetic value judgments guide the artist's choice of form and material; they also guide the observers' evaluations. This implies that art involves more than just objects. V.N. Voloshinov ([1926] 1987) argues that art is a creative "event of living communication" (107) involving the work, the artist, and the artist's audience. Artists create their works with an audience in mind, and audiences respond to these works as if the works were addressed to them. Sometimes their response is enthusiastic; sometimes it is highly critical. In addition, if aesthetic creation involves more than just the end product, such as a painting or a poem, attention needs to be paid to the process through which some product is made. James Vaughan (1973, 186) pointed out, for example, that the Margi of northeastern Nigeria do not appreciate a folktale as a story per se but rather enjoy the *performance* of it (see EthnoProfile 10.1: Margi).

To understand what Alland means by "transformation-representation," we can recall that the link between a symbol and what it represents is arbitrary. This means that symbols can be separated from the object or idea represented and appreciated for their own sake. They may also be used to represent a totally different meaning. Because transformation and representation depend on each other, Alland (1977, 35) suggests that they be referred to together (i.e., as transformation-representation). When a Javanese leather-puppet maker makes a puppet of the great mythic hero Arjuna, for example, he is representing the traditional form of the hero in his work, but he is also transforming a three-dimensional human form into a two-dimensional flat puppet made of buffalo hide, in which the colours, style, inclination of the head, and adornment stand for the internal state

of the hero at a specific moment (Figure 10.2). At the same time, he is carrying out this work more

For more on the people of Java, see EthnoProfile 9.1, on p. 247.

or less skillfully and is representing in his work the meanings that Arjuna carries for his Javanese audience.

Alland's definition of art attempts to capture something universal about human beings and cultural creativity. Similarly, anthropologist Shelly Errington (1998, 84) observes that all human cultures have "'symbolic forms': artifacts, activities, or even aspects of the landscape that humans view as densely meaningful." One dramatic example of this in Canada is the National War Memorial in Ottawa, which has a profound emotional impact on hundreds of thousands of people who visit it each year (see Figure 10.3). The memorial continues

**FIGURE 10.2** | One of the great mythic heroes of Javanese *wajang* is represented here in a beautifully painted flat leather shadow puppet. The colour of the image, the angle of the head, the shape of the eye, the position of the fingers, and the style, colour, and quantity of the clothing all represent the inner state of the hero.

## EthnoProfile 10.1

### Margi

**Region:** Western Africa

**Nation:** Nigeria

**Population:** 100,000 to 200,000 (1960s)

**Environment:** Mountains and plains

**Livelihood:** Farming, selling surplus in local markets

**Political organization:** Traditionally, kingdoms; today, part of a modern nation-state

**For more information:** Vaughan, James. 2006. *The Mandara Margi: A Society Living on the Cerge.* www.indiana.edu/~margi

**FIGURE 10.3 |** The National War Memorial in Ottawa recognizes the importance of those who have given up their lives in times of conflict.

to draw offerings from visitors, not just wreaths and flowers but also messages of all kinds remembering those memorialized.

## "But Is It *Art*?"

Many people—anthropologists included—have resisted the notion that art is only what a group of Western experts define as art. To highlight the ethnocentrism of Western art experts, they stressed that the division into categories of art and non-art is not universal. In many societies, there is no word that corresponds to *art*, nor is there a category of art distinct from other human activities. At the same time, anthropologists felt justified in speaking of art and of artists in non-Western societies, as they believed that all people were endowed with the same aesthetic capacities. Their goal was to recognize a fully human capacity for art in all societies and to redefine art until it became broad enough to include on an equal basis aesthetic products and activities that Western art experts would qualify, at best, as "primitive," "ethnic," or "folk" art.

For example, some anthropologists focused on the evaluative standards that artists use for their own work and other work in the same form and how these may differ from the standards used by people who do not themselves perform such work. Anthony Forge (1967), for example, noted that Abelam carvers in New Guinea discuss carvings in a language that is more incisive than that of non-carvers. Forge

and other anthropologists pointed out that artists in traditional non-Western societies created objects or engaged in activities that reinforced the central values of their culture. Thus, their work helped to maintain the social order, and the artists did not see themselves (nor were they understood to be) avant-garde critics of society as they often are in modern Western societies. Forge (1967) tells us that Abelam artworks are statements about male violence and warfare, male nurturance, and the combination of the two. These statements about the nature of men and their culture are not made by other means of communication, such as speech. Moreover, these statements are essential to Abelam social structure.

Recent work in the anthropology of art, however, has prompted many anthropologists to rethink this position. They have turned their attention to the way certain kinds of material objects made by tribal peoples flow into a global art market, where they are transformed into "primitive" or "ethnic" art. Some anthropologists, like Shelly Errington (1998), point out that even in the West many of the objects in fine arts museums today, no matter where they came from, were not intended by their makers to be "art." They were intended to be, for example, masks for ritual use, paintings for religious contemplation, reliquaries for holding the relics of saints, ancestor figures, furniture, jewellery boxes, architectural details, and so on. They are in fine arts museums today because at some point they were claimed to be art by someone with the authority to put them in the museum (Figure 10.4).

FIGURE 10.4 | Non-Western sculpture is transformed into art when it is displayed like Western art in a museum and viewed by members of the public who have the opportunity to look at it intensively (in this case, former French president Jacques Chirac).

For these reasons, Errington distinguishes "art by intention" from "art by appropriation." Art by intention includes objects that were made to be art, such as Impressionist paintings. Art by appropriation, however, consists of all the other objects that "became art" because at a certain moment certain people decided that they belonged to the category of art. Because museums, art dealers, and art collectors are found everywhere in the world today, it is now the case that potentially any material object crafted by human hands can be appropriated by these institutions as "art."

To transform an object into art, Errington (1998) argues, it must have *exhibition value*—someone must be willing to display it. Objects that somehow fit into the Western definition of art will be selected for the art market as "art." Looking at the objects that over the years have been defined as "art," Errington sees that the vast majority show certain elements to be embedded rather deeply in the Western definition of art: the objects are "portable (paintings, preferred to murals), durable (bronze preferred to basketry), useless for practical purposes in the secular West (ancestral effigies and Byzantine icons preferred to hoes and grain grinders), representational (human and animal figures preferred to, say, heavily decorated ritual bowls)" (116–17). In other words, for Errington, art requires that someone *intend* that the objects be art, but that someone does not have to be the object's creator.

It can be fruitful to talk about art as a kind of play. Like play, art presents its creators and participants with alternative realities, a separation of means from ends, and the possibility of commenting on and transforming the everyday world. In today's global art market, however, restrictions of an entirely different order also apply. Errington (1998, 268) observes that the people who make "primitive art" are no longer "tribal" but have become

> modern-day peasants or a new type of proletariat. . . . They live in rain forests and deserts and other such formerly out-of-the-way places on the peripheries . . . within national and increasingly global systems of buying and selling, of using natural and human resources, and of marketing images and notions about products. Some lucky few of them make high ethnic art, and sell it for good prices, and obtain a good portion of the proceeds. Others make objects classed as tourist or folk art, usually for much less money, and often through a middleperson.

Others fulfill orders from elsewhere, "producing either masses of 'folk art' or expensive handmade items designed by people in touch with world taste and world markets" (269). Errington points out the bitter irony that international demand for "exotic" objects is growing at the very moment when the makers of these objects are severely threatened by international economic policies and resource-extraction projects that impoverish them and undermine the ways of life that give the objects they make their "exotic" allure. It should also be noted that what counts as fashionable decoration this year—"world taste"—may be out of fashion next year, leaving the producers with very little to fall back on.

## "She's Fake": Art and Authenticity

Michelle Bigenho is an anthropologist and violinist whose multi-sited ethnography examines music performance in Bolivia, in part through her experiences performing with Música de Maestros (Figure 10.5). This ensemble performs the works of master Bolivian composers of the past and attempts to recreate accurate performances of contemporary original music that they have studied in the countryside (Bigenho 2002, 4). The ensemble included both classically trained and traditionally trained musicians, and three were foreigners: a Japanese musician who played the Andean flute, a Cuban musician who played violin, and Bigenho, an American, who also played violin. Along with a local dance ensemble, the musicians were invited to represent Bolivia in a folklore festival in France. As the bands were lining up, a member of the Belgian delegation walked over to Bigenho and announced, in French, "She's fake." The Belgian woman then "pointed to one of the Bolivian dancers dressed in her dancing costume with her long fake braids worked into her short brown hair. As she pointed, she said, 'She's real'" (88).

In this way, Bigenho (2002) raises the issue of the connection between "authenticity" and so-called folk art. How do the images that people in dominant nations have of "folk" or Indigenous peoples affect the production and circulation of Indigenous art? Can a Bolivian band include musicians from Japan, Cuba, and the United States and still be Bolivian? And who gets to decide what is authentic? Bigenho discusses a kind of authenticity that she calls "unique authenticity," which refers to the individual artist's new, innovative, and personal production, such as the original compositions of creative musicians. Unique authenticity is "the founding myth of modern concepts of authorship and copyright" (20). It concerns who owns cultural products and raises the issue of whether it is possible to talk about collective creation and ownership of the music of a community, a people, or an ethnic group.

Bigenho came face to face with this issue when she compiled a cassette of music from one of the villages in which she worked. While the villagers recognized that the music they played was composed by individuals, they felt strongly that ownership of the music was collective. In doing so, they moved from uniquely authentic individual compositions—intellectual property—to collective ownership of a "culturally authentic representation"—cultural property (Bigenho 2002, 217). She discussed with the villagers how to register the copyright on the cassette. When Bigenho went to La Paz to register the copyright, however, she found that it was impossible to register the cassette

**FIGURE 10.5** | Música de Maestros in costume performing in a folklore festival in France.

under collective authorship or ownership. Ironically, *she* as the compiler could register the work but the people who created the work could not, unless they were willing to be recognized as individuals. According to Bolivian law, the music on the cassette was legally folklore, "the set of literary and artistic works created in national territory by unknown authors or by authors who do not identify themselves and are presumed to be nationals of the country, or of its ethnic communities, and that are transmitted from generation to generation, constituting one of the fundamental elements of traditional cultural patrimony of the nation" (Bigenho 2002, 221). As a result, the music was part of the "national patrimony" and belonged to the nation-state. Given the context of Bolivian cultural and ethnic politics, Bigenho reports that the villagers decided to try to gain visibility and connections as a collective Indigenous entity, which they believed would provide them with possible economic advantages; whether this belief was accurate remains to be seen. But similar struggles over the relationship between art and authenticity can be found all over the world.

## What Is Myth?

We have suggested that play lies at the heart of human creativity. However, because the openness of play seems random, and thus just as likely to undermine the social order as to enhance it, societies tend to surround play with cultural rules, channelling it in directions that appear less destructive. Rules designed to discipline artistic expression are one result of this channelling process. As we have seen, artists in various media are permitted a wide range of expression as long as they adhere to rules governing the form that expression takes. Societies differ in how loose or strict the rules of artistic form may be. Artists who challenge the rules, however, are often viewed negatively by those in power, who believe they have the right to restrict artistic expressions that question social, religious, or sexual precepts that ought not to be questioned.

In fact, all societies depend on the willingness of their members to not question certain assumptions about the way the world works. Because the regularity and predictability of social life might collapse altogether if people were free to imagine and act upon their own understandings of the world, most societies find

ways to restrict the available options through the use of myth. Many people take the word *myth* to mean something that is false. But for anthropologists, myths are stories that recount how various aspects of the world came to be the way they are. The power of myths comes from their ability to make life meaningful for those who accept them. The truth of myths seems self-evident because they do such a good job of integrating personal experiences with a wider set of assumptions about how the world works. As stories that involve a teller and an audience, myths are products of high verbal art (and increasingly of cinematic art). Frequently, the official myth-tellers are the ruling groups in society: the elders, the political leaders, the religious specialists. They may also be considered master storytellers. The content of myths usually concerns past events (usually at the beginning of time) or future events (usually at the end of time). Myths are socially important because, if they are taken literally, they tell people where they have come from and where they are going and, thus, how they should live right now (Figure 10.6).

Societies differ in the degree to which they permit speculation about key myths. In complex Western societies like Canada, many different groups, each with its own mythic tradition, often live side by side. Multiculturalism is often toted as the dominant Canadian myth, which assumes that we are highly accepting of a wide variety of cultures and their beliefs. However, this is not always the case, and some groups appear to have higher status than others. For example, Canada's Official Languages Act gives English and French special status as the country's official languages and requires that government documents be prepared in both languages. In addition, our consumer packaging and labelling laws require that almost all items sold in Canada have labels that are written in both English and French. These laws uphold the power of the founding colonial powers, but they disregard the importance of First Nations and other groups in the country whose first language is neither English nor French.

Myths and related beliefs that are taken to be self-evident truths are sometimes codified in an explicit manner. When this codification is extreme and deviation from the code is treated harshly, we sometimes

> **myths** Stories that recount how various aspects of the world came to be the way they are and that make life meaningful for those who accept them.

**FIGURE 10.6** | A vase painting illustrating part of the Popol Vuh, the Mayan creation story.

speak of **orthodoxy** (or "correct doctrine"). Societies differ in the degree to which they require members to adhere to orthodox interpretations of key myths. But even societies that place little emphasis on orthodoxy are likely to exert some control over the interpretation of key myths because myths have implications for action. They may justify past action, explain present action, or generate future action. To be persuasive, myths must offer plausible explanations for our experience of human nature, human society, and human history.

The success of Western science has led many members of Western societies to dismiss non-scientific myths as flawed attempts at science or history. Only recently have some scientists come to recognize the similarities between scientific and non-scientific storytelling about such events as the origin of life on earth. Scientific stories about origins, *origin myths*, must be taken to the natural world to be matched against material evidence; the success of this match determines whether they are accepted or rejected. By contrast, non-scientific origin myths get their vitality from how well they match up with the social world.

## How Does Myth Reflect—and Shape—Society?

Early in the twentieth century, anthropologist Bronislaw Malinowski introduced a new approach to myth. He believed that to understand myths we must understand the social context in which they are embedded. Malinowski argued that myths serve as "charters" or "justifications" for present-day social arrangements. That is, the myth contains some "self-evident" truth that explains why society is as it is and why it cannot be changed. If the social arrangements justified by the myth are challenged, the myth can be used as a weapon against the challengers.

Malinowski's ([1926] 1948) famous example is of the origin myths of the Trobriand Islanders (see EthnoProfile 10.2: Trobriand Islanders). Members of every significant kinship grouping knew, marked, and retold the history of the place from which their

**orthodoxy** "Correct doctrine"; the prohibition of deviation from approved theories or beliefs.

**EthnoProfile 10.2**

## Trobriand Islanders

**Region:** Oceania

**Nation:** Papua New Guinea

**Population:** 8500 (1970s)

**Environment:** Tropical island

**Livelihood:** Yam growing

**Political organization:** Traditionally, chiefs and others of rank; today, part of a modern nation-state

**For more information:** Weiner, Annette. 1988. *The Trobrianders of Papua New Guinea*. New York: Holt, Rinehart, and Winston.

group's ancestress and her brother had emerged from the depths of the earth. These origin myths were set in the time before history began. Each ancestress-and-brother pair brought a distinct set of characteristics that included special objects and knowledge, as well as various skills, crafts, spells, and the like. On reaching the surface, the pair took possession of the land. That is why, Malinowski was told, the people on a given piece of land had rights to it. It is also why they possessed a particular set of spells, skills, and crafts. Because the original sacred beings were a woman and her brother, the origin myth could also be used to endorse present-day membership in a Trobriand clan, which depends on a person's ability to trace kinship links through women to that clan's original ancestress. A brother and a sister represent the prototypical members of a clan because they are both descended from the ancestress through female links. Should anyone question the wisdom of organizing society in this way, the myth could be cited as proof that this is indeed the correct way to live.

In Trobriand society, Malinowski found, clans were ranked relative to one another in terms of prestige. To account for this ranking, Trobrianders referred to another myth. In the Trobriand myth that explains rank, one clan's ancestor, the dog, emerged from the earth before another clan's ancestor, the pig, thus justifying ranking the dog clan highest in prestige. To believe in this myth, Malinowski asserted, is to accept a transcendent justification for the ranking of clans. Malinowski made it clear, however, that if social arrangements change, the myth changes too—in order to justify the new arrangements. At some point, the dog clan was replaced in prominence by the pig clan. This social change resulted in a change in the mythic narrative. The dog was said to have eaten food that was taboo. In so doing, the dog gave up its claim to higher rank. Thus, to understand a myth and its transformations, one must understand the social organization of the society that makes use of it.

Detailed descriptions of various ways in which different cultures define kinship relationships can be found in Chapter 13, on pp. 359–60.

## Do Myths Help Us Think?

Beginning in the mid-1950s, a series of books and articles by the French anthropologist Claude Lévi-Strauss (1967) transformed the study of myth. Lévi-Strauss argues that myths have meaningful structures that are worth studying in their own right, quite apart from the uses to which the myths may be put. He suggested that myths should be interpreted the way we interpret musical scores. In a piece of music, the meaning emerges not just from the melody but also from the harmony. In other words, the structure of the piece of music, the way in which each line of the music contributes to the overall sound and is related to other lines, carries the meaning.

For Lévi-Strauss, myths are tools for overcoming logical contradictions that cannot otherwise be overcome. They are put together in an attempt to deal with the oppositions of particular concern to a particular society at a particular moment in time. Using a linguistic metaphor, Lévi-Strauss argues that myths are composed of smaller units—phrases, sentences, words, relationships—that are arranged in ways that give both a linear, narrative (or "melodic") coherence and a multilevel, structural (or "harmonic") coherence. These arrangements represent and comment on aspects of social life that are thought to oppose each other. Examples include the opposition of men to women; opposing rules of residence after marriage (e.g., living with the groom's father or the bride's mother); the opposition of the natural world to the cultural world, of life to death, of spirit to body, of high to low, and so on.

The complex syntax of myth works to relate those opposed pairs to one another in an attempt to overcome their contradictions. However, these contradictions can never be overcome; for example, the opposition of death to life is incapable of any earthly resolution. But myth can transform an insoluble problem into a more accessible, concrete form. Mythic narrative can then provide the concrete problem with a solution. For example, a culture hero may bridge the opposition between death and life by travelling from the land of the living to the land of the dead and back. Alternatively, a myth might propose that the beings who transcend death are so horrific that death is clearly preferable to eternal life. Perhaps a myth describes the journey of a bird that travels from the earth, the home of the living, to the sky, the home of the dead. This is similar to Christian thought, where the death and resurrection of Jesus may be understood to resolve the opposition between death and life by transcending death.

From this point of view, myths do not just talk about the world as it is but also describe the world as it might be. To paraphrase Lévi-Strauss, myths are good to think with; mythic thinking can propose other ways to live our lives. Lévi-Strauss insists, however, that the alternatives that myths propose are ordinarily rejected as impossible. Thus, even though myths allow for play with self-evident truths, this play remains under strict control.

Is Lévi-Strauss correct? There has been a great deal of debate on this issue since the publication in 1955 of his article "The Structural Study of Myth" (see Lévi-Strauss 1967). But even those who are most critical of his analyses of particular myths agree that mythic structures are meaningful because they display the ability of human beings to play with possibilities as they attempt to deal with basic contradictions at the heart of human experience.

For Malinowski, Lévi-Strauss, and their followers, those who believe in myths are not conscious of how their myths are structured or of the functions their myths perform for them. More recent anthropological thinking takes a more reflexive approach. This research recognizes that ordinary members of a society often *are* aware of how their myths structure meaning, allowing them to manipulate the way myths are told or interpreted in order to make an effect, to prove a point, or to buttress a particular perspective on human nature, society, or history.

# What Is Ritual?

Play allows unlimited consideration of alternative perspectives on reality. Art permits consideration of alternative perspectives, but certain limitations restricting the form and content are imposed. Myth aims to narrow radically the possible perspectives and often promotes a single, orthodox perspective presumed to be valid for everyone. It thus offers a kind of intellectual indoctrination. But because societies aim to shape action as well as thought to orient all human faculties in the approved direction, art, myth, and ritual are often closely associated with one another. In this section,

we will look at ritual as a form of action in a variety of societies.

## How Can Ritual Be Defined?

For many people in Western societies, rituals are presumed to be religious—for example, weddings, Jewish bar mitzvahs, Hmong sacrifices to the ancestors, or the Catholic Mass. For anthropologists, however, rituals also include practices such as scientific experiments, college graduation ceremonies, procedures in a court of law, and children's birthday parties.

To capture this range of activities, our definition of **ritual** has four parts. First, ritual is a *repetitive social practice* composed of a sequence of symbolic activities in the form of dance, song, speech, gestures, the manipulation of certain objects, and so forth. Second, it is *set off from the social routines of everyday life*. Third, rituals in any culture *adhere to a characteristic, culturally defined schema*. This means that members of a culture can tell that a certain sequence of activities is a ritual even if they have never seen that particular ritual before. Fourth, ritual action is *closely connected to a specific set of ideas that are often encoded in myth*. These ideas might concern, for example, the relationship of human beings to the spirit world, how human beings ought to interact with one another, or the nature of evil. The purpose for which a ritual is performed guides how these ideas are selected and symbolically enacted. What gives rituals their power is that the people who perform them assert that the authorization for the ritual comes from outside themselves—from the state, society, a divine being, a god, the ancestors, or "tradition." They have not made up the ritual themselves; rather, it connects them to a source of power that they do not control but that controls them.

## How Is Ritual Expressed in Actions?

A ritual has a particular sequential ordering of acts, utterance, and events: that is, ritual has a *text*. Because ritual is action, however, we must pay attention to the way the ritual text is performed. The performance of a ritual cannot be separated from its text; text and performance shape each other. Through ritual performance, the ideas of a culture become concrete, take on a form, and, as Bruce Kapferer (1983) puts it,

**ritual** A repetitive social practice composed of a sequence of symbolic activities that is set off from the social routines of everyday life, adheres to a culturally defined ritual schema, and closely connects to a specific set of ideas that are often encoded in myth.

give direction to the gaze of participants. At the same time, ritual performers are not robots but active individuals whose choices are guided by, but not rigidly dictated by, previous ritual texts; ritual performance can serve as a commentary on the text and even transform it. For example, Jewish synagogue ritual following the reading from the Torah (the five books of Moses, the Hebrew Bible) includes lifting the Torah scroll, showing it to the congregation, and then closing it and covering it. In some synagogues, a man and a woman, often a couple, are called from the congregation to lift and cover the Torah: the man lifts it and, after he seats himself, the woman rolls the scroll closed, places the tie around it, and covers it with the mantle that protects it. One of the authors of this text once observed a performance of this ritual in which the woman lifted the Torah and the man wrapped it; officially, the ritual text was carried out, but the performance became a commentary on the text—on the role of women in Judaism, on the Torah as an appropriate subject of attention for women as well as for men, on the roles of men and women overall, and so on. The performance was noteworthy—indeed, many of the regular members of the congregation seemed quite surprised—precisely because it violated people's expectations and in so doing directed people's attention toward the role of men and women in religious ritual at the end of the twentieth century as well as toward the Torah as the central symbol of the Jewish people.

## What Are Rites of Passage?

Graduating from college, getting married, joining the military, and other "life cycle" rituals share certain important features, most notably that people begin the ritual as one kind of person (e.g., student, single, recruit), and by the time the ritual is over, they have been transformed into a different kind of person (e.g., graduate, spouse, soldier). These rituals are called rites of passage. At the beginning of the twentieth century, the Belgian anthropologist Arnold Van Gennep (1960) noted that certain kinds of rituals around the world had similar structures. These were rituals associated with the movement (or passage) of people from one position in the social structure to another. They took place at births, initiations,

confirmations, weddings, funerals, and the like (Figure 10.7).

Van Gennep (1960) found that all these rituals began with a period of *separation* from the old position and from normal time. During this period, the ritual passenger leaves behind the symbols and practices of his or her previous position. For example, military recruits leave their families behind and are moved to a new place. They are forced to leave behind the clothing, activities, and even the hairstyle that marked who they were in civilian life.

The second stage in rites of passage involves a period of *transition*, in which the ritual passenger is neither in the old life nor yet in the new one. This period is marked by rolelessness, ambiguity, and perceived danger. Often, the person involved is subjected to ordeal by those who have already passed through. In the military service, this is the period of basic training, in which recruits (not yet soldiers but no longer civilians) are forced to dress and act alike. They are subjected to a grinding-down process, after which they are rebuilt into something new.

During the final stage—*reaggregation*—the ritual passenger is reintroduced into society in his or her new position. In the military, this involves graduation from basic training and a visit home, but this time as a member of the armed forces, in uniform and on leave—in other words, as a new person. Other familiar rites of passage in youth culture in Canada include high school graduation and the informal yet significant ceremonies associated with the eighteenth birthday, both of which are understood as movements from one kind of person to another.

The work of Victor Turner greatly increased our understanding of rites of passage. Turner concentrated on the period of transition, which he saw as important both for the rite of passage and for social life in general. Van Gennep (1960) referred to this part of a rite of passage as the "liminal period," from the Latin *limen* ("threshold"). During this period, the individual is on the threshold, betwixt and between, neither here nor there, neither in nor out. Turner notes that the symbolism accompanying the rite of passage often expresses this

**rite of passage** A ritual that serves to mark the movement and transformation of an individual from one social position to another.

**FIGURE 10.7** | Rites of passage are rituals that enable people to move from one position in the social structure to another. An Apache girl, accompanied by her godmother and a helper, moves into adulthood through the Sunrise Dance.

ambiguous state. Liminality, he tells us, "is frequently likened to death, to being in the womb, to invisibility, to darkness, to bisexuality, to the wilderness, and to an eclipse of the sun or moon" (Turner 1969, 95). People in the liminal state tend to develop an intense comradeship with each other in which their non-liminal distinctions disappear or become irrelevant. Turner calls this kind of social relationship communitas, which is best understood as an unstructured or minimally structured community of equal individuals.

Turner (1969) contends that all societies need some kind of communitas as much as they need structure. Communitas gives "recognition to an essential and generic human bond, without which there could be no society" (Turner 1969, 97). That bond is the common humanity that underlies all culture and society. However, periods of communitas (often in ritual context) are brief. Communitas is dangerous, not just because it threatens structure but also because it threatens survival itself. During the time of communitas, the things that structure ensures—production of food and physical and social reproduction of the society—cannot be provided. But someone always has to take

out the garbage and clean up after the party. Thus, communitas gives way again to structure, which in turn generates a need for a new release of communitas. The feeling of communitas can also be attained by means of play and art. Indeed, it may well be that for people in contemporary nation-states the experience of communitas comes through participation in mass public events like Carnival in Rio de Janeiro, Carnaval de Quebec in Quebec City, or the Calgary Stampede; attendance at large-scale rock concerts; or even the climactic winning moments of a regional or national sports team (Figure 10.8).

## How Are Play and Ritual Complementary?

How does the logic of ritual differ from the logic of play? Play and ritual are complementary forms of metacommunication (Handelman 1977). The movement from non-play to play is based on the premise of metaphor ("Let's make believe"); the movement to ritual is based on the premise of literalness ("Let's believe"). From the perspective of the everyday social order, the result of these contrasting premises is the "inauthenticity" of play and the "truth" of ritual.

Because of the connection of ritual with self-evident truth, the metacommunication of the ritual frame ("This is ritual") is associated with an additional metacommunication: "All messages within this frame are true." It is ritual that asserts *what should be* to play's *what can be*.

**liminality**   The ambiguous transitional state in a rite of passage in which the person or persons undergoing the ritual are outside their ordinary social positions.

**communitas**   An unstructured or minimally structured community of equal individuals found frequently in rites of passage.

**FIGURE 10.8** | A crowd of hockey fans cheers on Team Canada during the 2010 Winter Olympic Games in Vancouver. These kinds of mass public events can create a feeling of communitas in today's nation-states.

The ritual frame is more rigid than the play frame. Consequently, ritual is the most stable liminal domain, whereas play is the most flexible. Players can move with relative ease into and out of play, but such is not the case with ritual.

Finally, play usually has little effect on the social order of ordinary life; as a result, play can safely create a wide range of commentary on the social order. Ritual is different: its role is explicitly to maintain the status quo, including the prescribed ritual transformations. Societies differ in the extent to which ritual behaviour alternates with everyday, non-ritual behaviour. When nearly every act of everyday life is ritualized and other forms of behaviour are strongly discouraged, we sometimes speak of **orthopraxy** ("correct practice"). Traditionally observant Jews and Muslims, for example, lead a highly ritualized daily life, attempting from the moment they awaken until the moment they fall asleep to carry out even the humblest of activities in a manner that is ritually correct. In their view, ritual correctness is the result of God's law, and it is their duty and joy to conform their every action to God's will.

Margaret Drewal (1992) argues that, at least among the Yoruba, play and ritual overlap (see EthnoProfile 10.3: Yoruba on page 287). Yoruba rituals combine spectacle, festival, play, sacrifice, and so on and integrate diverse media—music, dance, poetry, theatre, sculpture (Drewal 1992, 198). They are events that require improvisatory, spontaneous individual moves; as a result, the mundane order is not only inverted and reversed but may also be subverted through power play and gender play. For example, gender roles are rigidly structured in Yoruba society. Yoruba rituals, however, allow some cross-dressing by both men and women, providing institutionalized opportunities for men and women to cross gender boundaries and to express the traits that the Yoruba consider to be characteristic of the opposite sex, sometimes as parody but sometimes seriously and respectfully (Drewal 1992, 190).

## How Are World View and Symbolic Practice Related?

Our previous discussions of language, play, art, myth, and ritual provided an overview of some of the ways human beings use culture to construct rich understandings of everyday experiences. In this section, we build on those insights and describe how human beings use cultural creativity to make sense of the wider world on a more comprehensive scale as they construct encompassing pictures of reality called **world views**.

**orthopraxy** "Correct practice"; the prohibition of deviation from approved forms of behaviour.

**world views** Encompassing pictures of reality created by the members of societies.

## In Their Own Words

## Video in the Villages

*Patricia Aufderheide describes how Indigenous peoples of the Amazonian rain forest in Brazil have been able to master the video camera and use it for their own purposes.*

The social role and impact of video is particularly intriguing among people who are new to mass-communications technologies, such as lowlands Amazonian Indians. One anthropologist has argued persuasively that a naive disdain for commercial media infuses much well-meaning concern over the potential dangers of introducing mass media and that "Indigenous media offers a possible means—social, cultural, and political—for reproducing and transforming cultural identity among people who have experienced massive political, geographic, and economic disruption." . . . In two groups of Brazilian Indians, the Nambikwara and the Kayapo, this premise has been tested.

The Nambikwara became involved with video through Video in the Villages, run by Vincent Carelli at the Centro de Trabalho Indigenista in São Paulo. This project is one example of a trend to put media in the hands of people who have long been the subjects of ethnographic film and video. . . . While some anthropologists see this resort as a "solution" to the issue of ethnographic authority, others have focused on it as part of a struggle for Indigenous rights and political autonomy. . . . Many of the groups Carelli has worked with have seized on video for its ability to extensively document lengthy rituals that mark the group's cultural uniqueness rather than produce a finished product. . . .

Carelli coproduced a project with a Nambikwara leader, documenting a cultural ritual. After taping, the Nambikwara viewed the ritual and offered criticisms, finding it tainted with modernisms. They then repeated the ritual in traditional regalia and conducted, for the first time in a generation, a male initiation ceremony—taping it all. (This experience is recounted in a short tape, *Girls' Puberty Ritual*, produced by Carelli with a Nambikwara leader for outsiders.) Using video reinforced an emerging concept of "traditional" in contrast to Brazilian culture—a concept that had not, apparently, been part of the Nambikwara's repertoire before contact but that had practical political utility.

The Kayapo are among the best-known Brazilian Indians internationally, partly because of their video work, promoted as a tool of cultural identification by the anthropologist who works most closely with them. Like other tribes such as the Xavante who had extensive contact with Brazilian authorities and media, the Kayapo early seized on modern media technologies. . . . Besides intimidating authorities with the evidence of recording equipment . . . , the Kayapo quickly grasped the symbolic expectations of Brazilian mass media for Indians. They cannily played on the contrast between their feathers and body paint and their recording devices to get coverage. Even staging public events for the purpose of attracting television crews, they were able to insert, although not ultimately control, their message on Brazilian news by exploiting that contrast. . . . Using these techniques, Kayapo leaders became international symbols of the ironies of the postmodern age and not incidentally also the subjects of international agitation and fundraising that benefitted Kayapo over other Indigenous groups and some Kayapo over others.

Kayapo have also used video to document internal cultural ceremonies in meticulous detail; to communicate internally between villages; to develop an archive; and to produce clips and short documentaries intended for wide audiences. Their video work, asserts anthropologist Terence Turner, has not merely preserved traditional customs but in fact transformed their understanding of those customs as customs and their culture as a culture. Turner also found that video equipment, expertise, and products often fed into existing factional divisions. Particular Kayapo leaders used the equipment in their own interests, sometimes as a tool to subdue their enemies, sometimes as evidence of personal power.

## EthnoProfile 10.3

### Yoruba

**Region:** Western Africa

**Nation:** Nigeria

**Population:** 40,000,000

**Environment:** Coastal and forest

**Livelihood:** Farming, commerce, modern professions

**Political organization:** Traditionally, kingdoms; today, part of a modern nation-state

**For more information:** Bascom, William. 1969. *The Yoruba of Southwestern Nigeria.* New York: Holt, Rinehart, and Winston.

## What Are Symbols?

As they develop complex understandings of themselves and the wider world, people regularly devise symbols to organize this knowledge. As we saw earlier, a symbol—such as a word, an image, or an action—is something that stands for something else. Symbols signal the presence and importance of given domains of experience.

Some symbols, which anthropologist Sherry Ortner (1973, 1339) calls *summarizing symbols*, sum up, express, or represent for people "in an emotionally powerful ... way what the system means to them." Examples include the cross representing the Christian faith or the Canadian flag representing our country and its citizens as a whole. These symbols represent a complex collection of ideas and feelings, which they draw our attention to all at once. Yet summarizing symbols often mean different things to different people. For example, while the Canadian flag might stand for patriotism, democracy, and freedom to many citizens, to others it may stand for limitations on civil rights or a history of colonization.

Other symbols, which Ortner calls *elaborating symbols*, are essentially analytic. They allow people to sort out and label complex and undifferentiated feelings and ideas into comprehensible and communicable language and action. Elaborating symbols provide people with categories for thinking about how their world is ordered. For the Dinka, cattle herding people of eastern Africa, cattle are a key elaborating symbol. According to Godfrey Lienhardt (1961), cattle provide the Dinka with most of the metaphors they use for thinking about and responding to experience. For instance, Dinka perceptions of colour, light, and shade are connected to the colours they see in cattle. They even liken how their society is put together to how a bull is put together (Ortner 1973).

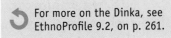 For more on the Dinka, see EthnoProfile 9.2, on p. 261.

## What Is Religion?

For many readers of this text, the most familiar form of world view is probably religion. The anthropological concept of religion, like many analytic terms, began as a description of a certain domain of Western culture. As a result, it has been very difficult for anthropologists to settle on a definition of religion that is applicable in all human societies. Scholars have often argued that a religion differs from other kinds of world views because it assumes the existence of a supernatural domain: an invisible world populated by one or more beings who are more powerful than human beings and able to influence events in the "natural" human world. The problem with this definition is that the distinction between "natural" and "supernatural" was originally made by non-religious Western observers in order to distinguish the real "natural" world from what they took to be the imaginary "supernatural" world. Many anthropologists who study different religious traditions believe that it is less distorting to begin with their informants' statements about what exists and what does not. In this way, they are in a better position to understand the range of forces, visible and invisible, that religious devotees perceive as being active in their world.

For these reasons, John Bowen proposes that anthropologists approach religion in a way that begins broadly but that allows for increasing specificity as we learn more about the details of particular religious traditions. Bowen (2008, 4) defines **religion** as "ideas and practices that postulate reality beyond that which is immediately available to the senses." In individual societies, this may take the shape of beliefs in spirits and gods, in impersonal forces that affect the world, in

**religion** "Ideas and practices that postulate reality beyond that which is immediately available to the senses" (Bowen 2008).

the correct practice of ritual, or in the awareness that people's ancestors continue to be active in the world of the living. It is important to note that this definition encompasses both practices and ideas; religions involve actions as well as beliefs (Figure 10.9). Indeed, anthropologist A.F.C. Wallace (1966) proposed a set of "minimal categories of religious behaviour" that describe many of the practices usually associated with religions. Several of the most important are as follows:

1. *Prayer.* Where there are personified cosmic forces, there is a customary way of addressing them, usually by speaking or chanting out loud. Often, people pray in public, at a sacred location, and with special apparatus: incense, smoke, objects (e.g., rosary beads or a prayer wheel), and so on.

2. *Physiological exercise.* Many religious systems have methods for physically manipulating psychological states to induce an ecstatic spiritual state. Wallace suggests four major kinds of manipulation: (1) drugs; (2) sensory deprivation; (3) mortification of the flesh by pain, sleeplessness, and fatigue; and (4) deprivation of food, water, or air. In many societies, the experience of ecstasy, euphoria, dissociation, or hallucination seems to be a goal of religious effort.

3. *Exhortation.* In all religious systems, certain people are believed to have closer relationships with the invisible powers than others have, and they are expected to use those relationships in the spiritual interests of others. They give orders, they heal, they threaten, they comfort, and they interpret.

4. *Mana.* Mana refers to an impersonal superhuman power that is sometimes believed to be transferable from an object that contains it to one that does not. The laying on of hands, in which the power of a healer enters the body of a sick person to remove or destroy an illness, is an example of the transmission of power. In Guider, Cameroon, some people believe that the ink used to copy passages from the Qur'an has power (see EthnoProfile 14.3: Guider). Washing the ink off the board on which the words are written and drinking the ink transfers the power of the words into the body of the drinker. All these examples illustrate the principle that sacred things are sometimes to be touched so that their power may be transferred to human beings.

5. *Taboo.* Objects or people that may not be touched are taboo. Some people believe that touching such objects or people may cause the cosmic power they contain to "drain away" or may injure the toucher. Many religious systems have taboo objects. Traditionally, Catholics were not to touch the Host (a form of sacred bread) during communion. Jews may not touch the handwritten text of the biblical scrolls. In ancient Polynesia, commoners could not touch the chief's body; even an accidental touch resulted in the death of the commoner. Food may also be taboo; many societies have elaborate rules

**FIGURE 10.9** | The joint pilgrimage by Hindu worshipers to the Ganges River illustrates the social, active nature of religion.

concerning the foods that may or may not be eaten at different times or by different kinds of people.

6. *Feasts*. Eating and drinking in a religious context is very common. The Holy Communion of Catholics and Protestants is a meal set apart by its religious context. The Passover Seder for Jews is another religious feast. For the Huichol of Mexico (EthnoProfile 10.4), the consumption of peyote is set apart from other meals by its religious context. Even everyday meals may be seen to have a religious quality if they begin or end with prayer.

7. *Sacrifice*. Giving something of value to the invisible forces or their agents is a feature of many religious systems. This may be an offering of money, goods, or services. It may also be the immolation of animals or, rarely, human beings. Sacrifices may be made in thanks to the cosmic forces, in hopes of influencing them to act in a certain way, or simply to gain general religious merit.

## How Do People Communicate in Religion?

Those who are committed to religious world views are convinced of the existence and active involvement in their lives of beings or forces that are ordinarily invisible. Some of the most highly valued religious practices, such as religious ecstasy or trance, produce outer symptoms that may be perceived by others; but their most powerful effects can be experienced only by the individual who undergoes them personally. What if you wanted to know what it felt like to experience religious ecstasy? What if you were someone who had had such an experience and wanted to tell others about it? What if you were convinced that the supreme power in the universe had revealed itself to you and you wanted to share this revelation with others? How would you proceed?

You might well begin by searching for metaphors based on experiences already well known to your audience. Thus, one Hindu Tamil worshiper in Kuala Lumpur who successfully went into trance during the festival of Thaipusam described his experience as "floating in the air, followed by the wind" (*Floating on the Air* 1973). And the Hebrew poet who wrote the twenty-third psalm of the Bible tried to express his experience of the power and love of his god by comparing his god to a shepherd and himself to a sheep. Many contemporary theologians argue that the language human beings use to talk about God is inevitably full of everyday metaphors (e.g., see Gillman 1992). Even those who claim to have had personal experience of the reality of God, of ancestral spirits, or of witchcraft will probably still find themselves forced to resort to poetic, metaphorical language if they want to explain that experience to other people—and perhaps even to themselves.

## How Are Religion and Social Organization Related?

Anthropological research suggests that members of many religious traditions base their understanding of the structure of the universe on the structure of the society in which they live. One consequence of this mode of understanding is that forces in the universe are personalized. Thus, people seeking to influence those forces must handle them as they would handle powerful human beings. Communication is perhaps the central feature of how we deal with human beings: when we address each other, we expect a response. The same is true when we address personalized cosmic forces.

Maintaining contact with invisible cosmic powers is a tremendously complex undertaking. It is not surprising, therefore, that some societies develop complex social practices to ensure that it is done properly. In

### EthnoProfile 10.4

### Huichol

**Region:** Latin America

**Nation:** Mexico

**Population:** 20,000

**Environment:** Mountainous terrain

**LivelihoodL:** Corn farming, deer hunting in recent past

**Political organization:** Traditionally, no formal organization, some men with influence; today, part of a modern nation-state

**For more information:** Myerhoff, Barbara. 1974. *Peyote Hunt*. Ithaca, NY: Cornell University Press.

other words, religion becomes institutionalized. Social positions are created for specialists who supervise or embody correct religious practice.

Anthropologists have identified two broad categories of religious specialists: shamans and priests. A **shaman** is a part-time religious practitioner who is believed to have the power to contact invisible powers directly on behalf of individuals or groups. Shamans are often thought to be able to travel to the cosmic realm to communicate with the beings or forces that dwell there. They often plead with those beings or forces to act in favour of their people and may return with messages for them. The Ju/'hoansi, for example, recognize that some people are able to develop an internal power that enables them to travel to the world of the spirits—to enter "half death"—in order to cure those who are sick. Among the Inuit, shamans known as *angakkuit* have traditionally been relied on to cure the sick and provide spiritual guidance; in recent times, this form of shamanism has been integrated with Christianity, and *angakkuit* have become intermediaries teaching traditional beliefs and Christian ideology (Laugrand and Oosten 2010).

For more on the Ju/'hoansi, see EthnoProfile 11.5, on p. 314. For more on shamanism and Christianity among Inuit societies in northern Canada, see Chapter 2, pp. 39–40.

In many societies, the training that a shaman receives is long and demanding and may involve the use of powerful psychotropic substances. Repeatedly entering altered states of consciousness can produce long-lasting effects on shamans themselves, and shamans may be viewed with suspicion or fear by others in the society. This is because contacting cosmic beings to persuade them to heal embodies dangerous ambiguities: someone who can contact such beings for positive benefits may also be able to contact them to produce negative outcomes like disease or death.

The term *shaman* comes from the Tungus of eastern Siberia, where, at a minimum, it referred to a religious specialist who has the ability to enter a trance through which he or she is believed to enter into direct contact with spiritual beings and guardian spirits for the purposes of healing, fertility, protection, and aggression in a ritual setting (Bowie 2006, 175; Hultkrantz

**shaman** A part-time religious practitioner who is believed to have the power to contact supernatural forces directly on behalf of individuals or groups.

1992, 10). The healing associated with Siberian shamanism was concerned with the idea that illness was caused by soul loss and healing through recovery of the soul (Figure 10.10). Thus, the shaman was responsible for dealing with spirits that were at best neutral and at worst actively hostile to human beings. The shaman could travel to the spirit world to heal someone by finding the missing soul that had been stolen by spirits. But a shaman who was jealous of a hunter, for example, was believed to be able to steal the souls of animals so that the hunter would fail, which could ultimately lead to starvation. In these societies, shamans are considered to be dangerous.

Shamanic activity takes place in the trance séance, which can be little more than a consultation between shaman and patient or a major public ritual, rich in drama. Becoming a shaman is not undertaken for personal development. In the societies in which shamanism is important, it is said that the shaman has no

**FIGURE 10.10 |** Using smoke from a juniper twig, Siberian shaman Vera heals a patient possessed by evil spirits.

**FIGURE 10.11** | The complex organization of the Roman Catholic Church was illustrated at the funeral for Pope John Paul II in 2005.

choice but to take on the role; the spirits demand it. It can take a decade or more to become fully recognized as a shaman, and it is assumed that the shaman will be in service to the society (for good or ill) for the rest of his or her life.

A priest, by contrast, is skilled in the practice of religious rituals, which are carried out for the benefit of the group or individual members of the group. Priests do not necessarily have direct contact with cosmic forces. Often their main role is to mediate such contact by ensuring that the required ritual activity has been properly performed. Priests are found in hierarchical societies, and they owe their ability to act as priests to the hierarchy of the religious institution (Figure 10.11). Status differences separating rulers and subjects in such societies are reflected in the unequal relationship between priest and laity.

## World Views in Operation: Two Case Studies

We have been discussing how world views are constructed, but most of us encounter them fully formed, both in our own society and in other societies. We face a rich tapestry of symbols, rituals, and everyday practices linked to one another in what often appears to be a seamless web. Where do we begin to sort things out? The following two case studies offer some insight.

### Coping with Misfortune: Witchcraft, Oracles, and Magic among the Azande

Anthropologist E.E. Evans-Pritchard, in his classic work *Witchcraft, Oracles, and Magic among the Azande* ([1937] 1976), showed how Azande beliefs and practices concerning witchcraft, oracles, and magic were related to one another (see EthnoProfile 10.5: Azande). He describes how Azande in the 1920s used witchcraft beliefs to explain unfortunate things that happened to them and how they employed oracles and magic to exert a measure of control over the actions of other people. Evans-Pritchard was impressed by the intelligence, sophistication,

**priest** A religious practitioner skilled in the practice of religious rituals, which he or she carries out for the benefit of the group.

**witchcraft** The performance of magic by human beings, often through innate supernatural powers, whether or not it is intentional or self-aware.

**oracles** Invisible forces to which people address questions and whose responses they believe to be truthful.

**magic** A set of beliefs and practices designed to control the visible or invisible world for specific purposes.

## EthnoProfile 10.5

### Azande

**Region:** Central Africa

**Nation:** Democratic Republic of the Congo, South Sudan, Central African Republic

**Population:** 1,100,000

**Environment:** Sparsely wooded savannah

**Livelihood:** Farming, hunting, fishing, chicken raising

**Political organization:** Traditionally, highly organized, tribal kingdoms; today, part of modern nation-states

**For more information:** Evans-Pritchard, E.E. [1937] 1976. *Witchcraft, Oracles, and Magic among the Azande*. Abridged ed. Oxford: Oxford University Press.

and skepticism of his Azande informants. For this reason, he was all the more struck by their ability to hold a set of beliefs that many Europeans would regard as superstitious.

## Azande Witchcraft Beliefs

The Azande Evans-Pritchard knew believed that *mangu* (translated by Evans-Pritchard as "witchcraft") was a substance in the body of witches, generally located under the sternum. Being a part of the body, the witchcraft substance grew as the body grew; therefore, the older the witch, the more potent his or her witchcraft. The Azande believed that children inherited witchcraft from their parents. Men or women might be witches. Men practised witchcraft against other men, women against other women. Witchcraft worked when its "soul" removed the soul of a certain organ in the victim's body, usually at night, causing a slow, wasting disease. Suffering such a disease was therefore an indication that an individual had been bewitched.

Witchcraft was a basic concept for the Azande, one that shaped their experience of adversity. All deaths were due to witchcraft and had to be avenged by magic. Other misfortunes were also commonly attributed to witchcraft unless the victim had broken a taboo, had

failed to observe a moral rule, or was believed to be responsible for his or her own problems. An incompetent potter whose pots break during the firing process may claim that witchcraft caused them to break, but everyone will laugh at the potter because they know he or she lacks skill. Witchcraft was believed to be so common that the Azande were neither surprised nor awestruck when they encountered it. Rather, their usual response was anger.

To the Azande, witchcraft was a completely natural explanation for events. Consider the classic case of the collapsing granary. Azande territory is hot, and people seeking shade often sit under traditional raised granaries, which rest on logs. Termites are common in Azande territory, and sometimes they destroy the supporting logs, making a granary collapse. Occasionally, when a granary collapses, people sitting under it are killed. Why does this happen? The Azande are well aware that the termites chew up the wood until the supports give way, but to them that is not answer enough. Why, after all, should that particular granary have collapsed at that particular moment? To skeptical observers, the only connection is coincidence in time and space. Western science does not provide any explanation for why these two chains of causation intersect. But the Azande did: witchcraft caused the termites to finish chewing up the wood at just that moment; thus, that witchcraft had to be avenged by magic.

## Dealing with Witches

To expose the witch, the Azande consulted oracles (invisible forces to which people address questions and whose responses they believe to be truthful). Preeminent among these was the poison oracle. The poison was a strychnine-like substance imported into Azande territory. The oracle "spoke" through the effect the poison had on chickens. When witchcraft was suspected, a relative of the afflicted person took some young chickens into the bush along with a specialist in administering the poison oracle. This person fed poison to one chicken, named a suspect, and asked the oracle to kill the chicken if that person were the witch. If the chicken died, a second chicken was fed poison, and the oracle was asked to spare the chicken if the suspect just named was indeed the witch. Thus, the Azande double-checked the oracle carefully; a witchcraft accusation was not made lightly.

People did not consult the oracle with a long list of names. They needed only to consider those who might wish them or their families ill: people who had quarreled with them, who were unpleasant, who were antisocial, or whose behaviour was somehow out of line. Indeed, witches were always neighbours because neighbours were the only people who know you well enough to wish you and your family ill.

Once the oracle identified the witch, the Azande removed the wing of the chicken and had it taken by messenger to the compound of the accused person. The messenger presented the accused witch with the chicken wing and said that he had been sent concerning the illness of so-and-so's relative. "Almost invariably the witch replies courteously that he is unconscious of injuring anyone, that if it is true that he has injured the man in question he is very sorry, and that if it is he alone who is troubling him then he will surely recover, because from the bottom of his heart he wishes him health and happiness" (Evans-Pritchard [1937] 1976, 42). The accused then called for a gourd of water, took some in his mouth, and sprayed it out over the wing. He said aloud, so the messenger could hear and repeat what he said, that if he was a witch he was not aware of it and that he was not intentionally causing the sick man to be ill. He addressed the witchcraft in him, asking it to become cool, and concluded by saying that he made this appeal from his heart, not just from his lips (42).

People accused of witchcraft were usually astounded; no Azande thought of himself or herself as a witch. However, the Azande strongly believed in witchcraft and in the oracles; and if the oracle said someone was a witch, then it must be so. The accused witch was grateful to the family of the sick person for being informed. Otherwise, if the accused had been allowed to murder the victim, all the while unaware of it, the witch would surely be killed later by vengeance magic. The witchcraft accusation carried a further message: the behaviour of the accused was sufficiently outside the bounds of acceptable Azande behaviour to have marked him or her as a potential witch. Only the names of people who you suspected of wishing you ill were submitted to the oracle. The accused witch, then, was being told to change his or her behaviour.

## Are There Patterns of Witchcraft Accusation?

Compared with the stereotypes of European American witchcraft—old hags dressed in black, riding on broomsticks, casting spells, causing milk to sour or people to sicken—Azande witchcraft seems quite tame. People whose impression of witchcraft comes from Western European images may believe that witchcraft and witch-hunting tear at the very fabric of society. Yet, anthropological accounts like Evans-Pritchard's suggest that practices such as witchcraft accusation can sometimes keep societies together. Anthropologist Mary Douglas (1970, xxvi–xxvii) looked at the range of witchcraft accusations worldwide and discovered that they fall into two basic types: in some cases, the witch is an evil outsider; in others, the witch is an internal enemy, either the member of a rival faction or a dangerous deviant. These different patterns of accusation perform different functions in a society. If the witch is an outsider, witchcraft accusations can strengthen in-group ties. If the witch is an internal enemy, accusations of witchcraft can weaken in-group ties; factions may have to regroup, communities may split, and the entire social hierarchy may be reordered. If the witch is a dangerous deviant, the accusation of witchcraft can be seen as an attempt to control the deviant in defence of the wider values of the community. Douglas concluded that how people understand witchcraft is based on the social relations of their society.

## Coping with Misfortune: Listening for God among Contemporary Evangelicals in the United States

Anthropologist T.M. Luhrmann spent several years studying the beliefs and practices of Vineyard Christian Fellowship evangelical churches in the United States—specifically, in the city of Chicago and the state of California. Luhrmann (2012) notes that the Vineyard movement came out of the turmoil and spiritual ferment of the 1960s and early 1970s, as some people were searching for a more direct experience of God. Specifically, when they prayed to God they expected an answer. Luhrmann's research was designed to address a significant issue in the study of religion—how might one know that God exists? "I set out many years ago to understand how God becomes real for modern people. I chose an example of the style of Christianity that would seem to make the cognitive burden of belief most difficult: the evangelical Christianity in which God is thought to be present as a person in someone's everyday life, and in which God's supernatural power is thought to be immediately accessible by that person" (Luhrmann 2012, xix). The people in the churches she attended were typically middle class, college educated, and white, although there were some very wealthy and very poor people and many members of visible minorities who belonged.

One of the striking characteristics of the church is that congregants expect to experience God immediately, directly, and personally. Members of the church told her that God is an intimate friend who wants to know everything about them, who is as concerned with the clothing they wear as he is with matters of life and death. For these Christians, God is transformed into someone with whom members of the church have a relationship. That relationship is cultivated through prayer, the act of talking with God, the performance of which must be learned (Luhrmann 2012, 47). For members of the church, prayer is modelled on the idea of a conversation between friends, and the hardest part of prayer training was learning to hear God's part of the communication.

The Vineyard Christian Fellowship fosters an intense individuality among its congregants, who were taught that God was to be addressed and listened to individually. God is an all-good, all-powerful, all-knowing friend. He will care for those who seek him and who learn to pray to him. He loves them unconditionally and answers prayer. But if this is so, how does this understanding of God explain why bad things happen in the world? Evil is a fundamental problem for all religions, because part of being human is suffering, often unjust. Theologians use the term *theodicy* to describe the field of study that proposes answers to the problem of evil. Luhrmann (2012, 268) points out that theologians have proposed three general solutions: (1) Evil is the lack of God's goodness, and humans create it when they do not choose God; (2) the world will be good in the

end, even if it isn't now; and (3) although it may not look like it to us right now, we live in the best of all possible worlds. So how does the Vineyard Church explain human suffering? According to Luhrmann, "Churches like the Vineyard handle the problem of suffering with a fourth solution: they ignore it. Then they turn the pain into a learning opportunity. When it hurts, you are supposed to draw closer to God. . . . When God is very close and very powerful and always very loving, there is no easy explanation when he does not deliver" (260). Luhrmann adds that modern believers don't need religion to explain misfortune or indeed anything else. "They have plenty of scientific accounts for why the world is as it is and why some bodies rather than others fall ill" (295).

But if prayer is not intended to find answers to suffering, then what do these congregants get from it? According to Luhrmann, what they get is God's role as a friend to help them through a difficult time. Members of the Vineyard do not generally speculate about why there is evil or misfortune. They turn to God as they would turn to a powerful and especially trusted friend to help them deal with pain or unhappiness, and God's friendship becomes its own reward. In other words, "People stay with this God not because the theology makes sense but because the practice delivers emotionally" (Luhrmann 2012, 268). So far, this seems to be a theology of the individual—"me and my relationship with God"—but Luhrmann points out that the congregational community is essential to the development of these individual relationships: "It takes a great deal of work for the community to teach people to develop these apparently private and personal relationships with God. . . . At the Vineyard, the community stood in for God when God seemed distant and particularly when he seemed unreal" (279). Thus, although the religious beliefs of these US evangelicals offer no cause for misfortune, their religious practice does offer a solution for misfortune: to strengthen their personal relationship with God with the aid of their community. "They want to hold on to hope, despite their doubt. They care about transforming their own suffering, not about explaining why suffering persists. Their faith is practical, not philosophical" (Luhrmann 2012, 299).

# How Do People Maintain and Change Their World View?

What makes a world view stable? Why is a world view rejected? Changes in world view are regularly connected to the practical, everyday experiences of people in a particular society. Stable, repetitive experiences reinforce the acceptability of any traditional world view that has successfully accounted for such experiences in the past. Connections to the land and traditional territories assist in keeping a world view strong. As Sarah King (2013) remarks, space and place are an important part of maintaining a stable world view for members of the Mi'kmaq First Nation in Atlantic Canada (EthnoProfile 10.6; see the "In Their Own Words" box on the importance of context in Mi'kmaq world views). When experiences become unpredictable, however, thinking people in any society may become painfully aware that past experiences can no longer be trusted as guides for the future, and traditional world views may be undermined (see Horton 1982, 252).

## How Do People Cope with Change?

Drastic changes in experience lead people to create new interpretations that will help them cope with the changes. Sometimes the change is an outcome of local or regional struggles. The Protestant Reformation, for example, adapted the Christian tradition to changing social circumstances in northern Europe during the Renaissance by breaking ties to the pope, turning church lands over to secular authorities, allowing clergy to marry, and so forth. Protestants continued to identify themselves as Christians, although many of their religious practices had changed.

In Guider, Cameroon, lone rural migrants to town have frequently abandoned their former religious practices and took on urban customs and a new identity through conversion to Islam. However, similar conflicts between new and old ways do not always lead to religious conversion. Sometimes the result is a creative synthesis of old religious practices and new ones, a process called syncretism. Under the pressure of Christian missionizing, Indigenous people of Central America identified some of their own pre-Christian, personalized superhuman beings with particular Catholic saints. Similarly, Africans brought to Brazil identified Catholic saints with African gods, to produce the syncretistic religion Candomblé.

Anthropologists have debated the nature of syncretistic practices, noting that while some may be viewed as a way of resisting new ideas imposed from above, others may be introduced from above by powerful outsiders deliberately making room for local beliefs within their own more encompassing world view. The Romans, for example, made room for local deities within their imperial pantheon, and post–Vatican II Catholicism explicitly urged non-European Catholics to worship using local cultural forms (Stewart and Shaw 1994).

When groups defend or refashion their own way of life in the face of outside encroachments, anthropologists sometimes describe their activities as revitalization—a deliberate, organized attempt by some members of a society to create a more satisfying culture (Wallace 1972, 75).

---

## EthnoProfile 10.6

### Mi'kmaq

**Region:** North Atlantic coast

**Nation:** Canada

**Population:** 35,000

**Environment:** Maritime

**Livelihood:** fishing, agriculture, foraging

**Political organization:** Traditionally, tribal systems; today, part of modern nation-state

**For more information:** Sable, Trudy, and Bernie Francis. 2012. *The Language of this Land, Mi'kma'ki*. Sydney, NS: Cape Breton University Press.

---

syncretism  The synthesis of old religious practices (or an old way of life) with new religious practices (or a new way of life) introduced from outside, often by force.

revitalization  A conscious, deliberate, and organized attempt by some members of a society to create a more satisfying culture in a time of crisis.

## In Their Own Words

### The Importance of Context in Mi'kmaq World Views

*Sarah King outlines the importance of context and place when studying Indigenous world views, drawing on examples from the Mi'kmaq First Nation living in Atlantic Canada.*

Context is the hallmark of Indigenous philosophies and religions, as these are ways of being in which things are seen as interconnected, and the world is viewed in a holistic fashion. Traditional Indigenous knowledge is contextual. . . . [For example, Sable and Francis (2012)] suggest that the Mi'kmaq understand themselves as sprouting from and rooted in the landscape, *weji-sqalia'timk* (17). The knowledge of the people is connected to the place where they live and to human . . . and non-human relations. . . .

[L]and is the context of Indigenous philosophy, culture, and religion, as the embodiment of relationships between many (human and other-than-human) relatives. . . . "*Weji-sqalia'timk* is about an embodied landscape—a landscape that is still integral to the cultural psyche of the Mi'kmaq today" (Sable and Francis 2012, 25). . . . Mi'kmaw stories reflect not only "the mapping skill of the Mi'kmaq" but also their knowledge

of "the sentient landscape" (Sable and Francis 2012, 42). [For example, t]he Mi'kmaq serpent dance teaches respect for the powers of the land and the medicines, and it also "teaches of the seasons, the directions, the stars, the nature of reptiles, the bird that leads one to the medicine and values of respect and care in collecting plants" (90). . . .

Taking the land seriously as a fundamental organizing principle of Indigenous ways of knowing means recognizing how this principle leads to immense diversity. Nations, tribes, and communities all become who and what they are because of the *particular* place in which they are at home. . . . Context matters, not simply because it illuminates the importance of land as a fundamental principle to Indigenous peoples across North America, but because it leads us to the diversity of thinking and practices that is characteristic of lived Indigenous experience.

Source: King 2013, 499–500. Excerpts from pp. 499–500.

Revitalization arises in times of crisis, most often among groups who are facing oppression and radical transformation, usually at the hands of outsiders (e.g., colonizing powers). In Canada, cultural revitalization continues to take place in many Aboriginal communities today. This process is perhaps most apparent in efforts to renew First Nations languages, provide traditional education for Aboriginal children, and revitalize aspects of Aboriginal spirituality. In fact, evidence shows that efforts to revitalize Aboriginal spirituality are actually increasing in many regions across Canada and the United States

(Fonda 2011; Kosmin et al. 2001). In many cases, these efforts have been highly successful, especially among young people. The process of spiritual revitalization often leads to healthier communities, an increased sense of well-being in individuals, and a higher level of self-reliance in youth. Not surprisingly, then, it has also been linked to reduced suicide rates in a number of Aboriginal communities in British Columbia and a more effective healing process among Aboriginal individuals incarcerated in Canadian jails.

Revitalization movements engage in a "politics of religious synthesis" that produces a range of outcomes (Stewart and Shaw 1994). Sometimes syncretism is embraced. Other times it is rejected in favour of **nativism**, or a return to the old ways. Some nativistic

**nativism** A return to the old ways; a movement whose members expect a messiah or a prophet who will bring back a lost golden age of peace, prosperity, and harmony.

movements expect a messiah or a prophet who will bring back a lost golden age of peace, prosperity, and harmony, a process often called *revivalism, millenarianism*, or *messianism*.

Nativistic movements often involve individuals in actively removing or avoiding any cultural practices associated with those who seek to dominate them. One such "anti-syncretistic" group is the Kwaio, who live on the island of Malaita in the Solomon Islands (see EthnoProfile 10.7: Kwaio). Almost all their neighbours have converted to Christianity, and the nation of which they are a part is militantly Christian. Members of other groups wear clothing, work on plantations or in tourist hotels, attend schools, and live in cities. The Kwaio have refused all this: "Young men carry bows and arrows; girls and women, nude except for customary ornaments, dig taro in forest gardens; valuables made of strung shell beads are exchanged at mortuary feasts; and priests sacrifice pigs to the ancestral spirits on whom prosperity and life itself depend" (Keesing 1982, 1).

Roger Keesing (1992) admits that he does not know exactly why the Kwaio responded in this way. He suspects that precolonial social and political differences between the Kwaio and their coastal neighbours influenced later developments. The colonial encounter itself was certainly relevant. In 1927, some Kwaio attacked a British patrol, killing the district officer and 13 Solomon Island troops. The subsequent massacre of many Kwaio by a police force made up of other Malaitans, followed by marginalization and persecution by the colonial government, also clearly contributed to Kwaio resistance.

It is important to emphasize that the Kwaio maintain their old ways deliberately, in the face of alternatives; their traditional way of life is therefore lived in a modern context. "In the course of anticolonial struggle, *kastomu* (custom) and commitment to ancestral ways have become symbols of identity and autonomy" (Keesing 1992, 240). In the eyes of the Kwaio, the many Solomon Islanders who became Christianized and acculturated lost their cultural ties and thereby their ties to the land and to their past, becoming outsiders in their own homeland. Maintaining traditional ways is thus a form of political protest. From this perspective, many contemporary anti-syncretistic movements in the world, from fundamentalism of various religions to movements for national identity and cultural autonomy, can be understood as having aims very similar to those of the Kwaio, sparked by many of the same forces.

## How Are World Views Used as Instruments of Power?

Within any particular cultural tradition, different world views often coexist. How then does a particular picture of reality become the "official" world view for a given society? And once that position is achieved, how is it maintained? To be in the running for the official picture of reality, a world view must be able, however minimally, to make sense of some people's personal and social experiences. Sometimes, however, it may seem to some members of society that barely credible views of reality have triumphed over alternatives that seem far more plausible. Thus, something more than persuasive ability alone must be involved, and that something is power. Powerless people may be unable to dislodge the official world view of their society. They can, however, refuse to accept the imposition of someone else's world view and develop an unofficial world view based on metaphors that reflect their own condition of powerlessness (Scott 1990).

### EthnoProfile 10.7

#### Kwaio

**Region:** Oceania (Melanesia)

**Nation:** Solomon Islands (Malaita)

**Population:** 7000 (1970s)

**Environment:** Tropical island

**Livelihood:** Horticulture and pig raising

**Political organization:** Traditionally, some men with influence but no coercive power; today, part of a modern nation-state

**For more information:** Keesing, Roger. 1992. *Custom and Confrontation*. Chicago: University of Chicago Press.

## In Their Own Words

## Custom and Confrontation

*In the following passage, the late Roger Keesing relays the words of one of his Kwaio informants, Dangeabe'u, who defends Kwaio custom.*

The government has brought the ways of business, the ways of money. The people at the coast believe that's what's important, and tell us we should join in. Now the government is controlling the whole world. The side of the Bible is withering away. When that's finished, the government will rule unchallenged. It will hold all the land. All the money will go to the government to feed its power. Once everything—our lands, too—are in their hands, that will be it.

I've seen the people from other islands who have all become Christians. They knew nothing about their land. The white people have gotten their hands on their lands. The whites led them to forget all the knowledge of their land, separated them from it. And when the people knew nothing about their land, the whites bought it from them and made their enterprises. . . .

That's close upon us too. If we all follow the side of the Bible, the government will become powerful here too, and will take control of our land. We won't be attached to our land, as we are now, holding our connections to our past. If the government had control of our land, then if we wanted to do anything on it, we'd have to pay them. If we wanted to start a business—a store, say—we'd have to pay the government. We reject all that. We want to keep hold of our land, in the ways passed down to us.

Source: Keesing 1992, 184.

How can world views be mobilized as instruments of power and control? First, a religious symbol can be invoked as a guarantee of self-evident truths when people in power seek to eliminate or impose certain forms of conduct. Holy books, like the Qur'an, may be used in this way. For example, a legal record from Guider, Cameroon, indicates that a son once brought suit against his father for refusing to repay him a certain amount of money. The father claimed that he had paid. Both father and son got into an increasingly heated argument in which neither would give ground. Finally, the judge in the case asked the father to take a copy of the Qur'an in his hand and swear that he was telling the truth. This he did. The son, however, refused to swear on the Qur'an and finally admitted that he had been lying. In this case, the status of the Qur'an as the unquestioned word of God, which implied the power of God to punish liars, controlled the son's behaviour.

Second, a symbol may be under the direct control of a person wishing to affect the behaviour of others.

Consider the role of official interpreters of religious or political ideology, such as priests or kings. Their pronouncements define the bounds of permissible behaviour. As Roger Keesing (1982, 219) points out:

Senior men, in Melanesia as elsewhere in the tribal world, have depended heavily on control of *sacred knowledge* to maintain their control of earthly politics. By keeping in their hands relations with ancestors and other spirits, by commanding magical knowledge, senior men could maintain a control mediated by the supernatural. Such religious ideologies served too, by defining rules in terms of ancient spirits and by defining the nature of men and women in supernatural terms, to reinforce and maintain the roles of the sexes—and again to hide their nature.

Keesing's observations remind us that knowledge, like power, is not evenly distributed throughout a society. Different kinds of people know different things. In some societies, what men know about their religious system is different from what women know and what older men know may be different from what younger men know. Keesing (1982, 14) suggested that men's control over women and older men's control over younger men are based on differential access to knowledge. It is not just that these different kinds of people know different things; rather, the different things they know (and do not know) enable them (or force them) to remain in the positions they hold in the society (Figure 10.12).

World views represent comprehensive ideas about the structure of the world and the place of one's own group, or one's own self, within that world. The ethnographic record offers a broad array of different world views, each testifying to the imaginative, meaning-making cultural capacity of humans. These models of the world, moreover, do not exist apart from everyday social practices; on the contrary, they are heavily implicated in our interactions with others. And when those interactions lead to crisis, humans respond by, among other things, seeking a way of making the crisis appear meaningful and therefore manageable. We are meaning-making, meaning-using, meaning-dependent organisms; and that is nowhere more clear than when a meaningful way of life is under assault.

**FIGURE 10.12** | Senior Dogon men carrying out fox trail divination. The knowledge and skills of elderly men, based on experience gained over a lifetime, provide their interpretations with an authority that those of people with less experience would not have.

## Chapter Summary

1. Play is a generalized form of behavioural openness: the ability to think about, speak about, and do different things in the same way or the same thing in different ways. Play can also be thought of as a way of organizing activities. We put a frame that consists of the message "This is play" around certain activities, thereby transforming them into play. Play also permits reflexive consideration of alternative realities by setting up a separate reality and suggesting that the perspective of ordinary life is only one way to make sense of experience. The functions of play include exercise, practice for the real world, increased creativity in children, and commentary on the real world. Play is likely linked to our evolution as modern humans capable of creativity and symbolic thought.

2. Art is a kind of play that is subject to certain culturally appropriate restrictions on form and content. It aims to evoke an aesthetic response from the artist and the observer. It succeeds when the form is culturally appropriate for the content and technically perfect in its realization. Aesthetic evaluations are culturally shaped value judgments. We recognize art in other cultures because of its family resemblance to what we call art in our own culture. Although people with other cultural understandings may not have produced art by intention, we can often successfully appreciate what they have created as art by appropriation. These issues are addressed in ethnographic studies that call into question received ideas about what counts as "authentic" art.

3.  Myths are stories whose truth seems self-evident because they do such a good job of integrating personal experiences with a wider set of assumptions about the way the world works. The power of myths comes from their ability to make life meaningful for those who accept them. As stories, myths are the products of high verbal art. A full understanding of myth requires ethnographic background information.

4.  Ritual is a repetitive social practice composed of sequences of symbolic activities such as speech, singing, dancing, gestures, and the manipulation of certain objects. In studying ritual, we pay attention not just to the symbols but also to how the ritual is performed. Cultural ideas are made concrete through ritual action. Rites of passage are rituals in which members of a culture move from one position in the social structure to another. These rites are marked by periods of separation, transition, and reaggregation. During the period of transition, individuals occupy a liminal position. All those in this position frequently develop an intense comradeship and a feeling of oneness, or communitas.

5.  Ritual and play are complementary. Play is based on the premise "Let us make believe," while ritual is based on the premise "Let us believe." As a result, the ritual frame is far more rigid than the play frame. Although ritual may seem overwhelming and all-powerful, individuals and groups can sometimes manipulate ritual forms to achieve non-traditional ends.

6.  Anthropological studies of religion tend to focus on the social institutions and meaningful processes with which it is associated. Followers of religions can address personalized forces symbolically and expect them to respond. Maintaining contact with cosmic forces is very complex, and societies have complex social practices designed to ensure that this is done properly. Two important kinds of religious specialists are shamans and priests.

7.  Many anthropologists have attempted to display the rich, coherent tapestries of symbols, rituals, and everyday practices that make up particular world views and to demonstrate the high degree to which world views vary from one another. They have also studied the ways in which drastic changes in people's experiences lead them to create new meanings to explain the changes and to cope with them. This can be accomplished through elaboration of the old system to fit changing times, conversion to a new world view, syncretism, revitalization, or resistance.

8.  Because religious knowledge is not distributed evenly among the members of societies, those who control such knowledge are often able to use it as an instrument of power to control other members of society.

## For Review

1.  Consider the definition of *play* in the running glossary on page 271, and explain the importance of each feature of this complex definition by examining Robert Park's research, as discussed on page 272.

2.  What is metacommunication? Can you provide an example of metacommunication? How do you use metacommunication in your own life?

3.  How do Elizabeth Chin's observations about African American girls and their dolls in Newhallville, New Haven, Connecticut, illustrate the importance of play for understanding human symbolic practices?

4.  What are the main components of the definition of *art* offered in this chapter, and why is each component important?

5.  What argument is made in this chapter concerning the role of "authenticity" in art? How does Michelle Bigenho's experience with Música de Maestros illustrate these points?

6.  What are myths? List some myths that you believe in. What would be an example of a Canadian myth?

7.  Compare Malinowski's view of myth with the view of Lévi-Strauss. How do the two relate to one another?

What are the advantages and potential drawbacks of each view?

8.  What are the major components of a ritual? In what ways might a child's birthday party be understood as a ritual?

9.  Describe each stage of a rite of passage. How do these stages apply to any rites of passage that you have undergone in your life?

10. Explain the differences anthropologists recognize between shamans and priests. Use the discussion of Inuit shamans to illustrate your answer.

11. Compare the Azande and the evangelicals of the Vineyard Christian Fellowship with regard to the way members of each group explain misfortune. In what ways are their explanations shaped by their world views?

12. Christianity and Islam are religions followed by vast numbers of people from many different societies. Are these religions followed in precisely the same way by each and every follower? Explain why or why not using examples from this chapter.

13. Explain how world views can be used as instruments of power.

# Key Terms

art 274
communitas 284
framing 272
liminality 284
magic 291
metacommunication 272
myths 279
nativism 296

oracles 291
orthodoxy 280
orthopraxy 285
play 271
priest 291
reflexivity 273
religion 287
revitalization 295

rites of passage 283
ritual 282
shaman 290
syncretism 295
witchcraft 291
world views 285

# Suggested Readings

Alland, Alexander. 1977. *The Artistic Animal: An Inquiry into the Biological Roots of Art.* New York: Doubleday Anchor. *An introductory look at the biocultural bases for art. This work is very well written, very clear, and fascinating.*

Boddy, Janice, and Michael Lambek, eds. 2013. *A Companion to the Anthropology of Religion.* Chichester, UK: John Wiley and Sons. *This book, edited by two professors from the University of Toronto, presents a collection of original, ethnographically based essays that explore the variety of beliefs, practices, and religious experiences in the contemporary world and examine how we think about religion as a subject of anthropological inquiry.*

Errington, Shelly. 1998. *The Death of Authentic Primitive Art and Other Tales of Progress.* Berkeley: University of California Press. *A sharp and witty book about the production, distribution, interpretation, and selling of "primitive art."*

Evans-Pritchard, E.E. [1937] 1976. *Witchcraft, Oracles, and Magic among the Azande.* Abridged ed. Oxford: Oxford University Press. *An immensely influential and very readable anthropological classic.*

Keesing, Roger. 1992. *Custom and Confrontation: The Kwaio Struggle for Cultural Autonomy.* Chicago: University of Chicago Press. *Based on thirty years of research, Keesing's final book provides a clear, readable, and committed discussion of Kwaio resistance.*

Lambek, Michael. 2008. *A Reader in the Anthropology of Religion.* 2nd ed. Malden, MA: Blackwell. *An excellent collection of classic and contemporary readings in the anthropology of religion.*

Laugrand, Frederic B., and Jarich G. Oosten. 2010. *Inuit Shamanism and Christianity: Transitions and Transformations in the Twentieth Century.* Montreal: McGill-Queen's University Press. *A collection of archival materials, oral testimonies from workshops held in in Nunavut, and insightful analysis that captures and explores the ongoing relationship between traditional Inuit beliefs and Christianity.*

Paper, Jordan. 2007. *Native North American Religious Traditions: Dancing for Life.* Westport, CT: Praeger. *An introduction to Native American religious traditions and rituals that examines a large diversity of ceremonies, including the Northwest Coast potlatch and Anishinaabe seasonal gatherings.*

Schwartzman, Helen. 1978. *Transformations: The Anthropology of Children's Play.* New York: Plenum. *A superlative work that considers how anthropologists have studied children's play, with some insightful suggestions about how they might continue to study children's play in the future.*

Turner, Victor. 1969. *The Ritual Process: Structure and Anti-structure.* Chicago: Aldine. *An important work in the anthropological study of ritual, this text is an eloquent analysis of rites of passage.*

Vogel, Susan M. 1997. *Baule: African Art/Western Eyes.* New Haven, CT: Yale University Press. *A book of extraordinary photographs and beautifully clear text, this work explores both Baule and Western views of Baule expressive culture.*

# *11*  *Why Do Anthropologists Study Economic Relations?*

▲ A vegetable market in Chichicastenango, Guatemala. Photo: AWL Images/Getty Images

## *Chapter Outline*

- How Do Anthropologists Study Economic Relations?
- How Do Anthropologists Study Production, Distribution, and Consumption?
- How Are Goods Distributed and Exchanged?
- Does Production Drive Economic Activities?
- Why Do People Consume What They Do?

- The Anthropology of Food and Nutrition
- Chapter Summary
- For Review
- Key Terms
- Suggested Readings

All human groups must organize themselves to make available to their members the material things they need for survival, such as food, shelter, and clothing. This chapter explores the variety of economic patterns human societies have developed over the millennia. It also draws attention to the way large-scale connections forged by trade or conquests continue to shape—and be reshaped by—the local economic practices of societies throughout the world.

Human beings are material organisms, and the seemingly endless meaningful ways we can imagine to live must always come to terms with the material realities of day-to-day existence. Culture contributes to the way human beings organize their social lives to meet such challenges. Social organization can be defined as the patterning of human interdependence in a given society through the actions and decisions of its members. This chapter and the two that follow will explore the ways anthropologists have investigated differences in human social organization in three key domains: economic relations, political relations, and more intimate forms of human relatedness associated with kin and families. The variation these forms of human social organization display across space and over time is truly remarkable, but that does not mean that people are free to do or be whatever they like. Rather, the adaptive flexibility of long-lived, large-brained social animals such as ourselves develops over the life cycle in response to a range of sometimes unpredictable experiences. This kind of developmental response would be impossible if human behaviour were rigidly programmed by genes, firmly circumscribed by environments, or strictly limited by technologies.

## How Do Anthropologists Study Economic Relations?

Forty years ago, I.M. Lewis (1967, 166ff.) pointed out that the northern Somalis and the Boran Galla lived next to each other in semiarid scrubland and even herded the same animals (goats, sheep, cattle, camels) (see EthnoProfile 11.1: Somalis [Northern] and EthnoProfile 11.2: Boran). Despite these similarities, the Somali and the Boran were quite different in social structure: The Boran engaged in much less fighting and feuding than did the Somali; Boran families split up to take care of the animals, whereas the Somali did not; and lineage organization was less significant among the Boran than it was among the Somali. Economic and political anthropologists have attempted to explain why this should be.

### EthnoProfile 11.1

**Somalis (Northern)**

**Region:** Eastern Africa

**Nation:** Somalia, Djibouti, Ethiopia, Kenya

**Population:** 600,000 (3,250,000 total; 2,250,000 in Somalia)

**Environment:** Harsh, semidesert

**Livelihood:** Herding of camels, sheep, goats, cattle, horses

**Political organization:** Traditionally, lineage-based, ad hoc egalitarian councils; today, part of modern nation-states

**For more information:** Lewis, I.M. 1967. *A Pastoral Democracy: A Study of Pastoralism and Politics among the Northern Somali of the Horn of Africa.* Oxford: Oxford University Press.

## What are the Connections between Culture and Livelihood?

Although our physical survival depends on our making adequate use of the resources around us, our culture tells us which resources to use and how to use them. Economic anthropologists study the many variations in human livelihood that anthropologists have found in different societies. Richard Wilk (1996, xv) has defined economic anthropology as "the part of the discipline that debates issues of *human nature* that relate directly to the decisions of daily life and making a living."

> **social organization** The patterning of human interdependence in a given society through the actions and decisions of its members.
>
> **economic anthropology** The part of the discipline of anthropology that debates issues of human nature that relate directly to the decisions of daily life and making a living.

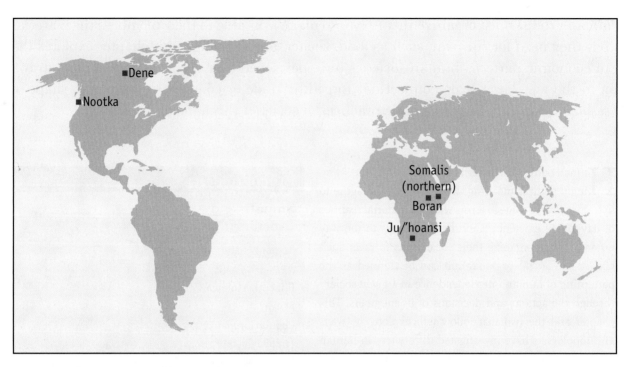

MAP 11.1 | Locations of societies whose EthnoProfiles appear in Chapter 11.

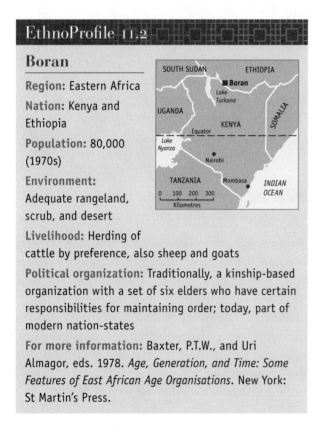

## EthnoProfile 11.2

### Boran

**Region:** Eastern Africa

**Nation:** Kenya and Ethiopia

**Population:** 80,000 (1970s)

**Environment:** Adequate rangeland, scrub, and desert

**Livelihood:** Herding of cattle by preference, also sheep and goats

**Political organization:** Traditionally, a kinship-based organization with a set of six elders who have certain responsibilities for maintaining order; today, part of modern nation-states

**For more information:** Baxter, P.T.W., and Uri Almagor, eds. 1978. *Age, Generation, and Time: Some Features of East African Age Organisations*. New York: St Martin's Press.

In ordinary conversation, when we speak of making a living, we usually mean doing what is necessary to obtain the material things—food, clothing, shelter—that sustain human life. Making a living thus encompasses what is generally considered to be economic activity. However, anthropologists and other social scientists disagree about just what the term *economy* ought to represent. The rise of the capitalist market led to one view of what economy might mean: buying cheap and selling high. That is, economy means maximizing utility—obtaining as much satisfaction as possible for the smallest possible cost. This is a Western perspective of economy and is based on the assumption of scarcity. Many economists and economic anthropologists believe that people's resources (e.g., money) are not, and never will be, great enough for them to obtain all the goods they want. This view of economy also assumes that economic analysis should focus on *individuals* who must maximize their utility under conditions of scarcity. An economizing individual is supposed to set priorities and to allocate resources according to those priorities: this is what economists mean by economic "rationality." To accept this view implies that economic anthropologists should clarify the different priorities set by different societies and study how these priorities affect the maximizing decisions of individuals who live in those societies.

Other economic anthropologists, however, regard this way of thinking about economic life as ethnocentric. They present evidence to show that different societies use different principles to organize economic life, and they argue that the job of economic anthropologists should be to describe and explain these cultural variations. This view of economy focuses on **institutions**: complex, variable, and enduring forms of cultural practice that organize social life. From an institutional point of view, a society's economy consists of the culturally specific processes its members use to provide themselves with material resources. Therefore, economic processes cannot be considered separate from the other cultural institutions in which they are embedded and by which they are sustained. And because institutional structures rely on human decisions—or choices—of daily life and making a living, economic anthropologists need to pay attention to the conditions that shape these

For a description of the concept of holism and its importance to the anthropological study of culture, see Chapter 2, p. 26.

choices. In essence, then, the anthropological study of economy and economic life requires a holistic approach.

## How Do Anthropologists Study Production, Distribution, and Consumption?

Anthropologists generally agree that economic activity is usefully subdivided into three distinct phases: *production*, *distribution*, and *consumption*. Production involves transforming nature's raw materials into products useful to human beings. Distribution involves getting those products to people. Consumption involves using up the products—for example, by eating food or wearing clothing. When analyzing economic activity in a particular society, however, anthropologists differ in the importance they attach to each phase. For example, the distributive process known as *exchange* is central to the functioning of capitalist free enterprise. Some anthropologists have assumed that exchange is equally central to the functioning of all economies and have tried to explain the economic life of non-Western societies in terms of exchange. Anthropologists influenced by the work of Karl Marx, however, have argued that exchange cannot be understood properly without first studying the nature of *production*. They point out that production shapes the context in which exchange can occur, determining which parties have how much of what kind of goods to exchange. Other anthropologists have suggested that neither production nor exchange

patterns make any sense without first specifying the *consumption* priorities of the people who are producing and exchanging. Consumption priorities, they argue, are certainly designed to satisfy material needs. But the recognition of needs and of appropriate ways to satisfy them is shaped by historically contingent cultural patterns. Finally, many would agree that patterns of production, exchange, and consumption are seriously affected by the kind of *storage* in use in a particular society (Figure 11.1).

## How Are Goods Distributed and Exchanged?

For a discussion of the links between storage and sedentism, see Chapter 8, pp. 217–20.

### Capitalism and Neoclassical Economics

The discipline of economics was born in the late 1700s, during the early years of the Industrial Revolution in Western Europe. At that time, such thinkers as Adam Smith and his disciples struggled to devise theories to explain the profound changes in economic and social life that European societies had recently begun to experience.

**Capitalism** differed in many ways from the feudal economic system that had preceded it, but perhaps the most striking difference was how it handled distribution. Feudal economic relations allotted goods and services to different social groups and individuals on the basis of status, or position in society. Because lords had high status and many obligations, they had a right to more goods and services. Peasants, with low status and few rights, were allowed far less. This distribution of goods was a time-honoured tradition not open to modification. The customs derived from capitalist economic relations, by contrast, were considered "free" precisely because they swept away all such traditional restrictions. As we shall see in our discussion of "Sedaka"

For our discussion of "Sedaka" Village, see Chapter 12, pp. 343–4.

Village, Malaysia, capitalism also swept away traditional protections. In any case, distribution under capitalism was negotiated between buyers and sellers in the market.

**institutions**  Complex, variable, and enduring forms of cultural practices that organize social life.

**capitalism**  An economic system dominated by the supply-demand-price mechanism called the "market"; an entire way of life that grew in response to and in service of that market.

**FIGURE 11.1** | (Below) A seventeenth-century drawing of storage warehouses built at the height of the Inka Empire. (Right) The plan of Huánuco Pampa, Peru, shows the location of these storage warehouses. Some anthropologists argue that food storage practices buffer a population from ecological fluctuations, making possible considerable cultural manipulation of the economic relations of consumption.

Capitalist market exchange of goods for other goods, for labour, or (increasingly) for cash was an important development in Western economic history. It is not surprising, therefore, that Western economic theory was preoccupied with explaining how the capitalist market worked. Markets clearly had a new, decisive importance in capitalist society, which they had not possessed in feudal times. Toward the end of the nineteenth century, the views of early economic thinkers like Adam Smith were transformed into **neoclassical economics**, which remains the foundation of formal economics today. As Hann and

Hart (2011) explain, neoclassical economics "still celebrated the market as the main source of increased economic welfare; but it replaced the classical view of economic value as an objective property of produced commodities, to be struggled over by the different classes, with a focus on the subjective calculations of individuals seeking to maximize their own utility" (37). This was a key turning point in the history of economics.

## What Are Modes of Exchange?

Some anthropologists argued that taking self-interested, materialistic decision making in the capitalist market as the prototype of human rationality was ethnocentric. They pointed out that the capitalist market is a relatively recent cultural invention in human history. Western

**neoclassical economics** A formal attempt to explain the workings of capitalist enterprise, with particular attention to distribution.

capitalist societies distribute material goods in a manner that is consistent with their basic values, institutions, and assumptions about human nature. So too non-Western, non-capitalist societies might be expected to have devised alternative modes of exchange that distribute material goods in ways that are in accord with their basic values, institutions, and assumptions about human nature. In the early twentieth century, for example, French anthropologist Marcel Mauss ([1950] 2000) contrasted non-capitalist gift exchanges (which are deeply embedded in social relations and always require a return gift) with impersonal commodity exchanges typical of the capitalist market (in which goods are exchanged for cash and exchange partners need have nothing further to do with one another). Later, Marshall Sahlins (1972) drew on the work of economic historian Karl Polanyi (e.g., 1977) to propose that three modes of exchange could be identified historically and cross-culturally: *reciprocity*, *redistribution*, and *market exchange*.

Reciprocity is likely the oldest mode of exchange, and it is characteristic of egalitarian societies, such as the Ju/'hoansi in southern Africa (see EthnoProfile 11.5: Ju/'hoansi). Sahlins identified three kinds of reciprocity. *Generalized reciprocity* is found when those who exchange do so without expecting an immediate return and without specifying the value of the return. Everyone assumes that the exchanges will eventually balance out. Generalized reciprocity usually characterizes the exchanges that occur between parents and their children. In Canada, for example, parents ordinarily do not keep a running tab on what it costs them to raise their children and then present their children with repayment schedules when they reach the age of 18. Instead, there is a social expectation that children will look after their parents as their parents age and require care. *Balanced reciprocity* is found when those who exchange expect a return of equal value within a specified time limit (e.g., when cousins exchange gifts of equal value with one another at Christmastime). Finally, *negative reciprocity* is an exchange of goods and services in which at least one party attempts to get something for nothing without suffering any penalties. These attempts can range from haggling over prices to outright seizure, as with cattle rustling.

Redistribution, the second mode of exchange, requires some form of centralized social organization. Those who control the central position receive economic contributions from all members of the group. It is then their responsibility to redistribute the goods they receive

## EthnoProfile 11.3

### Nootka (Nuu-chah-nulth)

**Region:** Northwestern North America

**Nation:** Canada (Vancouver Island)

**Population:** 6000 (1970s)

**Environment:** Rainy, relatively warm coastal strip

**Livelihood:** Fishing, hunting, gathering

**Political organization:** Traditionally, ranked individuals, chiefs; today, part of a modern nation-state

**For more information:** Rosman, Abraham, and Paula G. Rubel. 1971. *Feasting with Mine Enemy: Rank and Exchange among Northwest Coast Societies*. New York: Columbia University Press.

in a way that provides for every member of the group. In Canada, the income taxes that we pay to the government are probably the most recognizable form of redistribution. Everyone pays the government, which in turn redistributes the money for roads, schools, and various other social services. A classic anthropological example of redistribution is the *potlatch* of the Indigenous peoples of the northwest coast of Canada. In the highly stratified fishing and gathering society of the Nootka, for example,

**gift exchanges** Non-capitalist forms of economic exchange that are deeply embedded in social relations and always require a return gift.

**commodity exchanges** Impersonal economic exchanges typical of the capitalist market in which goods are exchanged for cash and exchange partners need have nothing further to do with one another.

**modes of exchange** Patterns according to which distribution takes place: reciprocity, redistribution, and market exchange.

**reciprocity** The exchange of goods and services of equal value. Anthropologists distinguish three forms of reciprocity: *generalized*, in which neither the time nor the value of the return is specified; *balanced*, in which a return of equal value is expected within a specified time limit; and *negative*, in which parties to the exchange hope to get something for nothing.

**redistribution** A mode of exchange that requires some form of centralized social organization to receive economic contributions from all members of the group and to redistribute them in such a way as to provide for every group member.

**FIGURE 11.2** | Items for sale at a market in Byblos, Lebanon. Markets can be found in many societies, but capitalism links markets to trade and money in a unique way.

nobles sought to outdo one another in generosity by giving away vast quantities of goods during the potlatch ceremony (see EthnoProfile 11.3: Nootka). The noble giving the potlatch accumulated goods produced in one village and redistributed them to other nobles attending the ceremony. When the guests returned to their own villages, they in turn redistributed the goods among their followers. In the late nineteenth century, the Canadian government outlawed this form of redistribution as a means of establishing control over the Indigenous peoples of Canada's northwest coast. The potlatch ban lasted until 1951, and it wasn't until 1952 that the first legal potlatch was celebrated on Vancouver Island.

**Market exchange**, invented in capitalist society, is the most recent mode of exchange, according to Polanyi (1977) (Figure 11.2). Polanyi was well aware that trade, money, and market institutions had developed independently of one another historically. He also knew that they could be found in societies outside the West. The uniqueness of capitalism was how all three institutions were linked to one another in the societies of early modern Europe.

According to Polanyi (1977), different modes of exchange often coexist within a single society, although only one structures the society's principal economy. Canada's economy, for example, is structured by the

market mode of exchange, yet redistribution and reciprocity have not disappeared. Within the family, parents who obtain income from the market redistribute that income, or goods obtained with that income, to their children. Generalized reciprocity also characterizes much exchange within the family: as noted earlier, parents regularly provide their children with food and clothing without expecting any immediate return.

Some economic anthropologists, however, have argued that exchange cannot properly be understood without a prior knowledge of production. Like earlier critics of capitalism, such as Karl Marx, they have insisted that people who meet to exchange have different kinds and amounts of resources to use in bargaining with one another. Those differences in resources, Marx argued, are shaped by the process of economic production.

## Does Production Drive Economic Activities?

Some economic anthropologists have argued that production is the driving force behind economic activity, creating supplies of goods that must accommodate people's demand, thereby determining levels of consumption. Anthropologists who take this view borrow their perspective, as well as many key concepts, from the works of Karl Marx. They argue that studying production explains important economic processes ignored by views that emphasize market exchange as the driving force of economic activity.

---

**market exchange**  The exchange of goods (trade) calculated in terms of a multipurpose medium of exchange and standard of value (money) and carried out by means of a supply–demand–price mechanism (the market).

## Labour

Anthropologists often emphasize the importance of labour (work) as a central concept of economic production. **Labour** is the activity linking human social groups to the material world around them: human beings must actively struggle together to transform natural substances into forms they can use. Human labour is therefore always *social* labour. Marx emphasized the importance of human physical labour in the material world, especially in the production of food, clothing, shelter, and tools. But Marx also recognized the importance of mental or cognitive labour: human intelligence allows us to reflect on and organize productive activities in different ways.

## Modes of Production

Marx attempted to classify the ways different human groups carry out production. Each way is called a **mode of production**. Anthropologist Eric Wolf (1982, 75) defined a mode of production as "a specific, historically occurring set of social relations through which labour is deployed to wrest energy from nature by means of tools, skills, organization, and knowledge." Tools, skills, organization, and knowledge constitute what Marx called the **means of production**. The social relations linking human beings who use a given means of production within a particular mode of production are called the **relations of production**. That is, different productive tasks (clearing the bush, planting, harvesting, and so on) are assigned to different social groups, which Marx called *classes*, all of which must work together for production to be successful. Wolf notes that Marx speaks of at least eight different modes of production in his own writings, although he focused mainly on the capitalist mode.

Wolf (1982) finds the concept of mode of production useful and suggests that three modes of production have been particularly important in human history: (1) a *kin-ordered mode* (Figure 11.3), in which social labour is deployed on the basis of kinship relations (e.g., husbands/fathers clear the fields, the whole family plants, mothers/wives weed, children keep animals out of the field); (2) a *tributary mode*, "in which the primary producer, whether cultivator or herdsman, is allowed access to the means of production while tribute [a payment of goods or labour] is exacted from him by political or military means" (79); and (3) the *capitalist mode*, which has three main features: the means of production

### EthnoProfile 11.4

## Dene

**Region:** Northern North America

**Nation:** Canada (Northwest Territories)

**Population:** 2000

**Environment:** Subarctic tundra and boreal forest

**Livelihood:** Fishing, hunting, and gathering

**Political organization:** Traditionally, ranked individuals, chiefs; today, part of a modern nation-state

**For more information:** Dokis, Carly. 2015. *Where the Rivers Meet: Pipelines, Participatory Resource Management, and Aboriginal–State Relations in the Northwest Territories.* Vancouver: UBC Press.

are private property owned by members of the capitalist class, workers must sell their labour power to the capitalists in order to survive, and surpluses of wealth are produced that capitalists may retain as profit or reinvest in production, to increase output and generate further surpluses and higher profits.

The kin-ordered mode of production is found among foragers and those farmers and herders whose political organization does not involve domination by one group. An example of this mode of production is found among the Dene in the Sahtu Region of the Northwest Territories (Dokis 2015) (see EthnoProfile 11.4). The tributary mode is found among farmers or herders living in a social system that is divided into classes of rulers and subjects. Subjects produce both for themselves and for their rulers, who take a certain proportion of their subjects' produce or labour as tribute. The capitalist mode, the most recent to develop,

**labour** The activity linking human social groups to the material world around them; from the point of view of Karl Marx, labour is therefore always social labour.

**mode of production** A specific, historically occurring set of social relations through which labour is deployed to obtain energy from nature by means of tools, skills, organization, and knowledge.

**means of production** The tools, skills, organization, and knowledge used to extract energy from nature.

**relations of production** The social relations linking the people who use a given means of production within a particular mode of production.

**FIGURE 11.3** | This drawing from 1562 shows Native American men breaking the soil and Native American women planting, a gender-based division of labour.

## In Their Own Words

### "So Much Work, So Much Tragedy . . . and for What?"

*Angelita P.C. (the author's surnames were initialed to preserve her anonymity) describes traditional labour for farmers' wives in Costa Rica during the 1930s. Her account was included in a volume of peasant autobiographies published in Costa Rica in 1979.*

The life of farmers' wives was more difficult than the life of day labourers' wives; what I mean is that we work more. The wife of the day labourer, she gets clean beans with no rubbish, shelled corn, pounded rice, maybe she would have to roast the coffee and grind it. On the other hand, we farm wives had to take the corn out of the husk, shuck it; and if it was rice, generally we'd have to get it out of the sack and spread it out in the sun for someone to pound it in the mortar. Although we had the advantage that we never lacked the staples: tortillas, rice, beans, and sugar-water. When you had to make tortillas, and that was every day, there were mountains of tortillas, because the people who worked in the fields had to eat a lot to regain their strength with all the effort they put out. And the tortilla is the healthiest food that was eaten—still is eaten—in the countryside. Another thing we had to do often was when you'd get the corn together to sell it, you always had to take it off the cob and dry it in the sun: the men spread it out on a tarp, maybe two or three sackfuls, and they would go and bring the corn,

still in the husks, up from the cornfield or the shack where it was kept. Well, we women had to guard it from the chickens or the pigs that were always in the house, but the rush we had when it started to rain and the men hadn't gotten back! We had to fill the sacks with corn and then a little later haul it in pots to finish filling them; that's if the rain gave us time. If not, all of us women in the house would have to pick up the tarps—sometimes the neighbour-women would get involved in all the bustle—to carry the corn inside. We looked like ants carrying a big worm! The thing was to keep the corn from getting wet.

It didn't matter if you threw out your spine, or if your uterus dropped, or you started hemorrhaging, or aborted, but since none of that happened immediately, it was the last thing we thought of. So much work, so much tragedy and that was so common that it seemed like just a natural thing, and for what? To sell corn at about 20 colones or at most at 24 colones per fanega [about 3 bushels] of 24 baskets! What thankless times for farm people!

Source: *Autobiografías Campesinas*. 1979, 36. (Translation from the original Spanish by Robert H. Lavenda).

can be found in the industrial societies of North America and Western Europe beginning in the seventeenth and eighteenth centuries. The concept of mode of production thus draws attention to many of the same features of economic life highlighted in traditional anthropological discussions of subsistence strategies. Yet, the concept emphasizes forms of social and political organization as well as material productive activities and shows how they are interconnected. That is, the kin-ordered mode of production is distinctive as much for its use of the kinship system to allocate labour to production as for the kind of production undertaken, such as farming. In a kin-ordered mode of production, the *relations of kinship* serve as the *relations of production* that enable a particular *mode of production* to be carried out. Farm labour organized according to kin-ordered relations of production, where labourers are relatives to whom no cash payment is due, is very different from farm labour organized according to capitalist relations of production, where labourers are often non-relatives who are paid a wage.

## What Is the Role of Conflict in Material Life?

Anthropologists traditionally have emphasized the important links between a society's organization (kinship groups, chiefdom, state) and the way that society meets its subsistence needs, either to demonstrate the stages of cultural evolution or to display the functional interrelationships between its parts. In both cases, however, the emphasis of the analysis has been on the harmonious fashion in which societies operate. For some observers, this carried the additional message that social stability was "natural" and should not be tampered with. Social change was possible, but it would take place in an orderly fashion, in the fullness of time, according to laws of development beyond the control of individual members of society.

Many anthropologists, however, have not been persuaded that social organization is naturally harmonious or that social change is naturally orderly. Instead, they tend to use Marxian approaches because these sorts of approaches recognize that conflict and disorder are a natural part of the human condition. The concept of mode of production makes a major contribution to economic anthropology precisely because it acknowledges that the potential for conflict is built into the mode of production itself. And the more complex and unequal is the involvement of different classes in a mode of production, the more intense is the struggle between them likely to be. The links between economic and political relations become particularly obvious and must be addressed.

For more on the intersections among economy, politics, and culture, see Chapter 12, p. 333.

## Why Do People Consume What They Do?

Consumption usually refers to the use of material goods necessary for human survival. These goods include—at a minimum—food, drink, clothing, and shelter; they can and often do include much more. Until quite recently, the study of consumption by economists and others has been much neglected, especially when compared to the study of distribution or production. To some extent, this is because many observers assumed that there were no interesting questions to ask about consumption. That is, it seemed clear either that people consume goods for obvious reasons (i.e., because they need to eat and drink to survive) or that they consume goods as a result of idiosyncratic personal preferences (e.g., "I like the flavour of licorice and so I eat a lot of it, but my neighbour hates the flavour and would never put it into his mouth"). In either case, studying consumption seemed unlikely to reveal any interesting cultural patterns. As we will see below, however, anthropologists have always noticed striking differences in consumption patterns in different societies that seemed hard to reconcile with accepted economic explanations. Historically, anthropologists have taken three basic approaches to account for these patterns: (1) the internal explanation, (2) the external explanation, and (3) the cultural explanation.

### The Internal Explanation: Malinowski and Basic Human Needs

The internal explanation for human consumption patterns comes from the work of Bronislaw Malinowski. Malinowski's version of functionalist anthropology explains social practices by relating them to the basic human needs that each practice supposedly fulfills. Basic human needs can be biological or psychological. Whatever their origin, if these needs go unmet, Malinowski argued, a society might not survive. Malinowski (1944) proposed

**consumption** The use of material goods necessary for human survival.

## In Their Own Words

## Making a Living: Place, Food, and Economy in an Inuit Community

*In her study among the Inuit of Puvirnituq in northern Quebec, Nicole Gombay considers the meaning of food in the context of the changing local economy.*

The Inuit economy, until relatively recently, has operated according to altogether other means than the Western market economy. . . . In most instances, Inuit are well aware of the means by which their food was produced. Because of people's participation not only in the eating of food, but also in the getting and distributing of it, they are generally aware both of its importance to them and of their wish to preserve their capacities to continue participating in these processes. For many Inuit, these processes are tied to their way of life. The production, distribution, exchange, and consumption of food is inexorably linked to how they conceive of and construct the world around them. These conceptions reflect not simply the mechanical processes involved in procuring food, but are linked to larger cosmological notions about the nature of existence and the place of humans in the world. These, in turn, are linked to a host of other processes: ideas about the role of the individual in relation to society, the experience of being in the elements rather than removed from them, notions of temporality and understandings of history grounded in place. An important component of these elements is that they developed and operated outside the market economy. Since time immemorial, without markets and without money, Inuit have managed to make a living and supply themselves with the necessities of life.

Try to imagine how you would have to live were you to be involved in producing everything you ate. Try to imagine how that would affect how you interacted with the world around you and how you spent your time. How would you relate to others and to the environment that provided you with food? How would you make your living? What would your day be filled with from morning to night, from season

to season, from year to year? Then think about what happens when the market economy comes into the equation. How would all these things be affected when you no longer had to produce everything you ate but could buy your food? Where would you get the money? How would you spend your time? How would this change in your circumstances affect your concerns about the world around you? These questions are inherently economic, and are intimately tied to the quality of our lives. . . . They are the questions Inuit society is confronting, at a fundamental level.

For Inuit, the economy operates in two fundamental realms, neither of which is isolated from the other, but each of which is informed by markedly different means of operating. First there is the local economic system that sprang from, and is a reflection of, Inuit beliefs and ways of working. Such an economy has been called variously an "indigenous" economy, a "community" economy, or an "informal" economy. All are, to varying degrees, used to describe economies that are related to systems that are particular to a place and its people. Such economies have often fallen under the umbrella of the term "subsistence," which is commonly used in relation to Inuit. The term, linked to the idea that people are eking out a bare existence, carries negative connotations that do not reflect reality. The notion also has the effect of freezing the Inuit in time, preventing them from commercial development. For these reasons, I have chosen to use the term "vernacular" economy to identify the economy associated with the ideas, processes, social relations, values, and institutions that Inuit link to the produce of hunting, fishing, and gathering. The term [acknowledges that the Inuit] are constantly changing, while at the

a list of basic human needs, which includes nourishment, reproduction, bodily comforts, safety, movement, growth, and health. Every culture responds in its own way to these needs with some form of the corresponding institutions: food-getting techniques, kinship, shelter, protection, activities, training, and hygiene (91).

Malinowski's approach had the virtue of emphasizing the dependence of human beings on the physical world in order to survive. In addition, Malinowski was

able to show that many customs that appear bizarre to uninitiated Western observers make sense once it is seen how they help people satisfy their basic human needs. However, Malinowski's approach fell short of explaining why all societies do not share the same consumption patterns. After all, some people eat wild fruit and nuts and wear clothing made of animal skins, others eat bread made from domesticated wheat and wear garments woven from the hair of domesticated sheep, and same time implying that such change has a local flavour . . . and that important links exist between economy and place.

The second economic realm in which Inuit now function is the market system that came with the arrival of non-Inuit to their region. It is an economy in which transactions rely on money as a medium of exchange. Under a market economy, prices are self-regulating, which means that markets must be allowed to function without interference. In the process, nature becomes interwoven with processes of commoditization as its products become fodder for the market. Each market exchange is discrete; there is no expectation that it will entail an ongoing social relationship. As a result, social relations become embedded in the economy rather than the economy being embedded in social relations.

These two economies, the market and the vernacular, have been operating in tandem—sometimes in apparent isolation, but in fact increasingly overlapping and mixing together, with the distinction between them becoming blurred. Inuit are not living in isolation from the market, but must come to terms with the fact that their economy exists within the market. The term that is commonly used to denote this is a "mixed economy," wherein neither of the two economic systems exists in a pristine state, but each must be understood as connected to the other. At issue for the Inuit is what this means for them and how they are making sense of the mixing. What I argue is that, in comprehending this process, we need to recognize that the Inuit economy is intimately linked to people's understandings of place, which, in turn, relates to such things as their experiences of time and history, their understandings of natural forces, their basic notions of value, and their conceptions of community and the social institutions that sustain it. . . .

On the one hand, Inuit have expressed a desire to hold on to their traditions of hunting, fishing, and trapping. This has been at the root of all Inuit land claims negotiated in Canada. On the other hand, they are aware that their economies cannot rely solely on traditions of the past. . . . They know they need money even to pursue the traditional elements of their economy. Bullets, rifles, gas, Ski-Doos, and canvas for tents, among other things, all cost money, and as far as money is concerned, one thing is clear: for many Inuit it is in short supply.

By southern standards, northern economies are based on a limited set of activities, so the options for gaining access to cash are few. Since the period of contact with Europeans, Inuit have earned cash through . . . the fur trade, whaling, the sale of arts and crafts, social transfer payments, and [limited] employment in and assortment of public and private ventures [e.g., public services, development activities]. These forms of income have generally proved either unsustainable or of limited impact, and are open only to a few. . . .

One potential way to expand the sources of cash income has been to sell the produce from people's hunting, fishing, and gathering commonly referred to as "country foods." This has led to a meeting of the two economic systems, the market and the vernacular. In the past, these economies generally operated separately, and under quite different rules. The vernacular economy of Inuit is predicated on sharing, . . . [while the] market economy . . . is predicated on monetary exchange. . . . How does a local economic system adjust itself to a global economic system when each is predicated on different concepts of value . . . and different concepts of access to and control over resources? In selling country foods, Inuit are obliged to confront these questions and learn how to accommodate the influx of new ideas and ways of living with [traditional] concepts about how the world operates. They are not alone: in their encounters with the forces of globalization, vernacular economies the world over have had to make similar adjustments.

Source: Gombay 2010, 10–14.

still others eat millet paste and meat from domesticated cattle and go naked. Why should these differences exist?

## The External Explanation: Cultural Ecology

A later generation of anthropologists was influenced by evolutionary and ecological studies. They tried to answer this question with an external explanation for the diversity of human consumption patterns. As we saw in earlier chapters, ecology has to do with how living species interact with one another and how they interact with their physical environment. To explain patterns of human consumption (as well as production and distribution), cultural ecologists tend to focus on the available resources in particular habitats that are exploited by particular human groups. Hence, the particular consumption patterns found in a particular society cannot depend just on the obvious, internal hunger drive, which is the same for all people everywhere; instead, people depend on the particular external resources present in the local habitat to which their members must adapt. Nicole Gombay's work with Inuit peoples in northern Quebec provides an excellent example of how a society has adapted to and thrived in a generally hostile environment (see the "In Their Own Words" box on making a living).

## How Is Consumption Culturally Patterned?

Why do people *X* raise peanuts and sorghum? The internal, Malinowskian explanation would be to meet their basic human need for food. The external, cultural ecological explanation would be because peanuts and sorghum are the only food crops available in their habitat that, when cultivated, will meet their subsistence needs. Both these answers sound reasonable, but they are also incomplete. To be sure, people must consume something to survive, and they will usually meet this need by exploiting plant and animal species locally available. However, these explanations seem to assume that patterns of consumption are shaped only by survival needs and environmental limits.

But we have seen that human beings (along with many other organisms) are able to actively construct their own niches, buffering themselves from some kinds of selection pressures while exposing themselves to other kinds. This means that human populations, even those with foraging technologies, are not passive in the face of environmental demands. On the contrary, people have the agency to produce a range of cultural inventions—tools, social relations, domesticated crops, agroecologies, and so on. Or as Marshall Sahlins (1976, 142) put it, human beings are *human* "precisely when they experience the world as a concept (symbolically). It is not essentially a question of priority but of the unique quality of human experience as meaningful experience. Nor is it an issue of the reality of the world; it concerns *which worldly dimension becomes pertinent*, and in what way, to a given human group" (emphasis added). Because human beings construct their own niches, they construct their patterns of consumption as well.

🔄 For a fuller discussion of niche construction by humans, see Chapter 3, pp. 62–3.

### *What Is the Original Affluent Society?*

Based on the perceptions of early colonial settlers, it was long believed by many Westerners that foraging peoples led the most miserable of existences, spending all their waking hours in a food quest that yielded barely enough to keep them alive. To test this assumption in the field, Canadian anthropologist Richard Lee, from the University of Toronto, went to live among the Dobe Ju/'hoansi, a foraging people of southern Africa (see EthnoProfile 11.5: Ju/'hoansi). Living in the central Kalahari Desert of southern Africa in the early 1960s, the Ju/'hoansi of Dobe were among the few remaining groups of the San peoples who returned to full-time foraging when economic ties with neighbouring herders became too onerous. Although full-time foraging has been impossible in the Dobe area since the 1980s and the Ju/'hoansi have had to make some difficult adjustments, Lee documented a way of life that contrasts vividly with their current settled existence.

Lee accompanied the Ju/'hoansi as they gathered and hunted in 1963, and he recorded the amounts and kinds of food they consumed. The results of his research were surprising. It turned out that the Ju/'hoansi provided themselves with a varied and well-balanced diet based on a selection from among the food sources available in their environment. At the time of Lee's fieldwork, the Ju/'hoansi classified more than 100 species of plants as edible, but only 14 were primary components of their diet (Lee 1992, 45ff.). Some 70 per cent of this diet consisted of vegetable foods; 30 per cent was meat. Mongongo nuts, a protein-rich food widely available throughout the Kalahari, alone made up more than one-quarter of the diet. Women provided about 55 per cent of the diet, and men provided

## EthnoProfile 11.5

### Ju/'hoansi (!Kung)

**Region:** Southern Africa

**Nation:** Botswana and Namibia

**Population:** 45,000

**Environment:** Desert

**Livelihood:** Hunting and gathering

**Political organization:** Traditionally, egalitarian bands; today, part of modern nation-states

**For more information:** Lee, Richard B. 1992. *The Dobe Ju/'hoansi*. 2nd ed. New York: Holt, Rinehart, and Winston.

FIGURE 11.4 | Ju/'hoansi women returning from foraging with large quantities of mongongo nuts.

45 per cent, including the meat. The Ju/'hoansi spent an average of 2.4 working days—or about 20 hours—per person per week in food-collecting activities. Ju/'hoansi bands periodically suffered from shortages of their preferred foods and were forced to consume less desired items. Most of the time, however, their diet was balanced and adequate and consisted of foods of preference (Lee 1992, 56ff.) (Figure 11.4).

Marshall Sahlins coined the expression "the original affluent society" to refer to the Ju/'hoansi and other foragers like them. In an essay published in 1972, Sahlins challenged the traditional Western assumption that the life of foragers is characterized by scarcity and near-starvation (see Sahlins 1972). Affluence, he argued, is having more than enough of whatever is required to satisfy consumption needs. There are two ways to create affluence. The first, to *produce much*, is the path taken by Western capitalist societies; the second, to *desire little*, is the option, Sahlins argues, that foragers have taken. Put another way, the Ju/'hoansi foragers used culture to construct a niche within which their wants were few but abundantly fulfilled by their local environment. Moreover, it is not that foragers experience no greedy impulses; rather, according to Sahlins, affluent foragers live in societies whose institutions do not reward greed. Sahlins concluded that, for these reasons, foragers

should not be considered poor, although their material standard of living is low by Western measures.

Original affluent foraging societies emphasize the long-standing anthropological observation that the concept of economic "needs" is vague (Douglas and Isherwood 1979). Hunger can be satisfied by beans and rice or steak and lobster. Thirst can be quenched by water or beer or soda pop. In effect, human beings in differently constructed niches define needs and provide for their satisfaction according to their own *cultural* logic, which is reducible to neither biology nor psychology nor ecological pressure. In every case, the human need for food is met selectively, and the selection humans make carries a social message. But what about cases of consumption that do not involve food and drink (e.g., consumption of wood to make ceremonial masks or paper to make money)?

## Banana Leaves in the Trobriand Islands

Anthropologist Annette Weiner travelled to the Trobriand Islands in the 1970s, more than half a century after Malinowski carried out his classic research there. To her

---

**affluence** The condition of having more than enough of whatever is required to satisfy consumption needs.

## *In Their Own Words*

### Fake Masks and Faux Modernity

*Christopher Steiner addresses the perplexing situation all of us face in the contemporary multicultural world: given mass reproduction of commodities made possible by industrial capitalism, how can anybody distinguish "authentic" material culture from "fake" copies? The encounter he describes took place in Ivory Coast, western Africa.*

In the Plateau market place, I once witnessed the following exchange between an African art trader and a young European tourist. The tourist wanted to buy a Dan face mask which he had selected from the trader's wooden trunk in the back of the market place. He had little money, he said, and was trying to barter for the mask by exchanging his Seiko wrist watch. In his dialogue with the trader, he often expressed his concern about whether or not the mask was "real." Several times during the bargaining, for example, the buyer asked the seller, "Is it really old?" and "Has it been worn?" While the tourist questioned the trader about the authenticity of the mask, the trader, in turn, questioned the tourist about the authenticity of his watch. "Is this the real kind of Seiko," he asked, "or is it a copy?" As the tourist examined the mask—turning it over and over again looking for the worn and weathered effects of time—the trader scrutinized the watch, passing it to other traders to get their opinion on its authenticity.

Although, on one level, the dialogue between tourist and trader may seem a bit absurd, it points to a deeper problem in modern transnational commerce: an anxiety over authenticity and a crisis of misrepresentation. While the shelves in one section of the Plateau market place are lined with replicas of so-called "traditional" artistic forms, the shelves in another part of the market place—just on the other side of the street—are stocked with imperfect imitations of modernity: counterfeit Levi jeans, fake Christian Dior belts, and pirated recordings of Michael Jackson and Madonna. Just as the Western buyer looks to Africa for authentic symbols of a "primitive" lifestyle, the African buyer looks to the West for authentic symbols of a modern lifestyle. In both of their searches for the "genuine" in each other's culture, the African trader and the Western tourist often find only mere approximations of "the real thing"—tropes of authenticity which stand for the riches of an imagined reality.

Source: Steiner 1994, 128–9.

For more on the Trobriand Islanders, see EthnoProfile 10.2, on p. 280.

surprise, she discovered a venerable local tradition involving the accumulation and exchange of banana leaves, which were known locally as "women's wealth" (Figure 11.5). Malinowski had never described this tradition, even though there is evidence from photographs and writing that it was in force at the time of his fieldwork. Possibly, Malinowski overlooked these transactions because they are carried out by women, and Malinowski did not view women as important actors in the economy. However, Malinowski might also have considered banana leaves to be an unlikely item of consumption because he recognized as "economic" only those activities that satisfied biological survival needs, and banana leaves are inedible. Transactions involving women's wealth, however, turn out to be crucial for the stability of Trobrianders' relationships to their relatives.

Banana leaves might be said to have a "practical" use because women make skirts out of them. These skirts are highly valued, but the transactions involving women's wealth more often involve the bundles of leaves themselves. Why bother to exchange great amounts of money or other goods to obtain bundles of banana leaves? This would seem to be a classic example of irrational consumption. Yet, "as an economic, political, and social force, women's wealth exists as the representation of the most fundamental relationships in the social system" (Weiner 1980, 289).

Trobrianders are *matrilineal* (i.e., they trace descent through women), and men traditionally prepare yam gardens for their sisters. After the harvest, yams from these gardens are distributed by a woman's brother to her husband. Weiner's

The different forms of descent, including patrilineal, matrilineal, and bilateral, are described in detail in Chapter 13, on pp. 353–9.

FIGURE 11.5 | In the Trobriand Islands, women's wealth, made from banana leaves, is displayed during a funeral ritual called the *sagali*, which serves to reaffirm the status of the women's kinship group.

research suggests that what Malinowski took to be the *redistribution* of yams, from a wife's kin to her husband, could be better understood as a *reciprocal exchange* of yams for women's wealth. The parties central to this exchange are a woman, her brother, and her husband. The woman is the person through whom yams are passed from her own kin to her husband and through whom women's wealth is passed from her husband to her own kin.

Transactions involving women's wealth occur when someone in a woman's kinship group dies. Surviving relatives must "buy back," metaphorically speaking, all the yams or other goods that the deceased person gave to others during his or her lifetime. Each payment marks a social link between the deceased and the recipient, and the size of the payment marks the importance of their relationship. All the payments must be made in women's wealth.

The dead person's status, as well as the status of her or his family, depends on the size and number of the payments made; and the people who must be paid can number into the hundreds. Women make women's wealth themselves and exchange store goods to obtain it from other women, but when someone in their matrilineage dies, they collect it from their husbands. Indeed, a woman's value is measured by the amount of women's wealth her husband provides. Furthermore, "if a man does not work hard enough for his wife in accumulating wealth for her, then her brother will not increase his labour in the yam garden. . . . The production in yams and women's wealth is always being evaluated and calculated in terms of effort and energy expended on

both sides of production. The value of a husband is read by a woman's kin as the value of his productive support in securing women's wealth for his wife" (Weiner 1980, 282).

Weiner argues that women's wealth upholds the kinship arrangements of Trobriand society. It balances out exchange relationships between lineages linked by marriage, reinforces the pivotal role of women and matriliny, and publicly proclaims, during every funeral, the social relationships that make up the fabric of Trobriand society. The system has been stable for generations, but Weiner suggests that it could collapse if cash ever became widely substitutable for yams. Under such conditions, men might buy food and other items on the market. If they no longer depended on yams from their wives' kin, they might refuse to supply their wives' kin with women's wealth. This had not yet happened at the time of Weiner's research, but she saw it as a possible future development.

## How Is Consumption Being Studied Today?

The foregoing examples focus attention on distinctive consumption practices in different societies and demonstrate why the Western market should not be used to measure all things related to economics. These studies also encourage respect for alternative consumption practices that, in different times and places, have worked as well as or better than capitalist markets to define needs and provide goods to satisfy those needs. But many anthropologists also draw attention to the way in which

## In Their Own Words

### Treating Your Food Good: Changing Natures and Economies in the Northwest Territories

*Carly Dokis from Nipissing University describes how the Dene people living in the Sahtu Region of the Northwest Territories form connections with their landscape and the food they rely on for sustenance.*

Dene people in the Sahtu Region of the Northwest Territories have drawn sustenance from their lands since time immemorial. While a vast majority of people in the Sahtu continue to hunt, fish, and gather plants and berries for most of their food, the sustenance that people obtain from their lands extends beyond material needs to include personal, subjective, emotive, and spiritual connections to the places and other-than-human beings who inhabit the landscape. Spending time "in the bush" allows for the development of skills and knowledge that people associate with being Dene; it connects people to the places and stories that explain how the world was created and how it will come to be in the future; it fosters community cohesion through the sharing of knowledge, food, and senses of common identity; and it is in the bush [that] Dene people are free of imposed systems of state control.

In contrast to the rendering of an objectified and insentient nature often presented in managerial ecology, for a majority of Sahtu Dene people, the landscape is composed of animate and affinitive beings imbued with power and agency. The land is seen as a leader (*k'aowe*), rather than a passive receptor of human management. In order to maintain proper relationships with the land and the other-than-human beings that dwell there, Dene people often

talk about maintaining a Universal Law, or *Dene ɂeɂah*, which is a set of moral codes that one ought to live by in order to be a good human being. Part of the Universal Law includes engaging in respectful and reciprocal relationships with other-than-human beings, including making offerings before travelling, hunting, fishing, or gathering; respecting the bodies of animals killed in the hunt or fish caught during fishing; a consideration not to take too much or to interfere in the lives of other-than-human beings; and . . . sharing—with other-than-human beings and with one another. As one Dene Elder put it, "if you treat your food good, it will treat you good too."

While there is a continued emphasis on the importance of spending time in the bush, and [on] maintaining the Universal Law, Dene people in the Sahtu face increased challenges to spending time on the land. Over the last half century, Dene people have witnessed a change from life lived primarily on the land to living primarily in permanent settlements. Young people now spend a majority of their time in town, where they attend school, and adults must obtain cash in order to pay for the high cost of housing, fuel, and other necessities. Somewhat ironically, the high price of gas, ammunition, and equipment such as snowmobiles and traps necessitates that people who continue to

the imposition of Western colonialism has regularly undermined such alternatives, attempting to replace them with new needs and goods defined by the capitalist market. This helps explain why, as Daniel Miller (1995) summarizes, "much of the early literature on consumption is replete with moral purpose," (144–5) emphasizing the ways in which vulnerable groups have resisted commodities or have developed ritual means of "taming" them, based on an awareness at some level of the capacity of those commodities to destroy. At the beginning of the twenty-first century, however, the consumption of market commodities occurs everywhere in the world. Moreover, not only are Western commodities sometimes embraced by those we might have expected to reject them (e.g., video technology by Indigenous peoples

of the Amazon), but this embrace frequently involves making use of these commodities for local purposes, to defend or to enrich local culture, rather than to replace it.

Daniel Miller has therefore urged anthropologists to recognize that these new circumstances require that they move beyond a narrow focus on the destructive potential of mass-produced commodities to a broader recognition of the role commodities play in a globalizing world. But this shift does not mean that concern about the negative consequences of capitalist practices disappears. In a global world in which everyone everywhere increasingly relies on commodities provided by a capitalist market, Miller (1995, 143) believes that critical attention must be refocused on "inequalities of access and the deleterious impact of contemporary economic spend time on the land, or their families, must also participate in a cash economy. This, of course, means that some people cannot travel great distances or for long periods of time because they have to come back to town to work.

The Sahtu Region has also experienced a significant increase in oil and gas exploration over the past twenty years. Some local people see the development of a hydrocarbon-based economy as an opportunity to provide jobs, business contracts, and increased revenue through access and benefits agreements, some of which could be used to support land-based activities. Others, however, express concerns about the impacts of oil and gas activities, including environmental contamination, changes in local lifeways such as decreased Slavey language use and greater influence of popular culture, and of course interferences with the ability to spend time in the bush. Importantly, increased extractive industries are also seen to seriously interfere in human–other-than-human relationships in ways that are moral in nature. That is, the impacts of oil and gas activities on moose or birds or fish are not just viewed as ecological, but may also come to bear on the responsibility that people have to maintain the Universal Law and proper relationships with the landscape.

When state agencies and regulators consider the potential impacts of extractive industries, even under systems of resource co-management, the impacts and risks associated with resource extraction are often evaluated in technocratic terms that serve to measure and quantify what for Sahtu Dene cannot be represented in graphs and tables—those subjective attachments that people have to their land and components of life that are associated with being Dene. Additionally, mitigation measures adopted to avoid the risks of extractive projects are often technical in nature, for example moving a pipeline right-of-way, rather than seriously questioning the desirability of the proposed project itself or the effects of the project on local subjectivities or relational and emotive connections to land. When mitigation cannot be accomplished, the proposed solution is often economic compensation, implying that trapping, hunting, and gathering plants and medicines are solely economic activities that have little or no connection to other realms of peoples' lives.

The state-driven assessment of extractive projects in the Sahtu and elsewhere raise[s] a series of important questions: How can environmental assessments account for the impacts of extractive industries in ways that reflect the moral relationships that Sahtu Dene people have with their land? In what ways does the assessment of extractive projects require a reconfiguration of how people talk about and define their relationships to the land? If regulators find no quantifiable evidence of risk, as most environmental assessments do, does this mean that there are "no significant impacts" on affected communities? And, if such impacts do exist, how do we place a value on the way of life of a people?

Source: Carly Dokis, Nipissing University, 2015. For more on this topic, see Dokis 2015.

institutions on much of the world's population." (For a contemporary example that relates to many of these themes, see the "In Their Own Words" box on changing natures and economies among the Dene people of the Northwest Territories.)

# The Anthropology of Food and Nutrition

One of the most recent areas of anthropological specialization centres on studies of food and nutrition. For some time biological anthropologists have carried out cross-cultural comparisons of nutrition and growth in different societies, and cultural anthropologists, such as Daniel Miller, have written detailed studies of particular local or ethnic food habits. Today, however, the anthropology of food and nutrition is increasingly concerned with the way the global capitalist food market works and the influence of political forces on how food is produced, distributed, and accessed around the world. For example, Alan and Josephine Smart (2011) of the University of Calgary have investigated how quarantines, health inspections, and import bans have been used as political tools to control the transport of beef across international borders, especially in North America. At the same time, exploring links between food and culture in a globally complex world reveals the many ways different kinds of food and cooking can be embraced by different groups is society to bolster their gender, sexual, racial, ethnic, class, or national identities.

Carole Counihan is a pioneering anthropologist of food and nutrition whose work was initially inspired by a feminist desire to give an ethnographic voice to women. She found that food was an aspect of culture that many women used to express themselves when other avenues were blocked. Beginning in 1970, she lived and worked in Italy for fourteen years. During this time she developed a "long-term relationship with a Florentine" she refers to as "Leonardo," and most of the data for her book *Around the Tuscan Table* (Counihan, 2004) comes "from 56 hours of food-centred life histories tape-recorded in Italian with Leonardo's 23 living relatives in 1982–84" (2).

Counihan began collecting food-centred life histories from women but eventually collected them from men as well. Because these life histories came from individuals from different generations, they reflected historical changes in the political economy of food that had shaped the lives of her interview subjects over time. For example, situating the food memories of the oldest members of her sample required reconstructing the traditional *mezzadria* sharecropping system in Tuscany. This system was based on large landholdings worked by peasant labourers whose households were characterized by a strict division of labour by gender: the patriarch (male head of the family) managed food production in the fields, and his wife supervised food preparation for the large extended family. The *mezzadria* system would

disappear in the early twentieth century, but it constituted the foundation of Tuscan food practices that would follow.

Counihan's interviewees ate a so-called "Mediterranean" diet consisting of "pasta, fresh vegetables, legumes, olive oil, bread, and a little meat or fish" (2004, 7) (Figure 11.6). Food was scarce in the first part of the twentieth century but more abundant after World War II. "This diet, however, was already being modified by the postmodern, ever-larger agro-food industry that continued to grow in 2003, but which Florentines and other Italians shaped by alternative food practices" (2004, 4).

The postwar capitalist market also drew younger Florentines into new kinds of paid occupations, which led to modifications of the earlier gendered division of labour, without eliminating it entirely. Counihan describes the struggles of Florentines of her generation, especially women, who needed to work for wages but who were still expected to maintain a household and a paying job at the same time and often could not count on assistance from their husbands with domestic chores, including cooking. Counihan is especially critical about Italian child-rearing practices that allow boys to grow up with no responsibilities around the house, learning to expect their sisters (and later their wives) to take care of them, explaining away their incompetence at housekeeping tasks as a natural absence of talent or interest. She also describes men who cook on a regular basis but who often do not take on the tasks of shopping for ingredients or cleaning

**FIGURE 11.6** | Tuscan women making pasta in a farm kitchen.

up and who tend to dismiss cooking as easy, thereby diminishing the status of work that has long been central to Florentine women's sense of self-worth.

Food-centred life histories from Counihan's oldest interviewees traced nearly a century of changing Tuscan food practices and revealed, surprisingly, older people's nostalgia for the more constrained patterns of food consumption in their youth. "When my older subjects were young before and during the Second World War, consumption was highly valued because it was scarce and precarious. Yet their children, born after the war in the context of the Italian economic miracle, grew up in a world where consumption was obligatory, taken for granted, and essential to full personhood—a transformation lamented by older people" (Counihan 2004, 5).

Even as Counihan's research documents continuities in Tuscan diet and cuisine, it also demonstrates the way deeply rooted consumption practices were upended by the Italian state under Mussolini in the 1920s and 1930s and by the international cataclysm of World War II. Anthropologists have long argued that economic life cannot be considered apart from political relations in any society.

## Chapter Summary

1. Contemporary cultural and economic anthropologists are interested in the material realities of peoples' day-to-day existence. They are also interested in the connections between culture and livelihood, and in the power that human beings have to reproduce or to change their social organization. Anthropological approaches can provide insights often overlooked by other disciplines.

2. Human economic activity is usefully divided into three phases—production, distribution, and consumption—and is often shaped in important ways by storage practices. Formal neoclassical economic theory developed in Europe to explain how capitalism works, and it emphasizes the importance of market exchange. Economic anthropologists have shown that non-capitalist societies regularly relied on non-market modes of exchange, such as reciprocity and redistribution, which still play restricted roles in societies dominated by the capitalist market.

3. Marxian economic anthropologists view production as more important than exchange in determining the patterns of economic life in a society. They classify societies in terms of their modes of production. Each mode of production contains within it the potential for conflict between classes of people who receive differential benefits and losses from the productive process.

4. In the past, some anthropologists tried to explain consumption patterns in different societies either by arguing that people produce material goods to satisfy basic human needs or by connecting consumption patterns to specific material resources available to people in the material settings where they lived. Ethnographic evidence demonstrates that both these explanations are inadequate because they ignore how culture defines our needs and provides for their satisfaction according to its own logic.

5. Particular consumption preferences that may seem irrational from the viewpoint of neoclassical economic theory may make sense when the wider cultural practices of consumers are taken into consideration. In the twenty-first century, those whom Western observers might have expected to reject Western market commodities often embrace them, frequently making use of them to defend or enrich their local culture rather than to replace it. In a global world in which everyone everywhere increasingly relies on commodities—including food—provided by a capitalist market, some anthropologists focus on inequalities of access and the negative impact of contemporary economic institutions on most of the world's population.

## For Review

1. Explain the connection between culture and livelihood.
2. Visit the website http://storyofstuff.org/movies/story-of-stuff. Then, create a flowchart that shows the steps of production, distribution, and consumption for an article of clothing you own. Note any international connections in your flowchart. What do these connections suggest about the modes of production operating in today's world?
3. Explain the significance of food storage and food sharing in economic activity.
4. Discuss the role of distribution in capitalism as explained by neoclassical economics.
5. According to Eric Wolf's definition of *mode of production* (see p. 309), what mode of production is in use in Canada today? Compare and contrast the Canadian mode of production with the other modes listed by Wolf in this chapter.
6. Consider Marxian approaches to economic theory and explain why these are favoured in anthropology.
7. Explain the complex interchange that occurs in the Canadian Arctic between the Inuit economy and the Western one, according to Nicole Gombay. Discuss which of the modes of exchange are at work in each economy.
8. Which of the three explanations of consumption do you agree with? Why?
9. Outline the key elements in Marshall Sahlin's argument about "the original affluent society." Do you agree with Sahlin? Why or why not?
10. This chapter offers two case studies on how consumption is culturally patterned—one about the Dobe Ju/'hoansi as the original affluent society, and one about the significance of banana leaves to the Trobriand Islanders. Explain how each of these case studies illuminates the cultural construction of human needs.
11. Discuss the connections between gender and food in Italy, as presented by Carole Counihan. How are gender roles framed by individuals' relationships with food and food preparation?

## Key Terms

affluence   314
capitalism   305
commodity exchanges   307
consumption   311
economic anthropology   303
gift exchanges   307

institutions   305
labour   309
market exchange   308
means of production   309
mode of production   309
modes of exchange   307

neoclassical economics   306
reciprocity   307
redistribution   307
relations of production   309
social organization   303

## Suggested Readings

Counihan, Carole. 2004. *Around the Tuscan Table: Food, Family, and Gender in Twentieth Century Florence.* New York: Routledge. *Food-centred life histories allow Counihan to re-create a century of changing food practices—and social relations—in central Italy. Counihan analyzes the historically changing food ways of Tuscany to reveal changes in Tuscan (and Italian) understandings of gender and family relations.*

Counihan, Carole, and Penny van Esterik, eds. 2013. *Food and Culture: A Reader.* 3rd ed. New York: Routledge. *A collection of classic and recent essays on a range of topics currently investigated by anthropologists who study the anthropology of food and nutrition.*

Douglas, Mary, and Baron Isherwood. 1996. *The World of Goods: Towards an Anthropology of Consumption.* Rev. ed. New York: Routledge. *A discussion of consumption, economic theories about consumption, and what anthropologists can contribute to the study of consumption.*

Ensminger, Jean, ed. 2002. *Theory in Economic Anthropology.* Walnut Creek, CA: AltaMira Press. *An introductory volume that addresses the contributions that economic anthropology can make to understanding a globalized world economy.*

Lee, Richard B. 2013. *The Dobe Ju/'hoansi.* 4th ed. Belmont, CA: Wadsworth. *This highly readable ethnography contains important discussions about foraging as a way of making a living and* traces political and economic changes in Ju/'hoansi life since Lee began fieldwork in Dobe in the 1960s.

Leonard, Annie. 2010. *The Story of Stuff: The Impact of Overconsumption on the Planet, Our Communities, and Our Health—And How We Can Make It Better.* New York: Free Press. *A highly accessible book that outlines current economic practices of acquiring, and quickly discarding, too much stuff. Leonard has also produced a companion website (www.story-ofstuff.org) that contains a number of related resources for those who are interested in learning or doing more.*

Sahlins, Marshall. 1972. *Stone Age Economics.* Chicago: Aldine. *A series of classic essays on economic life, written from a sub-stantivist position. Includes "The Original Affluent Society."*

Smart, Alan, and Josephine Smart, eds. 2006. *Petty Capitalists and Globalization: Flexibility, Entrepreneurship, and Economic Development.* New York: SUNY Press. *This collection of readings, edited by two researchers from the University of Calgary, uses ethnographic examples to show how small firms from around the world are competing in a transnational environment.*

Wilk, Richard R., and Lisa Cliggett. 2007. *Economies and Cultures: Foundations of Economic Anthropology.* 2nd ed. Boulder, CO: Westview. *A current, accessible "theoretical guidebook" to the conflicting views of human nature that underlie disputes in economic anthropology.*

▲ Migrant children from Syria stand behind a fence on the Serbian side of the recently closed Horgoš border crossing between Serbia and Hungary. The number of people leaving their homes in war-torn countries such as Syria marks the largest migration of people since World War II. Photo: Srdjan Stevanovic/Getty Images.

## Chapter Outline

Human societies are able to organize human interdependency successfully only if they find ways to manage relations of power among the different individuals and groups of which they are composed. In this chapter, we survey approaches anthropologist take to the study of political relations in different societies.

Anthropologists have long been interested in the role of power in human societies. Why are members of some societies able to exercise power on roughly equal terms, whereas other societies sharply divide the powerful from the powerless? In societies where access to power is unequal, how can those with little power gain more? What, in fact, *is* power?

Human societies are able to organize human interdependency successfully only if they find ways to manage relations of power among the different individuals and groups they comprise. Power may be understood broadly as "transformative capacity" (Giddens 1979, 88). When the choice affects an entire social group, scholars speak of *social power*. In this chapter, you will learn about the approaches anthropologists take to the study of political relations in different societies. Eric Wolf (1994) describes three different modes of social power: the first, *interpersonal power*, involves the ability of one individual to impose his or her will on another individual; the second, *organizational power*, highlights how individuals or social units can limit the actions of other individuals in particular social settings; the third, *structural power*, organizes social settings themselves and controls the allocation of social labour. To lay bare the patterns of structural power requires paying attention to the large-scale and increasingly global division of labour among regions and social groups, the unequal relations between these regions and groups, and the way these relations are maintained or modified over time. The way in which clothing is manufactured now—in factories in Indonesia or El Salvador, Romania or China—for markets in Europe, North America, and Japan is an example of structural power. People are hired to work long hours for low wages in unpleasant conditions to make clothing that they cannot afford to buy, even if it were available for sale in the communities where they live.

## How Are Culture and Politics Related?

The study of social power in human society is the domain of political anthropology. Current approaches to political anthropology date to the 1970s and 1980s, when political anthropologists began turning much of their attention to broad questions about power and inequality (Vincent 2002, 3). Under conditions of globalization, anthropologists interested in studying power have joined forces with scholars in other disciplines who share their concerns, and they have adopted ideas from influential political thinkers such as Antonio Gramsci and Michel Foucault to help them explain how power shapes the lives of those among whom they carry out ethnographic research. The cross-cultural study of political institutions reveals the paradox of the human condition. On the one hand, open cultural creativity allows humans to imagine worlds of pure possibility; on the other hand, all humans live in material circumstances that make many of those possibilities profoundly unrealistic. We can imagine many different ways to organize ourselves into groups, but, as Marx pointed out long ago, the past weighs like a nightmare on the brains of the living—and the opportunity to remake social organization is ordinarily quite limited.

Human beings actively work to reshape the environments in which they live to suit themselves. Because the resources available in any environment can be used to sustain more than one way of life, however, human beings must choose which aspects of the material world to depend on. This is why, inevitably, questions about human population growth and economic activity are

**power**  Transformative capacity; the ability to transform a given situation.

**political anthropology**  The study of social power in human society.

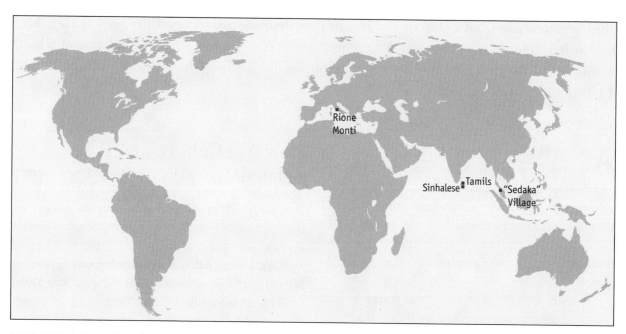

**MAP 12.1** | Location of societies whose EthnoProfiles appear in Chapter 12.

intimately intertwined with questions about the distribution of power in society. Some archaeologists have suggested that population growth is a constant aspect of the human condition that determines forms of social organization. As Marshall Sahlins (1976, 13) pointed out, however, population pressure determines nothing more than the number of people that can be supported when the environment is used in a particular way. Members of a society can respond to that pressure in any of various ways: they can try to get along on less, intensify food production by inventing new technology, reduce their numbers by inventing new social practices (infanticide or forms of birth control), or migrate elsewhere. Indeed, the manner in which a group might choose to implement any of these options is equally undetermined by population pressure. Which members of the group will have to do with less? Which members will control technological innovation? Who will be expected to migrate? And will the ultimate decision be imposed by force or voluntarily adopted?

The answers offered to these questions by members of any particular society describe the niche these individuals have constructed for themselves. By building social and political alliances and mobilizing technology and material resources in order to make a living, ways of life are maintained and sustained over time.

## How Do Anthropologists Study Politics?

### Coercion

Early in the twentieth century, political anthropologists were strongly influenced by Western philosophers who had assumed that the state was the prototype of "civilized" social power. For them, the absence of a state could mean only *anarchy*, disorderly struggles for power among individuals—what the English philosopher Thomas Hobbes (1588–1679) called the "war of all against all." This view assumes that power is best understood as physical force, or *coercion*. A fistfight might be seen as a typical, "natural" manifestation of attempts by individuals to exercise physical coercion. Although states that monopolize the use of force often perpetrated injustice or exploitation as a side effect, Hobbes and others viewed this as the necessary price for social order.

Their assumption was that co-operative social living is not natural for human individuals because they are born with **free agency**—instincts that lead them to pursue their own self-interest above everything else and to challenge one another for dominance.

Discussions of power as coercion tend to see political activity as competition between individual free agents over political control. When free agents make decisions, no larger groups, no historical obligations, no collective beliefs can or ought to stand in their way. Some believe that cultural evolution took a giant leap forward when our ancestors first realized that sticks and stones could be used as weapons not only against non-human predators but especially against human enemies. In this view, human history was driven by the production of better and better weapons, and civilizations were created and sustained by violence. But this is not the only way to understand human agency, as we will see.

### Coercion in Societies without States?

Early anthropologists such as Lewis Henry Morgan showed that kinship institutions could organize orderly social life in societies without states, and his observations were confirmed by later political anthropologists, such as E.E. Evans-Pritchard, based on his work among the Azande. Evans-Pritchard's description of social life among the Azande ([1937] 1976) in no way resembled a war of all against all, even though the Azande lived in a stateless society and held a complex set of beliefs about witchcraft, oracles, and magic. Evans-Pritchard observed that Azande people discussed witchcraft openly, and if they believed they were bewitched, they were likely to be angry rather than afraid. This kind of attitude made sense because most Azande subscribed to a world view in which witchcraft had a meaningful place. In addition, they did not feel helpless because their society also supplied them with practical remedies, like vengeance magic, that they could use to defend themselves if they thought they had been bewitched. Here, we see an example of what Wolf called *organizational power* that does not depend on state coercion. Instead, it depends on *persuasion*. Supported by particular social institutions and practices, the belief system continues to appear natural and rational to members of the society; this is why ordinary, rational people support it.

For a more detailed exploration of Azande beliefs about witchcraft, oracles, and magic, see Chapter 10, pp. 291–3.

### What Are Domination and Hegemony?

Anthropologists who consider both coercive and persuasive forms of power have to come to terms with the ambiguity of power both as a concept and as a phenomenon threaded into the fabric of everyday life. Perhaps people do submit to institutionalized power because they have been coerced and fear punishment. But perhaps they submit because they believe that the power structures in their society are legitimate, given their understandings of the way the world works. What could lead people to accept coercion by others as legitimate (Figure 12.1)? A world view that justifies the social arrangements under which people live is sometimes called an **ideology**. Karl Marx argued that rulers consolidate their power by successfully persuading their subjects to accept an ideology that portrays domination by the ruling class as legitimate; dominated groups who accept the ruling class ideology were said to suffer from *false consciousness*. The concept of false consciousness is problematic, however, since it views people as passive beings incapable of withstanding ideological indoctrination.

For an example of how humans actively engage with and revise their belief systems, see the discussion of culture change and cultural authenticity in Chapter 2, on pp. 39–40.

More promising is the approach taken by Antonio Gramsci (1971). Writing in the 1930s, Gramsci pointed out that coercive rule—what he called **domination**—is expensive and unstable. Rulers do better if they can persuade the dominated to accept their rule as legitimate, both by providing some genuine material benefits to their subjects and by using schools and other cultural institutions to disseminate an ideology

**free agency** The freedom of self-contained individuals to pursue their own interests above everything else and to challenge one another for dominance.

**ideology** A world view that justifies the social arrangements under which people live.

**domination** Ruling with coercive force.

**FIGURE 12.1** | Prior to colonial conquest by outsiders, Muslim emirs from northern Cameroon had coercive power.

The concept of hegemony is attractive to many anthropologists because it draws attention to the central role of cultural beliefs and symbols in struggles to consolidate social organization and political control. Gramsci's contrast between domination (rule by coercive force) and hegemony (rule by persuasion) was central to his own analysis of the exercise of power (Crehan 2002, 153), and it has been helpful to anthropologists who study the exercise of power in societies with and without traditional state institutions. In attempting to extend Gramsci's insights to non-state settings, anthropologists are able to avoid some of the implausible accounts of power that depend on fear of punishment or false consciousness. In place of such arguments, attention can be drawn to the verbal dexterity and personal charisma of leaders with limited coercive force at their disposal who can nonetheless persuade others to follow them by skillfully aligning shared meanings, values, and goals with a particular interpretation of events or proposed course of action.

Consider, for example, the Azande belief that people use witchcraft only against those they envy. The psychological insight embodied in this belief makes it highly plausible to people who experience daily friction with their neighbours. At the same time, however, this belief makes it impossible to accuse Azande chiefs of using witchcraft against commoners—because, as the Azande themselves say, why would chiefs envy their subjects? In this way, hegemonic ideology deflects challenges that might be made against those in power.

## Power and National Identity: A Case Study

Gramsci himself was particularly interested in how hegemony is (or is not) successfully established in state societies. In a postcolonial and globalizing world, where all people are presumed to be citizens of one or another nation-state, understanding the effects of decisions and actions of state authorities becomes crucial for making sense of many events at the local level. Anthropologists have often focused on the processes by which ruling groups in former colonies attempt to build a new national identity. For example, the British colony of Ceylon became independent in 1948, later changing its name to Sri Lanka. The residents of Ceylon belonged to two major populations: the Tamils, concentrated in the northern part of the island, and the larger population of Sinhalese, who lived everywhere else

justifying their rule. If they achieve all this—while also ensuring that none of these concessions seriously undermines their privileged position—they have established what Gramsci called **hegemony**. Hegemony is never absolute but always vulnerable to challenges: struggles may develop between rulers trying to justify their domination and subordinate groups who exercise agency by challenging "official" ideologies and practices that devalue or exclude them. Hegemony may be threatened if subordinate groups maintain or develop alternative, or *counterhegemonic*, cultural practices. Successful hegemony, by contrast, involves linking the understandings of dominant and subordinate groups into what appears to be mutual accommodation.

**hegemony** The persuasion of subordinates to accept the ideology of the dominant group by mutual accommodations that nevertheless preserve the rulers' privileged position.

## EthnoProfile 12.1

### Sinhalese

**Region:** Southern Asia

**Nation:** Sri Lanka
(city: Galle)

**Population:**
15,000,000
(population of Galle:
95,000)

**Environment:** Tropical
island

**Livelihood:** Farming, urban life

**Political organization:** Highly stratified state

**For more information:** Kapferer, Bruce. 1983.
*A Celebration of Demons.* Bloomington: Indiana
University Press.

## EthnoProfile 12.2

### Tamils

**Region:** South Asia

**Nation:** Sri Lanka

**Population:** 3,500,000
(several hundred
thousand have fled the
country)

**Environment:** Low
plains; tropical
monsoon climate

**Livelihood:** Planation agriculture, clothing
manufacture

**Political organization:** Modern nation-state. Long-
term armed dispute between government and Tamil
separatists.

**For more information:** Trawick, Margaret. 2002.
"Reasons for Violence: A Preliminary Ethnographic
Account of the LTTE." In *Conflict and Community in
Contemporary Sri Lanka*, ed. Siri Gamage and
I.B. Watson. Thousand Oaks, CA: Sage.

(see EthnoProfiles 12.1: Sinhalese and 12.2: Tamils).
After independence, however, new Sinhalese rulers
worked to forge a national identity rooted in their version of local history, which excluded the Tamils. In
1956, Sinhala was made the only official language; in
the 1960s and 1970s, Tamils' access to education was

restricted and they were barred from the civil service
and the army (Daniel 1997, 316). When some Tamils
began to agitate for a separate state of their own, the
Sri Lankan government responded in 1979 with severe,
violent repression against Tamils, sending many into
exile and stimulating the growth of the nationalist
Liberation Tigers of Tamil Eelam (LTTE), which grew
"into one of the most dreaded militant organizations
in the world" (Daniel 1997, 323). By May 2009, the Sri
Lankan government army had retaken all territory once
controlled by the Tamil Tigers (Figure 12.2); however,
since the 1980s, thousands have died in ethnic violence.

The exclusion of the Tamil residents from the
Sri Lankan state has exemplifies the use of violent coercion. But violence has also been used
by the government against Sinhalese citizens
who objected to state policies. Between 1987
and 1990, Indian troops were brought into Sri
Lanka to supervise a peace agreement between
Tamils and Sinhalese. These troops found
themselves fighting the LTTE in the north, but
they were also resisted violently in Sinhalese
areas, where the rest of the country was con-
vulsed by a wave of terror as young members of a group called the JVP (*Janata Vimukti
Peramuna*, or People's Liberation Front) attacked the government not only for betraying
the nation by allowing the Indian presence, but
also for its own unjust political and economic
policies. . . . The government responded with
a wave of terror, directed at young males in
particular, which reached its climax with the
capture and murder of the JVP leadership in
late 1989. As far as we can tell, the government
won the day by concentrated terror—killing
so many young people, whether JVP activists
or not, that the opposition ran out of resources
and leadership. (Spencer 2000, 124–5)

After 1990, violence directed by the state against
Sinhalese lessened, and in 1994, a new government
promised to settle the
ethnic conflict by peace-
ful means. But even
before then, Sri Lankan
government efforts to create national unity had not

For more on how ruling
groups have attempted to
build new national identities
in postcolonial settings,
see Chapter 14, pp. 419–22.

**FIGURE 12.2** | Sri Lankan Tamil civilians arrive at a government-controlled area in 2009 after fleeing territory controlled by the Liberation Tigers of Tamil Eelam (LTTE) separatist rebels in northeast Sri Lanka.

rested entirely on violence. Leaders also tried to exercise persuasive power to convince Sinhalese citizens that the state had their welfare in mind and was prepared to take steps to improve their lives. For example, anthropologist Michael Woost (1993) described how the government of Sri Lanka has used a wide range of cultural media (television, radio, newspapers, the school system, public rituals, and even a lottery) to link the national identity to development. National development strategies are presented as attempts to restore Sinhalese village society to its former glory under the precolonial rule of Sinhalese kings. The ideal village, in this view, is engaged in rice paddy cultivation carried out according to the harmonious principles of Sinhala Buddhist doctrine.

The villagers Woost knew could hardly escape this nationalist development discourse, but they did not resist it as an unwelcome imposition from the outside. On the contrary, all of them had incorporated development goals into their own values and had accepted that state-sponsored development would improve their lives. This might suggest that the state's attempt to establish hegemony had succeeded. But collaboration with the state was undermined as three different village factions selectively manipulated development discourse in their struggle to gain access to government resources. For example, nationalistic rhetoric connected development with "improvement of the land." One village faction claimed it had been the first in the village to "improve the land" by building houses or planting tree crops. A second faction claimed that it had "improved the land" first by introducing paddy cultivation in the village. A

third faction claimed it had "improved the land" first since its members had intermarried with other early settlers who had planted a large mango tree, a sign of permanent residence. Each faction made what the other factions interpreted as unjust claims, and each blamed the lack of village unity on the un-Buddhist greed of its opponents. These disagreements eventually led the state to withdraw its offer of resources, ultimately preventing the implementation of a village development scheme that all factions wanted!

Woost argues that the outcome of this political wrangling demonstrates the contradictory and fragile nature of the hegemonic process: paradoxically, the villagers' active appropriation of nationalist ideology undermined efforts to establish the very social order it was supposed to create. Gramsci himself was well aware that establishing successful hegemony in a nation-state was a difficult process whose outcome was not assured; it was the very inability of Italians to achieve this goal that stimulated many of his reflections on domination and hegemony. Indeed, Gramsci's own description of a *colonial* state, emphasized by Indian historian Ranajit Guha, as dominance *without* hegemony (Crehan 2002, 125) is brought to mind by the repeated resort of the Sri Lankan state to violent coercion.

## Biopower and Governmentality

Is there a way to bring into existence and sustain a peaceful, prosperous nation-state in places like Sri Lanka? French historian Michel Foucault (1991) looked at the way European thinkers from the end of the Middle Ages onward had posed (and attempted to answer) similar questions. Together with colleagues, he identified the emergence of a new form of power in the nineteenth century. This form of power he called biopower or *biopolitics*, and it was preoccupied with bodies, both the bodies of citizens and the social body itself (Hacking 1991, 183). As Colin Gordon (1991, 4–5) summarizes, biopower refers to "forms of power exercised over persons specifically insofar as they are thought of as living beings; a politics concerned with subjects as members of a *population*, in which issues of individual sexual and reproductive conduct interconnect with issues of national policy and power."

Before the 1600s, according to Foucault (1991), European states were ruled according to different political understandings. At that time, politics was focused on making sure that an absolute ruler maintained control of the state. Machiavelli's famous guide *The Prince* is the best known of a series of handbooks explaining what such an absolute ruler needed to do to maintain himself in power. But by the seventeenth century, this approach to state rule was proving increasingly inadequate. Machiavelli's critics began to speak instead about *governing* a state, likening such government to the practices that preserved and perpetuated other social institutions.

The example of household management was a preferred model of government. But running a state as if it were a household meant that rulers would need more information about the people, goods, and wealth that needed to be managed. How many citizens were there? What kinds of goods did they produce, and in what quantities? How healthy were they? What could a state do to manage the consequences of misfortunes such as famines, epidemics, and death? In the 1700s, state bureaucrats began to count and measure types of people and things subject to state control, thereby inventing what we would today refer to as *census taking*.

In this way, according to Foucault (1991), European states began to govern in terms of biopolitics, using statistics to manage the people, goods, and wealth within their borders. This, in turn, led to the birth of a new art of governing appropriate to biopolitics, which Foucault calls governmentality. Governmentality involves using the information encoded in statistics to govern in a way that promotes the welfare of populations within a state. To exercise governmentality, for example, state

bureaucrats might use statistics to determine that a famine was likely and to calculate how much it might cost the state in the suffering and death of citizens and in other losses. They would then come up with a plan of intervention—perhaps a form of insurance—designed to reduce the impact of famine on citizens, protect economic activity within the state, and thereby preserve the stability of the state and its institutions.

In contemporary states, governmentality functions as a form of power that relies on accurate counting and measurements of individuals within a state's borders, for example through national censuses (Figure 12.3). However, as Ian Hacking (1991, 183) suggests, people must remain aware that the statistical information governments collect is not always used with their best interests at heart. After all, governments want to tax

> **biopower** Forms of power preoccupied with bodies, both the bodies of citizens and the social body of the state itself.
>
> **governmentality** The art of governing appropriately to promote the welfare of populations within a state.

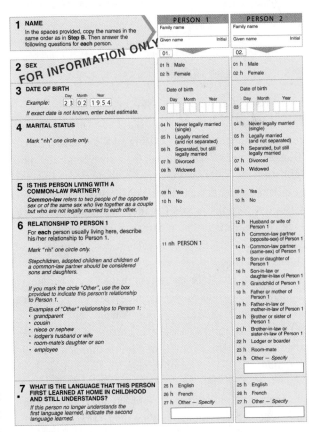

**FIGURE 12.3** | In order to govern, a state must know who it is governing. Censuses are one way in which the information a state believes it needs can be collected.

citizens, vaccinate and educate their children, restrict their activities to those that benefit the state, control their movements beyond (and sometimes within) state borders, and otherwise manage what they do. In the worst cases, detailed statistics can provide a government with the information it needs to act in stark opposition to the interests of a specific cultural, racial, or other group subject to its control. This was clearly the case in the late nineteenth century when the Canadian government forced thousands of Indigenous peoples off their traditional lands and onto reserves and began sending their children to residential schools, the effects of which continue to be felt by Indigenous peoples across Canada today. (See the "In

Their Own Words" box on the Idle No More movement for an example of how some Indigenous peoples in Canada and elsewhere are standing up for themselves, in opposition to government forces that threaten their ways of life.)

## Can Governmentality Be Eluded?

In a globalizing world full of nation-states, anthropologists are increasingly likely to encounter in their fieldwork both the pressures of governmentality and attempts to evade or manipulate governmentality. This was the experience of Aihwa Ong (2002), who carried out research among a dispersed population of wealthy Chinese merchant families. In explaining how these

## In Their Own Words

### Idle No More: Giving a Voice to the Voiceless

*Researcher and writer Febna Caven outlines the strengths of the women leaders of the Idle No More movement as well as the strengths of the movement itself—a personal, global, and spiritual movement aimed at "empowering Indigenous communities to stand up for their lands, rights, cultures, and sovereignty" (Caven 2013).*

On 11 December 2012, on International Human Rights Day, northern Ontario Attawapiskat Chief Theresa Spence began a hunger strike, calling on Canadian Prime Minister Stephen Harper and Governor General David Johnston to "initiate immediate discussions and the development of action plans to address treaty issues with First Nations across Canada." Her peaceful resistance, emphasizing the importance of dialogue, catapulted the Idle No More movement to a new level of urgency. . . .

The Idle No More movement began as a thread of emails between four women from Saskatchewan: Jessica Gordon, Sylvia McAdam, Nina Wilson, and Sheelah McLean, who decided to make a "sincere effort to make some change." The context for their resolution was the Canadian Bill C-45, the government's omnibus budget implementation bill that includes changes to land management on the reservations. It attacks the land base reserved for Indigenous people, removes protection for hundreds of waterways, and weakens Canada's environmental laws. The women started a Facebook page to brainstorm ideas and [create] a plan for action.

In December 2012, during the third week of her hunger strike, Attawapiskat Chief Theresa Spence meets with journalists in a teepee on Victoria Island in Ottawa, Ontario.

Gordon, who is from Pasqua 4 Treaty Territory, decided to name the page "Idle No More" as a reminder to "get off the couch and start working."

The movement's grassroots tactics were evident from the first major event, a mass teach-in at . . . an innovative community enterprise centre in Saskatoon, Saskatchewan, on 10 November 2012. Following the teach-in, . . . a series of rallies and protests spread across Saskatchewan to Manitoba and Alberta. Speaking to a reporter at one such rally, Wilson, a Nakota and Plains Cree from Treaty 4 White Bear territory said, "We are trying to help people get their voices back so that we can make more change and we are able to have more of a First Nations voice . . . not just

Chinese became so successful, Ong focused on the different forms of governmentality characteristic of nation-states, the capitalist market, and Chinese kinship and family. These three forms of governmentality possess rules for disciplining individual conduct in ways that are connected to the exercise of power appropriate to each of them. Ong argues that in the late nineteenth century, some Chinese citizens managed to evade the governmentality of Chinese kinship and family by moving out of China and into merchant cities under European imperial control elsewhere in Asia and Southeast Asia. Under these circumstances, the traditional obligations to one's lineage were effectively severed, and the individual family and its members,

under the control of males, became the principal focus of loyalty among kin. But such families had to deal with two other forms of governmentality in this new setting. One of these was the governmentality of particular states. Moving from one state to the next involved

For additional discussion of Ong's work, see Chapter 15, pp. 438–40.

making oneself or one's family subject to different forms of biopower: for example, for wealthy residents of Hong Kong, "citizenship becomes an issue of handling the diverse rules or 'governmentality' of host societies where they may be economically correct in terms of human capital, but culturally incorrect in terms of ethnicity" (2002, 340).

---

a First Nations [voice] but an Indigenous voice, and not just an Indigenous voice but a grassroots voice, because it affects us all." And it does affect us all, as it does the environment.

Though it was the omnibus C-45 bill that led to the movement, Idle No More is not just about legislation. It is also a call for renewal of the Indigenous identities and lifeways. The leaders and spokespersons of the movement have no hesitation linking the political to the personal, as the personal is very much a part of the movement. From her teepee on the frozen Ottawa River, a stone's throw away from Parliament Hill, [Chief] Spence spent 44 days on hunger strike and recently said, "I am in this resistance because the pain became too heavy. I just could not take it anymore." She explained how the alienation and pain she feels stems from her years in the residential schools. "It was a closed chapter, until one day you realize this generation is facing the same pain we felt at resident school. We want a life of freedom and not a life of pain and fear for the [next] generation.". . .

As McLean, who is the only non-Indigenous member in the initial group of four women, says "It is a very loving movement . . . and it's almost entirely female-led. Even though there are hundreds of men who support the movement, the vast majority of the movement's participants and organizers are women." The nature of the fluid, non-violent, and unifying movement is one that both reflects and engages women's agency. . . .

. . . Gordon, who has long served her community through non-profit organizations and by volunteering on committees and boards, has taken up the responsibility for monitoring the virtual space of the movement. She manages the movement's website, www.idlenomore.ca, and takes great care in ensuring that the events that get promoted and added to the Idle No More banner are all peaceful in nature. . . .

McAdam, who is from the Treaty 6 territory and a direct descendant of the treaty makers, is a scholar of Cree culture as well as law and human justice. . . . McAdam invokes Cree history and laws to unite the Indigenous people. She says ". . . when we say we are going to do something, the spirit world listens, your keepers listen, and our ancestors listen. When we say we are going to go 'support,' we mean *e we ni towh setohks ka ke yak*. This means we are doing more than supporting; our keepers [and our] spirits are going too. . . ."

Each of the four women leading Idle No More fills a valuable niche. But even as the movement has strong leadership . . ., the masses at the grassroots still retain their place at the core of the movement. As the movement leaders speak of disenfranchised communities left without potable drinking water, as the extended history of colonialism and violation of treaty rights are recalled, the focus still remains on dialogue so that solutions are sought together and not imposed. . . . Speaking up, dancing, and rallying together, co-creating, let's join too. Let us be Idle No More.

---

Source: Caven 2013, 6–7. Reprinted with permission from Cultural Survival.

Finally, the prosperity of these overseas Chinese families depended on doing business according to the governmentality of the capitalist market. But the governmentality of the market is hard to evade because it reaches beyond families or nation-states. As a result, overseas Chinese families would try whenever possible to move their members from country to country, as needed, to take advantage of fresh opportunities for business. Such mobility, in turn, depended on being able to evade or manipulate the bureaucratic rules of nation-states whenever these threatened to limit mobility. Thanks to their wealth, overseas Chinese families found this sort of evasion or manipulation was frequently possible: "international managers and professionals have the material and symbolic resources to manipulate global schemes of cultural difference, racial

## Anthropology in the Contemporary World

### Doing Business in Japan

Anthropologist Richard Reeves-Ellington (1993) designed and implemented a cross-cultural training program for a North American company doing business in Japan. He found that many of the traditional methods of anthropology—cultural understanding, ethnographic data, and participant-observation—helped managers conduct business in Japan. Reeves-Ellington began the training program by having employees first gather general cultural information artifacts ("How are things classified or what are the artifacts of an agreed classification system?"), social knowledge ("What are proper principles for behaviour? What are the values that drive the categories and artifacts?"), and cultural logic. Social knowledge or values are based on an underlying, taken-for-granted cultural logic. Coming to understand Japanese cultural logic is of great importance to foreigners wishing to live and work in Japan.

The managers at the company decided to learn how to carry out introductions, meetings, leave-taking, dinner, and drinking in Japan. Each practice was analyzed according to the framework of artifacts, social knowledge, and cultural logic and was taught by a combination of methods that included the general observations that the managers collected while visiting Japanese museums, theatres, shrines, baseball games, and business meetings. The managers analyzed these observations and discussed stories that show how badly things can go when cultural knowledge is not sufficient. For example, one thing Reeves-Ellington's students needed to learn about introductions involved the presentation of the business card (*meishi*). The proper presentation and use of the meishi is the central element in the practice of making introductions at business meetings. Reeves-Ellington explained that, to a Japanese businessperson, the meishi is an extension of the self. Damage to the card is damage to the individual. Therefore, mistreatment of a meishi will ruin

a relationship. Reeves-Ellington notes that his colleagues did not fully appreciate the consequences of these beliefs until he told them a story:

> A major US company was having problems with one of its distributors, and the parties seemed unable to resolve their differences. The president of the US company decided to visit Japan, meet with his counterpart in the wholesaler organization, and attempt to resolve their differences. The two had not met previously and, upon meeting, each followed proper *meishi* ritual. The American, however, did not put the Japanese counterpart's *meishi* on the table; instead he held on to it. As the conversation became heated, the American rolled up the *meishi* in his hand. Horror was recorded on the face of the Japanese businessman. The American then tore the *meishi* into bits. This was more than the Japanese could stand; he excused himself from the meeting. Shortly afterward the two companies stopped doing business with each other. (209)

Table 12.1 shows the information regarding introductions and the use of the meishi that Reeves-Ellington's students derived from their work based on their analytic framework of artifacts, social knowledge, and cultural logic.

On three critical measures—effective working relationships with Japanese executives, shortened project times, and improved financial returns—the anthropologically based training program that Reeves-Ellington designed was a success. Both employees and their Japanese counterparts felt more comfortable in working with each other. Prior to the program, joint projects required an average of fifteen months to complete;

projects run by executives applying the methodologies of the program cut completion time to an average of eight months. Financial returns based on contracts negotiated by personnel who had not participated in the program averaged gross income of 6 per cent of sales, whereas those negotiated by personnel applying the anthropological techniques averaged gross income equal to 18 per cent of sales.

**TABLE 12.1 | Introductions at Business Meetings**

| Artifacts | Social Knowledge | Cultural Logic |
|---|---|---|
| **Technology** • Business cards | • Once given, a card is kept—not discarded | **Human Relations** • Meishi provide understanding of appropriate relations between parties |
| • Meishi | • Meishi are not exchanged a second time unless there is a position change | • Meishi take uncertainty out of relationships |
| | • Before the next meeting between parties, the meishi are reviewed for familiarization with the people attending the meeting | |
| | • The meishi provides status for the owner | |
| **Visual Behaviour** • Presentation of meishi by presenting card, facing recipient | | **Environment** • Meishi help establish insider/outsider environment |
| • Senior people present meishi first | | • Meishi help establish possible obligations to environment |
| • Guest presents first, giving name, company affiliation, and bowing | | **Human Activity** |
| • Host presents meishi in same sequence | | • Meishi help to establish human activities |
| • Upon sitting at conference table, all meishi are placed in front of recipient to assure name use | | |

Source: Reeves-Ellington 1993.

hierarchy, and citizenship to their own advantage . . . in environments controlled and shaped by nation-states and capitalist markets" (Ong 2002, 339).

## How Are Politics, Gender, and Kinship Related?

Formal electoral politics in many countries seems to be the domain of men—few women run for office, and some countries have prohibited women from voting. Anthropologist Katherine Bowie (2008) has analyzed a local election in Thailand to show "how anthropological insights into kinship systems can provide important avenues into understanding the gender dynamics of electoral politics" (136). Her point is that it is impossible to understand local electoral politics in Thailand without paying attention to local practices of matrilocality and matrilineal kinship (Figure 12.4).

In northern Thailand, people belong to social groups called *matrilineages*, which are created by links made through women, and both men and women belong to the same matrilineage as their mother. People there also practise matrilocal residence after marriage—that is, a newly married couple goes to live with or near the wife's mother, a residence practice found in many matrilineal societies. Thus, when a man marries, he leaves his mother's house and goes to live in his wife's parents' home. Because

> ↻ Matrilineages are discussed at greater length in Chapter 13, on pp. 357–9.

**FIGURE 12.4** | A woman in northern Thailand votes. In local elections, kin relations are entangled with local electoral politics.

members of the same matrilineage tend to live near one another, entire sections of villages—and sometimes entire villages—are made up of related women and their in-marrying husbands.

Co-operative labour exchanges are essential for transplanting and harvesting rice, maintaining irrigation systems, and helping build houses in these communities. Because of the matrilocal residence pattern, it is the wife's matrilineal kinship network that provides labour and other resources for these activities, and labour exchanges are made both within and across matrilines. Kin groups also depend on one another to share the costs of various expensive ritual events. In any neighbourhood there, it is women who keep these connections harmonious and functioning well—after all, it is their matriline that is being maintained: the village or neighbourhood is composed of related women and their husbands, who are "strangers."

In-marrying men feel a certain stress as strangers: even though they have formal authority as

head of the household, they are dependent on their wives' families; and because everyone in the village is a stranger to them, they are isolated in the village. At the same time, stranger status frees men to engage in local politics, because men who are strangers have less at stake when engaging in political conflict at the village level. By contrast, women members of the local matrilineages appear neutral in local elections, which allows them to mediate the tensions that build as a result of the political activities of in-marrying men. They are able to transmit information and maintain networks, even while appearing to have no political interests of their own. In fact, they do have interests in mobilizing votes for specific candidates, but they are also committed to "their efforts to achieve unity within their villages and to heal divisions both within and across their villages" (Bowie 2008, 148).

In July 2005, Bowie was able to observe a local election to choose two village representatives from nine candidates. Almost everyone in the village was related to all nine candidates in some way. Villagers were willing to reveal that one of their votes would go to their closest relative, but they would not commit to the second vote, instead just describing each candidate's relative strengths. "When I delicately probed into who might win, the standard response was a politic refrain, 'depends on their kinship network'" (148). Indeed, Bowie argues that as women embedded male leaders within their matrilines, the political networks provided by wives, sisters, and mothers were fundamental to a successful campaign. "At the village level, the art of neutral partisanship enables women to pursue the broader interests of their matrilines and safeguard village harmony. . . . In the politics of matrilineal kinship, conflict is the arena for ignorant, drunken husbands and sons-in-law; resolving conflict is the arena for knowledgeable, sober wives and mothers. If formal politics is necessarily divisive, women's political role is in avoiding conflict and healing division. The processes are diametrically opposed, but each is political" (148).

Thus, kinship continues to play a significant role in people's political lives, even in contemporary settings, in which it would not necessarily be expected to do so. It is the holistic approach of anthropology that makes such connections visible. In the following "In Their Own Words" box, Kathryn Reese-Taylor (2009)

## In Their Own Words

## Mayan Queens: Rulers and Warriors

*Canadian archaeologist Kathryn Reese-Taylor and her colleagues from the University of Calgary have begun to identify the powerful roles that wealthy Mayan women played during the Classic period of Maya civilization (c. 200–900 CE). Their interpretations of inscriptions and hieroglyphic representations are helping to recognize how important women were in battles fought in the homelands of the Maya and how possible changes from a patrilineal to a matrilineal kinship system occurred.*

The importance of women in Maya society is no longer in question. Recent studies have highlighted the important roles played by women, particularly those in the royal courts. . . .

The results of our analysis have allowed us to greatly increase our understanding of Maya women's roles during the Classic period. Most significantly, we can now assert that during the later part of the seventh and early part of the eighth centuries, queens actually ruled independently, participated in battles, and captured enemies. In other words, for several women, the role of a Maya warrior queen was identical in all ways to that of warrior king.

Moreover, the visibility of women in the historic records grew after 623. The manner in which they were portrayed—conducting rituals, dedicating stelae [i.e., stone monuments], capturing prisoners—and, indeed, even the manner in which they were dressed, in the transgendered costume of the Maize God/Moon Goddess, all signify the power and authority royal women commanded in state politics. . . .

Our analysis has demonstrated that at the beginning of the seventh century, the roles of royal women in the central lowlands shifted dramatically. . . . [For example,] matrilineal descent appears to have become more important than patrilineal descent in the northern lowlands. We have also recognized an increased importance placed on matrilineal heritage in the texts and images of public art from 623 to 761. This implies a reformation in kinship systems during this period, at least among the elite of the central lowlands.

While additional research needs to be done to more fully understand Maya kinship systems, as well as gender identities, through this study we have detected a previously unrecognized link between the two. . . . Nonetheless, what is clear is that the shared representational systems—pictorial and textual—that existed in the corpus of Maya Lowland art are a rich source for continued investigation into gender roles, kinship systems, and expressions of political and military authority.

Source: Reese-Taylor et al. 2009, 39, 66–7.

demonstrates how even in the prehistoric Mayan culture, this relationship between kinship and political control was important.

## How Are Immigration and Politics Related in the New Europe?

One of the more interesting things about the early twenty-first century is that Europe—the continent that gave birth to the Enlightenment, to colonial empires, and (along with North America) to anthropology itself—has become a living laboratory for the study of some of the most complex social and cultural processes to be found anywhere in the world.

During the last half of the twentieth century, the countries of Europe, including Italy, were the target of large waves of migration from all over the world. Visitors to Rome regularly make stops at the ancient ruins in the centre of the city. One venerable working-class Roman neighbourhood, only a short walk from the Colosseum, is Rione Monti, which has a fascinating history of its own (EthnoProfile 12.3: Rione Monti; Figure 12.5). In 1999, anthropologist Michael Herzfeld (2003) moved into Rione Monti to explore social change in the uses of the past. Long-time residents of Monti share a common local culture, which includes use of the *romanesco* dialect rather than standard Italian and a strong sense of local identity that distinguishes them from "foreigners,"

## EthnoProfile 12.3

### Rione Monti (Rome)

**Region:** Europe

**Nation:** Italy

**Population:** 15,300

**Environment:** Central neighbourhood in Rome

**Livelihood:** Urban occupations, ranging from tourism and factory work to restaurants, small businesses, bureaucratic, executive

**Political organization:** Neighbourhood in a modern nation-state

**For more information:** www.rionemonti.net

including diplomats and non-Roman Italians. Their identity survived Mussolini's demolition of part of the neighbourhood in the early twentieth century. They successfully dealt with a local criminal underworld by mastering a refined urbane code of politeness. The underworld had faded away by the 1970s, but beginning in the 1980s, residents began to face two new challenges to their community. First, historic Roman neighbourhoods became fashionable, and well-to-do Italians began to move into Rione Monti, pushing many

workers into cheaper housing elsewhere. Second, in the 1990s, another group of newcomers arrived: immigrants from eastern Europe.

Italy is one of the more recent destinations of immigration into Europe, reversing the country's historical experience as a source, rather than a target, of immigration. However, after Germany, France, and Britain passed laws curtailing immigration in the 1970s, Italy became an increasingly popular destination for immigrants from Africa, Asia, and Latin America; after the end of the Cold War came immigrants from outside the European Union (EU), including eastern Europe. Until recently, laws regulating immigration were few, and the country appeared welcoming. But this is changing. "Italy has not historically been a racist country, but intolerant attitudes towards immigrants have increased. To a large extent, this seems to be the result of a longstanding underestimation of the magnitude of the changes and thus poor policy implementation for a lengthy period, in spite of the best intentions officially proclaimed" (Melotti 1997, 91).

Umberto Melotti (1997) contrasts the distinctive ways in which immigration is understood by the governments of France, Britain, and Germany. According to Melotti, the French project is "ethnocentric assimilationism": since early in the nineteenth century, when French society experienced a falling birth rate, immigration was encouraged and immigrants were promised all the rights and privileges of native-born

**FIGURE 12.5** | Rione Monti is a neighbourhood in central Rome, Italy, where longtime residents and new immigrants are negotiating new forms of relationship.

citizens as long as they adopted French culture completely, dropping other ethnic or cultural attachments and assimilating the French language and character (1997, 75). The British project, by contrast, is "uneven pluralism": that is, the pragmatic British expect immigrants to be loyal and law-abiding citizens, but they do not expect immigrants to "become British" and they tolerate private cultivation of cultural differences as long as these do not threaten the British way of life (79–80). (In many ways, Canadian immigration policy follows the British pattern, but multiculturalism is more firmly entrenched in our government policy and our national identity. At the same time, the practice of multiculturalism in Canada is somewhat uneven, as it privileges those who speak one of our two "official" languages [see Haque 2012], and it is not consistent in all regions [e.g., Quebec's policy of "interculturalism"; see Bouchard 2011].). Lastly, Melotti describes the German project as "the institutionalization of precariousness," by which he means that, despite the fact that Germany has within its borders more immigrants than any other European country and began receiving immigrants at the end of the nineteenth century, its government continues to insist that Germany is not a country of immigrants. Immigrants were always considered "guest workers," children born to guest workers were considered citizens of the country from which the worker came, and it remains very difficult for guest workers or their children born in Germany to obtain German citizenship.

Coming to terms with increasing numbers of Muslims living in countries where Christianity has historically been dominant is a central theme in political debates within Europe. Although almost all European states consider themselves secular in orientation (see Asad 2003), the relation between religion and state is far from uniform. France is unusual because of its strict legal separation between religion and state. In Britain, the combination of a secular outlook with state funding of the established Anglican Church has allowed citizens to support forms of religious inclusion that first involved state funding of Catholic schools for Irish immigrants and now involve state funding of Muslim schools for Muslim immigrants (Modood 1997; P. Lewis 1997). In Germany, where a secular outlook also combines with state-subsidized religious institutions, the state has devised curricula for elementary schools designed to teach all students about different religious traditions, including Islam, in ways that emphasize the possibility of harmonizing one's religious faith with one's obligations as a citizen. Although this approach may seem presumptuous or paternalistic, its supporters counter that its advantages outweigh its costs. Perhaps as a result of their own history, many contemporary Germans have less faith than the British that a civic culture of religious tolerance will automatically lead to harmony without state intervention and less faith than the French in the existence of a separate secular sphere of society from which religion can be safely excluded (Schiffauer 1997).

These are, of course, thumbnail sketches of more complex attitudes and practices. But they illustrate the fact that there is no single "European" approach to the challenges posed by immigration. In a way, each European state, with its own history and institutions, is experimenting with different ways of coping with the challenges immigration presents; and their failures and successes will influence the kinds of cultural institutions that develop in the twenty-first century. This is particularly significant in light of the fact that European nation-states have joined together in the EU, a continent-wide superstate with 28 members. Reconciling the diverse interests and needs of member states poses enormous challenges for EU members, and issues surrounding immigration are among them.

Tariq Modood (1997) points out, for example, that European multiculturalism requires supporting conceptions of citizenship that allow the "right to assimilate" as well as the "right to have one's 'difference' . . . recognized and supported in the public and the private spheres"; multiculturalism must recognize that "participation in the public or national culture is necessary for the effective exercise of citizenship" while at the same time defending the "right to widen and adapt the national culture" (20).

Anthropologist John Bowen's (2010) recent fieldwork in France documents the process Modood describes. Bowen has worked among the many French Muslims who are not interested in terrorism but "who wish to live fulfilling *and* religious lives in France" (4). He has paid particular attention to the work of a number of French Muslim religious teachers and scholars, whom he calls "Islamic public actors." Other French Muslims come to them for religious instruction and for advice about how to cope with the difficulties of living in a non-Muslim country. In turn, the Islamic public actors Bowen knew are working to craft solutions that, in their view, are true both to the laws of the French republic and to the norms and traditions of Islam.

For example, many French Muslims are concerned about how to contract a valid marriage in France. Ever since the French Revolution, France has refused to accept the legality of religious marriages and recognizes only civil marriages contracted at city hall (Figure 12.6). Yet Muslims who want to marry are often confused about whether a "secular" marriage at city hall is appropriate or necessary. Indeed, some Muslims have argued that city hall marriages are un-Islamic because they did not exist at the time of the Prophet Muhammad. But other Muslims, including some of Bowen's consultants, disagree with this position. They argue that there was no need for civil marriages at the time of the Prophet because, in those days, tribal life made it impossible to avoid the obligations of the marriage contract. But things are different today for Muslims in urban France: Bowen's consultants have seen many tragic outcomes when young women who thought they had a valid Muslim marriage were left by their husbands, only to discover that the French state did not recognize their marriage and could offer them no legal redress.

Because this was not the outcome that Islamic marriage was intended to produce, the Muslim scholars Bowen knew looked beyond traditional Islamic marriage practices in order to clarify the larger purposes that Islamic marriage was supposed to achieve. They then asked if these purposes could be achieved using the French institution of civil marriage. One scholar told Bowen: "I say that if you marry at the city hall, you have already made an Islamic marriage, because all the conditions for that marriage have been fulfilled" (2010, 167). Those conditions include the fact that both Islamic marriages and French civil marriages are contracts; that both require the consent of the spouses; and that the legal requirements imposed on the spouses by French civil marriage further the Islamic goal of keeping the spouses together. Given that this kind of reasoning is further strengthened by appealing to opinions on marriage drawn from the four traditional Sunni schools of Islamic law, many Islamic public intellectuals believe that a way can be found to craft acceptable practices for French Muslims in many areas of daily life.

Because Bowen agrees with Modood that accommodation has to go in both directions, he also shows how some French legal scholars are working to craft solutions to the challenges Muslim marriage practices present to French law. Most French judges agree, for example, that Islamic marriages or divorces contracted outside France remain valid when the parties involved move to France. But French judges can refuse to accept international rules for resolving legal conflicts if they decide that the solution would violate French "public order." Bowen found that the concept of public order is basic to the French legal system, referring "both to the conditions of social order and to basic values, and it limits the range of laws that a legislator may pass and the decisions that a judge may make" (2010, 173).

FIGURE 12.6 | A Turkish bride and groom in Clichy-sous-Bois, a poor suburb of Paris. Islamic and French legal scholars are both working to harmonize French and Islamic marriage practices.

Violations of public order may include customs from outside France that are judged to "offend the morality and values" of French law. Some French jurists argue that consequences following from Muslim practices of marriage and divorce should not be recognized in France if they violate French and European commitments to the equality of women and men. Other French jurists, however, point to the practical problems that this argument creates: not recognizing the validity of Islamic divorces in France, for example, would mean that a woman divorced according to Islamic law abroad could not remarry if she came to France. Similarly, refusing to recognize polygamous marriage in France would deprive the children of all but a man's first wife of their rights under French and European law. In recent years, Bowen reports, French judges have devised two ways of crafting a solution to these unwelcome consequences. One has been to modify the concept of public order by making so-called "practical exceptions" for Muslims who emigrate to France. The other is to be more flexible with Muslim marriage and family practices as long as these arrangements involve individuals who are not French citizens. These pragmatic solutions are an improvement over what Bowen calls the "more bluntinstrument approach" associated with the older understanding of public order. Bowen (2010) concludes that in France today, Muslim and French jurists alike are both struggling to craft "the legal conditions for common life that are capacious enough to 'reasonably accommodate' people living in differing conditions and with differing beliefs, yet unitary enough to retain the hope that such a common life is conceivable" (178).

As these examples suggest, the struggles and dilemmas facing residents of Rione Monti are widespread across the new Europe. But the specifics of these residents' situation and the cultural resources at their disposal have their own particularity. Thus, the traditionally left-wing Monti residents have resisted attempts by neo-fascist politicians to get them to turn against immigrant families in the neighbourhood. Longtime Monti residents were initially unhappy with the location of the Ukrainian church in a building that overlooks the neighbourhood's central square because the churchgoers gather there twice a week, invading "their" space. Herzfeld found that the residents of Monti, like other Romans, claimed not to be racist, and that they seemed less hostile to immigrants of colour than to Ukrainians. But Ukrainians were more numerous in

Monti, and more threatening, because they looked like local people but in fact were competing with locals for work and space in the neighbourhood (Herzfeld 2009, 230). Local and immigrant Monti residents eventually did find ways to get along with each other (231). Indeed, during the years when Herzfeld was doing his ethnography, the mix of residents in Monti was changing in other ways, as young professionals, including professors from the nearby university, began to rent apartments in local buildings. The low-income artisans who had traditionally lived in these buildings were finding, however, that rents were rising, even as entire apartment blocks remained empty. The owners of the apartment buildings in these blocks had concluded that it was worth their while to keep their buildings empty until real estate prices rose, even if this precipitated a housing shortage.

Prior to this period, struggles between renters, landlords, and the city government of Rome regarding building permits or over rental rates were common. Such disputes had usually been resolved by negotiations among all interested parties, and the negotiations had been carried out according to the mostly extralegal rules of a traditional neighbourhood "code." As a result, low-income renters had often managed to avoid eviction from their apartments. But in the early years of the twenty-first century, the rules changed, in large part because some of the key players changed. A lot of outside money was entering the Roman real estate market, deployed by businessmen who knew nothing and cared less about whether low-income renters ought to be allowed to stay in building in desirable locations.

Still, Monti residents were politically active, and they banded together when threatened with eviction. Herzfeld followed closely the back-and-forth negotiations that ensued when the renters in one particular building staged a rent strike, after the building's new owner threatened to evict current residents. This was the sort of action that, in the old days, would likely have been quietly resolved according to the neighbourhood code; and at first, the strikers were able to get the building's new owner to agree not to evict them. What nobody had counted on, however, was the clout of the wealthy outside buyers who had entered the Roman real estate market. The building's new owner then sold the building to another company, who then sold it to a third company, whose owners refused to honour the agreement that the original owner had made with the renters. The current owners then tried to sell the building to the city, which refused to pay the price they were asking. "It became clear that nothing further could be done; this company soon thereafter sold the property to yet another firm, one that was developing extensive interests in the neighbourhood, and the struggle finally came to an end" (2009, 297).

A key component contributing to this outcome was a change in the law that reflected struggles over what kinds of rights residents had to their homes. One of Herzfeld's informants, who had been active in Roman city government, explained to him that the power of the city to intervene in struggles against eviction had changed. In the past, the city had respected the view that people had a social right to their homes; but these rights were no longer legally protected: "under the national constitution, it was now the owner's rights that were protected. . . . A set of laws, promulgated at the national level by the coalition to which he had belonged at the city level, and reinforced by already existing constitutional guarantees for the rights of property owners, had now effectively undercut any serious prospect of resolving the dispute as an issue of the social right to a home" (2009, 297). At first the strikers refused to give up, but their legal position was weak; within a year, they had been evicted. There was much bitterness among those forced to leave, and even though all of them eventually did find other places to live, many had to leave Monti, which undermined their sense of community and identity.

The experiences of these Monti residents raise interesting and troubling questions about the rights of long-time residents in any place who discover that under the current regime of global neo-liberalism they apparently possess no rights that international capital is obliged to respect. Herzfeld observes that "the intense attachment to place that aroused my sympathies can also be the source of no less intense forms of cultural fundamentalism and racism" (2009, 301). These responses are not limited to Europe; they can be found in many countries around the world, including Thailand, where Herzfeld next carried out fieldwork. However, he insists that "there is no necessary connection between localism and racism and other forms of intolerance, and in fact what has impressed me throughout both field projects—one in Italy, the other in Thailand—has been the firmness with which some reject the seductions of intolerance in

the midst of their own sufferings, even as they recognize the bitterness that drives others in far less attractive directions" (2009, 302). He adds that "none of this will make much sense except in the further context of a consideration of the history of nationalism, both in Italy and elsewhere" (2009, 302).

# Hidden Transcripts and the Power of Reflection

The power that people have to invest their experiences with meanings of their own choosing suggests that a ruler's power of coercion is limited, which was Gramsci's key insight. Thought alone may be unable to alter the fact of material coercion, yet it has the power to transform the meaning of material coercion for those who experience it.

Any hegemonic establishment runs the risk that the dominated may create new, plausible accounts of their experiences of domination. Political scientist James Scott (1990) refers to these unofficial accounts as "hidden transcripts." Occasionally, those who are dominated may be able to organize themselves socially in order to transform their hidden transcripts into a counterhegemonic discourse aimed at discrediting the political establishment. Those who are dominated may be able to persuade some or all of those around them that their counterhegemonic interpretation of social experience is better than the hegemonic discourse of the current rulers. Such challenges to incumbent political power are frequently too strong to be ignored and too widespread to be simply obliterated by force. When coercion no longer works, what remains is a struggle between alternative accounts of experience.

Scott carried out two years of ethnographic research among peasant rice farmers in a Malaysian village called "Sedaka" (a pseudonym; see EthnoProfile 12.4: "Sedaka" Village). In "Sedaka," poor Malaysian peasants are at the bottom of a social hierarchy dominated locally by rich farmers and nationally by a powerful state apparatus. According to Scott (1987, 274), these peasants are not kept in line by some form of state-sponsored terrorism; rather, the context of their lives is shaped by what he calls "routine repression": "occasional arrests, warnings, diligent police work, legal restrictions, and an Internal Security Act that allows for indefinite preventive detention and proscribes much political activity."

EthnoProfile 12.4

## "Sedaka" Village

**Region:** Southeastern Asia

**Nation:** Malaysia

**Population:** 300

**Environment:** Lush paddy land

**Livelihood:** Rice cultivation

**Political organization:** Village within a modern nation-state

**For more information:** Scott, James. 1987. *Weapons of the Weak*. New Haven: Yale University Press.

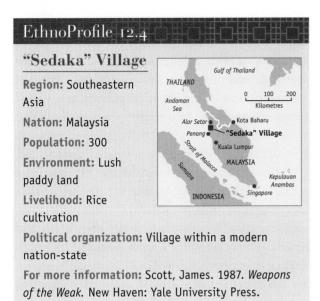

Scott wanted to find out how this highly restrictive environment affected political relations between members of dominant and subordinate classes in the village. He quickly realized that the poor peasants of "Sedaka" were not about to rise up against their oppressors. But this was not because they accepted their poverty and low status as natural and proper. For one thing, organized overt defence of their interests was difficult because local economic, political, and kinship ties generated conflicting loyalties. For another, the peasants knew that overt political action in the context of routine repression would be foolhardy. Finally, they had to feed their families. Their solution was to engage in what Scott (1987) calls "everyday forms of peasant resistance": this included "foot dragging, dissimulation, desertion, false compliance, pilfering, feigned ignorance, slander, arson, sabotage, and so forth" (xvi). These actions may have done little to alter the peasants' situation in the short run; however, Scott argues, in the long run they may have been more effective than overt rebellion in undercutting state repression.

What we find in everyday forms of peasant resistance are indirect attempts to challenge local hegemony. Scott (1987) says, "The struggle between rich and poor in Sedaka is not merely a struggle over work, property rights, grain, and cash. It is also a struggle over the appropriation of symbols, a struggle over how the past and present shall be understood and labelled, a struggle to identify causes and assess blame" (xvii). When peasants criticize rich landowners or rich landowners find fault with peasants, the parties involved are not just venting emotion. According to Scott, each side is simultaneously constructing a world view. Rich and poor alike are offering "a critique of things as they are as well as a vision of things as they should be. . . . [They are writing] a kind of social text on the subject of human decency" (23).

Scott describes the dynamics of this struggle during the introduction of mechanized rice harvesting in "Sedaka." Traditionally, rice harvesting was manual labour. It regularly allowed poor peasants to earn cash and receive grain from their employers as a traditional form of charitable gift (Figure 12.7). In the late 1970s, however, the introduction of combine harvesters

**FIGURE 12.7** | Until the late decades of the twentieth century, rice harvesting in rural Malaysia was manual labour that regularly allowed poor peasants to earn cash and receive charitable gifts of grain from their employers.

eliminated the rich farmers' need for hired labour, a loss that dealt poor families a severe economic blow. When the rich and poor talked about the harvesters, each side offered a different account of their effect on economic life in the village.

Scott tells us that both sides agreed that using the machines hurt the poor and helped the rich. When each side was asked whether the benefits of the machines outweighed their costs, however, consensus evaporated. The poor offered practical reasons against the use of combine harvesters: they claimed that the heavy machines were inefficient and that their operation destroyed rice paddies. They also offered moral reasons: they accused the rich of being "stingy," of ignoring the traditional obligation of rich people to help the poor by providing them with work and charity. The rich denied both the practical and the moral objections of the poor. They insisted that using harvesters increased their yield. They accused the poor people of bad faith. They claimed that the poor suffered because they were bad farmers or lazy, and they attributed their own success to hard work and prudent farm management.

Rich rice farmers would never have been able to begin using combine harvesters without the outside assistance of both the national government and the business groups that rented the machines to them at harvest time. Poor peasants were aware of this, yet they directed their critique at the local farmers and not at the government or outside business organizations. After all, the rich farmers "are a part of the community and therefore *ought* not to be indifferent to the consequences of their acts for their neighbors" (Scott 1987, 161). The stinginess of the rich did not just bring economic loss; it also attacked the social identity of the poor, who vigorously resisted being turned into non-persons. The poor insisted on being accorded the "minimal cultural decencies in this small community" (xviii). The only weapon they controlled in this struggle was their ability, by word and deed, to undercut the prestige and reputation of the rich.

This strategy worked in "Sedaka" because rich local farmers were not ready to abandon the traditional morality that had regulated relations between rich and poor. They had not yet become so Westernized that they no longer cared what other villagers thought of them. A shrewd campaign of character assassination may have caused at least some of the rich to hesitate before

ignoring their traditional obligations. The improvement might have been minor in strictly economic terms, but it would have been major in terms of the ability of the poor to defend their claims to citizenship in the local community. In addition, the wider political arena could always change in the future. Scott was convinced that many of the poor peasants he knew might well engage in open, active rebellion if routine repression disappeared.

When disputes are settled in this manner, experience is transformed. As Scott (1987) observes, "The key symbols animating class relations in "Sedaka"—generosity, stinginess, arrogance, humility, help, assistance, wealth, and poverty—do not constitute a set of given rules or principles that actors simply follow. They are instead the normative raw material that is created, maintained, changed, and above all manipulated by daily human activity" (309). World views articulated in language by different social subgroups aim "not just to convince but to control; better stated, they aim to control by convincing" (23).

The power to invest experience with one's own meanings is very real. Yet, many anthropologists are divided about the effectiveness of resistance as a solution to the problems of those at the very bottom of society. While there is much ethnographic evidence documenting the ability of some individuals and groups to assert themselves and their view of the world in the face of tremendous oppression, there is also much evidence that other individuals and groups have been destroyed by such oppression. Political anthropologist John Gledhill (1994, 198) has observed that it would be "dangerous to be over-optimistic. 'Counter-hegemonic' movements exist, but much of the world's population is not participating in them." He is particularly skeptical about the power of everyday forms of peasant resistance: the ability of such practices to undermine the local elite, he warns, may "merely provide the scenario for the replacement of one elite by another, more effective, dominant group" (92). At the beginning of the twenty-first century, with no utopian solutions in sight, the most that anthropologists may be able to do is agree with historian A.R. Tawney, who wrote about the agrarian disturbances in sixteenth-century England: "Such movements are a proof of blood and sinew and of a high and gallant spirit. . . . Happy the nation whose people has not forgotten how to rebel" (quoted in Wallerstein 1974, 357).

## Anthropology in the Contemporary World

### Human Terrain Teams and Anthropological Ethics

Recently, an ethical dispute has emerged among anthropologists about the Human Terrain System, a United States Army program that hires small teams of civilian anthropologists and other social scientists to become embedded with US combat brigades in Iraq and Afghanistan. These teams are intended to provide relevant sociocultural information about the particular neighbourhoods and village communities in which the US military is operating. Backed by an elaborate 24-hour research centre in the United States, the Human Terrain System attempts to improve relations between US military personnel and Iraqis and Afghans they might encounter, to gather information on development needs, and to generate culturally informed strategic advice. The hope is that providing US military forces with a greater understanding of social and cultural contexts will help reduce misunderstandings and unintentional insults and ultimately help prevent bloodshed. This program was instantly controversial, raising the question, "Is this an appropriate use of anthropological knowledge?"

A number of anthropologists have been concerned that the service of anthropologists in military units, almost like spies, could compromise the integrity of the discipline. Anthropologist Hugh Gusterson was quoted as saying, "The prime directive is you do no harm to informants . . . [but] data collected by [Human Terrain Team] members can also be accessed by military intelligence operatives who might use the same information for targeting Taliban operatives" (Caryl 2009). Indeed, it might be used to target *supposed* Taliban sympathizers. As Gusterson puts it, "The product generated by the Human Terrain Teams is inherently double-edged" (Caryl 2009). The interests of the military units may not be the same as the interests of the embedded anthropologists. How can these anthropologists prevent their research from being used for purposes to which they object? Could working for the military betray informants' trust?

Further, some have argued that the Human Terrain System may undermine anthropological research anywhere, all of which depends on the trust anthropologists develop with the people with whom they work. If some anthropologists are working for a foreign military, how can community members be sure that an anthropologist in their community is not also working for a foreign military?

An American civilian anthropologist talks to Afghan national army soldiers, who were providing security both for the April 2009 elections and for Human Terrain Team interviews with local people.

## Chapter Summary

1. Contemporary cultural anthropologists are interested in how cultures change, but they are suspicious of evolutionary schemes that give the impression that social arrangements could not have been—or could not be—other than the way they are. They also point out that no society anywhere is static. The power that human beings have to reproduce or to change their social organization is an important focus of political anthropology.

2. The ability to act implies power. The study of power in human society is the domain of political anthropology. In most societies at most times, power cannot be reduced to physical force, although this is the Western prototype of power. Power in society operates according to principles that are cultural creations. As such, those principles are affected by history and may differ from one society to another.

3. Western thinkers traditionally assumed that without a state social life would be chaotic, if not impossible. They believed that people were free agents who would not co-operate unless forced to do so. Anthropologists have demonstrated that power is exercised both by coercive and by persuasive means. They have been influenced by the works of Antonio Gramsci and Michel Foucault. Gramsci argued that coercion alone is rarely sufficient for social control, distinguishing coercive domination from hegemony. Rulers always face the risk that those they dominate may create counterhegemonic accounts of their experience of being dominated, acquire a following, and unseat their rulers. Foucault's concept of governmentality addresses practices developed in Western nation-states in the nineteenth century that aimed to create and sustain peaceful and prosperous social life by exercising biopower over persons who could be counted, whose physical attributes could be measured statistically, and whose sexual and reproductive behaviours could be shaped by the exercise of state power.

4. Anthropological research in societies without states has shown how social obligations can restrict individuals from pursuing their own self-interest to the detriment of the group. Individuals cannot be coerced but must be persuaded to co-operate. Individuals use the constraints and opportunities for action open to them, however limited they may be. They are not free agents, but they are empowered to resist conforming to another's wishes.

## For Review

1. Define *power*, and describe the three different kinds of power identified by Eric Wolf. How has each of these kinds of power influenced your life and the society in which you live?

2. Explain how power may be understood as physical force, or coercion. Do you agree that this is the best way to understand power? Why or why not?

3. Compare hegemony and domination. Why is *hegemony* a particularly useful term for anthropologists?

4. How can power influence an individual's or a group's sense of national identity? Why is dominance alone not enough to build a sense of national identity among the citizens of a nation-state? Consider the historical tensions in Sri Lanka as an example.

5. Following Foucault, how does *governing* a state differ from *ruling* a state?

6. Why is self-determination important for Canadian First Nations? Discuss the Canadian government's failures to promote the welfare of Aboriginal Canadians.

7. Summarize how kinship affects politics in northern Thailand. What does this example reveal about the complex relationships among power, politics, and interpersonal relationships?

8. Outline the key points concerning multicultural politics in contemporary Europe, with particular attention to the different ways in which the United Kingdom, France, and Germany deal with immigration. How can ethnographic research illuminate the challenges faced by immigrants in Europe and elsewhere?

9. What are hidden transcripts? Where do they come from and how do they function?

10. What are everyday forms of peasant resistance? How does James Scott connect them with the political relations of dominant and subordinate categories of people in "Sedaka," Malaysia? How effective do they seem to be in the context Scott describes? Do you think similar forms of resistance would have similar outcomes in other places?

11. Should anthropologists work for military organizations? Who "owns" anthropological knowledge? How might being aligned with one "side" affect the work that anthropologists do? What would you do if you were faced with the chance to do anthropological fieldwork in which you were required to collect information on locals and report back to a military organization?

## Key Terms

biopower   331
domination   327
free agency   327

governmentality   331
hegemony   328
ideology   327

political anthropology   325
power   325

## Suggested Readings

Arens, W., and Ivan Karp, eds. 1989. *Creativity of Power: Cosmology and Action in African Societies*. Washington, DC: Smithsonian Institution Press. *A collection of 13 essays exploring the relationship among power, action, and human agency in African social systems and cosmologies.*

Fogelson, Raymond D., and Richard N. Adams, eds. 1977. *The Anthropology of Power: Ethnographic Studies from Asia, Oceania, and the New World*. New York: Academic Press. *A classic collection of 28 ethnographic essays on the varied ways power is understood all over the world.*

Haque, Eva. 2012. *Multiculturalism within a Bilingual Framework: Language, Race, and Belonging in Canada*. Toronto: University of Toronto Press. *This remarkable study casts light on many issues in Canada that arise from the country's competing federal policies of bilingualism and multiculturalism.*

Herzfeld, Michael. 2009. *Evicted from Eternity: The Restructuring of Modern Rome*. Chicago: University of Chicago Press. *An extended study of the politics of the new Europe as experienced in one historic neighbourhood in Rome.*

Keesing, Roger. 1983. *Elota's Story: The Life and Times of a Solomon Islands Big Man*. New York: Holt, Rinehart, and Winston. *A fascinating autobiography of a Kwaio "Big Man" (i.e., community leader), with interpretive material by Keesing, that surveys political and kin relations as well as a variety of other aspects of Kwaio culture.*

Lewellen, Ted C. 2003. *Political Anthropology: An Introduction*. 3rd ed. New York: Praeger. *A standard introductory text in political anthropology, covering leading theories, scholars, and problems in the field.*

Vincent, Joan, ed. 2002. *The Anthropology of Politics: A Reader in Ethnography, Theory, and Critique*. New York: Wiley-Blackwell. *An excellent collection of works that illustrate the development of political anthropology over time and showcase important achievements by influential political anthropologists today.*

# 13 Where Do Our Relatives Come From and Why Do They Matter?

▲ Indigenous Canadian grandmothers, mothers, and daughters, North Vancouver, British Columbia, Canada. Photo courtesy of Red Works Photography, www.redworks.ca.

## Chapter Outline

One of the major ways in which people sustain their connections to each other is by asserting that they are in some way related. In this chapter, we will look at some important social rules and patterns that result from different ways of understanding human relatedness. In particular, we will explore varying views on such related topics as kinship, adoption, marriage, where to live after marriage, family, and sexuality.

Human life is group life. How we choose to organize ourselves is open to creative variation, as we have seen. But each of us was born into a society whose political, economic, and cultural practices were already well established when we arrived. These traditional practices make some kinds of social connections more likely than other kinds. As a result, much can be predicted about a child's probable path in life just by knowing the kind of social groups into which he or she is born. This chapter focuses on how such human experiences as sexuality, conception, birth, and nurturance are selectively interpreted and shaped into shared cultural practices that anthropologists call relatedness. Relatedness takes many forms—friendship, marriage, parenthood, shared links to a common ancestor, workplace associations, and so on. And these intimate everyday relationships are always embedded in, and shaped by, broader structures of power, wealth, and meaning.

For more than a century, anthropologists have studied those forms of relatedness believed to come from shared substance and its transmission (Holy 1996, 171). The substance believed to be shared may be a bodily one (blood, genes, or mother's milk, for example) or a spiritual one (soul, spirit, nurturance, or love, for example); sometimes more than one substance is thought to be shared. Systems of relatedness based on ideas of shared substance are called kinship systems. In the West as well as in many other parts of the world, people are thought to share a common substance because it was transmitted to them via the act of sexual intercourse between their parents that led to their conception and birth. Such ideas were close enough to Western beliefs for many anthropologists to conclude that all people everywhere based their kinship systems on the biology of reproduction. It was but a short step to conclude that Western beliefs about which people counted as one's "real" relatives were universally valid. In the early days, kinship studies in anthropology were based on the assumption that all societies recognized the same basic genealogical relationships between mothers and fathers, children and parents, sisters and brothers, and so on. But over the years, ethnographic evidence accumulated indicating that quite often people's understanding of kin ties was strikingly at odds with these genealogical relationships. In other cases, these genealogical relationships turned out to form but a small subset of the ways in which people created enduring connections with one another.

## What Is Kinship?

Anthropologists call culturally recognized relationships based on mating *marriage* and those based on birth *descent*. Although nurturance is ordinarily seen to be closely connected with mating and birth, it need not be, and all societies have ways of acknowledging a relationship based on nurturance alone, which is called "adoption" in English. Although marriage is based on mating, descent on birth, and adoption on nurturance, marriage is not the same thing as mating, descent is not the same thing as birth, and adoption is not the same thing as nurturance. This is because the human experiences of mating, birth, and nurturance are ambiguous. Systems of relatedness in different societies highlight some features of these experiences while

relatedness  The socially recognized ties that connect people in a variety of different ways.

kinship systems  Social relationships that are prototypically derived from the universal human experiences of mating, birth, and nurturance.

marriage  An institution that transforms the status of the participants, carries implications about permitted sexual access, perpetuates social patterns through the production or adoption of offspring, creates relationships between the kin of partners, and is symbolically marked.

descent  The principle based on culturally recognized parent–child connections that define the social categories to which people belong.

adoption  Kinship relationships based on nurturance, often in the absence of other connections based on mating or birth.

downplaying or even ignoring others. Europeans and North Americans know that in their societies mating is not the same as marriage, although a culturally valid marriage encourages mating between the married partners. Similarly, all births do not constitute valid links of descent: children whose parents have not been married according to accepted legal or religious specifications do not fit the cultural logic of descent, and many societies offer no positions that they can properly fill. Finally, not all acts of nurturance are recognized as adoption: consider, for example, foster parents in Canada, whose custody of foster children is officially temporary. Put another way, through culturally created ties of kinship, a society emphasizes certain aspects of human experience, constructs its own theory of human nature, and specifies "the processes by which an individual comes into being and develops into a complete (i.e., mature) social person" (Kelly 1993, 521).

Marriage, descent, and adoption are selective institutions. One society may emphasize women as the bearers of children and base its kinship system on this fact, paying little formal attention to the male's role in conception. Another society may trace connections through men, emphasizing the paternal role in conception and reducing the maternal role. A third society may encourage its members to adopt not only children but also adult siblings, blurring the link between biological reproduction and family creation. Even though they contradict one another, all three understandings can be justified with reference to the panhuman experiences of mating, birth, and nurturance.

## How Do We Define *Sex, Gender,* and *Kinship*?

Kinship is based on, but is not reducible to, biology. It is a cultural interpretation of the culturally recognized "facts" of human reproduction, and how one defines one's relatives changes with each culture. This is another example of how humans are biocultural organisms. One of the most basic of these "facts," recognized in some form in all societies, is that two different kinds of human beings must co-operate sexually to produce offspring (although what they believe to be the contribution of each party to the outcome varies from society to society). Anthropologists use the term *sex* to refer to the observable physical characteristics that distinguish the two kinds of human beings, females and males, needed for reproduction. People everywhere pay attention to *morphological sex* (the appearance of external genitalia and observable secondary sex characteristics, such as enlarged breasts in females). Scientists further distinguish females from males on the basis of *gonadal sex* (the presence of ovaries in females, testes in males) and *chromosomal sex* (two X chromosomes in females, one X and one Y chromosome in males).

At the same time, cross-cultural research repeatedly demonstrates that physical sex differences do not allow us to predict the roles that females or males will play in any particular society (Figure 13.1). Consequently, anthropologists distinguish sex from gender—the cultural construction of beliefs and behaviours considered appropriate for each sex. As Barbara Miller (1993, 5) puts it,

**FIGURE 13.1 |** Cross-cultural research repeatedly demonstrates that physical indicators of sex difference do not allow us to predict the roles that females or males will play in any particular society. In Otavalo, Ecuador, men were traditionally weavers (*a*). Indigenous Mayan culture has a strong tradition of female weavers—among the Tzotzil Maya, weaving is viewed as part of the essence of being a woman (*b*).

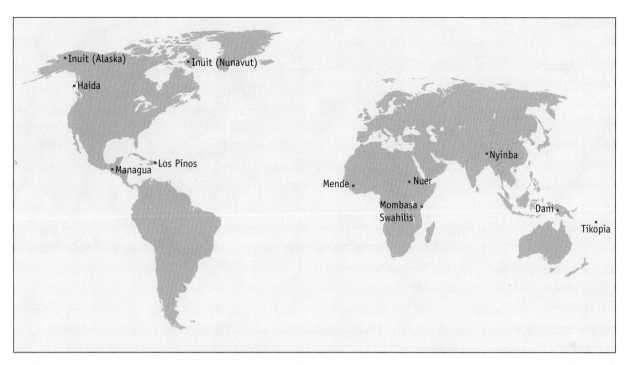

**MAP 13.1** | Location of societies whose EthnoProfiles appear in Chapter 13.

In some societies, people with XX chromosomes do the cooking, in others it is the XY people who cook, in others both XX and XY people cook. The same goes for sewing, transplanting rice seedlings, worshipping deities, and speaking in public. Even the exclusion of women from hunting and warfare has been reduced by recent studies from the level of a universal to a generality. While it is generally true that men hunt and women do not, and that men fight in wars and women do not, important counter cases exist.

> ↻ For a discussion of gender as a social category of inequality, see Chapter 14, pp. 396–7.

In fact, the outward physical features used to distinguish females from males may not be obvious either. Sometimes genetic or hormonal factors produce ambiguous external genitalia. In other cases, anthropologists have documented the existence of *supernumerary* (i.e., more than the standard two) sexes in cultures where the presence of ambiguous genitalia at birth seems to play no obvious role. In the Byzantine civilization of late antiquity, observable phenotypic differences were deliberately created in the case of eunuchs, whose testicles were removed or destroyed, often before puberty (Ringrose 1994). In the case of the *hijras* of Gujarat, India, adult males deliberately cut off both penis and

testicles in order to dedicate themselves to the mother goddess Bahuchara Mata (Nanda 1994). In both these cases, third gender roles distinct from traditional feminine and masculine gender roles are believed appropriate for third-sexed individuals.

Elsewhere, supernumerary gender roles developed that apparently had nothing to do with morphological sex anomalies. Perhaps the most famous case is that of the so-called *berdache* of North America, who are now often referred to as *two-spirited*. Will Roscoe (1994, 332) points out that "the key features of male and female berdache roles were, in order of importance, *productive specialization* (crafts and domestic work for male berdaches and warfare, hunting, and leadership roles in the case of female berdaches), *supernatural sanction* (in the form of an authorization and/or bestowal of powers from extrasocietal sources), and *gender variation* (in relation to normative cultural expectations for male and female genders)," commonly but not always marked by cross-dressing. Some berdaches may have engaged in sexual practices that most Westerners would interpret as "homosexual" or "bisexual." Berdaches were accepted and respected members of their communities, and their economic and religious pursuits seem to have been culturally more significant than their sexual practices.

The term *berdache* was a derogatory term used by the early French colonizers, which apparently meant "male prostitute." For this reason, many anthropologists and

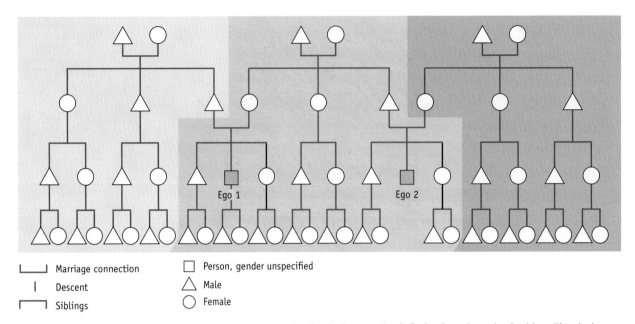

Marriage connection

| Descent

⌐ ⌐ Siblings

☐ Person, gender unspecified

△ Male

○ Female

**FIGURE 13.2 |** A bilateral kindred includes all recognized relatives on Ego's father's and mother's sides. The dark area in the centre indicates where the kindreds of Ego 1 and Ego 2 overlap. Note that anthropologists often use kinship diagrams such as this one to visually represent who is related to whom in any given society. In many ways, these diagrams are like family trees, but they are constructed with conventional symbols and lines, and the individual around whom the diagram is centred is labelled as "Ego".

First Nations peoples reject the term. However, many contemporary Indigenous societies want to reclaim this alternative gender role for themselves. Although no single term has yet reached universal acceptance, members of First Nations groups in Canada have begun to use the term *two-spirited*. Perhaps no single term is adequate; after all, male berdaches have been described in almost 150 Indigenous North American societies and female berdaches in perhaps half that number.

Gilbert Herdt's (1994) survey of ethnographic literature led him to conclude that it is difficult for societies to maintain more than two sexes or genders. Still, anthropologists can argue convincingly that a society possesses supernumerary sexes or genders when a culture defines for each "a symbolic niche and a social pathway of development into later adult life distinctly different from the cultural life plan set out by a model based on male/female duality" (1994, 68).

**bilateral descent** The principle that a descent group is formed by people who believe they are related to each other by connections made through their mothers *and* their fathers equally (sometimes called *cognatic descent*).

**unilineal descent** The principle that a descent group is formed by people who believe they are related to each other by connections made through *either* their mothers *or* their fathers.

# What Is the Role of Descent in Kinship?

In many societies, kinship practices, rather than written statutes, clarify for people what rights and obligations they owe one another. A central aspect of kinship is descent—the cultural principle that defines social categories through culturally recognized parent–child connections. Descent groups are defined by ancestry and consequently exist in time. Descent groups use parent–child links to transmit group identity and to incorporate new members. In some societies, descent group membership controls how people mobilize for social or political action.

Two major strategies are employed in establishing patterns of descent: bilateral descent and unilineal descent. In the first strategy, bilateral descent, the descent group is formed by people who believe they are just as closely related to their father's side of the family as to their mother's. The most common kind of bilateral descent group identified by anthropologists is called a *bilateral kindred*. This group includes all the people linked to an individual (or a group of siblings) through kin of both sexes on the mother's and the father's sides of the family—people conventionally called "relatives" in English (Figure 13.2). The bilateral

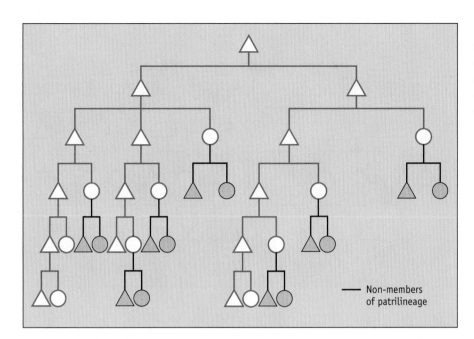

**FIGURE 13.3** | Patrilineal descent; all those who trace descent through males to a common male ancestor are indicated in white.

— Non-members of patrilineage

kindred is the kinship group that most Europeans and North Americans follow. In North American society, bilateral kindreds typically assemble when an individual undergoes a religious rite of passage (e.g., is baptized, is confirmed, or becomes a bar or bat mitzvah); when an individual graduates from high school, college, or university; or when an individual is married or buried. Bilateral kindreds centre on an individual (referred to as "Ego" in the terminology of kinship studies), and each member of that individual's bilateral kindred also has his or her own separate kindred.

Bilateral kindreds can be extended indefinitely to form broad overlapping networks of people who are somehow related to one another. Such flexible group boundaries offer advantages in an individualistic, capitalist society like that of Canada. However, flexible group boundaries can become a liability when social action requires the formation of groups with clear-cut memberships that are larger than individual families. This can happen, for example, when conflicting claims to land and labour must be resolved and groups seek to perpetuate limitations on membership over time. In societies that face such challenges, unilineal descent groups are usually formed.

## What Roles Do Lineages Play in Descent?

Unilineal descent is based on the assumption that a person's most significant kin relationships are aligned through one's mother or through one's father. **Lineages**

are unilineal descent groups whose members believe they can specify all the parent–child links that unite them. Lineages that are made up of links traced through a father are called *patrilineal*; those traced through a mother are called *matrilineal*. In a patrilineal society, women and men belong to a **patrilineage** formed by father–child links (Figure 13.3); similarly, in a matrilineal society, men and women belong to a **matrilineage** formed by mother–child connections (Figure 13.4). Lineages in some societies may have from 20 or 30 members to several hundred. Before 1949, some Chinese lineages contained more than 1000 members.

### Who Is a Member of a Lineage?

The most important feature of lineages is that they are *corporate* in organization—that is, a lineage has a single legal entity. The Ashanti, for example, think of a lineage as "one person," since (from the point of view of outsiders) all members of a lineage are equal *in law* to all others (Fortes 1953). For example, in the case of a blood feud, the death of any opposing lineage member

**lineages**  The consanguineal members of descent groups who believe they can trace their descent from known ancestors.

**patrilineage**  A social group formed by people connected by father–child links.

**matrilineage**  A social group formed by people connected by mother–child links.

**FIGURE 13.4** | Matrilineal descent; all those who trace descent through females to a common female ancestor are indicated in white.

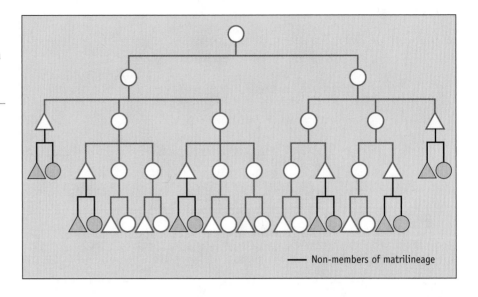

—— Non-members of matrilineage

avenges the death of the person whose death triggered the feud. Lineages are also corporate in that they control property, specifically land, as a unit. Such groups are found only in societies where rights to use land are crucial and must be monitored over time. Lineages are also the main political associations in the societies that have them; people living in such societies recognize that their individual political or legal status comes mainly through the lineage to which they belong.

In societies where lineages are found, the system of lineages can serve as a foundation for all social life. Lineage membership is transmitted in a direct line from father or mother to child. This means that in societies in which no other form of organization lasts, lineages can endure as long as people can remember from whom they are descended. Most lineages have a time depth of about five generations: grandparents, parents, Ego, children, and grandchildren. When members of a group believe that they can no longer accurately specify the genealogical links that connect them but believe that they are "in some way" connected, they form what anthropologists refer to as a "clan." A **clan** is usually made up of lineages that the society's members believe to be related to each other through links that go back into mythic times. Sometimes the common ancestor of each clan is said to be an animal that lived at the beginning of time. The distinguishing point is that lineage members can specify all the generational links back to

their common ancestor, whereas clan members ordinarily cannot. Thus a clan can be larger than any lineage and more diffuse in its membership.

## What Are Patrilineages?

The most common form of lineage organization is the patrilineage, which consists of all the people (male and female) who believe themselves to be related to each other because they are related to a common male ancestor by connections through men. The prototypical kernel of a patrilineage is the father–son pair. Although female members of patrilineages normally leave the lineages when they marry, they do not relinquish their interest in their own lineages. Indeed, in a number of societies, they play an active role in the affairs of their own patrilineages for many years.

A classic patrilineal system was found among the Nuer of Ethiopia and what is now South Sudan (see EthnoProfile 13.1: Nuer). At the time of his fieldwork in the 1930s, English anthropologist E.E. Evans-Pritchard (1940) noted that the Nuer were divided into at least twenty clans. EvansPritchard defined *clan* as the largest group of people who (1) trace their descent patrilineally from a common ancestor, (2) cannot marry each other, and (3) consider sexual relations within the group to be incestuous. The clan is subdivided, or segmented, into smaller lineages that are themselves linked to each other by presumed ties of patrilineal descent. The most basic level of lineage segmentation is the minimal lineage, which has a time depth of three to five generations (Figure 13.5).

**clan**   A descent group formed by members who believe they have a common (sometimes mythical) ancestor, even if they cannot specify the genealogical links.

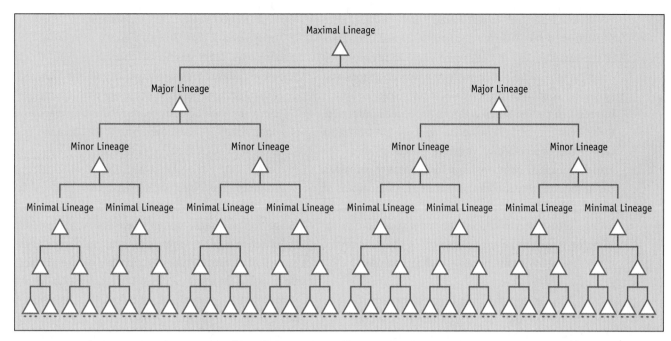

**FIGURE 13.5** | From a founder recognized by all descendants, lineages develop through *segmentation* across generations. The complexity of this segmentation is determined by the number and gender of the members of each generation.

Evans-Pritchard (1940) observed that the Nuer kinship system worked as a set of nested lineages: members of lineages A and B might consider themselves related because they believed that the founder of lineage A had been the older brother of the founder of lineage B. These two *minimal lineages*, as Evans-Pritchard called them, together formed a *minor lineage*—all those descended from a common father, believed to be the father of the two founders of A and B. Minor lineages connect to other minor lineages by yet another presumed common ancestor one more level back, forming *major lineages*. These major lineages are also believed to share a common ancestor and thus form a *maximal lineage*. The members of two maximal lineages believe their founders had been the sons of the clan ancestor; thus, all members of the clan are believed to be patrilineally related.

According to Evans-Pritchard (1940), disputes among the Nuer emerged along the lines created by lineages. Suppose a quarrel erupted between two men whose minimal lineages were in different minor lineages. Each man could recruit allies both from his own minimal lineage and from all the other minimal lineages that belonged in his major lineage. When members of the quarreling minor lineages acknowledged (or were made to acknowledge by a mediator) that they were all part of the same major lineage, the dispute would be resolved. Similarly, the minor lineages belonging to one major lineage would ally if a dispute broke out that involved members of another, opposed major lineage. This process of nested groups moving apart or coming together in order to oppose one another at different levels of a hierarchy is called segmentary opposition, and it is a very common social process.

**EthnoProfile 13.1**

## Nuer

**Region:** Eastern Africa

**Nation:** Ethiopia and South Sudan

**Population:** 300,000

**Environment:** Open grassland

**Livelihood:** Cattle herding and farming

**Political organization:** Traditionally, egalitarian tribes, no political offices; today, part of modern nation-states

**For more information:** Evans-Pritchard, E.E. 1940. *The Nuer.* Oxford: Oxford University Press; and Hutchinson, Sharon. 1996. *Nuer Dilemmas.* Berkeley: University of California Press.

**segmentary opposition** A mode of hierarchical social organization in which groups beyond the most basic emerge only in opposition to other groups on the same hierarchical level.

Evans-Pritchard (1940) noted that lineages were important to the Nuer for political purposes. Members of the same lineage in the same village were conscious of being in a social group with common ancestors and symbols, corporate rights in territory, and common interests in cattle. When a son in the lineage married, these lineage members helped provide the bridewealth cattle, the symbolically valuable goods paid to the bride's lineage in compensation for the loss of her services. If the son were killed, they—indeed, all members of his patrilineage, regardless of where they lived—would avenge him and would hold the funeral ceremony for him. Nevertheless, relationships among the members of a patrilineage were not necessarily harmonious:

> A Nuer is bound through balanced reciprocal exchange to his paternal kin from whom he derives aid, security, and status, but in return for these benefits he has many obligations and commitments. Their often indefinite character may be both evidence of, and a reason for, their force, but it also gives ample scope for disagreement. Duties

bridewealth  The transfer of certain symbolically important goods from the family of the groom to the family of the bride on the occasion of their marriage. It represents compensation to the wife's lineage for the loss of her labour and childbearing capacities.

and rights easily conflict. Moreover, the privileges of [patrilineal] kinship cannot be divorced from authority, discipline, and a strong sense of moral obligation, all of which are irksome to Nuer. They do not deny them, but they kick against them when their personal interests run counter to them. (Evans-Pritchard 1951, 162)

Although the Nuer were patrilineal, they recognized as kin people who were not members of their lineage. In the Nuer language, the word *mar* referred to "kin": all the people to whom a person could trace a relationship of any kind, including people on the mother's side as well as on the father's side. In fact, at such important ceremonial occasions as a bridewealth distribution after a woman in the lineage had been married, special attention was paid to kin on the mother's side. Certain important relatives, such as the mother's brother and the mother's sister, were given cattle. A man's mother's brother was his great supporter when he was in trouble. The mother's brother was kind to him as a boy and even provided a second home after he reached manhood. If he liked his sister's son, a mother's brother would even be willing to help pay the bridewealth so that he could marry. "Nuer say of the maternal uncle that he is both father and mother, but most frequently that 'he is your mother'" (Evans-Pritchard 1951, 162).

## In Their Own Words

### Outside Work, Women, and Bridewealth

*Judith M. Abwunza interviewed many women among the Logoli of western Kenya about their lives, and she allowed many of those women to speak for themselves in her 1997 book,* Women's Voices, Women's Power: Dialogues of Resistance from East Africa. *Here, Abwunza introduces us to Alice, a 24-year-old secondary school teacher.*

Alice's father is relatively affluent, as all his children are in school or working, his land is well-kept and fully utilized, and the yard has cows, chickens, and goats. Alice's motivation to get a job was that she wanted to assist her family. She said that everyone in the family depends upon her for money, a burden that she finds to be "overwhelming." Alice has been living with her husband, who is also a teacher, since January 1987. They have seven-month-old twins, a

boy and a girl. Uvukwi [bridewealth] discussion has taken place and her in-laws and her relatives have agreed on 23,000 shillings and five cows. A 3000 shilling "down payment" has been given, and her marriage occurred in January 1988. Alice discusses her situation in English:

> We live in a house supplied by the school. We have electricity and water and a gas cooker. We

have a small house plot in my husband's yard at Bunyore, and six acres in the scheme in Kitale. We hire people to dig there, as we are teaching. So far, we have not sold cash crops. We are only beginning. On the schemes, workers are paid between five and six hundred shillings a month to dig, so it is expensive. There is no need of paying uvukwi. Am I a farm to be bought? It is unfortunate the parents are poor. Parents ought to contribute to the newly married to start them off. But there is nothing we can do; it's a custom. Also uvukwi is not the end of assistance to parents. Some men mistreat after buying, that is paying uvukwi. Some men refuse to help parents any more after uvukwi, think that's enough. On the other hand, if you don't pay uvukwi, the husbands think you are not valued by parents. You are cheap. It's a tug of war.

People who get jobs in Kenya have been to school, these are the elite. They are able to integrate various situations. They are analytical and choosing courses of action. They have developed decision-making skills; this gives access to wage labour. Most women are not this; many men are not. Things have changed for women, but still it is very difficult; they must work very hard. In the old days, customs did not allow men in the kitchen; now they do. It's absurd to see milk boiling over in the kitchen while I'm taking care of the baby and he is reading. A more even distribution of labour is needed. Women need a word of appreciation for their hard work, in the home and caring for children. Here in Maragoli we cannot develop: the population is too high. The government is suggesting that maternity leave will not be given after the fourth child. This is a good thing but it has not been passed yet. I will not be abused in my marriage. I will leave. My job is difficult. Children are beaten, sent from school for fees, for harambee this, harambee that. Seldom do I have my entire class to teach. Some are always missing. I have had to chase them for fees. This is not my role; my job is to teach them, so they may better their lives. I refuse to beat them. I try not to upset them. I want them to learn. But many do not want to. Girls only want to chase boys, and boys the girls. But a few learn. Teaching is difficult.

Alice takes a different position from most Logoli women. She complains of having to follow traditional ways in these difficult economic times, even as she adheres to them. Although many people complained about the "high cost" of uvukwi, on no other occasion did women suggest that parents should assist a newly married couple and not follow the custom of uvukwi. Alice's feeling is not typical of Logoli people. It comes about at least in part because Alice's uvukwi is quite high and both she and her husband will have to contribute to its payment, as she says, "at the expense of our own development." She sees that she is caught in a bind. Not following the traditions will place her in a position of being without a good reputation and thus at risk in the community.

Source: Abwunza 1997, 77–8.

## What Are Matrilineages?

In matrilineages, descent is traced through women rather than through men. Recall that in a patrilineage, a woman's children are not in her lineage. In a matrilineage, a man's children are not in his.

Certain features of matrilineages make them more than just mirror images of patrilineages. First, the prototypical kernel of a matrilineage is the sister–brother pair; a matrilineage may be thought of as a group of brothers and sisters connected through links made by women. Brothers marry out and often live with the family of their wives, but they maintain an active interest in the affairs of their lineage. Second, the most important man in a boy's life is not his father (who is not in his lineage) but his mother's brother, from whom he will receive his lineage inheritance. Third, the amount of power women exercise in matrilineal societies is still hotly debated in anthropology. A matrilineage is not the same thing as a *matriarchy* (a society in which women rule); brothers often retain what appears to be a controlling interest in the lineage. Some anthropologists claim that the male members of a matrilineage run the lineage even though there is more autonomy for women in matrilineal societies than in patrilineal ones—that the day-to-day exercise of power tends to be carried out by the brothers or sometimes the husbands. A number of studies, however, have questioned the validity of these generalizations. Saying anything about matrilineal societies in general is difficult. The ethnographic evidence suggests that matrilineages must be examined on a case-by-case basis.

The Haida of Canada's northwest coast are a matrilineal people (see EthnoProfile 13.2: Haida), with each matrilineage belonging to either the Raven or the Eagle *k'waalaa* (clan). Strong feelings of reciprocity and social responsibility exist between the Ravens and the Eagles, and membership in a particular matrilineage and its *k'waalaa* shapes individuals' identities as well as social relationships (Krmpotich 2010). The Haida use matrilineal identity to navigate such matters as their participation in potlatches, their use of property, whom they should marry, their social status, and whom they can ask for economic support. As all things in Haida society are either owned by or a part of either the Raven or the Eagle *k'waalaa*, belonging to a matrilineage is both humbling and empowering.

A Haida matrilineage can be thought of as a broad network of families linked through ancestry, property, and common social responsibilities. The most closely related members of a matrilineage tend to share the strongest bonds, which are based on love, friendship, history, obligations, shared work, and commitment. Indeed, matrilineal kin form the basis of each person's sense of family, and they play integral roles in major life events—for example, by leading rites of passage; by preparing feasts, potlatches, weddings, and other celebrations; and by mourning the deceased (Krmpotich 2010, 162). At the same time, individuals are generally encouraged to marry outside of their *k'waalaa*, a practice that facilitates non-matrilineal kinship bonds (e.g., between children and fathers).

Haida often wear crests to represent the matrilineage to which they belong. The designs of these crests are owned and inherited by members of the *k'waalaa* to which they correspond, and they can be painted or embroidered onto garments and even tattooed onto a person (Figure 13.6). These material expressions perpetuate a sense of belonging and continuity of family and lineages. A significant factor in Haida kinship is the relationships between the living and the dead. Ancestors are often considered as guides for the living, providing opportunities and companionship.

**EthnoProfile 13.2**

## Haida

**Region:** Northwest coast of North America

**Nation:** Canada

**Population:** 60,000

**Environment:** Maritime, cool

**Livelihood:** Fishing, whaling, collecting plants

**Political organization:** Traditionally, clans, public consensus; today, a tribal council within a modern nation-state

**For more information:** Boelscher, Marianne. 1988. *The Curtain within: Haida Social and Political Discourse.* Vancouver: University of British Columbia Press.

**FIGURE 13.6** | Haida wear crests to physically represent the matrilineages to which they belong. Here, Haida elders wear full ceremonial regalia at the dedication ceremony for a new canoe on Graham Island, part of the Queen Charlotte Islands in British Columbia.

The recently deceased often accompany a relative for days or months after their death. Thus kinship relationships are not only part of the living world; they transcend into the past, solidifying the matrilineal ties among the Haida (Krmpotich 2010, 163).

## What Are Kinship Terminologies?

People everywhere use special terms to refer to people they recognize as related to them. Kinship terminologies suggest both the external boundaries and the internal divisions of kinship groups, and they outline the structure of rights and obligations assigned to different members of the society. They also provide clues about how the vast and undifferentiated world of potential relations may be divided.

### What Criteria Are Used for Making Kinship Distinctions?

Anthropologists have identified several criteria that people use to indicate how people are related to one another. From the most common to the least common, these criteria include the following:

- *Generation.* Kin terms distinguish relatives according to the generation to which the relatives belong. In English, the term *cousin* conventionally refers to a non-sibling relative of the same generation as Ego.
- *Gender.* The gender of an individual is used to differentiate kin. In Spanish, *primo* refers to a male cousin and *prima* to a female cousin. In English, cousins are not distinguished on the basis of gender, but *uncle* and *aunt* are distinguished on the basis of both generation and gender.
- *Affinity.* A distinction is made on the basis of connection through marriage, or affinity. This criterion is used in Spanish when *suegra* (Ego's spouse's mother) is distinguished from *madre* (Ego's mother). In matrilineal societies, Ego's mother's sister and Ego's father's sister are distinguished from one another on the basis of affinity. The mother's sister is a direct, lineal relative; the father's sister is an affine; and they are called by different terms.
- *Collaterality.* A distinction is made between kin who are believed to be in a direct line and those who are "off to one side," linked to Ego through a lineal relative. In English, the distinction of collaterality is exemplified by the distinction between *mother* and *aunt* or *father* and *uncle*.
- *Bifurcation.* The distinction of bifurcation is employed when kinship terms referring to the mother's side of the family differ from those referring to the father's side.
- *Relative age.* Relatives of the same category may be distinguished on the basis of whether they are older or younger than Ego. Among the Ju/'hoansi, for example, speakers must separate "older brother" (*!ko*) from "younger brother" (*tsin*).
- *Gender of linking relative.* This criterion is related to collaterality. It distinguishes *cross relatives* (usually cousins) from *parallel relatives* (also usually cousins). Parallel relatives are linked through two brothers or two sisters. Parallel cousins, for example, are Ego's father's brother's children or Ego's mother's sister's children. Cross relatives are linked through a brother-sister pair. Thus, cross cousins are Ego's mother's brother's children or Ego's father's sister's children. The gender of either Ego or the cousins does not matter; rather, the important factor is the gender of the linking relative (Figure 13.7).

By the early 1950s, kinship specialists in anthropology had identified six major patterns of kinship terminology, based on how cousins were classified. In recent years, however, anthropologists have become quite skeptical of the value of these idealized models, in large measure because they are highly formalized, neglect all kin categories except cousins, and fail to consider the full range of people's actual kinship practices. Perhaps the main value to come from formal kinship studies is

**affinity** Connection through marriage.

**collaterality** A criterion employed in the analysis of kinship terminologies in which a distinction is made between kin who are believed to be in a direct line and those who are "off to one side," linked to the speaker by a lineal relative.

**bifurcation** A criterion employed in the analysis of kinship terminologies in which kinship terms referring to the mother's side of the family are distinguished from those referring to the father's side.

**parallel cousins** The children of a person's parents' same-gender siblings (a father's brother's children or a mother's sister's children).

**cross cousins** The children of a person's parents' opposite-gender siblings (a father's sister's children or a mother's brother's children).

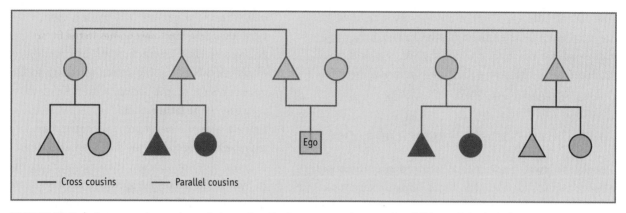

**FIGURE 13.7** | Cross cousins and parallel cousins. Ego's cross cousins are the children of Ego's father's sister and Ego's mother's brother. Ego's parallel cousins are the children of Ego's father's brother and Ego's mother's sister.

the fact that they took seriously the ways other people classified their relatives and were able to display the logic that informed such classifications.

## What Is Adoption?

Kinship systems sometimes appear to be fairly rigid sets of rules that use the accident of birth to thrust people into social positions laden with rights and obligations they cannot escape. Social positions that people are assigned at birth are sometimes called ascribed statuses, and positions within a kinship system have long been viewed as the prototypical ascribed statuses in any society. Ascribed statuses are often contrasted with achieved statuses, those social positions that people may attain later in life, often as the result of their own (or other people's) effort, such as becoming a spouse or college graduate. All societies have ways of incorporating outsiders into their kinship groups, however, which they achieve by converting supposedly ascribed kinship statuses into achieved ones, thus undermining the distinction between them. We will use the term *adoption* to refer to these practices that allow people to transform relationships based on nurturance into relations of kinship.

### Adoption and Naming among the Inuit of Nunavut

In some societies, like that of ancient Rome, people distinguish between Ego's biological father (or *genitor*)

**ascribed statuses** Social positions people are assigned at birth.

**achieved statuses** Social positions people may attain later in life, often as the result of their own (or other people's) effort.

**EthnoProfile 13.3**

## Inuit (Nunavut)

**Region:** North American Arctic

**Nation:** Canada

**Population:** 100,000

**Environment:** Arctic archipelago, tundra, shrub tundra

**Livelihood:** Hunting, fishing

**Political organization:** Traditionally, band societies; today, self-governing as part of a modern nation-state

**For more information:** McElroy, Ann. 2008. *Nunavut Generations: Change and Continuity in Canadian Inuit Communities.* Long Grove, IL: Waveland Press.

and Ego's social father (or *pater*); they may also distinguish between Ego's biological mother (or *genetrix*) and Ego's social mother (or *mater*). Social parents are those who nurture a child, and they are often the child's biological parents as well. Among the Inuit of Nunavut, these distinguishing factors are not strongly acknowledged (see EthnoProfile 13.3). Rather, the Inuit view of extended family encompasses the concept of "custom adoption"—a traditional form of adoption in which the adoptee maintains flexible relationships with her or his birth and adoptive families. As Valerie Alia (2007, 35) has observed, in Nunavut communities, "children move daily among the homes of birth and adoptive parents . . .

**FIGURE 13.8** | An Inuit mother carries her daughter in her *amauti* on Baffin Island, Nunavut.

receiving care, food, and companionship." Alia further notes that this form of adoption is generally considered to be "more welcoming and less stigmatized than adoption among *Qallunaat* [i.e., southerners]" (36). According to Alia's informants, "adoptions are a part of everyday life," and "giving a child for adoption is a way of making sure every *amauti* (or *amautik*) (the baby-carrying hood on a woman's parka, or *amautik*) carries a child" (36) (Figure 13.8). This practice of adoption encourages the formation of families, which contributes to a strong sense of community and provides families with many hands to help with hunting, fishing, preparing food, maintaining homes, and other sustenance tasks. Moreover, as Alia notes, "[w]hen communities are small and communication is open, adopted children grow up well nurtured and loved" (36).

To understand the cultural significance of custom adoption, it is important to understand the Inuit tradition of naming. According to the highly intricate *sauniq* naming system, Inuit parents and other relatives (usually women, sometimes men) assign the adoptee the name of a deceased relative. This act not only commemorates the deceased but also forms a vital, symbolic connection between the adoptee and her or his namesake, allowing the namesake to "live on" in the community. To the Inuit, the giving of a *sauniq* name is an act of extreme importance. As Alia (2007, 37) notes, "naming is a—perhaps *the*—central component of Inuit culture. It is often viewed literally as reincarnation—the embodiment of continuity from person to person and generation to generation." Guemple (1979, 51) offers additional insight into the connections between naming and relatedness:

In Inuit society, children are not thought to be extensions of and therefore in some sense

"owned" by their parents . . . [T]heir identity is . . . introduced into their bodies in the form of a name spirit . . . The bond between parents and child is the bond of "love" and the only persons whose personal sense of self-worth is affected by the actions of the child are his [or her] ritual relatives, most importantly his [or her] namesakes. (qtd in Alia 2007, 36)

## How Are New Reproductive Technologies Changing Western Concepts of Kinship?

The development and increasing use of relatively new reproductive technologies such as in vitro fertilization (IVF) has created challenges for Western concepts of kinship (Figure 13.9). Marilyn Strathern (1992) observes that in the Western world, kinship is usually understood as the social construction of natural facts, a logic that both combines and separates the social and natural worlds. That is, Europeans and North Americans typically recognize kin related by blood and kin related by marriage, but they also believe that procreation—the process that brings kin into existence—is part of nature. "The rooting of social relations in natural facts traditionally served to impart a certain quality to one significant dimension of kin relations . . . these relations were at base non-negotiable" (Strathern 1992, 28). Yet, the new reproductive technologies make clear that everything is

**FIGURE 13.9** | Zain Rajani, pictured here with his parents in Toronto, Ontario, in May 2015, was the first baby born using a new method of IVF that focuses on improving the health of a woman's eggs. In recent decades, treatments such as IVF have altered many peoples' perceptions of what it means to be a "natural" parent.

negotiable: even the world of natural facts is subject to social intervention.

Ambiguities surrounding kinship in Canada and elsewhere have put pressure on courts to decide what constitutes biological parenthood and how it is related to legal parenthood. Janet Dolgin (1995) has examined two sets of court cases arising in the United States, the first involving the paternal rights of unwed supposed fathers and the second focusing on the rights of parties involved in surrogate motherhood agreements. In two cases involving supposed unwed fathers, courts reasoned that biological maternity automatically made a woman a social mother, but biological paternity did not automatically make a man a social father. Because the men in these two cases had failed to participate in rearing their children, their paternity rights were not recognized. In another case, the biological father had lived with his child and her mother for extended periods during the child's early years and had actively participated in her upbringing. However, the child's mother had been married to another man during this period, and the law proclaimed her legal husband to be the child's father. Although the genitor had established a supportive relationship with his daughter, the court labelled him "the adulterous natural father," arguing, in effect, that a genitor can never be a pater unless he is involved in an ongoing relationship with the child's mother, something that was impossible because she was already married to someone else.

The surrogacy cases demonstrate directly the complications that can result from new reproductive technologies. The "Baby M" situation was a traditional surrogacy arrangement in which the surrogate, Mary Beth Whitehead, was impregnated with the sperm of the husband in the couple who intended to become the legal parents of the child she bore. Whitehead was supposed to terminate all parental rights when the child was born, but she refused to do so. The court faced a dilemma. Existing law backed Whitehead's maternal rights, but the court was also concerned that the surrogacy agreement looked too much like baby selling or womb rental, which were against the law. The court's opinion focused on Whitehead's attempt to break the surrogacy contract to justify terminating her legal rights, although she was awarded visitation rights.

More complicated than traditional surrogacy, *gestational surrogacy* deconstructs the role of genetrix into two roles that can be performed by two different women. In a key case, the Calverts, a childless married couple, provided eggs and sperm that were used in the laboratory to create an embryo, which was then implanted in Anna Johnson's uterus. But when Johnson gave birth to the baby, she refused to give it up. As Dolgin (1995, 58) points out, this case "provided a context in which to measure the generality of the assumption that the gestational role both produces and constitutes maternity." As we have seen, other court cases emphasized the role of gestation in forming an indissoluble bond between mother and child. In this case, however, the court referred to Anna Johnson "as a 'gestational carrier,' a 'genetic hereditary stranger' to the child, who acted like a 'foster parent'" (Dolgin 1995, 59). The court declared the Calverts and the child a family unit on genetic grounds and ruled that the Calverts were the baby's "natural" and legal parents.

Dolgin notes that in all of these cases the courts awarded legal custody to those parties whose living arrangements most closely approximated the traditional middle-class, North American two-parent family. "Biological facts were called into judicial play only . . . when they justified the preservation of traditional families" (Dolgin 1995, 63). Biological facts that might have undermined such families were systematically overlooked. Perhaps the clear-cut biological basis of North American kinship is not so clear-cut after all.

## How Do We Define Marriage?

Marriages and households represent another form of relatedness that provides significant forms of social support that enable people to take part in wider patterns of social life. In many places, they also facilitate important economic and political exchanges between the kinship groups to which the marriage partners belong. Even when marriage is not connected with lineage or clan relations, marriage patterns provide frameworks for linking previously unrelated people to one another, embedding individuals within groups, and organizing individual emotional commitments and economic activities.

*Marriage* and *family* are two terms anthropologists use to describe how mating and its consequences are understood and organized in different societies. Marriage involves more than living together and having sexual relations. In most societies, marriage also requires involvement and support from the wider social groups to which the spouses belong—first and foremost, from their families. While not all cultural groups define marriage in exactly the same way, we can identify five criteria that are common in most societies: (1) marriage transforms the status of the participants; (2) marriage stipulates the degree of sexual access the married partners are expected to have to each other, ranging from exclusive to preferential; (3) marriage perpetuates social patterns through the production or adoption of offspring, who also have rights and obligations; (4) marriage creates relationships between the kin of the partners; and (5) marriage is symbolically marked in some way.

Many societies have long considered the prototypical marriage to involve a man and a woman. But as the following cases illustrate, marriage can take many forms.

## Woman Marriage and Ghost Marriage among the Nuer

Among the Nuer, as E.E. Evans-Pritchard observed during his fieldwork in the 1930s, a woman could marry another woman and become the "father" of the children the wife bore (see EthnoProfile 13.1: Nuer). This practice, which also appears in some other parts of Africa, involves the distinction between pater and genitor. The female husband (the pater) had to have some cattle of her own to use for bridewealth payments to the wife's lineage. Once the bridewealth had been paid, the marriage was established. The female husband then got a male kinsman, friend, or neighbour (the genitor) to impregnate the wife and to help with certain tasks around the homestead that the Nuer believed could be done only by men.

Generally, Evans-Pritchard (1951) noted, a female husband was unable to have children herself "and for this reason counts in some respects as a man." Indeed, she played the social role of a man. She could marry several wives if she was wealthy. She could demand damage payment if those wives engaged in sexual activity without her consent. She was the pater of her wives' children. On the marriage of her daughters, she received the portion of the bridewealth that traditionally went to the father, and her brothers and sisters received the portions appropriate to the father's side. Her children

were named after her, as though she were a man, and they addressed her as "Father." She administered her compound and her herds as a male head of household would, and she was treated by her wives and children with the same deference shown a male husband and father.

More common in Nuer social life was what Evans-Pritchard called the "ghost marriage." The Nuer believed that a man who died without male heirs left an unhappy and angry spirit who might trouble his living kin. The spirit was angry because a basic obligation of Nuer kinship was for a man to be remembered through and by his sons: his name had to be continued in his lineage. To appease the angry spirit, a kinsman of the dead man—a brother or a brother's son—would often marry a woman "to his name." Bridewealth cattle were paid in the name of the dead man to the patrilineage of a woman. She was then married to the ghost of the dead man but lived with one of his surviving kinsmen. In the marriage ceremonies and afterward, this kinsman acted as though he were the true husband. The children of the union were referred to as though they were the kinsman's, but officially they were not. That is, the ghost husband was their pater and his kinsman, their genitor. As the children got older, the name of their ghost father became increasingly important to them. The ghost father's name, not his stand-in's name, would be remembered in the history of the lineage. The social union between the ghost and the woman took precedence over the sexual union between the ghost's surrogate and the woman.

Ghost marriage serves to perpetuate social patterns. Although it was common for a man to marry a wife "to his kinsman's name" before he himself married, it became difficult, if not impossible, for him to marry later in his own right. His relatives would tell him he was "already married" and that he should allow his younger brothers to use cattle from the family herd so they could marry. Even if he eventually accumulated enough cattle to afford to marry, he would feel that those cattle should provide the bridewealth for the sons he had raised for his dead kinsman. When he died, he died childless because the children he had raised were legally the children of the ghost. He was then an angry spirit, and someone else (in fact, one of the sons he had raised for the ghost) had to marry a wife to *his* name. Thus, the pattern continued, as, indeed, it does to the present day.

**FIGURE 13.10** | Marriage is a social process that creates social ties and involves more than just the people getting married. Family and friends recognize the new couple after the formal ceremony in Venice.

## Why Is Marriage a Social Process?

Like all formal definitions, our definition of marriage is somewhat rigid. Thinking of marriage as a social process rather than a rigid form, however, is more inclusive of all forms of marriage, even those that may not perfectly fit the definition (Figure 13.10). For example, mating alone does not create in-laws, nor does it set up a way of locating the offspring in space and time as members of a particular social group. Marriage does both; it embeds human mating within an elaborately constructed social and cultural niche. A marriage sets up new relationships that bring together the kin of both spouses. These are called **affinal relationships** (based on *affinity*—relationships created via marriage) and contrast with **consanguineal relationships** (based on "blood" ties, i.e., on descent).

Marriage mediates relationships based on affinity and consanguinity and thus can play an important role in the formation of social groups. Marriage marks

a major transformation of social position. It affects not only the newly married couple and their families but also the wider community, which is responsible for acknowledging the legitimacy of every new union. Every society has its own forms of matchmaking. Sometimes marriages must be contracted within a particular social group, a pattern called **endogamy**. In other cases, marriage partners must be found outside a particular group, a pattern called **exogamy**. In Nuer society, for example, a person had to marry outside his or her lineage. In Canada, where the ideology of individualism leads many people to conclude that they can marry whomever they want, statistically people tend to marry within the bounds of certain groups. For example, young people are often told to marry "your own kind," which usually means someone in their own ethnic, racial, or religious group or social class. Until recently, legal definitions of marriage in Canada also prohibited marriage between individuals of the same sex (see the "In Their Own Words" box on Marriage in Canada) (Figure 13.11). In all societies, some close kin are off limits as spouses or as sexual partners. This exogamous pattern is known as the *incest taboo*.

## Patterns of Residence after Marriage

Once married, a couple must live somewhere. There are four major patterns of postmarital residence. Most familiar to North Americans is **neolocal residence**, in which the new couple sets up an independent household at a

---

**affinal relationships**  Kinship connections through marriage, or affinity.

**consanguineal relationships**  Kinship connections based on descent.

**endogamy**  Marriage within a defined social group.

**exogamy**  Marriage outside a defined social group.

**neolocal residence**  A postmarital residence pattern in which a married couple sets up an independent household at a place of their own choosing.

**FIGURE 13.11** | Definitions of marriage have evolved in Canada, with civil marriage of same-sex couples becoming legal in 2005 across the country. Here, Michael Leshner and Michael Stark, the first same-sex couple to marry in Canada, display their wedding bands.

## In Their Own Words

### Marriage in Canada: The Evolution of a Fundamental Social Institution

*Nicholas Bala, a professor in the Faculty of Law at Queen's University, reflects on the evolution of marriage laws in Canada generally, and on the shift to legal recognition of same-sex marriage in particular, as a consequence of changing social attitudes toward marriage and constitutional reform.*

Marriage is one of the oldest social institutions, predating recorded history, law, and perhaps even religion. Marriage has not been a static social or legal institution, but rather has changed over the course of history in response to changing religious beliefs, social values and behaviours, technology, and even demographics. Similarly, there is great variation today in marital behaviours, attitude, and laws about marriage in different countries.

. . . Despite profound changes in the legal and social nature of marriage, marriage has remained a fundamental social institution, with primary responsibility for the nurturing and care of children. As society changes, the question which must be faced is whether the legal rules that were developed in the past to govern the definition of marriage and spousal relationships continue to best meet current social, economic, cultural, and spiritual needs and circumstances. . . .

. . . [R]eligion historically established the legal basis of marriage throughout much of the world. In Canada and the United States, marriage law was largely based on Christian doctrine about marriage, in particular as reflected in English common law. . . . In both Canada and the United States, the laws and expectations for husbands and wives within marriage have changed dramatically over the past half century, setting the stage for the possible redefinition of marriage to include same-sex partners. . . . [M]arriage is now regarded as a "partnership of equals." . . . Laws no longer refer to "husbands" and "wives," but are generally written in gender-neutral terms. . . . Fathers and mothers are, in statutes, presumed to be equally capable of caring for their children. . . . Spouses are viewed as legally equal. Gender roles in marriage are no longer *legally* prescribed. . . .

Historically in Canada, . . . there was great social [criticism] attached to adults who were "living in sin"—cohabiting without being married—and there was no legal recognition given to this type of relationship. Changing social mores in the 1960s and 1970s led to wider social acceptance of opposite-sex cohabitation outside of marriage and an increase in the incidence of what is often referred to in Canada as "common-law marriage." By 2001, 14 per cent of all Canadian opposite-sex couples residing together were unmarried,

Continued

an increase from 6 per cent in 1981. . . . [Between 1972 and 1992,] almost every province enacted legislation giving limited recognition to unmarried opposite-sex partners for a range of legal purposes such as spousal support. . . .

[At the same time, s]tarting in 1977, provincial legislatures in Canada began to amend their human rights codes to add a prohibition of discrimination on the basis of sexual orientation. . . . After the introduction of the Canadian Charter of Rights and Freedoms in 1982, most politicians and members of the Canadian public were prepared to accept that it was wrong to overtly discriminate against individuals on the basis of their sexual orientation in regard to such issues as employment. . . . In a number of decisions starting in 2002, lower courts in most jurisdictions in Canada recognized that it is a violation of the Charter to deny same-sex partners the right to marry. By early 2005, courts in eight provinces and two territories had issued such rulings. . . .

. . . [T]he government brought the Civil Marriage Act (Bill C-38) to Parliament in February 2005, to define a "civil marriage" as "the lawful union of two persons to the exclusions of all others." In the spring of 2005, there was intense lobbying of members of Parliament over same-sex marriage, with demonstrations, advertising, and letter-writing campaigns. Much of the anti–same-sex marriage advocacy was undertaken by conservative, faith-based groups. . . . More liberal faith groups and civil liberties organizations supported changing the definition of marriage to allow same-sex partners to marry. There were Parliamentary Committee hearings and extensive media debates over same-sex marriage. . . . [Bill C-38] was passed by the House of Commons by a vote of 158 to 133 on 28 June 2005. The new marriage law came into force on 20 July 2005, after passage by the Senate. . . .

The introduction of same-sex marriage in Canada has been motivated by a desire to respect the equality and human dignity of all Canadians, and in particular to recognize the social and emotional importance of the conjugal relationships of homosexuals. This development also has considerable social value, as it promotes the interests of children who are being parented by same-sex partners, and it shifts some burdens which might otherwise fall on the state onto private shoulders [e.g., through allowances for spousal and child support]. . . . [T]he recognition of same-sex marriage is of profound symbolic significance . . . . The court decisions about same-sex marriage and the ultimate government response recognize the fundamental right of gays and lesbians to full equality under the law and provide important social validation of these relationships.

Source: Bala 2005, 195–220.

place of their own choosing. Neolocal residence tends to be found in societies that are more or less individualistic in their organization.

When the married couple lives with (or near) the husband's father's family, the pattern is called **patrilocal residence**, which is observed by more societies in the contemporary world than any other residence pattern. It produces a characteristic social grouping of related men: a man, his brothers, and their sons (along with in-marrying wives) all live and work together. This pattern is common in both herding and farming societies; some anthropologists argue that survival in such societies depends on activities that are best carried out by groups of men who have worked together all their lives.

When the married couple lives with (or near) the family in which the wife was raised, the pattern is called **matrilocal residence**, which is usually found in association with matrilineal kinship systems. Here, the core of the social group consists of a woman, her sisters, and their daughters (along with in-marrying husbands). This pattern is most common among groups practising extensive agriculture.

Less common, but also found in matrilineal societies, is the pattern known as **avunculocal residence**. Here, the married couple lives with (or near) the husband's mother's brother. The most significant man in a boy's matrilineage is his mother's brother, from whom he will inherit. Avunculocal residence emphasizes this relationship.

**patrilocal residence**   A postmarital residence pattern in which a married couple lives with (or near) the husband's father.

**matrilocal residence**   A postmarital residence pattern in which a married couple lives with (or near) the wife's mother.

**avunculocal residence**   A postmarital residence pattern in which a married couple lives with (or near) the husband's mother's brother (from *avuncular*, "of uncles").

**FIGURE 13.12 |** The wives and children of a polygynous family.

## Single and Plural Spouses

The number of spouses a person may have varies cross-culturally. Anthropologists distinguish forms of marriage in terms of how many spouses a person may have. Monogamy is a marriage form in which a person may have only one spouse at a time, whereas polygamy is a marriage system that allows a person to have more than one spouse at a time. Within the category of polygamy are two subcategories: polygyny, or multiple wives, and polyandry, or multiple husbands. Of the two, polygyny is far more common in societies around the world.

### *Monogamy*

Monogamy is the most common spousal pattern in Canada and most industrialized nations. There are variations in the number of times a monogamous person can be married. Before the twentieth century, people in western European societies generally married only once unless death intervened. Today, some observers suggest that we practise *serial monogamy*—we may be married to several different people but only one at a time.

### *Polygyny*

Polygynous societies vary in the number of wives a man may have. Islam permits a man to have as many as four wives but only on the condition that he can support them equally. Some Muslim authorities today argue, however, that equal support must be emotional and affective, not just financial. Convinced that no man can feel the same toward each of his wives, they have concluded that monogamy must be the rule. Other polygynous societies have no limit on the number of wives a man may have. Nevertheless, not every man can be polygynous. There is a clear demographic problem: for every man with two wives, there is one man without a wife. Men can wait until they are older to marry and women can marry very young, but this imbalance cannot be eliminated. Polygyny is also expensive, for a husband must support all his wives as well as their children (Figure 13.12).

### *Polyandry*

Polyandry is the rarest of the three marriage forms. In some polyandrous societies, a woman may marry several brothers. In others, she may marry men who are not related to each other and who all will live together in a single household. Sometimes a woman is allowed to

---

**monogamy** A marriage pattern in which a person may be married to only one spouse at a time.

**polygamy** A marriage pattern in which a person may be married to more than one spouse at a time.

**polygyny** A marriage pattern in which a man may be married to more than one wife at a time.

**polyandry** A marriage pattern in which a woman may be married to more than one husband at a time.

marry several men who are not related, but she will live only with the one she most recently married. Studies of polyandry have shed new light on the dynamics of polygyny and monogamy, as well.

The traditional anthropological prototype of polyandry is based on marriage practices among some groups in Nepal and Tibet, where a group of brothers marry one woman. This is known as *fraternal polyandry*. During a wedding, one brother, usually the oldest, serves as the groom. All brothers (including those yet to be born to the husbands' parents) are married by this wedding, which establishes public recognition of the marriage. The wife and her husbands live together, usually patrilocally. All brothers have equal sexual access to the wife, and all act as fathers to the children. In some cases—notably among the Nyinba of Nepal (Levine 1980, 1988)—each child is recognized as having one particular genitor, who may be a different brother from the genitor of his or her siblings (see EthnoProfile 13.4: Nyinba). In other cases, all the brothers are considered jointly as the father, without distinguishing the identity of the genitor.

There appears to be little sexual jealousy among the men, and the brothers have a strong sense of solidarity with one another. Levine (1988) emphasizes this point for the Nyinba. If the wife proves sterile, the brothers may marry another woman in hopes that she may be fertile. All brothers also have equal sexual access to the new wife and are treated as fathers by her children.

## EthnoProfile 13.4

### Nyinba

**Region:** Central Asia

**Nation:** Nepal

**Population:** 1200

**Environment:** Valleys

**Livelihood:** Agriculture, herding

**Political organization:** Traditionally, headmen; today, part of a modern nation-state

**For more information:** Levine, Nancy. 1988. *The Dynamics of Polyandry: Kinship, Domesticity, and Population on the Tibetan Border.* Chicago: University of Chicago Press.

In societies that practise fraternal polyandry, marrying sisters (or *sororal polygyny*) may be preferred or permitted. In this system, a group of brothers could marry a group of sisters.

According to Levine, Nyinba polyandry is reinforced by a variety of cultural beliefs and practices (1988, 158ff.). First, it has a special cultural value. Nyinba myth provides a social charter for the practice because the legendary ancestors are polyandrous, and they are praised for the harmony of their family life. Second, the solidarity of brothers is a central kinship ideal. Third, the corporate, landholding household, central to Nyinba life, presupposes the presence of a single wife with multiple husbands. Fourth, the closed corporate structure of Nyinba villages is based on a limited number of households, and polyandry is highly effective at checking the proliferation of households. Fifth, a household's political position and economic viability increase when its resources are concentrated.

***The Distinction between Sexuality and Reproductive Capacity.*** Polyandry demonstrates how a woman's sexuality can be distinguished from her reproductive capacity. This distinction is absent in monogamous or purely polygynous systems, in which polyandry is not permitted; such societies resist perceiving women's sexual and reproductive capacities as separable (except, perhaps, in prostitution), yet they usually accept such separation for men without question. "It may well be a fundamental feature of the [world view] of polyandrous peoples that they recognize such a distinction for both men and women" (Levine and Sangree 1980, 388). In the better-known polyandrous groups, a woman's sexuality can be shared among an unlimited number of men, but her childbearing capacities cannot. Indeed, among the Nyinba (Levine 1980), a woman's childbearing capacities are carefully controlled and limited to one husband at a time. But she is free to engage in sexual activity outside her marriage to the brothers as long as she is not likely to get pregnant.

## How Is Marriage an Economic Exchange?

In many societies, marriage is accompanied by the transfer of certain symbolically important goods. Anthropologists have identified two major categories of marriage payments, called *bridewealth* or *dowry*.

**FIGURE 13.13** | This photo from Santa Cruz Island (in the Solomon Islands) from 1906 shows bridewealth—in the foreground, reels of feather money on a rod, and in the background, other items of bridewealth carried on the women's heads.

Bridewealth is most common in patrilineal societies that combine agriculture, pastoralism, and patrilocal marriage, although it is found in other types of societies as well (Figure 13.13). When it occurs among matrilineal peoples, a postmarital residence rule (avunculocal, for example) usually takes the woman away from her matrilineage.

As we noted earlier, the goods exchanged as bridewealth have significant symbolic value to the people concerned. They may include shell ornaments, ivory tusks, brass gongs, bird feathers, cotton cloth, and animals. Cash may also be used. Bridewealth in animals is prevalent in eastern and southern Africa, where cattle have the most profound symbolic and economic value. In these societies, a man's father, and often his entire patrilineage, give a specified number of cattle (often in installments) to the patrilineage of the man's bride. Anthropologists view bridewealth as a way of compensating the bride's relatives for the loss of her labour and childbearing capacities. When the bride leaves her home, she goes to live with her husband and his lineage. She will be working and producing children for his people, not her own.

Bridewealth transactions create affinal relations between the relatives of the wife and those of the husband. The wife's relatives, in turn, may use the bridewealth they receive to find a bride for her brother in yet another kinship group. In many societies in eastern and southern Africa, a woman gains power and influence over her brother because her marriage brings the cattle that allow him to marry and continue their lineage. This is why Jack Goody and Stanley Tambiah (1973, 17) describe bridewealth as "a societal fund, a circulating pool of resources, the movement of which corresponds to the movement of rights over spouses, usually women." Or, as the Southern Bantu put it, "cattle beget children" (Kuper 1982, 3).

Dowry, by contrast, is typically a transfer of family wealth, usually from parents to their daughter, at the time of her marriage. It is found primarily in the agricultural societies of Europe and Asia but has been brought to some parts of Africa with the arrival of religions like Islam that support the practice. In societies where both women and men are seen as heirs to family wealth, dowry is sometimes regarded as the way women receive their inheritance. Dowries are often considered the wife's contribution to the establishment of a new household, to which the husband may bring other forms of wealth. In stratified societies, the size of a woman's dowry often ensures that when she marries she will continue to enjoy her accustomed style of life. The goods included in dowries vary in different societies and may or may not include land (Goody and Tambiah 1973).

**dowry**  The wealth transferred, usually from parents to their daughter, at the time of a woman's marriage.

## In Their Own Words

### Dowry Too High. Lose Bride and Go to Jail

*In some parts of the world, discussions of bridewealth or dowry seem so divorced from reality as to appear "academic." But elsewhere, these topics remain significant indeed. In May 2003, news media all over the world reported the story of a bride in India who called the police when a battle erupted over demands for additional dowry payments at her wedding. The* New York Times *reports.*

Noida, India, 16 May—The musicians were playing, the 2000 guests were dining, the Hindu priest was preparing the ceremony, and the bride was dressed in red, her hands and feet festively painted with henna.

Then, the bride's family says, the groom's family moved in for the kill. The dowry of two televisions, two home theatre sets, two refrigerators, two air-conditioners, and one car was too cheap. They wanted $25,000 in rupees, now, under the wedding tent.

As a free-for-all erupted between the two families, the bartered bride put her hennaed foot down. She reached for the royal blue cellphone and dialed 100. By calling the police, Nisha Sharma, a 21-year-old computer student, saw her potential groom land in jail and herself land in the national spotlight as India's new overnight sensation.

"Are they marrying with money, or marrying with me?" Ms Sharma asked today, her dark eyes glaring under arched eyebrows. In the next room a fresh wave of reporters waited to interview her, sitting next to the unopened boxes of her wedding trousseau.

After fielding a call from a comic-book artist who wanted to bring her act of defiance last Sunday night to a mass market, she said, "I'm feeling proud of myself."

"It Takes Guts to Send Your Groom Packing," a headline in *The Times of India* read.

*Rashtriya Sahara*, a major Hindi daily, said in a salute, "Bravo: We're Proud of You."

"She is being hailed as a New Age woman and seen as a role model to many," the newspaper *Asian Age* wrote next to a front-page drawing of Ms Sharma standing in front of red and green wedding pennants while flashing a V sign to cameras and wearing a sash over her blue sari with the words *Miss Anti-Dowry*.

"This was a brave thing for a girl dressed in all her wedding finery to do," said Vandana Sharma, president of the Women's Protection League, one of many women's rights leaders and politicians to make a pilgrimage this week to this eastern suburb of Delhi. "This girl has taken a very dynamic step." India's new 24-hour news stations have

Nisha Sharma, surrounded by some of the dowry with which her family had intended to endow her.

propelled Nisha Sharma to Hindi stardom. One television station set up a service allowing viewers to "send a message to Nisha." In the first two days, 1500 messages came in.

Illegal for many decades in India, dowries are now often disguised by families as gifts to give the newlyweds a start in life. More than a media creation, Ms Sharma and her dowry defiance struck a chord in this nation, whose expanding middle class is rebelling against a dowry tradition that is being overfed by a new commercialism.

"Advertisements now show parents giving things to make their daughters happy in life," Brinda Karat, general secretary of the All India Democratic Women's Association, a private group, said, referring to television commercials for products commonly given in dowries.

"It is the most modern aspects of information technology married to the most backward concepts of subordination of women," Ms Karat continued in a telephone interview. Last year, she said, her group surveyed 10,000 people in 18 of India's 26 states. "We found an across-the-board increase in dowry demand," she said.

Much of the dowry greed is new, Ms Karat added. In a survey 40 years ago, she noted, almost two-thirds of

Indian communities reported that the local custom was for the groom to pay the bride's family, the reverse of the present dominant custom. According to government statistics, husbands and in-laws angry over small dowry payments killed nearly 7000 women in 2001.

When Ms Sharma's parents were married in 1970, "my father-in-law did not demand anything," her mother, Hem Lata Sharma, said while serving hot milk tea and cookies to guests.

For the Sharma family, the demands went far beyond giving the young couple a helping hand.

Dev Dutt Sharma, Nisha's father, said his potential in-laws were so demanding that they had stipulated brands. "She specified a Sony home theatre, not a Philips," Mr Sharma, an owner of car battery factories, said of Vidya Dalal, the mother of the groom, Munish Dalal, 25.

Sharma Jaikumar, a telecommunications engineer and friend of the Sharma family, said as the press mob ebbed and flowed through the house: "My daughter was married recently and there was no dowry. But anyone can turn greedy. What can be more easy money than a dowry? All you have to do is ask."

Source: Brooke 2003.

## What Is a Family?

A minimal definition of a family would be that it consists of a woman and her dependent children. While some anthropological definitions of family require the presence of an adult male, related by either marriage or descent (husband or brother, for example), recent feminist and primatological scholarship has called this requirement into question. As a result, some anthropologists prefer to distinguish the conjugal family, which is a family based on marriage—at its minimum, a husband and a wife (a spousal pair) and their children—from the non-conjugal family, which consists of a woman and her children. In a non-conjugal family, the husband/father may be occasionally present or completely absent. Non-conjugal families are never the only form of family organization in a society and, in fact, cross-culturally are usually rather infrequent. In some large-scale industrial societies, including Canada, however, non-conjugal families have become increasingly common. In most societies, the conjugal family is co-resident—that is, spouses live in the same dwelling, along with their children—but there are some matrilineal societies in which the husband lives with his matrilineage, the wife and children live with theirs, and the husband visits his wife and children.[1]

---

[1] In Canada today, where many men as well as women are single parents, the view that a man with his children constitute a family is widely shared. This illustrates the ongoing reconfiguration of North American family relations, other features of which are described below.

## What Is the Nuclear Family?

The structure and dynamics of neolocal monogamous families are familiar to North Americans. These families are called *nuclear families*, and it is often assumed that most people in Canada live in them (although in 2010 only about one-quarter of the Canadian population did). For anthropologists, a nuclear family is made up of two generations: the parents and their unmarried children. Each member of a nuclear family has a series of evolving relationships with every other member: husband and wife, parents and children, and children with each other. These are the lines along which jealousy, competition, controversy, and affection develop in neolocal monogamous families; sibling rivalry, for example, is a form of competition characteristic of nuclear families that is shaped by the relationships between siblings and between siblings and their parents.

## What Is the Polygynous Family?

A polygynous family includes, at a minimum, the husband, all his wives, and their children. Polygynous families are significantly different from nuclear families

family  Minimally, a woman and her dependent children.

conjugal family  A family based on marriage; at a minimum, a spousal pair and their children.

non-conjugal family  A woman and her children; the husband/father may be occasionally present or completely absent.

nuclear family  A family pattern made up of two generations: the parents and their unmarried children.

## In Their Own Words

### Law, Custom, and Crimes against Women

*John van Willigen and V.C. Channa describe the social and cultural practices surrounding dowry payments that appear to be responsible for violence against women in some parts of India.*

A 25-year-old woman was allegedly burnt to death by her husband and mother-in-law at their East Delhi home yesterday. The housewife, Mrs Sunita, stated before her death at the Jaya Prakash Narayana Hospital that members of her husband's family had been harassing her for bringing inadequate dowry.

The woman told the Shahdara subdivisional magistrate that during a quarrel over dowry at their Pratap Park house yesterday, her husband gripped her from behind while the mother-in-law poured kerosene over her clothes.

Her clothes were then set ablaze. The police have registered a case against the victim's husband, Suraj Prakash, and his mother.

—*Times of India*, 19 February 1988

This routinely reported news story describes what in India is termed a "bride-burning" or "dowry death." Such incidents are frequently reported in the newspapers of Delhi and other Indian cities. In addition, there are cases in which the evidence may be ambiguous, so that deaths of women by fire may be recorded as kitchen accidents, suicides, or murders. Dowry violence takes a characteristic form. Following marriage and the requisite giving of dowry, the family of the groom makes additional demands for the payment of more cash or the provision of more goods. These demands are expressed in unremitting harassment of the bride, who is living in the household of her husband's parents, culminating in the murder of the woman by members of her husband's family or by her suicide. The woman is typically burned to death with kerosene, a fuel used in pressurized cook stoves, hence the use of the term "bride-burning" in public discourse.

Dowry death statistics appear frequently in the press and parliamentary debates. Parliamentary sources report the following figures for married women 16 to 30 years of age in Delhi: 452 deaths by burning for 1985; 478 for 1986, and 300 for the first six months of 1987. There were 1319 cases reported nationally in 1986 (*Times of India*, 10 January 1988). Police records do not match hospital records for third-degree burn cases among younger married women; far more violence occurs than the crime reports indicate.

There is other violence against women related both directly and indirectly to the institution of dowry. For example, there are unmarried women who commit suicide so as to relieve their families of the burden of providing a dowry. A recent case that received national attention in the Indian press involved the triple suicide of three sisters in the industrial city of Kanpur. A photograph was widely published showing the three young women hanging from ceiling fans by their scarves. Their father, who earned about 4000 Rs [rupees] per month, was not able to negotiate marriage for his oldest daughter. The grooms were requesting approximately 100,000 Rs. Also linked to the dowry problem is selective female abortion made possible by amniocentesis. This issue was brought to national attention with a startling statistic reported out of a seminar held in Delhi in 1985. Of 3000 abortions carried out after sex determination through amniocentesis, only one involved a male fetus. As a result of these developments, the government of the state of Maharashtra banned sex determination tests except those carried out in government hospitals.

Source: van Willigen and Channa 1991, 369–70.

in their internal dynamics. Each wife has a relationship with her co-wives as individuals and as a group (Figure 13.14). Co-wives, in turn, individually and collectively, interact with the husband. In addition, an important distinction is made between children with the same mother and children with a different mother. Where there is a significant inheritance, these relationships serve as the channels for jealousy and conflict. The children of the same mother, and especially the children of different mothers, compete with one another

**FIGURE 13.14** | Cowives in polygynous households frequently co-operate in daily tasks, such as food preparation.

for their father's favour. Each mother tries to protect the interests of her own children, sometimes at the expense of her cowives' children.

### Competition in the Polygynous Family

Although the relationships among wives in a polygynous society may be very close, among the Mende of Sierra Leone, co-wives eventually compete with each other (see EthnoProfile 13.5: Mende). Caroline Bledsoe (1993) explains that this competition is often focused on children: how many each wife has and how likely it is that each child will obtain things of value, especially education. Husbands in polygynous Mende households are supposed to avoid overt signs of favouritism, but their wives do not all have equal status. To begin with, wives are ranked by order of marriage. The senior wife is the first wife in the household, and she has authority over junior wives.

## EthnoProfile 13.5

### Mende

**Region:** Western Africa

**Nation:** Sierra Leone

**Population:** 12,000,000

**Environment:** Forest and savannah

**Livelihood:** Slash-and-burn rice cultivation, cash cropping, diamond mining

**Political organization:** Traditionally, a hierarchy of local chiefdoms; today, part of a modern nation-state

**For more information:** Little, Kenneth. 1967. *The Mende of Sierra Leone*. London: Routledge and Kegan Paul.

Marriage-order ranking structures the household but also lays the groundwork for rivalries. Wives are also ranked, however, in terms of the status of the families from which they came. Serious conflicts arise if the husband shows favouritism by paying for the education of the children of a wife from a high-status family before educating the older children of other wives or the children of wives higher in the marriage-order ranking.

The level of her children's education matters intensely to a Mende woman because her principal claim to her husband's land or cash and her expectations of future support after he dies come through her children. She depends not only on the income that a child may earn to support her but also on the rights her children have to inherit property and positions of leadership from their father. Nevertheless, education requires a significant cash outlay in school fees, uniforms, books, and so on. A man may be able to send only one child to school, or he may be able to send one child to a prestigious private school only if he sends another to a trade apprenticeship. These economic realities make sense to husbands but can lead to bitter feuds among cowives and even divorce when wives blame their husband for disparities in the accomplishments of their children. In extreme cases, cowives are said to use witchcraft to make their rivals' children fail their exams. To avoid these problems, children are frequently sent to live with relatives who will send them to school. Such competition is missing in monogamous households unless they include adopted children or spouses who already have children from a previous marriage.

## What Are Extended and Joint Families?

Within any society, certain patterns of family organization are considered proper. In Canadian nuclear families, two generations live together. In some societies, three generations—parents, married children, and grandchildren—are expected to live together in a vertical extended family. In still other societies, the extension is horizontal: brothers and their wives (or sisters and their husbands) live together in a joint family. These are ideal patterns, which all families may not be able or willing to emulate. It is important to emphasize that extended families do not operate the way joint families operate, and neither can be understood as just several nuclear families that happen to overlap. Extended and joint families are fundamentally different from nuclear families with regard to the rights and obligations they engender among their members.

# How Are Families Transformed over Time?

Families change over time: they have a life cycle and a life span. The same family takes on different forms and provides different opportunities for the interaction of members at different points in its development. New households are formed and old households change through divorce, remarriage, the departure of children, and the breakup of extended families.

## Divorce and Remarriage

Most societies make it possible for married couples to separate. In some societies, the process is long, drawn out, and difficult, especially when bridewealth must be

extended family   A family pattern made up of three generations living together: parents, married children, and grandchildren.

joint family   A family pattern made up of brothers and their wives or sisters and their husbands (along with their children) living together.

returned; a man who divorces a wife in such societies or whose wife leaves him expects some of the bridewealth back. But for the wife's family to give the bridewealth back, a whole chain of marriages may have to be broken up. Brothers of the divorced wife may have to divorce to get back enough bridewealth from their in-laws. Sometimes a new husband will repay the bridewealth to the former husband's line, thus relieving the bride's relatives of this expense.

### Grounds for Divorce

Depending on the society, nagging, quarreling, cruelty, stinginess, or adultery may be cited as causes for divorce. In almost all societies, childlessness is grounds for divorce as well. For the Ju/'hoansi, most divorces are initiated by women, mainly because they do not like their husbands or do not want to be married (Lee 1992; Shostak 1981). After what is often considerable debate, a couple that decides to break up merely separates. There is no bridewealth to return, no legal contract to be renegotiated. Mutual consent is all that is necessary. The children stay with the mother. Ju/'hoansi divorces are cordial, Richard Lee (1992) tells us, at least compared with the Western norm. Ex-spouses may continue to joke with each other and even live next to each other with their new spouses.

For more on the Ju/'hoansi, see EthnoProfile 11.5, on p. 314.

### Separation among the Inuit

Among the northwestern Inuit, the traditional view is that all kin relationships, including marital ones, are permanent (Burch 1970) (see EthnoProfile 13.6: Alaskan Inuit). Thus, although it is possible to deactivate a marriage by separating, a marriage can never be permanently dissolved. (Conversely, re-establishing the residence tie is all that is needed to reactivate the relationship.) A husband and wife who stop living together and having sexual relations with each other are considered to be separated and ready for another marriage. If each member of a separated couple remarried, the two husbands of the wife would become cohusbands, and the two wives of the husband would become cowives; the children of the first and second marriages would become cosiblings. In effect, a "divorce" among the Inuit results in more, not fewer, connections.

## EthnoProfile 13.6

### Inuit (Alaska)

**Region:** North American Arctic

**Nation:** United States (northwestern Alaska)

**Population:** 11,000 (1960s)

**Environment:** Arctic: mountains, foothills, coastal plain

**Livelihood:** Hunting, wage labour, welfare

**Political organization:** Traditionally, families; today, part of a modern nation-state

**For more information:** Burch, Ernest S., Jr. 1975. *Eskimo Kinsmen: Changing Family Relationships in Northwest Alaska.* American Ethnological Society Monograph, no. 59. St Paul: West.

### *Blended Families*

In recent years, anthropologists have observed the emergence of a new family type in Canada: the **blended family**. A blended family is created when previously divorced or widowed people marry, bringing with them children from their previous marriages. The internal dynamics of the new family—which can come to include his children, her children, and their children—may resemble the dynamics of polygynous families, as the relations among the children and their relations to each parent may be complex and negotiated over time.

## How Does International Migration Affect the Family?

Migration to find work in another country has become increasingly common worldwide and has important effects on families. Anthropologist Eugenia Georges (1990) examined its effects on people who migrated to the United States from Los Pinos, a small town in the Dominican Republic (see EthnoProfile 13.7: Los Pinos). Migration divided these families, with some members moving to New York and some remaining in Los Pinos. Some parents stayed in the Dominican Republic while their children went to the United States. A more common pattern was for the husband to migrate and the

## EthnoProfile 13.7

### Los Pinos

**Region:** Caribbean

**Nation:** Dominican Republic

**Population:** 1000

**Environment:** Rugged mountain region

**Livelihood:** Peasant agriculture (tobacco, coffee, cacao) and labour migration

**Political organization:** Part of a modern nation-state

**For more information:** Georges, Eugenia. 1990. *The Making of a Transnational Community: Migration, Development, and Cultural Change in the Dominican Republic.* New York: Columbia University Press.

wife to stay home. Consequently, many households in Los Pinos were headed by women. In most cases, however, the spouse in the United States worked to bring the spouse and children in Los Pinos there.

This sometimes took several years because it involved completing paperwork for the visa and saving money beyond the amount regularly sent to Los Pinos. Children of the couple who were close to working age also came to the United States, frequently with their mother, and younger children were sent for as they approached working age. Finally, after several years in the United States, the couple who started the migration cycle would often take their savings and return home to the Dominican Republic. Their children stayed in the United States and continued to send money home. Return migrants tended not to give up their residence visas and, therefore, had to return to the United States annually. Often, they stayed for a month or more to work. This also provided them with the opportunity to buy household goods at a more reasonable cost, as well as other items—clothing, cosmetics, and the like—to sell to neighbours, friends, and kin in the Dominican Republic (Figure 13.15).

Georges observes that the absent family member maintained an active role in family life despite the

**blended family** A family created when previously divorced or widowed people marry, bringing with them children from their previous families.

**FIGURE 13.15** | As migration from the Dominican Republic to the United States has increased, more Dominicans are staying and bringing their families or creating families in the United States. Such celebrations of ethnic pride as the Dominican Day Parade in New York City have increased in recent years.

heavy psychological burden of separation. Although he might be working in a hotel in New York, for example, the husband was still the breadwinner and the main decision maker in the household. He communicated by visits, letters, and occasional telephone calls. Despite

the strains of migration, moreover, the divorce rate was actually slightly lower in migrant families than in families whose members never migrated. This was in part because the exchange of information between Los Pinos and New York was both dense and frequent but also because strong ties of affection connected many couples. Finally, "the goal of the overwhelming majority of the migrants [from Los Pinos] I spoke with was permanent return to the Dominican Republic. Achievement of this goal was hastened by sponsoring the migration of dependents, both wives and children, so that they could work and save as part of the reconstituted household in the United States" (Georges 1990, 201). This pressure also helped keep families together.

In recent years, the Internet has come to play an increasingly important role in the lives of families that are separated by migration, education, work, and so on. Daniel Miller and Don Slater (2000) studied Internet use in Trinidad, finding that email and instant messaging have considerably strengthened both nuclear and extended families, allowing closer relations between distant parents and children, among siblings, and among other relatives.

## Anthropology in the Contemporary World

### Caring for Infibulated Women Giving Birth in Norway

Female genital cutting (FGC) has generated enormous publicity—and enormous conflict. Coping with this practice across difference is complex. People in Western societies often have very little grasp of how the operation fits into the cultural practices of those who perform it. Even women from societies with the tradition find themselves on opposing sides: Some seek asylum to avoid it, while others are prosecuted because they seek to have it performed on their daughters. Many governments have declared it a human rights violation.

Norway has struggled with these issues ever since 1991, when it became the home of a large number of refugees from civil war in Somalia. Norwegian health care is free, and Norway has one of the lowest infant mortality rates in the world. Nevertheless, despite the efforts of dedicated health care workers to be culturally sensitive, outcomes for Somali women are not always optimal.

Medical anthropologist R. Elise B. Johansen tried to find out why (Johansen 2006, 516).

In contemporary Norway, Johansen reports, giving birth is considered a positive, "natural" process that women are expected to be able to handle with minimal medical intervention. As a result, "midwives are preferred to obstetricians, medication and incisions are avoided whenever possible, partners are allowed to be present in the delivery room to support the birthing mother, newborns are immediately placed on the mother's belly, and mothers are encouraged to breast feed immediately" (2006, 521). At the same time, Norwegian health workers believe that giving birth "naturally" is hard for Norwegian women, because their "natural female essence" is "buried under layers of modernity" (521). Norwegian women nevertheless support "natural" birth practices out of concern for the health of the child, and they expect to manage the pain of unmedicated labour assisted by nothing more than their own physical stamina. Midwives also usually leave women alone until the expulsion phase of labour begins, a practice connected to their idea of what constitutes a "natural" delivery: "Women are expected to take charge of their own deliveries. Health workers explained restricted interference as a gesture of respect for women's strength and ability to deliver by themselves," an attitude that is possibly also reinforced by the Norwegian values of independence and privacy (538).

What happens when midwives with these expectations encounter Somali women about to give birth? The high value they place on "natural" birthing has led some to regard African immigrant women as "more natural than most Norwegians" and "in closer contact with their female essence" (2006, 521). As a result, health care workers sometimes assume that African women are "naturally" equipped with the skills they need to deliver and care for their babies. Only "modern" Norwegian women require such things as medication or child care instruction.

At the same time, Somali women present a paradox: They are African, but they have been infibulated, and infibulation is thought by most health workers to be "the ultimate expression of female oppression and male dominance" (522). As a result, "infibulated women in the delivery ward present a confusing mixture because 'the natural wild' has culturally constructed genitals." Johansen saw this paradox as "central to understanding the challenges facing health workers in looking after infibulated women during delivery" (522).

Midwives thought of infibulation as a social stigma: It marked infibulated women "as incomplete, disfigured, and oppressed." Johansen concludes that health care workers are at once troubled by infibulation and concerned that this discomfort not interfere with their "professionalism." Their solution is simply *not to speak about infibulation*, a decision that "seems to increase discomfort in both health workers and birthing women. It also reduces the parties' chances of exchanging vital information" (523).

Although the midwives Johansen interviewed knew about infibulation, they had not been formally trained to provide care for infibulated women giving birth, because guidelines were not yet available. This lack of training, coupled with the midwives' unwillingness to talk with Somali women about infibulation, had two unfortunate, interconnected effects. First, it made many Somali women unsure about whether they would be properly cared for during their deliveries, adding to their own anxieties about childbirth. Second, it allowed health care workers to draw their own silent, *mistaken* conclusions about the "cultural meaning" of infibulation for Somali women. Midwives

assumed without asking, for example, that Somali women would not want to be deinfibulated—that is, to have the infibulation scar cut to widen the vaginal opening. They further assumed without asking that Somali women would also oppose the use of *episiotomies*—cuts used to widen the vaginal passage for the child during delivery. Such cuts, which are sewn up afterwards, are a fairly common practice in Western obstetrics.

Since many health care workers assumed that Somali values dictated that Somali women remain infibulated through life, they were concerned that deinfibulation would violate those values. Why had one midwife chosen to perform three episiotomies to avoid deinfibulating one Somali woman, even though episiotomies involve cutting through muscular and blood-filled tissue? Had the midwife asked the woman if she preferred deinfibulation? The surprised midwife replied, "No! Of course she wants to remain the way she is" (526). Because the midwife assumed that Somali women want to remain infibulated and because the midwife wanted to respect this wish, to ask this Somali woman if she wanted deinfibulation made no sense to the midwife.

Had the midwives actually spoken with Somali women, Johansen reports, much discomfort and misunderstanding could have been avoided on both sides. Midwives would have learned that almost all Somali women *wanted* to be deinfibulated and *did not want* to be reinfibulated—and that nearly two-thirds of their husbands did not want their wives to be reinfibulated either (527). Midwives would also have learned that Somali infibulation practices were different from infibulation practices elsewhere in Africa. As we saw from Janice Boddy's ethnography in Chapter 2 (see pp. 32–35), lifelong infibulation is a traditional practice in Sudan. Johansen discovered that "infibulation as practised in Sudan has been taken to represent infibulation in general, so that the practice of reinfibulation in Sudan is taken as evidence that reinfibulation must also be common in all other societies practising infibulation. However, as we have seen, this is not always the case" (529).

Johansen's research shows how even attempts to be culturally sensitive can generate a wall of misconceptions. These can circumvent actual conversation with those individuals whose culture is the focus of attention. There is no question that the midwives were trying to do right by the women they attended. Ironically, however, from a Norwegian perspective, to respect the dignity and autonomy of Somali women meant that one left Somali women alone and *did not ask them questions*. In situations like this, medical anthropologists can play an important role as cultural brokers who see situations from a fresh perspective, ease the friction, and help to build a bridge across difference.

## Families by Choice

In spite of the range of variation in family forms that we have surveyed, some readers may still be convinced that family ties depend on blood and that blood is thicker than water. It is therefore instructive to consider the results of research carried out by Kath Weston (1991) on family forms among gay and lesbian individuals in the San Francisco Bay Area during the 1980s. A lesbian herself, Weston knew that a turning point in the lives of most gays and lesbians was the decision to announce their sexual orientation to their parents and siblings. If blood truly were thicker than water, this announcement should not destroy family bonds; and many parents have indeed been supportive of their children after the announcement. Often enough, however, shocked parents have turned away, declaring that this person is no longer their son or daughter. Living through—or even contemplating—such an experience has been enough to force gays and lesbians to think seriously about the sources of family ties.

By the 1980s, some North American gays and lesbians had reached two conclusions: (1) that blood ties *cannot* guarantee the "enduring diffuse solidarity" supposedly at the core of North American kinship (Schneider 1968); and (2) that new kin ties *can* be created over time as friends and lovers demonstrate their genuine commitment to one another by creating families of choice. "Like their heterosexual counterparts, most gay men and lesbians insisted that family members are people who are 'there for you,' people you can count on emotionally and materially" (Weston 1991, 113). Some gay kinship ideologies now argue that "whatever endures is real" as a way of claiming legitimacy for chosen families. Such a definition of family is compatible with understandings of kinship based on nurturance. In the 1980s and early 1990s, long before the legalization of same-sex marriage in either Canada or the United States, many lesbian and gay activists used this similarity as a resource in their struggles to obtain for long-standing families by choice some of the same legal rights enjoyed by traditional families, such as hospital visiting privileges, joint adoption, and property rights (Weston 1995, 99).

**friendship** The relatively "unofficial" bonds that people construct with one another that tend to be personal, affective, and often a matter of choice.

## Friendship

Anthropologist Robert Brain (1976, 15) cites a dictionary definition of *friend* as "one joined to another in intimacy and mutual benevolence independent of sexual or family love." He quickly points out that the Western belief that friendship and kinship are separate phenomena often breaks down in practice. Today, for example, some husbands and wives in Western societies consider each other "best friends." Similarly, we may become friends with some of our relatives while treating others the same way we treat non-relatives. Indeed, as we have just seen, families can become constituted by friendship—"that which endures is real," as Kath Weston's informants told her (Weston 1991, 113). Presumably, we can be friends with people over and above any kinship ties we might have with them. Indeed, primatologist Joan Silk (2003, 42) points out that close human friendships, especially the kind we find in Western societies, are unlike relationships called "friendship" in primate species like baboons and do not correspond to any of the classic patterns of reciprocity recognized in formal evolutionary models. "People establish close co-operative relationships with non-relatives, care about reciprocity, but avoid keeping careful count of benefits given and received" (51). Although this would seem to make us vulnerable to exploitation, Silk is impressed by evidence that human beings are nevertheless strongly committed to friendships with exactly these attributes.

Sandra Bell and Simon Coleman suggest that typical "markers" for friendship are the relatively "unofficial" bonds that people construct with one another (see Figure 13.16). These bonds tend to be personal, affective, and, to a varying extent from society to society, a matter of choice. The line between friendship and kinship is often a very fuzzy one since there may be an affective quality to kinship relations (we can like our cousins and do the same things with them that we would do with friends), since sometimes friends are seen after a long time as being related, and since some societies have networks of relatedness that can be activated or not for reasons of sentiment, not just for pragmatic reasons. Friendship has been difficult for some anthropologists to study since in the past they have concentrated on trying to find regular long-term patterns of social organization in societies with non-centralized forms of political organization (Bell and Coleman 1999, 4). Bell

**FIGURE 13.16** | Friendships are based on "unofficial" bonds between people that vary from society to society. Here, a group of friends share a laugh in London.

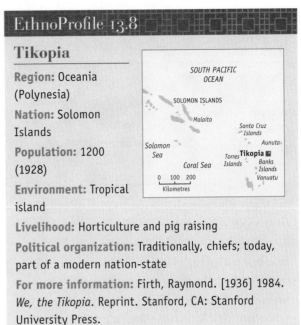

**EthnoProfile 13.8**

**Tikopia**

**Region:** Oceania (Polynesia)

**Nation:** Solomon Islands

**Population:** 1200 (1928)

**Environment:** Tropical island

**Livelihood:** Horticulture and pig raising

**Political organization:** Traditionally, chiefs; today, part of a modern nation-state

**For more information:** Firth, Raymond. [1936] 1984. *We, the Tikopia*. Reprint. Stanford, CA: Stanford University Press.

and Coleman also note that the importance of friendship seems to be increasing: "In many shifting social contexts, ties of kinship tend to be transformed and often weakened by complex and often contradictory processes of globalization. At the same time new forms of friendship are emerging" (5). This is illustrated in a striking way in Rio de Janeiro by Claudia Barcellos Rezende (1999), who observed the ways in which middle-class women and their maids could come to refer to each other as "friends." Within this hierarchical relationship, the distinctions that separated the women were not questioned in themselves, but the "friendship" consisted of the affection, care, and consideration that both sets of women valued in their work relationship. It was a way of establishing trust: "What friendship invokes . . . is the affinity that brings these people together as parts of the same social world" (93).

## How Are Sexual Practices Organized?

Some anthropologists seem to regard marriage as an abstract formal system and say little about human **sexual practices**, the emotional or affectional relationships between sexual partners and the physical activities they engage in with one another. But sexual intercourse is part of almost all marriages. And because in many societies marriage is the formal prerequisite for becoming sexually active (at least for females), a desire for sex is a strong motivation for getting married (Spiro 1977, 212).

### Ranges of Heterosexual Practices

The range of sexual practice in the world is vast. In many Oceanian societies—Tikopia, for example—the young could expect to have a great deal of sexual experience before marriage (see EthnoProfile 13.8: Tikopia). In the early twentieth century, anthropologist Raymond Firth observed that young men and young women began having sexual relations at an early age, and having several lovers was considered normal for the young. Getting married, however, was a key move toward adulthood and represented a great change for both partners. The woman was to give up sexual freedom, but she replaced it with what Firth called "a safe and legalized sexual cohabitation" ([1936] 1984, 434). The man was theoretically free to continue to have affairs, but in practice he also "settled down." This pattern is quite common cross-culturally, but it is not universal.

Karl Heider's research (1979) among the Dani, a people of highland New Guinea, revealed yet another pattern (see EthnoProfile 13.9: Dani). Heider discovered that the Dani had extraordinarily little interest in sex. For five years after the birth of a child, the parents did not have sexual intercourse with each other. This practice, called a *postpartum sex taboo*, is found in all cultures, but in most societies it lasts for a few weeks

**sexual practices** Emotional or affectional relationships between sexual partners and the physical activities they engage in with one another.

## EthnoProfile 13.9

### Dani

**Region:** Oceania (New Guinea)

**Nation:** Indonesia (Irian Jaya)

**Population:** 100,000 (1960s)

**Environment:** Valley in central highlands

**Livelihood:** Horticulture and pig raising

**Political organization:** Traditionally, some men with influence but no coercive power; today, part of a modern nation-state

**For more information:** Heider, Karl. 1979. *Grand Valley Dani*. New York: Holt, Rinehart, and Winston.

or months. (In North America, we say that the mother needs time to heal; other societies have other justifications.) What could explain a postpartum sex taboo that lasts five years? Heider points out that Westerners assume that the sex drive is so powerful that if it is not satisfied directly in sexual activity, then some other outlet will be found. In fact, some suggest that the Dani's high levels of outgroup aggression may be connected with their low level of sexual intercourse. The Dani were not celibate, and they certainly had sexual intercourse often enough to reproduce biologically; yet, they did not seem very interested in sex (Heider 1979, 78–81). The Dani represent an extreme in the cultural construction of sexuality.

## Other Sexual Practices

The traditional anthropological focus on what European Americans call "heterosexual relationships" is understandable. People in every society are concerned about perpetuating themselves, and most have developed complex ideological and ritual structures to ensure that this occurs. The fact that elaborate cultural constructions seem necessary to encourage heterosexual practices, however, suggests that human sexual expression would resist such confinement if it were not under strict control. For example, anthropologists Evelyn Blackwood and Saskia Wieringa have studied the cultural shaping of female desires. They found that female bodies are assigned different cultural meanings

in different historical and ethnographic settings and that those meanings affect the way females constitute their relations with other females. Their research further revealed a wide range of "varied and rich cultural identities and same-sex practices between those with female bodies" (Blackwood and Wieringa 1999, ix). This sort of research does not assume that having a male body or a female body necessarily determines any individual's traits, feelings, or experiences (x). As a result, it provides a vital comparative context that can illuminate our understanding of sexual practices that European Americans commonly call "homosexuality" and "bisexuality."

### Female Sexual Practices in Mombasa

Anthropologist Gil Shepherd (1987) shows that traditional patterns of male–female interaction among Swahili Muslims in Mombasa, Kenya, make male and female same-sex relationships there intelligible (see EthnoProfile 13.10: Mombasa Swahilis). For one thing, men and women in Muslim Mombasa live in very different subcultures. For women, the most enduring relationship is between a mother and her daughter, mirrored in the relationship between an older married sister and a younger unmarried sister. By contrast, relationships between mothers and sons and between brothers and sisters are more distant. Except in the

## EthnoProfile 13.10

### Mombasa Swahilis

**Region:** Eastern Africa

**Nation:** Kenya

**Population:** 50,000 Swahili among 350,000 total population of city (1970s)

**Environment:** Island and mainland port city

**Livelihood:** Various urban occupations

**Political organization:** Part of a modern nation-state

**For more information:**
Shepherd, Gil. 1987. "Rank, Gender, and Homosexuality: Mombasa as a Key to Understanding Sexual Options." In *The Cultural Construction of Sexuality*, ed. Pat Caplan, 240–70. London: Tavistock.

case of young, modern, educated couples, the relationship between husband and wife is often emotionally distant as well. Because the worlds of men and women overlap so little, relationships between the sexes tend to be one-dimensional. Men and women join a variety of sex-segregated groups for leisure-time activities such as dancing or religious study. Within these same-sex groups, individuals compete for social rank.

Of the some 50,000 Swahili in Mombasa, about 5000 could be called "homosexual." The number is misleading, however, because men and women shift between having sexual relationships with same- and opposite-sex partners throughout their lives. Women are allowed to choose other women as sexual partners only after they have been married. Therefore, all women in Mombasa who form sexual relationships with other women are married, widowed, or divorced. Both men and women are open about their same-sex relationships, and "nobody would dream of suggesting that their sexual choices had any effect on their work capabilities, reliability, or religious piety" (Shepherd 1987, 241). Moreover, many women were quite clear about the practical reasons that had led them into sexual relationships with other women. Women with little money are unlikely to marry men who can offer them jewellery, shoes, new dresses, status, or financial security, but a wealthy female lover can offer them all these things. Also, a poor young woman in an unhappy marriage may have no way to support herself if she leaves her husband unless she has a female lover.

According to Islamic law, a wealthy, high-ranking Muslim woman can marry only a man who is her equal or superior. A marriage of this kind brings a great deal of seclusion, and her wealth is administered by her husband. The wealthy partner in a lesbian relationship, however, is freed from these constraints. "Thus if she wishes to use her wealth as she likes and has a taste for power, entry into a lesbian relationship, or living alone as a divorced or widowed woman, are virtually her only options" (Shepherd 1987, 257). Financial independence for a woman offers the chance to convert wealth to power. If she pays for the marriages of other people or provides financial support in exchange for loyalty, a woman can create a circle of dependants. Shepherd points out that a few women, some lesbians, have achieved real political power in Mombasa in this way (257).

Still, it is not necessary to be a lesbian to build a circle of dependents. Why do some women follow this route? The answer, Shepherd tells us, is complicated. It is not entirely respectable for a woman under 45 or 50 to be unmarried. Some women can maintain autonomy by entering into a marriage of convenience with a man who already lives with a wife and then living apart from him. Many women, however, find this arrangement both lonely and sexually unsatisfying. Living as a lesbian is less respectable than being a second, non-resident wife, but it is more respectable than not being married at all. The lesbian sexual relationship does not reduce the autonomy of the wealthy partner "and indeed takes place in the highly positive context of the fond and supportive relationships women establish among themselves anyway" (Shepherd 1987, 258).

Shepherd suggests that the reason sexual relationships between men or between women are generally not heavily stigmatized in Mombasa is that social rank takes precedence over all other measures of status. Rank is a combination of wealth, the ability to claim Arab ancestry, and the degree of Muslim learning and piety. Rank determines marriage partners as well as relations of loyalty and subservience, and both men and women expect to rise in rank over a lifetime. Although lesbian couples may violate the prototype for sexual relations, they do not violate relations of rank. Shepherd suggests that a marriage between a poor husband and a rich wife might be more shocking than a relationship between a dominant rich woman and a dependent poor one. It is less important that a woman's lover be a male than it is for her to be a good Arab, a good Muslim, and a person of wealth and influence.

Anthropologists working in Africa have described a range of relations between females (e.g., woman marriage) that have been likened to European or North American models of lesbian relationships, but disputes have arisen about whether such relationships always include an erotic involvement between the female partners. In a survey of this evidence, Wieringa and Blackwood note that woman marriage can take many forms, some of which are more likely than others to include sexuality between the female partners. Among those where such sexual relations appear more likely are cases like that described by Shepherd, "in which a woman of some means, either married (to a man) or unmarried, pays bride-price for a wife and establishes her own compound" (Wieringa and Blackwood 1999, 5).

Such evidence is not merely of academic interest. In the contemporary world of intensified global communication and exchange, Western and non-Western same-sex practices are becoming increasingly entangled with one another, leading to the emergence of local movements for "lesbian" and "gay" rights in Africa and elsewhere. In this context, in the late 1990s, the presidents of Zimbabwe, Kenya, and Namibia declared that "homosexuality" is "un-African." Based on the ethnographic evidence, however, Wieringa and Blackwood side with those arguing that, on the contrary, it is homophobia that is "un-African": "President Mandela from South Africa is a striking exception to the homophobia of his colleagues. The South African constitution specifically condemns discrimination on the basis of sexual orientation" (1999, 27).

### Male Sexual Practices in Nicaragua

Anthropologist Roger Lancaster spent many months during the 1980s studying the effects of the Sandinista Revolution on the lives of working people in Managua, Nicaragua (see EthnoProfile 13.11: Managua). While he was there, he learned about *cochones*. *Cochón* could be translated into English as "homosexual," but this would be highly misleading. As Lancaster discovered, working-class Nicaraguans interpret sexual relations between men differently than North Americans do, and their interpretation is central to the traditional Nicaraguan ideas about masculinity that have been called *machismo*.

## EthnoProfile 13.11

### Managua

**Region:** Central America

**Nation:** Nicaragua

**Population:** 1,000,000 (1995 est.)

**Environment:** Tropical city

**Livelihood:** Modern stratified city

**Political organization:** City in modern nation-state

**For more information:** Lancaster, Roger. 1992. *Life Is Hard: Machismo, Danger, and the Intimacy of Power in Nicaragua.* Berkeley: University of California Press.

To begin with, a "real man" (or *macho*) is widely admired as someone who is active, violent, and dominant. In sexual terms, this means that the penis is seen as a weapon used violently to dominate one's sexual partner, who is thereby rendered passive, abused, and subordinate. North Americans typically think of machismo as involving the domination of men over women, but as Lancaster describes, the system may also be defined by the domination of men over other men. Indeed, a "manly man" in working-class Nicaragua is defined as one who is the active, dominant, penetrating sexual partner in encounters with women *and* men. A "passive" male who allows a "manly man" to have sexual intercourse with him in this way is called a *cochón*.

A North American gay man himself, Lancaster found that Nicaraguan views of male–male sexual encounters differed considerably from contemporary North American ideas about male "homosexuality." In Nicaragua, for example, the people Lancaster knew assumed that men "would naturally be aroused by the idea of anally penetrating another male" (1992, 241). Only the "passive" *cochón* is stigmatized, whereas males who always take the "active" role in sexual intercourse with other males and with females are seen as "normal." Nicaraguans, moreover, find hate crimes such as gay-bashing inconceivable: *cochones* may be made fun of, but they are also much admired performers during Carnival. In Canada, by contrast, the active–passive distinction does not exist, and anal intercourse is not the only form that sexual expression between two males may take. Both partners in same-sex encounters are considered "homosexual" and may be equally stigmatized, and gay-bashing is a sometimes deadly reality, probably because it is *not* assumed that "normal" males will naturally be aroused by the idea of sex with another man.

In Nicaragua, public challenges for dominance are a constant of male–male interaction even when sexual intercourse is not involved. The term *cochón* may be used as an epithet not only for a man who yields publicly to another man but also for cats that do not catch mice or, indeed, anything that somehow fails to perform its proper function. In Lancaster's view, *cochones* are made, not born: "Those who consistently lose out in the competition for male status . . . discover pleasure in the passive sexual role or its social status: these men are made into *cochones*. And those who master the rules of conventional masculinity . . . are made into *machistas*" (1992, 249).

These ideas about gender and sexuality created an unanticipated roadblock for Sandinistas who wanted to improve the lives of Nicaraguan women and children. The Sandinista government passed a series of New Family Laws, which were designed to encourage men to support their families economically and to discourage irresponsible sex, irresponsible parenting, and familial dislocation. When Lancaster interviewed Nicaraguan men to see what they thought of these laws, however, he repeatedly got the following response: "First the interrogative: 'What do the Sandinistas want from us? That we should all become *cochones*?' And then the tautological: 'A man has to be a man.' That is, a man is defined by what he is not—a *cochón*" (1992, 274).

## Sexuality and Power

The physical activity that we call "sexual intercourse" is not just doing what comes naturally. Like so much else in human life, sex does not speak for itself, nor does it have only one meaning. Sexual practices can be used to give concrete form to more abstract notions we have about the place of men and women in the world. They may serve as a metaphor for expressing differential power within a society. This is particularly clear in the sexual practices that embody Nicaraguan machismo or North American date rape and family violence. That is, sexual practices can be used to enact, in unmistakable physical terms, the reality of differential power. This is equally clear in the arguments regarding same-sex marriage in North America and elsewhere, since marriage in a nation-state has legal consequences and protections, as well as embodying the legitimacy of the couple's commitment to each other. This reminds us that marriages, families, and sexual practices never occur in a vacuum but are embedded in other social practices such as food production, political organization, kinship, and friendship.

## Chapter Summary

1. Human life is group life; we depend upon one another to survive. People organize their interdependence by means of various forms of relatedness, including friendship, marriage, parenthood, shared links to a common ancestor, workplace associations, and so on. Forms of relatedness are always embedded in, and shaped by, politics, economics, and world views.

2. One of the key forms of relatedness studied by anthropologists is kinship. Kinship systems focus on ideas about shared substance and its transmission, often thought to take place in the process of sexual reproduction. Cross-cultural comparison, however, shows that kinship is not a direct reflection of biology. Kinship principles are based on, but not reducible to, the universal biological experiences of mating, birth, and nurturance. Kinship systems help societies maintain social order without central government. Although female–male duality is basic to kinship, many societies have developed supernumerary sexes or genders.

3. Descent links members of different generations with one another. Patterns of descent in kinship systems are selective. Bilateral descent results in the formation of groups called "kindreds" that include all relatives from both parents' families. Unilineal descent results in the formation of groups called "lineages" that trace descent through either the mother or the father. Unlike kindreds, lineages are corporate groups. Lineages control important property, such as land, that collectively belongs to their members. In many societies, the language of lineage is the idiom of political discussion and lineage relationships are of political significance.

4. Kinship terminologies pay selective attention to certain attributes of people that are then used to define different classes of kin. The attributes most often recognized include, from most to least common, generation, gender, affinity, collaterality, bifurcation, relative age, and the gender of the linking relative. Achieved kinship statuses can be converted into ascribed ones by means of adoption, a kinship relationship based on nurturance rather than mating or birth.

5. Marriage may be defined as a social process that transforms the status of the participants, stipulates the degree of sexual access the married partners are expected to have to each other, perpetuates social patterns through the production or adoption of offspring, and creates relationships between the kin of the partners. Woman marriage and ghost marriage among the Nuer demonstrate that the social roles of husband and father or wife and mother may be independent of the gender of the persons who fill them. There are four major patterns of postmarital residence: neolocal, patrilocal, matrilocal, and avunculocal.

6. A person may be married to only one person at a time (*monogamy*) or to several (*polygamy*). Polygamy can be

further subdivided into *polygyny*, in which a man is married to two or more wives, and *polyandry*, in which a woman is married to two or more husbands. The study of polyandry reveals how a society may distinguish a married woman's sexuality from her reproductive capacity, a distinction not found in monogamous or polygynous societies. Most human societies permit marriages to end by divorce, although it is not always easy. In most societies, childlessness is grounds for divorce. Sometimes nagging, quarreling, adultery, cruelty, and stinginess are causes. In some societies, only men may initiate a divorce.

7.  Bridewealth is a payment of symbolically important goods by the husband's lineage to the wife's lineage. Anthropologists see this as compensation to the wife's family for the loss of her productive and reproductive capacities. A woman's bridewealth payment may enable her brother to pay bridewealth to get a wife. Dowry is typically a transfer of family wealth from parents to their daughter at the time of her marriage. Dowries are often considered the wife's contribution to the establishment of a new household.

8.  Different family structures produce different internal patterns and tensions. There are three basic family types: nuclear, extended, and joint. Families may change from one type to another over time and with the birth, growth, and marriage of children. Families have developed ingenious ways of keeping together even when some members live abroad for extended periods. As illustrated by the concept of "families by choice," individuals who find themselves without the support of a traditional family may also devise creative family structures based on nurturance and the principle that "whatever endures is real."

9.  Friendship is a form of relatedness that is apparently unique to human beings. In some societies, the link between best friends may be ritually confirmed. Under conditions of globalization, older forms of relatedness such as kinship are transformed and new forms of friendship are developing.

10. Sexual practices vary greatly worldwide. In some societies, young men and women begin having free sexual relations from an early age until they are married. Sexual practices that North Americans commonly call "homosexuality" or "bisexuality" may be understood very differently in different societies. In the contemporary globalizing world, Western and non-Western same-sex practices are becoming increasingly entangled with one another, leading to the emergence of local movements for "lesbian" and "gay" rights on many continents.

## For Review

1.  What is relatedness? What form of relatedness does your family use for establishing family ties? How do concepts of relatedness reflect the idea that humans are biocultural organisms?

2.  Define *kinship*, *marriage*, and *adoption*, and explain how each of these relationships is based on, but not reducible to, biology.

3.  How have anthropologists traditionally distinguished between sex and gender? What factors might influence how a society defines and reinforces gender roles?

4.  Compare bilateral kindreds and unilineal descent groups. What might be some advantages or disadvantages to membership in either type of group?

5.  Prepare a chart of the key criteria used to distinguish different categories of kin, and provide a brief explanation and an example for each criterion.

6.  Explain the differences between ascribed status and achieved status. In what situations might the distinctions between these categories be unclear?

7.  What is the difference between *pater* and *genitor*, and between *mater* and *genetrix*? How do these concepts relate to most Westerners' understands of adoption? How are they understood among the Nuer, in relation to woman marriage and ghost marriage?

8.  Distinguish between endogamy and exogamy. In what ways might these practices simplify or complicate the task of finding a marriage partner?

9.  Summarize the four main residence patterns that newly married couples may be expected to observe in different societies. What might be some advantages and disadvantages to each type of arrangement?

10. Discuss how different marriage patterns reflect variation in social understandings of male and female sexuality.

11. Explore the economic characteristics of marriage. Do you think that marriage is driven primarily by economic forces in Canadian society? Why or why not?

12. Summarize the major forms of a family discussed in this chapter. How would you describe your family structure?

13. Discuss the ways in which families and family structures change over time. How has the structure of your family changed over time?

14. Compare and contrast friendship and kinship. In what situations might these concepts overlap? What qualities do you consider necessary in a relationship to calls someone a friend?

15. Using the case studies in this chapter, discuss how anthropologists understand human sexual practices.

## Key Terms

| | | |
|---|---|---|
| achieved statuses 360 | cross cousins 359 | monogamy 367 |
| adoption 349 | descent 349 | neolocal residence 364 |
| affinal relationships 364 | dowry 369 | non-conjugal family 371 |
| affinity 359 | endogamy 364 | nuclear family 371 |
| ascribed statuses 360 | exogamy 364 | parallel cousins 359 |
| avunculocal residence 366 | extended family 373 | patrilineage 353 |
| bifurcation 359 | family 371 | patrilocal residence 366 |
| bilateral descent 352 | friendship 378 | polyandry 367 |
| blended family 375 | joint family 373 | polygamy 367 |
| bridewealth 356 | kinship systems 349 | polygyny 367 |
| clan 354 | lineages 353 | relatedness 349 |
| collaterality 359 | marriage 349 | segmentary opposition 355 |
| conjugal family 371 | matrilineage 353 | sexual practices 379 |
| consanguineal relationships 364 | matrilocal residence 366 | unilineal descent 352 |

## Suggested Readings

Alia, Valerie. 2007. *Names and Nunavut: Culture and Identity in the Inuit Homeland.* New York: Berghahn Books. *This book looks at Inuit ways of naming, both themselves and the landscape they live in, focusing on how identity and politics closely align with the process of naming and how the effects on the Inuit of the Canadian government program "Project Surname."*

Bamford, Sandra, and James Leach, eds. 2009. *Kinship and Beyond: The Genealogical Model Reconsidered.* New York: Berghahn Books. *This collection features detailed ethnographic work and analysis that explores how assumptions based on the genealogical model of kinship affects our understanding of personhood, ethnicity, and property relations.*

Carsten, Janet, ed. 2000. *Cultures of Relatedness: New Approaches to the Study of Kinship.* Cambridge: Cambridge University Press. *An excellent collection of fairly current articles on relatedness.*

Ginsburg, Faye D. 1998. *Contested Lives: The Abortion Debate in an American Community.* Updated ed. Berkeley: University of California Press. *A study of gender and procreation in the context of the abortion debate in Fargo, North Dakota, in the 1980s.*

Ginsburg, Faye D., and Rayna Rapp, eds. 1995. *Conceiving the New World Order: The Global Politics of Reproduction.* Berkeley: University of California Press. *An important collection of articles by anthropologists who address the ways human reproduction is structured across social and cultural boundaries.*

Kahn, Susan Martha. 2000. *Reproducing Jews: A Cultural Account of Assisted Conception in Israel.* Durham, NC: Duke University Press. *An exceptionally interesting ethnographic study of the effects of new reproductive technologies on kinship in Israel.*

Lancaster, Roger N. 1992. *Life Is Hard: Machismo, Danger, and the Intimacy of Power in Nicaragua.* Berkeley: University of California Press. *A stunning analysis of machismo in Nicaragua, in which sexual practices that North Americans consider "homosexual" are interpreted very differently.*

McElroy, Ann. 2008. *Nunavut Generations: Change and Continuity in Canadian Inuit Communities.* Long Grove, IL: Waveland Press. *A brief ethnography documenting the political and social change in Nunavut as it was recognized as a new territory of Canada.*

Parkin, Robert, and Linda Stone, eds. 2004. *Kinship and Family: An Anthropological Reader.* Malden, MA: Blackwell. *A distinguished collection of classic and contemporary articles.*

Shostak, Marjorie. 1981. *Nisa: The Life and Words of a !Kung Woman.* New York: Vintage. *The story of a Ju/'hoansi (!Kung) woman's life in her own words. Shostak provides background for each chapter. There is much here on marriage and everyday life.*

Stone, Linda. 2013. *Kinship and Gender.* 5th ed. Boulder, CO: Westview Press. *A recent discussion of human reproduction and the social and cultural implications of male and female reproductive roles.*

Suggs, David N., and Andrew W. Miracle, eds. 2004. *Culture, Biology, and Sexuality.* Athens, GA: University of Georgia Press. *A collection of important articles from a variety of theoretical perspectives on the nature and culture of human sexuality.*

# Cultural Anthropology: Ethnographic Methods

## How Do We Study and Understand Other Cultures?

Nineteenth-century Euro-American anthropology was ethnocentric, predominantly biased, and largely shaped by the opinions of upper-class white men who did "armchair" research—that is, they conducted research from the comfort of their own armchairs by reading existing reports prepared by Western explorers, colonial officers, and missionaries rather than going out into the field and interacting directly with the peoples they were studying. This sort of indirect study often led researchers to conclude that there was a fundamental dichotomy between "them" (i.e., non-white, non-Western peoples) and "us" (i.e., white Westerners). From this ethnocentric point of view, "they" were marginalized "savages" who were not equal to "civilized" people and who could be easily dismissed and displaced from their lands. Thankfully, this viewpoint is not shared by contemporary ethnographers. Instead, these researchers try to take a culturally relativistic point of view, which allows them to focus on the human condition with as little bias as possible.

Today's ethnographers recognize that all peoples and cultures must be respected. They also take seriously their responsibility to describe their participants' worlds as fully and as accurately as possible. As such, they place great emphasis on the *context* in which they make their observations. This context consists of not only the circumstances that surround an event but also the backgrounds and perceptions of both the people involved and the ethnographer who is making observations. Being aware of context can help fill in the blanks where the significance of an interaction is unclear or miscommunication has occurred. So, anthropologists must begin their research by understanding the *context* in which social events, day-to-day interactions, and even special occasions take place. This is an essential first step in conducting field work, as is clarifies ambiguity and creates a framework for making valid observations.

## Making Observations in the Field

To practise making observations and taking notes from an anthropological perspective, go to your favourite coffee shop or restaurant and record what you see. Begin by sketching a map of the location. Draw in the walls, the furniture, the people, and any other objects or features you can see. Then, spend about an hour observing and taking notes on what is going on around you. Who else is there? How are the people grouped? Is anyone sitting alone? What are the various people doing? As you record your observations, be sure to record the context in which what you observe is happening. Also make notes about your own mental state, which can influence how you see the world around you. Once you have finished, repeat the same process in a library or a study hall, and compare the observations you made in each setting. What similarities and differences did you observe? Consider what you observed others doing, and also reflect on your own actions and perceptions. You may want share your observations with others in your class and discuss any similarities or differences you can identify in terms of your observations or approaches.

## Working in the Field

Traditionally, anthropologists have learned about the peoples in whose ways of life they are interested by conducting fieldwork. Fieldwork involves working closely with research participants, observing their daily lives, and making detailed notes on these observations. While the exact methods an ethnographer will employ while engaging in fieldwork can vary greatly depending on the nature of the study and the research questions being asked, the following discussion offers an overview of some principal approaches and concerns.

Before entering the field, researchers must obtain permission and funding for their project. They must also develop a research question and make practical arrangements for their time in the field. These tasks require researchers to collect preliminary information on the peoples with whom they will be working. This process involves reviewing and critically assessing the accounts of any other anthropologists who have studied the particular group of interest. It also involves examining the work of other scholars familiar with the area of the world where they will be doing their research, in order to achieve a general understanding of the group's place in the world. Preparing in this way has the added benefit of helping researchers guard against culture shock.

It used to be believed that, before entering the field, ethnographic fieldworkers needed to identify (and overcome) any personal, theoretical, or other biases that could interfere with their work. Ideally, a researcher would be able to step into the field and make observations entirely free from the influence of bias. Today, however, following many decades of reflection on the fieldwork process, sociocultural anthropologists are aware that it is not possible to free oneself from all one's biases. The best we can hope for is to be as aware as we can be of our own preconceived notions that can affect how we see the world around us. For the past forty years at least, ethnographers have been taught to cultivate reflexivity as an essential fieldwork skill. Reflexivity—active reflection on one's own experience, thinking about the way one thinks— is essential, not only in the field, but also every time one returns to one's field notes to write about that field experience. Indeed, reflexivity is stimulated by the ongoing dialogues that fieldworkers have with the people they meet during their research, which offer opportunities to reflect on the similarities and differences in the way their consultants think about the topics under investigation. It helps researchers identify ambiguities and misunderstandings that might otherwise go unnoticed. Reflexive awareness forces researchers to look at their own observations from different perspectives, and it can allow them to identify the significance of social or cultural factors that they had downplayed or ignored. The more thoroughly contextualized one's research becomes, the more accurate and reliable it becomes, not only in the eyes of one's anthropological colleagues, but also from the perspective of the people with whom one has worked.

A final step many researchers take in the preparatory stages is establishing the persona they will project when in the field. In general, this persona should be professional yet approachable. It should also reflect local customs and conventions of behaviour. For example, a researcher who tends to be loud and boisterous when interacting with friends at home might need to adopt a more reserved persona when entering a community in which silence and self-restraint are respected. Or, a young, single researcher who is accustomed to living alone may need to join and live with a family in the field setting in order to be accepted by the local community. Advance research can help researchers identify the type of persona they will need to adopt in the field; however, they must still remain open and flexible in adjusting this persona once fieldwork has begun. It is not until they have begun to live in a new community with specific sociocultural expectations that fieldworkers will truly begin to learn about the varied and complex ways they will be perceived by others.

## Adopting a Persona

What sorts of personas might the following individuals want to adopt in order to fit in with the communities they are hoping to study?

- a single woman from Halifax who is in her early twenties and wants to study a patriarchal society in Southeast Asia
- a clean-cut male anthropology student from Vancouver who wants to study the religious ceremonies of an Aboriginal society in northern British Columbia
- a middle-aged, heavily tattooed man who wants to study workplace hierarchies in a top accounting firm in metropolitan Toronto

Why is one's persona an important factor to consider when conducting field research? What problems might a researcher encounter when adopting a persona?

**culture shock**  The feeling, akin to panic, that develops in people living in an unfamiliar society when they cannot understand what is happening around them.

Once in the field, ethnographers typically collect data by engaging in participant observation—fieldwork in which the researcher not only *observes* but also *participates in* the lives of his or her informants. Participant observation typically involves living with members of the community and taking part in social events in order to better understand the society's rules, practices, customs, and so on. This sort of fieldwork can help researchers build close social relationships and achieve an intimate understanding of the context in which they are making their observations. Participant observation typically relies on full disclosure in which the members of a society are well aware of the researcher's role and purpose for being among them. This sort of disclosure is essential to building trust, and it is often an ethical requirement of studies being conducted in association with a university or a professional organization.

In order to gain access to a society, anthropologists typically rely on informants—members of the society who are willing to work closely with researchers to provide them with insights about local ways of life. The relationship between a researcher and an informant must be based on mutual respect and trust. The informant needs to trust that the researcher will not misrepresent his or her society, while the researcher needs to trust that the information the informant provides is reliable. Informants often act as translators, and they can explain subtleties of cultural practices that may not be obvious to outsiders. They also often act as facilitators to the relationships that anthropologists continue to make as they work to get a fuller, more accurate picture of the society. In some cases, informants may be the only individuals who are fully aware of the researcher's reasons for interacting with members of the community. Most contemporary ethnographers strive to develop egalitarian working relationships with their informants, with the result that many of them have dropped the term *informants* entirely, replacing it with other terms such as *respondents*, *consultants*, or even, simply, *the people with whom I work*.

## Thinking about Participant Observation

What might be some advantages and disadvantages of participant observation? Do the apparent advantages outweigh the potential disadvantages? What is the purpose of full disclosure? What are some potential drawbacks to this approach? When might partial disclosure or even covert forms of participant observation be preferable? What sorts of ethical considerations might arise when members of the community are not fully aware of the researcher's purpose for being among them?

The most significant and revealing data ethnographers collect often come from the conversations they have with people in the field. Canadian anthropologist Andrew Walsh (2007, 207), who has done extensive fieldwork in Madagascar, stresses the importance of seemingly mundane conversations:

> The simple fact that anthropological work, and ethnographic fieldwork in particular, necessitates conversations and enables collaborations among people who would otherwise have no reason to associate with one another must surely be one of its most valuable and attractive features. Like unlikely comparisons, unlikely conversations and collaborations can bear unexpected fruit.

In contrast to formal interviews, which are more structured and thus less likely to uncover unexpected information, informal conversations can lead to a fuller understanding of what is important to informants. Informal conversations allow anthropologists and those with whom they work to encounter one another on a more equal footing, which permits the consultants more freedom to direct the course the discussion takes and elaborate on points they feel to be critical to their experiences. By establishing the researcher as an equal participant rather than a leader in the interaction, conversations also encourage informants to feel more at ease and thus more willing to reveal the intimate details of their lives.

**participant observation**  A method of data collection in which a researcher lives and works closely with the people whose way of life she or he is studying while participating in their lives as much as possible.

Anthropologists working in the field must find a balance between professionalism and friendship when establishing relationships with the people with whom they carry out their fieldwork. Friendship often arises naturally between people who work closely for an extended period of time, but maintaining focus on an end goal is necessary to the success of a research project. At the same time, this focus should not be so rigid that it forces a static structure upon the researcher's interactions with others. Human interaction is subject to variation, and the most authentic discoveries are often a result of the unexpected.

## Recording Data

Fieldwork involves more than participating and observing—it also involves recording what happened in the field. Effective note taking is essential to fieldwork because researchers cannot trust their memories to keep track of the vast amount of information that comes at them in the field. Fieldworkers often carry around a notebook and a pencil to jot down brief notes about what they are seeing, hearing, doing, or thinking, as well as the context in which significant events take place. Notes about context are essential because they can communicate important but subtle details that are easily forgotten. These days, fieldworkers also often use digital cameras and audio recorders to document what they are seeing and hearing. Whichever method a researcher chooses to use, data recording should take place as unobtrusively as possible, to avoid interfering with the natural course of events or making participants feel as though their actions are under scrutiny. On the other hand, fieldworkers may sometimes find that participants want their activities to be recorded and may even solicit the researcher's involvement.

Creating field notes is a two-step process. Step one is taking brief jottings (or making digital recordings) in the field. Step two involves turning those brief jottings (or recordings) into detailed field notes. As a result, anthropologists tend to spend a lot of time in front of their computers, writing as complete and coherent a set of notes as possible. Most ethnographers try to write up field notes on a daily basis. As they do, places for further inquiry become plain, and a back-and-forth process begins. The ethnographer collects information, writes it down, thinks about it, analyzes it, and then takes new questions and interpretations back to the people with

whom he or she is working to see if the new questions and interpretations are more accurate than the previous ones.

When writing up field notes—and even when making brief jottings in the field—researchers must always remain aware of their own role as a participant and an observer. The relationships anthropologists form with their informants and other members of the community can influence the results of the ethnography. So too can anthropologists' feelings and personal impressions affect what details they record and how they interpret what they have seen and experienced. Here is a setting where ethnographers can explicitly engage in a reflexive exploration of their own field experiences as well as the perspectives of those with whom they have been working.

The ability to do fieldwork and then write about it in a productive and coherent manner is an art that anthropologists strive to perfect throughout their careers. It requires field researchers to remain dedicated to their project, attentive to many sorts of details, and open to the unfamiliar. As important as these personal qualities are, however, researchers must always remember that they are not alone in the field. The success of their endeavours depends on the willingness of others to share aspects of their lives with them. In return for this great gift of time and resources, anthropologists are obligated—at the very least—to depict their informants' ways of life as accurately and faithfully as possible.

## Questions of Authority

Fifty years ago, many Western readers of ethnographies often assumed that the most reliable accounts of non-Western ways of life were those written by anthropologists or other social scientists. Today, most members of the academic community recognize that the people at the centre of a study are in fact the ultimate authority on their own experiences. This change in perspective accompanied the recognition that the content of ethnography is a joint production of conversations in which ethnographers and the people with whom they work are equal partners. As a result, contemporary ethnographers try to work *with* communities to include individuals' voices within their texts.

Michael J. Kral and Lori Idlout (2006) describe how these approaches are exemplified in the Unikkaartuit

Project—a **participatory action research (PAR)** project focussed on Inuit communities in Nunavut. An important part of this project has been the merging of anthropological and Inuit understandings. This objective was achieved through the inclusion of members of the communities under investigation as researchers, and through the collection of community members' stories, as told by the people themselves. This focus on individuals' stories was so integral to the research approach that it gave the project its name—*unikkaartuit* means "the people's stories" (Kral and Idlout 2006, 60).

Kral and Idlout identify the central "problem" with traditional ethnographic work as a lack of effort "to involve communities in the design and planning of the research," which "too often fail[s] to provide results in forms that are useful to the people studied" (2006, 56). Although anthropologists try to provide accounts of other ways of life that are accurate and trustworthy, it has often been the case that their research projects have been shaped primarily by controversies within their academic discipline. This state of affairs has often meant that projects have involved no prior consultation with the people who will be the focus of the research. By not allowing community members to articulate their own interests at all stages of the research, anthropologists risk misrepresenting and misinterpreting key aspects of social life. They also risk allowing their own research interest to inordinately shape the outcomes of their fieldwork. Ultimately, this sort of one-sided approach can lead to a largely false representation of the society as a whole. Today, more and more ethnographers are consulting with the people whose way of life they study to identify research projects that build on issues of central concern to people themselves. This kind of prior consultation, which allows ethnographers and their consultants to locate a research focus where their interests coincide, avoids creating a hierarchy of authority in which the researcher is at the top. The inequalities engendered by such a hierarchy risk creating tension and animosity between the researcher and members of the community. Involving members of the community not only in developing and executing the research plan

**participatory action research (PAR)** A type of fieldwork that aims to bring about social change through the collection of data and the empowerment of community members as researchers in the projects.

## Conducting an Informal Interview

Find a partner whose way of life you would like to learn more about. Meet with that person to identify a research question that relates to his or her lifestyle (e.g., "How does your partner's cultural background influence the types of foods she or he likes to prepare for dinner?"). Once you have decided on a research question, conduct an informal interview in which you discuss topics relevant to your question. As the discussion progresses, take brief notes to record what your partner says and any contextualizing factors that could be relevant to your study. Throughout the process, try to make your partner feel at ease, and be as unobtrusive as possible while taking notes. When you feel that you have fully explored your research question, thank your partner for his or her time, and begin the process of turning your brief notes into detailed field notes. As you write, try to recall exactly what your partner said, and keep the following questions in mind: What impact could the setting have had on the interview process? Was the setting formal or informal? Familiar or unfamiliar? Quiet or noisy? Did your mental state influence the way in which you interacted with your partner? Did any of your partner's responses make you feel uncomfortable in any way? How might your actions and reactions—either verbal or non-verbal—have influenced what your partner decided to tell you? How might your pre-existing relationship with your partner have affected the discussion? Did the interview feel like a discussion between equals, or did one of you have more power than the other? Were any of your partner's responses surprising to you, and did any take the conversation in an entirely unanticipated direction?

but also in analyzing and disseminating the outcomes of the research project disrupts this hierarchy, allowing for the inclusion of more perspectives. As a result, a more accurate, nuanced ethnographic account can be developed.

A related problem with traditional ethnographic approaches is that they establish a hierarchy of authority in which the researcher is at the top, followed by the informants with whom she or he works most closely, and finally the members of the wider society who are less directly involved in the research. This hierarchy often creates tension and animosity between the researcher and members of the community. Involving members of the community in developing and executing the research plan and in analyzing and disseminating the outcomes of the research project dissolves this hierarchy, allowing for the inclusion of more perspectives. As a result, a truer, more nuanced reflection of reality can develop.

Kral and Idlout describe how researchers and community members drew on the principles of PAR in carrying out the Unikkaartuit Project, the main purpose of which was "to help understand the context for the high incidence of suicide in Nunavut" (2006, 59). The idea for the project arose at a conference on suicide prevention, out of a discussion involving Inuit and non-Inuit, "including northerners, frontline mental health workers in the North and South, and academics" (ibid.). All involved agreed that the project should involve collaborative approaches that embraced contributions from members of the affected communities. The planning of the study was undertaken by a "multidisciplinary academic research team" in conjunction with a "steering committee" made up of Inuit "youth, elders, and others involved in community health and wellness" (60). After the team had secured funding, the team worked together to design and conduct semi-structured and open-ended interviews meant to "reveal Inuit meanings and experiences of wellness, happiness, health, unhappiness, and healing" and also "explicate local understandings of causes and consequences of suicide" (61). Throughout the interview process, the Inuit and non-Inuit fieldworkers met with local community leaders to review their findings. In the end, by integrating the voices of the researched equally with the voices of the researchers, the study uncovered a vast amount of information that benefitted the discipline of anthropology and the Inuit communities alike.

## Key Terms

culture shock   387
participant observation   388

participatory action research   390

▲ A Roma woman and her child guard their belongings as they wait to be relocated after authorities tore down their ramshackle house in Craica, a shantytown on the outskirts of Baia Mare, Romania. Photo: AFP/Stringer/Getty Images

## Chapter Outline

N ot all human groups are equal to one another in terms of wealth, power, or prestige. Indeed, in complex human societies, a variety of forms of social inequality are regularly passed on from generation to generation. This chapter looks at forms of social inequality based on gender, class, caste, race, ethnicity, and nationalism. We also explore some of the ways different societies regularly attempt to justify forms of inequality by attempting to make them appear unchangeable and eternal, rather than the outcome of historically contingent cultural and political practices.

I n Chapter 12, we observed that most people in the world today come under the authority of one or another nation-state and that all nation-states are socially stratified. But inequality within nation-states may be constructed out of multiple categories arranged in different, and sometimes contradictory, hierarchies of stratification. We shall focus in this chapter on six such categories: gender, class, caste, race, ethnicity, and nationality. It is important to emphasize from the outset that *every one of these categories is a cultural invention* designed to create boundaries around one or another imagined community. *None* of these categories maps onto permanent biological subdivisions within the human species, although members of societies that employ these categories often will invoke "nature" to shore up their legitimacy.

Some of these patterns of inequality (e.g., gender, class, caste) reach back thousands of years into human history. Others (e.g., race, ethnicity, and nationality) are closely associated with European colonialism beginning some five hundred years ago. The spread of capitalism and colonial powers around the world reshaped forms of stratification that predated their arrival, as well as introducing new types of stratification into formerly independent, egalitarian societies. Anthropologists and other social scientists have argued with one another about how these categories should be defined and whether they can be usefully applied cross-culturally, and we will look at some of their arguments. But these observations are quite abstract, so we begin with an ethnographic example to illustrate the issues involved.

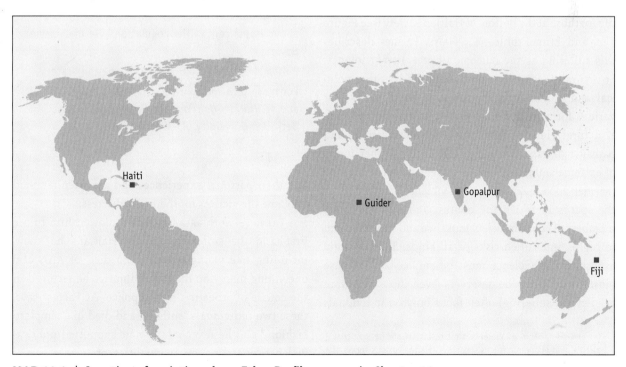

**MAP 14.1** | Location of societies whose EthnoProfiles appear in Chapter 14.

# Inequality and Structural Violence in Haiti

The entire world focused on Haiti in January 2010, when a devastating earthquake struck the country, killing more than a thousand people, rendering more than a million people homeless, and turning much of the built environment to rubble. Paul Farmer is an anthropologist and medical doctor who has been involved with aid work in Haiti since 1983. The organization he co-founded, Partners in Health (PIH), provided care to many who suffered in the earthquake and is active in efforts to rebuild and improve medical facilities that were lost (see PIH's website for details: www.pih.org/country/haiti/; also see PIH Canada's website for information on how Canadians are contributing to PIH's efforts in Haiti: http://pihcanada.org/our-work/haiti). Today, the organization continues to be involved in strengthening Haiti's health care systems in various ways, including partnering with the Haitian government to help build the University Hospital in Mirebalais and train a new generation of doctors, nurses, and health care workers.

One reason the effects of the earthquake were so devastating is that most Haitians live under precarious circumstances, with child mortality rates around 87 per 1000 live births. Farmer's activities as a physician have exposed him to extreme forms of human suffering that have long been taken-for-granted aspects of everyday life for those at the bottom of Haitian society (see Figure 14.1 and EthnoProfile 14.1: Haiti). Farmer describes this suffering as the outcome of **structural violence**. Structural violence is a product of the way that political and economic forces structure people's risks for various forms of suffering within a population. Much structural violence takes the form of infectious and parasitic disease. But it can also include other forms of extreme suffering, such as hunger, torture, and rape (Farmer 2002, 424). Structural violence circumscribes the spaces in which the poorest and least powerful members of Haitian society must live and subjects them to highly intensified risks of all kinds. The *structural* aspect of this violence must be emphasized because most Western outside observers (even those who want to alleviate suffering) often focus only on individuals

**structural violence** Violence that results from the way that political and economic forces structure risk for various forms of suffering within a population.

**FIGURE 14.1** | Dr. Paul Farmer with an AIDS patient at a medical clinic in a rural Haitian village. Political and economic forces structure people's risks for various forms of suffering in Haiti as elsewhere.

## EthnoProfile 14.1

### Haiti

**Region:** Caribbean

**Nation:** Haiti

**Population:** 7,500,000

**Environment:** Rough, mountainous terrain; tropical to semiarid climate

**Livelihood:** Varied; about 80 per cent of the population lives in extreme poverty

**Political organization:** Multi-party nation-state

**For more information:** Farmer, Paul. 1992. *AIDS and Accusation: Haiti and the Geography of Blame.* Berkeley: University of California Press.

and their personal experiences and are often tempted to blame the victims for their own distress.

Farmer's work as a physician allowed him to see first-hand the suffering of poor Haitians he knew, including one young woman who died of AIDS and one young man who died from injuries he received in the course of a beating by the police. As Farmer says, these two individuals "suffered and died in exemplary fashion," and he reveals how state-supported political violence operating on inequalities of gender, social class, and race conspired "to constrain agency" and "crystallize into the sharp, hard surfaces of individual suffering" (2002, 425).

Acéphie Joseph was the woman who died of AIDS at 25, in 1991, one of the first in her rural village. Her parents had been prosperous peasant farmers selling produce in village markets until 1956, when the fertile valley in which they lived was flooded after a dam was built to generate electricity. They lost everything and became "water refugees," forced to try to grow crops on an infertile plot in the village where they were resettled. Farmer writes that Acéphie's "beauty and her vulnerability may have sealed her fate as early as 1984" (2002, 426). She began to help her mother carry produce to the market along a road that went past the local military barracks, where soldiers like to flirt with the passing women, and one soldier in particular approached her. "Such flirtation is seldom unwelcome, at least to all appearances. In rural Haiti, entrenched poverty made the soldiers—the region's only salaried men—ever so much more attractive" (427). Although Acéphie knew he had a wife and children, she nevertheless did not rebuff him; indeed, he visited her family, who approved of their liaison. "I could tell that the old people were uncomfortable, but they didn't say no. . . . I never dreamed he would give me a bad illness . . . it was a way out, that's how I saw it," Acéphie explained. Only a few weeks after the beginning of their sexual relationship, the soldier died. Eventually, Acéphie found work as a maid, began a relationship with a young man, and planned to marry. After three years, Acéphie became pregnant and went home to her village to give birth, but she had a very difficult delivery; when she finally sought medical help for a series of infections, she was diagnosed with AIDS. After her death, her father hanged himself.

Chouchou Louis grew up in a village on the Central Plateau of Haiti. He attended primary school briefly and then worked with his father and older sister to raise produce after his mother died. In the 1980s, times were especially difficult under the repressive dictatorship of Jean-Claude Duvalier. Those Haitians who tried to flee by boat to the United States were termed *economic* rather than *political* refugees and, thanks to an existing treaty between the two countries, were promptly returned to Haiti. By 1986, a pro-democracy movement had grown powerful enough in Haiti to force Duvalier to leave the country, but he was replaced in power by the military. Although the US government based its hopes for the introduction of democracy on this military government and supplied it with over $200 million in aid, poor peasants like Chouchou Louis and his family continued to be subject to military violence. An election in 1990 brought the popular leader Father Jean-Bertrand Aristide to power with over 70 per cent of the vote, but in 1991 he was ousted in a coup. Anger in the countryside at this coup "was soon followed by sadness, then fear, as the country's repressive machinery, dismantled during the seven months of Aristide's tenure, was hastily reassembled under the patronage of the army" (Farmer 2002, 429). Soon thereafter Chouchou was riding in a truck when he made a remark about the poor state of the roads that might have been interpreted as a veiled criticism of the coup. On the same truck was an out-of-uniform soldier, who, at the next checkpoint, had Chouchou dragged from the truck and beaten. Although he was let go, he lived in fear of another arrest, which came several months later, with no explanation, when he was visiting his sister. He was taken to the nearest military checkpoint and tortured. Three days later, he was dumped in a ditch to die; the day after, Farmer was brought in to treat him, but his injuries were too severe. He died three days later.

Acéphie and Chouchou are individuals, so it is natural to ask how representative their experiences might be. Farmer's experience among many poor women with AIDS allowed him to recognize that all of their cases, including Acéphie's, showed "a deadly monotony." Farmer observes that "the agony of Acéphie and Chouchou was, in a sense, 'modal' suffering. In Haiti, AIDS and political violence are two leading causes of death among young adults" (2002, 431). And all the key events that contributed to their deaths, from the flooding of the valley to the funding of the Haitian army, were the consequences of human agency. Because of this,

> the agency of Acéphie and Chouchou was . . . curbed at every turn. These grim biographies suggest that the social and economic forces that have helped to shape the AIDS epidemic are, in every sense, the same forces that led to Chouchou's death and to the larger repression in which it was eclipsed. What is more, both were "at risk" of such a fate long before they met the soldiers who altered their destinies. *They* were both, from the outset, victims of structural violence. (431)

The deaths of Acéphie and Chouchou can be explained if their ethnographic and historical context is articulated, as Farmer tries to do. It is also important to identify specifically the relations of power in which each of them was embedded, for these contributed to the likelihood that their suffering and death would take the forms they took. For example, "gender helps explain why Acéphie died of AIDS whereas Chouchou died from torture . . . also . . . why the suffering of Acéphie is much more commonplace than that of Chouchou" (433). Race or ethnicity helps explain why illness is more likely to be suffered by the descendants of enslaved Africans, and social class helps explain why they were more likely to be poor. To understand why the Haitian state should need or receive aid from other countries, as well as why it should use violence against its citizens, requires a consideration of the structure of the Haitian state and its position within a global system of nation-states. In what follows, we explore each of these dimensions of inequality—and a bit more besides.

## Gender

Anthropological research on issues involving sex and gender increased enormously in the later part of the twentieth century, especially in the work of feminist anthropologists, who focused not only on reproductive roles and sexuality but also on the question of gender inequality. Beginning in the 1970s, feminist anthropologists dissatisfied with gender inequality in their own societies closely examined the ethnographic record to determine whether male dominance was a feature of all human societies. Early work seemed to suggest that male dominance was in fact universal. For example, Sherry Ortner (1974) suggested that male dominance was rooted in a form of binary cultural thinking that opposed male to female; males were ranked higher than females because females were universally seen as "closer to nature" by virtue of the fact that they gave birth and nursed their young. Yet Jane Collier, Michelle Rosaldo, and Sylvia Yanagisako (1997) were able to show that the roles of men and women within families—even the very idea of what constituted a "family"—varied enormously, cross-culturally and historically. They concluded that the "nuclear family" of father, mother, and children was far from universal and, in fact, was best understood as a relatively recent historical consequence of the rise of industrial capitalism in western European societies. Attention to history also led Marxist-feminist anthropologists like Eleanor Leacock to argue that women's subordination to men was not inevitable but rather was connected explicitly to Western capitalist colonization, the beginnings of private property ownership, and the emergence of the state. She used ethnographic and historical evidence from North America and South America, Melanesia, and Africa to show how Western capitalist colonization had transformed egalitarian pre-colonial Indigenous gender relations into unequal, male-dominated gender relations (Leacock 1983). And more support for the existence of a vast variety of gender roles in prehistory are being revealed by archaeologists like Joan Gero, Rosemary Joyce, and Kathryn Reese-Taylor.

> ⟲ For a review of the differences between gender and sex, see Chapter 13, pp. 350–2; for a discussion of archaeological evidence that is being used to infer gender roles in the past, see Chapter 7, pp. 185–7.

Marilyn Strathern (1988) has argued that the particular relations between males and females in society need to be recognized as just one example of gender symbolism. In her work, she defines *gender* as "those categorizations of persons, artifacts, events sequences, and so on which draw upon sexual imagery—upon the ways in which the distinctiveness of male and female characteristics make concrete people's ideas about the nature of social relations" (1988, ix). Thinking of gender in this way helps make sense of the fact that in some societies gendered forms of inequality not only are applied to phenotypic males and females but also may be used to structure relations between different categories of men, as in the Nicaraguan contrast between "manly men" and *cochones* described in Chapter 13. Similarly, Roy Richard Grinker found that male village-dwelling Lese householders of the Democratic Republic of Congo distinguished themselves from their forest-dwelling Efe pygmy trading partners using the same unequal gender categories that they used to distinguish themselves from their wives. From the point of view of Lese men, Efe partners and Lese wives were subordinate to them because both had been incorporated within the households of Lese men (Grinker 1994).

Anthropologist Ann Stoler (1997) studied the effects of Dutch colonialism in Indonesia and has compared it with colonialism elsewhere. She described how the relationship between white European colonizers and the non-white Indigenous males was regularly conceived in terms both of "racial" inequality and of gender inequality. That is, colonizers constructed a "racial" divide between colonizer and colonized that ranked "white" colonial males above "non-white" Indigenous males. At the same time, by violently punishing any hint of sexual involvement between Indigenous males and "white" women, while allowing themselves unrestricted sexual access to Indigenous women, white male colonizers "feminized" Indigenous males—constructing them as less than fully male because they had been unable to defend either their land or "their women" from more powerful white colonizers. In Canada, First Nations women and men were treated in a similar way during the country's period of colonization. European men who were explorers and colonizers commonly partnered with First Nations women, but First Nation men were not allowed to speak with European women. Moreover, children of First Nations women and European men were stigmatized, denied the rights and privileges of other Indigenous children, and referred to as "Metis" or "mixed blood."

Haiti began as a colony of France and achieved its independence following a successful revolt of black slaves against their white colonial masters. As Nina Glick Schiller and Georges Fouron (2001, 133) argue, however, "Haiti has its own particular and mixed messages about gender that give to women and men both rights and responsibilities to family and nation." Women appear in official stories about the Haitian Revolution, and some of them are even portrayed as heroines; most, however, are usually portrayed as silent wives and mothers. Moreover, the founders of the Haitian state borrowed from their former French masters "a patriarchal idea of family as well as a civil code that gave men control of family life, wealth, and property" (134). Women belonged to the Haitian nation, but "state officials and the literate elite envisioned women as able to reproduce the nation only in conjunction with a Haitian man" (134). Until recently, Haitian women who married foreigners lost their Haitian citizenship. High-status Haitian women are those who are supported economically by their Haitian husbands and who stay home with their children. Schiller and Fouron argue that many Haitians "still believe that to live by these values is to uphold not only family but also national honor" (135) (Figure 14.2).

By contrast, Haitian women who cannot live by these values are accorded low status. On the one hand, this means that they are not confined to the domestic

FIGURE 14.2 | The founders of the Haitian state borrowed from their former French masters an idea of gender that gave men control of family life and political power. Until recently, Haitian women who married foreigners lost their Haitian citizenship, and their children were not considered Haitians.

sphere. On the other hand, for this very reason, they are assumed to be always sexually available. "Men in Haiti see women alone or in the workplace as willing and able to trade their sexuality for other things they need. Men may ask rather than take, but often they are making an offer that women cannot afford to refuse" (Schiller and Fouron 2001, 139–40). This describes well the structural constraints with which Acéphie Joseph had to contend; options open to women of higher social position were not available to her. To understand why, however, we need to look more closely at what anthropologists have to say about the connections between social class and social inequality.

## Class

In general, classes are hierarchically arranged social groups defined on economic grounds. That is, members of higher-ranked social classes have disproportionately high access to sources of wealth in the society, whereas members of lower-ranked classes have much more limited access to wealth (Figure 14.3).

The concept of class has a double heritage in modern anthropology, one stemming from Europe and the other from North America. European social scientists lived in states with a long history of social class divisions reaching back into the Middle Ages and, in some cases, even earlier times. In their experience, social classes were well-entrenched and relatively closed groups. In the late

FIGURE 14.3 | Members of different social classes often live within easy sight of one another. Here, luxury apartments and squatter settlements rub shoulders in Rio de Janeiro, Brazil.

1700s, both the Industrial Revolution and the French Revolution promised to end the oppressive privileges of the ruling class and to equalize everyone's access to wealth. However, class divisions did not wither away in Europe during the nineteenth century; they just changed their contours. Followers of Karl Marx judged that, at best, an old ruling class had been displaced by a new one: feudal aristocrats had been replaced by bourgeois capitalists. The lowest level in European societies—rural peasants—were partially displaced as well, with the appearance of the urban working class. But the barriers separating those at the top of the class hierarchy from those at the bottom seemed just as rigid as ever.

Marx defines classes in terms of their members' different relations to the means of production. This means that as long as a particular set of unequal productive relations flourishes in a society, the classes defined by these unequal roles in the division of labour will also persist. The French Revolution had triggered the displacement of aristocrats and peasants who had played the key roles in European feudalism. They were replaced by new key classes—industrial entrepreneurs and the industrial working class—who were linked together within the capitalist mode of production. In time, Marx predicted, these industrial workers would

> For a discussion of Marxist ideas about classes in relation to the means of production, see Chapter 11, pp. 308–311.

become the new "leading class," rising up to oust capitalists when the socialist revolution came.

As Marx was well aware, all those who are linked to the means of production in the same way (e.g., as workers) often do not recognize what they have in common and may therefore fail to develop the kind of solidarity among themselves—the "class consciousness"—that could, in Marx's view, lead to revolution. Indeed, the possibility of peasant- or working-class solidarity in many of the stratified societies studied by anthropologists is actively undercut by institutions of clientage. According to anthropologist M.G. Smith ([1954] 1981, 31), clientage "designates a variety of relationships, which all have inequality of status of the associated persons as a common characteristic." Clientage is a relationship between *individuals* rather than groups. The party of superior status is the patron, and the party of inferior status is the client. Stratified societies united by links of clientage can be very stable. Low-status clients believe their security depends on finding a high-status individual who can protect them. For example, clientage is characteristic of *compadrazgo*, or ritual coparenthood relationships, found throughout Latin America. The Latin American societies in which compadrazgo flourishes are class societies, and parents who are peasants or workers often seek landowners or factory owners to serve as *compadres*, or godparents, at the baptism of their children. When the baptism ritual is completed, the parents and godparents of the child have a new, more relaxed relationship. They call each other "compadre" and can feel freer to seek

clientage   The institution linking individuals from upper and lower levels in a stratified society.

one another out for support in times of need. While the lower-status biological parents may seek out their higher-status compadres for economic relief, the higher-status individuals might seek out their lower-status compadres for political support.

Marx's view of class is clearly different from the hegemonic view of class in Canada and the United States. For generations, Canadians and Americans have believed that they may pursue wealth, power, and prestige unhampered by the unyielding class barriers characteristic of traditional European societies. As a result, many social scientists trained in Canada and the United States (including cultural anthropologists) have tended to define social classes primarily in terms of income level and to argue that such social classes are open, porous, and permeable, rather than rigid and exclusionary. Upward class mobility is supposed to be, in principle, attainable by all people, regardless of how low their social origins are.

But the promise of equal opportunity for upward class mobility has not been realized by all those living in either Canada or the United States. In the early twentieth century, social scientists concluded that an unyielding "colour bar" prevented upward class mobility in both North American countries. In Canada, this colour bar had a particularly limiting effect on individuals with Aboriginal ancestry; in the United States, it had the greatest negative effect on those with African ancestry. One participant in these studies, an American sociologist named W. Lloyd Warner, argued in 1936 that the colour bar looked more like the rigid barrier reported to exist between castes in India than the supposedly permeable boundary separating social classes in North America. That is to say, membership in a caste is ascribed at birth, and each ranked caste is closed such that individuals are not allowed to move from one caste into another. Membership in social classes is also ascribed at birth, according to Warner; but unlike castes, classes are not closed and individual social mobility from one class into another is possible (Sharma 1999, 15; Harrison 1995, 1998; Warner 1936). Warner's distinction between *caste* and *class* became standard for decades in North American cultural anthropology.

## Caste

The word *caste* comes from the Portuguese word *casta*, meaning "chaste." Portuguese explorers applied it to the stratification systems they encountered in South

Asia in the fifteenth century. They understood that these societies were divided into a hierarchy of ranked subgroups, each of which was "chaste" in the sense that sexual and marital links across group boundaries were forbidden. That is, in anthropological terms, castes were endogamous, and many anthropologists agree that caste is fundamentally a form of kinship (Guneratne 2002). Most Western scholars have taken the stratification system of India as the prototype of caste stratification, and some insist that caste cannot properly be said to exist outside India. However, anthropologists often use the term *caste* to describe societies outside India when they encounter one of two features: (1) endogamous occupational groupings whose members are looked down on by other groups in the society or (2) an endogamous ruling elite who set themselves above those they rule. Anthropologist James Vaughan (1970; see also Tamari 1991) reviewed the data on caste systems in western Africa. The presence of endogamous, stigmatized occupational groupings was common in all societies of the Sahara as well as all societies located within a band of territory bordered by Senegal to the west, Lake Chad to the east, the Sahara to the north, and the coastal rain forest to the south. Vaughan also found castes in a second cultural area located in the mountain ranges that lie along the modern border between Nigeria and Cameroon. In this region, many societies had endogamous groups of "blacksmiths" whose status was distinct from that of other members of society. These "blacksmiths" were not despised, however; if anything, they were feared or regarded with awe.

The concept of "caste" was also used by anthropologist Jacques Maquet (1970) to describe the closed, endogamous ranked strata of Tutsi, Hutu, and Twa in the central African kingdom of Rwanda prior to 1959. Pierre van den Berghe (1970) documents the history of caste-like relationships dating from the beginnings of white settlement in southern Africa that culminated in the twentieth-century "colour caste" system distinguishing Whites, Asians, Coloureds, and Bantu that was enforced in apartheid South Africa. De Vos and Wagatsuma (1966) used the term *caste* to describe the

**caste** A ranked group within a hierarchically stratified society that is closed, prohibiting individuals to move from one caste to another.

*burakumin* of Japan, low-ranking endogamous groups traditionally associated with polluting occupations, who have been subjected to dehumanizing stereotypes and residential segregation from other Japanese. Andrea Geiger (2011), from Simon Fraser University, has used the term *caste* in a similar way in her study of lower-class Japanese immigrants' experiences in Canada and the United States in the late nineteenth and early twentieth centuries, in which she notes that the *race*-based discrimination that these recent immigrants faced in North America was very similar to the *caste*-based discrimination they had faced in their homeland. Ursula Sharma (1999, 85–6) suggests that the concept of "caste" might also be used to characterize the relations between the Rom of Europe and their non-Rom neighbours, who for centuries have subjected the Rom to stigmatization, social segregation, and economic exclusion. To better understand why these examples of social inequality have been called "caste," we will look more closely at the best-studied example of caste in the ethnographic literature.

## Caste in India

The term *caste*, as most Western observers use it, combines two distinct south Asian concepts. The first concept, labelled as *varna*, is the widespread Hindu notion that Indian society is ideally divided into priests, warriors, farmers, and merchants—four functional subdivisions analogous to the estates of medieval and early modern Europe (Sharma 1999; Guneratne 2002). The second concept is the existence of *jati*, which are localized, named, endogamous groups. Although jati names are frequently the names of occupations (e.g., farmer, saltmaker), there is no universally agreed-upon way to group the many local jatis within one or another of the four varnas. This is why members of different jatis can disagree about where their own jatis ought to belong. In any case, varna divisions are more theoretical in nature, whereas jati is the more significant term in most of the local village settings where anthropologists have traditionally conducted fieldwork.

Villagers in the southern Indian town of Gopalpur defined a jati for anthropologist Alan Beals (1962)

## In Their Own Words

### Burakumin: Overcoming Hidden Discrimination in Japan

*Tomoe Kawasaki is a college staff member in Japan and identifies herself as a Buraku. While the Japanese government has passed laws prohibiting discrimination against Burakumin, prejudice remains. Here, Tomoe tells her story.*

My parents didn't tell me much about Buraku, and they raised me as far away from the Buraku as possible. They didn't want me to suffer any discrimination. Upon taking a class about Buraku issues in college, I started to face my family roots—roots that I was forgetting. I sometimes wrestled with my parents' protective love, and it made me anxious; I wondered if other people would accept me having a Buraku origin. At the same time, it was overwhelmingly joyful for me to learn so much about myself in the contexts of history, culture, and people. Now I often visit my hometown, the Buraku [town] where I lived until the age of 7. Now I am weaving a story that leads to me through the people I was reunited with there. When I took the plunge and faced my roots, and then leaped further into my past, I found a world so wonderful.

Tomoe Kawasaki

Source: Kawasaki 2011. Personal statement. In "Inside Japan's 'Gentleman's Agreement'" [photo essay compiled by Masaru Goto]. www.majiroxnews.com/2011/02/07/inside-japans-gentlemen-agreement.

## EthnoProfile 14.2

## Gopalpur

**Region:** Southern Asia

**Nation:** India

**Population:** 540 (1960)

**Environment:** Centre of a plain, some fertile farmland and pasture

**Livelihood:** Intensive millet farming, some cattle and sheep herding

**Political organization:** Caste system in a modern nation-state

**For more information:** Beals, Alan. 1962. *Gopalpur, a South Indian Village*. New York: Holt, Rinehart, and Winston.

(see EthnoProfile 14.2: Gopalpur). They said it was "a category of men thought to be related, to occupy a particular position within a hierarchy of jatis, to marry among themselves, and to follow particular practices and occupations" (Beals 1962, 25). Beals's informants compared the relationship between jatis of different rank to the relationship between brothers. Ideally, they said, members of low-ranking jatis respect and obey members of high-ranking jatis, just as younger brothers respect and obey older brothers.

Villagers in Gopalpur were aware of at least fifty different jatis, although not all were represented in the village. Because members of jatis have different occupational specialties that they alone can perform, villagers were sometimes dependent on the services of outsiders. For example, there was no member of the Washerman jati in Gopalpur. As a result, a member of that jati from another village had to be employed when people in Gopalpur wanted their clothes cleaned ritually or required clean cloth for ceremonies.

Jatis are distinguished in terms of the foods they eat as well as their traditional occupations. These features have a ritual significance that affects interactions between members of different jatis. In Hindu belief, certain foods and occupations are classed as pure and others as polluting. In theory, all jatis are ranked on a scale from purest to most polluted. Ranked highest of all are the vegetarian Brahmins, who are pure enough to approach the gods. Carpenters and Blacksmiths, who also eat a vegetarian diet, are also assigned a high rank. Below the vegetarians are those who eat "clean," or "pure," meat. In Gopalpur, this group of jatis included Saltmakers, Farmers, and Shepherds, who eat sheep, goats, chicken, and fish but not pork or beef. The lowest-ranking jatis are "unclean" meat eaters, who include Stoneworkers and Basketweavers (who eat pork) as well as Leatherworkers (who eat pork and beef). Occupations that involve slaughtering animals or touching polluted things are themselves considered to be polluting. Jatis that traditionally carry out such activities as butchering and washing dirty clothing are ranked below jatis whose traditional work does not involve polluting activities (Figure 14.4).

Hindu dietary rules deal not only with the kinds of food that may be eaten by different jatis but also with the circumstances in which members of one jati may accept food prepared by members of another. Members of a lower-ranking jati may accept any food prepared by members of a higher-ranking jati. Members of a higher-ranking jati may accept only certain foods prepared by a lower-ranking jati. In addition, members of different jatis should not eat together.

In practice, these rules are not as confining as they appear. In Gopalpur, "'food' referred to particular kinds of food, principally rice. 'Eating together' means eating from the same dish or sitting on the same line. . . .

**FIGURE 14.4** | Gautam Ganu Jadhao, a city worker, removes a cart full of sewage waste from a Bombay (Mumbai) neighbourhood in July 2005. People like him whose occupations are characterized as polluting are ranked at the bottom of the Hindu caste system.

Members of quite different jatis may eat together if they eat out of separate bowls and if they are facing each other or turned slightly away from each other" (Beals 1962, 41). Members of jatis that are close in rank and neither at the top nor at the bottom of the scale often share food and eat together on a daily basis. Strict observance of the rules is saved for ceremonial occasions.

The way in which non-Hindus were incorporated into the jati system in Gopalpur illuminates the logic of the system. For example, Muslims have long ruled the region surrounding Gopalpur; thus, political power has been a salient attribute of Muslim identity. In addition, Muslims do not eat pork or the meat of animals that have not been ritually slaughtered. These attributes, taken together, led the villagers in Gopalpur to rank Muslims above the Stoneworkers and Basketweavers, who eat pork. All three groups were considered to be eaters of unclean meat, however, because Muslims do eat beef.

There is no direct correlation between the status of a jati on the scale of purity and pollution and the class status of members of that jati. Beals (1962, 37) noted, for example, that the high status of Brahmins meant that "there are a relatively large number of ways in which a poor Brahmin may become wealthy." Similarly, members of low-status jatis may find their attempts to amass wealth curtailed by the opposition of their status superiors. In Gopalpur, a group of Farmers and Shepherds attacked a group of Stone workers who had purchased good rice land in the village. Those Stoneworkers were eventually forced to buy inferior land elsewhere in the village. In general, however, regardless of jati, a person who wishes to advance economically "must be prepared to defend his gains against jealous neighbours. Anyone who buys land is limiting his neighbour's opportunities to buy land. Most people safeguard themselves by tying themselves through indebtedness to a powerful landlord who will give them support when difficulties are encountered" (Beals 1962, 39).

Although the interdependence of jatis is explained in theory by their occupational specialties, the social reality is a bit different. For example, Saltmakers in Gopalpur are farmers and actually produce little salt, which can be bought in shops by those who need it. It is primarily in the context of ritual that jati interdependence is given full play. Recall that Gopalpur villagers required the services of a Washerman when they needed ritually clean garments or cloth; otherwise, most villagers washed their own clothing.

To arrange a marriage, to set up the doorway of a new house, to stage a drama, or to hold an entertainment, the householder must call on a wide range of jatis. The entertainment of even a modest number of guests requires the presence of the Singer. The Potter must provide new pots in which to cook the food; the Boin from the Farmer jati must carry the pot; the Shepherd must sacrifice the goat; the Crier, a Saltmaker, must invite the guests. To survive, one requires the co-operation of only a few jatis; to enjoy life and do things in the proper manner requires the co-operation of many. (Beals 1962, 41)

Beals's study of Gopalpur documented three dimensions of caste relations in India that have become increasingly significant over time. First, Beals describes a rural village in which jati membership mattered most on ritual occasions. In the last thirty or so years, cultural practices associated with caste have become even more attenuated or have disappeared as increasingly large numbers of Indians have moved to large cities where they are surrounded by strangers whose caste membership they do not know (Sharma 1999, 37). Migrants still use the idiom of purity and pollution to debate the status of particular castes, but otherwise their understanding of caste usually has nothing to do with ritual status.

Second, Beals describes members of middle-ranking jatis in Gopalpur who treated one another as equals outside of ritual contexts. Subrata Mitra (1994, 61) points out that "[b]y the 1960s, electoral mobilization had led to a new phenomenon called horizontal mobilization whereby people situated at comparable levels within the local caste hierarchy came together in caste associations," many of which formed new political parties to support their own interests. Moreover, increased involvement of Indians in capitalist market practices has led to "a proliferation of modern associations that use traditional ties of *jati* and *varna* to promote collective economic well-being" (65). For example, a housing trust set up for Brahmins in the Indian state of Karnataka recruits Brahmins from throughout the Karnataka region in an effort to overcome "*jati*-based division into quarrelling sects of Brahmins" (66). The interests that draw jatis into coalitions of this kind "often turn out to be class interests. . . . This does not mean that caste and class are the same, since commentators note caste[s] as blurring class divisions as often as they express them. Rather, it tells us that class and caste are not 'inimical' or antithetical" (Sharma 1999, 68).

Third, Beals showed that middle-ranking jatis in Gopalpur in the 1960s were willing to use violence to block the upward economic mobility of members of a low-ranking jati. Similar behaviour was reported in the work of other anthropologists, like Gerald Berreman, who did fieldwork in the late 1950s in the peasant village of Sirkanda in the lower Himalayas of north India. Berreman (1962, 15–16) observed that low-caste people in Sirkanda "do not share, or are not heavily committed to, the 'common official values' which high-caste people affect before outsiders. . . . Low-caste people resent their inferior position and the disadvantages which inhere in it" while "high castes rely heavily on threats of economic and physical sanctions to keep their subordinates in line," such that when low-caste people do publicly endorse "common official values," they do so only out of fear of these sanctions.

In recent years, a number of low-caste groups in urban India have undertaken collective efforts to lift themselves off the bottom of society, either by imitating the ritual practices of higher castes (a process called "Sanskritization") or by converting to a non-Hindu religion (e.g., Buddhism or Christianity) in which caste plays no role. According to Dipankar Gupta, this should not surprise us. His research has shown that "castes are, first and foremost, discrete entities with deep pockets of ideological heritage" and that "the element of caste competition is, therefore, a characteristic of the caste order and not a later addition. . . . This implies that the caste system, as a system, worked primarily because it was enforced by power and not by ideological acquiescence" (2005, 412–13). These challenges have had no effect on changing the negative stereotypes of so-called untouchables held by the so-called clean castes. However, the constitution of India prohibits the practice of untouchability, and the national government has acted to improve the lot of the low castes by passing legislation designed to improve their economic and educational opportunities. In some cases, these measures seem to have succeeded, but violent reprisals have been common. In rural areas, many disputes continue to be over land, as in Gopalpur. However, even worse violence has been seen in urban India, as in 1990, when unrest was triggered by publication of a report recommending increases in

the numbers of government jobs and reserved college places set aside for members of low castes. At the end of the twentieth century, relations between low-caste and high-caste Hindus were described as "conflictual rather than competitive in some localities," with "caste violence . . . recognized as a serious problem in contemporary India" (Sharma 1999, 67).

A key element recognized by all anthropologists who use the concept of "caste" is the endogamy that is enforced, at least in theory, on the members of each ranked group. As van den Berghe (1970, 351) put it, membership in such groups is "determined by birth and for life." Sharma (1999, 85) notes the significance of this link between descent and caste, observing that "in societies where descent is regarded as a crucial and persistent principle (however reckoned, and whatever ideological value it is given) almost any social cleavage can become stabilized in a caste-like form". She suggests the term *castification* to describe a political process by which ethnic or other groups become part of a ranked social order of some kind, probably managed from the top, but which need not develop into a caste system (92–3).

But the principle of descent has also played a central role in the identification and persistence of race, ethnicity, and nation. As noted above, these three categories are all closely bound up with historical developments over the past five hundred years that built the modern world. Indeed, these categories are particularly significant in nation-states, and many contemporary nation-states are of very recent, postcolonial origin. Clearly, to make sense of contemporary postcolonial forms of social stratification, we also need to look more closely at the categories of race, ethnicity, and nation.

## Race

The concept of "race" developed in the context of European exploration, colonization, and conquest, beginning in the fifteenth century. Europeans conquered Indigenous peoples in the Americas and around the world, establishing colonial political economies that were based on the premise of *"terra nullius"*—that is, the idea that the land had not belonged to anyone before their arrival. Because colonialists did not consider the Indigenous peoples who were already living in these areas to be "people," they concluded that the land was "free" to live on. In taking control of the land, the colonizers forced huge numbers of Indigenous peoples to relocate and alter their ways of life; as a result, many died of starvation or disease. By the end of the nineteenth century, light-skinned Europeans had established colonial rule over large territories inhabited by darker-skinned peoples, marking the beginnings of a global racial order (see Smedley 1995, 1998; Harrison 1995; Sanjek 1994; Trouillot 1994; Köhler 1978). Some European intellectuals argued at that time that the human species was subdivided into "natural kinds" of human beings called "races" that could be sharply distinguished from one another on the basis of outward phenotypic appearance. All individuals assigned to the same race were assumed to share many other common features, such as language or intelligence, of which phenotype was only the outward index. *Race* was used both to explain human diversity and to justify the domination of Indigenous peoples and the enslavement of Africans.

## In Their Own Words

### Racism, Colonialism, and Indigeneity in Canada

*Professors Martin Cannon and Lina Sunseri have examined the continuing racism against Aboriginal peoples in Canada. The following text is an excerpt from the conclusion to their edited volume* Racism, Colonialism, and Indigeneity in Canada *(2011).*

On 27 September 2009, Prime Minister Stephen Harper announced to members of the G20 Summit—and the international community—that Canada is unique in being a country unmarked by histories of colonialism. "We . . . have no history of colonialism," he told world leaders, "so we have all of the things that many people admire about the great powers, but none of the things that threaten or bother them." Indigenous peoples and [non-Indigenous] Canadians alike listened in shock and disbelief. In saying these words, the prime minister seemed to contradict his own apology made to residential school survivors in Parliament about colonialism in June 2008. Moreover, his suggestion was that Indigenous efforts to challenge and rupture colonialism and dispossession are merely a "bother" and "threat" to the great powers of the world.

It is not uncommon to hear sentiments like these in Canadian society. Regrettably, they are not limited only to this country's leaders. In the classes we teach, we hear from educated Canadians that colonialism is a thing of the past, entirely disconnected from the present. These attitudes reflect a common sense or taken-for-granted set of assumptions about the nature of colonial dominance, the nature of history, and the making of the nation. In some cases, these attitudes are shaped by hostility toward Indigenous peoples, anti-Indian organizing, and unwillingness to acknowledge histories of land dispossession, even institutionalized racism. On the other hand, these attitudes stem from misunderstanding, ignorance about contemporary colonialism, and a lack of clear vision informed by original nation-to-nation principles.

In writing this anthology, we have hoped to provide readers with a more thorough understanding of the racism that structures the colonial present. We have hoped to show that it is no longer possible to ignore Canada's origins as a colonial creation of both British and French settlers. . . . In summary, we also hope this book will spur readers to further contemplate and reflect on some of our major conclusions, including:

1. That neither racism nor Indigenous peoples are disappearing into the twenty-first century;

2. That the options available for repairing the mistrust and disavowal structuring modern colonial consciousness have already been set out in early historical and nation-to-nation-based agreements, such as the Guswentah or Two Row Wampum;

3. That poverty and economic marginalization continue as obstacles, requiring us to revisit colonial legacies and—in the first historical instance—the dispossession of lands before fully understanding, repairing, and eradicating them;

4. That Indigenous peoples continue to face serious disparities in educational attainments despite ameliorative efforts, the nature of which require us to consider histories of difference-making, anti-racist, and anti-colonial pedagogies, along with—and sometimes even before—strategies aimed at cultural awareness and revitalization . . .;

5. That institutionalized racism is not disappearing, especially as this has been directed toward Indigenous women, men, and nations through the Indian Act, Indian status distinctions, proposed amendments to the Indian Act . . ., and other interlocking systems of oppression based on sexism, colonialism, and patriarchy;

6. That racialized violence (e.g., Stonechild, Stolen Sisters, Ipperwash, Caledonia, Burnt Church, and Gustafsen Lake) continues to take place in Canada, embodying, in itself, the ongoing physical—and symbolic—removal of Indigenous peoples from their lands into the twenty-first century; and

7. That our resistance and resilience as peoples is not disappearing, as is evidenced by the contributions we continue to make in reformulating academia . . ., the arts, sports, and legal reform in Canada.

Dismantling colonial dominance requires breaking with cycles of oppression founded in the first instance upon histories of racism and sex discrimination. . . . Racialization, sexism, and heteronormativity have . . . intersected historically to place Indigenous men and women at a disadvantage relative to the state, the justice system, and each other. We therefore suggest that any meaningful discussions about racism and Indigeneity in Canada take these complex interrelationships into account, as they profoundly shape and structure the experiences of Indigenous peoples.

Colonial injustice racialized injustice. . . . [T]he Indian Act set into motion a way of thinking about identity, governance, and nationhood in racialized terms. . . . For better or worse, racism shapes the everyday experience of Indigenous peoples in Canada, but it does not prevent us from naming and then resisting its parameters.

Source: Cannon and Sunseri 2011, 263–5.

European thinkers, including many early anthropologists, devised schemes for ranking the "races of mankind" from lowest to highest. Not surprisingly, the "white" northern Europeans at the apex of imperial power were placed at the top of this global hierarchy. Darker-skinned peoples, like the Indigenous inhabitants of the Americas or of Asia, were ranked somewhere in the middle. But Africans, whom Europeans bought and sold as slaves and whose homelands in Africa were later conquered and incorporated into European empires, ranked lowest of all. In this way, the identification of races was transformed into *racism*: the systematic oppression of one or more socially defined "races" by another socially defined "race" that is justified in terms of the supposedly inherent biological superiority of the rulers and the supposed inherent biological inferiority of those they rule. It is important to emphasize once again that all the so-called races of human beings are *imagined communities*. There are no major biological discontinuities within the human species that correspond to the supposed racial boundaries created by nineteenth-century European scientists. In other words, the traditional concept of biological "race" in Western society is incoherent and biologically meaningless.

For an overview of the history of the concept of race in anthropology, see Chapter 1, pp. 6–8; for discussion of why race is not considered a biological category, see Chapter 4, p. 71.

Nevertheless, racial thinking persists at the beginning of the twenty-first century, suggesting that racial categories have their origins not in biology but in society. Anthropologists have long argued that race is a culturally constructed social category whose members are identified on the basis of certain selected phenotypic features (e.g., skin colour) that all are said to share. The end result is a highly distorted but more or less coherent set of criteria that members of a society can use to assign people they see to one or another culturally defined racial category. Once these criteria exist, members of society can treat racial categories *as if* they reflect biological reality, using them to build institutions that include or exclude particular culturally defined races. In this way, race can become "real" in its consequences, even if it has no reality in biology.

The social category of "race" is a relatively recent invention. Audrey Smedley (1998, 693) reminds us that in the worlds of European classical antiquity and through the Middle Ages, "no structuring of equality . . . was associated with people *because of their skin colour*" (emphasis in original), and Faye Harrison (1995, 51) points out that "phenotype prejudice was not institutionalized before the sixteenth century." By the nineteenth century, most Europeans (including some early anthropologists) were attempting to classify all humans in the world into a few mutually exclusive racial categories.

**FIGURE 14.5 |** In the late nineteenth and early twentieth centuries, Canada's immigration policy began targeting farmers and other labourers from Eastern Europe. The Ukrainian family pictured here arrived in Quebec City in 1911.

Significantly, from that time until today, as Harrison (1998, 612) emphasizes, "darker skin has come to symbolize the social bottom" (see also Smedley 1998, 694–5).

White domination of European and North American racial hierarchies has been a constant, but some anthropologists who study the cultural construction of whiteness point out that even in North America "whiteness" is not monolithic and that the cultural attributes supposedly shared by "white people" have varied in different times and places. Most often, these attributes vary across class lines, with upper-class white people distancing themselves from lower-class white people. In terms of gender, white men have often had greater status and power than white women have had. And in different periods and places, white people of certain ethnicities or national origins have held greater status and power than others have had. Similarly, the status of those defined by any of the colour categories that have been applied to groups of people across modern history has varied according to shifting ideas about class, ethnic, or national origins.

A great example of how the lines between race, ethnicity, and nationality as sources of inequality may blur can be found in the history of Canada's immigration policy since the late nineteenth century. As Peter Li (2003, 15) notes, the Canadian government has used its immigration policy both "as a means to address the problems of labour shortages and economic development, and to regulate the social, cultural, and symbolic boundary of the nation." Around the end of the nineteenth century, most immigrants to Canada came from the United Kingdom and the United States (both of which had predominantly white populations at the time), and Canada's immigration policy remained fairly open. The first clear exception came in 1885, when the Canadian government passed an act imposing a "head tax" on Asian immigrants from China. When immigration from the United Kingdom and Western Europe started to dry up, Canada began to actively recruit immigrants from the predominantly white nations of Eastern and Southern Europe (Figure 14.5). Around the same time, the Canadian government enacted legislation that restricted immigration from any non-European nation, especially the nations of Southeast Asia and Africa. During this period, Canadians with British or American ancestry were considered to be of higher social standing than immigrants from Eastern or Southern Europe, who in turn were considered to be of higher social standing than non-white immigrants. Even with various reforms between the end of World War II and today, many of which were ostensibly made to avoid excluding people based on race, our immigration policy remains highly selective, favouring immigrants from the United States and certain European nations (including the United Kingdom) over immigrants from less wealthy, typically non-white countries.

## Colourism in Nicaragua

American anthropologist Roger Lancaster (1992, 215) argues that racism exists in Nicaragua but that it is "not as absolute and encompassing a racism as

## In Their Own Words

### Racialized Bodies, Disabling Worlds: Storied Lives of Immigrant Muslim Women

*Parin Dossa reveals the lives of immigrant Muslim women living in Vancouver who are discriminated against not only because they are new to Canada but also because they have physical disabilities. Dossa describes how storytelling provides a way for these women to affirm their identities and their value as human beings.*

My project . . . is to interrogate structures of exclusion and oppression by invoking the words and worlds of racialized women who have disabilities. I seek to demonstrate that people on the margins of society remake their world to affirm their agency and to avoid being perceived as helpless victims. . . . My goal is to bring to the fore issues of social justice and equality. . . .

In their everyday lives, persons with disabilities are given the societal message that they are lesser human beings. . . . My work aims to show that race and gender matter and that these social markers of difference cannot be dismissed under the seemingly neutral category of disability. . . . My data are derived from women in two communities in metropolitan Vancouver: South Asian Muslims from East Africa . . . and Iranian Muslims. Through their individual stories and testimonials I acquired an in-depth understanding of my key research question: What is it like to have a racialized body in a disabling world?". . . Exclusion and the social erasure of racialized individuals with disabilities have compromised their humanity. . . . Stories restore our humanity because they provide flesh to what may otherwise remain abstract (Jackson 2006). The participants in this study carry out this task of reconstituting personhood through speaking about their struggles, aspirations, and accomplishments. . . .

. . . For the women in this study, the starting point of their journeys is Canadian immigration policy, which has excluded them. . . . The premise at the root of this exclusion is that racialized persons who have disabilities cannot meet the labour skills criterion of the immigration policy; they are seen to be an anomaly. No value is

attached to their desire to undertake waged work; instead, they are cast as a population that consumes public services and therefore a drain on the system. . . .

. . . [T]he women in this study take it upon themselves to define their identities and claim the humanity denied them in their everyday lives. This is social justice at work. The women in this study speak in a testimonial voice, fully aware that their stories are links in a chain made up of many stories, each with its thread woven into the larger tapestry in the making. Furthermore, the women in this study do not refer to gender, race, and disability in exclusive terms. With varying emphasis, they interconnect these markers of difference in their lived realities. They are keen to ensure that their activist work, defined in their own terms, does not remain within the discrete spaces of their communities. They speak to advance the cause of a just society. . . .

The women bring forth their embodied, experiential knowledge of what it is like to be discriminated in a disabling world. They show how this world can be transformed into an enabling environment that is inclusive, where people can develop their potential as active citizens. . . . [Their] narratives reveal [their] desire to take their place in Canadian society in a way that positively acknowledges their differences of nationality, abilities, and gendered and race-based identities. The realization of this goal calls for the re-visioning of our social world: this is the mammoth task that the women pursue contextually and on the basis of their knowledge from the margins of society. From their special entry points into the dominant system, they see, hear, and question what others take as given reality.

Source: Dossa 2009, 4–8. © University of Toronto Press, 2009.

that which one encounters in the United States" even though it remains, in his opinion, "a significant social problem." One dimension of Nicaraguan racism contrasts the Spanish-speaking *mestizo* (or "mixed" European and Indigenous) majority of the

highlands with the Indigenous Miskitos and African Caribbeans along the Atlantic coast. The highland mestizos Lancaster knew tended to regard these coastal groups as backward, inferior, and dangerous. These notions were overlaid with political suspicions

**FIGURE 14.6** | This photograph of Nicaraguan children shows a range of skin tones. In some parts of Latin America, such as Nicaragua and Brazil, such variation is used to create a system of classification based on lightness or darkness of skin tone that assigns people with relatively lighter skin to higher status, a phenomenon that anthropologist Roger Lancaster calls *colourism*.

deriving from the fact that Lancaster's informants were Sandinistas and that some Miskito factions had fought with the Contras against the Sandinistas after the Sandinistas deposed the dictator Anastasio Somoza in 1979.

But Lancaster came to see racism toward the coastal peoples as simply an extension of the pattern of race relations internal to highland mestizo culture that he calls colourism: a system of colour identities negotiated situationally along a continuum between white and black (Figure 14.6). In colourism, no fixed race boundaries exist. Instead, individuals negotiate their colour identity anew in every social situation they enter, with the result that the colour they might claim or be accorded changes from situation to situation.

Lancaster's informants used three different systems of colour classification. The first, or "phenotypic," system has three categories—*blanco* (white), *moreno* (brown), and *negro* (black)—that people use to describe the various skin tones that can be seen among Nicaraguan mestizos: "Nicaraguan national culture is mestizo; people's physical characteristics are primarily Indigenous; and in the terms of this phenotypic system, most people are moreno. In this system, *negro* can

denote either persons of African ancestry or sometimes persons of purely Indigenous appearance, whether they are culturally classified as Indio or mestizo" (Lancaster 1992, 217).

Lancaster calls the second system Nicaraguans use the "polite" system, in which all the colours in the phenotypic system are "inflated." That is, Europeans are called *chele* (a Mayan word meaning "blue," referring to the stereotypically blue eyes of people of European ancestry), morenos are called *blanco*, and negros are called *moreno*. Polite terms are used in the presence of the person about whom one is speaking, and Lancaster was told that it was "a grave and violent offence to refer to a black-skinned person as *negro*" (1992, 217). In rural areas, for similar reasons, Indians are called *mestizos* rather than *Indios*.

Lancaster calls the third system of colour terms the "pejorative and/or affectionate" system. This system has only two terms, *chele* (fairer skin and lighter hair) and *negro* (darker skin, darker hair). For example, when the less powerful man in an interaction feels he is being imposed upon by the more powerful man, the former might express his displeasure by addressing the latter as *chele* or *negro*, both of which would be seen as insulting. Paradoxically, members of families call one another *negro* or *negrito mio* as affectionate and intimate terms of address, perhaps precisely because these terms are "informal" and violate the rules of polite discourse (1992, 218).

**colourism** A system of social identities negotiated situationally along a continuum of skin colours between white and black.

## On the Butt Size of Barbie and Shani: Dolls and Race in the United States

*Anthropologist Elizabeth Chin writes about race and Barbie dolls, based on some hands-on research.*

The Shani line of dolls introduced by Mattel in 1991 reduces race to a simulacrum consisting of phenotypical features: skin colour, hair, and butt. Ann DuCille . . . has discussed much of their complex and contradictory nature, highlighting two central issues: derriere and hair. According to DuCille's interviews with Shani designers, the dolls have been remanufactured to give the illusion of a higher, rounder butt than other Barbies. This has been accomplished, they told her, by pitching Shani's back at a different angle and changing some of the proportions of her hips. I had heard these and other rumours from students at the college where I teach: "Shani's butt is bigger than the other Barbies' butts," "Shani dolls have bigger breasts than Barbie," "Shani dolls have bigger thighs than Barbie." DuCille rightly wonders why a bigger butt is necessarily an attribute of blackness, tying this obsession to turn-of-the-century strains of scientific racism.

Deciding I had to see for myself, I pulled my Shani doll off my office bookshelf, stripped her naked, and placed her on my desk next to a naked Barbie doll that had been cruelly mutilated by a colleague's dog (her arms were chewed off and her head had puncture wounds, but the rest was unharmed). Try as I might, manipulating the dolls in ways both painful and obscene, I could find no difference between them, even after prying their legs off and smashing their bodies apart. As far as I have been able to determine, Shani's bigger butt is an illusion (see photo). The faces of Shani and Barbie dolls are more visibly different than their behinds, yet still, why these differences could be considered natural indicators of race is perplexing. As a friend of mine remarked acidly, "They still look like they've had plastic surgery." The most telling difference between Shani and Barbie is at the base of the cranium, where Shani bears a raised mark similar to a branding iron scar: © 1990 MATTEL INC. Barbie's head reads simply

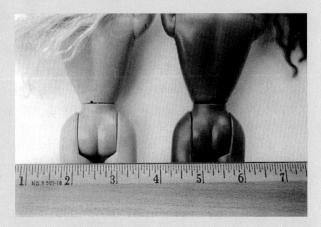

Barbie and Shani from behind.

© MATTEL INC. Despite claims of redesign, both Barbie and Shani's torsos bear a 1966 copyright, and although DuCille asserts that Shani's legs are shaped differently than Barbie's, their legs are imprinted with the same part numbers. This all strongly suggests that despite claims and rumors to the contrary, Shani and Barbie are the same from the neck down.

These ethnically correct dolls demonstrate one of the abiding aspects of racism: that a stolid belief in racial difference can shape people's perceptions so profoundly that they will find difference and make something of it, no matter how imperceptible or irrelevant its physical manifestation might be. If I had to smash two dolls to bits in order to see if their butts were different sizes, the differences must be small indeed: holding them next to each other revealed no difference whatsoever—except colour—regardless of the positioning (crack to crack or cheek to cheek). With the butt index so excruciatingly small, its meaning as a racial signifier becomes frighteningly problematic. Like the notion of race itself, Shani's derriere has a social meaning that is out of all proportion to its scientific measurement.

Source: Chin 1999, 311–13. Reproduced by permission of the American Anthropological Association from *American Anthropologist*, Volume 101, Issue 2, Pages 305–21, June 1999. Not for sale or further reproduction.

Lancaster discovered that "Whiteness is a desired quality, and polite discourse inflates its descriptions of people" (1992, 219). People compete in different settings to claim whiteness. In some settings, individuals may be addressed as *blanco* if everyone else has darker skin; but in other settings, they may have to yield the claim of whiteness to someone else with skin lighter than theirs and accept classification as *moreno*.

Because it allows people some freedom of manoeuvre in claiming higher-status colour for themselves, Nicaraguan colourism may seem less repressive than the rigid black–white racial dichotomy traditional in various other countries. Lancaster points out, however, that all three systems of colourist usage presuppose white superiority and black inferiority. "Africanos, Indios, and lower-class mestizos have been lumped together under a single term—*negro*—that signifies defeat" (1992, 223). Lancaster is not optimistic about the possibilities of successfully overturning this system any time soon in Nicaragua.

## Ethnicity

For anthropologists, **ethnic groups** are social groups whose members distinguish themselves (and/or are distinguished by others) in terms of **ethnicity**—that is, in terms of distinctive cultural features, such as language, religion, or dress. Ethnicity, like race, is a culturally constructed concept. Many anthropologists today would agree with John and Jean Comaroff (1992, 55–7) that ethnicity is created by historical processes that incorporate distinct social groups into a single political structure under conditions of inequality (see also Williams 1989, Alonso 1994). The Comaroffs recognize that ethnic consciousness existed in precolonial and precapitalist societies; however, they and most contemporary anthropologists have been more interested in forms of ethnic consciousness that were generated under capitalist colonial domination.

**ethnic groups** Social groups that are distinguished from one another on the basis of ethnicity.

**ethnicity** A principle of social classification used to create groups based on selected cultural features such as language, religion, or dress.

Ethnicity develops as members of different groups try to make sense of the material constraints they experience within the single political structure that confines them. This is sometimes described as a struggle between *self-ascription* (i.e., insiders' efforts to define their own identity) and *other-ascription* (i.e., outsiders' efforts to define the identities of other groups). In the Comaroffs' view, furthermore, the ruling group turns both itself and the subordinated groups into *classes* because all subordinated social groupings lose independent control "over the means of production and/or reproduction" (1992, 56).

One outcome of this struggle is the appearance of new ethnic groups and identities that are not continuous with any single earlier cultural group (Comaroff and Comaroff 1992, 56). In northern Cameroon, for example, successive German, French, and British colonial officials relied on local Muslim chiefs to identify for them significant local social divisions and adopted the Muslim practice of lumping together all the myriad non-Muslim peoples of the hills and plains and calling them *Haabe* or *Kirdi*—that is, "Pagans." To the extent, therefore, that Guidar, Daba, Fali, Ndjegn, or Guiziga were treated alike by colonial authorities and came to share a common situation and set of interests, members of these groups developed a new, more inclusive level of ethnic identity, like the young man we (Emily A. Schultz and Robert H. Lavenda) met in Guider who introduced himself to us as "just a Kirdi boy." This new, postcolonial "Kirdi" identity, like many others, cannot be linked to any single precolonial cultural reality but has been constructed out of cultural materials borrowed from a variety of non-Muslim Indigenous groups who were incorporated as "pagans" within the colonial political order (see Figure 14.7 and EthnoProfile 14.3: Guider). In a similar vein, francophone Québécois are an ethnic group that did not exist in precolonial times. This unique ethnicity represents a reframed culture, based on a modified form of the French culture and a distinct Québécois language.

The Comaroffs argue that a particular structure of nesting opposed identities was quite common throughout European colonies in Africa. The lowest and least inclusive consisted of local groups, often called "tribes," who struggled to dominate one another within separate colonial states. The middle levels consisted of a variety of entities that crossed local boundaries, sometimes called "supertribes" or "nations." For example,

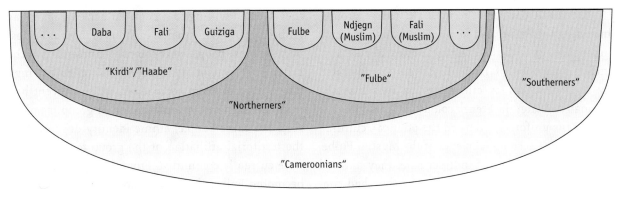

**FIGURE 14.7 | Nesting identities in northern Cameroon (1976).**

the British administered the settler colony of southern Rhodesia (later to become Zimbabwe) according to the policy of "indirect rule," which used Indigenous "tribal" authorities to maintain order on the local level. The effect of indirect rule was thus both to reinforce "tribal" identities where they already existed and to create them where they had been absent in precolonial times. Two such tribal identities, those of the Shona and the Ndebele, became pre-eminent, and each gave rise to its own "(supratribal) nationalist movement."

Both movements joined together in a "patriotic front" to win a war of independence fought against white settlers. This confrontation took place at the highest level of the ethnic hierarchy, which the Comaroffs call "race." At this level, "Europeans" and "Africans"

opposed one another, and each group developed its own encompassing ethnic identity. For example, Africans dealing regularly with Europeans began to conceive of such a thing as "African culture" (as opposed to European culture) and "pan-African solidarity" (to counter the hegemony of the European colonizers). Conversely, in the British settler colonies of southern and eastern Africa, European immigrants defined themselves in opposition to Africans by developing their own "settler-colonial order" based on a caricature of aristocratic Victorian English society (Comaroff and Comaroff 1992, 58).

Because ethnic groups are incorporated into the colony on unequal terms (and, if we follow the Comaroffs, in different class positions), it is not surprising to discover that many individuals in colonies attempted to achieve upward mobility by manipulating their ethnicity. Anthropological studies of such attempts at ethnic mobility constitute, as the Comaroffs put it, "the very stuff of the ethnography of urban Africa" (1992, 63); and one of us (Emily A. Schultz) investigated ethnic mobility in the northern Cameroonian town of Guider.

Guider began as a small settlement of non-Muslim Guidar. In 1830, it was brought into the Muslim Fulbe empire of Yola and remained a Fulbe stronghold under subsequent colonial rule. The Fulbe remained numerically dominant in town until after World War II; by 1958, however, individuals from over a dozen non-Fulbe groups had migrated to town, primarily from the surrounding countryside. By 1976, 83 per cent of household heads in town were recent migrants, and 74 per cent did not claim Fulbe origins.

**EthnoProfile 14.3**

## Guider

**Region:** Western Africa

**Nation:** Cameroon

**Population:** 18,000 (1976)

**Environment:** Savannah

**Livelihood:** Farming, commerce, civil service, cattle raising

**Political organization:** Traditionally, an emirate; today, part of a modern nation-state

**For more information:** Schultz, Emily. 1984. "From Pagan to Pullo: Ethnic Identity Change in Northern Cameroon." *Africa* 54 (1): 46–64.

In the Comaroffs' terms, all these groups, including the Fulbe, had lost political and economic independence with the coming of colonial rule and, under conditions of inequality, were incorporated by the colonizers as ethnic groups into first the German and later the French colony of Cameroon. The Europeans uniformly admired the political, cultural, and religious accomplishments of the Muslim Fulbe. In their own version of indirect rule, they allowed Fulbe chiefs to administer territories they had controlled prior to colonization and, in some cases, handed over to them additional territories whose residents had successfully resisted Fulbe domination in precolonial times.

In 1976, the local ethnic hierarchy in Guider placed Fulbe at the top and recent non-Muslim, non–Fulfulde-speaking migrants from rural areas at the bottom. But in the middle were numerous individuals and families of Fulfulde-speaking Muslims who could claim, and in some cases be accorded, recognition as Fulbe by others in the town. For example, two young men whom Schultz hired as field assistants first described themselves to her as "100 per cent Fulbe." As she got to know them better, however, she learned that the family of one was Ndjegn and the family of the other was Fali. Neither young man saw anything contradictory about being both Fulbe and Ndjegn or Fulbe and Fali. In fact, each ethnic identity was emphasized in different situations. Ndjegn and Fali ethnicity mattered to them in the domain of family and kinship; these ethnic identities nested within the broader Fulbe ethnicity that mattered in urban public settings, especially high-status ones associated with education and cash salaries.

Indeed, by 1976, Fulbe identity had become an achieved status; it was the ethnicity claimed by the upwardly mobile in Guider. It was therefore possible for people born outside the dominant Fulbe ethnic group to achieve Fulbe status in their lifetimes (Schultz 1984). To do this, they had to be successful at three tasks: they had to adopt the Fulbe language (Fulfulde), they had to adopt the Fulbe religion (Islam), and they had to adopt the Fulbe "way of life," which was identified with urban customs and the traditional Muslim high culture of the western Sudan. Many Fulbe claimed that descent from one or another Fulbe lineage was needed in order to claim Fulbe identity. Nevertheless,

they seemed willing to accept "Fulbeized Pagans" as Fulbe (e.g., by giving their daughters to them as brides) because those people were committed defenders of the urban Fulbe way of life. Those who were "Fulbeizing," however, came from societies in which descent had never been an important criterion of group membership. For these people, ethnic identity depended on the territorial affiliation of the group to which they were currently committed. From their perspective, in becoming Fulbe, they had simply chosen to commit themselves to Fulfulde, Islam, and life in "Fulbe territory," the town.

This example illustrates some of the key attributes often associated with ethnicity: it is fluid, malleable, something that can be voluntarily embraced or successfully ignored in different situations. Ambitious individuals and groups in an ethnically stratified society can manipulate ethnicity as a resource in order to pursue their interests. When nesting identities are present, people may regularly alternate between different identities in different contexts. Ethnic Fulbeization in northern Cameroon might be described as the formation of a "supertribe." Like the formation of caste alliances in India, it involves the expansion of group boundaries, allowing for the creation of stronger solidarity links among more people of different backgrounds. When such expanded alliances actually achieve increased success in political, economic, and social struggles, they may affect the very structures that gave rise to them (as the Shona–Ndebele alliance did in Zimbabwe) (Comaroff and Comaroff 1992, 61).

For dominant groups, however, defence of ethnic identity can be a way of defending privilege. Those who dominate may be threatened rather than flattered by subordinate groups who master elite cultural practices. Members of the dominant ethnic group may stress their cultural superiority and question the eligibility (and even the humanity) of subordinate groups who challenge them. It is at this point that anthropologists like Faye Harrison would argue that ethnicity becomes *racialized*. In her view, race differs from ethnicity precisely because it is used to "mark and stigmatize certain peoples as essentially and irreconcilably different, while treating the privileges of others as normative. This quality of difference, whether constructed through a biodeterminist or a culturalist idiom, is what constitutes the social category and material phenomenon of 'race'" (Harrison 1998, 613). Racialization in Western societies would thus bear a family resemblance to castification in South Asian societies.

Harrison (1995, 52) argues that by the middle of the nineteenth century, white northern Europeans, connecting their growing colonial power with their whiteness, began to racialize ethnic, religious, or class stereotypes associated with other Europeans (e.g., Irish, Jews, Italians, Poles, Slavs), viewing them as less human or, at any rate, differently human from themselves and attributing this difference to biologically inherited factors. Conversely, some racialized ethnic groups, such as the Irish, were able to reverse this process once they moved to North America, shedding their stigma and *ethnicizing* into just another "ordinary" Canadian or American ethnic group. Some social scientists might argue, or at any rate hope, that all racialized groups should be able to ethnicize sooner or later. But such a perspective risks ignoring the plight of racialized groups whose status never seems to change. Historians argue, for example, that the Irish were able to ethnicize precisely because they accepted the racialization of Aboriginal peoples and individuals of African descent (see Allen 1997). Indeed, operating under material conditions that presuppose white privilege, members of non-white races living in white-dominated countries are typically ranked below recent white immigrants on race- or ethnicity-based social hierarchies (see Harrison 1995, 49; see also Smedley 1998, 690).

For these reasons, Harrison argues that attempts to interpret race relations as ethnic relations in all contexts have "euphemized if not denied race" by failing to address the social, political, and economic factors responsible for keeping racialized groups excluded and stigmatized at the bottom of society (1995, 48). Harrison agrees that certain racialized groups do engage in "ethnicizing practices emphasizing cultural heritage," but in her view such practices have never been able to overcome the "caste-like assumptions of the most systematically oppressive racial orders" (1998, 613; 1995, 54; see also Sharma 1999, 91).

As we have seen, anthropologists have argued about which technical terms ought to be used to describe which forms of identity under which circumstances. We agree with Ursula Sharma (1999, 93) that social scientists should use a particular term only if it highlights a dimension of social relationships that would otherwise

go unnoticed. Thus, ethnicity probably needs to be supplemented by the notion of race in order to distinguish the dehumanizing confinement of certain social groups to the bottom layers of society, and caste's emphasis on endogamy and hierarchical ranking highlights features of social organization that elude the usual scope of race, class, or ethnicity. Anthropologist Pnina Werbner (1997) further builds on these distinctions when she argues that in order to make progress in analyzing ethnic violence as a social force, practices of "everyday" ethnic identification need to be distinguished from racism.

Based on her research on multicultural social relations in Britain, Werbner distinguishes two different social processes: objectification and reification. *Objectification* simply refers to the intentional construction of a collective public identity; it is the process that produces "everyday" or "normal" ethnicity. Ethnic identities are distinguished by the fact that they are "evoked situationally, . . . highlighted pragmatically, and objectified relationally and contingently" and by the fact that they focus on two key issues: "a demand for ethnic rights, including religious rights, and a demand for protection against racism" (1997, 241). Social relations between objectified ethnic groups are based on a "rightful performance" of multiple, shifting, highly valued forms of collective identification, based on religion, dress, food, language, and politics. Interaction between groups that differentiate themselves along such lines ordinarily does not lead to violent confrontations (229). *Reification*, by contrast, is a form of negative racial or ethnic absolutism that encourages the violent elimination of targeted groups and is central to the practice of racism. Reification "distorts and silences"; it is "essentialist in the pernicious sense" (229). It is violence that differentiates racism from everyday ethnicity; and if ethnic confrontation becomes violent, then it turns into a form of racism (234–5). For Werbner, making this distinction is crucial in multiethnic situations because when people fail to distinguish non-violent forms of everyday ethnicity from racism, they are, in effect, criminalizing valid ethnic sentiments and letting racists off the hook (233).

In many ways, the multicultural policy of Canada promotes what Werbner calls *objectification* while attempting to prevent what she calls *reification*. In practice, however, this policy is not always successful in preventing conflict. Ethnic tensions exist across Canada everywhere that diverse cultural systems coexist. While

## Anthropology in the Contemporary World

### Diverse Experiences with Intimate Relationships and Dating among South Asian Youth in the Greater Toronto Area

In a recent paper, Arshia Zaidi and colleagues (2014) asked the question, "How do ethnic identification, religion, religiousness, and gender intersect to shape second-generation South Asian youth's experiences of intimate relationships in Canada?" As background to their project, the researchers noted that, as recently as 2005, Canada was ranked seventh in the world in terms of the number of immigrants it receives; moreover, a significant number of these immigrants live in the Greater Toronto Area (GTA), making up just over 40 per cent of its population. Consequently, Toronto is often described as a "world in a city" (Siemiatycki 2011, quoted in Zaidi et al. 2014, 29). Many of these immigrants hail from South Asian countries such as India, Pakistan, Nepal, and Bangladesh, to name only a few.

The researchers also note that second-generation South Asian youth are often caught between the traditional value systems of their heritage countries and the contemporary value systems of their current homes, a difficulty that can sometimes lead to intergenerational conflict (28–9). In most "traditional" South Asian families, both those living in their original country and those living in Canada, young men and young women are strongly discouraged from forming intimate relationships with cross-gender peers before they are officially engaged or, in some cases, married (30). In addition, marriages are typically arranged by family members, and a heightened focus is placed on the preservation of premarital virginity to preserve a family's honour (ibid.). These cultural norms and

expectations tend to be heavily gendered—women are expected to stay at home and be sexually conservative, while men are encouraged to venture out into the world and learn to support themselves and their families (31). In Canadian society, however, it is generally acceptable for youths to date cross-gender peers of their own choice, and there is a greater sense of gender equality in relation to dating.

In attempting to answer the central question of their paper, the researchers interviewed 56 unmarried second-generation South Asian youth between the ages of 18 and 25. The sample consisted of 30 females and 26 males, with equal numbers of Hindus and Muslims (20 each) and fewer Christians (only 16). The families of most of the youth originated in Sri Lanka, Pakistan, or India (36). The researchers' findings indicated that there was a gradual acceptance of and experience with intimate relationships, mainly among Hindus, followed in number by Christians and, lastly, Muslims. In addition, those youth whose ethnic identities most closely reflected the norms, values, and practices of their heritage countries and whose levels of religiosity were high, regardless of their faith, tended not to approve of premarital intimate relationships (48). Consequently, the researchers concluded that multiple factors relating to ethnicity, gender, and religious beliefs influence the degree to which second-generation immigrant youth accept their new country's values regarding dating and forming intimate cross-gender relationships.

these tensions may not escalate into the sorts of large-scale ethnic conflicts we hear about in countries like Rwanda or Sudan, they do cause conflict, particularly when differing views on gender roles, religious beliefs, and sexuality are involved. And these tensions cause conflict not only between people of different ethnicities but also among members of the same ethnic group who interpret and express their ethnicity differently. Arshia Zaidi and her colleagues (2014) have examined these latter sorts of conflicts among South Asian youth in Canada. For a discussion of this work, see the "Anthropology in the Contemporary World" box on the

experiences of South Asian youth living in Canada with forming intimate relationships and dating.

## Nation and Nationalism

As we saw earlier, state societies are not new social forms. Nation-states, however, are a far more recent invention. Prior to the French Revolution, European states were ruled by kings and emperors whose access to the throne was officially believed to have been ordained by God. After the French Revolution in 1789, which thoroughly discredited the divine right of kings, rulers needed to find a new basis on which to found legitimate state authority. The solution that was eventually adopted rooted political authority in **nations**: groups of people believed to share the same history, culture, language, and even physical substance. Nations were associated with territories, as were states, and a **nation-state** came to be viewed as an ideal political unit in which national identity and political territory coincided.

The building of the first nation-states is closely associated with the rise and spread of capitalism and its related cultural institutions during the nineteenth century. Following the demise of European colonial empires and the end of the Cold War, the final decades of the twentieth century witnessed a scramble in which former colonies or newly independent states struggled to turn themselves into nation-states capable of competing successfully in what anthropologist Liisa Malkki (1992) has called a "transnational culture of nationalism."

On the one hand, the ideology of the nation-state implies that every nation is entitled to its own state. On the other hand, it also suggests that a state containing heterogeneous populations *might be made into a nation* if all peoples within its borders could somehow be made to adopt a common **nationality**: a sense of identification with and loyalty to the nation-state. The attempt made by government officials and state institutions to instill into the citizens of a state this sense of nationality has been called **nation building**, or **nationalism**.

As we learned in our discussion of ethnicity, states are the very political structures that generate ethnic identities among the various cultural groupings that are incorporated within them on unequal terms. Thus, anthropologists studying state formation often find themselves studying ethnicity as well as nationalism (Alonso 1994). However, groups with different forms of identity that continue to persist within the boundaries of the nation-state often are viewed as obstacles to nationalism. If such groups successfully resist assimilation into the nationality that the state is supposed to represent, their very existence calls into question the legitimacy of the state. Indeed, if their numbers are sufficient, they might well claim that they are a separate nation, entitled to a state of their own.

The separatist movement in Quebec provides an example of a group that has been resisting assimilation into the wider nation by claiming to have a unique identity. This movement gained momentum in the late 1960s and early 1970s, and in 1976 the people of Quebec elected the recently formed Parti Québécois (PQ), the provincial separatist party then led by René Lévesque, to form Quebec's provincial government. The PQ's main platform was the forming of a distinct, sovereign state of Quebec, which it promoted as a way of protecting Quebec's distinctive French language and culture. On two occasions, in 1980 and then again in 1995, the PQ held a provincial referendum on Quebec's secession from Canada. However, despite the party's best efforts, on both occasions the people of Quebec voted to remain a part of Canada. Shortly before the second referendum, a federal French Canadian nationalist party, the Bloc Québécois (BQ), was formed with Lucien Bouchard as its leader, and in 1993 the BQ gained enough support to be elected as the official opposition in the federal government. Today, the Quebec separatist movement does not have the support that it had in the past. However, Quebec nationalists have succeeded in preserving Québécois peoples' unique cultural identity, especially through laws that promote French language and culture within the province (Figure 14.8).

To head off the possibility of any particular group breaking off and forming its own nation, nationalist ideologies typically include some cultural features of subordinate cultural groups. Thus, although nationalist traditions are invented, they are not created out of thin air. The prototype of national identity is usually based on attributes of the dominant group, into which are integrated specially chosen elements of the cultural practices of other, subordinated groups. That is, those who control the nation-state will try to define nationality in ways that "identify and ensure loyalty among citizens . . . the goal is to create criteria of inclusion and exclusion to control and delimit the group" (Williams 1989, 407). The hope seems to be that if at least some aspects of their ways of life are acknowledged as essential to national identity, subordinated groups will

**nation** A group of people believed to share the same history, culture, language, and even physical substance.

**nation-state** An ideal political unit in which national identity and political territory coincide.

**nationality** A sense of identification with and loyalty to a nation-state.

**nation building (or nationalism)** The attempt made by government officials to instill into the citizens of a state a sense of nationality.

**FIGURE 14.8 |** While Quebec did not ultimately separate from Canada following either the 1980 or the 1995 referendum, the preservation of a distinct cultural identity remains important to many people in the province. Pride in Quebec's unique history and culture is evident in the festivities that take place on Saint-Jean-Baptiste Day, officially known in Quebec as "la fête nationale" ("the national holiday"), celebrated annually on 24 June.

identify with and be loyal to the nation. Following Antonio Gramsci, Brackette Williams (1989, 429, 435) calls this process a transformist hegemony in which nationalist ideologues are attempting to "create purity out of impurity."

National leaders will measure the trustworthiness and loyalty of citizens by how closely they copy (or refuse to copy) the cultural practices that define national

> **transformist hegemony**  A nationalist program to define nationality in a way that preserves the cultural domination of the ruling group while including enough cultural features from subordinated groups to ensure their loyalty.

identity (Williams 1989, 407). Unfortunately, the practices of subordinated groups that are not incorporated into nationalist ideology are regularly marginalized and devalued. Continued adherence to such practices may be viewed as subversive, and practitioners may suffer persecution and even extermination. Other groups, by contrast, may be totally ignored. Alonso points out, for example, that Mexican nationalism is "mestizo nationalism" rooted in the official doctrine that the Mexican people are a hybrid of European whites and the Indigenous people they conquered. African slaves were also a part of early colonial Mexican society, but nationalist ideology erases their presence entirely (Alonso 1994, 396).

## Australian Nationalism

Australia began its existence as a settler colony of Great Britain. Over the past two hundred years, the prototype of Australian national identity was based on the racial and cultural features of the settler population. The phenotypically distinct Indigenous people, called "Aborigines" by the settlers, were completely excluded from citizenship. As in most colonized regions, settlers' claims to land and other resources rested on the doctrine of *terra nullius*: the idea that, before their arrival, the land had been owned by nobody. In European capitalist terms, "ownership" meant permanent settlement and "improvement" of the land by clearing it and planting crops or grazing animals. Since the Aborigines living on the continent of Australia were foraging peoples who did not depend on domesticated plants or animals, European settlers felt justified in displacing them and "improving" the land as they saw fit. Aborigines were viewed as a "dying race," and white settler domination was taken as a foregone conclusion.

But times change, and in recent decades Australians have been seriously rethinking the nature of Australian national identity. Indeed, according to Robert Tonkinson (1998), two kinds of nation building are going on at the same time. First, an intense national debate has developed that would favour creating a new Australian republic whose constitution would affirm the existence and rights of the country's Indigenous peoples. For that to happen, however, "the nation as a whole must reimagine itself via a myth-making process, in which the search for distinctively Australian national symbols may well include elements drawn from Indigenous cultures" (287–8).

And this will not be easy because such a myth-making process (or transformist hegemony) immediately runs up against the second, alternative myth-making process generated by Australia's Indigenous minorities, who have for decades struggled to construct for themselves a sense of "pan-Aboriginal" identity. Since the 1970s, a central theme in this struggle has been the demand for land rights, which was given an enormous boost by the decision handed down by the High Court of Australia in 1992 in the case of Eddie Mabo and others versus the State of Queensland. The so-called Mabo decision rejected the doctrine of *terra nullius*. It proclaimed that the right of Australia's Indigenous peoples to ownership of their original lands was protected by Australian common law.

The symbolic significance of the Mabo decision has been enormous. For those Australians who want to remake Australian nationalism, Mabo clears ground for constructing a multicultural national identity. The Australian federal government has therefore made reconciliation with Indigenous minorities a major policy goal, well aware that "unless Australia achieves a formal and lasting reconciliation with its Indigenous people, its self-image as a fair and just land will continue to be mocked by the history of its oppression of them" (Tonkinson 1998, 291). Many white Australians and the national government are seeking ways of incorporating Aboriginality into Australian national identity. A measure of success is indicated by increasing interest on the national level in the artistic, literary, and athletic accomplishments of Aboriginal people. As a popular reconciliation slogan puts it, "White Australia has a Black History" (Figure 14.9).

While all this might augur favourably for a reconstructed Australian national identity that includes Aboriginal people, many problems remain. Some come from white Australians who reject a multicultural national identity or who see their economic interests threatened by the Mabo decision. But even Aboriginal people whom it is supposed to help criticize the Mabo decision because of its limitations and unresolved complexities. For example, the only lands eligible for Indigenous claims turn out to be those that have demonstrable historical connection to contemporary Aboriginal groups who continue to practise "traditional" Aboriginal customs. This not only exempts most of Australia from Indigenous land claims but also means

**FIGURE 14.9** | Australian Aboriginal people marching in protest over the Australian Bicentennial celebrations in 1988 that, they argued, did not pay appropriate attention to them.

that most of Australia's quarter of a million Aboriginal people will be barred from making land claims because they live in Australia's large towns and cities and have for generations been separated from the lands of their ancestors.

Following the Mabo decision, expressions of Aboriginality seemed to be moving toward "a more culture-centred—and to non-Aboriginal Australians more easily accommodated—emphasis on Aboriginal commonalities, continuity, and survival" (Tonkinson 1998, 289). The Mabo decision had ratified the legitimacy and revival of not only Aboriginal land rights but also Aboriginal customs. This stimulated an explosion of Aboriginal cultural expression that white Australians came to appreciate, as well as numerous programs that have brought urban Aboriginals into remote areas to work, to learn about rural Aboriginal traditions, and to contribute to the growth of biculturalism among rural Aboriginal people.

Writing in 1998, Tonkinson was hopeful that, "despite the limitations of Mabo . . . its symbolic force is such that it may provide the basis for reconciliation between Indigenous and other Australians" (300). Over a decade later, those hopes have experienced a setback. When John Howard became Liberal prime minister in 1996, he entered office with a record of opposition to the recognition of Native title, to the unique status of Aboriginal people, and to the Aboriginal and Torres Strait Islander Commission (ATSIC), established in 1990 as a political structure through which Indigenous Australians might participate in self-government (Dodson 2007). One of Howard's first acts as prime minister was to slash the

ATSIC budget and to introduce legislation to abolish it, which passed in 2005.

The Howard government was also responsible, in 2007, for the highly controversial Northern Territory National Emergency Response. The Australian government justified this intervention by citing a report titled *Little Children Are Sacred*, which documented widespread child sexual abuse and neglect in Aboriginal communities in the Northern Territory. For several reasons, however, many Aboriginal activists and their allies have found this justification for the intervention unpersuasive (Behrendt 2007). First, the kinds of problems the intervention was intended to address were not new; some Aborigines initially thought the intervention was a belated attempt to reverse decades of government neglect. Second, the actions taken during the intervention ignored virtually all the recommendations made by the *Little Children Are Sacred* report, emphasizing instead unilateral changes in welfare and land tenure policies that were implemented without using evidence-based research and without consulting Aboriginal communities. Finally, the Australian government suspended its own *Racial Discrimination Act* in order to implement some of these policies.

As John Sanderson (2007, 35) observed, "It is true that only about 20 per cent of Indigenous people now live on the land that is the source of their Dreaming. . . . But . . . respect for the relationship with the land and the culture that sustained Aboriginal people . . . remains the source of their well-being." Melinda Hinkson (2007, 6) concluded that the intervention "is aimed at nothing short of the production of a newly oriented, 'normalised' Aboriginal population, one whose concerns with custom, kin, and land will give way to the individualistic aspirations of private home ownership, career, and self-improvement."

When a new Labour government took power in 2007, many Aborigines and their allies hoped that the intervention would be reversed. For example, the new prime minister, Kevin Rudd, and both houses of the Australian parliament offered a formal apology in 2008 for the "stolen generations" of Aboriginal children forcibly removed from their homes in the nineteenth and twentieth centuries as a consequence of government policy. Still, Indigenous Australians complained to the United Nations about the provisions of the Northern Territory intervention, and the United Nations communicated with the Rudd government in March 2009, pointing out that suspension of the *Racial Discrimination Act* put Australia in violation of two international human rights conventions that it had signed. In April 2009, Rudd endorsed the United Nations *Declaration on the Rights of Indigenous Peoples*; in November 2009, the Rudd government introduced a bill in Parliament to reinstate the *Racial Discrimination Act*. The bill passed in June 2010.

## Naturalizing Discourses

We have emphasized more than once in this chapter that the social categories of class, caste, race, ethnicity, and nationality are culturally created and cannot be justified with reference to biology or nature. At the same time, many members of the societies anthropologists study argue just the opposite, employing what some anthropologists call **naturalizing discourses**. That is, they regularly represent particular identities as if they were rooted in biology or nature, rather than in history and culture, thereby making them appear eternal and unchanging.

Naturalizing discourses rely on the imaginary reduction, or *conflation*, of identities to achieve persuasive power (Williams 1989). For example, every one of the forms of identity we have discussed in this chapter has been described or justified by someone at some time in terms of *shared bodily substance*. Thus, living within the same borders is conflated with having the same ancestors and inheriting the same culture, which is conflated with sharing the same blood or the same genes. Culture is reduced to blood, and "the magic of forgetfulness and selectivity, both deliberate and inadvertent, allows the once recognizably arbitrary classifications of one generation to become the given inherent properties of reality several generations later" (Williams 1989, 431).

Nation-states frequently use trees as national symbols, rooting the nation in the soil of its territory (Figure 14.10). Sometimes they use kinship imagery, referring to the nation-state as a "motherland" or "fatherland"; sometimes the territory of a nation-state itself can be a unifying image, especially when portrayed on a

**naturalizing discourses**   The deliberate representation of particular identities (e.g., caste, class, race, ethnicity, and nationality) as if they were a result of biology or nature, rather than history or culture, making them appear eternal and unchanging.

**FIGURE 14.10** | Nation-states frequently use trees as national symbols, rooting the nation in the soil of its territory. The treelike symbol at the centre of the Mexican national seal (the cactus on which an eagle perches holding a snake in its beak) is a pre-conquest Aztec symbol. Other versions of the image are encircled by the Spanish words *Estados Unidos Mexicanos* (United Mexican States). These combined elements stand for the officially mixed—*mestizo*—Mexican people the state is supposed to represent, the offspring of Spanish conquerors.

map (Alonso 1994). The case of Australia shows, however, that doctrines like *terra nullius* enable newcomers to deny the "natural" links to the land of Indigenous inhabitants while specifying how newcomers may proceed to establish their own "natural" links to the land through "improvement."

## The Paradox of Essentialized Identities

The struggle of Aboriginal people to defend themselves and claim their rights after centuries of exploitation and neglect was extraordinarily important in making the Mabo decision possible. In response to dominant groups that attempted to conflate their humanity with a narrow, unflattering stereotype, they chose to accept the racial designation but to view it as a positive *essence*, an "inner something or distinctive 'spirituality' possessed by everyone who is Aboriginal" (Tonkinson 1998, 294–95). Similar kinds of essentialist rhetoric have helped many stigmatized groups build a positive self-image and unite politically.

Many anthropologists and other observers would argue that the essentialist rhetoric of Aboriginal activists does not, in fact, reflect their beliefs about Aboriginality at all. They would describe what the activists are promoting as *strategic essentialism*: that is, essentialist rhetoric is being used as a conscious political strategy. Many activists are perfectly aware that essentialized racial or ethnic identities have no biological validity. Nevertheless, they press their claims, hoping that by stressing their difference they may be able to extract concessions that the national government cannot refuse without violating its own laws and sense of justice. The concessions may be substantial, as in the case of the Mabo decision. At the same time, strategic essentialism is troubling to many observers and participants in these struggles, for those who promote it as a political strategy risk "reproducing the same logic that once oppressed them" (Hale 1997, 567); and, rather than bringing about a more just society, it may simply "serve to perpetuate an ethnically ordered world" (Comaroff and Comaroff 1992, 62).

## Nation Building in a Postcolonial World: The Example of Fiji

Nation building involves constructing a shared public identity, but it also involves establishing concrete legal mechanisms for taking group action to influence the state. That is, as John Kelly and Martha Kaplan (2001) argue, nation-states are more than imagined communities; they are also *represented* communities. For this reason, nation building involves more than constructing an image of national unity; it also requires institutions of political representation that channel the efforts of citizens into effective support for the state. But what happens when citizens of a nation-state do not agree about exactly what nation they are building or what kinds of legal and political structures are necessary to bring it about? One answer to these questions can be seen in the South Pacific island nation of Fiji, which became independent from Britain in 1970 and has experienced two political coups since 1987 (see EthnoProfile 14.4: Fiji).

At independence, the image of the Fijian nation was that of a "three-legged stool," each "leg" being a separate category of voters: "general electors" (a minority of the population including Europeans), "Fijians" (ethnic Fijians, descended from the original inhabitants of the island), and "Indians" (or Indo-Fijians, descendants of indentured labourers brought to Fiji by the British from Bombay [Mumbai] and Calcutta [Kolkata] in the nineteenth century). Kelly and Kaplan (2001) show that these three categories have deep roots in the colonial period, where they were said to correspond to separate "races." In the British Empire, race was an accepted way to categorize subordinated peoples, even though in many cases—as in the case of the Indo-Fijians—the people so labelled had shared no common identity prior to their arrival in Fiji.

These racial distinctions were concretized in colonial law, and the legal status of ethnic Fijians was different from the legal status of Indo-Fijians. The status of ethnic Fijians was determined by the Deed of Cession, a document signed by some Fijian chiefs with the British in 1874, which linked ethnic Fijians to the colonial government through their hierarchy of chiefs. The status of Indo-Fijians, by contrast, was determined by the contracts of indenture (*girmit*) that each individual labourer had signed in order to come to Fiji. Thus, ethnic Fijians were accorded a hierarchical, collective legal identity, whereas Indo-Fijians had the status of legal individuals, with no legally recognized ties to any collectivity.

Inspired by the Freedom Movement in India in the early twentieth century, Indo-Fijians began to resist racial oppression and struggle for equal rights in Fiji; but their efforts were repeatedly quashed by the British. When it became possible for them to vote after 1929, for example, Indo-Fijians lobbied for equal citizenship and

the abolition of separate racial voting rolls, and they lost: the voting rolls were divided by race in order to limit representation for Indo-Fijians in government. At the time of World War II, Indo-Fijians agreed to serve in the armed forces but only if they were treated as equals with white soldiers, and their efforts were resisted: they spent the war serving in a labour battalion for very low wages, while ethnic Fijians joined the Fijian Defence Force. It was primarily Indo-Fijians who pushed for independence in the late 1960s, and once again they engaged in difficult negotiations for equal citizenship and a common voting roll but finally consented to separate race-based voting rolls in 1969 in order to obtain independence.

Thus, when Fiji's independence became real in 1970, the constitution insisted that races still existed in Fiji and that they had to vote separately. Since then, political parties have generally and increasingly followed racial lines and the army has remained an enclave of Indigenous Fijians. When political parties backed mostly by Indo-Fijian voters won Fiji's 1987 election, the army staged a coup and took over the country after only a month. The constitution that was then installed in 1990 returned to even more naked discrimination against Indo-Fijians with regard to voting rights (Kelly and Kaplan 2001, 77).

The constitution was revised yet again, in a manner that favoured ethnic Fijian chiefly interests and seemed guaranteed to prevent parties backed by Indo-Fijian voters from winning control of the government in the 1999 election. To everyone's surprise, parties backing ethnic Fijians lost again. On 19 May 2000 came a second coup. Finally, after new elections in 2001, ethnic Fijians won control of the government.

The new government lasted until a December 2006 military takeover. One of the military's demands was an end to the "race-based" voting system, to be replaced by a new "one citizen, one vote" system. Elections were planned for 2009, but in April of that year the president suspended the constitution and appointed himself head of state. In September 2009, the British Commonwealth expelled Fiji for its failure to schedule democratic elections by 2010. Finally, in September 2013, a revised constitution put an end to the race-based voting system, and general elections in which each citizen had an equal vote occurred in 2014 (Figure 14.11).

What lessons does this history suggest about nation building in postcolonial states? The issues are many and complex. But one key factor emphasized by Kelly and

**FIGURE 14.11** | A Fijian citizen contemplates the list of candidates in anticipation of the 2014 national election.

Kaplan (2001) is that the image of a united Fijian nation, projected at independence, was severely undermined by legal mechanisms of political representation carried over from the colonial period, particularly the race-based voting rolls. What became apparent in the years after independence was the fact that Indo-Fijians and ethnic Fijians had imagined very different national communities. Indo-Fijians had supported the image of a nation in which all citizens, Indo-Fijian and ethnic Fijian and "general elector," would have equal status, voting on a single roll, working together to build a constitutional democracy. However, "few among the ethnic Fijians have yet come to see themselves as partners with immigrants" (2001, 41). Ever since independence, and particularly after each coup, ethnic Fijians worked to construct an image of the nation based solely on chiefly traditions in which Indo-Fijians had no meaningful place. Thus, Kelly and Kaplan conclude, in Fiji (and in many other parts of the world) "'the nation' is a contested idea, not an experienced reality" (142).

## Nation Building in a Postcolonial World: The Example of Nunavut

In Canada today, many Aboriginal Canadians are struggling to achieve a nation-building goal very different from that of the Indo-Fijians. The First Nations, Inuit, and Metis peoples of Canada have long sought recognition of their nationhood and their inherent right to self-determination. They want to regain control of their affairs and to make their own decisions concerning the preservation and development of their distinct cultures. Many Aboriginal groups seek an officially recognized form of self-government that would enable them to have more control over affairs within their communities and the power to deliver programs and services such as education, child welfare, and health care initiatives that align with their values.

Anthropologists have devoted considerable attention in their research to traditional forms of leadership and government among Canadian Aboriginal peoples. For example, there have been studies of the Iroquois Confederacy (a confederation of First Nations tribes that flourished in the seventeenth and early eighteenth centuries), chief-led governance among individual bands of the Northern Ojibwa and Cree, and the complexities of the Kwakiutl (Kwakwaka'wakw) and Haida sociopolitical groups of the northwest coast of North America. These studies demonstrate clearly that Aboriginal people have always been quite capable of managing their own internal affairs without the interference of colonial administrators. Since the early days of Confederation, Aboriginal people have expressed their desire to govern themselves once again in a way that they choose, so that they can participate in a more equitable power-sharing arrangement with Ottawa and the provinces. This aim would require the creation of another level of government that recognizes Aboriginal peoples as members of distinct groups that had an important and unique role in contributing to the formation of Canada.

Some of this power was finally granted in 1982, under section 35 of the Constitution Act, when the Canadian government recognized Aboriginal peoples' right to determine matters related to their culture, identity, traditions, and language. However, because each nation is so unique, negotiations for more specific arrangements have been conducted on a nation-by-nation basis. For example, self-government arrangements have been settled with the Selchelt of British Columbia, the Cree-Naskapi of Quebec, and various Yukon First Nations. At the same time, many non-Aboriginal Canadians have been resistant to making such arrangements, as they feel that the Canadian government has already made too many concessions to Aboriginal peoples. Yet these concerns seem unwarranted, as recent research demonstrates that those First Nations communities whose members have been given greater autonomy in managing their own social programs and education have proven to be more efficient and less burdensome on the federal and provincial governments (Hedican 2008). Moreover, within these communities, resources have become more focused on the most important needs of First Nations groups, and Aboriginal peoples have received more effective training for administrative positions.

Perhaps the most successful outcome of Canadian Aboriginal peoples' fight for self-determination has been the creation of Nunavut, which became independent of the Northwest Territories on 1 April 1999 (Map 14.2). Inuit groups had been petitioning the federal government to create a separate territory for Inuit peoples since the mid-1970s. While formal negotiations began in the early 1980s, it wasn't until 1993 that the official

documents—the Nunavut Act and the Nunavut Land Claims Agreement—were signed to create the new territory. (See EthnoProfile 13.3 for more information on the Inuit of Nunavut) The latter of these documents, which was signed by representatives of the Inuit governmental organization known as the Tunngavik Federation of Nunavut as well as the Canadian government and the government of the Northwest Territories, granted Inuit peoples a variety of rights and powers, including: land title to 350,000 square kilometres of land, mineral rights to 35,000 square kilometres of land, equal representation of Inuit on environmental and wildlife boards, the right to harvest wildlife, a share of royalties from oil and gas and mineral development on Crown land, and the right to create their own self-governing body (PolarNet 2015). This land claim settlement represented the largest in Canadian history, and it marked the beginning of new relationships between Inuit peoples and the government of Canada. Many Aboriginal peoples, both in Canada and around the world, also hope that it may provide a model for their own self-determination endeavours in the future.

## Nationalism and Its Dangers

The most horrifying consequence of nation building movements in the twentieth century has been the discovery of just how far the ruling groups of some nation-states are willing to go in order to enforce their version of national identity.

After World War II, the world was shocked to learn about Nazi programs to "liquidate" Jews, "Gypsies" (Romani), and other groups that failed to conform to Nazi ideals of Aryan purity (Linke 1997). Many people hoped that the Nazi Holocaust was exceptional, but subsequent developments suggest that it may have been only the most dramatic example of an exterminationist temptation that accompanies all drives to nationalism. Sociologist Zygmunt Bauman argued in his book *Modernity and the Holocaust* (1989) that modern nation-states with rationalized bureaucracies and industrial technology were the first societies in history to make efficient mass extermination of deviants technically possible. In a transnational culture of nationalism, not to belong to a nation-state made up of loyal, ambitious, like-minded citizens is a severe, possibly fatal handicap. Using violence against all citizens who undermine claims of national homogeneity and common

**MAP 14.2 | Nunavut** became an independent Canadian territory on 1 April 1999. *Nunavut* means "our land" in Inuktitut, one of the major languages of the Inuit peoples. Approximately 85 per cent of those who occupy this area of the eastern Arctic are Inuit.

**FIGURE 14.12** | Relatives of the more than eight thousand Muslim men and boys slaughtered in the 1995 Srebrenica massacre walk between rows of coffins next to freshly dug graves, looking for those belonging to their relatives, in a field in the town of Srebrenica, Bosnia and Herzegovina, on 31 March 2003.

purpose may thus be a peculiarly modern way for insecure rulers of embattled nation-states to try to bring about solidarity and stability. In the late twentieth century, warring nationalities in the former Yugoslavia deployed selective assassinations and forced migration to rid their fledgling nation-states of unwanted "others," a policy known as *ethnic cleansing* (Figure 14.12). Thus, rather than relics of a barbarian past, ethnic cleansing, *ethnocide* (the destruction of a culture), and *genocide* (the extermination of an entire people) may constitute a series of related practices that are all signs of things to come. All are measures of the high stakes for which rulers of these nation-states see themselves competing.

Inevitably, such policies create populations of immigrants and refugees whose social status is anomalous and ambiguous in a world of nation-states and whose presence as new pockets of heterogeneity in a different nation-state sets the stage for new rounds of social struggle that may lead to violence. As we will see in the next chapter, the economic, political, and cultural processes that made such developments possible have undergone important shifts in the last few years.

## Chapter Summary

1. All people in the world today must deal with the authority of one or another nation-state, each of which contains multiple and sometimes contradictory hierarchies of stratification. Every one of these hierarchies is a cultural invention designed to create boundaries around different kinds of imagined communities. Some patterns of stratification may reach back thousands of years, but others are closely associated with the rise of European capitalism and colonialism.

2. Gender stratification draws on sexual imagery to create and rank categories of people. Stratification by gender regularly subordinates phenotypic females to phenotypic males, but it is often applied more widely to other categories of people, artifacts, or events: to structure relations between different categories of men, for example, or between different ethnic groups or "races."

3. The concept of "class" in anthropology has a double heritage: Europeans tended to view class boundaries as closed and rigid, whereas North Americans tended to view them as open and permeable. Class solidarity may be undercut by clientage relations that bind individuals to one another across class boundaries.

4. The stratification system of India has been taken as the prototype of caste stratification, although anthropologists also have applied the concept of *caste* to social hierarchies encountered elsewhere in the world. Local caste divisions (jatis) in rural India adhere to rules of purity and pollution that are defined in terms of the occupations their members perform and the foods they

eat and that govern whom they may marry. Members of jatis of similar rank do not observe most of these distinctions with one another, especially in urban settings. Caste associations in large cities of India use jati ties to promote their members' economic well-being. The use of violence by higher-ranking jatis to block the advance of lower-ranking jatis has increased in recent years. Contemporary anthropologists reject views of caste in India that portray it as internally harmonious and uncontested by those at the bottom of the hierarchy, pointing to the rise in caste violence in recent years.

5. The contemporary concept of "race" developed in the context of European exploration and conquest beginning in the fifteenth century as light-skinned Europeans came to rule over darker-skinned peoples in different parts of the world. The so-called races whose boundaries were forged during the nineteenth century are imagined communities; human biological variation does not naturally clump into separate populations with stable boundaries. Despite variations in opinions and practices regarding race over the centuries, a global hierarchy persists in which whiteness symbolizes high status and blackness symbolizes the social bottom.

6. Although ethnic consciousness existed in precolonial and precapitalist societies, contemporary anthropologists have been most interested in forms of ethnicity that were generated under capitalist colonial domination, when different groups were subordinated within a single political structure under conditions of inequality. This process can produce ethnic groups not continuous with any single earlier group and is often characterized by nesting, opposed identities that individuals often manipulate in

order to achieve upward mobility. When dominant ethnic groups feel threatened, they may attempt to stigmatize subordinate groups by "racializing" them.

7. Nation-states were invented in nineteenth-century Europe, but they have spread throughout the world along with capitalism, colonialism, and eventual political decolonization. Nationalist thinking aims to create a political unit in which national identity and political territory coincide, and this has led to various practices designed to force subordinate social groups to adopt a national identity defined primarily in terms of the culture of the dominant group. When subordinate groups resist, they may become the victims of genocide or ethnic cleansing. Alternatively, the dominant group may try to recast its understanding of national identity in a way that acknowledges and incorporates cultural elements belonging to subordinate groups. If the creation of such an imagined hybrid identity is not accompanied by legal and political changes that support it, however, the end result may be political turmoil, as shown in the recent history of Fiji.

8. Because membership in social categories such as gender, class, caste, race, ethnicity, and nationality can determine enormous differences in peoples' life chances, much is at stake in defending these categories, all of which are rooted in culture and history rather than biology or nature. Conceptualizing these forms of identity as essences can be a way of stereotyping and excluding, but it has also been used by many stigmatized groups to build a positive self-image and as a strategic concept in struggles with dominant groups. Although strategic essentialism may be successful in such struggles, it also risks repeating the same logic that justifies oppression.

## For Review

1. Explain structural violence, using the example of Haiti. How have different socially constructed hierarchies of power contributed to the situation in Haiti?

2. How is gender used as a tool of structural violence in various societies? Why are power differences often characterized in terms of gender even when the differences are between individuals of the same gender?

3. Does Canada have a class system? What would Marx say of Canadian society?

4. How does caste differ from class? Do you think that caste can be said to exist outside India? Why or why not?

5. Summarize the key arguments in the discussion of race in this chapter. Why does racism continue to be a problem even in societies where "race" is widely recognized to be a cultural construction?

6. In what ways is colourism in Nicaragua similar to and different from racism in Canada?

7. Summarize the main arguments in the discussion of ethnicity in this chapter. Describe how ethnicity is recognized in Canada.

8. Are ethnicity and race related? If so, how?

9. What is a nation? Discuss the relationship between nation-states and nationalism.

10. What are naturalizing discourses? Give an example.

11. Outline some of the issues with strategic essentialism. What are some of the potential drawbacks for marginalized groups who attempt to gain power and/or recognition through strategically essentializing their collective identities?

12. List some of the dangers associated with nationalism and nation building described in this chapter. Which of these dangers have arisen in the Canadian context? Give specific examples.

## Key Terms

| | | |
|---|---|---|
| caste   399 | ethnicity   410 | nation-state   415 |
| clientage   398 | nation   415 | naturalizing discourses   418 |
| colourism   408 | nation building (or nationalism)   415 | structural violence   394 |
| ethnic groups   410 | nationality   415 | transformist hegemony   416 |

## Suggested Readings

Anderson, Benedict. 1991. *Imagined Communities: Reflections on the Origin and Spread of Nationalism*. Rev. ed. London: Verso. *The classic discussion of the cultural processes that create community ties between people—such as citizens of a nation-state—who have never seen one another, producing the personal and cultural feeling of belonging to a nation.*

Cannon, Martin J., and Lina Sunseri, eds. 2011. *Racism, Colonialism, and Indigeneity in Canada*. Toronto, Oxford University Press Canada. *A collection of papers that outline how the history of colonization and racism in Canada has created the marginalization of Indigenous peoples in Canada today.*

Farmer, Paul. 2003. *Pathologies of Power: Health, Human Rights, and the New War on the Poor*. Berkeley: University of California Press. *Paul Farmer, a physician and an anthropologist, uses his experiences in several different parts of the world to show how patterns of disease and suffering are shaped by social and political policies that violate human rights, creating landscapes of "structural violence."*

Geiger, Andrea. 2011. *Subverting Exclusion: Transpacific Encounters with Race, Caste, and Borders, 1885–1928*. New Haven, CT: Yale University Press. *An examination of the history of Japanese immigrants in the North American West in the late nineteenth and early twentieth centuries and their experiences with two separate conditions of exclusion, one based in caste and the other in race.*

Hinton, Alexander Laban, ed. 2002. *Annihilating Difference: The Anthropology of Genocide*. Berkeley: University of California Press. *A collection of articles probing the ways in which anthropology can help explain and perhaps contribute to the prevention of genocide. Case studies include Nazi Germany, Cambodia under the Khmer Rouge, Rwanda, Guatemala, and the former Yugoslavia.*

Malkki, Liisa. 1995. *Purity and Exile: Violence, Memory, and National Cosmology among Hutu Refugees in Tanzania*. Chicago: University of Chicago Press. *This ethnography chronicles a fairly recent example in Africa of the bloody consequences of nationalist politics and explores the connections between the conditions of refugee resettlement and the development of refugee identities.*

Nash, Manning. 1989. *The Cauldron of Ethnicity in the Modern World*. Chicago: University of Chicago Press. *Nash looks at ethnicity in the postcolonial world, examining the relations between Ladinos and Maya in Guatemala, Chinese and Malays in Malaysia, and Jews and non-Jews in the United States.*

Sharma, Ursula. 1999. *Caste*. Philadelphia: Open University Press. *A brief survey of relatively recent anthropological scholarship dealing with caste in South Asia.*

Smedley, Audrey, and Brian D. Smedley. 2012. *Race in North America: Origin and Evolution of a Worldview*. 4th ed. Boulder, CO: Westview Press. *This book offers a comprehensive historical overview of the development of the concept of race in North America, beginning in the late eighteenth century. Smedley shows how the concept of "race" is a cultural construct that over time has been used in different ways, for different purposes.*

Strathern, Marilyn. 1988. *The Gender of the Gift*. Berkeley: University of California Press. *This is a challenging volume but a classic. Strathern expands the notion of "gender" beyond the traditional bounds of feminist anthropology in order to make sense of the complexities of Melanesian cultural practices.*

# 15 What Can Anthropology Tell Us about Globalization?

▲ Cargo ships in Kowloon Bay, Hong Kong, China. Photo: © XPACIFICA/Corbis.

## Chapter Outline

A very popular term these days is *globalization*. But what does it mean? In this chapter, we will look at how anthropologists study globalization by following global flows of information, people, and commodities. You will learn how anthropologists approach debates about such contemporary matters as international migration, multiculturalism, and human rights. We will also show how cultural anthropology's traditional ethnographic focus can make unique contributions to our understanding of globalization.

In this chapter, we take up again the story of relations between the West and the rest of the world, how those relations have changed over the last fifty or so years, and with what consequences. We look at ourselves as much as we look at the traditional subjects of anthropological research.

## What Happened to the Global Economy after the Cold War?

In 1989, the Cold War came to an end. The Soviet Union and its satellite states collapsed, and China began to encourage some capitalist economic practices. These radical changes in the global political economy left no part of the world unaffected. For some, this period of uncertainty offered a chance to challenge long-unquestioned truths about development and underdevelopment that had guided government policies throughout the Cold War. From new social movements such as the *rondas campesinas* of Peru to squatter movements in cities to movements defending the rights of women and various minority groups to movements to preserve rain forests, people attempted to construct entirely new social institutions that often bypassed national governments or development agencies (see Figure 15.1). Anthropologist Arturo Escobar (1992) argued that the new social movements in Latin America were struggles over meanings as well as over material conditions.

This work promoted the hope that new social movements might succeed in promoting less exploitative forms of society in generations to come. But the world toward which such arguments were aimed was already disappearing. The breakdown of communism led to a crisis of confidence among many who had been inspired by key tenets of Marxist thought. At the same

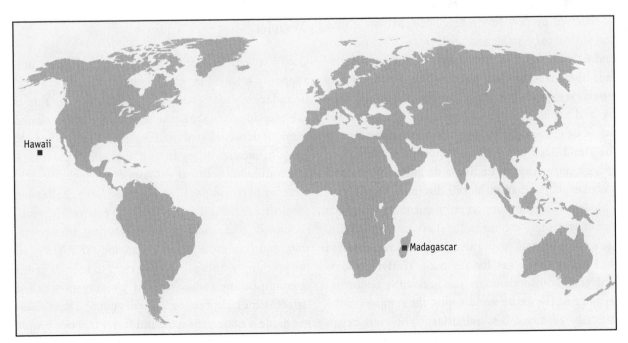

**MAP 15.1** | Location of societies whose EthnoProfiles appear in Chapter 15.

**FIGURE 15.1** | Beginning in the mid-1970s, peasants in the highlands of northern Peru developed rural justice groups called *rondas campesinas* ("peasant rounds"). These were armed groups of peasants who walked the paths around their villages at night, keeping an eye out for animal rustlers. During the 1980s, they spread throughout the north and became an alternative justice system, with assemblies to resolve problems ranging from wife-beating to land disputes. This social movement, concludes anthropologist Orin Starn (1999), gave Peruvian peasants the vision of an alternative modernity and renewed among them a powerful sense of independent identity. Here a group of *ronderos* pose with a stolen donkey recovered from rustlers in 1986.

time, the apparent triumph of capitalism reanimated the former proponents of a Cold War theory called "modernization," which held that there were a series of stages of economic growth that successful countries like Britain or Canada had gone through and that should be followed by new, "underdeveloped" nations if they, too, wished to be stable and prosperous. These scholars and political figures now defended a new view called "neo-liberalism." Under neo-liberalism, no nation-state would be expected to rely on itself to achieve prosperity and avoid communist revolution. Instead, states would be encouraged by international institutions like the World Bank and the International Monetary Fund to seek prosperity by finding a niche in the growing global capitalist market. Market discipline would force state bureaucrats to support economic enterprises that would earn them income in the market and to eliminate expensive state institutions and subsidies that had provided a safety net for the poor. Western leaders embraced with enthusiasm the beckoning opportunity to bring the entire world within the compass of the capitalist economy. Less enthusiastic observers began to suspect that forces unleashed at the end of the Cold War were remaking the global political economy in unprecedented new ways, with outcomes that no one could predict or control.

## Cultural Processes in a Global World

Cold War–era economic and political theories presupposed a world in which geographic and cultural boundaries were relatively clear-cut: only if this is the case does it make sense to distinguish developed from underdeveloped nations, cores from peripheries, or local cultures from global social processes. The worldwide political, economic, and technological changes of recent decades, however, have challenged the utility of these distinctions. The cybernetics revolution led to advances in manufacturing, transportation, and communications technology that removed the seemingly unbreakable barriers to long-distance communication and contact, a phenomenon called "space–time compression" (Harvey 1990). These changes made it easier, cheaper, and faster to move people and things around the world than ever before; they also made it possible to stretch social relationships of all kinds over huge distances that previously would have been unbridgeable (Giddens 1990). And with the end of the Cold War, no part of the globe was blocked from the effects of these changes. The outcome has been the widely recognized phenomenon of globalization: the reshaping of local conditions by powerful global forces on an ever-intensifying scale. Globalization suggests a "world full of movement and mixture, contacts and linkages, and persistent cultural interaction and exchange" (Inda and Rosaldo 2002, 2).

Globalization is understood and evaluated differently by different observers. Anthropologists ordinarily approach globalization from the perspective of those among whom they do their research, and this approach reveals a variety of unlikely connections, such as the link between ecotourism and the sapphire trade in Madagascar (see EthnoProfile 15.1) or the link between the industrialization of textile work and the end of foot binding in China (see the "In Their Own Words" boxes on the following pages for more on these topics.) From this point of view, it has been apparent for some time that the effects of globalization are *uneven*: "large expanses of the planet are only tangentially tied to the webs of interconnection that encompass the globe" (Inda and Rosaldo 2002, 4). As a result, global processes are interpreted

## EthnoProfile 15.1

### Madagascar

**Region:** Indian Ocean

**Nation:** Madagascar

**Population:** 22,005,222 (2012 estimate)

**Environment:** Mix of tropical and semi-arid regions

**Livelihood:** Agriculture and ecotourism

**Political organization:** Modern nation-state with a parliamentary system

**For more information:** Gezon, Lisa L. 2014. "Who Wins and Who Loses? Unpacking the 'Local People' Concept in Ecotourism: A Longitudinal Study of Community Equity in Ankarana, Madagascar." *Journal of Sustainable Tourism* 22 (5): 821–38.

and experienced in contradictory ways by different groups and actors.

**globalization** Reshaping of local conditions by powerful global forces on an ever-intensifying scale.

## In Their Own Words

### Sapphires, Ecotourism, and the Global Bazaar in Madagascar

*Andrew Walsh is an associate professor at Western University. He has done extensive work with people in Madagascar whose lives have been impacted by global forces that drive the sapphire trade and ecotourism in their country.*

What do sapphires and ecotourist attractions have in common? More than you might imagine. I have recently done work on Madagascar's sapphire and ecotourist trades that illustrates how the sometimes unlikely comparisons inspired by anthropological research can reveal "unexpected associations and unconsidered entanglements, and encourage new ways of thinking about what ties and divides people in a shared world" (Walsh 2012: xvi).

I first travelled to Madagascar in the early 1990s to do research on the political organization and rituals

of a kingdom in the far north of this large island in the Indian Ocean. Known as "Antankarana" or "the people of the rocks," the constituents of this traditional Malagasy kingdom take their name from the immense limestone massif that dominates the local landscape (see photo). The Ankarana massif is more than just a landmark to Antankarana people, however. It is a sacred place where they have sought protection from conflict in the past, and where many of their ancestors lie entombed at sites that are regularly and carefully tended to.

Continued

Ankarana massif in Madagascar.

It is not only Antankarana people who consider this place special, however. In the late 1990s, I turned my attention to two other groups of people whose interest in the Ankarana massif and its surrounding forests had only recently been sparked: first, the large numbers of Malagasy and foreign gem-prospectors and traders who flooded the region following the discovery of sapphires there in late 1996, and second, the large numbers of foreign ecotourists who began arriving around the same time in hopes of experiencing the spectacular caves, forests, lemurs, chameleons, and other attractions on offer in a newly accessible conservation area centred on the massif.

Over more than a decade, I traced the parallel development of the region's sapphire and ecotourist trades, conducting research with gemstone miners and traders as well as with foreign ecotourists and their Malagasy guides. What I learned was that although these two trades have different impacts on local landscapes, it would be a mistake to imagine them only as contradictory. While it is true that, as conservationists warn, small-scale mining in and around conservation areas poses a threat to the region's ecosystems, and that, as promoters of ecotourism's promise worry, the region's mining industry thus poses a threat to the region's ecotourism industry, it is also true that, as was clear to the local observers with whom I did my research, the region's sapphire and ecotourist trades exist for one and the same reason: because of foreign demand for what can be found in Ankarana. Simply put, if it weren't for foreign consumers wanting

to buy the natural sapphires coming out of this region and foreign ecotourists seeking direct access to the region's other natural attractions, neither of the local trades on which I focused my attention would ever have come into being. What's more, as I learned by expanding my focus to include the *global* sapphire and ecotourism industries, foreign sapphire consumers and ecotourists are often looking for and finding precisely the same thing in Ankarana.

What *do* Ankarana's sapphires and ecotourist attractions have in common? As I have come to understand them, both might be described as "natural wonders" (2012: 93)—that is, as commodities that are valued in large part because of their affective, inspirational, and sometimes even awe-inspiring naturalness. Foreign consumers have the option of buying cheap, synthetic sapphires produced in a lab, or of visiting lemurs and chameleons in a zoo—and many of them do just that. For the foreign consumers who have made Ankarana's sapphire and ecotourist trades possible, however, such alternatives are nowhere near as valuable or satisfying as what Ankarana offers. The natural gemstones coming out of Ankarana and the ecotourist attractions that bring visitors into the region are alike in how they are marketed and consumed as one-of-a-kind, irreproducible products of nature.

Obviously, Malagasy people working in Ankarana's sapphire and ecotourist trades are not alone in being marginal, but absolutely essential, players in global industries. That doesn't mean, however, that we should ignore the specifics that anthropological research on the working lives and perspectives of people in places like Ankarana reveals. In fact, it is often these apparently marginal perspectives and places that offer us the clearest views of how the global economy actually functions. Seen from the margins, the global economy is not the orderly and rational system of well-integrated markets that many of us imagine it to be. From the perspective of many of the people with whom I work in Ankarana, the global economy looks more than anything like a global bazaar—an economic system that "presents a world of choices to [relatively wealthy] consumers and a world of paradoxes and limited possibilities to people in places like Ankarana" (2012: 104).

Source: Andrew Walsh, Associate Professor, Western University, 2015. For more on this topic, see Walsh 2012.

## *In Their Own Words*

## Connections between Foot Binding and Rural Women's Household Work in China

*Laurel Bossen of McGill University and her colleagues provide a new and interesting perspective on the practice of foot binding in rural China. In their research, they connect the decline of this practice to the increased industrialization and modernization of textile production fostered by the forces of globalization in the early decades of the twentieth century.*

Binding young girls' and women's feet in order to make them smaller was once very widespread in China. . . . The process took years to complete, but permanently changed the feet so that later unbinding could not restore their natural form. Foot binding greatly inhibited the mobility of Chinese girls and women for the rest of their lives. It permanently stopped their running, slowed their walking, and reduced their balance. It limited their ability to do many kinds of physical work outside the home. . . .

. . . Scholars have proposed numerous theories about the reasons for foot binding and its persistence. Reflecting on the experiences of urban, elite women, some interpret foot binding as an expression of male dominance or as a demonstration that families did not need their women's labour. Still others interpret foot binding through the lenses of sexuality, fashion, prestige, and beauty. . . . Yet foot binding was not practised only by elite or urban populations, it was also widespread among *rural* women whose families could hardly dispense with their labour for fashion, prestige, beauty, or the foot as erotic plaything. . . .

Foot binding, we propose, was more than a symbol of beauty; it was an integral part of an economic system depending on women's intensive domestic handwork in textiles. The young woman with bound feet was "attractive" to her husband's family in part because her small feet and handmade shoes proved she was already accustomed to sedentary handwork. Different forms of handwork, varying by locality, were very common in preindustrial China. They included transforming fibers (silk, cotton, hemp, and others) into yarn, thread, cloth, shoes, and nets, as well as making straw and wicker mats and baskets. Many of these products were not just for home use, but entered into circuits of local and long-distance trade. Women's heavy workload meant that they had to enlist their daughters' help at a young age, and mothers-in-law needed to know that their daughters-in-law had the skills and diligence for textile work. . . .

. . . [Early in the twentieth century, however, the] value of [handmade] cotton products changed dramatically

An elderly Chinese woman displays one of her feet, which were permanently reshaped by the foot-binding process she underwent as a young girl.

because industrial thread and cloth could be produced on a large scale with much less labour and because these industrial products and improved technologies were now reaching the interior. More remote rural locations . . ., which had formerly relied on human and animal carriers to bring in cotton for hand spinning and weaving, had high transport costs that [now] made their goods uncompetitive on the market. Where formerly a huge labour force of women was needed to produce clothing in the villages, now factory-made textiles could be brought to them for almost the same price as raw cotton. It no longer paid to spin or weave. . . . As textile work proved incapable of adding to family income, families had to question the conventions that confined girls and women to the courtyard economy and limited their participation in the more physically demanding agricultural tasks faced by all farming households. . . . As the household textile economy was destroyed, women had little incentive to keep their daughters busy at the spinning wheel or loom if it did not help to support the family. They thus had little reason to continue foot binding, a change in behaviour no doubt encouraged by social and political forces pushing in the same direction.

Source: Bossen et al. 2011, 348–9, 373–6.

Faye Ginsburg and Rayna Rapp (1995, 3), for example, describe a global process they call "stratified reproduction," in which some categories of people are empowered to nurture and reproduce while others are not: "Low-income African American mothers, for example, often are stereotyped as undisciplined 'breeders' who sap the resources of the state through incessant demands on welfare. But historically and in the present, they were 'good enough' nurturers to work as childcare providers for other, more privileged class and ethnic groups." Globalization has created new opportunities for some groups, like the Kayapó of Brazil and other Indigenous peoples, to build worldwide organizations to defend their interests (Kearney 1995, 560) (Figure 15.2). At the same time, global forces can also reinforce old constraints. Evaluating the record of new social movements in Latin America, for example, John Gledhill (1994, 198) writes that "to date the challenge that popular forces have been able to mount to the remorseless progress of the neo-liberal, neo-modernization agenda has remained limited."

It would be difficult to find any research project in contemporary cultural anthropology that does not in some way acknowledge the ways in which global forces affect the local societies in which anthropologists work. In this respect, globalization studies emphasize the ways in which *the global articulates with the local*: anthropological studies of globalization aim to show "how globalizing processes exist in the context of, and must come to terms with, the realities of particular societies" (Inda and Rosaldo 2002, 4). In other words, "while everyone might continue to live local lives, their phenomenal worlds have to some extent become global" (9).

Globalization is seen in the growth of transnational corporations that relocate their manufacturing operations from core to periphery or that appropriate local cultural forms and turn them into images and commodities to be marketed throughout the world (Figure 15.3). It is seen in tourism, which has grown into the world's largest industry, and in migration from periphery to the core on such a massive scale that observers now speak of the "de-territorialization" of peoples and cultures that, in the past, were presumed to be firmly attached to specific geographic locations. Not only that: de-territorialized people always "re-territorialize" in a new location. Such re-territorialization regularly sparks social conflicts and generates new forms of cultural identity, as nation-states try to retain control over citizens who have migrated beyond their borders and as relocated populations struggle both for recognition in their new homes and for influence

**FIGURE 15.2 |** To publicize their opposition to a proposed hydroelectric dam complex that threatened to flood their traditional territories, Indigenous Amazonian peoples, under the leadership of the Kayapó, engaged in a variety of activities. Here, Kayapó chief Paiakan (left) and British rock star Sting (right) hold a press conference.

**FIGURE 15.3 |** One dimension of globalization involves the appropriation of local cultural forms and the use of these forms in a variety of widely sold commodities. Dreamcatchers, for example, are sacred among many Aboriginal groups in North America, although they are now manufactured and sold on a massive scale.

in their places of origin. An example of this sort of migration *within* the borders of a country is the movement of Canadian First Nations peoples between cities and their reserves. Often, Aboriginal centres are created in urban settings to facilitate and encourage cultural practices that were common on Aboriginal reserves and to create a sense of belonging and connectedness within cities (Darnell 2011).

Heterogeneous and unstable cultural spaces created by re-territorialization call into question views like Wallerstein's (1974) that portray global processes as part of a coherent world system. Anthropologist Arjun Appadurai (1990) claims, to the contrary, that ever-intensifying global flows of people, technology, wealth, images, and ideologies are highly contradictory, generating global processes that are fundamentally disorganized and unpredictable. Jonathan Friedman (1994), by contrast, argues that the disorder may be real but that it is also a predictable consequence of the breakdown of Western global hegemony, with the dissolution of European colonial empires and the decentralization of capitalist economic accumulation from Europe and North America to parts of the world such as the Pacific Rim. In his view, these developments exemplify a pattern of global commercial expansion and contraction that began at least 5000 years ago with the rise of the first commercial civilizations—world systems in Wallerstein's sense—each of which was characterized by its own form of "modernity." Recognition of this pattern makes Friedman even more pessimistic than Wallerstein about possibilities for the future.

Not all anthropologists accept Friedman's conclusions. But even if Friedman's overall schema of civilizational cycles seems plausible, it cannot by itself account for the "local structures" and "autonomous cultural schemes" that appear at any point in the cycle. It is this historically specific local detail—what Inda and Rosaldo (2002, 27) call "the conjunctural and situated character of globalization"—that anthropologists aim to document and analyze. In the rest of this chapter, we examine three important areas of study in the anthropology of globalization: the effect of global forces on nation-states, human rights as the emerging discourse of globalization, and debates about cultural hybridization and cosmopolitanism.

# How Does Globalization Affect the Nation-State?

## Are Global Flows Undermining Nation-States?

In the second half of the twentieth century, one of the fundamental suppositions about global social organization was that it consisted of an international order of independent nation-states. This assumption has roots that can be traced back to nineteenth-century nationalist struggles in Europe, but it seems to have come fully into its own after World War II, with the final dissolution of European empires, as former colonies achieved independence (Figure 15.4). The United Nations (UN), created in 1945, presupposed a world of nation-states.

The flow of wealth, images, people, things, and ideologies unleashed by globalization, however, has undermined the ability of nation-states to police their boundaries effectively and has seemed to suggest that the conventional ideas about nation-states require revision. Many observers have suggested that globalization inevitably undermines the power and sovereignty of nation-states. National governments are virtually powerless to control what their citizens read or watch in the media: satellite services, telecommunications, and the Internet elude state-ordered censorship. Nation-states allow migrants, students, and tourists to cross their borders because they need their labour, tuition, or vacation expenditures; but in

**FIGURE 15.4** | Queen Elizabeth II at Nigerian independence ceremonies, January 1956.

so doing, states must contend with the political values, religious commitments, or families that these outsiders bring with them. Some people have argued that to weaken boundaries between states is a good thing since border restrictions and censorship need to be overcome. Since 1989, however, as we witness the ways that forces of globalization have made weakened states vulnerable to chaos and violence, the ability of the nation-state to protect its citizens from such destruction has led some to ask whether stronger nation-states might not have at least some points in their favour.

Massive global displacements of people have characterized Western modernity, starting with the slave trade and the movement of indentured labour to the colonies. In the nineteenth century, as developing

## In Their Own Words

### Cofan: Story of the Forest People and the Outsiders

*Randy Borman is president of the Centro Cofan Zabalo. He was born to missionary parents and grew up in Cofan culture in the Ecuadorian Amazon. Borman briefly attended school in North America and then returned to Ecuador to become a leader in the Cofan fight for economic and cultural survival. He has written in Cultural Survival Quarterly about the development of ecotourism in the Cofan area of Ecuador. The results of tourism elsewhere in the world are not always as positive as they have been for the Cofan people, in part because tourism is often imposed from the outside. To find out more about the Cofan people, visit www.cofan.org.*

I had the fortune to grow up as a forest person, enjoying the clean rivers and unlimited forests, learning the arts and skills of living comfortably in a wonderland of the marvellous, beautiful, and deadly. I experienced firsthand both the good and the bad of a world which will never again be possible, at least in the foreseeable future. And I also experienced the crushing physical, psychological, and spiritual impact of the invasion of the outside that erased our world.

In 1955, the Cofan people were the sole inhabitants of more than 1,000,000 hectares of pristine forest in northeastern Ecuador. By 1965, oil exploration and exploitation had begun. And by 1975, the forest was fast disappearing before a massive mestizo colonization, which was brought in by roads created to access vast quantities of oil. The rivers were fouled with chemicals and raw crude; the animals disappeared; boom towns sprung up all over; and the Cofan struggled to survive on less than 15,000 hectares of badly degraded forest. The old life was gone forever, and my companions and I faced the numbing prospect of discarding our culture and way of life, and becoming peasant farmers like so many others, trying to eke out a living from crops and animals which were never meant to grow in this environment. We had been powerless to maintain our forests in the face of outsider pressures to make every given piece of land profitable. If we were to save anything from the wreckage we needed alternatives, and quickly . . . .

[As the only member of his community with an outsider education, Borman worked with the community in trying to develop strategies for community survival, including those associated with marketing forest products. These strategies did not work.]

As we were wrestling with these possible alternatives, we were also acting as boatmen for the slowly increasing economy on the river. Several of us had managed to buy outboard motors with carefully saved returns from corn fields, animal skins, and short stints as trail makers with the oil companies. We had a long tradition of carving dugouts, and soon our canoes were travelling up and down the rivers with loads of lumber, corn, and coffee; occasional trips carrying cattle provided excitement and variety. This was not an alternative for the entire community, and it was only viable until roads were built, but it worked as a stop-gap measure for some of us. And unexpectedly, it led us directly into the alternative, which we have adopted as our own in the years since.

Travellers were coming to our region. The roads made it easier than at any previous time, and people from First World countries—the USA, Canada, England, Germany, Israel, Italy—began to come, searching for the vanishing rain forest. Most of them were primarily interested in seeing wildlife. This fit with our view of the situation precisely. We had our motorboats. There was still a lot of good forest out there, but it was hard to access with regular paddling and poling expeditions. So when these travellers arrived and wanted to go to "wild jungle," we were delighted to take them. They paid the transportation cost, and we took our shotguns and spears along to go hunting. Our attitude was that if the traveller wanted to go along with us, and didn't mind that we were hunting, why, we were happy to have them along to help carry the game home! From such a pragmatic beginning, we slowly developed our concept of tourism.

There were changes. We soon learned that the traveller had a lot more fun if we modified our normal hunting pattern a bit, and we even got paid extra for it. We found out that the average tourist didn't mind if we shot birds that looked like chickens, even if they were rare. But if we shot a toucan they were outraged, despite the fact that toucans are very common. Tourists preferred a board to a stick as a seat in the canoe, and a pad made them even happier. Tourists' food needed to be somewhat recognizable, such as rice, rather than the lumpy, thick manioc beer we normally eat and drink. But the community as a whole decided early that our role would be that of guides and service providers for tourists interested in the forest. We would not dress up and do dances, or stage fake festivals, or in any way try to sell our traditions and dress. We would not accept becoming the objects of tourism—rather, we would provide the skills and knowledge for the tourist to understand our environment. We would sell our education, at a price that was in line with the importance to the outsiders who wanted to buy it, such as lawyers, biologists, doctors, teachers, and other professionals the world over do.

Being guides for the tourism experience, not the objects of it, has provided both a very real economic alternative and a very solid incentive for the younger generation to learn the vast body of traditional knowledge, which lies at the heart of our culture. A deep conservation ethic—the roots of which lie at the hearts of most cultures who maintain a viable relation with their environments—has helped the Cofan community to create a number of projects which combine outsider science with our traditional knowledge. Interestingly enough, this has also turned out to be an economic success, as many of our projects began to receive funding in recognition of their innovation and replicability in other communities throughout Amazonia . . . .

Tourism is not for everyone. Some of our experiences have been negative. One of our biggest and most constant headaches is effective commercialization. To operate a community-based tourism business while maintaining our cultural heritage is not possible using the outsider formula of a tour operator. The implied hierarchy of manager, finance department, buyers, transport specialists, etc., all working eight hours a day, five days a week, with an office and a fax machine is clearly not applicable. Instead, we rely on teams, which rotate in their work, leaving time for farms, family duties, crafts, fishing, hunting, and the garden. But the lack of a full-time office makes it difficult to commercialize effectively, and we walk the precarious line between too much tourism (no time left over to live a normal life, and possible loss of our cultural way of life) and too little (not enough jobs, not enough income, lack of attraction for a forest-based life, and education for our young people). If we commercialize effectively, we run the risk of the operation snowballing, with more and more tourists arriving, and eventually, we are all wealthy in outsider goods and income but without our culture's wealth of time and interpersonal relationships that we all value so much now. If we don't commercialize effectively, we will wake up tomorrow back at the beginning, with the need to destroy our forest for short-term survival.

But in the overall scheme of things, our experiment with tourism has been overwhelmingly positive. Contact with people who wish to know what we can teach, who value our forests and are willing to pay to help us maintain them has been very important. Our increased awareness of the conservation imperatives facing us has led to many changes in our way of life, all aimed at preserving core values for future generations.

Source: Borman 1999, 48–50.

---

capitalist markets pushed and pulled waves of European and Asian emigrants out of their homelands and installed them in different parts of the globe, colonial authorities revived the institution of indentured labour to rearrange populations within their dominions.

A hundred years ago, when volumes of immigration were lower and moved at a slower pace and jobs were plentiful, assimilation into the society of reterritorialization was often possible. Today, however, desperate economic and political situations in migrants' home territories plus ease of transportation have increased the volume and speed of migration, while market crises in the countries where migrants have settled have sharply reduced the economic opportunities available to them once they arrive.

Migrants often find themselves caught. On the one hand, they now form sizeable minority populations in their countries of settlement, which still offer them better opportunities for economic survival and political security than the nations from which they came, factors that encourage them to stay where they are. On the other hand, local economic crises and their visibility in enclaves of settlement, often in the poorer areas of cities, increases the hostility and sometimes violence directed against them by locals whenever there is an economic downturn. Many migrants thus conclude that the possibility of permanent assimilation is unrealistic, which encourages them to maintain ties to their homeland or to other communities of migrants located elsewhere.

## Migration, Transborder Identities, and Long-Distance Nationalism

The term *diaspora* is commonly used to refer to migrant populations with a shared identity who live in a variety of different places around the world, but Nina Glick Schiller and Georges Fouron point out that not all such populations see themselves in the same way. Schiller and Fouron describe different types of "transborder identities" that characterize different groups of migrants. They prefer to use the term *diaspora* to identify a form of transborder identity that does not focus on nation building. Should members

diaspora Migrant populations with a shared identity who live in a variety of different locales around the world; a form of transborder identity that does not focus on nation building.

long-distance nationalists Members of a diaspora organized in support of nationalist struggles in their homeland or to agitate for a state of their own.

transborder state A form of state in which it is claimed that those people who left the country and their descendants remain part of their ancestral state, even if they are citizens of another state.

transborder citizenry A group made up of citizens of a country who continue to live in their homeland plus the people who have emigrated from the country and their descendants, regardless of their current citizenship.

of a diaspora begin to organize in support of nationalist struggles in their homeland or to agitate for a state of their own, they become long-distance nationalists (Schiller and Fouron 2002, 360–1). The term *long-distance nationalism* was coined by political scientist Benedict Anderson to describe the efforts of émigrés to offer moral, economic, and political support to the nationalist struggles of their countries of origin. In his original discussion, Anderson (1992, 13) emphasized the dangerous irresponsibility of the "citizenshipless participation" of the long-distance nationalist: "while technically a citizen of the state in which he comfortably lives, but to which he may feel little attachment, he finds it tempting to play identity politics by participating (via propaganda, money, weapons, any way but voting) in the conflicts of his imagined *Heimat* [homeland]" (quoted in Schiller and Fouron 2002, 269–70). Schiller and Fouron argue, however, that the conditions of globalization have led to new forms of long-distance nationalism that do not correspond to Anderson's original description but that have led to the emergence of the transborder state: a form of state "claiming that its emigrants and their descendants remain an integral and intimate part of their ancestral homeland, even if they are legal citizens of another state" (357).

The idea of a transborder state did not characterize earlier periods of mass emigration in the nineteenth and twentieth centuries (e.g., the period of the late nineteenth and early twentieth centuries in which a massive influx of Eastern Europeans settled in Western Canada). At that time, nations sending emigrants abroad regarded permanent settlement of emigrants elsewhere as national betrayal and encouraged them to think of migration as temporary, expecting them eventually to return home with new wealth and skills to build the nation. But in today's global world, political leaders of many states sending emigrants not only accept the likelihood that those emigrants will settle permanently elsewhere but also insist that such permanently settled émigrés retain full membership in the nation-state from which they came. This form of long-distance nationalism creates what Schiller and Fouron (2002, 358) call a transborder citizenry: "Citizens residing within the territorial homeland and new emigrants and their descendants are part of the nation, whatever legal citizenship the émigrés may have."

Transborder states and transborder citizenries are more than symbolic identities: they have become concretized in law. For example, several Latin American countries, including Mexico, Colombia, the Dominican Republic, Ecuador, and Brazil, permit emigrants who have become naturalized citizens in countries such as the United States to retain dual nationality and even voting rights in their country of origin. Special government ministries are set up to address the needs of citizens living abroad. In Canada, a form of transborder citizenry exists for foreign workers who are awarded a visa through the national Temporary Foreign Workers Program. Under the rules of this program, temporary migrant workers must come to Canada alone, and they must leave once their specified term of employment is over. These workers have been essential for the growth of Canada's economy in places like Alberta and Ontario, where labourers are in short supply; however, their stay in Canada is temporary and citizenship is rarely an option (Figure 15.5). These forms of transborder citizenry are very different from Anderson's notion of "citizenshipless participation." Schiller and Fouron (2002, 359) stress that transborder states and citizenries spring "from the life experiences of migrants of different classes" and are "rooted in the day to day efforts of people in the homeland to live lives of dignity and self-respect that compel them to include those who have migrated."

But some transborder citizenries face difficulties. First, their efforts at nation building are sometimes blocked by political forces in the homeland that do not welcome their contributions. This has been the case

for Haitians living abroad while Haiti was ruled by the Duvalier family dictatorship and for Cubans living abroad whose efforts have been blocked by the Castro revolutionary government. Second, the states in which immigrants have settled may not welcome the continued involvement of transborder citizens in the affairs of another state. Yet, in an era of globalization, attempts to control migration threaten to block the flows of people that keep the global economy going. Moreover, the vulnerability of transborder citizens in these circumstances often increases the appeal of long-distance nationalism (Schiller and Fouron 2002, 359–60).

The globalizing forces that produce long-distance nationalism and transborder states and citizens have undermined previous understandings of what a world made up of nation-states should look like. In addition, unacknowledged contradictions and weaknesses of actual nation-states are revealed. For example, the existence and strength of transborder states and citizenries show that some nation-states—especially those sending migrants—are actually what Schiller and Fouron (2002, 363) call "apparent states": they have all the outward attributes of nation-states (government bureaucracies, armies, a seat in the UN), but in fact they are unable to meet the needs of their people. The strength of long-distance nationalism and transborder citizenries also exposes inconsistencies and paradoxes in the meaning of citizenship in the nation-states where migrants settle.

Schiller and Fouron contrast legal citizenship with what they call "substantive citizenship" and point out that, for transborder citizens, the two often do not

**FIGURE 15.5** | Migrant workers harvest raspberries in Milton, Ontario.

coincide. As we saw, legal citizenship is accorded by state laws and can be difficult for migrants to obtain. But even those transborder citizens who obtain legal citizenship often experience a gap between what the legal citizenship promises and the way they are treated by the state. For example, women and visible minorities who are Canadian citizens are not treated by the state the same way white male citizens are treated. By contrast, substantive citizenship is defined by the actions people take, regardless of their legal citizenship status, to assert their membership in a state and to bring about political changes that will improve their lives. Some transborder citizenries call for the establishment of full-fledged transnational nation-states. That is, "they challenge the notion that relationships between citizens and their state are confined within that territory" and work for the recognition of a new political form that contradicts the understandings of political theory but reflects the realities of their experiences of national identity (Schiller and Fouron 2002, 359).

## How Can Citizenship Be Flexible?

Schiller and Fouron's observations about the way globalization has undermined the stability of conventional nation-states expose contradictory and ambiguous practices associated with such basic concepts as "national identity" and "citizenship." Their contrast between formal and substantive citizenship suggests that conventional notions of citizenship that previously seemed straightforward begin to break down in the context of globalization. Another way of speaking about these contradictions and ambiguities is suggested by anthropologist Aihwa Ong (2002, 174), who speaks of flexible citizenship: "the strategies and effects of mobile managers, technocrats, and

---

legal citizenship  The rights and obligations of citizenship accorded by the laws of a state.

substantive citizenship  The actions people take, regardless of their legal citizenship status, to assert their membership in a state and to bring about political changes that will improve their lives.

transnational nation-state  A nation-state in which the relationships between citizens and the state extend to wherever citizens reside.

flexible citizenship  The strategies and effects employed by managers, technocrats, and professionals who move regularly across state boundaries and seek both to circumvent and to benefit from different nation-state regimes.

---

professionals seeking both to circumvent *and* benefit from different nation-state regimes by selecting different sites for investment, work, and family relocation." Ong's research concerns diaspora communities of elite Chinese families who have played key roles in the economic successes of the Pacific Rim in recent years. Although their success is often attributed by outsiders to "Chinese culture," Ong's research calls this simplistic explanation into question. Ong documents the ways in which Chinese families have responded creatively to opportunities and challenges they have encountered since the end of the nineteenth century as they found ways to evade or exploit the governmentality of three different kinds of institutions: Chinese kinship and family, the nation-state, and the marketplace.

For an earlier discussion of Ong's work, see Chapter 12, p. 333.

The break from mainland Chinese ideas of kinship and Confucian filial piety came when Chinese first moved into the capitalist commercial circuits of European empires. Money could be made in these settings, but success required Chinese merchant families to cut themselves off from ties to mainland China and to reinforce bonds among family members and business partners in terms of *guanxi* ("relationships of social connections built primarily upon shared identities such as native place, kinship, or attending the same school" [Smart 1999, 120]). The family discipline of overseas Chinese enabled them to become wealthy and provided the resources to subvert the governmentality of the nation-state. The orientation of these wealthy families toward national identity and citizenship, Ong explains, is "market-driven." In Hong Kong, for example, in the years leading up to its return to mainland China in 1997, many wealthy Chinese thought of citizenship "not as the right to demand full democratic representation, but as the right to promote familial interests apart from the well-being of society" (Ong 2002, 178). None of the overseas Chinese she knew expressed any commitment to nationalism, either local or long-distance. This understanding of citizenship could not be more different from the committed transborder citizenship of long-distance nationalists described by Schiller and Fouron.

Relying on family discipline and loyalty and buttressed by considerable wealth and strong interpersonal ties, these families actively worked to evade the governmentality of nation-states. For example, Chinese from Hong Kong who wanted to migrate to Britain in

**FIGURE 15.6** | Overseas Chinese are to be found in many parts of the world. Many of them run small businesses such as those that make up this Chinatown in Kuala Lumpur, Malaysia.

the 1960s were able to evade racial barriers that blocked other "coloured" immigrants because of their experience with capitalism and their reputation for peaceful acquiescence to British rule. When the British decided to award citizenship to some Hong Kong residents in the 1990s, they used a point system that favoured applicants with education, fluency in English, and training in professions of value to the economy, such as accountancy and law. These attributes fitted well the criteria for citizenship valued under the government of Margaret Thatcher, while other applicants for citizenship who lacked such attributes were excluded. Citizenship, or at least a passport, could be purchased by those who had the money: "well-off families accumulated passports not only from Canada, Australia, Singapore, and the United States but also from revenue-poor Fiji, the Philippines, Panama, and Tonga (which required in return for a passport a down payment of US $200,000 and an equal amount in installments)" (Ong 2002, 183) (Figure 15.6).

Although wealthy overseas Chinese families had thus managed to evade or subvert the governmentality of both Chinese kinship and nation-states, they remained vulnerable to the discipline of the capitalist market. To be sure, market discipline under globalization was very different from the market discipline typical in the 1950s and 1960s. Making money in the context of globalization required the flexibility to take advantage of economic opportunities wherever and whenever they appeared. Ong describes one family in which the eldest son remained in Hong Kong to run part of the family

hotel chain located in the Pacific region while his brother lived in San Francisco and managed the hotels located in North America and Europe. Children can be separated from their parents when they are, for example, installed in one country to be educated while their parents manage businesses in other countries on different continents.

These flexible business arrangements are not without costs. "Familial regimes of dispersal and localization ... discipline family members to make do with very little emotional support; disrupted parental responsibility, strained marital relations, and abandoned children are such common circumstances that they have special terms" (Ong 2002, 185). At the same time, individual family members truly do seem to live comfortably as citizens of the world. A Chinese banker in San Francisco told Ong that he could live in Asia, Canada, or Europe: "I can live anywhere in the world, but it must be near an airport" (190).

The values and practices to which overseas Chinese adhere and which seem to be responsible for their tremendous achievements in a globalized capitalist economy suggest to Ong that, for these elite Chinese, the concept of nationalism has lost its meaning. Instead, she says, they seem to subscribe to a **postnational ethos** in which they submit to the governmentality of the capitalist market while trying to evade the governmentality of nation-states, ultimately because their only true loyalty

**postnational ethos** An attitude toward the world in which people submit to the governmentality of the capitalist market while trying to evade the governmentality of nation-states.

is to the family business (2002, 190). Ong notes, however, that flexible citizenship informed by a postnational ethos is not an option for non-elite migrants: "whereas for bankers, boundaries are always flexible, for migrant workers, boat people, persecuted intellectuals and artists, and other kinds of less well-heeled refugees, this ... is a harder act to follow" (190).

She points out that, on the way to their success, contemporary Chinese merchants "have also revived premodern forms of child, gender, and class oppression, as well as strengthened authoritarianist regimes in Asia" (2002, 190). Yet, neither the positives nor the negatives should, she insists, be attributed to any "Chinese" essence; instead, she thinks these strategies are better understood as "the expressions of a habitus that is finely tuned to the turbulence of late capitalism" (191).

## Are Human Rights Universal?

Globalization has stimulated discussions about human rights: powers, privileges, or material resources to which people everywhere, by virtue of being human, are justly entitled. Rapidly circulating capital, images, people, things, and ideologies juxtapose different understandings about what it means to be human or what kinds of rights people may be entitled to. The context within which human-rights discourse becomes relevant is often described as multiculturalism: living permanently in settings surrounded by people with cultural backgrounds different from your own and struggling to define with them the degree to which the wider society should accord respect and recognition to the cultural beliefs and practices of different groups. It is precisely in multicultural settings—found everywhere in today's globalized world—that questions of rights become salient and different cultural understandings of what it means to be human, and what rights humans are entitled to, become the focus of contention.

Essentially, the ideology of multiculturalism defines Canada as a modern nation-state. Canada was

human rights  Powers, privileges, or material resources to which people everywhere, by virtue of being human, are justly entitled.

multiculturalism  Living permanently in settings surrounded by people with cultural backgrounds different from one's own and struggling to define with them the degree to which the cultural beliefs and practices of different groups should or should not be accorded respect and recognition by the wider society.

FIGURE 15.7 | In 2013, demonstrators in Quebec marched against the province's proposed Charter of Values, which sought to prohibit public-sector employees from wearing or displaying religious symbols, including the hijab. Many people opposed the bill on the grounds that a number of its provisions violated individuals' fundamental rights to religious freedom and expression of beliefs.

one of the first countries in the world to introduce a federal multiculturalism policy (in 1971), and as a result Canada's version of multiculturalism has been adopted internationally. Over the past forty years, Canada's culturally inclusive immigrant-integration policies have become the cornerstone for maintaining the country's economic success and growth. Yet, as in other multicultural societies, the close proximity of people with different cultural values and beliefs has led to various debates over what constitute a "human right" (Figure 15.7).

### Human-Rights Discourse as the Global Language of Social Justice

Discourses about human rights have proliferated in recent decades, stimulated by the original UN Universal Declaration of Human Rights in 1948 and followed by numerous subsequent declarations. For example, in 1992, the Convention on the Elimination of All Forms of Discrimination against Women (CEDAW) declared that violence against women was a form of gender discrimination that violated the human rights of women. This declaration was adopted by the UN General Assembly in 1993 and became part of the rights platform at the Fourth World Conference on Women in Beijing, China, in 1995. Anthropologist Sally Merry (2001, 36–7) observes that this declaration "dramatically demonstrates the creation of new rights—rights which depend on the state's failure to protect women rather than its active violation of rights" and that "the emergence of violence against women as a distinct human-rights violation depends on redefining the family so that it is no longer shielded from legal scrutiny."

Although CEDAW has proved particularly contentious, other human-rights documents have been signed without controversy by many national governments. Signing a human-rights declaration supposedly binds governments to take official action to implement changes in local practices that might be seen to violate the rights asserted in the declaration. Human-rights discourses are common currency in all societies, at all levels.

Because of the wide adoption of human-rights discourses throughout the world, some people have come to speak of an emerging "culture of human rights," which has now become "the pre-eminent global language of social justice" (Merry 2001, 38). As Jane Cowan, Marie Bénédicte Dembour, and Richard Wilson (2001, 5) write, it is "no use imagining a 'primitive' tribe which has not yet heard of human rights . . . . [W]hat it means to be 'Indigenous' is itself transformed through interaction with human-rights discourses and institutions." These developments mean that anthropologists need to take note of the important influence this human-rights discourse is having in the various settings where they do their research.

What counts as "human rights" has changed over time, not only because of the action of international bodies like the UN but also because of the efforts of an increasing number of non-governmental organizations (NGOs) that have become involved in various countries of the world, many of them deeply committed to projects designed to improve people's lives and protect their rights (Figure 15.8). As Merry (2001, 35) says, these developments "have created a new legal order" that has given birth to new possibilities throughout the world for the elaboration and discussion of what human rights are all about.

In addition, because the "culture of human rights" is increasingly regarded, in one way or another, as the "culture of globalization," it would seem to be a topic well-suited to anthropological analysis in itself. This is because, as we shall see, human-rights discourse is not as straightforward as it seems. On the face of things, defending human rights for all people would seem unproblematic. Few people who are aware of the devastation wrought by colonial exploitation, for example,

**FIGURE 15.8** | Women's shelters run by NGOs in Afghanistan provide a variety of services. Here, classmates applaud a fellow student after she stood up to read in a literacy class at one such shelter.

would want to suggest that the victims of that exploitation did not have rights that needed to be protected at all costs. Yet, when we look closely at particular disputes about human rights, the concept no longer seems so simple.

Cowan and her colleagues have noted that there are two major arguments that have developed for talking about the way human rights and culture are related. The first involves the idea that *human rights are opposed to culture* and that the two cannot be reconciled. The second involves the idea that a key universal human right is precisely one's *right to culture*. We will consider each in turn.

## Rights versus Culture?

Arguments that pit human rights against culture depend on the assumption that "cultures" are homogeneous, bounded, and unchanging sets of ideas and practices and that each society has only one culture, which its members are obligated to follow. This view of culture has been severely criticized by cultural anthropologists, but it is very much alive in many human-rights disputes. For if people have no choice but to follow the rules of the culture into which they were born, international interference with customs said to violate human rights would seem itself to constitute a human-rights violation. Outsiders would be

For a discussion of why cultural anthropologists have criticized this view of "cultures," see Chapter 2, pp. 37–8.

disrupting a supposedly harmonious way of life and preventing those who are committed to such a way of life from observing their own culturally specific understandings about rights. Thus, it is concluded, cultures should be allowed to enjoy absolute, inviolable protection from interference by outsiders. This has been the position adopted, for example, by some national governments that have refused to sign the CEDAW declaration that violence against women violates women's human rights. "Many states have opposed this conception of human rights on cultural or religious grounds and have refused to ratify treaties" (Merry 2001, 37). Nevertheless, by 2015, 189 countries had ratified CEDAW (UN 2015b).

Sometimes representatives of non-Western nation-states may feel free to dismiss rights talk as an unwelcome colonial imposition of ideas that, far from being universal, reflect ethnocentric European preoccupations. But such a dismissal of human-rights discourse needs to be closely examined. In the case of the right of women to protection from violence, for example, Merry points out that although some forms of violence against women may be culturally sanctioned in some societies, there are many forms that violence against women can take even in those societies, and not all of these are accorded the same amount of cultural support. For example, the cultural practice of female genital cutting could be justified in the past in some circumstances as an appropriate cultural action, but it is now being questioned and even outlawed in the societies where it was traditional. This suggests that "culture values" cannot be held responsible for everything that people do in any society and that members of the same society can disagree about these matters and sometimes change their minds.

For a more thorough discussion of female genital cutting, see Chapter 2, pp. 31–2.

As talk about human rights has become incorporated into local cultural discussions in recent decades, anthropologists are not surprised to discover that the notion undergoes transformation as people try to make sense of what it means in their own local contexts (Cowan et al. 2001, 8). Being forced to choose between rights and culture, however, seems increasingly unviable in a globalizing, multicultural world. In their own anthropological work on these matters, Cowan and her colleagues (2001) are convinced that the rights-versus-culture debate exaggerates cultural differences. Like many cultural anthropologists today,

they find that "it is more illuminating to think of culture as a field of creative interchange and contestation" (2001, 4). Such a view of culture makes it possible to find points of connection between the defence of certain human rights and the defence of particular cultural values.

Finally, it is worth asking if "culture" is sometimes used as a scapegoat to mask the unwillingness of a government to extend certain rights to its citizens for reasons that have nothing to do with culture. Cowan and colleagues observe that states like Indonesia and Singapore, which position themselves as stout defenders of "Asian values," have welcomed Western industrial capitalism. To reject human-rights discourse because it contradicts "Asian values" would, at the very least, suggest "an inconsistent attitude toward westernization," which in turn feeds suspicions that the defence of "Asian values" may be a political tactic designed "to bolster state sovereignty and resist international denunciations of internal repression and political dissent" (Cowen et al. 2001, 6–7).

## Rights to Culture?

A second popular argument about the relationship between rights and culture begins from very different premises. This argument does not view universal "human rights" as alien and opposed to "cultures." Instead, it says that all peoples have a universal human right to maintain their own distinct cultures. The *right to culture* has already been explicit in a number of international rights documents.

This argument is interesting because it seems to concede that such things as universal human rights do exist after all. The list of universal rights is simply amended to include the right to one's culture. It draws strength from the idea that cultural diversity is intrinsically valuable and that people should be able to observe their own cultural practices free from outside interference. However, it calls into question the common understanding that people frequently cannot enjoy their full human rights until they are *freed* from the constraints of local cultures. A right to culture, therefore, shows how the very idea of rights and culture is transformed and contested by globalization.

One key issue in the struggle to protect the right to culture is shared by *any* claim to human rights. It concerns the kinds of legal mechanisms needed to ensure protection. The great promise of international documents like the UN Universal Declaration of Human Rights seems to be that people are now free to bring allegations of human-rights abuses to an international forum to seek redress. But in fact this is not the case. As human-rights activists have discovered, human rights are legally interpreted as *individual* rights, not group rights. This means that people must demand that the *governments of the nation-states in which they are citizens* recognize and enforce the individual rights defended in international documents. International institutions like the UN have been unwilling to challenge the sovereignty of individual nation-states.

The defence of all human rights, including a right to culture, thus depends on the policies of national governments. Some activists see this as a serious contradiction in human-rights discourse that undermines its effectiveness. Talal Asad recounts, for example, how human rights activist Malcolm X argued in the 1960s that African Americans who wanted redress for abuses of their human rights should go directly to the UN and press their case against the government of the United States: "When you expand the civil-rights struggle to the level of human rights, you can then take the case of the black man in [the United States] before the nations in the UN" (quoted in Asad 2003, 141).

In fact, however, this is not the way the system was intended to work. Asad reminds us that

> *The Universal Declaration of Human Rights* begins by asserting "the inherent dignity" and the "equal and inalienable rights of all members of *the human family*," and then turns immediately to the state. In doing so, it implicitly accepts the fact that the universal character of the rights-bearing person is made the responsibility of sovereign states. (137)

In this legal universe, African Americans (and similarly situated groups in other nation-states) occupied an anomalous position: they bore neither national rights nor human rights (144). The recognition of the human rights of African Americans thus depended on persuading the *United States government* to recognize those rights; the UN might use its persuasive power to urge such changes, but it had no coercive power to force the United States—or any other national government—to come into compliance.

Martin Luther King's strategy, Asad points out, took a very different tack, using arguments drawn from prophetic religious discourse and the discourse of American liberalism. His movement aimed at "mobilizing American public opinion for change," and it was effective at pressing for progressive social change in a way that, among other things, was compatible with the division of labour set forth by the UN Universal Declaration of Human Rights (Asad 2003, 146). In a globalizing world, however, this division of human-rights labour—international bodies propose, but nation-states implement—is being challenged. For example, transborder citizenries lack any forum in which their status and their demands are clearly accorded legitimacy. The right-to-culture movement has succeeded in recent years in highlighting such anomalies and eroding the traditionally recognized right of nation-states to determine the kinds of rights their citizens will be accorded (Cowan et al. 2001, 8–9). As in the case of the rights-versus-culture argument, however, the right-to-culture argument can be "called upon to legitimate reactionary projects as easily as progressive ones ... the uses to which culture can be put in relation to rights are evidently multiple" (10).

Anthropological disciplinary commitments have allowed anthropologists to approach debates about rights and culture in ways that contribute something new to the discussion. These anthropological contributions can be seen in two ways. First, anthropologists have addressed the ways in which human-rights discourse can itself be seen as culture. Second, their own struggles with the concept of "culture" allow them to mount a critique of some of the ways that this concept has been mobilized in discussions of human rights.

## Are Rights Part of Culture?

Anthropological approaches are well suited for investigating the so-called culture of human rights that appears to have emerged in recent years. As in the cultures traditionally studied by anthropologists, the culture of human rights is based on certain ideas about human beings, their needs, and their ability to exercise agency, as well as the kinds of social connections between human beings that are considered legitimate and illegitimate. The entire question of "legitimacy" in human-rights discourse points to the central role played by *law*, both as a way of articulating specific human rights and as a tool for defending those rights. Cowan and colleagues (2001) have drawn on earlier anthropological work in which systems of law were analyzed as cultural systems.

One important source has been the "law and culture" framework developed by anthropologists Clifford Geertz, Laura Nader, and Lawrence Rosen and non-anthropologists like Boaventura de Sousa Santos. In this framework, "law is conceived as a worldview or structuring discourse . . . . 'Facts' . . . are socially constructed through rules of evidence, legal conventions, and the rhetoric of legal actors" (Cowan et al. 2001, 11). Analysts who talk about a "culture of human rights" as the new culture of a globalizing world point out that the key features of the human-rights worldview clearly indicate its origins in Western secular discourse. That is, it focuses on the rights of individuals, it proposes to relieve human suffering through technical rather than ethical solutions, and it emphasizes rights over duties or needs (2001, 11–12).

In the meantime, most anthropologists would probably agree that anthropology can clarify the idea of a "culture of human rights" (Cowan et al. 2001, 13). An understanding of culture as open, heterogeneous, and supple could be effective in helping us understand how human-rights processes work.

## Anthropology in the Contemporary World

### Anthropology and Indigenous Rights

Anthropologists are increasingly participating in organizations for the defence of human rights. In particular, they have contributed to the recognition by human-rights legal advocates that the collective rights of groups (such as Indigenous groups) deserve as much attention as the rights of individuals do. In Canada, there have been numerous opportunities for anthropologists to work as advocates for First Nations groups to promote their rights as Indigenous peoples. One of the first arose during the 1970s in response to a proposal to construct an oil and gas pipeline that would run from Alaska through the Mackenzie Valley to the southern United States. The proposed project would have taken away and altered the traditional lands of the Dene and other First Nations groups living along its route. Concerned about the negative social and environmental consequences of the project, the Canadian government commissioned an inquiry and charged Thomas Berger, a Supreme Court judge, with leading the investigation. Over the course of the investigation, which came to be known as the Berger Inquiry (Berger 1977), numerous anthropologists and First Nations peoples provided evidence to substantiate claims that the lands in question were essential to the wellbeing of the Dene and other Indigenous peoples and that these peoples' ways of life were not "becoming extinct." In the end, Berger recommended that the project be put on hold for ten years in order for land claims and environmental concerns to be assessed.

Another early example arose in the 1970s when numerous anthropologists, mostly from McGill University, were asked to work with the James Bay Cree as they negotiated for rights to their traditional hunting lands, an area of about 380,000 square kilometres that the Quebec government planned to develop for a hydroelectric plant. Harvey Feit (1995) and Richard Salisbury (1986) were among the first anthropologists invited to advocate for and assist the James Bay Cree. Feit was called upon by the Cree Grand Council to use his doctoral research on Cree ecological land use to defend their claims against the Quebec and federal governments. Between 1973 and 1978, multiple negotiations took place with numerous anthropologists advocating for the Cree's Indigenous rights. Their work led to the establishment of the James Bay and Northern Quebec Agreement, which was, at the time, the most comprehensive land claims settlement ever reached in Canada. The settlement included not only rights to land but also authority over education, health services, housing, and other social services as well as a role in future development plans in the area.

Since the late 1980s, anthropologist Ronald Niezen (2003) has spent much of his time involved in community-based research with the eastern James Bay Cree in northern Quebec as well as the Cross Lake Cree in Manitoba. As his involvement with these groups increased, Niezen found that the Cree valued his ability to provide a link between their own Aboriginal government and the government of Canada. He was called on to perform many roles in addition to that of participant-observer, acting at various times "as an observer, witness, advocate, author— roles that were pretty much informally developed as needs became felt" (Niezen 2003, xiv).

As his work with the Cree evolved, and he moved back and forth from reservation to government meetings, Niezen came to realize that a global movement of Indigenous peoples had come into existence and was getting noticed at places such as the United Nations. His earlier research in Mali also became relevant in a new way when, during one of his trips to Geneva, he encountered delegates from West Africa who were coming to identify themselves as Indigenous peoples and who were working "to develop human-rights standards appropriate to their concerns" (Niezen 2003, xiv). So, in 1994, he travelled as an observer delegate with the Grand Council of the Cree to a meeting of the Working Group on Indigenous Populations at the United Nations in Geneva, Switzerland. People on Aboriginal reservations were also learning via the Internet about the struggles of other Indigenous communities for rights, and some community leaders were starting to "see themselves as leading a cause for justice directly analogous to (and without distinguishing among) a variety of liberation movements, including the American civil rights movement and resistance to South African apartheid" (Niezen 2003, xiii).

Indigeneity is supposed to refer to a primordial identity that preceded the establishment of colonial states. Yet the very possibility that groups from West Africa, Latin America, and North America might come together as Indigenous peoples "is predicated upon global sameness of experience, and is expressed through the mechanisms of law and bureaucracy" (Niezen 2003, 2–3). "Indigenous peoples" is not just a badge of identity, but also a legal term that has been included in international conventions issued by the International Labour Organization.

According to Niezen (2003), it is important to distinguish what he calls *ethnonationalism* from *indigenism*. Ethnonationalism, he believes, describes a movement of people who "have defined their collective identities with clear cultural and linguistic contours and who express their goals of autonomy from the state with the greatest conviction and zeal, sometimes with hatreds spilling over into violence" (8). For example, in Canada the advocates of sovereignty for Quebec have pushed for an independent French-speaking nation-state (8). Indigenism, by contrast, "is not a particularized identity but a global one, . . . grounded in international networks" (9). What connects specific groups to this identity, whether they live in dictatorships or democratic states, "is a sense of illegitimate, meaningless, and dishonourable suffering" (13).

Unlike ethnonationalists, Indigenous-rights activists do not seek to form breakaway states of their own. Their approach is entirely different: Indigenous representatives lobby for their rights before international bodies such as the United Nations, attempting to hold states accountable for abusing their Indigenous citizens. In Niezen's (2003, 16) opinion, the strategy "shows some Indigenous leaders to be, despite their limited power and resources, some of the most effective political strategists on the contemporary national and international scenes." Their goal is to get nation-states to live up to their responsibilities and promises to Indigenous people, which are often explicitly stated in treaties. Thus, they seek affirmation of their rights to land and compensation for past losses and suffering; they seek cultural self-determination and political sovereignty. The goal of Indigenous liberation thus involves the recognition of *collective rights*.

While Niezen (2003, 23) urges us to acknowledge the daring and effectiveness of the Indigenous movement, he also warns against romanticizing it: "Significant obstacles remain to be overcome before a new order of relations between Indigenous peoples and the state can be said to have truly arrived." For example, the United Nations has been less responsive than many Indigenous delegates might have hoped, because some of its member states continue to equate the movement for Indigenous sovereignty with ethnonationalism. Hence the UN Permanent Forum on Indigenous Issues is not called the UN Permanent Forum on Indigenous *Peoples* (160–4).

Some liberal human-rights theorists are also concerned that the recognition of collective rights would serve as a green light to despotic governments, who could use the rights of distinct cultures as an excuse for repression. Niezen (2003, 219–21) concluded that

> if Indigenous claims to self-determination are to avoid playing into the hands of despotic governments, they must have individual rights built into them . . . . Human rights do not offer protection of cultural practices that themselves violate individual rights. The concept of "Indigenous peoples" developed principally within Western traditions of scholarship and legal reform . . . has transcended its symbolic use by acquiring legal authority . . . . It has been taken control of by its living subjects—reverse-engineered, rearticulated, and put to use as a tool of liberation.

## How Can Culture Help in Thinking about Rights?

To use the culture concept as a tool for analyzing human-rights processes means looking for "patterns and relationships of meaning and practice between different domains of social life" that are characteristic of the culture of human rights (Cowan et al. 2001, 13). Since human rights are articulated in legal documents and litigated in courts, one of the most important patterns that become visible in the culture of human rights is the way these rights are shaped to accommodate the law. Groups and individuals who assert that their human rights have been violated regularly take their cases to courts of law. But this means that in order to get the courts to take them seriously, they need to understand how the law operates. A key feature of this understanding involves a realistic awareness of the kinds of claims that the law pays attention to and the kinds of claims that it dismisses.

Looking at human-rights law as culture reveals that only certain kinds of claims are admissible. As we saw above, the culture of human rights as currently constituted is best suited to redress the grievances of individuals, not groups. It also provides technical, not ethical, remedies, and it emphasizes rights over duties or needs. Plaintiffs are therefore likely to have a difficult time if they want to claim that their group rights have been violated, that they want the violator exposed and punished, or that the state itself has failed to fulfill its responsibilities toward them. Part of the human-rights process therefore involves learning how to craft cases that will fit the laws. This can be tricky if the categories and identities recognized in human-rights law do not correspond to categories and identities that are meaningful to the plaintiffs.

Anthropologists have worked with many social groups struggling with national governments to practise their culture freely. These political struggles regularly include claims about distinct and unchanging values and practices. These kinds of arguments for a right to culture are often cases of "strategic essentialism." That is, the unity and unchanging homogeneity of a particular "culture" is deliberately constructed in order to build group solidarity and to engage the state in a focused and disciplined way. But the "essentialism" that often comes to dominate discussions of

group rights is not due entirely to the strategies of activists. Once they choose to make their case in a court of law, they become subject to the "essentializing proclivities of the law" (Cowan et al. 2001, 11). Because human-rights law recognizes only certain kinds of violations, groups with grievances must tailor those grievances to fit.

According to Merry, for example, groups like the Hawaiian Sovereignty Movement have successfully achieved some of their political goals by making claims based on the requirements of their "traditional culture" (Figure 15.9). But this is because they live in a society that is "willing to recognize claims on the basis of cultural authenticity and tradition but not reparations based on acts of conquest and violation" (Merry 2001, 42–3). Outside the courtroom, many members of Indigenous groups think of their culture the way contemporary anthropologists think about culture: there are some common patterns, but culture is basically unbounded, heterogeneous, and open to change. The conflict between these two understandings of culture has the potential to reshape their ideas about what their culture is. Groups that enter into the human-rights process, thus, are entering into ethically ambiguous territory that is "both enabling and constraining" (Cowan et al. 2001, 11).

### Human Rights in Hawaii: Violence against Women

Merry (2001) has studied how changing legal regimes in Hawaii over nearly two centuries have reshaped local understandings of Hawaiian culture (see EthnoProfile 15.2: Hawaii). Part of her work has addressed the ways "local human-rights activists are struggling to create a new space which incorporates both cultural differences and transnational conceptions of human rights" (32). Hawaii is a particularly interesting setting for such a study, since for much of the nineteenth century it was located "at the crossroads of a dizzying array of peoples and at the centre of a set of competing cultural logics" (44)—in a setting that is very much like the globalized, multicultural settings that are increasingly common today. Over the course of the century, Hawaiian law went through two important periods of "legal transplantation:" the first, 1820–1844, involved the adoption of a Christianized Hawaiian law; and the second, 1845–1852, involved the adoption of a secularized Western law. Although

**FIGURE 15.9** | The Hawaiian Sovereignty Movement has emphasized traditional culture and has taken action more broadly. Here members lead a march protesting the Asian Development Bank.

these legal transformations involved colonial imposition, they also depended upon active collaboration by Hawaiian elites (43–4). Indeed, Merry says that these legal changes are best understood as a process of *transculturation* in which subjugated Hawaiians received and adopted forms of self-understanding imposed by the Christian West, even as the Christian West was modified in response to this reception and adoption. Because the Hawaiians were not passive in this process and tried to make use of Christianity and Western ideas for purposes of their own, the process, Merry argues, was fraught with frustration and failure. Missionaries and rulers who wanted to turn Hawaii into a "civilized" place were forced to try to impose their will in stages, rather than all at once, and the end result still bore many Hawaiian traces that, to their dismay, seemed to evade the civilizing process.

This process of cultural appropriation is uncertain: change comes in fits and starts, constantly requiring adjustment as circumstances vary. Merry (2001, 46–7) argues that humanrights discourse is being appropriated by contemporary Hawaiians in much the same way. For the past decade, she

has studied a feminist program in Hilo, Hawaii, that "endeavours to support women victims of violence and retrain male batterers" (48). This program is based on one originally created in the state of Minnesota, and it works closely with the courts. In 1985, the courts adopted the language of rights in dealing with violence against women. This means that the law supports the notion of gender equality and, when husbands are found guilty of battering their wives, calls for separation of the couple. By contrast, Hawaiian couples who participate in the program are often conservative Christians who do not believe in divorce. It might seem that this is a classic example of the conflict between "rights" and "culture," but in fact "local adaptations of the rights model do take place" (47). This was done by tailoring the program's curriculum to local circumstances using Hawaiian images and examples. Particularly interesting was the way the part of the program designed to teach anger management to batterers was made locally relevant by combining Christian ideas with ideas from Hawaiian activists that connected male anger to the losses Hawaiians have suffered as a consequence of conquest. Merry visited a similar

## EthnoProfile 15.2

### Hawaii

**Region:** Polynesia

**Nation:** United States

**Population:** 1,244,000 (2002 census)

**Environment:** Tropical Pacific island

**Livelihood:** Agriculture, industry, tourism, service, state and local government

**Political organization:** A state within a modern nation-state

**For more information:** Merry, Sally Engle. 1999. *Colonizing Hawai'i*. Princeton: Princeton University Press.

kind of program in New Zealand based on the same Minnesota model, which had been locally modified for Maori men in a way that linked their anger to Maori experiences of racism and loss. "Although all of these programmes share a similar commitment to a rights-based approach that works in conjunction with the criminal justice system, each has developed a local accommodation of the curriculum, a reframing which takes into account local problems and cultural practices" (49).

These examples suggest two important conclusions: first, it is possible to find ways of accommodating the universal discourse of human rights to the particularities of local conditions; second, no single model of the relationship between rights and culture will fit all cases. Moreover, as the culture of human rights becomes better established, it increasingly becomes enmeshed in political and legal institutions that go beyond the local level. As activists become more experienced operating in globalized circumstances, moreover, they are likely to become more sophisticated about making use of these different settings as they plan their human-rights strategies (Cowan et al. 2001, 21). Struggles over human rights are hardly likely to go away;

indeed, along with struggles over global citizenship, they can be seen as the prime struggles of our time (Mignolo 2002). Anthropologists are well positioned to help make sense of these complex developments as they unfold.

## Cultural Imperialism or Cultural Hybridity?

The impact of the global spread of images, ideas, people, things, and ideologies in local social settings has clearly been profound, as illustrated by the preceding examples. But how should anthropologists characterize the processes by which these changes have come about?

### What Is Cultural Imperialism?

One explanation, formulated during the Cold War, was called cultural imperialism. Cultural imperialism is based on two notions. First is the idea that some cultures dominate other cultures. In recent history, it is the culture(s) of Europe, or "the West," that are seen to have come to dominate all other cultures of the world, due to the spread of colonialism and capitalism. Second, domination by one culture is said to lead inevitably to the destruction of subordinated cultures and their replacement by the culture of those in power. Thus, Western cultural imperialism is seen as responsible for destroying, for example, local music, technology, dress, and food traditions and replacing them with rock and roll, radios, flashlights, cellphones, T-shirts, blue jeans, McDonald's hamburgers, and Coca-Cola. The inevitable outcome of Western cultural imperialism is seen to be "the cultural homogenization of the world," with the unwelcome consequence of "dooming the world to uniformity" (Inda and Rosaldo 2002, 13–14) (Figure 15.10).

The idea of cultural imperialism developed primarily outside anthropology, but anthropologists could not ignore it because it claimed to describe what was happening to the people they studied. Anthropologists, too, were aware that Western music, fashion, food, and technology had spread among those they worked with. But cultural imperialism did not seem to be a satisfactory explanation for this spread, for at least three reasons (Inda and Rosaldo 2002, 22–4). First, the discourse of cultural imperialism denies *agency* to non-Western peoples who make use of Western cultural forms. It assumes that they are passive and without the resources

cultural imperialism The idea that some cultures dominate others and that domination by one culture leads inevitably to the destruction of subordinated cultures and their replacement by the culture of those in power.

**FIGURE 15.10 |** A McDonald's restaurant sits beneath traditional architecture in the Old Town district of Shanghai, China.

to resist anything of Western origin that is marketed to them. Second, cultural imperialism assumes that non-Western cultural forms never move "from the rest to the West." But this is clearly false. Non-Western music, food, and material culture have large and eager followings in Western Europe, Canada, and the United States. Third, cultural imperialism ignores that cultural forms and practices sometimes move from one part of the non-Western world to other parts of the non-Western world, bypassing the West entirely. For example, movies made in India have been popular for decades in northern Nigeria (Larkin 2002), Mexican soap operas have large followings in the Philippines, and karaoke is popular all over the world.

## What Is Cultural Hybridity?

Dissatisfied with the discourse of cultural imperialism, anthropologists began to search for alternative ways of understanding global cultural flows. From the days of Franz Boas and his students, anthropologists had recognized the significance of cultural borrowing. They had also emphasized that borrowing cultural forms or practices from elsewhere always involves *borrowing-with-modification*. That is, people never adopt blindly but always adapt what they borrow for local purposes. Put another way, people rarely accepted ideas or practices or objects from elsewhere without *domesticating* or *indigenizing* them—that is, finding a way of reconciling them with local practices in order to serve local purposes.

In the 1980s, for example, weavers in Otavalo, Ecuador, were making a lot of money selling textiles to tourists. They could then organize small production firms and purchase television sets to entertain their employees while they worked at their looms. In addition, some men had so much business that they encouraged their wives to take up weaving, even though women were not traditionally weavers. In order to spend more time weaving, women started to use indoor cookstoves, which relieved them from the time-consuming labour of traditional meal preparation over an open fire (Colloredo-Mansfeld 1999). From the perspective of anthropologist Rudi Colloredo-Mansfeld, these uses of Western technology could not be understood as the consequences of Western cultural imperialism because they clearly had nothing to do with trying to imitate a Western lifestyle. It made more sense to interpret these changes as Otavalan domestication or indigenization of televisions and cookstoves, since these items from elsewhere were adopted precisely in order to promote Indigenous Otavalan weaving. Put yet another way, borrowing-with-modification always involves customizing that which is borrowed to meet the purposes of the borrowers, which may be quite remote from the purposes of those among whom the form or practice originated (Inda and Rosaldo 2002, 16). This form of cultural change is very different from having something from elsewhere forced on you against your will (Figure 15.11).

At the same time, the consequences of borrowing-with-modification can never be fully controlled. Thus, Otavalan weavers may start watching television because local reruns of old American television series relieve the tedium of weaving. However, once television watching becomes a habitual practice, it also exposes them to advertising and news broadcasts, which may stimulate other local changes that nobody can predict.

**FIGURE 15.11** | Musical performance has become an important part of the Otavalo economy, as musicians from Otavalo travel throughout the world performing and selling woven goods. Otavalans have domesticated CD production as well and have been quite successful at selling CDs of their music to tourists in Otavalo and listeners abroad.

The domestication or indigenization of cultural forms from elsewhere *both* makes it possible to do old things in new ways *and* leaves open the possibility of doing new things as well. Put another way, cultural borrowing is double-edged; borrowed cultural practices are both amenable to domestication and yet able to escape it. No wonder that cultural borrowing is often viewed with ambivalence.

The challenges are particularly acute in globalizing conditions, colonial or postcolonial, where borrowed ideas, objects, or practices remain entangled in relationships with donors even as they are made to serve new goals by recipients (Thomas 1991). People in multicultural

**cultural hybridization (or cultural hybridity)** Cultural mixing.

settings must deal on a daily basis with tempting cultural alternatives emanating from more powerful groups. It is therefore not surprising that they regularly struggle to control processes of cultural borrowing and to contain domesticated cultural practices within certain contexts or in the hands of certain people only.

Many social scientists have borrowed a metaphor from biology to describe this complex process of globalized cultural exchange and speak of **cultural hybridization** or **cultural hybridity**. Both these concepts were meant to highlight forms of cultural borrowing that produced something new that could not be collapsed or subsumed, either within the culture of the donor or within the culture of the recipient. In addition, they stressed the positive side of cultural mixing: rather than indicating a regrettable loss of original purity, they draw attention to positive processes of cultural creativity.

Furthermore, if cultural hybridization is a normal part of all human social experience, then the idea that "authentic" traditions never change can legitimately be challenged. For members of a social group who wish to revise or discard cultural practices that they find outmoded or oppressive, hybridity talk is liberating. Choosing to revise or discard, borrow or invent *on terms of one's own choosing* also means that one possesses *agency*, the capacity to exercise at least some control over one's life. And exercising agency calls into question charges that one is succumbing to cultural imperialism or losing one's cultural "authenticity."

## Are There Limits to Cultural Hybridity?

However, as anthropologist Nicholas Thomas (1996, 9) puts it, "hybridity is almost a good idea, but not quite." Close examination of talk about cultural hybridization reveals at least three problems. First, it is not clear that this concept actually frees anthropologists from the modernist commitment to the existence of bounded, homogeneous, unchanging "cultures." That is, the idea of cultural hybridity is based on the notion of cultural mixing. But what is it that is mixed? Two or more non-hybridized, original, "pure," cultures! But such "pure" homogeneous, bounded, unchanging cultures are not supposed to exist. Thus, we are caught in a paradox. For this reason, Jonathan Friedman, among others, is highly critical of discussions of cultural hybridity; in his view, cultures have *always* been hybrid and it is the existence of *boundaries*, not cultural borrowing, that anthropologists need to explain. Besides, hybrid cultural mixtures often get transformed into new, unitary cultural identities, as with the Métis in Canada, who until recently were considered neither Aboriginal nor white. Friedman (1997) also points out that hybrid identities are not liberating when they are thrust upon people rather than being adopted freely. He draws attention to cases in Latin America where the "mestizo" identity has been used "as a middle-/upper-class tool" against Indigenous groups. "We are all part-Indian, say members of the elite who have much to lose in the face of minority claims" (81–2).

These examples highlight a second difficulty with hybridity talk: those who celebrate cultural hybridization often ignore the fact that its effects are experienced differently by those with power and those without power. As Friedman (1997, 81) says, "the question of class becomes crucial." The complexity of this issue appears in many popular discussions of "multiculturalism" that celebrate cultural hybridization and turn hybridity into a marketable commodity. The commodification of hybridity is problematic because it smooths over differences in the experience of cultural hybridization, offering multiculturalism as an array of tempting consumables for outsiders. "Multiculturalism is aimed at nourishing and perpetuating the kind of differences which do not [threaten]," writes Nira Yuval-Davis (1997, 197). International folk festivals, festivals of nations, and the like—events that emphasize costume, cuisine, music, and dance—spring to mind (Figure 15.12). But the troubling fact is that cultural hybridity is experienced as both non-threatening and very threatening, depending on the terms on which it is available.

**FIGURE 15.12 |** Dancers from Macedonia perform at a folklore festival in Zagreb, Croatia.

Because of power differences among groups challenged by cultural hybridization, any globalized "multicultural" setting reveals active cultural hybridization together with active *resistance* to cultural hybridization (Werbner 1997, 3). Werbner observes that cultural hybridization is unobjectionable when actors perceive it to be under their own control but resisted when it is "perceived by actors themselves to be potentially threatening to their sense of moral integrity" (12). The threat of cultural hybridization is greatest for those with the least power, who feel unable to control forms of hybridity that threaten the fragile survival structures on which they depend in an unwelcoming multicultural setting.

And this leads to a third problem with the concept of cultural hybridization. Fashionable hybridity talk hides the differences between elite and non-elite experiences of multiculturalism. Anthropologist John Hutnyk (1997, 122), for example, deplores the way "world music" is marketed to middle-class consumers because such sales strategies divert attention "from the urgency of anti-racist politics." That is, when cultural hybridization becomes fashionable, it easily turns the experiences of hybridized elites into a hegemonic standard, suggesting that class exploitation and racial oppression are easily overcome or no longer exist. But to dismiss or ignore continuing non-elite struggles with cultural hybridization can spark dangerous confrontations that can quickly spiral out of control.

Anthropologist Peter van der Veer argues that such a dynamic ignited the furor in Britain that followed the publication of Salman Rushdie's novel *The Satanic Verses*. Rushdie is an elite, highly educated South Asian migrant to Britain who experienced cultural hybridity as a form of emancipation from oppressive religious and cultural restrictions. His novel contained passages describing Islam and the Prophet Muhammad that, from this elite point of view, embodied a liberating form of cultural "transgression." But migrants from South Asia in Britain are not all members of the elite. Most South Asian Muslim immigrants in Britain are workers, and they saw *The Satanic Verses* not as a work of artistic liberation but as a deliberate attempt to mock their beliefs and practices. "These immigrants, who are already socially and culturally marginalized, are thus double marginalized in the name of an attack on 'purity' and Islamic 'fundamentalism'" (van der Veer 1997, 101–2).

Even more important, however, may be the way popular interpretations of their objections in the press and among Western intellectuals ignored these immigrants' own, very different but very real, non-elite experiences of cultural hybridization. Put simply, elites experience cultural hybridization in ways that are often very different from the ways non-elites experience cultural hybridization. To ignore this difference is not only politically short-sighted but also bad social science.

## Can We Be at Home in a Global World?

The era of globalization in which we live is one of uncertainty and insecurity. Possibilities for emancipatory new ways of living are undercut by sharpening economic and political differences and the looming threat of violence. Is it possible, in the midst of all this confusion and conflict, to devise ways of coping with our circumstances that would provide guidance in the confusion, moderation to the conflict? No one expects such efforts to be easy. But anthropologists and other concerned scholars are currently struggling to come up with concepts and practices that might be helpful.

### What Is Cosmopolitanism?

Our era is not the first to have faced such challenges. Walter Mignolo (2002) argues that multiculturalism was born in the sixteenth century when Iberian conquest in the New World first raised troubling issues among Western thinkers about the kinds of relationships that were possible and desirable between the conquerors and the Indigenous peoples whom they conquered. During the ensuing centuries, the challenges posed by a multicultural world did not disappear. In the context of eighteenth-century Enlightenment promises of human emancipation based on the "rights of man and the citizen," philosopher Immanuel Kant concluded that the achievements of the Enlightenment offered individuals new opportunities for developing ways of being at home in the world wherever they were.

> cosmopolitanism   Being at ease in more than one cultural setting.
>
> friction   The awkward, unequal, unstable aspects of interconnection across difference.

To identify this orientation, he revived a concept that was first coined by the Stoic philosophers of ancient Rome: cosmopolitanism (Mignolo 2002). Historically, cosmopolitanism "by and large meant being versed in Western ways and the vision of 'one world' culture was only a sometimes unconscious, sometimes unconscionable, euphemism for 'First World' culture" (Abbas 2002, 210).

But is it possible to rework our understandings of cultural hybridity to stretch the notion of cosmopolitanism beyond its traditional association with privileged Western elites? Many anthropologists have become comfortable talking about "alternative" or "minority" modernities that depart from the Western European norm. In a similar fashion, any new anthropological understanding of cosmopolitanism would have to be plural, not singular, and would have to include non-elite experiences of cultural hybridization.

### What Is Friction?

Anthropologist Anna Lowenhaupt Tsing (2005, 4) has worked in Indonesia for many years, investigating what she calls friction, "the awkward, unequal, unstable aspects of interconnection across difference." Tsing seeks to understand how capitalist interests brought about the destruction of the Indonesian rain forests in the 1980s and 1990s as well as how environmental movements emerged to defend the forests and the people who live in them. Discussions of cultural imperialism assume that processes of global change will be smooth and unstoppable, that "globalization can be predicted in advance" (3). After the Cold War, for example, a number of politicians and social theorists predicted "an inevitable, peaceful transition" to global integration of the capitalist market (11). On the contrary, Tsing's research showed that the encounters between Japanese lumber traders and Indonesia government officials that turned Indonesia into the world's largest tropical lumber producer by 1973 were "messy and surprising" (3). She points out that "Indonesian tropical rain forests were not harvested as industrial timber until the 1970s" because "large-scale loggers prefer forests in which one valuable species predominates; tropical rain forests are just too biologically diverse" (14). However, in the 1970s the Japanese trading companies that began negotiations with the Indonesian New Order regime of President Suharto did not want access to valuable hardwoods;

instead, they wanted "large quantities of cheaply produced logs," which they intended to turn into plywood.

The Japanese traders did not get what they wanted right away, however. Rather, as Tsing points out, this could not happen until two specific transformations had occurred. First, the forest had to be "simplified." Japanese lumber traders and Indonesian officials ignored species diversity, recognizing as valuable only those species that could be turned into plywood and regarding everything else—"the rest of the trees, fungi, and fauna ... the fruit orchards, rattans, and other human-tended plants of forest dwellers"—as waste (Tsing 2005, 16). Second, to make such forest simplification politically palatable, forests were reconfigured as a "sustainable resource" that could be replaced later by industrial tree plantations. However, once the Japanese traders were successful, Indonesian businessmen built their own plywood industry, based on the Japanese model. This led to the development of links between destruction of the forest and nation-building, as the state came to depend on income from selling forest concessions to favoured political cronies. Once this alliance was forged, legal and illegal forms of forest exploitation could no longer be distinguished from one another, and it became impossible for forest dwellers to defend their own, pre-existing property rights. "Either official or unofficial alone could be challenged, but together they overwhelmed local residents . . . . Together they transform the countryside into a free-for-all frontier" (Tsing 2005, 17). But the production of such a frontier was not inevitable. It was the outcome of contingent encounters that people reworked in order to produce desired outcomes, along with additional, unintended consequences.

In response to rain forest destruction, a strong Indonesian environmental movement came into existence (Figure 15.13). Once again, however, this cannot be understood as a simple, predictable extension of Western environmentalist practices into Indonesia. On the contrary, "the movement was an amalgam of odd parts: engineers, nature lovers, reformers, technocrats" (Tsing 2005, 17). In fact, activists who were dissatisfied with other features of President Suharto's New Order regime decided to focus on environmental issues, because these seemed to be issues less likely to trigger government censorship and repression. In any case, as Tsing says, "the movement was organized around difference" (17). It was not centralized, but "imagined itself as coordinating already existing but scattered and disorganized rural complaints. Activists' jobs, as they imagined it, involved translating subaltern demands into the languages of the powerful" and "translating back to let people know their rights" (18). It was messy, but this did not deter activists. "Within the links of awkwardly transcended difference, the environmental movement has tried to offer an alternative to forest destruction and the erosion of Indigenous rights" (18).

Like the alliance between businessmen and New Order government officials, the environmental movement emerged out of relationships forged by unlikely parties who struggled to find ways of working together

**FIGURE 15.13** | Heavy logging activity has led to destruction of the rain forest in Kalimantan and to the emergence of a strong Indonesian environmental movement.

to achieve overlapping but non-identical goals. Thus, friction in the struggle to bridge differences makes new things possible: "Rubbing two sticks together produces heat and light; one stick alone is just a stick. As a metaphorical image, friction reminds us that heterogeneous and unequal encounters can lead to new arrangements of culture and power" (Tsing 2005, 3–5). And these arrangements, while potentially dangerous, may also be seen as a source of hope: "Just as the encounter of Japanese trading companies and Indonesian politicians produced simplified dipterocarp forests, these activist-inspired encounters may yet produce different kinds of forests" (18).

## What Is Border Thinking?

Tsing's understanding of "friction" as an unavoidable and productive feature of the process of cultural hybridization has much in common with what Walter Mignolo calls "border thinking." For Mignolo, in a globalized world, concepts like "democracy" and "justice" can no longer be defined within a single Western logic—or, for that matter, from the perspective of the political left or the political right. Border thinking involves detaching these concepts from their hegemonic "Western" meanings and practices and using them as *connectors*, tools for imagining and negotiating new, cosmopolitan forms of democracy or justice informed by the ethical and political judgments of non-elites (Mignolo 2002, 179, 181).

Finally, in reimagining what cosmopolitanism might mean, it is important to go beyond not only Kantian limitations but also standard anthropological orientations to other ways of life. The hope is that border thinking can produce a *critical cosmopolitanism* capable of negotiating new understandings of human rights and global citizenship in ways that can dismantle the barriers of gender and race that are the historical legacies of colonialism (Mignolo 2002, 161, 180) (Figure 15.14). In many cases, attempts to overcome power differentials and threats to moral integrity experienced by non-elites may lead to serious revision of Western modernist ideas and practices. But because cosmopolitanism involves border thinking, ideals and practices with Enlightenment credentials may also turn out to be valuable counterweights to extremism and violence. For example, relationships between Hindus and Muslims in India took a severe turn for the worse after Hindu vandals destroyed a mosque in the city of Ayodhya in 1992. Arjun Appadurai, who followed these developments closely, noted that the brutal Hindutva movement pushing to turn India into a Hindu state "violates the ideals of secularism and interreligious harmony enshrined in the constitution" (Appadurai 2002, 273–4). Appadurai writes of Indian citizens of Mumbai (formerly Bombay), India, from many walks of life—rich and poor, Muslim and Hindu—who have shown "extraordinary displays of courage and critical imagination in Mumbai," who have "held up powerful images of a cosmopolitan, secular, multicultural Bombay." Their "radical moderation" in resisting violent religious polarization is, he argues, neither naive nor nostalgic: "These utopian visions and critical practices are resolutely modernist in their visions of

**FIGURE 15.14** | Cosmopolitanism is no longer only for Western elites. Here, Otavalo tourist José María Cotachaci visits the San Francisco Bay Area in the United States in November 2000. Otavalos have created their own forms of modernity.

equity, justice, and cultural cosmopolitanism" (2002, 279). Secularism, of course, is a notion with impeccable European Enlightenment credentials. As anthropologist Talal Asad (2003, 5) explains, the concept of "secular citizenship" developed in Europe following the post-Reformation wars of religion and aimed to "transcend the different identities built on class, gender, and religion, replacing conflicting perspectives by unifying experience. In a sense, this transcendent mediation *is* secularism." Secularism arrived in India with British colonialism. Yet it has become, over time, a "situated secularism"—indigenized, customized, domesticated, *Indian* secularism, opposed to *Indian* interreligious violence. Appadurai and many other Indian citizens see Indian secularism as a key element of Indian cosmopolitanism that has been effective in preventing religious strife in the past and may be able to do so again.

Many of the cases in this chapter demonstrate the human ability to cope creatively with changed life circumstances. They remind us that human beings are not passive in the face of the new, that they actively and resiliently respond to life's challenges. Nevertheless, successful outcomes are never ensured. Modes of livelihood that may benefit some human groups can overwhelm and destroy others. Western capitalism and modern technology have exploded into a vortex of global forces that resist control. A critical cosmopolitanism involving concerted practical action to lessen violence and exploitation has perhaps never been more necessary.

## Why Study Anthropology?

Studying anthropology, even at the introductory level, can have a powerful effect on students. It brings students into contact with different ways of life. It makes them aware of just how arbitrary their own understanding of the world is as they learn how other people have developed satisfying but different ways of living. In addition, if they are from Western countries that were responsible for colonialism and its consequences, it makes them painfully aware of just how much their own tradition has to answer for in the modern world.

Knowing and experiencing cultural variety gives rise, perhaps inevitably, to doubt. We come to doubt the ultimate validity of the central truths of our own cultural tradition, which have been ratified and sanctified by the generations who preceded us. We doubt because a familiarity with alternative ways of living makes the ultimate meaning of any action, of any object, a highly ambiguous matter. Ambiguity is part of the human condition. Human beings have always coped with ambiguity by using culture, which places objects and actions in contexts and thereby makes their meanings plain. This doubt can lead to anxiety, but it can also be liberating.

All human beings, ourselves included, live in culturally shaped worlds, enmeshed in webs of interpretation and meaning that we have spun. It has been the particular task of anthropology and its practitioners to go out into the world to bear witness to and record the vast creative diversity in world-making that has been the history of our species. In our lifetimes, we will witness the end of many of those ways of life—and if we are not careful, of all ways of life. This loss is tragic, for as these worlds disappear, so too does something special about humanity: variety, creativity, and awareness of alternatives.

Our survival as a species and our viability as individuals depend on the possibility of choice, of perceiving and being able to act on alternatives in the various situations we encounter during our lives. If, as a colleague has suggested, human life is a minefield, then the more paths we can see and imagine through that minefield, the more likely we are to make it through—or at least to have an interesting time trying. As alternatives are destroyed, wantonly smashed, or thoughtlessly crushed, our own human possibilities are reduced. A small group of men and women have for the last century laboured in corners of the world, both remote and nearby, to write the record of human accomplishment and bring it back and teach it to others.

Surely our greatest human accomplishment is the creation of the sometimes austerely beautiful worlds in which we all live. Anthropologists have rarely given in to the romantic notion that these other worlds are all good, all life-enhancing, all fine or beautiful. They are not. Ambiguity and ambivalence are, as we have seen, hallmarks of the human experience. There are no guarantees that human cultures will be compassionate rather than cruel or that people will agree they are one or the other. There are not even any guarantees that our species will survive. But all anthropologists have

## The Anthropological Voice

*American anthropologist Annette Weiner traces the history of anthropological challenges to colonialism and Western capitalism, pointing out why the perspective of anthropologists has so often been ignored.*

Colonialism brought foreign governments, missionaries, explorers, and exploiters face-to-face with cultures whose values and beliefs were vastly different. As the harbingers of Western progress, their actions were couched in the rhetoric of doing something to and for "the natives"—giving them souls, clothes, law—whatever was necessary to lift them out of their "primitive" ways. Anthropologists were also part of the colonial scene, but what they came to "do" made them different from those who were carrying out the expectations of missions, overseas trade, and government protectorates. Anthropologists arrived in the field determined to understand the cultural realities of an unfamiliar world. The knowledge of these worlds was to serve as a warning to those in positions of colonial power by charging that villagers' lives were not to be tampered with arbitrarily and that changing the lives of powerless people was insensitive and inhumane, unless one understood and took seriously the cultural meanings inherent in, for example, traditional land ownership, the technologies and rituals surrounding food cultivation, myths, magic, and gender relations.

All too often, however, the anthropologist's voice went unnoticed by those in power, for it remained a voice committed to illuminating the cultural biases under which colonialists operated. Only recently have we witnessed the final demise of colonial governments and the rise of independent countries. Economically, however, independence has not brought these countries the freedom to pursue their own course of development. In many parts of the world, Western multinational corporations, often playing a role not too dissimilar from colonial enterprises, now determine the course of that freedom, changing people's lives in a way that all too often is harmful or destructive. At the same time, we know that the world's natural resources and human productive capabilities can no longer remain isolates. Developed and developing countries are now more dependent on one another than ever before in human

history. Yet this interdependency, which should give protection to Indigenous peoples, is often worked out for political ends that ignore the moral issues. Racism and the practice of discrimination are difficult to destroy, as evidenced by the United States today, where we still are not completely emancipated from assumptions that relegate blacks, women, Asians, Hispanics, and other minorities to second-class status. If we cannot bridge these cultural differences intellectually within our own borders, then how can we begin to deal politically with Third World countries—those who were called "primitives" less than a century ago—in a fair, sensitive, and meaningful way?

This is the legacy of anthropology that we must never forget. Because the work of anthropology takes us to the neighbourhoods, villages, and campsites—the local level—we can ourselves experience the results of how the world's economic and political systems affect those who have no voice. Yet once again our voices too are seldom heard by those who make such decisions. Anthropologists are often prevented from participating in the forums of economic and government planning. Unlike economists, political scientists, or engineers, we must stand on the periphery of such decision making, primarily because our understanding of cultural patterns and beliefs forces on others an awareness that ultimately makes such decisions more formidable.

At the beginning of the twentieth century, anthropologists spoke out strongly against those who claimed that "savage" societies represented a lower level of biological and social development. Now, as we face the next century, the anthropological approach to human nature and human societies is as vital to communicate as ever. We face a difficult, potentially dangerous, and therefore complex future. A fundamental key to our future is to make certain that the dynamic qualities of human beings in all parts of the world are recognized and that the true value of cultural complexities is not ignored. There is much important anthropology to be done.

Source: Weiner 1990, 392–3.

believed that these are human worlds that have given those who have lived in them the ability to make sense out of their experiences and to derive meaning for their lives, that we are a species at once bound by our culture and free to change it.

This is a perilous and fearsome freedom, a difficult freedom to grasp and to wield. Nevertheless, the freedom is there, and in this tension of freedom and constraint lies our future. It is up to us to create it.

## Chapter Summary

1. Globalization is understood and evaluated differently by different observers, but most anthropologists agree that the effects of globalization are uneven. In a globalizing world, wealth, images, people, things, and ideologies are deterritorialized. Some groups in some parts of the world benefit from global flows, contacts, and exchanges, whereas others are negatively affected or bypassed entirely. Anthropologists disagree about whether global processes are or are not systemic and whether they are only the latest in a series of expansions and contractions that can be traced back to the rise of the first commercial civilizations several thousand years ago. But none of these overall schemas can by itself account for the historically specific local details of the effects of global forces in local settings, which is what most anthropologists aim to document and analyze.

2. The flows unleashed by globalization have undermined the ability of nation-states to police their boundaries effectively, suggesting that conventional ideas about nation-states require revision. Contemporary migrants across national borders have developed a variety of transborder identities. Some become involved in long-distance nationalism that leads to the emergence of transborder states claiming emigrants as transborder citizens of their ancestral homelands even if they are legal citizens of another state. Some transborder citizenries call for the establishment of full-fledged transnational nation-states. Struggles of these kinds can be found all over the globe.

3. The contrasts between formal and substantive citizenship suggest that conventional notions of citizenship are breaking down in the context of globalization. Diaspora communities of elite Chinese families have developed a strategy of flexible citizenship that allows them to both circumvent and benefit from different nation-state regimes by investing, working, and settling their families in different sites. For these elite Chinese, the concept of nationalism has lost its meaning, and they seem to subscribe instead to a postnational ethos in which their only true loyalty is to the family business.

4. Discussions of human rights have intensified as global flows juxtapose and at least implicitly challenge different understandings of what it means to be human or what kinds of rights people may be entitled to under radically changed conditions of everyday life. But different participants in this discourse have different ideas about the relationship between human rights and culture. As talk about human rights becomes incorporated into local cultural discussions, the notion is transformed to make sense in local contexts. Sometimes, "culture" may be used as a scapegoat for a government unwilling to extend certain rights to its citizens.

5. Some arguments about human rights include the right to one's culture. One of the key issues involved concerns the kinds of legal mechanisms needed to ensure such protection. But most international human-rights documents protect only individual human rights, not group rights. And even those who seek to protect their individual rights are supposed to appeal to the governments of their own nation-states to enforce rights defended in international documents. Many activists and others view this factor as a serious contradiction in human-rights discourse that undermines its effectiveness.

6. Some anthropologists argue that a "culture of human rights" has emerged in recent years that is based on certain ideas about human beings, their needs, and their abilities that originated in the West. Some consider this culture of human rights to be the culture of a globalizing world that emphasizes individual rights over duties or needs and that proposes only technical rather than ethical solutions to human suffering. Anthropologists disagree about the value of such a culture of human rights in contemporary circumstances.

7. Groups and individuals who assert that their human rights have been violated regularly take their cases to courts of law. But because human-rights law recognizes only certain kinds of rights violations, groups with grievances must tailor those grievances to fit the violations that human-rights law recognizes. Groups that enter into the human-rights process are entering into

ethically ambiguous territory that is both enabling and constraining. Debates about women's rights in Hawaii show both that it is possible to accommodate the universal discourse of human rights to local conditions and that no single model of the relationship between rights and culture will fit all cases.

8. The discourse of cultural imperialism, which developed primarily outside anthropology, tried to explain the spread of Western cultural forms outside the West. But anthropologists reject cultural imperialism as an explanation because it denies agency to non-Western peoples, because it assumes that cultural forms never move "from the rest to the West," and because it ignores flows of cultural forms that bypass the West entirely.

9. Anthropologists have developed alternatives to the discourse of cultural imperialism. They speak about borrowing-with-modification, domestication, indigenization, or customization of practices or objects imported from elsewhere. Many anthropologists describe these processes as examples of cultural hybridization or hybridity.

Talk of cultural hybridization has been criticized because the very attempt to talk about cultural mixtures assumes that "pure" cultures existed prior to mixing. Others object to discussions of cultural hybridization that fail to recognize that its effects are experienced differently by those with power and those without power. Cultural hybridization is unobjectionable when actors perceive it to be under their own control but resisted when they see it threatening their moral integrity.

10. Some anthropologists would like to revive the notion of "cosmopolitanism" originally associated with Western elite forms of cultural hybridization and rework it in order to be able to speak about alternative or discrepant cosmopolitanisms that reflect the experiences of those who have been the victims of modernity. The ideal end result would be a critical cosmopolitanism capable of negotiating new understandings of human rights and global citizenship in ways that can dismantle barriers of gender and race that are the historical legacies of colonialism.

## For Review

1. How is globalization defined in this chapter? What are the key features of the anthropological approach to the study of globalization?

2. Discuss the effects of migration on the nation-state. How are these effects apparent in Canada?

3. What does it mean to talk about a "transborder citizenry"? What are some of the forms that this sort of citizenry can take?

4. What is "flexible citizenship," and how is it used to describe Chinese diaspora communities?

5. How and why do anthropologists study human rights?

6. What is the "rights versus culture" debate? In what ways does it differ from the "right to culture" debate? What are some of the major objections to each approach?

7. Explain how the anthropological concept of culture can help clarify issues in discussions of human rights.

8. What are the key points in the case study of violence against women in Hawaii? Describe how programs to deal with violence against women in Hawaii and elsewhere in the world are connected to globalization.

9. What is cultural imperialism? What are three difficulties that anthropologists have found with this concept?

10. Discuss cultural hybridity, paying particular attention to the idea of *borrowing-with-modification*. What are the difficulties associated with the concept of cultural hybridity?

11. What does it mean to be cosmopolitan? Why do many anthropologists resist using the traditional interpretation of cosmopolitanism in their work? In what ways might a "plural" understanding of cosmopolitanism be more useful for describing various peoples' experiences in our increasingly connected modern world?

12. Summarize Anna Tsing's discussion of "friction." Can you think of any examples from the Canadian context in which the sort of friction Tsing describes has led to "new arrangements of culture and power"?

13. Describe border thinking. What are some advantages—both for anthropologists and for others—of being able to detach concepts like "democracy" and "justice" from their typical "Western" meanings?

## Key Terms

cosmopolitanism 452
cultural hybridization
  (or hybridity) 450
cultural imperialism 448
diaspora 436
flexible citizenship 438

friction 452
globalization 429
human rights 440
legal citizenship 438
long-distance nationalists 436
multiculturalism 440

postnational ethos 439
substantive citizenship 438
transborder citizenry 436
transborder state 436
transnational nation-state 438

## Suggested Readings

Goodale, Mark, ed. 2009. *Human Rights: An Anthropological Reader.* Malden, MA: Wiley-Blackwell. *An excellent collection of historical and contemporary readings about human rights.*

Hobart, Mark, ed. 1993. *An Anthropological Critique of Development: The Growth of Ignorance.* London: Routledge. *Anthropologists from Britain, Holland, and Germany challenge the notion that Western approaches to development have been successful. They use ethnographic case studies to demonstrate how Western experts who disregard Indigenous knowledge contribute to the growth of ignorance.*

Inda, Jonathan Xavier, and Renato Rosaldo, eds. 2007. *The Anthropology of Globalization: A Reader.* 2nd ed. Malden, MA: Blackwell. *A comprehensive collection of articles by anthropologists who address the process of globalization from varied points of view and different ethnographic situations.*

Lewellen, Ted C. 2002. *The Anthropology of Globalization: Cultural Anthropology Enters the Twenty-First Century.*

Westport, CT: Bergin & Garvey. *An introduction to key issues in the anthropology of globalization, situating it historically in terms of earlier views of the global political economy, such as modernization theory and dependency theory.*

Tsing, Anna Lowenhaupt. 2005. *Friction: An Ethnography of Global Connection.* Princeton, NJ: Princeton University Press. *An innovative multi-sited ethnography illustrating how a global environmental movement formed across different kinds of boundaries, for different reasons, and prevented rainforest destruction in one region of Indonesia for a number of years in the 1980s.*

Walsh, Andrew. 2012. *Made in Madagascar: Sapphires, Ecotourism, and the Global Bazaar.* Toronto: University of Toronto Press. *An ethnographic study of the northern Malagasy that looks at how the global bazaar today values some groups while devaluing the work of others at the sources of some of the world's most precious commodities.*

# Glossary

**absolute dating methods** See **chronometric dating methods**.

**acclimatization** A change in the way the body functions in response to physical stress.

**Acheulean tradition** A Lower Paleolithic stone-tool tradition associated with *Homo erectus* and characterized by stone bifaces, or "hand axes."

**achieved statuses** Social positions people may attain later in life, often as the result of their own (or other people's) effort.

**adaptation** (1) The mutual shaping of organisms and their environments. (2) The shaping of a useful feature of an organism by natural selection for the function it now performs.

**adoption** Kinship relationships based on nurturance, often in the absence of other connections based on mating or birth.

**affinal relationships** Kinship connections through marriage, or affinity.

**affinity** Connection through marriage.

**affluence** The condition of having more than enough of whatever is required to satisfy consumption needs.

**agriculture** The systematic modification of the environments of plants and animals to increase their productivity and usefulness.

**agroecology** The systematically modified environment (or constructed niche) that becomes the only environment within which domesticated plants can flourish.

**alleles** All the different forms that a particular gene might take.

**anagenesis** The slow, gradual transformation of a single species over time.

**anatomically modern human beings** Hominins assigned to the species *Homo sapiens* with anatomical features similar to those of living human populations: short and round skulls, small brow ridges and faces, prominent chins, and gracile skeletal build.

**anthropoid** The primate evolutionary grade that includes monkeys, apes, and humans.

**anthropology** The study of human nature, human society, human language, and the human past.

**anthropomorphism** The attribution of human characteristics to non-human animals.

**applied anthropology** The subfield of anthropology in which anthropologists use information gathered from the other anthropological specialties to solve practical cross-cultural problems.

**aptation** The shaping of any useful feature of an organism, regardless of that feature's origin.

**archaeological record** All material objects and structures created by humans and our hominin ancestors.

**archaeology** The specialty of anthropology that is interested in learning about the human past by analyzing material remains left behind by earlier societies.

**archaeology** The specialty of anthropology that studies the human past by analyzing material remains left behind by earlier societies.

**archaic *Homo sapiens*** Hominins dating from 500,000 to 200,000 years ago that possessed morphological features found in both *Homo erectus* and *Homo sapiens*.

**art** Play with form producing some aesthetically successful transformation-representation.

**artifacts** Objects that have been deliberately and intelligently shaped by humans or our hominin ancestors.

**ascribed statuses** Social positions people are assigned at birth.

**assemblage** Artifacts and structures from a particular time and place in an archaeological site.

**australopiths** An informal term used to refer to all hominins that appeared before those of the genus *Homo*.

**avunculocal residence** A postmarital residence pattern in which a married couple lives with (or near) the husband's mother's brother (from *avuncular*, "of uncles").

**band** The characteristic form of social organization found among foragers. Bands are small, usually no more than 50 people, and labour is divided ordinarily on the basis of age and sex. All adults in band societies have roughly equal access to whatever material or social valuables are locally available.

**bifurcation** A criterion employed in the analysis of kinship terminologies in which kinship terms referring to the mother's side of the family are distinguished from those referring to the father's side.

**bilateral descent** The principle that a descent group is formed by people who believe they are related to each other by connections made through their mothers *and* their fathers equally (sometimes called *cognatic descent*).

**bioarchaeology** The study of human remains from prehistory to provide information about the human past.

**biocultural organisms** Organisms (in this case, human beings) whose defining features are codetermined by biological and cultural factors.

**biological anthropology (or physical anthropology)** The specialty of anthropology that looks at human beings as biological organisms and tries to discover what characteristics make them different from other organisms and what characteristics they share.

**biopower** Forms of power preoccupied with bodies, both the bodies of citizens and the social body of the state itself.

**biostratigraphic dating** A relative dating method that relies on patterns of fossil distribution in different rock layers.

**bipedalism** Walking on two feet.

**blades** Sharp-edged stone tools that are at least twice as long as they are wide.

**blended family** A family created when previously divorced or widowed people marry, bringing with them children from their previous families.

**bloodwealth** Material goods paid by perpetrators to compensate their victims for their loss.

**body language** Movements and postures that communicate attitudes and feelings non-verbally.

**bridewealth** The transfer of certain symbolically important goods from the family of the groom to the family of the bride on the occasion of their marriage. It represents compensation to the wife's lineage for the loss of her labour and child-bearing capacities.

**broad-spectrum foraging** A subsistence strategy based on collecting a wide range of plants and animals by hunting, fishing, and gathering.

**capitalism** An economic system dominated by the supply-demand–price mechanism called the "market"; an entire way of life that grew in response to and in service of that market.

**caste** A ranked group within a hierarchically stratified society that is closed, prohibiting individuals to move from one caste to another.

**chiefdom** A form of social organization in which a leader (the chief) and close relatives are set apart from the rest of the society and allowed privileged access to wealth, power, and prestige.

**chromosomes** Sets of paired bodies in the nucleus of cells that are made of DNA and contain the hereditary genetic information that organisms pass on to their offspring.

**chronometric dating methods (or "absolute" dating methods)** Dating methods based on laboratory techniques that assign age in years to material evidence.

**cladogenesis** The birth of a variety of descendant species from a single ancestral species.

**clan** A descent group formed by members who believe they have a common (sometimes mythical) ancestor, even if they cannot specify the genealogical links.

**class** A ranked group within a hierarchically stratified society whose membership is defined primarily in terms of wealth, occupation, or other economic criteria.

**clientage** The institution linking individuals from upper and lower levels in a stratified society.

**cline** The gradual intergradation of genetic variation from population to population.

**coevolution** The interconnected relationship between biological processes and symbolic cultural processes, in which each makes up an important part of the environment to which the other must adapt.

**collaterality** A criterion employed in the analysis of kinship terminologies in which a distinction is made between kin who are believed to be in a direct line and those who are "off to one side," linked to the speaker by a lineal relative.

**colourism** A system of social identities negotiated situationally along a continuum of skin colours between white and black.

**commodity exchanges** Impersonal economic exchanges typical of the capitalist market in which goods are exchanged for cash and exchange partners need have nothing further to do with one another.

**common ancestry** Darwin's claim that similar living species must all have had a common ancestor.

**communicative competence** A term coined by anthropological linguist Dell Hymes to refer to the mastery of adult rules for socially and culturally appropriate speech.

**communitas** An unstructured or minimally structured community of equal individuals found frequently in rites of passage.

**comparison** A characteristic of the anthropological perspective that requires anthropologists to study similarities and differences across as many human societies as possible before generalizing about human beings and their activities.

**complex societies** Societies with large populations, an extensive division of labour, and occupational specialization.

**composite tools** Tools such as bows and arrows in which several different materials are combined (e.g., stone, wood, bone, ivory, antler) to produce the final working implement.

**concentrations of particular artifacts** Sets of artifacts indicating that particular social activities took place at a particular area in an archaeological site when that site was inhabited in the past.

**conjugal family** A family based on marriage; at a minimum, a spousal pair and their children.

**consanguineal relationships** Kinship connections based on descent.

**consumption** The use of material goods necessary for human survival.

**continuous variation** A pattern of variation involving polygeny in which phenotypic traits grade imperceptibly from one member of the population to another without sharp breaks.

**cosmopolitanism** Being able to move with ease from one cultural setting to another.

**cosmopolitanism** Being at ease in more than one cultural setting.

**cranial capacity** The size of the braincase.

**cranium** The bones of the head, excluding the jaw.

**creole** (1) A complex language with native speakers that has developed over one or more generations from two or more distinct languages. (2) A complex language that has developed from two or more distinct languages and that is used as a main language, whether or not it has native speakers.

**cross cousins** The children of a person's parents' opposite-gender siblings (a father's sister's children or a mother's brother's children).

**cultural anthropology** The specialty of anthropology that shows how variation in the beliefs and behaviours of members of different human groups is shaped by sets of learned behaviours and ideas that human beings acquire as members of society—that is, by culture.

**cultural hybridity** See **cultural hybridization**.

**cultural hybridization (or cultural hybridity)** Cultural mixing.

**cultural imperialism** The idea that some cultures dominate others and that domination by one culture leads inevitably to the destruction of subordinated cultures and their replacement by the culture of those in power.

**cultural relativism** Understanding another culture in its own terms sympathetically enough so that the culture appears to be a coherent and meaningful design for living.

**culture** Sets of learned behaviour and ideas that human beings acquire as members of society. Human beings use culture to adapt to and transform the world in which they live.

**culture shock** The feeling, akin to panic, that develops in people living in an unfamiliar society when they cannot understand what is happening around them.

**Denisovans** A population of Pleistocene hominins known only from ancient DNA recovered from two tiny, 41,000-year-old fossils deposited in Denisova Cave in Siberia. Denisovans and Neanderthals are thought to share a common ancestor that left Africa 500,000 years ago. Parts of the Denisovan genome resemble the genomes of modern humans from New Guinea.

**dentition** The sizes, shapes, and number of an animal's teeth.

**descent** The principle based on culturally recognized parent–child connections that define the social categories to which people belong.

**diaspora** Migrant populations with a shared identity who live in a variety of different locales around the world; a form of transborder identity that does not focus on nation building.

**discontinuous variation** A pattern of phenotypic variation in which the phenotype (e.g., flower colour) exhibits sharp breaks from one member of the population to the next.

**discourse** A stretch of speech longer than a sentence united by a common theme.

**diurnal** Active during the day.

**DNA (deoxyribonucleic acid)** The structure that carries the genetic heritage of an organism as a kind of blueprint for the organism's construction and development.

**domestication** Human interference with the reproduction of another species, with the result that specific plants and animals become more useful to and dependent on people.

**domination** Ruling with coercive force.

**dowry** The wealth transferred, usually from parents to their daughter, at the time of a woman's marriage.

**Early Stone Age (ESA)** The name given to the period of Oldowan and Acheulean stone-tool traditions in Africa.

**ecofacts** Biological remains that are likely associated with food consumption or other human activities.

**ecological niche** A species' unique position within the ecosystem in which it exists, which is shaped by its way of life (e.g., what it eats and how it finds mates, raises its young, relates to companions, and protects itself from predators).

**economic anthropology** The part of the discipline of anthropology that debates issues of human nature that relate directly to the decisions of daily life and making a living.

**egalitarian social relations** Social relations in which no great differences in wealth, power, or prestige divide members from one another.

**enculturation** The process by which humans living with one another must learn to come to terms with the ways of thinking and feeling that are considered appropriate in their respective cultures.

**endogamy** Marriage within a defined social group.

**ethnic groups** Social groups that are distinguished from one another on the basis of ethnicity.

**ethnicity** A principle of social classification used to create groups based on selected cultural features such as language, religion, or dress. Ethnicity emerges from historical processes that incorporate distinct social groups into a single political structure under conditions of inequality.

**ethnoarchaeology** The study of the way present-day societies use artifacts and structures and how these objects become part of the archaeological record.

**ethnocentrism** The opinion that one's own way of life is natural or correct and, indeed, the only true way of being fully human.

**ethnography** An anthropologist's written or otherwise recorded description of a particular culture.

**ethnology** The comparative study of two or more cultures.

**ethnopragmatics** The study of language use that relies on ethnography to illuminate the ways in which speech is both constituted by and constitutive of social interaction.

**evolution** (1) The process of change over time. (2) A characteristic of the anthropological perspective that requires anthropologists to place their observations about human beings and their activities in a temporal framework that takes into consideration change over time.

**evolutionary niche** Sum of all the natural selection pressures to which a population is exposed.

**evolutionary theory** The set of testable hypotheses that assert that living organisms can change over time and give rise to new kinds of organisms, with the result that all organisms ultimately share a common ancestry.

**exaptation** The shaping of a useful feature of an organism by natural selection to perform one function and the later reshaping of that feature by different selection pressures to perform a new function.

**excavation** The systematic uncovering of archaeological remains through removal of the deposits of soil and other material covering them and accompanying them.

**exogamy** Marriage outside a defined social group.

**extended family** A family pattern made up of three generations living together: parents, married children, and grandchildren.

**family** Minimally, a woman and her dependent children.

**features** Non-portable items created by humans, such as house walls or ditches.

**feminist archaeology** A research approach that explores why women's contributions have been systematically written out of the archaeological record and suggests new approaches to the human past that include such contributions.

**fieldwork** An extended period of close involvement with the people in whose way of life anthropologists are interested, during which anthropologists ordinarily collect most of their data.

**flexible citizenship** The strategies and effects employed by managers, technocrats, and professionals who move regularly across state boundaries and seek both to circumvent and to benefit from different nation-state regimes.

**formal models** Mathematical formulas to predict outcomes of particular kinds of human interactions under different hypothesized conditions.

**framing** A cognitive boundary that marks certain behaviours as "play" or as "ordinary life."

**free agency** The freedom of self-contained individuals to pursue their own interests above everything else and to challenge one another for dominance.

**friction** The awkward, unequal, unstable aspects of interconnection across difference.

**friendship** The relatively "unofficial" bonds that people construct with one another that tend to be personal, affective, and often a matter of choice.

**gender** The cultural construction of beliefs and behaviours considered appropriate for each sex.

**gender archaeology** Archaeological research that draws on insights from contemporary gender studies to investigate how people come to recognize themselves as different from others, how people represent these differences, and how others react to such claims.

**gene** The portion or portions of the DNA molecule that code for proteins that shape phenotypic traits.

**gene flow** The exchange of genes that occurs when a given population experiences a sudden expansion due to in-migration of outsiders from another population of the species.

**gene frequency** The frequency of occurrence of the variants of particular genes (i.e., of alleles) within the gene pool.

**gene pool** All the genes in the bodies of all members of a given species (or a population of a species).

**genetic drift** Random changes in gene frequencies from one generation to the next due to a sudden reduction in population size as a result of disaster, disease, or the out-migration of a small subgroup from a larger population.

**genetics** The scientific study of biological heredity.

**genome** The sum total of all the genetic information about an organism, carried on the chromosomes in the cell nucleus.

**genotype** The genetic information about particular biological traits encoded in an organism's DNA.

**genus** The level of the Linnaean taxonomy in which different species are grouped together on the basis of their similarities to one another. In modern taxonomies, genus is ranked between family (less specific) and species (more specific).

**gift exchanges** Non-capitalist forms of economic exchange that are deeply embedded in social relations and always require a return gift.

**globalization** Reshaping of local conditions by powerful global forces on an ever-intensifying scale.

**governmentality** The art of governing appropriately to promote the welfare of populations within a state.

**grammar** A set of rules that aim to describe fully the patterns of linguistic usage observed by speakers of a particular language.

**grave goods** Objects buried with a corpse.

**hegemony** The persuasion of subordinates to accept the ideology of the dominant group by mutual accommodations that nevertheless preserve the rulers' privileged position.

**heterozygous** Describes a fertilized egg that receives a different particle (or allele) from each parent for the same trait.

**historical archaeology** The study of archaeological sites associated with written records; frequently, the study of post-European contact sites.

**historical linguistics** The study of relationships between languages and how they change over time.

**holism** (1) A characteristic of the anthropological perspective that describes, at the highest and most inclusive level, how anthropology tries to integrate all that is known about human beings and their activities. (2) A perspective on the human condition that assumes that mind and body, individuals and society, and individuals and the environment interpenetrate and even define one another.

**hominins** Humans and their immediate ancestors.

**hominoid** The primate evolutionary grade that includes apes and humans.

*Homo* The genus to which taxonomists assign large-brained hominins approximately 2 million years old and younger.

*Homo erectus* The species of large-brained, robust hominins that lived between 1.8 and 0.3 mya.

**homology** Genetic inheritance resulting from common ancestry.

**homoplasy** Convergent, or parallel, evolution, as when two species with very different evolutionary histories develop similar physical features as a result of adapting to a similar environment.

**homozygous** Describes a fertilized egg that receives the same particle (or allele) from each parent for a particular trait.

**human agency** Human beings' ability to exercise of at least some control over their lives.

**human rights** Powers, privileges, or material resources to which people everywhere, by virtue of being human, are justly entitled.

**ideology** A world view that justifies the social arrangements under which people live.

**informants** People in a particular culture who work with anthropologists and provide them with insights about the local way of life. Also called *respondents, collaborators, teachers,* or *friends*.

**institutions** Complex, variable, and enduring forms of cultural practices that organize social life.

**intrusions** Artifacts made by more recent populations that find their way into more ancient strata as the result of natural forces.

**isotopic dating** Dating methods based on scientific knowledge about the rate at which various radioactive isotopes of naturally occurring elements transform themselves into other elements by losing subatomic particles.

**joint family** A family pattern made up of brothers and their wives or sisters and their husbands (along with their children) living together.

**kinesics** The study of body movement, gestures, and facial expressions as a form of communication.

**kinship systems** Social relationships that are prototypically derived from the universal human experiences of mating, birth, and nurturance.

**labour** The activity linking human social groups to the material world around them; from the point of view of Karl Marx, labour is therefore always social labour.

**language** The system of arbitrary symbols people use to encode their experience of the world and of others.

**language ideology** A marker of struggles between social groups with different interests, revealed in what people say and how they say it.

**Late Stone Age (LSA)** The name given to the period of highly elaborate stone-tool traditions in Africa in which blades were important, 40,000 to 10,000 years ago.

**law of superposition** A principle of geological interpretation stating that layers lower down in a sequence of strata must be older than the layers above them and, therefore, that objects embedded in lower layers must be older than objects embedded in upper layers.

**legal citizenship** The rights and obligations of citizenship accorded by the laws of a state.

**liminality** The ambiguous transitional state in a rite of passage in which the person or persons undergoing the ritual are outside their ordinary social positions.

**lineages** The consanguineal members of descent groups who believe they can trace their descent from known ancestors.

**linguistic anthropology** The specialty of anthropology concerned with the study of human languages.

**linguistic competence** A term coined by linguist Noam Chomsky to refer to the mastery of adult grammar.

**linguistic relativity principle** A position, associated with Edward Sapir and Benjamin Whorf, that asserts that language has the power to shape the way people see the world.

**linguistics** The scientific study of language.

**long-distance nationalists** Members of a diaspora organized in support of nationalist struggles in their homeland or to agitate for a state of their own.

**macroevolution** A subfield of evolutionary studies that focuses on long-term evolutionary changes, especially the origins of new species and their diversification across space and over millions of years of geological time.

**magic** A set of beliefs and practices designed to control the visible or invisible world for specific purposes.

**mandible** The lower jaw.

**market exchange** The exchange of goods (trade) calculated in terms of a multipurpose medium of exchange and standard of value (money) and carried out by means of a supply–demand–price mechanism (the market).

**marriage** An institution that transforms the status of the participants, carries implications about permitted sexual access, perpetuates social patterns through the birth of offspring, creates relationships between the kin of partners, and is symbolically marked.

**material culture** Objects created or shaped by humans and given meaning through cultural practices.

**matrilineage** A social group formed by people connected by mother–child links.

**matrilocal residence** A postmarital residence pattern in which a married couple lives with (or near) the wife's mother.

**means of production** The tools, skills, organization, and knowledge used to extract energy from nature.

**medical anthropology** The specialty of anthropology that concerns itself with human health—the factors that contribute to disease or illness and the ways that human populations deal with disease or illness.

**meiosis** The way sex cells make copies of themselves, which begins like mitosis, with chromosome duplication and the formation of two daughter cells. However, each daughter cell then divides again without chromosome duplication and, as a result, contains only a single set of chromosomes rather than the paired set typical of body cells.

**Mendelian inheritance** The view that heredity is based on non-blending, single-particle genetic inheritance.

**Mesopotamia** The area made up of the Tigris–Euphrates river system, corresponding to modern-day Iraq, Kuwait, the northeastern section of Syria, and parts of Turkey and Iran. Often referred to as the "cradle of civilization" where early complex societies developed.

**metacommunication** Communication about the process of communication.

**microevolution** A subfield of evolutionary studies that devotes attention to short-term evolutionary changes that occur within a given species over relatively few generations of ecological time.

**Middle Stone Age (MSA)** The name given to the period of Mousterian stone-tool tradition in Africa, 200,000 to 40,000 years ago.

**mitosis** The way body cells make copies of themselves. The pairs of chromosomes in the nucleus of the cell duplicate and line up along the centre of the cell. The cell then divides, each daughter cell taking one full set of paired chromosomes.

**mode of production** A specific, historically occurring set of social relations through which labour is deployed to wrest energy from nature by means of tools, skills, organization, and knowledge.

**modes of exchange** Patterns according to which distribution takes place: reciprocity, redistribution, and market exchange.

**monogamy** A marriage pattern in which a person may be married to only one spouse at a time.

**monumental architecture** Architectural constructions of a greater-than-human scale, such as pyramids, temples, and tombs.

**morphology** (1) The physical shape and size of an organism or its body parts. (2) In linguistics, the study of the minimal units of meaning in a language.

**mosaic evolution** A process of change over time in which different phenotypic traits, responding to different selection pressures, may evolve at different rates.

**Mousterian tradition** A Middle Paleolithic stone-tool tradition associated with Neanderthals in Europe and southwestern Asia and with anatomically modern human beings in Africa.

**multiculturalism** Living permanently in settings surrounded by people with cultural backgrounds different from one's own and struggling to define with them the degree to which the cultural beliefs and practices of different groups should or should not be accorded respect and recognition by the wider society.

**mutation** The creation of a new allele for a gene when the portion of the DNA molecule to which it corresponds is suddenly altered.

**myths** Stories that recount how various aspects of the world came to be the way they are and that make life meaningful for those who accept them.

**nation** A group of people believed to share the same history, culture, language, and even physical substance.

**nation building (or nationalism)** The attempt made by government officials to instill into the citizens of a state a sense of nationality.

**nationalism** See **nation building**.

**nationality** A sense of identification with and loyalty to a nation-state.

**nation-state** An ideal political unit in which national identity and political territory coincide.

**native speaker** A person who has spoken a particular language since early childhood.

**nativism** A return to the old ways; a movement whose members expect a messiah or a prophet who will bring back a lost golden age of peace, prosperity, and harmony.

**natural selection** A two-step, mechanistic explanation of how descent with modification takes place: (1) every generation, variant individuals are generated within a species because of genetic mutation, and (2) those variant individuals best suited to the current environment survive and produce more offspring than do other variants.

**naturalizing discourses** The deliberate representation of particular identities (e.g., caste, class, race, ethnicity, and nationality) as if they were a result of biology or nature, rather than history or culture, making them appear eternal and unchanging.

**Neanderthals** An archaic species of *Homo* that lived in Europe and western Asia 230,000 to 27,000 years ago.

**neoclassical economics** A formal attempt to explain the workings of capitalist enterprise, with particular attention to distribution.

**Neolithic** The "New Stone Age," which began with the domestication of plants 10,300 years ago.

**neolocal residence** A postmarital residence pattern in which a married couple sets up an independent household at a place of their own choosing.

**niche construction** When organisms actively perturb the environment in ways that modify the selection pressures experienced by subsequent generations of organisms.

**nocturnal** Active during the night.

**non-conjugal family** A woman and her children; the husband/father may be occasionally present or completely absent.

**non-isotopic dating** Chronometric dating methods that assign age in years to material evidence but not by using rates of nuclear decay.

**non-verbal communication** The process of sending and receiving messages without the use of words (e.g., through gestures, facial expressions, or non-verbal vocalizations).

**norm of reaction** A table or graph that displays the possible range of phenotypic outcomes for a given genotype in different environments.

**nuclear family** A family pattern made up of two generations: the parents and their unmarried children.

**occupational specialization** Specialization in various occupations (e.g., weaving or pot making) or in new social roles (e.g., king or priest) that is found in socially complex societies.

**Oldowan tradition** A stone-tool tradition named after the Olduvai Gorge (in Tanzania), where the first specimens of the oldest human tools were found.

**omnivorous** Eating a wide range of plant and animal foods.

**oracles** Invisible forces to which people address questions and whose responses they believe to be truthful.

**orthodoxy** "Correct doctrine"; the prohibition of deviation from approved theories and beliefs.

**orthopraxy** "Correct practice"; the prohibition of deviation from approved forms of behaviour.

**paleoanthropology** The study of human fossils and associated remains to understand our evolutionary history.

**pangenesis** A theory of heredity suggesting that an organism's physical traits are passed on from one generation to the next in the form of multiple distinct particles given off by all parts of the organism, different proportions of which get passed on to offspring via sperm or egg.

**parallel cousins** The children of a person's parents' same-gender siblings (a father's brother's children or a mother's sister's children).

**participant observation** A method of data collection in which a researcher lives and works closely with the people whose way of life she or he is studying while participating in their lives as much as possible.

**participatory action research** A type of fieldwork that aims to bring about social change through the collection of data and the empowerment of community members as researchers in the projects.

**patrilineage** A social group formed by people connected by father–child links.

**patrilocal residence** A postmarital residence pattern in which a married couple lives with (or near) the husband's father.

**phenotype** The observable, measurable, overt characteristics of an organism.

**phenotypic plasticity** Physiological flexibility that allows organisms to respond to environmental stresses, such as temperature changes.

**phonology** The study of the sounds of language.

**phyletic gradualism** A theory arguing that one species gradually transforms itself into a new species over time, yet the actual boundary between species can never be detected but only drawn arbitrarily.

**physical anthropology** See **biological anthropology**.

**pidgin** (1) A language with no native speakers that develops in a single generation between members of communities that possess distinct native languages. (2) A shared secondary language in a speech community in which speakers also use some other main language.

**play** A framing (or orienting context) that is (1) consciously adopted by the players, (2) somehow pleasurable, and (3) systemically related to what is non-play by alluding to the non-play world and by transforming the objects, roles, actions, and relations of ends and means characteristic of the non-play world.

**pleiotropy** The phenomenon whereby a single gene may affect more than one phenotypic trait.

**political anthropology** The study of social power in human society.

**polyandry** A marriage pattern in which a woman may be married to more than one husband at a time.

**polygamy** A marriage pattern in which a person may be married to more than one spouse at a time.

**polygeny** The phenomenon whereby many genes are responsible for producing a phenotypic trait, such as skin colour.

**polygyny** A marriage pattern in which a man may be married to more than one wife at a time.

**polymorphous** Describes alleles that come in a range of different forms.

**population genetics** A field that uses statistical analysis to study short-term evolutionary change in large populations.

**postcranial skeleton** The bones of the body, excluding those of the head.

**postnational ethos** An attitude toward the world in which people submit to the governmentality of the capitalist market while trying to evade the governmentality of nation-states.

**power** Transformative capacity; the ability to transform a given situation.

**pragmatics** The study of language in the context of its use.

**prehensile** The ability to grasp, with fingers, toes, or tail.

**priest** A religious practitioner skilled in the practice of religious rituals, which he or she carries out for the benefit of the group.

**primatology** The study of non-human primates, the closest living relatives of human beings.

**principle of independent assortment** A principle of Mendelian inheritance in which each pair of particles (genes) separates independently of every other pair when germ cells (egg and sperm) are formed.

**principle of segregation** A principle of Mendelian inheritance in which an individual gets one particle (gene) for each trait (i.e., one-half of the required pair) from each parent.

**prosimian** The least complex evolutionary grade of the primates, which includes lemurs, lorises, and tarsiers.

**provenance** The three-dimensional position of an artifact within the matrix of an archaeological site.

**proxemics** The study of how different societies perceive and use space.

**punctuated equilibrium** A theory claiming that most of evolutionary history has been characterized by relatively stable species coexisting in an equilibrium that is occasionally punctuated by sudden bursts of speciation, when extinctions are widespread and many new species appear.

**races** Social groupings that allegedly reflect biological differences.

**racism** The systematic oppression of members of one or more socially defined "races" by members of another socially defined "race" that is justified in terms of the supposed inherent biological superiority of the rulers and the supposed inherent biological inferiority of those they rule.

**reciprocity** The exchange of goods and services of equal value. Anthropologists distinguish three forms of reciprocity: *generalized*, in which neither the time nor the value of the return is specified; *balanced*, in which a return of equal value is expected within a specified time limit; and *negative*, in which parties to the exchange hope to get something for nothing.

**redistribution** A mode of exchange that requires some form of centralized social organization to receive economic contributions from all members of the group and to redistribute them in such a way as to provide for every group member.

**reflexivity** Critical thinking about the way one thinks; reflection on one's own experience.

**regional continuity model** The hypothesis that evolution from *Homo erectus* to *Homo sapiens* occurred gradually throughout the traditional range of *H. erectus*.

**relatedness** The socially recognized ties that connect people in a variety of different ways.

**relations of production** The social relations linking the people who use a given means of production within a particular mode of production.

**relative dating methods** Dating methods that arrange material evidence in a linear sequence, each object in the sequence being identified as older or younger than other objects.

**religion** "Ideas and practices that postulate reality beyond that which is immediately available to the senses" (Bowen 2008).

**replacement model** The hypothesis that only one subpopulation of *Homo erectus*, probably located in Africa, underwent a rapid spurt of evolution to produce *Homo sapiens* 200,000 to 100,000 years ago. After that time, *H. sapiens* would itself have multiplied and dispersed, gradually populating the globe and eventually replacing any remaining populations of *H. erectus* or their descendants.

**revitalization** A conscious, deliberate, and organized attempt by some members of a society to create a more satisfying culture in a time of crisis.

**rite of passage** A ritual that serves to mark the movement and transformation of an individual from one social position to another.

**ritual** A repetitive social practice composed of a sequence of symbolic activities that is set off from the social routines of everyday life, adheres to a culturally defined ritual schema, and closely connects to a specific set of ideas that are often encoded in myth.

**sedentism** The process of increasingly permanent human habitation in one place.

**segmentary opposition** A mode of hierarchical social organization in which groups beyond the most basic emerge only in opposition to other groups on the same hierarchical level.

**semantics** The study of meaning in language.

**seriation** A relative dating method based on the assumption that artifacts that look alike must have been made at the same time.

**sex** Observable physical characteristics that distinguish two kinds of humans, females and males, needed for biological reproduction.

**sexual dimorphism** Observable phenotypic differences between males and females of the same species.

**sexual practices** Emotional or affectional relationships between sexual partners and the physical activities they engage in with one another.

**shaman** A part-time religious practitioner who is believed to have the power to contact supernatural forces directly on behalf of individuals or groups.

**site** A precise geographical location of the remains of past human activity.

**social organization** The patterning of human interdependence in a given society through the actions and decisions of its members.

**social stratification** A form of social organization in which people have unequal access to wealth, power, and prestige.

**socialization** The process by which humans as material organisms, living together with other similar organisms, cope with the behavioural rules established by their respective societies.

**sodalities** Special-purpose groupings that may be organized on the basis of age, sex, economic role, or personal interest.

**species** A distinct segment of an evolutionary lineage. Different biologists, working with living and fossil organisms, have devised different criteria to identify boundaries between species. For Linnaeus, a species is a Platonic "natural kind" defined in terms of its essence. For modern biologists, a species is a reproductive community of populations (reproductively isolated from others) that occupies a specific niche in nature.

**species selection** A process in which natural selection is seen to operate among variant, related species within a single genus, family, or order.

**state** A stratified society that possesses a territory that is defended from outside enemies with an army and from internal disorder with police. A state, which has a separate set of governmental institutions designed to enforce laws and to collect taxes and tribute, is run by an elite that possesses a monopoly on the use of force.

**status** A particular social position in a group.

**stereoscopic vision** A form of vision in which the visual field of each eye of a two-eyed (binocular) animal overlaps with the other, producing depth perception.

**strata** Layers; in geological terms, a stratum is a layer of rock and soil.

**stratigraphic superposition** A relative dating method that relies on the depth of strata and associated artifacts and fossils.

**structural violence** Violence that results from the way that political and economic forces structure risk for various forms of suffering within a population.

**subsistence strategy** The ways that people in a particular society go about meeting their basic material survival needs.

**substantive citizenship** The actions people take, regardless of their legal citizenship status, to assert their membership in a state and to bring about political changes that will improve their lives.

**surplus production** The production of amounts of food that exceed the basic subsistence needs of the population.

**survey** The physical examination of a geographical region in which promising sites are most likely to be found.

**symbol** Something that stands for something else. A symbol often signals the presence of an important domain of experience.

**syncretism** The synthesis of old religious practices (or an old way of life) with new religious practices (or a new way of life) introduced from outside, often by force.

**syntax** The arrangement of words (or morphemes) into sentences.

**taphonomy** The study of the various processes that objects undergo in the course of becoming part of the fossil and archaeological records.

**taxon** Each species, as well as each group of species related at any level in a taxonomic hierarchy.

**taxonomy** In biology, a classification system used to organize various kinds of organisms.

**transborder citizenry** A group made up of citizens of a country who continue to live in their homeland plus the people who have emigrated from the country and their descendants, regardless of their current citizenship.

**transborder state** A form of state in which it is claimed that those people who left the country and their descendants remain part of their ancestral state, even if they are citizens of another state.

**transformist hegemony** A nationalist program to define nationality in a way that preserves the cultural domination of the ruling group while including enough cultural features from subordinated groups to ensure their loyalty.

**transnational nation-state** A nation-state in which the relationships between citizens and the state extend to wherever citizens reside.

**tribe** A society that is generally larger than a band, whose members usually farm or herd for a living. Social relations in a tribe are still relatively egalitarian, although there may be a chief who speaks for the group or organizes certain group activities.

**unilineal descent** The principle that a descent group is formed by people who believe they are related to each other by connections made through *either* their mothers *or* their fathers.

**variational evolution** The Darwinian theory of evolution, which assumes that variant members of a species respond differently to environmental challenges. Those variants that are more successful ("fitter") survive and reproduce more offspring, who inherit the traits that made their parents fit.

**witchcraft** The performance of magic by human beings, often through innate supernatural powers, whether or not it is intentional or self-aware.

**Woloff's law** The principle that a living person's bones adapt to the stress or load to which they are subjected, such that greater stress or load will lead to denser bones and less stress or load will lead to less dense bones.

**world views** Encompassing pictures of reality created by the members of societies.

# References

Abbas, Akhbar. 2002. "Cosmopolitan Description: Shanghai and Hong Kong." In *Cosmopolitanism*, edited by Carol Breckenridge, Sheldon Pollock, Homi Bhaba, and Dipeesh Chakrabarty, 209–28. Durham, NC: Duke University Press.

Abu El-Haj, Nadia. 2007. "The Genetic Reinscription of Race." *Annual Review of Anthropology* 36: 283–300.

Abusharaf, Rogaia Mustafa. 2000. "Female Circumcision Goes beyond Feminism." *Anthropology News* 41 (March): 17–18.

Abwunza, Judith M. 1997. *Women's Voices, Women's Power: Dialogues of Resistance from East Africa*. Peterborough, ON: Broadview Press.

Adams, Robert. 1981. *Heartland of Cities*. Chicago: University of Chicago Press.

Adams, Robert, and Hans Nissen. 1972. *The Uruk Countryside*. Chicago: University of Chicago Press.

Adams, Thomas, and R. Elphin Smith. 1962. "The Effect of Chronic Local Cold Exposure on Finger Temperature Responses." *Journal of Applied Physiology* 17 (2): 317–22.

Adovasio, J.M., J.D. Gunn, J.L. Donahue, and R. Stuckenrath. 1978. "Meadowcroft Rockshelter, 1977: An Overview." *American Antiquity* 43: 632–51.

Aiello, Leslie C. 1986. "The Relationships of the Tarisiiformes: A Review of the Case for the Haplorhini." In *Major Topics in Primate and Human Evolution*, edited by B. Wood, L. Martin, and P. Andrews, 47–65. Cambridge: Cambridge University Press.

——. 1993. "The Fossil Evidence for Modern Human Origins in Africa: A Revised View." *American Anthropologist* 95: 73–96.

Akmajian, Adrian, Richard A. Demers, Ann K. Farmer, and Robert M. Harnish. 1997. *Linguistics: An Introduction to Language and Communication*. 4th ed. Cambridge, MA: MIT Press.

Alia, Valerie. 2007. *Names and Nunavut: Culture and Identity in Arctic Canada*. New York: Berghahn Books.

Alland, Alexander. 1977. *The Artistic Animal*. New York: Doubleday Anchor.

Allen, Theodore. 1997. *The Invention of the White Race*. London: Verso.

Alonso, Ana María. 1994. "The Politics of Space, Time, and Substance: State Formation, Nationalism, and Ethnicity." *Annual Review of Anthropology* 23: 379–405.

Alverson, Hoyt. 1977. "Peace Corps Volunteers in Rural Botswana." *Human Organization* 36 (3): 274–81.

Anderson, Benedict. 1992. "The New World Disorder." *New Left Review* 193: 3–14.

Anderson, Richard L. 1990. *Calliope's Sisters: A Comparative Study of Philosophies of Art*. Englewood Cliffs, NJ: Prentice Hall.

Appadurai, Arjun. 1990. "Disjuncture and Difference in the Global Cultural Economy." In *Global Culture*, edited by Mike Featherstone, 295–310. London: Sage.

——. 2002. "Grassroots Globalization and the Research Imagination." In *The Anthropology of Politics*, edited by Joan Vincent, 271–84. Malden, MA: Blackwell.

Arbour, L., S. Rezazadeh, J. Eldstrom, G. Weget-Simms, R. Rupps, Z. Dyer, G. Tibbits, et al. 2008. "A KCNQ1 V205M Missense Mutation Causes a High Rate of Long QT Syndrome in a First Nations Community of Northern British Columbia: A Community-Based Approach to Understanding the Impact." *Genetics in Medicine* 10: 545–50.

Arnold, Jeanne E. 1995. "Social Inequality, Marginalization, and Economic Process." In *Foundations of Social Inequality*, edited by T. Douglas Price and Gary M. Feinman. New York: Plenum.

Arsuaga, Juan-Luis, Ignacio Martinez, Ana Gracia, José-Miguel Carretero, and Eudald Carbonell. 1993. "Three New Human Skulls from the Sima de los Huesos, Middle Pleistocene Site in Sierra de Atapuerca, Spain." *Nature* 362: 534–37.

Asad, Talal. 2003. *Formations of the Secular: Christianity, Islam, Modernity*. Palo Alto, CA: Stanford University Press.

Asch, Michael. 1984. *Home and Native Land: Aboriginal Rights and the Canadian Constitution*. Toronto: Methuen.

——. 2014. *On Being Here to Stay: Treaties and Aboriginal Rights in Canada*. Toronto: University of Toronto Press.

Asfaw, Berhane, Tim White, Owen Lovejoy, Bruce Latimer, Scott Simpson, and Gen Suwa. 1999. "*Australopithecus Garbi*: A New Species of Early Hominid from Ethiopia." *Science* 284 (5414): 629–35.

Asquith, Pamela. 2011. "Of Bonds and Boundaries: What Is the Modern Role of Anthropomorphism in Primatological Studies?" *American Journal of Primatology* 73 (3): 238–44.

Aufderheide, Patricia. 1993. "Latin American Grassroots Video: Beyond Television." *Public Culture* 5 (3): 579–92.

*Autobiografías Campesinas*. 1979. Vol. 1. Heredia, Costa Rica: Editorial de la Universidad Nacional.

Baer, Hans, Merrill Singer, and Ida Susser. 2003. *Medical Anthropology and the World System*. 2nd ed. Westport, CT: Praeger.

Bailey, Wendy J., David H.A. Fitch, Danilo A. Tagle, John Czelusniak, Jerry L. Slightom, and Morris Goodman. 1991. "Molecular Evolution of the Psi-Eta-Globin Gene Locus: Gibbon Phylogeny and the Hominoid Slowdown." *Molecular Biology and Evolution* 8: 155–84.

Bakhtin, Mikhail M. 1981. *The Dialogic Imagination: Four Essays*. Edited by Michael Holquist. Translated by Michael Holquist and Caryl Emerson. Austin: University of Texas Press.

Bala, Nicholas. 2005. "The Debates about Same-Sex Marriage in Canada and the United States: Controversy over the Evolution of a Fundamental Social Institution." *Brigham Young University Journal of Public Law* 20 (2): 195–231.

Banning, E.B. 2011. "So Fair a House." *Current Anthropology* 52 (5): 619–60.

Barkow, Jerome H., Leda Cosmides, and John Tooby. 1992. *The Adapted Mind: Evolutionary Psychology and the Generation of Culture*. New York: Oxford University Press.

Bar-Yosef, Ofer. 1989. "Geochronology of the Levantine Middle Paleolithic." In *The Human Revolution*, edited by P.A. Mellars and C. Stringer, 586–610. Princeton, NJ: Princeton University Press.

—— and Mordechai Kislev. 1989. "Early Farming Communities in the Jordan Valley." In *Foraging and Farming: The Evolution of Plant Exploitation*, edited by David Harris and Gordon Hillman, 632–42. Vol. 13 of *One World Archaeology*. London: Unwin Hyman.

—— and Steven L. Kuhn. 1999. "The Big Deal about Blades: Laminar Technologies and Human Evolution." *American Anthropologist* 101 (2): 322–28.

Bass, William M. 1995. *Human Osteology: A Laboratory and Field Manual*. 3rd ed. Columbia: Missouri Archaeological Society.

Bateson, Gregory. 1972. "A Theory of Play and Fantasy." In *Steps to an Ecology of Mind*, edited by Gregory Bateson, 177–93. New York: Ballantine Books.

Battiste, Marie. 1986. "Micmac Literacy and Cognitive Assimilation." In *The Legacy*, edited by Jean Barman, Yvonne Hebert, and Don McCaskill, 23–44. Vol. 1 of *Indian Education in Canada*. Vancouver: UBC Press.

——. 2012. "Enabling the Autumn Seed: Toward a Decolonized Approach to Aboriginal Knowledge, Language, and Education." In *Schooling in Transition: Readings in Canadian History of Education*, edited by S.Z. Burke and P. MIlewski, 275–86. Toronto: University of Toronto Press.

Bauman, Zygmunt. 1989. *Modernity and the Holocaust*. Cambridge: Polity Press.

Beals, Alan. 1962. *Gopalpur: A South Indian Village*. New York: Holt, Rinehart, and Winston.

Bearder, Simon K. 1987. "Lorises, Bushbabies, and Tarsiers: Diverse Societies in Solitary Foragers." In *Primate Societies*, edited by Barbara Smuts, Dorothy Cheney, Robert Seyfarth, Richard Wrangham, and Thomas Struhsaker, 11–24. Chicago: University of Chicago Press.

Beattie, Owen, Brian Aplaud, Erik Blake, James A. Cosgrove, Sarah Gaunt, Sheila Greer, Alexander Mackie, et al. 2000. "The Kwaday Dan Ts'inchi Discovery from a Glacier in British Columbia." *Canadian Journal of Archaeology* 24, 129–47.

Behrendt, Larissa. 2007. "The Emergency We Had to Have." In *Coercive Reconciliation: Stabilise, Normalise, Exit Aboriginal Australia*, edited by Jon Altman and Melinda Hinkson, 15–20. North Carlton, Australia: Arena Publications Association.

Belfer-Cohen, Anna. 1988. *The Natufian Settlement at Hayonim Cave*. Ph.D. diss. Jerusalem: Hebrew University.

——. 1991. "The Natufian in the Levant." *Annual Review of Anthropology* 20: 167–86.

Bell, Sandra, and Simon Coleman. 1999. "The Anthropology of Friendship: Enduring Themes and Future Possibilities." In *The Anthropology of Friendship*, edited by Sandra Bell and Simon Coleman, 1–19. Oxford: Berg.

Bender, Barbara. 1977. "Gatherer–Hunter to Farmer: A Social Perspective." *World Archaeology* 10: 204–22.

Benefit, Brenda, and Monte L. McCrossin. 1995. "Miocene Hominoids and Hominid Origins." *Annual Review of Anthropology* 24: 237–56.

Berger, Lee R., Darryl J. de Ruiter, Steven E. Churchill, Peter Schmid, Kristian J. Carlson, Paul H.G.M. Dirks, and Job M. Kibii. 2010. "*Australopithecus Sediba*: A New Species of *Homo*-Like Australopith from South Africa." *Science* 328: 195–204.

Berger, Richard L. 1988. "Unity and Heterogeneity within the Chavín Horizon." In *Peruvian Prehistory*, edited by Richard W. Keatinge, 99–144. Cambridge: Cambridge University Press.

Berger, Thomas R. 1977. *Northern Frontier, Northern Homeland: Report of the Mackenzie Valley Pipeline Inquiry*. 2 vols. Ottawa: Supply and Services Canada.

Bermúdez de Castro, J.M., J.L. Arsuaga, E. Carbonell, A. Rosas, I. Martinez, and M. Mosquera. 1997. "A Hominid from the Lower Pleistocene of Atapuerca, Spain." *Science* 276 (5317): 1392–95.

Berreman, Gerald D. 1962. *Behind Many Masks: Ethnography and Impression Management in a Himalayan Village*. Lexington, KY: Society for Applied Anthropology.

Bherer, Claude, Damian Labuda, Marie-Helene Roy-Gagnon, Lous Houde, Marc Tremblay, and Helene Vézina. 2011. "Admixed Ancestry and Stratification of Quebec Regional Populations." *American Journal of Physical Anthropology* 144: 432–441. doi:10.1002/ajpa.21424.

Bigenho, Michelle. 2002. *Sounding Indigenous: Authenticity in Bolivian Music Performance*. New York: Palgrave.

Binford, Lewis R., and Chuan Kun Ho. 1985. "Taphonomy at a Distance: Zhoukoudian, 'the Cave Home of Beijing Man'?" *Current Anthropology* 26 (4): 413–29.

Bisson, Michael S., and Bolduc, P. 1994. "Previously Undescribed Figurines from the Grimaldi Caves." *Current Anthropology*, 458–68.

Blackwood, Evelyn, and Saskia E. Wieringa. 1999. Preface to *Female Desires: Same-Sex Relations and Transgender Practices across Cultures*, edited by Evelyn Blackwood and Saskia E. Wieringa, ix–xiii. New York: Columbia University Press.

Bledsoe, Caroline. 1993. "The Politics of Polygyny in Mende Education and Child Fosterage Transactions." In *Sex and Gender Hierarchies*, edited by Barbara Diane Miller, 170–92. Cambridge: Cambridge University Press.

Boaz, Noel T. 1995. "Calibration and Extension of the Record of Plio-Pleistocene Hominidae." In *Biological Anthropology: The State of the Science*, edited by Noel T. Boaz and Linda Wolfe, 23–47. Bend, OR: International Institute for Human Evolutionary Research.

Boddy, Janice. 1997. "Womb as Oasis: The Symbolic Context of Pharaonic Circumcision in Rural Northern Sudan." In *The Gender/Sexuality Reader*, edited by Roger Lancaster and Micaela De Leonardo, 309–24. New York: Routledge.

——. 2007. "Gender Crusades: The Female Circumcision Controversy in Cultural Perspective." In *Transcultural Bodies: Female Genital Cutting in Global Context*, edited by Ylva Hernlund and Bettina Shell-Duncan. New Brunswick, NJ: Rutgers University Press.

Boesch-Achermann, Hedwige, and Christophe Boesch. 1994. "Hominization in the Rainforest: The Chimpanzee's Piece of the Puzzle." *Evolutionary Anthropology* 3 (1): 9–16.

Bogin, Barry. 1995. "Growth and Development: Recent Evolutionary and Biocultural Research." In *Biological Anthropology: The State of the Science*, edited by Noel T. Boaz and Linda Wolfe, 49–70. Bend, OR: International Institute for Human Evolutionary Research.

Bökönyi, Sandor. 1989. "Definitions of Animal Domestication." In *The Walking Larder: Patterns of Domestication, Pastoralism, and Predation*, edited by Juliet Clutton-Brock, 22–27. Vol. 14 of *One World Archaeology*. London: Unwin Hyman.

Borman, Randy. 1999. "Cofán: Story of the Forest People and the Outsiders." *Cultural Survival Quarterly* 23 (2): 48–50.

Bossen, Laurel, Wang Xurui, Melissa J. Brown, and Hill Gates. 2011. "Feet and Fabrication: Footbinding and Early Twentieth-Century Rural Women's Labor in Shaanxi." *Modern China* 37 (4): 247–83.

Boudreau, Annette, and Lise Dubois. 2007. "Francais, Acadien, Acadjonne: Competing Discourse on Language Preservation along the Shores of the Baie Sainte-Marie," in *Discourses of Endangerment*, edited by Alexandre Duchene and Monica Heller, 99–120. New York: Continuum Publishers.

Bowen, John R. 2008. *Religions in Practice: An Approach to the Anthropology of Religion*. 4th ed. Needham Heights, MA: Allyn and Bacon.

———. 2010. *Can Islam be French? Pluralism and Pragmatism in a Secularist State*. Princeton, NJ: Princeton University Press.

Bowie, Fiona. 2006. *The Anthropology of Religion: An Introduction*. 2nd ed. Malden, MA: Blackwell.

Bowie, Katherine. 2008. "Standing in the Shadows: Of Matrilocality and the Role of Women in a Village Election in Northern Thailand." *American Ethnologist* 35 (1): 136–53.

Boyd, Robert, and Peter J. Richerson. 1985. *Culture and the Evolutionary Process*. Chicago: University of Chicago Press.

Brain, C.K. 1985. "Interpreting Early Hominid Death Assemblages: The Rise of Taphonomy since 1925." In *Hominid Evolution: Past, Present, and Future*, edited by P.V. Tobias, 41–6. New York: Alan R. Liss.

——— and A. Sillen. 1988. "Evidence from the Swartkrans Cave for the Earliest Use of Fire." *Nature* 336: 464–66.

Brain, Robert. 1976. *Friends and Lovers*. New York: Basic Books.

Bräuer, Günter. 1989. "The Evolution of Modern Humans: A Comparison of the African and Non-African Evidence." In *The Human Revolution*, edited by P.A. Mellars and C. Stringer, 123–54. Princeton, NJ: Princeton University Press.

Brenneis, Donald, and Ronald Macaulay, eds. 1996. *The Matrix of Language: Contemporary Linguistic Anthropology*. Boulder, CO: Westview Press.

Brinton, Laurel J., and Leslie K. Arnovick. 2011. *The English Language: A Linguistic History*. 2nd ed. Toronto: Oxford University Press.

Brooke, James. 2003. "Dowry Too High: Lose Bride and Go to Jail." *New York Times*, May 17, A1, A7.

Brown, Keri A., and Terence A. Brown. 2013. "Biomolecular Archaeology." *Annual Review of Anthropology* 42: 159–74.

Browne, Malcolm. 1994. "Asian Fossil Prompts New Ideas on Evolution." *New York Times*, February 24, A1, A9.

Brunet, Michel, Alain Beauvilain, Yves Coppens, Emile Heintz, Aladji H.E. Moutaye, and David Pilbeam. 1995. "The First Australopithecine 2500 Kilometers West of the Rift Valley (Chad)." *Nature* 378: 273–5.

———, Franck Guy, David Pilbeam, Hassane Taisso Mackaye, Andossa Likius, Djimdoumalbaye Ahounta, Alain Beauvilain, et al. 2002. "A New Hominid from the Upper Miocene of Chad, Central Africa." *Nature* 418: 145–51.

Bruno, Maria C. 2009. "Practice and History in the Transition to Food Production." *Current Anthropology* 50 (5): 703–6.

Bryn, Brandon. 2011. "Science: Genalogy Reveals Reproductive Success of Quebec's Early Pioneers." *American Association for the Advancement of Science*, November 3. http://www.aaas.org/news/science-genealogy-reveals-reproductive-success-quebec%E2%80%99s-early-pioneers.

Burch, Ernest. 1970. "Marriage and Divorce among the North Alaska Eskimos." In *Divorce and After*, edited by Paul Bohannan, 152–81. Garden City, NY: Doubleday.

Burling, Robbins. 2005. *The Talking Ape: How Language Evolved*. New York: Oxford University Press.

CAA (Canadian Archaeological Association). 2015. "Principles of Ethical Conduct." http://canadianarchaeology.com/caa/principles-ethical-conduct.

Callow, Chris. 2006. "Reconstructing the Past in Medieval Iceland." *Early Medieval Europe* 14 (3): 297–324.

Canadian Museum of Civilization. 2011. "Repatriation Policy." http://www.historymuseum.ca/wp-content/uploads/2011/09/REPATRIATION-POLICY.pdf.

Cann, Rebecca L., Mark Stoneking, and Allan C. Wilson. 1987. "Mitchondrial DNA and Human Evolution." *Nature* 325: 31–6.

Cannon, Martin J., and Lina Sunseri, eds. 2011. *Racism, Colonialism, and Indigeneity in Canada: A Reader*. Toronto: Oxford University Press.

Carneiro, Robert. 1970. "A Theory of the Origin of the State." *Science* 169: 733–8.

Cartmill, Matt. 1972. "Arboreal Adaptations and the Origin of the Order Primates." In *The Functional and Evolutionary Biology of Primates*, edited by R. Tuttle, 97–122. Chicago: Aldine-Atherton.

Caryl, Christian. 2009. "Reality Check: Human Terrain Teams." *Foreign Policy*, September 8. http://www.foreignpolicy.com/articles/2009/09/08/reality_check_human_terrain_teams.

Cavalli-Sforza, Luigi Luca, and Marcus W. Feldman. 1981. *Cultural Transmission and Evolution: A Quantitative Approach*. Princeton, NJ: Princeton University Press.

Caven, Febna. 2013. "Being Idle No More: The Women Behind the Movement." *Cultural Survival Quarterly* 37 (1): 6–7.

Center for Reproductive Rights. 2015. "Female Genital Mutilation (FGM): Legal Prohibitions Worldwide." http://www.reproductiverights.org/document/female-genital-mutilation-fgm-legal-prohibitions-worldwide.

Chaplin George. 2004. "Geographic Distribution of Environmental Factors Influencing Human Coloration." *American Journal of Physical Anthropology* 125: 292–302.

Chase, A.F., D.Z. Chase, C.T. Fisher, S.J. Leisz, and J.F. Weishampel. 2012. "Geospatial Revolution and Remote Sensing LiDAR in Mesoamerican Archaeology." *Proceedings of the National Academy of Sciences USA* 109 (32): 12916–21.

Chase, Philip G. 1989. "How different was Middle Palaeolithic Subsistence? A Zooarchaeological Perspective on the Middle to Upper Palaeolithic Transition." In *The Human Revolution*, edited by P.A. Mellars and C. Stringer, 321–7. Princeton, NJ: Princeton University Press.

Chatters, James C., Douglas J. Kennett, Yemane Asmerom, Brian M. Kemp, Victor Polyak, Alberta Nava Blank, Patricia A. Beddows, et al. 2014. "Late Pleistocene Human Skeleton and mtDNA Link Paleoamericans and Modern Native Americans." *Science* 344 (6185): 750–4.

Chauchat, Claude. 1988. "Early Hunter–Gatherers on the Peruvian Coast." In *Peruvian Prehistory*, edited by Richard W. Keatinge, 41–66. Cambridge: Cambridge University Press.

Chazan, Michael. 2014. *World Prehistory and Archaeology*. Toronto: Pearson Education Canada.

Cheney, Dorothy L., Robert M. Seyfarth, Barbara B. Smuts, and Richard W. Wrangham. 1987. "The Study of Primate Societies." In *Primate Societies*, edited by Barbara Smuts, Dorothy Cheney, Robert Seyfarth, Richard Wrangham, and Thomas Struhsaker, 1–10. Chicago: University of Chicago Press.

Cheverud, James M. 2004. "Darwinian Evolution by the Natural Selection of Heritable Variation: Definition of Parameters and Application to Social Behaviors." In *The Origins and*

*Nature of Sociality*, edited by Robert W. Sussman and Audrey R. Chapman, pp. 140–60. New York: Aldine de Gruyter.

Chimpanzee Sequencing and Analysis Consortium. 2005. "Initial Sequence of the Chimpanzee Genome and Comparison with the Human Genome. *Nature* 437: 69–87. doi:10.1038/nature04072.

Chin, Elizabeth. 1999. "Ethnically Correct Dolls: Toying with the Race Industry." *American Anthropologist* 101 (2): 305–21.

Chomsky, Noam. 1957. *Syntactic Structures*. Cambridge, MA: MIT Press.

——. 1965. *Aspects of the Theory of Syntax*. Cambridge, MA: MIT Press.

CIHR (Canadian Institutes of Health Research). 2010. "CIHR Guidelines for Health Research Involving Aboriginal People." http://www.cihr-irsc.gc.ca/e/29134.html.

Clayman, Steven E. 2001. "Answers and Evasions." *Language in Society* 30 (3): 403–42.

Cochran P.A., C.A. Marshall, C. Garcia-Downing, E. Kendall, D. Cook, L. McCubbin, and R.M. Gover. 2008. "Indigenous Ways of Knowing: Implications for Participatory Research and Community." *American Journal of Public Health* 98: 22–7.

Collard, Mark, Briggs Buchanan, April Ruttle, and Michael J. O'Brien. 2011. "Niche Construction and the Toolkits of Hunter-Gatherers and Food Producers." *Biological Theory* 6 (3): 251–9.

—— and Mana Dembo. 2013. "Modern Human Origins." In *A Companion to Paleoanthropology*, edited by David Begun, 557–81. West Sussex, UK: John Wiley and Sons.

Collier, Jane, Michelle Z. Rosaldo, and Sylvia Yanagisako. 1997. "Is There a Family? New Anthropological Views." In *The Gender/Sexuality Reader*, edited by R. Lancaster and M. Di Leonardo, 71–81. New York: Routledge.

Colloredo-Mansfeld, Rudi. 1999. *The Native Leisure Class: Consumption and Cultural Creativity in the Andes*. Chicago: University of Chicago Press.

Colwell-Chanthaphonh, Chip. 2009. "The Archaeologist as World Citizen: On the Morals of Heritage Preservation and Destruction." In *Cosmopolitan Archaeologies*, edited by Lynn Meskell, 140–65. Durham, NC: Duke University Press.

Comaroff, Jean, and John Comaroff. 1992. *Ethnography and the Historical Imagination*. Boulder, CO: Westview.

Common, R.W., and L.G. Frost. 1988. "The Implications of the Mismeasurement of Native Students' Intelligence through the Use of Standardized Intelligence Tests." *Canadian Journal of Native Education* 15 (1): 18–30.

Conkey, Margaret W., and Joan M. Gero. 1991. "Tensions, Pluralities, and Engendering Archaeology: An Introduction to Women and Prehistory." In *Engendering Archaeology*, edited by Joan M. Gero and Margaret W. Conkey, 3–30. Oxford: Blackwell.

Conklin, William J., and Michael E. Moseley. 1988. "The Patterns of Art and Power in the Early Intermediate Period." In *Peruvian Prehistory*, edited by R. Keatinge, pp. 145–63. Cambridge: Cambridge University Press.

Cords, Marina. 1987. "Forest Guenons and Patas Monkeys: Male–Male Competition in One-Male Groups." In *Primate Societies*, edited by Barbara Smuts, Dorothy Cheney, Robert Seyfarth, Richard Wrangham, and Thomas Struhsaker, 98–111. Chicago: University of Chicago Press.

Counihan, Carole M. 2004. *Around the Tuscan Table: Food, Family, and Gender in Twentieth-Century Florence*. New York: Routledge.

Cowan, Jane, Marie-Bénédicte Dembour, and Richard A. Wilson. 2001. Introduction to *Culture and Rights: Anthropological Perspectives*, edited by Jane Cowan, Marie-Bénédicte Dembour, and Richard A. Wilson, 1–26. Cambridge: Cambridge University Press.

Crate, Susan A., and Mark Nuttall, eds. 2009. *Anthropology and Climate Change: From Encounters to Actions*. Walnut Creek, CA: Left Coast Press.

Creanza, Nicole, Lauren Fogarty, and Marcus Feldman. 2013. "Exploring Cultural Niche Construction from the Paleolithic to Modern Hunter-Gatherers." In *Dynamics of Learning in Neanderthals and Modern Humans*. Volume 1. 211–28. Springer Japan.

Crehan, Kate. 2002. *Gramsci and Cultural Anthropology*. Berkeley: University of California Press.

Cross, Alan, and Mark Collard. 2011. "Estimating Surface Area in Early Hominins." *PLOS ONE* 6 (1): e16107.

——, Mark Collard, and Andrew Nelson. 2008. "Body Segment Differences in Surface Area, Skin Temperatures and 3-D Displacement and the Estimation of Heat Balance During Locomotion in Hominins." *PLOS ONE* 3 (6): e2464.

Daly, Mary. 1978. *Gyn/Ecology: The Metaethics of Radical Feminism*. Boston: Beacon Press.

D'amours, Annie. 2011. "Must We Put Dogsleds on Wheels for the Tourist Season? Inuit Heritage, Tourism and Respecting the Community in Kangiqsujuaq." In *Polar Tourism: A Tool for Regional Development*, edited by Alain Grenier and Dieter Müller, 109–25. Montreal: Presses de l'Université du Québec.

Daniel, E. Valentine. 1997. "Suffering Nation and Alienation." In *Social Suffering*, edited by Arthur Kleinman, Veena Das, and Margaret Lock, 309–58. Berkeley: University of California Press.

Darnell, Regna. 1992. "The Boasian Text Tradition and the History of Canadian Anthropology." *Culture* 17: 39–48.

——. 1998. "Toward a History of Canadian Departments of Anthropology: Retrospect, Prospect, and Common Cause." *Anthropologica* 40 (2): 153–69.

——. 2000. "Canadian Anthropologists, the First Nations, and Canada's Self-Image at the Millennium." *Anthropologica* 42 (2): 165–74.

——. 2011. "Nomadic Legacies and Urban Contexts." In *Aboriginal Peoples in Canadian Cities: Transformations and Continuities*, edited by Heather Howard and Craig Proulx, 39–52. Waterloo: Wilfrid Laurier University Press.

Day, Michael H. 1985. "Pliocene Hominids." In *Ancestors: The Hard Evidence*, edited by Eric Delson, 91–3. New York: Alan R. Liss.

——. 1986. "Bipedalism: Pressures, Origins, and Modes." In *Major Topics in Primate and Human Evolution*, edited by Bernard A. Wood, Lawrence B. Martin, and Peter Andrews, 188–202. Cambridge: Cambridge University Press.

Deacon, Terrence. 1997. *The Symbolic Species: The Co-evolution of Language and the Brain*. New York: W.W. Norton.

——. 2003. "The Hierarchic Logic of Emergence: Untangling the Interdependence of Evolution and Self-Organization." In *Evolution and Learning: The Baldwin Effect Reconsidered*, edited by Bruce H. Weber and David J. Depew, 273–308. Cambridge, MA: MIT Press.

Defleur, Alban, Olivier Dutour, Helene Valladas, and Bernard Vandermeersch. 1993. "Cannibals among the Neanderthals?" *Nature* 362: 214.

——, Tim White, Patricia Valensi, Ludovic Slimak, and Evelyne Cregut-Bonnoure. 1999. "Neanderthal Cannibalism at Moula-Guercy, Ardeche, France." *Science* 286: 128–31.

de Heinzelin, Jean, J. Desmond Clark, Tim White, William Hart, Paul Renne, Giday Woldegabriel, Yonas Beyene, and Elisabeth Vrba. 1999. "Environment and Behavior of 2.5-Million-Year-Old Bouri Hominids." *Science* 284 (5414): 625–9.

de Meer, K., R. Bergman, and J.S. Kusner. 1993. "Differences in Physical Growth of Aymara and Quechua Children Living at High Altitude in Peru." *American Journal of Physical Anthropology* 90: 59–75.

Department of Communications, Information Technology, and the Arts. 2005. *Return of Indigenous Cultural Property Program*. Canberra: Government of Australia. http://www.dcita.gov.au/arts/councils/return_of_indigenous_cultural_property_(ricp)_program.

Depew, David J., and Bruce H. Weber. 1989. "The Evolution of the Darwinian Research Tradition." *Systems Research* 6 (3): 255–63.

De Vos, George, and Hiroshi Wagatsuma. 1966. *Japan's Invisible Race*. Berkeley: University of California Press.

de Waal, Frans. 1989. *Peacemaking among Primates*. Cambridge, MA: Harvard University Press.

Dibble, Harold L. 1989. "The Implications of Stone Tool Types for the Presence of Language during the Lower and Middle Palaeolithic." In *The Human Revolution*, edited by P.A. Mellars and C. Stringer, 415–32. Princeton, NJ: Princeton University Press.

Dillehay, Thomas D. 2000. *The Settlement of the Americas*. New York: Basic Books.

Dodson, Mick. 2007. "Bully in the Playground: A New Stolen Generation?" In *Coercive Reconciliation: Stabilise, Normalise, Exit Aboriginal Australia*, edited by Jon Altman and Melinda Hinkson. North Carlton, Australia: Arena Publications Association.

Dokis, Carly. 2015. *Where the Rivers Meet: Pipelines, Participatory Resource Management, and Aboriginal–State Relations in the Northwest Territories*. Vancouver: UBC Press.

Dolgin, Janet. 1995. "Family Law and the Facts of Family." In *Naturalizing Power*, edited by Sylvia Yanagisako and Carol Delaney, 47–67. New York: Routledge.

Doll, Maurice F.V., Robert S. Kidd, and John P. Day. 1988. *The Buffalo Lake Metis Site: A Late Nineteenth Century Settlement in the Parkland of Central Alberta*. Human History Occasional Paper No. 4. Edmonton: Provincial Museum of Alberta.

Dossa, Parin. 2009. *Racialized Bodies, Disabling Worlds: Storied Lives of Immigrant Muslim Women*. Toronto: University of Toronto Press.

Douglas, Mary. 1970. Introduction to *Witchcraft Confessions and Accusations*, edited by Mary Douglas, vi–xxxviii. London: Tavistock.

—— and Baron Isherwood. 1979. *The World of Goods: Towards an Anthropology of Consumption*. New York: W.W. Norton.

Drapeau, Michelle S.M. 2012. "Forelimb Adaptations in Australopithecus Afarensis." In *African Genesis: Perspectives on Hominin Evolution*, edited by Sally C. Reynolds and Andrew Gallagher. Cambridge: Cambridge University Press.

Drewal, Margaret Thompson. 1992. *Yoruba Ritual: Performers, Play, Agency*. Bloomington: Indiana University Press.

Driscoll, Bernadett. 1980. *The Inuit Amautik: I Like My Hood to Be Full*. Winnipeg: Winnipeg Art Gallery.

Dukepoo, Frank C. 1999. "It's More than the Human Genome Diversity Project." *Politics and the Life Sciences* 18: 293–7.

Duranti, Alessandro. 1994. *From Grammar to Politics: Linguistic Anthropology in a Western Samoan Village*. Berkeley: University of California Press.

Durham, William H. 1991. *Coevolution: Genes, Culture, and Human Diversity*. Stanford: Stanford University Press.

Eldredge, Niles. 1985. *Time Frames: The Rethinking of Darwinian Evolution and the Theory of Punctuated Equilibria*. New York: Simon and Schuster.

—— and Ian Tattersall. 1982. *The Myths of Human Evolution*. New York: Columbia University Press.

Elliot, Alison. 1981. *Child Language*. Cambridge: Cambridge University Press.

Engle, Karen. 2001. "From Skepticism to Embrace: Human Rights and the American Anthropological Association from 1947–1999." *Human Rights Quarterly* 23 (3): 536–9.

Errington, Shelly. 1998. *The Death of Authentic Primitive Art and Other Tales of Progress*. Berkeley: University of California Press.

Escobar, Arturo. 1992. "Culture, Economics, and Politics in Latin American Social Movements Theory and Research". In *The Making of Social Movements in Latin America*, edited by Arturo Escobar and Sonia Alvarez, 62–85. Boulder, CO: Westview Press.

Evans-Pritchard, E.E. 1940. *The Nuer*. Oxford: Oxford University Press.

——. 1951. *Kinship and Marriage among the Nuer*. Oxford: Oxford University Press.

——. 1963. *Social Anthropology and Other Essays*. New York: Free Press.

——. (1937) 1976. *Witchcraft, Oracles, and Magic among the Azande*. Abridged ed., prepared by Eva Gillies. Oxford: Oxford University Press.

Fagan, Brian. 1990. *The Journey from Eden*. London: Thames and Hudson.

—— and Christopher DeCorse. 2005. *In the Beginning: An Introduction to Archaeology*. 11th ed. New York: HarperCollins.

Fagen, Robert. 1981. *Animal Play Behavior*. New York: Oxford University Press.

——. 1992. "Play, Fun, and the Communication of Well-Being." *Play and Culture* 5 (1): 40–58.

——. 2005. "Play, Five Gates of Evolution, and Paths to Art." In *Play: An Interdisciplinary Synthesis*, edited by F.F. McMahnon, Donald E. Lytle, and Brian Sutton-Smith, 9–42. Vol. 6 of *Play and Culture Studies*. Lanham, MD: University Press of America.

Farmer, Paul. 2002. "On Suffering and Structural Violence: A View from Below." In *The Anthropology of Politics*, edited by Joan Vincent, 424–37. Malden, MA: Blackwell.

——. 2003. *Pathologies of Power: Health, Human Rights, and the New War on the Poor*. Berkeley: University of California Press.

Fedigan, Linda M. 1986. "The Changing Role of Women in Models of Human Evolution." *Annual Review of Anthropology* 15: 25–66.

Feibel, Craig S., Neville Agnew, Bruce Latimer, Martha Demas, Fiona Marshall, Simon A.C. Waane, and Peter Schmid.

1995/96. "The Laetoli Hominid Footprints: A Preliminary Report on the Conservation and Scientific Restudy." *Evolutionary Anthropology* 4 (5): 149–54.

Feit, Harvey A. 1995. "Hunting and the Quest for Power: The James Bay Cree and Whitemen in the Twentieth Century." In *Native Peoples: The Canadian Experience,* 2nd ed., edited by R.B. Morrison and C.R. Wilson. Toronto: McClelland and Stewart.

Fewkes, J.W. 1923. *Designs of Prehistoric Pottery from the Mimbres Valley, New Mexico.* Washington, DC: Smithsonian Institution Press.

Firth, Raymond. (1936) 1984. *We, the Tikopia.* Reprint, Stanford, CA: Stanford University Press.

Fleagle, John G. 1995. "Origin and Radiation of Anthropoid Primates." In *Biological Anthropology: The State of the Science,* edited by Noel T. Boaz and Linda Wolfe, 1–21. Bend, OR: International Institute for Human Evolutionary Research.

———. 2013. *Primate Adaptation and Evolution.* 3rd ed. Amsterdam: Elsevier/Academic Press.

*Floating on the Air, Followed by the Wind.* 1973. Film distributed by Indiana University Instructional Support Services, Gunter Pfaff (cinematographer) and Ronald A. Simons (psychiatric consultant). East Lansing: Michigan State University.

Foley, Robert. 1995. *Humans before Humanity.* Oxford: Blackwell.

Fonda, Marc. 2011. "Canadian Census Figures on Aboriginal Spiritual Preferences: A Revitalization Movement?" *Religious Studies and Theology* 30 (2): 171–87.

Forge, Anthony. 1967. "The Abelam Artist." In *Social Organization: Essays Presented to Raymond Firth,* edited by Maurice Freedman, 65–84. London: Cass.

Fortes, Meyer. 1953. The Structure of Unilineal Descent Groups. *American Anthropologist* 55: 25–39.

Foucault, Michel. 1991. "Governmentality." In *The Foucault Effect: Studies in Governmentality,* edited by Graham Burchell, Colin Gordon, and Peter Miller, 87–104. Chicago: University of Chicago Press.

Franklin, Sarah. 1995. "Science as Culture, Cultures of Science." *Annual Review of Anthropology* 24: 163–84.

———. 2003. "Re-thinking Nature–Culture: Anthropology and the New Genetics." *Anthropological Theory* 3: 65–85.

Frayer, David, Milford Wolpoff, Alan G. Thorne, Fred H. Smith, and Geoffrey G. Pope. 1993. "Theories of Modern Human Origins: The Paleontological Test." *American Anthropologist* 95 (1): 14–50.

Freeman, Leslie G. 1981. "The Fat of the Land: Notes on Paleolithic Diet in Iberia." In *Omnivorous Primates,* edited by Robert S.O. Harding and Geza Teleki, 104–65. New York: Columbia University Press.

Friedman, Jonathan. 1994. *Cultural Identity and Global Process.* London: Sage.

———. 1997. "Global Crises, the Struggle for Cultural Identity and Intellectual Porkbarrelling: Cosmopolitans versus Locals, Ethnics and Nationals in an Era of Dehegemonisation." In *Debating Cultural Hybridity: Multicultural Identities and the Politics of Anti-racism,* edited by Pnina Werbner and Tariq Modood, 70–89. London: Zed Books.

Gallivan, Martin, and Danielle Moretti-Langholtz. 2007. "Civic Engagement at Werowocomoco: Reasserting Native Narratives from a Powhatan Place of Power." In *Archaeology as a Tool of Civic Engagement,* edited by Barbara J. Little and Paul A. Shackel, 47–66. Lanham, MD: AltaMira Press.

Gamble, Clive. 1994. *Timewalkers.* Cambridge, MA: Harvard University Press.

Gardner, Howard. 2000. *Intelligence Reframed: Multiple Intelligences for the Twenty-First Century.* New York: Basic Books.

Geertz, Clifford. 1973. *The Interpretation of Cultures.* New York: Basic Books.

Geiger, Andrea. 2011. *Subverting Exclusion: Transpacific Encounters with Race, Caste, and Borders, 1885–1928.* New Haven: Yale University Press.

Gentner, Dedre, and Susan Goldin-Meadow. 2003. "Whither Whorf?" In *Language in Mind: Advances in the Study of Language and Thought,* edited by Dedre Gentner and Susan Goldin-Meadow, 3–14. Cambridge, MA: MIT Press.

Georges, Eugenia. 1990. *The Making of a Transnational Community: Migration, Development, and Cultural Change in the Dominican Republic.* New York: Columbia University Press.

Gero, Joan M. 1991. "Genderlithics: Women's Roles in Stone Tool Production." In *Engendering Archaeology,* edited by Margaret Conkey and Joan Gero, 163–93. Oxford: Blackwell.

Giddens, Anthony. 1979. *Central Problems in Social Theory.* Berkeley: University of California Press.

———. 1990. *The Consequences of Modernity.* Stanford: Stanford University Press.

Gillman, Neil. 1992. *Sacred Fragments: Recovering Theology for the Modern Jew.* New York: Jewish Publication Society.

Ginsburg, Faye, and Rayna Rapp. 1995. *Conceiving the New World Order: The Global Politics of Reproduction.* Berkeley: University of California Press.

Gledhill, John. 1994. *Power and Its Disguises.* London: Pluto Press.

Gombay, Nicole. 2010. *Making a Living: Place, Food, and Economy in an Inuit Community.* Saskatoon, SK: Purich Publishing.

Goodman, M., D.A. Tagle, D.H.A. Fitch, W. Bailey, J. Czelusniak, B.F. Koop, P. Benson, and J. L. Slighton. 1990. "Primate Evolution at the DNA Level and a Classification of the Hominoids." *Journal of Molecular Evolution* 30: 260–6.

Goody, Jack, and Stanley Tambiah. 1973. *Bridewealth and Dowry.* Cambridge: Cambridge University Press.

Gordon, Colin. 1991. "Governmental Rationality: An Introduction." In *The Foucault Effect: Studies in Governmentality,* edited by Graham Burchell, Colin Gordon, and Peter Miller, 1–52. Chicago: University of Chicago Press.

Gould, Stephen J. 1987. *Time's Arrow, Time's Cycle.* Cambridge, MA: Harvard University Press.

———. 1996. *Full House: The Spread of Excellence from Plato to Darwin.* New York: Harmony Books.

———. 2002. *The Structure of Evolutionary Theory.* Cambridge, MA: Harvard University Press.

——— and Niles Eldredge. 1977. "Punctuated Equilibria: The Tempo and Mode of Evolution Reconsidered." *Paleobiology* 3: 115–51.

——— and Elisabeth Vrba. 1982. "Exaptation—A Missing Term in the Science of Form." *Palaeobiology* 8: 4–15.

Gramsci, Antonio. 1971. *Selections from the Prison Notebooks.* Translated by Q. Hoare and G.N. Smith. New York: International Publishers.

Green, Richard E., Johannes Krause, Adrian W. Briggs, Tomislav Malicic, Udo Stenzel, Martin Kircher, Nick Patterson, et al. 2010. "A Draft Sequence of the Neandertal Genome." *Science* 328 (5979): 710–22.

Greenfield, Haskel J., Itzhaq Shai, and Aren Maeir. 2012. "Being an 'Ass': An Early Bronze Age Burial of a Donkey from Tell Es-Safi/Gath, Israel." *Bioarchaeology of the Near East* 6: 21–52.

Greenwood, David, and William Stini. 1977. *Nature, Culture, and Human History*. New York: Harper and Row.

Greska, Lawrence P. 1990. "Developmental Responses to High-Altitude Hypoxia in Bolivian Children of European Ancestry: A Test of the Developmental Adaptation Hypothesis." *American Journal of Human Biology* 2: 603–12.

Grinker, Roy Richard. 1994. *Houses in the Rainforest: Ethnicity and Inequality among Farmers and Foragers in Central Africa*. Berkeley: University of California Press.

Guemple, D. Lee. 1979. "Inuit Socialization: A Study of Children as Social Actors in an Eskimo Community." In *Childhood and Adolescence in Canada*, edited by Karigoudar Ishwaran, 39–53. Toronto: McGraw-Hill Ryerson.

Guneratne, Arjun. 2002. "Caste and State." In *South Asian Folklore: An Encyclopedia*, edited by Peter Claus and Margaret Mills. New York: Garland.

Gupta, Dipankar. 2005. "Caste and Politics: Identity over System." *Annual Review of Anthropology* 34: 409–27.

Hacking, Ian. 1991. "How Should We Do the History of Statistics?" In *The Foucault Effect: Studies in Governmentality*, edited by Graham Burchell, Colin Gordon, and Peter Miller, 181–96. Chicago: University of Chicago Press.

Hager, Lori D., ed. 1997. *Women in Human Evolution*. London: Routledge.

Haig-Brown, Celia. 1988. *Resistance and Renewal: Surviving the Indian Residential School*. Vancouver: Tillacum Library.

Haile-Selassie, Yohannes. 2001. "Late Miocene Hominids from Middle Awash." *Nature* 412: 178–81.

———, Gen Suwa, and Tim D. White. 2004. "Late Miocene Teeth from Middle Awash, Ethiopia, and Early Hominid Dental Evolution." *Science* 303: 1503–5.

Hale, Charles. 1997. "Cultural Politics of Identity in Latin America." *Annual Review of Anthropology* 26: 567–90.

Hall, Edward T. 1966. *The Hidden Dimension*. New York: Anchor Books.

Halperin, Rhoda H. 1994. *Cultural Economies: Past and Present*. Austin: University of Texas Press.

Handelman, Don. 1977. "Play and Ritual: Complementary Frames of Meta-communication." In *It's a Funny Thing, Humour*, edited by Antony J. Chapman and Hugh C. Foot, 185–92. London: Pergamon.

Hanks, William. 1996. *Language and Communicative Practices*. Boulder, CO: Westview Press.

Hann, Chris, and Keith Hart. 2011. *Economic Anthropology: History, Ethnography, Critique*. Malden, MA: Polity Press.

Haque, Eve. 2012. *Multiculturalism within a Bilingual Framework: Language, Race, and Belonging in Canada*. Toronto: University of Toronto Press.

Haraway, Donna. 1989. *Primate Visions*. New York: Routledge.

Harris, David. 1989. "An Evolutionary Continuum of People–Plant Interaction." In *Foraging and Farming: The Evolution of Plant Exploitation*, edited by David Harris and Gordon Hillman, 1–30. Vol. 13 of *One World Archaeology*. London: Unwin Hyman.

Harrison, Faye. 1995. "The Persistent Power of 'Race' in the Cultural and Political Economy of Racism." *Annual Review of Anthropology* 24: 47–74.

———. 1998. "Introduction: Expanding the Discourse on 'Race.'" *American Anthropologist* 100 (3): 609–31.

Harrison, Julia, and Regna Darnell, eds. 2006. *Historicizing Canadian Anthropology*. Vancouver: UBC Press.

Harvey, David. 1990. *The Condition of Postmodernity*. Malden, MA: Blackwell.

Hayden, Brian. 1981. "Subsistence and Ecological Adaptations of Modern Hunter/Gatherers." In *Omnivorous Primates*, edited by Robert S.O. Harding and Geza Telecki, 344–421. New York: Columbia University Press.

———. 1995. "Pathways to Power." In *Foundations of Social Inequality*, edited by T. Douglas Price and Gary Feinman, 15–86. New York, Springer.

———, Neil Canuel, and Jennifer Shanse. 2013. "What Was Brewing in the Natufian? An Archaeological Assessment of Brewing Technology in the Epipaleolithic." *Journal of Archaeological Method and Theory* 20 (1): 102–50.

Hedican, Edward. 2008. *Applied Anthropology in Canada: Understanding Aboriginal Issues*. 2nd ed. Toronto: University of Toronto Press.

Heider, Karl. 1979. *Grand Valley Dani*. New York: Holt, Rinehart, and Winston.

Henry, Donald. 1989. *From Foraging to Agriculture: The Levant and the End of the Ice Age*. Philadelphia: University of Pennsylvania Press.

Herdt, Gilbert, ed. 1994. *Third Sex, Third Gender: Beyond Sexual Dimorphism in Culture and History*. New York: Zone Books.

Herrnstein, Richard, and Charles Murray. 1994. *The Bell Curve*. New York: Free Press.

Herskovits, Melville. 1973. *Cultural Relativism*. New York: Vintage Books.

Herzfeld, Michael. 2003. "Competing Diversities: Ethnography in the Heart of Rome." *Plurimundi* 3 (5): 147–54.

———. 2009. *Evicted from Eternity: The Restructuring of Modern Rome*. Chicago: University of Chicago Press.

Hill, Jane, and Judith Irvine, eds. 1992. *Responsibility and Evidence in Oral Discourse*. Cambridge: Cambridge University Press.

Hillman, Gordon. 1989. "Late Paleolithic Plant Foods from Wadi Kubbaniya in Upper Egypt: Dietary Diversity, Infant Weaning, and Seasonality in a Riverine Environment." In *Foraging and Farming: The Evolution of Plant Exploitation*, edited by David Harris and Gordon Hillman, 207–39. Vol. 13 of *One World Archaeology*. London: Unwin Hyman.

Hinkson, Melinda. 2007. "Introduction: In the Name of the Child." In *Coercive Reconciliation: Stabilise, Normalise, Exit Aboriginal Australia*, edited by Jon Altman and Melinda Hinkson, 1–12. North Carlton, Australia: Arena Publications Association.

Hockett, Charles F. 1966. "The Problems of Universals in Language." In *Universals of Language*, edited by Joseph H. Greenberg, 1–29. Cambridge, MA: MIT Press.

Hodder, Ian. 1982. *Symbols in Action*. Cambridge: Cambridge University Press.

Hoffman, Michael A. 1991. *Egypt before the Pharaohs: The Prehistoric Foundations of Egyptian Civilization*. Rev. ed. Austin: University of Texas Press.

Hogberg, A. 2008. "Playing with Flint: Tracing a Child's Imitation of Adult Work in a Lithic Assemblage." *Journal of Archaeological Method and Theory* 15 (1): 112–31.

Holm, John. 1988. *Theory and Structure. Vo. 1 of Pidgins and Creoles*. Cambridge: Cambridge University Press.

Holy, Ladislav. 1996. *Anthropological Perspectives on Kinship*. London: Pluto Press.

Horton, Robin. 1982. "Tradition and Modernity Revisited." In *Rationality and Relativism*, edited by M. Hollis and Steven Lukes, 201–60. Cambridge, MA: MIT Press.

Huang, Alice. 2009. "Languages: Aboriginal Languages in Canada." http://indigenousfoundations.arts.ubc.ca/home/culture/languages.html.

Hublin, J., F. Spoor, M. Braun, F. Zonneveld, and S. Condemi. 1996. "A Late Neanderthal Associated with Upper Palaeolithic Artifacts." *Nature* 381: 224–6.

Hultkrantz, Åke. 1992. *Shamanic Healing and Ritual Drama: Health and Medicine in Native North American Religious Traditions*. New York: Crossroads.

Hunter, David, and Phillip Whitten. 1976. *Encyclopedia of Anthropology*. New York: Harper and Row.

Hutnyk, John. 1997. "Adorno at Womad: South Asian Crossovers and the Limits of Hybridity-Talk." In *Debating Cultural Hybridity: Multicultural Identities and the Politics of Anti-racism*, edited by Pnina Werbner and Tariq Modood, 106–36. London: Zed Books.

Hyde, Sandra. 2007. *Eating Spring Rice: The Cultural Politics of AIDS in Southwest China*. Berkeley: University of California Press.

Hymes, Dell. 1972. "On Communicative Competence." In *Sociolinguistics: Selected Readings*, edited by J.B. Pride and Janet Holmes, 269–93. Baltimore: Penguin.

Inda, Jonathan Xavier, and Renato Rosaldo. 2002. "Introduction: A World in Motion." In *The Anthropology of Globalization*, edited by Jonathan Xavier Inda and Renato Rosaldo. Malden, MA: Blackwell.

Ingold, Tim. 1983. "The Significance of Storage in Hunting Societies." *Man* 18: 553–71.

——. 1994. General introduction to *Companion Encyclopedia of Anthropology*, edited by Tim Ingold, xiii–xxii. London: Routledge.

Isaac, Glynn L., and Diana C. Crader. 1981. "To What Extent Were Early Hominids Carnivorous? An Archaeological Perspective." In *Omnivorous Primates*, edited by Robert S.O. Harding and Geza Teleki, 37–103. New York: Columbia University Press.

Isbell, William H. 1988. "City and State in Middle Horizon Huari." In *Peruvian Prehistory*, edited by Richard W. Keatinge, 164–89. Cambridge: Cambridge University Press.

Jablonski, Nina G. 2004. "The Evolution of Human Skin and Skin Color." *Annual Review of Anthropology* 33: 585–623.

—— and George Chaplin. 2000. "The Evolution of Skin Coloration." *Journal of Human Evolution* 39: 57–106.

Jackson, Michael. 2006. *The Politics of Storytelling: Violence, Transgression, and Intersubjectivity*. Copenhagen: Museum Tusculanum Press.

Jarman, M.R., G.N. Bailey, and H.N. Jarman, eds. 1982. *Early European Agriculture: Its Foundations and Development*. Cambridge: Cambridge University Press.

Jenness, Diamond. 1922. *The Life of the Copper Eskimos*. Ottawa: FA Ackland.

Johansen, R.E. 2006. "Care for Infibulated Women Giving Birth in Norway: An Anthropological Analysis of Health Workers' Management of a Medically and Culturally Unfamiliar Issue." *Medical Anthropology Quarterly* 20 (4): 516–44.

Johanson, Donald, and Maitland A. Edey. 1981. *Lucy: The Beginnings of Humankind*. New York: Simon and Schuster.

Johnson, Matthew. 1999. *Archaeological Theory: An Introduction*. Oxford: Blackwell Publishers.

Jolly, Alison. 1985. *The Evolution of Primate Behaviour*. 2nd ed. New York: Macmillan.

Jones, J.S. 1986. "The Origin of *Homo Sapiens*: The Genetic Evidence." In *Major Topics in Primate and Human Evolution*, edited by B. Wood, L. Martin, and P. Andrews, 317–30. Cambridge: Cambridge University Press.

Jourdan, Christine. 1991. "Pidgins and Creoles: The Blurring of Categories." *Annual Review of Anthropology* 20: 187–209.

Joyce, Rosemary A. 2000. "Girling the Girl and Boying the Boy: The Production of Adulthood in Ancient Mesoamerica." *World Archaeology* 31 (3): 473–83.

——. 2008. *Ancient Bodies, Ancient Lives: Sex, Gender, and Archaeology*. New York: Thames and Hudson.

Kapferer, Bruce. 1983. *A Celebration of Demons*. Bloomington: Indiana University Press.

Karp, Ivan. 1990. Guest editorial in *Cultural Anthropology: A Perspective on the Human Condition*, by Emily Schultz and Robert Lavenda, 74–5. 2nd ed. St Paul, MN: West.

Kawasaki, Tomoe. 2011. Personal statement. In "Inside Japan's 'Gentleman's Agreement'" [photo essay compiled by Masaru Goto]. http://www.majiroxnews.com/2011/02/07/inside-japans-gentlemen-agreement.

Kearney, Michael. 1995. "The Local and the Global: The Anthropology of Globalization and Transnationalism." *Annual Review of Anthropology* 24: 547–65.

Keatinge, Richard W. 1988. "A Summary View of Peruvian Prehistory." In *Peruvian Prehistory*, edited by Richard W. Keatinge, 303–16. Cambridge: Cambridge University Press.

Keesing, Roger. 1982. *Kwaio Religion: The Living and the Dead in a Solomon Island Society*. New York: Columbia University Press.

——. 1992. *Custom and Confrontation: The Kwaio Struggle for Cultural Autonomy*. Chicago: University of Chicago Press.

Kelly, John D., and Martha Kaplan. 2001. *Represented Communities: Fiji and World Decolonization*. Chicago: University of Chicago Press.

Kelly, Raymond. 1993. *Constructing Inequality: The Fabrication of a Hierarchy of Virtue among the Etoro*. Ann Arbor: University of Michigan Press.

Kimbel, William H., Donald C. Johanson, and Yoel Rak. 1994. "The First Skull and Other New Discoveries of *Australopithecus Afarensis* at Hadar, Ethiopia." *Journal of Human Evolution* 31: 549–61.

King, Sarah J. 2013. "Context Matters: Studying Indigenous Religions in North America." *Religion Compass* 7 (11): 498–507.

King, Turi, Gloria Gonzalez Fortes, Patricia Balaresque, Mark G. Thomas, David Balding, Pierpaolo Maisano Delser, Rita Neumann, et al. 2014. "Identification of the Remains of King Richard III." *Nature Communications* 5. http://www.nature.com/ncomms/2014/141202/ncomms6631/full/ncomms6631.html.

Kipp, Rita Smith, and Edward M. Schortman. 1989. "The Political Impact of Trade in Chiefdoms." *American Anthropologist* 91: 370–85.

Kitcher, Philip. 1982. *Abusing Science*. Cambridge, MA: MIT Press.

Klein, Richard G. 2009. *The Human Career: Human Biological and Cultural Origins*. 3rd ed. Chicago: University of Chicago Press.

Koehler, Elizabeth M. 2007. "Repatriation of Cultural Objects to Indigenous Peoples: A Comparative Analysis of US and Canadian Law." *International Lawyer* 41 (1): 103–26.

Köhler, Gernot. 1978. *Global Apartheid*. New York: Institute for World Order.

Kosmin, Barry A., Egon Mayer, and Ariela Keysar. 2001. *American Religious Identification Survey*. The Graduate Center of the City University of New York.

Kral, Michael J., and Lori Idlout. 2006. "Participatory Anthropology in Nunavut," in *Critical Inuit Studies: An Anthology of Contemporary Arctic Ethnography*, edited by Pamela Stern and Lisa Stevenson, 54–69. Lincoln: University of Nebraska Press.

Krause, Johannes, Carles Lalueza-Fox, Ludovic Orlando, Wolfgang Enard, Richard E. Green, Hernan A. Burbano, Jean-Jacques Hublin, et al. 2007. "The Derived FOXP2 Variant of Modern Humans Was Shared with Neandertals." *Current Biology* 17: 1–5.

Krings, Matthias, Helga Geisart, Ralf W. Schmitz, Heike Krainitzki, and Svante Pääbo. 1999. "DNA Sequence of the Mitochondrial Hypervariable Region II from the Neandertal Type Specimen." *Proceedings of the National Academy of Sciences* 95: 5581–5.

——, Anne Stone, Ralf W. Schmitz, Heike Krainitzki, and Mark Stoneking. 1997. "Neandertal DNA Sequences and the Origin of Modern Humans." *Cell* 90: 19–30.

Krmpotich, Cara. 2010. "Remembering and Repatriation: The Production of Kinship, Memory and Respect." *Journal of Material Culture* 15 (2): 157–79.

Kuhn, Thomas. 1979. "Metaphor in Science." In *Metaphor and Thought*, edited by Andrew Ortony, 409–19. Cambridge: Cambridge University Press.

Kuper, Adam. 1982. *Wives for Cattle: Bridewealth and Marriage in Southern Africa*. London: Routledge and Kegan Paul.

——. 1999. *Culture: The Anthropologist's Account*. Cambridge, MA: Harvard University Press.

Laberge, A.M., J. Michaud, A. Richter, E. Lemyre, M. Lambert, B. Brais, and G.A. Mitchell. 2005. "Population History and Its Impact on Medical Genetics in Quebec," *Clinical Genetics* 68 (4): 287–301.

Labrecque, Marie France. 2012. "Gender Mainstreaming and Market Fundamentalist in Rural Yucatan Mexico." In *Confronting Capital: Critique and Engagement in Anthropology*, edited by Pauline Gardiner Barber, Belinda Leach, and Winnie Lem, 222–38. New York: Routledge.

Lahr, Marta, and Robert Foley. 1994. "Multiple Dispersals and Modern Human Origins." *Evolutionary Anthropology* 2: 48–60.

Lakoff, George, and Mark Johnson. 1980. *Metaphors We Live By*. Berkeley: University of California Press.

Lalueza-Fox, Carles, Holger Rompeler, David Caramelli, Claudia Staubert, Giulio Catalano, David Hughes, Nadin Rohland, et al. 2007. "A Melanocortin 1 Receptor Allele Suggests Varying Pigmentation among Neanderthals." *Science* 318: 1453–5.

——, Antonio Rosas, Almudena Estalrrich, Elena Gigli, Paula F. Campos, Antonio Garcia-Tabernero, Samuel Garcia-Vargas, et al. 2010. "Genetic Evidence for Patrilocal Mating Behavior among Neandertal Groups." *PNAS* 108 (1): 250–3. doi:10.1073/pnas.1011553108.

——, Maria Lourdes Sampietro, David Caramelli, Yvonne Puder, Martina Lari, Francesc Calafell, Cayetana Martinez-Maza, et al. 2005. "Neandertal Evolutionary Genetics: Mitochondrial DNA Data from the Iberian Peninsula." *Molecular Biology and Evolution* 22: 1077–81.

Lancaster, Roger. 1992. *Life Is Hard: Machismo, Danger, and the Intimacy of Power in Nicaragua*. Berkeley: University of California Press.

Larkin, Brian. 2002. "Indian Films and Nigerian Lovers: Media and the Creation of Parallel Modernities." In *The Anthropology of Globalization*, edited by Jonathan Xavier Inda and Renato Rosaldo, 350–78. Malden, MA: Blackwell.

Laugrand, Frédéric B., and Jarich G. Oosten. 2010. *Inuit Shamanism and Christianity: Transitions and Transformations in the Twentieth Century*. Montreal: McGill-Queen's University Press.

Lea, Joanne, and Karolyn Smardz Frost. 2012. "Public Archaeology in Canada." In *New Perspectives in Global Public Archaeology*, edited by Katsuyuki Okamura and Akira Matsuda, 57–76. Springer: New York.

Leacock, Eleanor. 1983. "Interpreting the Origins of Gender Inequality: Conceptual and Historical Problems." *Dialectical Anthropology* 7 (4): 263–84.

Leakey, Meave G., Craig S. Feibel, Ian McDougall, and Alan C. Walker. 1995. "New Four-Million-Year-Old Hominid Species from Kanapoi and Allia Bay, Kenya." *Nature* 376: 565–71.

Leca, Jean-Baptiste, Michael A. Huffman, and Paul L. Vasey, eds. 2012. *The Monkeys of Stormy Mountain: Sixty Years of Primatological Research on the Japanese Macaques of Arashiyama*. Cambridge Studies in Biological and Evolutionary Anthropology, no. 61. Cambridge: Cambridge University Press.

Lee, Richard B. 1974. "Male–Female Residence Arrangements and Political Power in Human Hunter–Gatherers." *Archaeology of Sexual Behavior* 3: 167–73.

——. 1992. *The Dobe Ju/'hoansi*. 2nd ed. New York: Holt, Rinehart, and Winston.

—— and Irven DeVore, eds. 1968. *Man the Hunter*. Chicago: Aldine.

Lee, Sandra Soo-Jin, Deborah A. Bolnick, Troy Duster, Pilar Ossorio, and Kimberly Tallbear. 2009. "The Illusive Gold Standard in Genetic Ancestry Testing." *Science* 325: 38–39.

Le Gros Clark, W.E. 1963. *The Antecedents*. 2nd ed. New York: Harper and Row.

Leighton, Donna Robbins. 1987. "Gibbons: Territoriality and Monogamy." In *Primate Societies*, edited by Barbara Smuts, Dorothy Cheney, Robert Seyfarth, Richard Wrangham, and Thomas Struhsaker, 135–45. Chicago: University of Chicago Press.

Leonard, W.R., R.L. Leatherman, J.W. Carey, and R.B. Thomas. 1990. "Contributions of Nutrition versus Hypoxia to Growth in Rural Andean Populations." *American Journal of Human Biology* 2: 612–26.

Lepage, Jean-François, and Jean-Pierre Corbeil. 2013. *The Evolution of English–French Bilingualism in Canada from 1961 to 2011*. Ottawa: Statistics Canada. http://www.statcan.gc.ca/pub/75-006-x/2013001/article/11795-eng.pdf.

Lepofsky, Dana. 2011. "Everyone Loves Archaeology: Bridging Communities through Archaeological Research." *The SAA Archaeological Record* 11 (5): 17–19.

Lerner, I. Michael, and William J. Libby. 1976. *Heredity, Evolution, and Society.* 2nd ed. San Francisco: W.H. Freeman.

Leslie, Paul W., and Michael Little. 2003. "Human Biology and Ecology: Variation in Nature and the Nature of Variation." *American Anthropologist* 105 (1): 28–37.

Levine, Nancy. 1980. "Nyinba Polyandry and the Allocation of Paternity." *Journal of Comparative Family Studies* 11 (3): 283–8.

———. 1988. *The Dynamics of Polyandry: Kinship, Domesticity, and Population on the Tibetan Border.* Chicago: University of Chicago Press.

——— and Walter Sangree. 1980. "Women with Many Husbands: Polyandrous Alliance and Marital Flexibility in Africa and Asia." *Journal of Comparative Family Studies* 11 (3): 325–34.

Levins, Richard, and Richard Lewontin. 1985. *The Dialectical Biologist.* Cambridge, MA: Harvard University Press.

Lévi-Strauss, Claude. 1967. *Structural Anthropology.* Translated by Claire Jacobson and Brooke Grundfest Schoepf. New York: Doubleday Anchor.

Lewis, I.M. 1967. *A Pastoral Democracy: A Study of Pastoralism and Politics among the Northern Somali of the Horn of Africa.* Oxford: Oxford University Press.

Lewis, Philip. 1997. "Arenas of Ethnic Negotiations: Cooperation and Conflict in Bradford." In *The Politics of Multiculturalism in the New Europe: Racism, Identity, and Community,* edited by Tariq Modood and Pnina Werbner, 126–46. London: Zed Books.

Lewin, Roger. 1989. *Human Evolution.* 2nd ed. Boston: Blackwell Scientific Publications.

Lewis-Williams, J. David. 1984. "Ideological Continuities in Prehistoric Southern Africa: The Evidence of the Rock Art." In *Past and Present in Hunter–Gatherer Studies,* edited by Carmel Schrire, 225–52. New York: Academic Press.

Lewontin, Richard. 1972. "The Apportionment of Human Diversity," *Evolutionary Biology* 6: 381–98.

———. 1982. *Human Diversity.* New York: Scientific American Books.

Lieberman, Daniel E., and Dennis M. Bramble. 2007. "The Evolution of Marathon Running." *Sports Medicine* 37 (4/5): 288–90.

Lienhardt, Godfrey. 1961. *Divinity and Experience.* Oxford: Oxford University Press.

Linke, Uli. 1997. "Gendered Difference, Violent Imagination: Blood, Race, Nation." *American Anthropologist* 99 (3): 559–73.

Little, Barbara J., and Paul A. Shackel, eds. 2007. *Archaeology as a Tool of Civic Engagement.* Walnut Creek, CA: AltaMira.

Little, Michael. 1995. "Adaptation, Adaptability, and Multidisciplinary Research." In *Biological Anthropology: The State of the Science,* edited by Noel T. Boaz and Linda Wolfe, 121–47. Bend, OR: International Institute for Human Evolutionary Research.

Liu, Jennifer. 2012a. "Aboriginal Fractions: Enumerating Identity in Taiwan." *Medical Anthropology* 31 (4): 329–46.

———. 2012b. "Asian Regeneration? Technohybridity in Taiwan's biotech." *East Asian Science, Technology and Society* 6 (3): 401–14.

Livingstone, Frank B. 1958. "Anthropological Implications of Sickle Cell Gene Distribution in West Africa." *American Anthropologist* 60: 533–62.

———. 1964. "On the Nonexistence of Human Races." In *The Concept of Race,* edited by M.F. Ashley-Montagu, 46–60. New York: Collier.

Lordkipanidze, David, Marcia S. Ponce de Leon, Ann Margvelashvili, Yoel Rak, G. Philip Rightmire, Abesalom Vekua, and Christopher P.E. Zollikofer. 2013. "A Complete Skull from Dmanisi, Georgia, and the Evolutionary Biology of Early *Homo*," *Science* 342: 326–31.

Lovejoy, Arthur O. (1936) 1960. *The Great Chain of Being.* New York: Harper Torchbooks.

Lovell, Nancy C., and Aaron A. Dublenko. 1999. "Further Aspects of Fur Trade Life Depicted in the Skeleton," *International Journal of Osteoarchaeology* 9 (4): 248–56.

Luhrmann, T.M. 2012. *When God Talks Back: Understanding the American Evangelical Relationship with God.* New York: Vintage Books.

McCoid, Catherine Hidge, and LeRoy D. McDermott. 1996. "Toward Decolonizing Gender: Female Vision in the Upper Paleolithic." *American Anthropologist* 98 (2): 319–26.

McCorriston, Joy, and Frank Hole. 1991. "The Ecology of Seasonal Stress and the Origins of Agriculture in the Near East." *American Anthropologist* 93: 46–69.

McDougall, Ian, Francis H. Brown, and John G. Fleagle. 2005. "Stratigraphic Placement and Age of Modern Humans from Kibish, Ethiopia," *Nature* 433: 733–6.

McHenry, Henry. 1985. "Implications of Postcanine Megadontia for the Origin of *Homo*." In *Ancestors: The Hard Evidence,* edited by E. Delson, 178–83. New York: Alan R. Liss.

——— and L.R. Berger. 1998. "Body Proportions in *Australopithecus Afarensis* and *A. Africanus* and the Origin of the Genus *Homo*." *Journal of Human Evolution* 35: 1–22.

McInnes, Roderick. 2011. "2010 Presidential Address: Culture: The Silent Language Geneticists Must Learn." *American Journal of Human Genetics* 88 (3): 254–61.

McKinnon, Susan, and Sydel Silverman, eds. 2005. *Complexities: Beyond Nature and Nurture.* Chicago: University of Chicago Press.

MacLeod, Carol E., Karl Zilles, Axel Schleicher, James K. Rilling, and Kathleen R. Gibson. 2003. "Expansion of the Neocerebellum in Hominoidea." *Journal of Human Evolution* 44 (4): 401–29.

Malinowski, Bronislaw. 1944. *A Scientific Theory of Culture and Other Essays.* Oxford: Oxford University Press.

———. (1926) 1948. *Magic, Science, and Religion, and Other Essays.* New York: Doubleday Anchor.

Malkki, Liisa. 1992. "National Geographic: The Rooting of Peoples and the Territorialization of National Identity among Scholars and Refugees." *Cultural Anthropology* 7 (1): 24–44.

Mann, Alan E. 1981. "Diet and Human Evolution." In *Omnivorous Primates,* edited by Robert S.O. Harding and Geza Teleki, 10–36. New York: Columbia University Press.

Manson, S.M. 1989. "Alcohol Study: Emphasis on Its Ethical and Procedural Aspects." *American Indian and Alaska Native Mental Health Research* 2: 5–6.

Maquet, Jacques. 1970. "Rwanda Castes." In *Social Stratification in Africa,* edited by Arthur Tuden and Leonard Plotnikov. New York: Free Press.

Marks, Jonathan. 1995. *Human Biodiversity.* New York: Aldine.

———. 2009. *Why I Am Not a Scientist: Anthropology and Modern Knowledge.* Berkeley: University of California Press.

——. 2011. *The Alternative Introduction to Biological Anthropology.* New York: Oxford University Press.

——. 2013. "The Nature/Culture of Genetic Facts." *Annual Review of Anthropology* 42: 247–67. doi: 10.1146/annurev-anthro-092412-155558.

Martin, R.D. 1986. "Primates: A Definition." In *Major Topics in Primate and Human Evolution*, edited by Bernard Wood, Lawrence Martin, and Peter Andrews, 1–31. Cambridge: Cambridge University Press.

——. 1993. "Primate Origins: Plugging the Gaps." *Nature* 363 (20 May): 223–34.

Marx, Karl. 1963. *The Eighteenth Brumaire of Louis Bonaparte.* New York: International Publishers.

Mauss, Marcel. (1950) 2000. *The Gift: The Form and Reason for Exchange in Archaic Societies.* New York: W.W. Norton.

Mayne Correia, Pamela, and Own Beattie. 2002. "A Critical Look at Methods for Recovering, Evaluating, and Interpreting Cremated Human Remains." In *Advances in Forensic Taphonomy: Method, Theory, and Archaeological Perspectives*, edited by William D. Haglund and Marcella H. Sorg, 435–50. Baton Rouge: CRC Press.

Mayr, Ernst. 1982. *The Growth of Biological Thought.* Cambridge, MA: Harvard University Press.

Mellars, Paul. 1996. *The Neandertal Legacy.* Princeton, NJ: Princeton University Press.

—— and Christopher Stringer. 1989. Introduction to *The Human Revolution*, edited by P.A. Mellars and C. Stringer, 1–14. Princeton, NJ: Princeton University Press.

Melotti, Umberto. 1997. "International Migration in Europe: Social Projects and Political Cultures." In *The Politics of Multiculturalism in the New Europe: Racism, Identity and Community*, edited by Tariq Modood and Pnina Werbner, 73–92. London: Zed Books.

Merry, Sally Engle. 2001. "Changing Rights, Changing Culture." In *Culture and Rights: Anthropological Perspectives*, edited by Jane Cowan, Marie-Bénédicte Dembour, and Richard A. Wilson, 31–55. Cambridge: Cambridge University Press.

——. 2003. "Human-Rights Law and the Demonization of Culture." *Anthropology Newsletter* 44 (2).

Meskell, Lynn, ed. 2009. *Cosmopolitan Archaeologies.* Durham, NC: Duke University Press.

Mielke, James H., Lyle W. Konigsberg, and John H. Relethford. 2011. *Human Biological Variation.* New York: Oxford University Press.

Mignolo, Walter D. 2002. "The Many Faces of Cosmo-polis: Border Thinking and Critical Cosmopolitanism." In *Cosmopolitanism*, edited by Carol Breckenridge, Sheldon Pollock, Homi Bhaba, and Dipeesh Chakrabarty, 157–87. Durham, NC: Duke University Press.

Miller, Barbara Diane. 1993. "The Anthropology of Sex and Gender Hierarchies." In *Sex and Gender Hierarchies*, edited by Barbara Diane Miller, 3–31. Cambridge: Cambridge University Press.

Miller, Daniel. 1995. "Consumption and Commodities." *Annual Review of Anthropology* 24: 141–61.

——. 2010. *Stuff.* Cambridge: Polity Press.

—— and Don Slater. 2000. *The Internet: An Ethnographic Approach.* Oxford: Berg.

Milton, Katherine. 1993. "Diet and Primate Evolution." *Scientific American* 269 (2): 86–93.

Mitra, Subrata. 1994. "Caste, Democracy and the Politics of Community Formation in India." In *Contextualizing Caste: Post-Dumontian Approaches*, edited by Mary Searle-Chatterjee and Ursula Sharma, 49–71. Oxford: Blackwell Publishers/Sociological Review.

Modood, Tariq. 1997. "Introduction: The Politics of Multiculturalism in the New Europe." In *The Politics of Multiculturalism in the New Europe: Racism, Identity, and Community*, edited by Tariq Modood and Pnina Werbner, 1–25. London: Zed Books.

Mohatt, Gerald V., Kelly L. Hazel, James Allen, Mary Stachelrodt, Chase Hensel, and Robert Fath. 2004. "Unheard Alaska: Culturally Anchored Participatory Action Research on Sobriety with Alaska Natives." *American Journal of Community Psychology* 33: 263–73.

Molnar, Stephen. 1992. *Human Variation: Races, Types, and Ethnic Groups.* 3rd ed. Englewood Cliffs, NJ: Prentice Hall.

——. 2001. *Human Variation.* New York: Prentice-Hall.

Montgomery, Marc. 2014. "Hot Flashes—Unique to Human Females." Radio Canada International. http://www.rcinet.ca/en/2014/01/08/hot-flashes-unique-to-human-females.

Moore, Sally Falk. 2005. "Comparisons: Possible and Impossible." *Annual Review of Anthropology* 34: 1–11.

Morbeck, Mary Ellen. 1997. "Life History, the Individual and Evolution." In *The Evolutionary Female: A Life-History Perspective*, edited by Mary Ellene Morbeck, Alison Galloway, and Adrienne Zihlman, 3–14. Princeton, NJ: Princeton University Press.

Moreau, Claudia, Claude Bhérer, Hélène Vézina, Michèle Jomphe, Damian Labuda, and Laurent Excoffier. 2011. "Deep Human Genealogies Reveal a Selective Advantage to Be on an Expanding Wave Front," *Science* 334: 1148–50.

Morgan, Lewis Henry. (1877) 1963. *Ancient Society.* Cleveland, OH: Meridian Books.

Morin, Eugene, 2008. "Evidence for Declines in Human Population Densities During the Early Upper Paleolithic in Western Europe." *Proceedings of the National Academy of Sciences* 105 (1): 48–53.

Morris, Craig. 1988. "Progress and Prospect in the Archaeology of the Inca." In *Peruvian Prehistory*, edited by Richard W. Keatinge, 233–56. Cambridge: Cambridge University Press.

Nanda, Serena. 1994. "An Alternative Sex and Gender Role." In *Third Sex, Third Gender*, edited by Gilbert Herdt, 373–417. New York: Zone Books.

Niezen, Ronald. 2003. *The Origins of Indigenism: Human Rights and the Politics of Identity.* Berkeley: University of California Press.

Nishida, Toshisada, and Mariko Hiraiwa-Hasegawa. 1987. "Chimpanzees and Bonobos: Cooperative Relationships among Males." In *Primate Societies*, edited by Barbara Smuts, Dorothy Cheney, Robert Seyfarth, Richard Wrangham, and Thomas Struhsaker, 165–77. Chicago: University of Chicago Press.

Nissen, Hans J. 1988. *The Early History of the Ancient Near East, 9000–2000 BC.* Chicago: University of Chicago Press.

Norris, Mary Jane. 2007. "Aboriginal Languages in Canada: Emerging Trends and Perspectives on Second Language Acquisition," *Canadian Social Trends* 83 (Summer): 20.

Nowell, April. 2013. "All Work and No Play Left Little Time for Art." *New Scientist* 217 (2905): 28–9.

Nuttall, Mark. 2009. "Living in a World of Movement: Human Resilience to Environmental Instability in Greenland." In *Anthropology and Climate Change: From Encounters to Actions*, edited by Susan A. Crate and Mark Nuttall, 292–310. Walnut Creek, CA: Left Coast Press.

Ochs, Elinor. 1986. Introduction to *Language Socialization across Cultures*, edited by Bambi Schieffelin and Elinor Ochs, 1–13. Cambridge: Cambridge University Press.

Odling-Smee, F. John. 1994. "Niche Construction, Evolution and Culture." In *Companion Encyclopedia of Anthropology: Humanity, Culture, and Social Life*, edited by Tim Ingold. London: Routledge.

——, Kevin L. Laland, and Marcus W. Feldman. 2003. *Niche Construction: The Neglected Process in Evolution*. Princeton, NJ: Princeton University Press.

Omohundro, John. 2000. *Careers in Anthropology*. New York: McGraw-Hill.

Ong, Aihwa. 2002. "The Pacific Shuttle: Family, Citizenship, and Capital Circuits." In *The Anthropology of Globalization*, edited by Jonathan Xavier Inda and Renato Rosaldo, 172–97. Malden, MA: Blackwell.

Ortner, Sherry. 1973. "On Key Symbols." *American Anthropologist* 75 (5): 1338–46.

——. 1974. "Is Female to Male as Nature Is to Culture?" In *Woman, Culture, and Society*, edited by Michelle Zimbalist Rosaldo and Louise Lamphere. Stanford, CA: Stanford University Press.

Ortony, Andrew. 1979. "Metaphor: A Multidimensional Problem." In *Metaphor and Thought*, edited by Andrew Ortony, 1–18. Cambridge: Cambridge University Press.

Ottenheimer, Harriet Joseph. 2013. *The Anthropology of Language: An Introduction to Linguistic Anthropology*. 3rd ed. Belmont, CA: Wadsworth.

Oyama, Susan, Paul E. Griffiths, and Russel D. Gray, eds. 2001. *Cycles of Contingency: Developmental Systems and Evolution*. Cambridge, MA: MIT Press.

Park, Robert W. 1998. "Size Counts: The Miniature Archaeology of Childhood in Inuit Societies." *Antiquity* 72 (276): 269–81.

——. 1999. "The Archaeology of Childhood." *Discovering Archaeology* 1 (2): 81–93.

Parkin, David. 1990. Guest editorial in *Cultural Anthropology: A Perspective on the Human Condition*, by Emily Schultz and Robert Lavenda, 90–1. 2nd ed. St Paul, MN: West.

Parsons, Jeffrey R., and Charles M. Hastings. 1988. "The Late Intermediate Period." In *Peruvian Prehistory*, edited by Richard W. Keatinge, 190–229. Cambridge: Cambridge University Press.

Pennington, Renee. 1992. "Did Food Increase Fertility? Evaluation of !Kung and Herero History." *Human Biology* 64: 497–501.

Pfeiffer, Susan, and Louis Lesage. 2014. "The Repatriation of Wendat Ancestors, 2013." *Canadian Journal of Archaeology* 38: 5–12.

Pineda, Rosa Fung. 1988. "The Late Preceramic and Initial Period." In *Peruvian Prehistory*, edited by Richard W. Keatinge, 67–96. Cambridge: Cambridge University Press.

Polanyi, Karl. 1977. *The Livelihood of Man*. New York: Academic Press.

PolarNet. 2015. "Welcome to Nunavut." http://www.polarnet.ca/polarnet/nunavut.htm.

Potts, Richard. 1993. "Archaeological Interpretations of Early Hominid Behavior and Ecology." In *The Origin and Evolution of Humans and Humanness*, edited by D. Tab Rasmussen, 49–74. Boston: Jones and Bartlett.

——. 1996. *Humanity's Descent*. New York: William Morrow.

——. 2012. "Evolution and Environmental Change in Early Human Prehistory," *Annual Review of Anthropology* 41: 151–67.

Powis, Terry G., W. Jeffrey Hurst, María del Carmen Rodríguez, Ortíz C. Ponciano, Michael Blake, David Cheetham, Michael D. Coe, and John G. Hodgson. 2008. "The Origins of Cacao Use in Mesoamerica." *Mexicon 30*: 35–8.

Price, T. Douglas. 1995. "Social Inequality at the Origins of Agriculture." In *Foundations of Social Inequality*, edited by T. Douglas Price and Gary M. Feinman. New York: Plenum Press.

—— and Anne Birgitte Gebauer, eds. 1995. *Last Hunters, First Farmers*. Santa Fe, NM: SAR Press.

Pringle, Heather. 2008. "The Messenger." *Canadian Geographic* (December): 73.

Pullman, Daryl, and Laura Arbour. 2009. "Genetic Research and Culture: Where Does the Offense Lie?" In *The Ethics of Cultural Appropriation*, edited by James O. Young and Conrad G. Brunk, 115–39. Hoboken, NJ: Wiley-Blackwell.

Rackow, Frank. 2013. "The Upside to Menopause." *Homestretch*. CBC Radio One. http://www.cbc.ca/player/Radio/Local+Shows/Alberta/The+Homestretch/ID/2415513090/.

Raff, Jennifer A., and Deborah A. Bolnick. 2014. "Palaeogenomics: Genetic Roots of the First Americans." *Nature 506*: 162–3. doi:10.1038/506162a.

Rasmussen, Morten, Sarah L. Anzick, Michael R. Waters, Pontus Skoglund, Michael DeGiorgio, Thomas W. Stafford Jr, Simon Rasmussen, et al. 2014. "The Genome of a Late Pleistocene Human from a Clovis Burial Site in Western Montana," *Nature 506*: 225–9.

Raymond, J. Scott. 1988. "A View from the Tropical Forest." In *Peruvian Prehistory*, edited by Richard W. Keatinge, 279–300. Cambridge: Cambridge University Press.

Reese-Taylor, Kathryn, Peter Mathews, Julia Guernsey, and Marlene Fritzler. 2009. "Warrior Queens among the Classic Maya." In *Blood and Beauty: Organized Violence in the Art and Archaeology of Mesoamerica and Central America*, edited by Heather Orr and Rex Koontz, 39–72. Los Angeles: Cotsen Institute of Archaeology Press.

Reeves-Ellington, Richard H. 1993. "Using Cultural Skills for Cooperative Advantage in Japan." *Human Organization* 52 (2): 203–16.

Relethford, John. 2001. *Genetics and the Search for Modern Human Origins*. New York: Wiley.

——. 2008. *The Human Species: An Introduction to Biological Anthropology*. 7th ed. New York: McGraw-Hill.

Remie, Cornelius H.W., and Jarich Oosten. 2002. "The Birth of a Catholic Inuit Community: The Transition to Christianity in Pelly Bay, Nunavut, 1935–1950," *Inuit Studies* 26 (1): 109–41.

Renfrew, Colin, and Paul Bahn. 2004. *Archaeology: Theories, Methods and Practice*. 4th ed. London: Thames and Hudson.

——. 2008. *Archaeology: Theories, Methods and Practice*. 5th ed. London: Thames and Hudson.

Rezende, Claudia Barcellos. 1999. "Building Affinity through Friendship." In *The Anthropology of Friendship*, edited by Sandra Bell and Simon Coleman, 79–97. Oxford: Berg.

Richerson, Peter, and Robert Boyd. 2005. *Not by Genes Alone: How Culture Transformed Human Evolution*. Chicago: University of Chicago Press.

—— and Joseph Henrich. 2003. "Cultural Evolution of Human Cooperation." In *Genetic and Cultural Evolution of Cooperation*, edited by Peter Hammerstein, 357–88. Cambridge, MA: MIT Press.

Rick, John W. 1988. "The Character and Context of Highland Preceramic Society." In *Peruvian prehistory*, edited by Richard W. Keatinge, 3–40. Cambridge: Cambridge University Press.

Rightmire, G. Philip. 1990. *The Evolution of* Homo Erectus. Cambridge: Cambridge University Press.

——. 1995. "Diversity within the Genus *Homo*." In *Paleoclimate and Evolution, with Emphasis on Human Origins*, edited by Elisabeth Vrba, George Denton, Timothy Partridge, and Lloyd Burckle. 483–92. New Haven, CT: Yale University Press.

Rindos, David. 1984. *The Origins of Agriculture: An Evolutionary Perspective*. New York: Academic Press.

Ringrose, Katheryn. 1994. "Living in the Shadows: Eunuchs and Gender in Byzantium." In *Third Sex, Third Gender*, edited by Gilbert Herdt, 85–109. New York: Zone Books.

Rogers, Alan R., David Iltis, and Stephen Wooding. 2004. "Genetic Variation at the MC1R Locus and the Time Since Loss of Human Body Hair." *Current Anthropology* 45: 105–7.

Romaniuk, Tanya. 2009. "The 'Clinton Cackle': Hillary Rodham Clinton's Laughter in News Interviews." *Crossroads of Language, Interaction, and Culture* 7: 17–49.

Rosas, Antonio, Cayetana Martinez-Maza, Markus Bastir, Antonio Garcia-Tabernero, Carles Lalueza-Fox, Rosa Huguet, José Eugenio Ortiz, et al. 2006. "Paleobiology and Comparative Morphology of a Late Neandertal Sample from El Sidron, Asturias, Spain." *Proceedings of the National Academy of Sciences* 103: 15266–71.

Roscoe, Will. 1994. "How to Become a Berdache: Toward a Unified Analysis of Gender Diversity." In *Third Sex, Third Gender*, edited by Gilbert Herdt, 329–72. New York: Zone Books.

Rose, Kenneth. 1994. "The Earliest Primates." *Evolutionary Anthropology* 3 (5): 159–73.

Rothwell, Norman V. 1977. *Human Genetics*. Englewood Cliffs, NJ: Prentice-Hall.

Rouhani, Shahin. 1989. "Molecular Genetics and the Pattern of Human Evolution: Plausible and Implausible Models." In *The Human Revolution*, edited by Robert S.O. Mellars and C. Stringer, 47–61. Princeton, NJ: Princeton University Press.

Royal C.D., J. Novembre, S.M. Fullerton, D.B. Goldstein, J.C. Long, M.J. Bamshad, A.G. Clark. 2010. "Inferring Genetic Ancestry: Opportunities, Challenges, and Implications." *American Journal of Human Genetics* 86: 661–73.

Roy-Gagnon, Marie-Hélène, Claudia Moreau, Claude Beherer, Pascal St-Onge, Daniel Sinnett, Catherine Laprise, Hélène Vézina, and Damian Labuda. 2011. "Genomic and Genealogical Investigation of the French Canadian Founder Population Structure," *Human Genetics* 129 (5): 521–31.

Rubertone, Patricia. 2007. "The Scrapbook Exercise: Teaching Archaeology of Death as Critical Thinking." In *Archaeology to Delight and Instruct*, edited by Heather Burke and Claire Smith, 255–65. Walnut Creek, CA: Left Coast Press.

Sable, Trudy, and Bernie Francis. 2012. *The Language of This Land, Mi'kma'ki*. Sydney, NS: Cape Breton University Press.

Sahlins, Marshall. 1972. *Stone Age Economics*. Chicago: Aldine.

——. 1976. *Culture and Practical Reason*. Chicago: University of Chicago Press.

Salisbury, Richard F. 1986. *A Homeland for the Cree: Regional Development in James Bay 1971–1981*. Montreal: McGill-Queen's University Press.

——, N. Elberg, and R.H. Schneider. 1974. *Development? Attitudes to Development among the Native Peoples of the Mackenzie District*. Montreal: McGill Programme in the Anthropology of Development.

——, F. Filion, F. Rawji, and D.A. Stewart. 1972. *Development and James Bay: Social Implications of the Proposals for the Hydroelectric Scheme*. Montreal: McGill Programme in the Anthropology of Development.

Sanderson, John. 2007. "Reconciliation and the Failure of Neo-liberal Globalisation." In *Coercive Reconciliation: Stabilise, Normalise, Exit Aboriginal Australia*, edited by Jon Altman and Melinda Hinkson, 31–6. North Carlton, Australia: Arena Publications Association.

Sanjek, Roger. 1994. "The Enduring Inequalities of Race." In *Race*, edited by Stephen Gregory and Roger Sanjek, 1–17. New Brunswick, NJ: Rutgers University Press.

Sapir, Edward. (1933) 1966. *Culture, Language, and Personality*, edited by David Mandelbaum. Berkeley: University of California Press.

Schiffauer, Werner. 1997. "Islam as a Civil Religion: Political Culture and the Organisation of Diversity in Germany." In *The Politics of Multiculturalism in the New Europe: Racism, Identity, and Community*, edited by Tariq Modood and Pnina Werbner, 147–66. London: Zed Books.

Schiller, Nina Glick, and Georges Fouron. 2001. *Georges Woke Up Laughing: Long-Distance Nationalism and the Search for Home*. Durham, NC: Duke University Press.

——. 2002. "Long-Distance Nationalism Defined." In *The Anthropology of Politics*, edited by Joan Vincent, 356–65. Malden, MA: Blackwell.

Schneider, David. 1968. *American Kinship: A Cultural Account*. Englewood Cliffs, NJ: Prentice-Hall.

Schreyer, Christine. 2011. "Media, Information, Technology, and Language Planning: What Can Endangered Language Communities Learn from Created Language Communities?" *Current Issues in Language Planning* 12 (3): 403–25.

Schultz, Emily. 1984. "From Pagan to Pullo: Ethnic Identity Change in Northern Cameroon." *Africa* 54 (1): 46–64.

——. 1990. *Dialogue at the Margins: Whorf, Bakhtin, and Linguistic Relativity*. Madison: University of Wisconsin Press.

——. 2009. "Resolving the Anti-antievolutionism Dilemma: A Brief for Relational Evolutionary Thinking in Anthropology." *American Anthropologist* 111 (2): 224–37.

Schwartzman, Helen. 1978. *Transformations: The Anthropology of Children's Play*. New York: Plenum Press.

Scott, James. 1987. *Weapons of the Weak*. New Haven, CT: Yale University Press.

——. 1990. *Domination and the Arts of Resistance*. New Haven, CT: Yale University Press.

Semaw, S., J. Renne, J.W.K. Harris, C.S. Feibel, R.L. Bernor, N. Fesseha, and K. Mowbray. 1997. "2.5-Million-Year-Old Stone Tools from Gona, Ethiopia." *Nature* 385: 333–6.

Senut, Brigitte, Martin Pickford, Dominique Gommery, Pierre Mein, Kiptalam Cheboi, and Yves Coppens. 2001. "First Hominid from the Miocene (Lukeino Formation, Kenya)." *Comptes Rendus Des Seances de l'Academie Des Sciences* 332: 137–44.

Service, Elman. 1962. *Primitive Social Organization*. New York: Random House.

Shanks, Michael, and Christopher Tilley. 1987. *Social Theory and Archaeology*. Oxford: Polity Press.

Sharma, Ursula. 1999. *Caste*. Buckingham, UK: Open University Press.

Shepherd, Gil. 1987. "Rank, Gender, and Homosexuality: Mombasa as a Key to Understanding Sexual Options." In *The Cultural Construction of Sexuality*, edited by Pat Caplan, 240–70. London: Tavistock.

Shipman, Pat. 1984. "Scavenger Hunt." *Natural History* (April): 22–7.

Shostak, Marjorie. 1981. *Nisa: The Life and Words of a !Kung Woman*. New York: Vintage.

Silcox, Mary T. 2013. "Primate Origins." in *A Companion to Paleoanthropology*, edited by D.R. Begun, 339–57. Oxford: Blackwell.

Silk, Joan. 2003. "Cooperation without Counting: The Puzzle of Friendship." In *Genetic and Cultural Evolution of Cooperation*, edited by Peter Hammerstein, 37–54. Cambridge, MA: MIT Press.

Silverstein, Michael. 1976. "Shifters, Linguistic Categories, and Cultural Description." In *Meaning in Anthropology*, edited by Keith Basso and Henry Selby, 11–55. Albuquerque: University of New Mexico Press.

——. 1985. "The Functional Stratification of Language and Ontogenesis." In *Culture, Communication, and Cognition: Vygotskian Perspectives*, edited by James Wertsch, 205–35. Cambridge: Cambridge University Press.

Simons, Elwyn L. 1985. "Origins and Characteristics of the First Hominids." In *Ancestors: The Hard Evidence*, edited by E. Delson, 37–41. New York: Alan R. Liss.

—— and D. Tab Rasmussen. 1994. "A Whole New World of Ancestors: Eocene Australopithecines from Africa." *Evolutionary Anthropology* 3 (4): 129–39.

Singer, Merrill. 1998. "The Development of Critical Medical Anthropology: Implications for Biological Anthropology." In *Building a New Biocultural Synthesis*, edited by Alan H. Goodman and Thomas L. Leatherman, 93–123. Ann Arbor: University of Michigan Press.

Singer, Natasha. 2007. "Is Looking Your Age Now Taboo?" *New York Times*, March 1, E1, E3.

Skinner, Mark, Heather P. York, and Melissa A. Connor. 2002. "Postburial Disturbance of Graves in Bosnia-Herzegovina." In *Advances in Forensic Taphonomy: Method, Theory, and Archaeological Perspectives*, edited by William D. Haglund and Marcella H. Sorg, 293–308. Boca Raton, FL: CRC Press.

Skinner, Matthew M., Bernard A. Wood, Christophe Boesch, Anthony J. Olejnczak, Antonio Rosas, Tanya M. Smith, and Jean-Jacques Hublin. 2008. "Dental Trait Expression at the Enamel-Dentine Junction of Lower Molars in Extant and Fossil Hominoids." *Journal of Human Evolution* 54: 173–86.

Slobin, Dan. 1987. "Thinking for Speaking." *Proceedings of the Berkeley Linguistics Society* 13: 435–44.

——. 2003. "Language and Thought Online: Cognitive Consequences of Linguistic Relativity." In *Language in Mind: Advances in the Study of Language and Thought*, edited by Dedre Gentner and Susan Goldin-Meadow, 157–91. Cambridge, MA: MIT Press.

Smart, Alan. 1999. "Expressions of Interest: Friendship and Guanzi in Chinese Societies." In *The Anthropology of Friendship*, edited by Sandra Bell and Simon Coleman, 119–36. Oxford: Berg.

—— and Josephine Smart. 2011. "(Im)mobilizing Technology: Slow Science, Food Safety, and Borders," *Identities: Global Studies in Culture and Power* 18 (6): 529–50.

Smedley, Audrey. 1995. *Race in North America: Origin and Evolution of a Worldview*. Boulder, CO: Westview Press.

——. 1998. "'Race' and the Construction of Human Identity." *American Anthropologist* 100 (3): 690–702.

Smith, Bruce. 1995. *The Emergence of Agriculture*. New York: Scientific American Library.

Smith, Gavin A., and R. Brooke Thomas. 1998. "What Could Be: Biocultural Anthropology for the Next Generation." In *Building a New Biocultural Synthesis*, edited by Alan H. Goodman and Thomas L. Leatherman, 451–73. Ann Arbor: University of Michigan Press.

Smith, M.G. (1954) 1981. Introduction to *Baba of Karo*, by Mary Smith. New Haven, CT: Yale University Press.

Smith, Patricia Elaine. 1998. "When Small Pots Speak: The Stories They Tell." Master's thesis, McMaster University.

So, Joseph K. 1980. "Human Biological Adaptation to Arctic and Subarctic Zones." *Annual Review of Anthropology* 9: 63–82.

Sonntag, Selma K. 2003. *The Local Politics of Global English*. Lanham, MD: Lexington Books.

Spector, Janet D. 1993. *What This Awl Means*. St Paul: Minnesota Historical Society Press.

Spencer, Jonathan. 2000. "On Not Becoming a 'Terrorist': Problems of Memory, Agency, and Community in the Sri Lankan Conflict." In *Violence and Subjectivity*, edited by Veena Das, Arthur Kleinman, Mamphela Ramphele, and Pamela Reynolds, 120–40. Berkeley: University of California Press.

Spiro, Melford. 1977. *Kinship and Marriage in Burma: A Cultural and Psychodynamic Account*. Berkeley: University of California Press.

Stammbach, Eduard. 1987. "Desert, Forest and Montane Baboons: Multilevel Societies." In *Primate Societies*, edited by Barbara Smuts, Dorothy Cheney, Robert Seyfarth, Richard Wrangham, and Thomas Struhsaker, 112–20. Chicago: University of Chicago Press.

Stanley, Steven M. 1981. *The New Evolutionary Timetable*. New York: Basic Books.

Starn, Orin. 1999. *Nightwatch: The Making of a Movement in the Peruvian Andes*. Durham, NC: Duke University Press.

Statistics Canada. 2012. *Aboriginal Languages in Canada*. Catalogue no. 98-314-X2011003. Ottawa: Statistics Canada. http://www12.statcan.gc.ca/census-recensement/2011/as-sa/98-314-x/98-314-x2011003_3-eng.pdf.

Steegmann, A.T. 1977. "Finger Temperatures During Work in Natural Cold: The Northern Ojibwa." *Human Biology* 49 (3): 349–62.

Steiner, Christopher. 1994. *African Art in Transit*. Cambridge: Cambridge University Press.

Stewart, Charles, and Rosalind Shaw. 1994. *Syncretism/Anti-syncretism*. London: Routledge.

Stewart, Kelly J, and Alexander H. Harcourt. 1987. "Gorillas: Variation in Female Relationships." In *Primate Societies*, edited by Barbara Smuts, Dorothy Cheney, Robert Seyfarth, Richard Wrangham, and Thomas Struhsaker, 155–64. Chicago: University of Chicago Press.

Stock, Jay, and Susan Pfeiffer. 2001. "Linking Structural Variability in Long Bone Diaphyses to Habitual Behaviors: Foragers from the Southern African Later Stone Age and the Andaman Islands." *American Journal of Physical Anthropology* 115: 337–48.

Stoler, Ann L. 1997. "Making Empire Respectable: The Politics of Race and Sexual Morality in Twentieth-Century Colonial Cultures." In *Situated Lives*, edited by Louise Lamphere, 373–99. New York: Routledge.

Strathern, Marilyn. 1988. *The Gender of the Gift*. Berkeley: University of California Press.

——. 1992. *Reproducing the Future: Anthropology, Kinship, and the New Reproductive Technologies*. New York: Routledge.

Stringer, Chris. 2012. *Lone Survivors: How We Came to Be the Only Humans on Earth*. New York: Holt.

—— and Peter Andrews. 2005. *The Complete World of Human Evolution*. London, New York: Thames and Hudson.

Struhsaker, T., and L. Leland. 1987. "Colobines: Infanticide by Adult Males." In *Primate Societies*, edited by Barbara Smuts, Dorothy Cheney, Robert Seyfarth, Richard Wrangham, and Thomas Struhsaker, 83–97. Chicago: University of Chicago Press.

Strum, Shirley, Donald G. Lindburg, and David Hamburg, eds. 1999. *The New Physical Anthropology: Science, Humanism, and Critical Reflection*. Upper Saddle River, NJ: Prentice Hall.

Summers, Lawrence H. 2005. "Remarks at NBER Conference on Diversifying the Science and Engineering Workforce." Cambridge, MA: President and Fellows of Harvard College. http://www.harvard.edu/president/speeches/summers_2005/nber.php.

Suplee, Curt. 1997. "Find May Rewrite America's Prehistory." *Washington Post*, February 11, A2.

Susman, Randall L., Jack T. Stern Jr, and William L. Jungers. 1985. "Locomotor Adaptations in the Hadar Hominids." In *Ancestors: The Hard Evidence*, edited by E. Delson, 184–92. New York: Alan R. Liss.

Sussman, Robert. 1991. "Primate Origins and the Evolution of Angiosperms." *American Journal of Physical Anthropology* 23: 209–23.

—— and Paul A. Garber. 2004. "Rethinking Sociality: Cooperation and Aggression among Primates." In *The Origins and Nature of Sociality*, edited by Robert W. Sussman and Audrey R. Chapman, 161–90. New York: Aldine de Gruyter.

Szathmáry, Emőke. 1986. "Diabetes in Arctic and Subarctic Populations Undergoing Acculturation." *Collegium Antropologium* 10: 145–158.

Tamari, Tal. 1991. "The Development of Caste Systems in West Africa." *Journal of African History* 32: 221–50.

Tannen, Deborah. 1990. *You Just Don't Understand: Women and Men in Conversation*. New York: William Morrow.

Tattersall, Ian. 2012. *Masters of the Planet: The Search for Our Human Origins*. New York: Palgrave-Macmillan.

——. 1998. *Becoming Human: Evolution and Human Uniqueness*. San Diego: Harcourt Brace.

——. 2009. *The Fossil Trail*. 2nd ed. New York: Oxford University Press.

—— and Rob DeSalle. 2011. *Race? Debunking a Scientific Myth*. College Station: Texas A and M Press.

Thomas, David Hurst, Robert L. Kelly, and Peter C. Dawson. 2009. *Archaeology*. 1st Canadian ed. Toronto: Nelson Education.

Thomas, Nicholas. 1991. *Entangled Objects*. Cambridge, MA: Harvard University Press.

——. 1996. "Cold Fusion." *American Anthropologist* 98: 9–25.

Thorne, Alan G., and Milford H. Wolpoff. 1992. The Multiregional Evolution of Humans. *Scientific American* (April): 76–83.

Tonkinson, Robert. 1998. "National Identity: Australia after Mabo." In *Pacific Answers to Western Hegemony: Cultural Practices of Identity Construction*, edited by Jürg Wassmann, 287–310. Oxford: Berg.

Trawick, Margaret. 2002. "Reasons for Violence: A Preliminary Ethnographic Account of the LTTE." In *Conflict and Community in Contemporary Sri Lanka*, edited by Siri Gamage and I.B. Watson, 153–80. Thousand Oaks, CA: Sage.

Treble, Patricia. 2015. "Canada's Connection to King Richard III: The Inside Story." *Maclean's*, 22 March, i. http://www.macleans.ca/society/canadas-connection-to-king-richard-iii-the-inside-story.

Trigger, Bruce. 1993. *Early Civilizations: Ancient Egypt in Context*. Cairo: American University in Cairo Press.

Trouillot, Michel-Rolph. 1991. "Anthropology and the Savage Slot: The Poetics and Politics of Otherness." In *Recapturing Anthropology*, edited by Richard Fox, 17–44. Santa Fe, NM: SAR Press.

——. 1994. "Culture, Color and Politics in Haiti." In *Race*, edited by Stephen Gregory and Roger Sanjek, 146–74. New Brunswick, NJ: Rutgers University Press.

Truth and Reconciliation Commission of Canada. 2015. "Honouring the Truth, Reconciling for the Future: Summary of the Final Report of the Truth and Reconciliation Commission of Canada." http://www.trc.ca/websites/trcinstitution/File/2015/Exec_Summary_2015_06_25_web_0.pdf.

Tsing, Anna Lowenhaupt. 2005. *Friction: An Ethnography of Global Connection*. Princeton, NJ: Princeton University Press.

Turner, Victor. 1969. *The Ritual Process*. Chicago: Aldine.

Tylor, E.B. (1871) 1958. *Primitive Culture*. New York: Harper and Row.

UN (United Nations). 2015a. "International Day of Zero Tolerance for Female Genital Mutilation." http://www.un.org/en/events/femalegenitalmutilationday.

UN (United Nations). 2015b. "United Nations Treaty Collection: Convention on the Elimination of All Forms of Discrimination against Women." https://treaties.un.org/Pages/ViewDetails.aspx?src=TREATY&mtdsg_no=IV-8&chapter=4&lang=en.

Underwood, Jane H. 1979. *Human Variation and Human Microevolution*. Englewood Cliffs, NJ: Prentice-Hall.

US Department of Energy. 2014. "Human Genome Project Information Archive 1990–2003." http://web.ornl.gov/sci/techresources/Human_Genome/index.shtml.

Valdez, Lidio M., Katrina J. Bettcher, and J. Ernesto Valdez. 2010. "Production of Maize Beer at a Wari Site in the Ayacucho Valley, Peru." *Arqueología Iberoamericana* 5: 25–35.

van den Berghe, Pierre. 1970. "Race, Class, and Ethnicity in South Africa." In *Social Stratification in Africa*, edited by Arthur Tuden and Leonard Plotnikov, 345–71. New York: Free Press.

van der Veer, P.T. 1997. "'The Enigma of Arrival': Hybridity and Authenticity in the Global Space." In *Debating Cultural Hybridity: Multicultural Identities and the Politics of Anti-racism*, edited by Pnina Werbner and Tariq Modood, 90–105. London: Zed Books.

Van Gennep, Arnold. 1960. *The Rites of Passage*. Chicago: University of Chicago Press.

van Willigen, John, and V.C. Channa. 1991. "Law, Custom, and Crimes against Women." *Human Organization* 50 (4): 369–77.

Vasey, Paul, and Doug VanderLaan. 2012. "Is Female Homosexual Behavior in Japanese Macaques Truly Sexual?" In *The Monkeys of Stormy Mountain: Sixty Years of Primatological Research on the Japanese Macaques of Arashiyama,* edited by Jean-Baptiste Leca, Michael A. Huffman, and Paul L. Vasey, 153–72. Cambridge: Cambridge University Press.

Vaughan, James. 1970. "Caste Systems in the Western Sudan." In *Social Stratification in Africa,* edited by Arthur Tuden and Leonard Plotnikov, 59–92. New York: Free Press.

———. 1973. "Engkyagu as Artists in Marghi Society." In *The Traditional Artist in African Societies,* edited by Warren d'Azevedo, 162–93. Bloomington: Indiana University Press.

Vessey, Rachelle. 2014. "Borrowed Words, Mock Language, and Nationalism in Canada." *Language and Intercultural Communication* 14 (2): 176–90.

Vincent, Joan. 2002. Introduction to *The Anthropology of Politics,* edited by Joan Vincent, 1–13. Malden, MA: Blackwell.

Voloshinov, V.N. (1926) 1987. "Discourse in Life and Discourse in Art." In *Freudianism,* edited translated by I.R. Titunik, in collaboration with Neil H. Bruss, 93–116. Bloomington: Indiana University Press.

Wade, Nicholas. 2014. *A Troublesome Inheritance: Genes, Race and Human History.* New York: Penguin Press.

Waldram, James B. 2010. "Engaging Engagement: Critical Reflections on a Canadian Tradition." *Anthropologica* 52 (2): 225–32.

Walker, Alan. 1993. "The Origin of the Genus *Homo.*" In *The Origin and Evolution of Humans and Humanness,* edited by D. Tab Rasmussen. Sudbury, MA: Jones and Bartlett.

Wallace, Anthony F.C. 1966. *Religion: An Anthropological View.* New York: Random House.

———. 1972. *The Death and Rebirth of the Seneca.* New York: Vintage.

Wallerstein, Immanuel. 1974. *The Modern-World System: Capitalist Agriculture and the Origins of the European World-Economy in the Sixteenth Century.* New York: Academic Press.

Wallmann, Joel. 1992. *Aping Language.* Cambridge: Cambridge University Press.

Walsh, Andrew. 2007. "Ethnographic Alchemy: Perspectives on Anthropological Work from Northern Madagascar." In *Anthropology Put to Work,* edited by Les W. Field and Richard G. Fox, 201–16. New York: Berg.

———. 2012. *Made in Madagascar: Sapphires, Ecotourism, and the Global Bazaar.* Toronto: University of Toronto Press.

Walsh, Michael. 2005. "Will Indigenous Languages Survive?" *Annual Review of Anthropology* 34: 293–315.

Warner, W. Lloyd. 1936. "American Caste and Class." *American Sociological Review* 42 (2): 237–57.

Washburn, Sherwood, and C.S. Lancaster. 1968. "The Evolution of Hunting." In *Man the Hunter,* edited by R. Lee and I. DeVore, 293–303. Chicago: Aldine.

Waters, Michael R., Steven L. Forman, Thomas A. Jennings, Lee C. Nordt, Steven G. Driese, Joshua M. Feinberg, Joshua L. Keene, et al. 2011. "The Buttermilk Creek Complex and the Origins of Clovis at the Debra L. Friedkin Site, Texas." *Science* 331: 1599–1603.

Weatherford, Jack. 1988. *Indian Givers: How the Indians of the Americas Transformed the World.* New York: Fawcett.

Weaver, Sally M. 1997. "An Assessment of the Federal Self-Government Policy." In *Justice for Natives: Searching for Common Ground,* edited by Andrea P. Morrison. Montreal: McGill-Queen's University Press.

Webster, David. 1975. "Warfare and the Evolution of the State: A Reconsideration." *American Antiquity* 40: 471–75.

Weiner, Annette. 1980. "Stability in Banana Leaves: Colonization and Women in Kiriwina, Trobriand Islands." In *Women and Colonization: Anthropological Perspectives,* edited by Mona Etienne and Eleanor Leacock, 270–93. New York: Praeger.

———. 1990. Guest editorial in *Cultural Anthropology: A Perspective on the Human Condition,* by Emily Schultz and Robert Lavenda, 392–3. 2nd ed. St Paul, MN: West.

Wellcome Trust. 2014. "Genomes of Richard III and His Living Descendants to Be Sequenced." http://www.wellcome.ac.uk/News/Media-office/Press-releases/2014/WTP055654.htm.

Wenke, Robert J. 1999. *Patterns in Prehistory: Humankind's First Three Million Years.* 4th ed. Oxford: Oxford University Press.

——— and Deborah I. Olszewski. 2007. *Patterns in Prehistory: Humankind's First Three Million Years.* 5th ed. New York: Oxford University Press.

Werbner, Pnina. 1997. "Introduction: The Dialectics of Cultural Hybridity." In *Debating Cultural Hybridity: Multi-cultural Identities and the Politics of Anti-racism,* edited by Pnina Werbner and Tariq Modood. 1–26. London: Zed Books.

West-Eberhard, Mary Jane. 2003. *Developmental Plasticity and Evolution.* Oxford: Oxford University Press.

Weston, Kath. 1991. *Families We Choose: Lesbians, Gays, Kinship.* New York: Columbia University Press.

———. 1995. "Forever Is a Long Time: Romancing the Real in Gay Kinship Ideologies." In *Naturalizing Power,* edited by Sylvia Yanagisako and Carol Delaney, 87–110. New York: Routledge.

White, Leslie. 1949. *The Science of Culture.* New York: Grove Press.

White, Tim D., B. Asfaw, Y. Beyene, Y. Haile-Selassie, C.O. Lovejoy, G. Suwa, and G. Wolde-Gabriel. 2009. "*Ardipithecus Ramidus* and the Paleobiology of Early Hominids." *Science* 326: 64, 75–86.

———, Berhane Asfaw, David DeGusta, Henry Gilvert, Gary D. Richards, Gen Suwa, and F. Clark Howell. 2003. "Pleistocene *Homo Sapiens* from Middle Awash, Ethiopia." *Nature* 423: 742–7.

———, Gen Suwa, and Berhane Asfaw. 1994. "*Australopithecus Ramidus,* a New Species of Early Hominid from Aramis, Ethiopia." *Nature* 371: 306–12.

———, Gen Suwa, William K. Hart, Robert C. Walter, Giday WoldeGabriel, Jean de Heinzelin, J. Desmond Clark, Berhane Asfaw, and Elisabeth Vrba. 1993. "New Discoveries of *Australopithecus* at Maka in Ethiopia." *Nature* 366: 261–5.

Whitten, Patricia L. 1987. "Infants and Adult Males." In *Primate Societies,* edited by Barbara Smuts, Dorothy Cheney, Robert Seyfarth, Richard Wrangham, and Thomas Struhsaker, 343–57. Chicago: University of Chicago Press.

Whorf, Benjamin Lee. 1956. *Language, Thought, and Reality.* Cambridge, MA: MIT Press.

Wieringa, Saskia, and Evelyn Blackwood. 1999. Introduction to *Female Desires: Same-Sex Relations and Transgender Practices across Cultures,* edited by Evelyn Blackwood and Saska Wieringa, 1–38. New York: Columbia University Press.

Wilgosh, L., R. Mulcahy and, B. Watters. 1986. "Assessing Intellectual Performance of Culturally Different, Inuit Children with the WISC-R." *Canadian Journal of Behavioural Science* 18 (3): 270–7.

Wilk, Richard. 1996. *Economies and Cultures: Foundations of Economic Anthropology.* Boulder, CO: Westview Press.

Williams, Brackette F. 1989. "A Class Act: Anthropology and the Race to Nation across Ethnic Terrain." *Annual Review of Anthropology* 18: 401–44.

Willoughby, Pamela. 2007. *The Evolution of Modern Humans in Africa: A Comprehensive Guide.* Lanham, MD: AltaMira Press.

——. and Benjamin Collins. 2010. "The Faunal Analysis of Magubike and Mlambalasi, Two MSA-LSA Archaeological Sites from Iringa District, Tanzania." *Journal of Taphonomy* 8 (1): 33–68.

Wilson, Allan C., and Rebecca L. Cann. 1992. "The Recent African Genesis of Humans." *Scientific American* (April): 68–73.

Wilson, David Sloan. 2002. *Darwin's Cathedral: Evolution, Religion, and the Nature of Society.* Chicago: University of Chicago Press.

Wilson, E.O. 1980. *Sociobiology: The New Synthesis.* Cambridge, MA: Harvard University Press.

Wittfogel, Karl. 1957. *Oriental Despotism: A Comparative Study of Total Power.* New Haven, CT: Yale University Press.

Wolcott, Harry F. 1999. *Ethnography: A Way of Seeing.* Walnut Creek, CA: AltaMira Press.

Wolf, Eric. 1982. *Europe and the People without History.* Berkeley: University of California Press.

——. 1994. "Facing Power: Old Insights, New Questions." In *Assessing Cultural Anthropology*, edited by Robert Borofsky, 218–28. New York: McGraw-Hill.

Wolfe, Linda. 1995. "Current Research in Field Primatology." In *Biological Anthropology: The State of the Science*, Noel T. Boaz and Linda Wolfe, 149–67. Bend, OR: International Institute for Human Evolutionary Research.

Wolpoff, Milford H. 1985. "Human Evolution at the Peripheries: The Pattern at the Eastern Edge." In *Hominid Evolution: Past, Present and Future*, edited by P.V. Tobias, 355–65. New York: Alan R. Liss.

——. 1989. "Multiregional Evolution: The Fossil Alternative to Eden." In *The Human Revolution*, edited by P.A. Mellars and C. Stringer, 62–108. Princeton, NJ: Princeton University Press.

Woodward, V. 1992. *Human Heredity and Society.* St Paul, MN: West.

Woolard, Kathryn A. 1998. "Introduction: Language Ideology as a Field of Inquiry." In *Language Ideologies: Practice and Theory*, edited by Bambi Schieffelin, Kathryn Woolard, and Paul V. Kroskrity, 3–47. New York: Oxford University Press.

Woost, Michael D. 1993. "Nationalizing the Local Past in Sri Lanka: Histories of Nation and Development in a Sinhalese Village." *American Ethnologist* 20 (3): 502–21.

Wrangham, Richard. 2009. *Catching Fire: How Cooking Made Us Human.* New York: Basic Books.

Yin, Steph. 2011. "Scientist Sunday: Leakey's Angels Part III, Biruté Galdikas." *Ink-Chroma.* http://inkchromatography.wordpress.com/2011/12/20/scientist-sunday-leakeys-angels-part-iii-birute-galdikas/.

Yuval-Davis, Nira. 1997. "Ethnicity, Gender Relations, and Multiculturalism." In *Debating Cultural Hybridity: Multicultural Identities and the Politics of Anti-racism*, edited by Pnina Werbner and Tariq Modood, 193–208. London: Zed Books.

Zaidi, Arshia U., Amanda Couture-Carron, Eleanor Maticka-Tyndale, and Mehek Arif. 2014. "Ethnic Identity, Religion, and Gender: An Exploration of Intersecting Identities Creating Diverse Perceptions and Experiences with Intimate Cross-Gender Relationships amongst South Asian Youth In Canada." *Canadian Ethnic Studies* 46 (2): 27–54.

Zeder, Melinda A., and Bruce D. Smith. 2009. "A Conversation on Agricultural Origins." *Current Anthropology* 50 (5): 681–91.

# Credits

Fig. 1.1:     Pornchai Kittiwongsakul/AFP/Getty Images
Fig. 1.3a:    Riley Brandt/University of Calgary
Fig. 1.3b:    © University of Alberta. Photo: by John Ulan
Fig. 1.4:     Emily A. Schultz, Robert H. Lavenda, and Roberta Robin Dods. 2015. *Cultural Anthropology: A Perspective on the Human Condition*. Toronto: Oxford University Press Canada, p. 28.
Fig. 1.5:     Courtesy Robert Lavenda
Fig. 1.6:     UBCO Media Services
Fig. 1.7:     Courtesy of Michael Brown.
Fig. 1.8:     © Sulejman Omerbasic/Demotix/Corbis
Fig. 1.9:     Courtesy Andrea Wiley
Fig. 2.1:     © Keith Levit/Alamy Stock Photo
Fig. 2.2:     Courtesy Robert H. Lavenda
Fig. 2.3:     © Markrhiggins/Dreamstime.com
Fig. 2.4:     Courtesy of Daniel Lavenda
Fig. 2.5:     © Anthony Bannister/Gallo Images/Corbis
Fig. 2.6:     Courtesy of Daniel Lavenda
Fig. 2.7:     Woohae Cho/Bloomberg/Getty Images
Fig. 2.8:     National Anthropological Archives, Smithsonian Institution, Negative MNH 8304
Fig. 3.2:     Digoarpi/Thinkstock.com
Fig. 3.4:     © Bettmann/Corbis
Fig. 3.5:     © Katherine Feng/Minden Pictures/Corbis
Fig. 3.6:     Wellcome Library, London. Charles Robert Darwin. Photograph by the London Stereoscopic & Photographic Company
Fig. 3.7:     kjorgen/Thinkstock.com
Fig. 3.8:     © iStock/amit erez
Fig. 3.11:    santiphotois/Thinkstock.com
Fig. 3.12:    © Tim Hale/Alamy Stock Photo
Fig. 3.13:    © iStock/WoodyUpstate
Map 4.1:      Chaplin, G. 2004. "Geographic Distribution of Environmental Factors Influencing Human Skin Coloration," *American Journal of Physical Anthropology* 125: 292–302; map updated in 2007. With permission from John Wiley and Sons.
Fig. 4.1a:    © Clouds Hill Imaging Ltd./Corbis
Fig. 4.1b:    © Howard Sochurek/Corbis
Fig. 4.2:     © Lou Linwei/Alamy Stock Photo
Fig. 4.3:     tratong/shutterstock.com
Fig. 4.5:     © Razvanjp/Dreamstime.com
Fig. 4.6:     © imageBROKER/Alamy Stock Photo
Fig. 4.8:     © Maher Attar/Sygma/Corbis
Fig. 5.1a:    RKO/The Kobal Collection
Fig. 5.1b:    Courtesy Universal Studies Media Licensing
Fig. 5.4:     Edwin Butter/Shutterstock.com
Fig. 5.5:     © Frans Lanting/Corbis
Fig. 5.6:     *The Human Career: Human Biological and Cultural Origins*, third edition by Richard G. Klein. Copyright © 2009 by the University of Chicago Press
Fig. 5.7:     © imageBROKER/Alamy Stock Photo
Fig. 5.8:     © Stephenmeese/Dreamstime.com
Fig. 5.9:     © ZUMA Press, Inc./Alamy Stock Photo
Fig. 5.10:    © Anup Shah/Corbis

Fig. 5.12:    *The Human Career: Human Biological and Cultural Origins*, third edition by Richard G. Klein. Copyright © 2009 by the University of Chicago Press
Fig. 5.14:    Martin D. Robert. *Primate Origins and Evolution: A Phylogenetic Reconstruction*, 1990, reprinted by permission of Princeton University Press
Fig. 5.15:    Courtesy Peabody Museum on Natural History, Yale University
Fig. 6.2:     Courtesy David L Brill
Fig. 6.3:     John Reader/Science Source
Fig. 6.4:     John Reader/Science Source
Map 6.6:      Reprinted by permission from Macmillan Publishers Ltd. Raff, Jennifer A., and Deborah A. Bolnick. "Palaeogenomics: Genetic Roots of the First Americans", *Nature* 506: 162–3, copyright © 2014.
Fig. 6.8a:    Pascal Goetgheluck/Science Source
Fig. 6.8b:    Pascal Goetgheluck/Science Source
Fig. 6.9:     Pascal Goetgheluck/Science Source
Fig. 6.10:    John Reader/Science Source
Fig. 6.11:    Kristie Cannon-Bonventre/AnthroPhoto
Fig. 6.12a:   F.E. Grine, SUNY, Stony Brook
Fig. 6.12b:   F.E. Grine, SUNY, Stony Brook
Fig. 6.13:    National Museums of Kenya, Nairobi
Fig. 6.15:    Pascal Goetgheluck/Science Source
Fig. 6.17:    Pascal Goetgheluck/Photo Researchers
Fig. 6.20:    Image # 39686, American Museum of Natural History, Library
Fig. 6.21:    Lionel Bonaventure/AFP/Getty Images
Fig. 6.22:    © Carolina Biological/Visuals Unlimited/Corbis
Fig. 6.23:    *The Human Career: Human Biological and Cultural Origins*, third edition by Richard G. Klein. Copyright © 2009 by the University of Chicago Press
Fig. F1.3:    Biophoto Associates/Science Source
Fig. F1.4:    Courtesy of the Hunterian Museum at the Royal College of Surgeons of England
Fig. 7.1a:    Courtesy Dr Payson D. Sheets
Fig. 7.1b:    Courtesy Dr Payson D. Sheets
Fig. 7.2:     Arlen F. Chase, Diane Z. Chase, John F. Weishampel, Jason B. Drake, Ramesh L. Shrestha, K. Clint Slatton, Jaime J. Awe, and William E. Carter. 2011 "Airborne LiDAR, Archaeology, and the Ancient Maya Landscape at Caracol, Belize," Journal of Archaeological Science 38:387–398.
Fig. 7.5:     © Gary Braasch/Corbis
Fig. 7.6:     © Reuters/Corbis
Fig. 7.7:     © Pilar Olivares/Reuters/Corbis
Fig. 7.8:     Photo courtesy of Andy Wilson
Fig. 7.9a:    © Reuters/Corbis
Fig. 7.9b:    © Reuters/Corbis
Fig. 7.10:    © Alfredo Dagli Orti/The Art Archive/Corbis
Fig. 7.11:    © Robert Bird/Alamy Stock Photo
Fig. 7.12:    Daniel Arsenault; copyright: Avataq Cultural Institute.
Fig. F2.1:    Martin M303/Shutterstock.com
Fig. 8.1:     © Igorj/Dreamstime.com

Fig. 8.2:     © Aivoges/Dreamstime.com
Fig. 8.3:     © Penny Tweedie/Alamy Stock Photo
Fig. 8.4:     *The Emergence of Agriculture* by Bruce Smith. Copyright 1995 by Scientific American Library. With permission of Springer.
Fig. 8.7:     Courtesy Pictures of Record
Fig. 8.8:     Israel Ancient Art and Architecture Collection Ltd./Bridgeman Images
Fig. 8.9:     Hoberman/UIG/ Maxx Images
Fig. 8.10:    © Corbis
Fig. 8.11:    © Ted Spiegel/Corbis
Fig. 8.13:    © iStock/ SkyF
Fig. 8.14:    © SimonDannhauer/Dreamstime.com
Fig. 8.15:    © Bettmann/Corbis
Fig. 8.16:    NASA
Fig. 8.17:    © Charles & Josette Lenars/Corbis
Fig. 8.18:    British Museum, London, UK/Bridgeman Images
Fig. 8.19:    © Keren Su/Corbis
Fig. 8.20:    © HO/Reuters/Corbis
Fig. 9.1:     © Blaine Harrington III/Alamy Stock Photo
Fig. 9.3:     Marty Bucella/Cartoonstock.com
Fig. 9.4:     Courtesy Robert H. Lavenda
Fig. 9.5:     Image Source White/Thinkstock.com
Fig. 9.6:     © Janine Wiedel Photolibrary/Alamy Stock Photo
Fig. 9.7:     Courtesy Robert H. Lavenda
Fig. 9.8:     iStock/PeopleImages
Fig. 9.9:     Library and Archives Canada, PA-134110
Fig. 10.1:    Courtesy Robert H. Lavenda
Fig. 10.2:    © Owen Franken/Corbis
Fig. 10.3:    © Ken Gillespie/Design Pics/Corbis
Fig. 10.4:    © Bernard Bisson/Sygma/Corbis
Fig. 10.5:    Courtesy Michelle Bigenho
Fig. 10.6:    Courtesy Justin Kerr/Kerr Associates
Fig. 10.7:    © Anders Ryman/Corbis
Fig. 10.8:    Rick Madonik/GetStock.com
Fig. 10.9:    © Reuters/Corbis
Fig. 10.10:   Abbas/Magnum Photos
Fig. 10.11:   © Alessandro Bianchi/Reuters/Corbis
Fig. 10.12:   © B&C Alexander/Arcticphoto
Fig. 11.1b:   *Peruvian Prehistory: An Overview of Pre-Inca and Inca Society*, ed. Richard W. Keatinge, Cambridge: Cambridge University Press, 1988, p. 240.
Fig. 11.2:    © Edwardkaraa/Dreamstime.com
Fig. 11.3:    © Bettman/Corbis
Fig. 11.4:    Marjorie Shostak/AnthroPhoto
Fig. 11.5:    © Caroline Penn/Corbis
Fig. 11.6:    © Macduff Everton/Corbis
Fig. 12.1     Courtesy Robert H. Lavenda
Fig. 12.2     © Str/Sri Lanka/Reuters/Corbis
Fig. 12.3     Emily A. Schultz, Robert H. Lavenda, and Roberta Robin Dods. 2015. *Cultural Anthropology: A Perspective on the Human Condition*. Toronto: Oxford University Press Canada, p. 279.
Fig. 12.4     © Sukree Sukplang/Reuters/Corbis
Fig. 12.5     Courtesy Robert H. Lavenda
Fig. 12.6     © Alexandra Boulat/VII/Corbis
Fig. 12.7     © iStock/HowenSia
Fig. 13.1a:   © Owen Franken/Corbis
Fig. 13.1b:   © Lena Wurm/Alamy Stock Photo
Fig. 13.5:    Emily A. Schultz, Robert H. Lavenda and Roberta Robin Dods, *Cultural Anthropology: A Perspective*

on the *Human Condition*. © Oxford University Press Canada 2015. Reprinted by permission of the publisher.
Fig. 13.6:    © Dewitt Jones/Corbis
Fig. 13.8:    RyersonClark/Getty Images
Fig. 13.9:    David Cooper/Toronto Star
Fig. 13.10:   Courtesy Robert H. Lavenda
Fig. 13.11:   Michael Stuparyk/Toronto Star/Getty Images
Fig. 13.12:   Courtesy Robert H. Lavenda
Fig. 13.13:   The British Museum Images
Fig. 13.13:   Courtesy Robert H. Lavenda
Fig. 13.15:   © David Grossman/Alamy Stock Photo
Fig. 13.16:   william87/Thinkstock.com
Fig. 14.1:    Gilles Peress/Magnum Photos
Fig. 14.2:    © Jake Lyell/Alamy Stock Photo
Fig. 14.3:    © iStock/Cesar Okada
Fig. 14.4:    © Shawn Baldwin/Corbis
Fig. 14.5:    William James Topley/Library and Archives Canada / PA-010401
Fig. 14.6:    © Philip Scalia/Alamy Stock Photo
Fig. 14.8:    meunierd/ Shutterstock.com
Fig. 14.9:    © Matthew McKee/Eye Ubiquitous/Corbis
Fig. 14.11:   PETER PARKS/AFP/Getty Images
Fig. 14.12:   © Reuters/Corbis
Fig. 15.1:    Courtesy Orin Starn
Fig. 15.2:    © Reuters/Corbis
Fig. 15.3:    sharonotai/ Thinkstock.com
Fig. 15.4:    © Bettmann/Corbis
Fig. 15.5:    Tannis Toohey/GetStock.com
Fig. 15.6:    © Tanawatpontchour/Dreamstime.com
Fig. 15.7:    © Darren Ell/Demotix/Corbis
Fig. 15.8:    Reuters/Lucy Nicholson (Afghanistan Society Education)
Fig. 15.9:    © Reuters/Corbis
Fig. 15.10:   © iStock/ fotoVoyager
Fig. 15.11:   Courtesy Lynn Meisch
Fig. 15.12:   Zvonimir Atletic/Shutterstock.com
Fig. 15.13:   © Kazuyoshi Nomachi/Corbis
Fig. 15.14:   Courtesy Lynn Meisch

## Unnumbered Figures

page 58:    Figure reprinted from McInnes, Roderick, R. "Culture: The Silent Language Geneticists Must Learn" *American Journal of Human Genetics* 88 (3); 254–61, 2011, with permission from Elsevier.
page 77:    Map from: Moreau, Claudia, Claude Bhérer, Hélène Vézina, Michèle Jomphe, Damian Labuda, and Laurent Excoffier. 2011. "Deep Human Genealogies Reveal a Selective Advantage to Be on an Expanding Wave Front," *Science* 334: 1148–50. Reprinted with permission from AAAS.
page 82:    Photo courtesy of Carl Vivian. University of Leicester.
page 105:   Photo © A & J Visage/Alamy Stock Photo
page 142:   Photo courtesy of April Nowell
page 332:   Photo © Chris Wattie/Reuters/Corbis
page 345:   Photo by Marco Di Lauro/Getty Images
page 370:   Photo © Amit Bhargava/Corbis

# Index